Introduction to Maple

Second Edition

Springer
New York
Berlin
Heidelberg
Barcelona
Budapest
Hong Kong
London
Milan
Paris
Santa Clara
Singapore
Tokyo

André Heck

Introduction to Maple

Second Edition

With 190 Illustrations

Springer

André Heck
University of Amsterdam
CAN Expertise Center
Nieuwe Achtergracht 170
1018 WV Amsterdam
The Netherlands

Maple is a registered trademark of Waterloo Maple Inc.

Library of Congress Cataloging-in-Publication Data
Heck, A. (André)
    Introduction to Maple / André Heck.—2nd ed.
      p.   cm.
    Includes bibliographical references and index.
    ISBN 0-387-94535-0 (hardcover : alk. paper)
      1. Maple (Computer file)   2. Algebra—Data Processing.   I. Title.
    QA155.7.E4H43   1996
    510´.285´53—dc20   96-5914

Printed on acid-free paper.

Production managed by Bill Imbornoni; manufacturing supervised by Jacqui Ashri.
Camera-ready copy prepared from the author's TEX files.
Printed and bound by R.R. Donnelley & Sons, Harrisonburg, VA.
Printed in the United States of America.

9 8 7 6 5 4 3 2 (Corrected second printing, 1997)

ISBN 0-387-94535-0 Springer-Verlag New York Berlin Heidelberg   SPIN 10644929

Preface to the Second Edition

The first edition of this book has been very well received by the community. The new version 4 of Maple V contains so many new mathematical features and improvements in the user interface that Waterloo Maple Inc. markets it as "the Power Edition." These two facts have made it necessary to write a second edition within a short period of the first. I corrected typographical errors, rephrased text, updated and improved many examples, and added much new material. Hardly any chapter has been left untouched. Substantially changed or added sections and chapters address the assume facility, I/O, approximation theory, integration, composite data types, simplification, graphics, differential equations, and matrix algebra. Tables summarize features, command options, etc., and constitute a quick reference. The enlarged index of the book has been carefully compiled to make locating search items quick and easy. Many new examples have been included showing how to use Maple as a problem solver, how to assist the system during computations, and how to extend its built-in facilities.

About the Maple Version Used

The second edition of this book is fully revised and updated to Maple V Release 4. More precisely, the second edition of this book was produced with Maple V Release 4, beta 3 on a SUN SPARCstation 20, Model 71. There should be hardly any difference between this beta version and the final release; only minor differences in the user interface are not excluded. Maple V Release 4 is available on many computer platforms, but most of the book should be system independent as it focuses on the mathematical contents of the system.

About the Production of the Second Edition

The manuscript has been typeset in LaTeX. The Maple version was customized by Waterloo Maple Inc. to make the production of LaTeX code out of Maple sessions easier. Essentially, the authoring tools provided by Stan Devitt from Waterloo Maple Inc. work in the same way as the `Export to` LaTeX button of the Maple worksheet. In this way, "true Maple sessions" interleaved with comments, remarks, and explanations were easily produced and, what is more important, you can be sure that you can reproduce the results on your terminal screen or on paper.

Source Code of Maple Sessions

Readers connected to the Internet can obtain the source code of all Maple sessions by anonymous ftp from `ftp.can.nl`, or through the WWW server `http://www.can.nl`.

Notation

The following notation is used throughout the book: Maple keywords are in `typewriter font` and references to Maple procedures are in **bold type**.

Acknowledgments

I am grateful to many people that have contributed to this book. My thanks go first to the developers of Maple. They have created a wonderful tool for scientists and engineers; Release 4 of Maple is a major improvement in mathematical contents and in ease of use. Writing the new edition of the book has been an exciting tour through the new facilities. The new edition would not have appeared so early without the support from Chris Howlett and Stan Devitt of Waterloo Maple Inc. They provided me with early versions of the software and the authoring tools, encouraged me, and were always willing to listen to my comments and answer my questions. Special thanks go to Gaston Gonnet for giving me access to the research version of Maple at ETH Zürich, so that I can keep abreast of developments in the software.

I wish to thank all readers of the first edition who sent me corrections of errors, helpful ideas, or expressions of appreciation. Their email reports and letters have encouraged me to write this corrected, updated, and expanded edition.

I would like to thank Rüdiger Gebauer and Betty Sheehan from Springer-Verlag for their interest in and support for this book. I am indebted to the CAN Foundation that made it possible to free myself from daily CAN affairs for a while and work full-time on the new edition.

And last, but not least, I wish to thank Rudi Hirschfeld from CWI and my colleagues at CAN, notably Leendert van Gastel and Roderik Lindenbergh, for their careful and thorough reading of early drafts of the new edition. They gave many valuable comments and greatly improved the quality of the book. Dick Verkerk from CAN Diensten encouraged and supported me.

Despite all the help I got, I am sure that users of this book will come up with remarks, suggestions, corrections, etc. Please send them to

University of Amsterdam
CAN Expertise Center
Attn. André Heck
Nieuwe Achtergracht 170
1018 WV Amsterdam
The Netherlands

or to the electronic mail address

heck@can.nl

Preface to the First Edition

In symbolic computation on computers, also known as computer algebra, keyboard and display replace the traditional pencil and paper in doing mathematical computations. Interactive computer programs, which are called computer algebra systems, allow their users to compute not only with numbers, but also with symbols, formulae, equations, and so on. Many mathematical computations such as differentiation, integration, series expansion of functions, and inversion of matrices with symbolic entries can be carried out quickly, with emphasis on exactness of results and without much human effort.

Computer algebra systems are powerful tools for mathematicians, physicists, chemists, engineers, technicians, psychologists, sociologists—in short, for anybody who needs to do mathematical computations. Computer algebra systems are indispensable in modern pure and applied scientific research and education.

This book is a gentle introduction to one of the modern computer algebra systems, viz., Maple. Primary emphasis is on learning what can be done with Maple and how it can be used to solve (applied) mathematical problems. To this end, the book contains many examples and exercises, both elementary and more sophisticated. They stimulate you to use Maple and encourage you to find your way through the system. My advice is read this book in conjunction with the Maple system, try the examples, make variations of them, and try to solve the exercises.

In this book, emphasis is on understanding the basic principles and ideas of Maple so that you can use it effectively to solve your mathematical problems. Factual knowledge or information about every built-in Maple facility can be obtained from the on-line help system or from the Maple documentation that comes along with the software. This book does not teach mathematics; it is understood that you know the theory behind the examples. By choosing a variety of problems and showing how Maple can be used to solve them, you should get an idea of the capabilities of the system.

In this book, the usage of Maple as a programming language is not discussed at a higher level than that of defining simple procedures and using simple language constructs. However, the Maple data structures are discussed in great detail because good understanding of them is necessary for manipulating and simplifying expressions effectively. This also forms a good starting point to acquaint you further with Maple as a programming language.

About the Maple Version Used

It is assumed that you use Maple V Release 2; it is available on many computer platforms, ranging from mainframes and workstations to desktop computers such as Macintosh, NeXT, Amiga, IBM PC, and compatibles. Most of the book should be system independent.

About the Production of the Book

This book was produced with Maple V Release 2 on a Silicon Graphics Indigo Server. The Maple version was customized by Waterloo Maple Software to allow the capture in PostScript format of Maple output of separate commands. These PostScript results were embedded while typesetting the manuscript with TEX. In this way, "true Maple sessions" interleaved with comments, remarks, and explanations were produced. Therefore, you can be sure that you can reproduce the results on your terminal screen or on paper. Maple I/O has been typeset in Courier font so that you can easily distinguish it from other text fragments. Maple procedures have been typeset in bold face characters to distinguish them from ordinary words. The book was prepared in camera-ready format on the phototypesetter at CWI at a resolution of 1200 dots per inch.

About the Origin of the Book

In 1987 the author started to develop introductory Maple courses at the University of Nijmegen. Several revisions and updates of course material have appeared since then. The most important of these was the 1990 course book *Introductie in het gebruik van maple*, which was the joint work of Ernic Kamerich from the University of Nijmegen and the author. In this course book, the existing material was restructured, updated, extended, and many parts were rewritten. The present book is based on the 1990 course book, but the appearance of Maple V Release 2 has made many alterations and extensions in the text inevitable. Furthermore, many examples of practical usage of Maple have been included. Nevertheless, Ernic Kamerich's collaboration should be regarded as one of the most important steps toward readability and usability of this book.

Acknowledgments

Many people have contributed to this book. First of all, I would like to thank my friends and colleagues of the Symbolic Computation Group at the University of Waterloo and of Waterloo Maple Software for their support, encouragement, and willingness to answer my questions throughout the past few years. I would like to thank Rüdiger Gebauer from Springer-Verlag for his interest in this book and his patience with me. I am greatly indebted to Darren Redfern and Bruce Barber for their careful and thorough reading of the book, and for improving my English and my style of writing. Michael Monagan's comments, suggestions, and criticism were invaluable. I would like to thank Ron Sommeling for the many discussions we had about Maple and the course material. Nancy Blachman and Bert Ruitenburg commented on an earlier draft of book. Jan Schipper's help in getting the manuscript in camera-ready format is acknowledged. Marc van Leeuwen's advice on using TeX was indispensable. And last, but not least, I wish to thank my colleagues of the CAN Foundation and at the CAN Expertise Center, notably Arjeh Cohen, Jan Sanders, and Leendert van Gastel, for reminding me of the fact that books must be published and for handling CAN affairs while I was working on the book.

Despite all the help I got, I am sure that users of this book will come up with remarks, suggestions, corrections, etc. Please send them to

University of Amsterdam
CAN Expertise Center
Attn. André Heck
Nieuwe Achtergracht 170
1018 WV Amsterdam
The Netherlands

or to the electronic mail address

heck@can.nl

Contents

List of Tables

1
Introduction to Computer Algebra

This chapter briefly describes what computer algebra is about, presents a little history of computer algebra systems, gives some examples of computer algebra usage, and discusses some advantages and limitations of this new technological tool. We end with a sketch of the design of the Maple system.

The examples in this first chapter are sometimes of a rather advanced mathematical level. Starting with the second chapter, we give a detailed, step-by-step exposition of Maple as a symbolic calculator. The rest of the book does not depend much on this chapter. Thus, anyone who is so eager to learn Maple that he or she cannot wait any longer may skip this chapter and return to it at any moment.

1.1 What is Computer Algebra?

Historically the verb *compute* has mostly been used in the sense of "computing with numbers." Numerical computation is not only involved with basic arithmetic operations such as addition and multiplication of numbers, but also with more sophisticated calculations like computing numerical values of mathematical functions, finding roots of polynomials, and computing numerical eigenvalues of matrices. It is essential in this type of computation that arithmetic operations are carried out on numbers and on numbers only. Furthermore, computations with numbers are in most cases not exact because in applications one is almost always dealing with floating-point numbers. Simple computations can be done with pencil and paper or with a pocket calculator; for large numerical computations, mainframes serve as "number crunchers." In the last fifty years numerical computation on computers flourished to such an extent that for many scientists mathematical computation on computers and numerical computation have become synonymous.

But mathematical computation has another important component, which we shall call *symbolic and algebraic computation*. In short, it can be defined as computation with symbols representing mathematical objects. These symbols may represent numbers like integers, rational numbers, real and complex numbers, and algebraic numbers, but they may also be used for mathematical objects like polynomials and rational functions, systems of equations, and even more abstractly for algebraic structures like groups, rings, and algebras, and elements thereof. Moreover, the adjective *symbolic* emphasizes that in many cases the ultimate goal of mathematical problem solving is expressing the answer in a closed formula or finding a symbolic approximation. By *algebraic* we mean that computations are carried out exactly, according to the rules of algebra, instead of using the approximate floating-point arithmetic. Examples of symbolic and algebraic computations are factorization of polynomials, differentiation, integration, and series expansion of functions, analytic solution of differential equations, exact solution of systems of equations, and simplification of mathematical expressions.

In the last twenty-five years great progress has been made regarding the theoretical background of symbolic and algebraic algorithms; moreover, tools have been developed to carry out mathematical computations on computers [19, 46, 79, 195]. This has led to a new discipline, which is referred to by various names: symbolic and algebraic computation, symbolic computation, symbolic manipulation, formula manipulation, and computer algebra, to name a few. Tools for mathematical computation on a computer are given as many names as the discipline itself: symbolic computation programs, symbol crunchers, symbolic manipulation programs, and computer algebra systems. Unfortunately, the term *symbolic computation* is used in many different contexts, like logic programming and artificial intelligence in its broadest sense, which have very little to do with mathematical computation. To avoid misunderstanding, we shall henceforth adopt the term *computer algebra* and we shall speak of *computer algebra systems*.

1.2   Computer Algebra Systems

In this section, we shall give a very short, incomplete, and subjective overview of present-day computer algebra systems. For a more thorough overview we refer to [42] and to WWW-servers dedicated to computer algebra [199]. Computer algebra systems can be conveniently divided into two categories: *special purpose systems* and *general purpose systems.*

Special purpose systems are designed to solve problems in one specific branch of physics and mathematics. Some of the best-known special purpose systems used in physics are SCHOONSCHIP ([178] high-energy physics), CAMAL ([9] celestial mechanics), and SHEEP and STENSOR ([65, 104, 134] general relativity). Examples of special purpose systems in the mathematical arena are Cayley and GAP ([28, 31, 165] group theory), PARI, SIMATH, and KANT ([12, 85, 103, 156] number theory), CoCoA ([34, 78] commutative algebra), Macaulay ([86, 173] algebraic geometry and commutative algebra), and LiE ([127] Lie theory). Our interest will be in the general purpose system Maple [38, 39, 40, 187, 188], but the importance of special purpose systems should not be underestimated: they have played a crucial role in many scientific areas [19, 30, 106]. Often they are more handsome and efficient than general purpose systems because of their use of special notations and data structures, and because of their implementation of algorithms in a low-level programming language.

General purpose systems please their users with a great variety of data structures and mathematical functions, trying to cover as many different application areas as possible (q.v., [95]). The oldest general purpose computer algebra systems still in use are MACSYMA [136] and REDUCE [97]. Both systems were born in the late 1960s and were implemented in the programming language LISP. MACSYMA is a full-featured computer algebra system with a wide range of auxiliary packages, but its demands on computer resources are rather high and it is only available on a limited number of platforms. The release of the PC version of MACSYMA in 1992 has caused a revival of this system. REDUCE began as a special purpose program for use in high-energy physics, but gradually transformed into a general purpose system. Compared to MACSYMA the number of user-ready facilities in REDUCE is modest, but on the other hand it is a very open system (the complete source code is distributed!) making it easily extensible and modifiable. REDUCE is still under active development: REDUCE 3.6 is from October 1995. It runs on a very wide range of computers and is well documented.

In the eighties, MuMATH [197] and its successor DERIVE [176] were the first examples of compact nonprogrammable symbolic calculators, designed for use on PC-type computers. DERIVE has a friendly menu-driven interface with graphical and numerical features. Considering its compactness and the limitations of DOS computers, DERIVE offers an amazing amount of user-ready facilities. Version 3 of 1994 also has limited programming facilities. Many of DERIVE's features have been built into the TI-92 calculator (Texas Instruments, 1995), thus making computer algebra available on small-size computers.

Most modern computer algebra systems are implemented in the programming language C. This language allows developers to write efficient, portable computer programs, which really exploit the platforms for which they are designed. Many of these computer algebra systems work on a variety of computers, from supercomputers down to desktop computers.

In §1.6 we shall sketch the design of Maple [38, 39, 40, 187, 188]. Another notable modern general purpose system is *Mathematica* [196]. *Mathematica* is the first system in which symbolics, numerics, and graphics are incorporated in such a way that it can serve as a user-friendly environment for doing mathematics. There exists on certain machines (such as Macintosh, NeXT, PC running MS-Windows) the notebook interface, which is a tool to create a structured text in which ordinary text is interwoven with formulas, programs, computations, and graphics. Another feature of *Mathematica* is the well-structured user-level programming language. With the publicity and marketing strategy that went into the production of *Mathematica*, commerce has definitely made its entry into the field of computer algebra, accompanied by less realistic claims about capabilities (q.v., [175]). On the positive side, the attention of many scientists has now been drawn to computer algebra and to the use of computer algebra tools in research and education. Another advantage has been the growing interest of developers of computer algebra systems in friendly user interfaces, good documentation, and ample user support. A wealth of information and user's contributions can be found at the WWW server of Wolfram Research, Inc., and more specifically at the electronic library MathSource [137]. A major new version of Mathematica, with new front end and mathematical features, is expected in 1996.

The aforementioned general purpose systems manipulate formulae if the entire formula can be stored inside the main memory of the computer. This is the only limit to the size of formulae. The symbolic manipulation program FORM [99, 148, 184] has been designed to deal with formulae of virtually infinite size (q.v., [185]). On the other hand, the size of the set of instructions in FORM is somewhat limited.

Magma [17, 18, 32] is the successor of Cayley, released in 1994, and designed around the algebraic notions of structure and morphism. Its aim is to support computation in algebra, number theory, geometry, and algebraic combinatorics. This is achieved through the provision of extensive machinery for groups, rings, modules, algebras, geometric structures, and finite incidence structures (designs, codes, graphs). Two basic design principles are the strong typing scheme derived from modern algebra whereby types correspond to algebraic structures and the integration of algorithmic and database knowledge.

MuPAD [67, 68] stands for Multi Processing Algebra Data Tool. It is is a system for symbolic and numeric computation, parallel mathematical programming, and mathematical visualization. MuPAD is freely distributed for noncommercial use. It is still in active development at the University of Paderborn and its mathematical contents is growing fast: version 1.2.2 has been released in July 1995.

A portable system for parallel symbolic computation through Maple exists as well; it is called ‖MAPLE‖ (speak: parallel MAPLE) [168]. The system is built as an interface between the parallel declarative language Strand [64] and the sequential computer algebra system Maple, thus providing the elegance of Strand and the powerfulness of the existing sequential algorithms in Maple.

Last (but not least) in the row is AXIOM [54, 55, 108, 109, 179]. It is a powerful general purpose system developed in the 1980s at the IBM Thomas J. Watson Research Laboratory under the name of "Scratchpad." In contrast to most other general purpose systems, which only allow calculations in a specific algebraic domain, e.g., the field of rational numbers or the ring of polynomials over the integers, AXIOM allows its users to define and handle distinct types of algebraic structures. Version 2.0 from 1995 is only available on large IBM RS/6000, SUN, and HP9000/700 machines.

1.3   Some Properties of Computer Algebra Systems

Computer algebra systems differ from one another, but they share many properties. We shall illustrate common properties with examples from Maple.

Computer algebra systems are *interactive* programs that, in contrast to numerical computer programs, allow mathematical computations with *symbolic* expressions. Typically, the user enters a mathematical expression or an instruction, which the computer algebra system subsequently tries to execute. Given the result of the computation the user may enter a new instruction. This may lead to a fruitful computer algebra session. As an easy example of the use of Maple, we shall compute the stationary point of the real function

$$x \mapsto \arctan\left(\frac{2x^2 - 1}{2x^2 + 1}\right),$$

as well as the value of the function at this point. As we shall see later on in this section, Maple can compute the minimum on its own. Here, we only use the example to show some of the characteristics of computer algebra systems. On the next page is a screen dump of a complete work session with Maple V Release 4, on a Unix-type computer running the worksheet interface.

Let us take a closer look at this example. When Maple is started under the X Window System with **xmaple**, an empty worksheet appears, except that the system prints the greater-than symbol ">" on the first line in order to prompt the user to enter an instruction. The symbol ">" is called the *Maple prompt*.

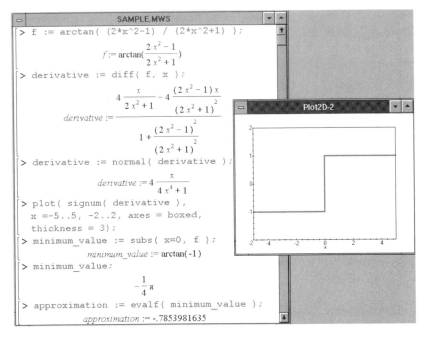

FIGURE 1.1. Example of Maple worksheet.

In the first command we enter the formula f, ending the input line with a semicolon, and pressing the RETURN key. The last two key strokes signal Maple to start to work. In this case, the formula is shown in two-dimensional mathematical notation of textbook quality. What strikes one most is that the system allows the use of symbols like x. In most numerical programming languages this would immediately cause an error; but not in systems for *symbolic* computations!

Each time Maple has executed an instruction, it prints the prompt and waits for another command. We decide to consider f as a function, **differen**-tiate it, and assign the result to the variable called *derivative*. Maple's answer is a rather complicated expression. So, we **normal**ize the rational function. The answer is a simple expression of which the sign can be plotted. From this plot we immediately conclude that the original function has a minimum at $x = 0$. The minimum value $-\frac{1}{4}\pi$ is obtained by **subst**itution of $x = 0$ in f. We obtain an approximate floating-point result by use of the command **evalf**. The name **evalf** — short for "**eval**uate using **f**loating-point arithmetic" — is already the fourth example that shows Maple's general philosophy in choosing names: Use a short, easy-to-remember name for a procedure that describes its functionality. In addition to this, we have given meaningful names to variables, which describe their use.

We see that Maple leaves it to us to find our way through the computation. *We* must decide, on the basis of the second result, to try and find a less complicated formula for the derivative. One may wonder why the system itself does not perform this more or less obvious simplification. But remember, it is not always clear when and how to simplify. In many cases more than one simplification is possible and it is the mathematical context that actually determines which simplification is appropriate. For example, the rational expression

$$\frac{(x^2 - 1)(x^2 - x + 1)(x^2 + x + 1)}{(x - 1)^6}$$

can be transformed into the compact expression

$$\frac{x^6 - 1}{(x - 1)^6},$$

but also into a form suitable for integration, viz.,

$$1 + \frac{6}{(x - 1)^5} + \frac{15}{(x - 1)^4} + \frac{20}{(x - 1)^3} + \frac{15}{(x - 1)^2} + \frac{6}{x - 1}.$$

Another problem with automatic simplification is that in many computations one cannot predict the size and shape of the results and therefore must be able to intervene at any time. A procedure that works fine in one case might be a bad choice in another case. For example, one might think that it is always a good idea to factorize an expression. For example, the factorization of

$$x^8 + 8x^7 + 28x^6 + 56x^5 + 70x^4 + 56x^3 + 28x^2 + 8x + 1$$

is

$$(x + 1)^8.$$

However (surprise!) apart from being expensive, the factorization of the relatively simple

$$x^{26} + x^{13} + 1$$

yields

$$(x^{24} - x^{23} + x^{21} - x^{20} + x^{18} - x^{17} + x^{15} - x^{14} + x^{12} - x^{10} + x^9 - x^7 + x^6 - x^4 + x^3 - x + 1)(x^2 + x + 1).$$

For these reasons, Maple only applies automatic simplification rules when there is no doubt about which expression is simpler: $x + 0$ should be simplified to x, $3x$ is simpler than $x + x + x$, x^3 is better than $x \times x \times x$, and $\sin(\pi)$ should be simplified to 0. Any other simplification is left to the user's control; Maple only provides the tools for such jobs.

Automatic simplification sometimes introduces loss of mathematical correctness. For example, the automatic simplification of $0 \times f(1)$ to 0 is not always correct. An exception is the case $f(1)$ is undefined or infinity. The automatic simplification is only wanted if $f(1)$ is finite but difficult to compute. In cases like this, designers of computer algebra systems have to choose between rigorous mathematical correctness and usability/efficiency of their systems (q.v., [60]). In Maple and many other systems the scales sometimes tip to simplifications that are not 100% safe in every case.

Another remarkable fact in the first example is that Maple computes the exact value $-\frac{1}{4}\pi$ for the function in the origin and does not return an approximate value like 0.785398. This is a second aspect of computer algebra systems: the emphasis on *exact arithmetic*. In addition, computer algebra systems can carry out floating-point arithmetic in a *user-defined precision*. For example, in Maple the square $\tan^2(\pi/12)$ can be computed exactly, but the numerical approximation in 25-digit floating-point notation can also be obtained.

```
>   real_number := tan(Pi/12)^2;
```
$$real\_number := (\,2 - \sqrt{3}\,)^2$$

```
>   real_number := expand( real_number );
```
$$real\_number := 7 - 4\sqrt{3}$$

```
>   approximation := evalf( real_number, 25 );
```
$$approximation := .07179676972449082589 0216$$

Computer algebra systems like Maple contain a substantial amount of built-in mathematical knowledge. This makes them good mathematical assistants. In calculus they differentiate functions, compute limits, and compute series expansions. Integration (both definite and indefinite), is one of the highlights in computer calculus. Maple uses nonclassical algorithms such as the Risch algorithm for integrating elementary functions [76], instead of the heuristic integration methods that are described in most mathematics textbooks.

With the available calculus tools, one can easily explore mathematical functions. In the Maple session below we shall explore the previously defined function f. The *sharp symbol* # followed by text is one of Maple's ways of allowing comments during a session; in combination with the names of variables and Maple procedures, this should explain the script sufficiently. If an input line is ended by a colon instead of a semicolon, then

Maple does not print its results. Spaces in input commands are optional, but at several places we have inserted them to make the input more readable.

```
>  f := arctan( (2*x^2-1) / (2*x^2+1) ); # enter formula
```
$$f := \arctan\left(\frac{2\,x^2 - 1}{2\,x^2 + 1}\right)$$

```
>  df := normal( diff( f, x ) ); # differentiate f
```
$$df := 4\,\frac{x}{4\,x^4 + 1}$$

```
>  F := integrate( df, x ); # integrate derivative
```
$$F := \arctan(2\,x^2)$$

```
>  normal( diff( F - f, x  ) ); # verify F = f + Pi/4
```
$$0$$

```
>  eval( subs( x=0, F - f ) );
```
$$\frac{1}{4}\,\pi$$

```
>  roadlib( extrema ): # load library function
>  extrema( f, {}, x, stationary_points );
```
$$\left\{-\frac{1}{4}\,\pi\right\}$$

```
>  stationary_points;
```
$$\{\{x = 0\}\}$$

```
>  # this value was assigned by the call of `extrema`
>  solve( f=0, x ); # compute the zero's of f
```
$$\frac{1}{2}\,\sqrt{2}, -\frac{1}{2}\,\sqrt{2}$$

```
>  # compute the Taylor series approximation of f
>  series( f, x=0, 15 );
```
$$-\frac{1}{4}\,\pi + 2\,x^2 - \frac{8}{3}\,x^6 + \frac{32}{5}\,x^{10} - \frac{128}{7}\,x^{14} + O(x^{15})$$

```
>  # load package for numerical approximation of functions
>  with( numapprox ):
>  pade( f, x, [6,4] );
```
$$\frac{1}{12}\,\frac{-15\,\pi + 120\,x^2 - 36\,\pi\,x^4 + 128\,x^6}{5 + 12\,x^4}$$

```
>   # compute the Chebyshev-Pade approximation of f
>   chebpade( f, x, [2,2] );
```

$$\frac{-.007904471007\,T(0,x)+.4715125862\,T(2,x)}{T(0,x)+.4089934686\,T(2,x)}$$

```
>   # compute limit of f when x goes to infinity
>   limit( f, x=infinity );
```

$$\frac{1}{4}\pi$$

```
>   # compute the asymptotic form of f
>   series( f, x=infinity );
```

$$\frac{1}{4}\pi-\frac{1}{2}\frac{1}{x^2}+O\left(\frac{1}{x^6}\right)$$

```
>   # finally, draw the graphs of f and df.
>   f_plot := plot( f, x=-5..5, linestyle=0 ):
>   df_plot := plot( df, x=-5..5, linestyle=4 ):
>   plots[display]( {f_plot, df_plot},
>     title=`graph of f and f´` );
```

The graph is shown in Figure 1.2.

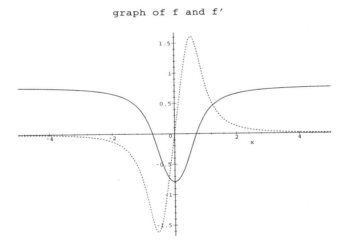

FIGURE 1.2. Graph of $(x,y)\mapsto\arctan\left(\frac{2x^2-1}{2x^2+1}\right)$ and its derivative.

Other impressive areas of computer algebra are polynomial calculus, the solution of systems of linear and nonlinear equations, the solution of recurrence equations and differential equations, calculations on matrices with numerical and symbolic coefficients, and tensor calculus. Various tools for manipulation of formulae are present: selection and substitution of parts of expressions, restricted simplification, simplification rules, pattern matching, and so on. We may call computer algebra systems *mathematical expert systems* with which mathematical problems can be solved in a more productive and accurate way than with pencil and paper.

In addition to functioning as symbolic and algebraic calculators, most computer algebra systems can be used as *programming languages* for implementing new mathematical algorithms. By way of illustration we write a Maple program that computes the Bessel polynomials $y_n(x)$. Recall [90] that they can be recursively defined by

$$
\begin{aligned}
y_0(x) &= 1, \\
y_1(x) &= x+1, \\
y_n(x) &= (2n-1)\,x\,y_{n-1}(x) + y_{n-2}(x), \quad \text{for } n > 1.
\end{aligned}
$$

```
>   Y := proc( n::nonnegint, x::name )
>      if n=0 then 1
>      elif n = 1 then x+1
>      else Y(n,x)  := expand( (2*n-1)*x*Y(n-1,x) + Y(n-2,x) )
>      fi
>   end:
>   Y(5,z);
```

$$945\,z^5 + 945\,z^4 + 420\,z^3 + 105\,z^2 + 15\,z + 1$$

The Maple programming language is reminiscent of Algol68 without declarations, but also includes several functional programming paradigms.

1.4   Advantages of Computer Algebra

The long-term goal of computer algebra is to automate as much as possible the mathematical problem solving process. Although present computer algebra systems are far from being automatic problem solvers, they are already useful, if not indispensable, tools in research and education. Of course, it takes time to familiarize oneself with a computer algebra system, but this time is well spent. In this section, some of the more important reasons for learning and using a computer algebra system will be illustrated with Maple examples, a few of which are rather advanced mathematically. All computations will be carried out with Maple V Release 4, on a SUN SPARCstation 20 M71 running SunOS 4.1.3, with a 75-Mhz Super SPARC II processor, and having 64-MB main memory plus 128-MB swap space. This does not imply that the same results could not have been obtained on a much smaller machine, but the timings would be different.

The main advantage of a computer algebra system is its ability to carry out large algebraic computations. Although many calculations are straightforward standard manipulations that can be calculated with pencil and paper, the larger the formulae the harder the work and the less the chance of success. For this kind of computation a computer algebra system is an excellent tool. The next three examples demonstrate this.

The first example is one of the problems posed by R. Pavelle [154] as a challenge for computer algebra systems. The object is to prove that

$$\frac{\sin\left(\dfrac{nz\sqrt{x^2+y^2+z^2}}{\sqrt{y^2+z^2}}\right)}{\sqrt{x^2+y^2+z^2}}$$

is a solution of the fourth-order partial differential equation

$$\left(\frac{\partial^2}{\partial x^2}\left(\frac{\partial^2}{\partial x^2}+\frac{\partial^2}{\partial y^2}+\frac{\partial^2}{\partial z^2}\right)+n^2\left(\frac{\partial^2}{\partial x^2}+\frac{\partial^2}{\partial y^2}\right)\right)f=0.$$

The simplification procedures of Maple are powerful enough to solve this problem in a few seconds.

```
>   settime := time():    # start timing
>   f := sin( n*z*sqrt(x^2+y^2+z^2) / sqrt(y^2+z^2) ) /
>     sqrt(x^2+y^2+z^2);
```

$$f := \frac{\sin(\dfrac{n\,z\,\sqrt{x^2+y^2+z^2}}{\sqrt{y^2+z^2}})}{\sqrt{x^2+y^2+z^2}}$$

```
>   simplify( diff( diff(f,x$2) + diff(f,y$2) + diff(f,z$2),
>     x$2 ) + n^2 * ( diff(f,x$2) + diff(f,y$2) ) );
```

$$0$$

```
>   cpu_time = (time()-settime) * seconds; # computing time
```

$$cpu\_time = 20.450 \; seconds$$

In the second example, the objective is find the generating function for dimensions of representations of the Lie group of type G_2 (q.v., [43, 44]). So, the attempt is made to find a rational function $F(x, y)$ such that

$$F(x,y) = \sum_{k,l\geq 0} G2(k,l)x^k y^l,$$

where $G2(k, l)$ is the following polynomial expression.

```
>   G2 := (k,l) -> 1/5! * (k+1) * (l+1) * (k+l+2) *
>     (k+2*l+3) * (k+3*l+4) * (2*k+3*l+5);
```

$$G2 := (k,l) \rightarrow \frac{1}{120}(k+1)(l+1)(k+l+2)(k+2l+3)$$
$$(k+3l+4)(2k+3l+5)$$

Here, we have used Maple's arrow notation for functional operators. In this way $G2$ is a function with values defined in terms of its arguments instead of just a formula. Maple has a package called genfunc for manipulating rational generating functions. We use it to solve our problem.

```
>  with( genfunc ):   # load genfunc package
>  settime := time():   # start timing
>  F := rgf_encode( rgf_encode( G2(k,1), k, x), l, y ):
>  F := sort( factor( F ) );
```

$$F := (x^4 y^4 + 8 x^4 y^3 + x^3 y^4 + 8 x^4 y^2 - 26 x^3 y^3 + x^4 y - 41 x^3 y^2$$
$$+ 15 x^2 y^3 - 6 x^3 y + 78 x^2 y^2 - 6 x y^3 + 15 x^2 y - 41 x y^2 + y^3$$
$$- 26 x y + 8 y^2 + x + 8 y + 1) / ((x - 1)^6 (y - 1)^6)$$

```
>  cpu_time = (time()-settime) * seconds; # computing time
```

$$cpu\_time = 1.200 \ seconds$$

An example taken from scientific life where Maple could have played the role of mathematical assistant can be found in [198]. In this paper the Laplace-Beltrami operator Δ in hyperspherical coordinates is wanted. To this end, the Jacobian of the coordinate mapping, the metric tensor, and its inverse are calculated. Following are quotations from the paper:

"It is not difficult to compute $\dfrac{\partial \mathbf{Y}}{\partial q_i}$, and it is not difficult, but tedious, to compute the traces in Eq.(32B). After quite some algebra we find, ..."

"It is also tedious to invert $\mathbf{g}$. After several pages of computation of minors we find, ..."

These remarks are indeed true when one carries out these calculations with pencil and paper; but not if one lets Maple carry out the computations! Below is the Maple calculation, as much as possible in the notation of [198]. Don't worry if you do not fully understand individual commands: details will be provided later in this book.

The first step in the computation is to define the coordinate mapping Y and to build the metric tensor G. This turns out to be the most time-consuming step in the computation.

```
>  settime := time():   # start timing
>  with( linalg ): # load linear algebra package
```

Warning, new definition for norm
Warning, new definition for trace

```
> R[z] := x -> array( [ [ cos(x), -sin(x), 0 ],
>                        [ sin(x),  cos(x), 0 ],
>                        [      0,       0, 1 ] ] ):
> `R[z](phi)´ = R[z](phi);
```

$$R_z(\phi) = \begin{bmatrix} \cos(\phi) & -\sin(\phi) & 0 \\ \sin(\phi) & \cos(\phi) & 0 \\ 0 & 0 & 1 \end{bmatrix}$$

```
> R[y] := x -> array( [ [ cos(x), 0, -sin(x) ],
>                        [      0, 1,       0 ],
>                        [ sin(x), 0,  cos(x) ] ] ):
> `R[y](phi)´ = R[y](phi);
```

$$R_y(\phi) = \begin{bmatrix} \cos(\phi) & 0 & -\sin(\phi) \\ 0 & 1 & 0 \\ \sin(\phi) & 0 & \cos(\phi) \end{bmatrix}$$

```
> T := x -> array( [ [ cos(x) + sin(x), 0, 0 ],
>                     [ 0, cos(x) - sin(x), 0 ],
>                     [ 0,              0, 0 ] ] ):
> `T(phi)´ = T(phi);
```

$$T(\phi) = \begin{bmatrix} \cos(\phi)+\sin(\phi) & 0 & 0 \\ 0 & \cos(\phi)-\sin(\phi) & 0 \\ 0 & 0 & 0 \end{bmatrix}$$

```
> # define macros for greek characters
> macro( a=alpha, b=beta, c=gamma, f=phi, t=theta ):
> # coordinate mapping Y is a product of matrices
> Y := evalm(  r/sqrt(2) * ( R[z](a) &* R[y](b) &* R[z](c/2)
>    &* T(t/2) &* R[z](f/2) ) ):
> # compute the metric tensor G
> Y1 := map( diff, Y, r ):   Y2 := map( diff, Y, a ):
> Y3 := map( diff, Y, b ):   Y4 := map( diff, Y, c ):
> Y5 := map( diff, Y, t ):   Y6 := map( diff, Y, f ):
> # build the metric tensor
> G := array( symmetric, 1..6, 1..6 ):
> for i to 6 do for j from i to 6 do
>   G[i,j] := simplify( trace( transpose(Y.i) &* Y.j ) )
> od od:
> intermediate_cpu_time = (time() - settime) * seconds;
```

$$intermediate\_cpu\_time = 11.900\ seconds$$

Now, we apply some simplification procedures to obtain the formulae in
[198]. To shorten the output of the session, we continue to suppress most
results. We also show a slightly polished session, admittedly not the first
interactive session when the problem was solved.

```
> G := subs( cos(t/2)^2 = 1/2 + 1/2*cos(t),
>    cos(c/2)^2 = 1/2 + 1/2*cos(c), sin(t/2) = sin(t) /
>    ( 2*cos(t/2) ), sin(c/2) = sin(c) / ( 2*cos(c/2) ),
>    eval(G)):
```

```
>  G := map( normal, G ): # normalize each matrix entry
>  G[2,2] := normal( subs( -1/2*r^2*cos(c) * sin(t) =
>     -1/2*r^2*(cos(b)^2 + sin(b)^2) * cos(c) * sin(t),
>     G[2,2] ) ):
>  G := map( factor, G ):  # this the formula in the paper!
>  G[2,2] := subsop( 1=-op(1,G[2,2]), 3=-op(3,G[2,2]),
>     G[2,2] ): # get nice signs for entry 2,2
>  print(G);   # this the formula in the paper!
```

$$\Big[1,0,0,0,0,0 \Big]$$

$$\Big[0, \frac{1}{2} r^2 \left(\cos(\beta)^2 + 1 - \sin(\theta)\cos(\gamma)\sin(\beta)^2 \right) ,$$
$$\frac{1}{2}\sin(\gamma) r^2 \sin(\beta)\sin(\theta), \frac{1}{2} r^2 \cos(\beta), 0, \frac{1}{2} r^2 \cos(\beta)\cos(\theta) \Big]$$

$$\Big[0, \frac{1}{2}\sin(\gamma) r^2 \sin(\beta)\sin(\theta), \frac{1}{2} r^2 (1 + \sin(\theta)\cos(\gamma)), 0,0,0 \Big]$$

$$\Big[0, \frac{1}{2} r^2 \cos(\beta), 0, \frac{1}{4} r^2, 0, \frac{1}{4} r^2 \cos(\theta) \Big]$$

$$\Big[0,0,0,0, \frac{1}{4} r^2, 0 \Big]$$

$$\Big[0, \frac{1}{2} r^2 \cos(\beta)\cos(\theta), 0, \frac{1}{4} r^2 \cos(\theta), 0, \frac{1}{4} r^2 \Big]$$

Due to the screen width and the length of expressions Maple was not able to produce a nice layout, but it can translate the formulae automatically into a format suitable for text processing programs like LATEX [124].

```
>  latex( G, ´metric_tensor´ ):
```

The LATEX code is not shown, but the result after typesetting is

$$\begin{bmatrix} 1 & 0 & 0 & 0 & 0 & 0 \\ 0 & \frac{r^2(\cos(\beta)^2+1-\sin(\theta)\cos(\gamma)\sin(\beta)^2)}{2} & \frac{r^2\sin(\gamma)\sin(\beta)\sin(\theta)}{2} & \frac{r^2\cos(\beta)}{2} & 0 & \frac{r^2\cos(\beta)\cos(\theta)}{2} \\ 0 & \frac{r^2\sin(\gamma)\sin(\beta)\sin(\theta)}{2} & \frac{r^2(1+\sin(\theta)\cos(\gamma))}{2} & 0 & 0 & 0 \\ 0 & \frac{r^2\cos(\beta)}{2} & 0 & \frac{r^2}{4} & 0 & \frac{r^2\cos(\theta)}{4} \\ 0 & 0 & 0 & 0 & \frac{r^2}{4} & 0 \\ 0 & \frac{r^2\cos(\beta)\cos(\theta)}{2} & 0 & \frac{r^2\cos(\theta)}{4} & 0 & \frac{r^2}{4} \end{bmatrix}$$

Let us compute the Jacobian.

```
>  determinant := simplify( det( G ) ):
>  determinant := normal( subs( cos(b)^2 = 1 - sin(b)^2,
>     cos(t)^4 = cos(t)^2 * (1 - sin(t)^2), determinant) ):
>  assume( 0<=r, 0<=t, t<=Pi/2, 0<=b, b<=Pi ):
>  Jacobian :=  subs( cos(t) = sin(2*t) / (2*sin(t)),
>     sqrt( determinant ) );
```

$$Jacobian := \frac{1}{32}\, r^{\sim 5} \sin(\, 2\,\theta^{\sim}\,) \sin(\,\beta^{\sim}\,)$$

This is formula (33) in the paper. The assumptions on the hyperspherical coordinates were necessary to have the square root expression automatically simplified by Maple. The tildes next to the variables indicate that some assumptions have been made about them.

Now we compute the inverse of the metric tensor.

```
>   GINV := map( simplify, inverse( G ) ):
>   GINV := subs( cos(t)^2 = 1 - sin(t)^2,
>      cos(b)^2 = 1 - sin(b)^2, eval( GINV ) ):
>   cpu_time = (time()-settime) * seconds; # computing time
```

$$cpu\_time = 14.934 \; seconds$$

We do not show the inverse metric tensor, but all entries except GINV[4,4] are in the shape of formula (34) in the paper. Casting GINV[4,4] into good shape is not difficult; we skip this last part of the computation. Anyway, the calculation can easily be done in about 15 seconds of computing time and paper-ready formulae are obtained too!

Another example from science where computer algebra enables the researcher to finish off a proof of a mathematical result that requires a lot of straightforward but tedious computations can be found in [45]. There, a purely algebraic problem, related to proving the existence of a certain finite subgroup of a Lie group, could be reduced to the problem of solving a set of linear equations in 240 variables with coefficients from the field of 1,831 elements. This system of linear equations was easily shown to have a unique solution by computer. By pencil and paper this is almost impossible, but by computer this is quite feasible. The role of Maple in this computation is described in [131].

In the last two worked-out examples we have used Maple to determine a generating function and to compute a metric tensor and its inverse, respectively. Now, one may not think much of mathematical results obtained by a computer program, but remember that there are many independent ways to check the answers. One may even use Maple itself to check the answers or to enlarge one's confidence in the results; e.g., one can compute the first terms of the Taylor series and compare them with the original coefficients, and one can multiply the metric tensor and its inverse as an extra check on the answers.

Symbolic and algebraic computation often precedes numerical computation. Mathematical formulae are first manipulated to cast them into good shape for final numerical computation. For this reason, it is important that a computer algebra system provides a good interface between these two types of computation. Maple can generate FORTRAN and C expressions from Maple expressions. Double precision arithmetic and code optimization are optional. For example, the submatrix of the metric tensor G in the previous example consisting of the first two rows can be converted into FORTRAN as shown below. Two technicalities play a role: You have to get rid of the link between Euler's constant and the Greek character γ in Maple, and you must use named arrays instead of nested lists for matrices.

```
>   `evalf/constant/gamma` := proc() args end:
>   H := submatrix( G, 2..3, 1..6 );
```

$H :=$

$$\left[0, \frac{1}{2}r^2 \left(\cos(\beta)^2 + 1 - \sin(\theta)\cos(\gamma)\sin(\beta)^2 \right) , \right.$$

$$\frac{1}{2}\sin(\gamma)r^2\sin(\beta)\sin(\theta), \frac{1}{2}r^2\cos(\beta), 0, \frac{1}{2}r^2\cos(\beta)\cos(\theta) \right]$$

$$\left[0, \frac{1}{2}\sin(\gamma)r^2\sin(\beta)\sin(\theta), \frac{1}{2}r^2\left(1 + \sin(\theta)\cos(\gamma)\right), 0, 0, 0 \right]$$

```
>   fortran( H, `optimized`, precision = double );
          t1 = r**2
          t2 = sin(theta)
          t4 = t2*cos(gamma)
          t5 = sin(beta)
          t6 = t5**2
          t8 = cos(beta)
          t9 = t8**2
          t15 = t1*sin(gamma)*t5*t2
          t16 = t1*t8
          H(1,1) = 0.D0
          H(1,2) = t1*(-t4*t6+t9+1.D0)/2.D0
          H(1,3) = t15/2.D0
          H(1,4) = t16/2.D0
          H(1,5) = 0.D0
          H(1,6) = t16*cos(theta)/2.D0
          H(2,1) = 0.D0
          H(2,2) = t15/2.D0
          H(2,3) = t1*(t4+1.D0)/2.D0
          H(2,4) = 0.D0
          H(2,5) = 0.D0
          H(2,6) = 0.D0
```

The answers obtained with a computer algebra system are either exact or in a user-defined precision. They can be more accurate than hand calculations [116]; and can lead to many corrections to integral tables. Below, we give two examples of integrals incorrectly tabulated in one of the most popular tables, viz., Gradshteyn and Ryzhik [84]:

1. Formula 2.269

$$\int \frac{1}{x\sqrt{(bx+cx^2)^3}}\,dx = \frac{2}{3}\left(-\frac{1}{bx}+\frac{4c}{b^2}-\frac{8c^2x}{b^3}\right)\frac{1}{\sqrt{bx+cx^2}}.$$

2. Formula 3.828(19)

$$\int_0^\infty \frac{\sin^2(ax)\,\sin^2(bx)\,\sin(2cx)}{x}\,dx =$$

$$\frac{\pi}{16}\left(1+\mathrm{sgn}(c-a+b)+\mathrm{sgn}(c-b+a)-2\mathrm{sgn}(c-a)-2\mathrm{sgn}(c-b)\right),$$

where $a, b, c > 0$.

As shown below Maple does not only give correct answers but also more information on conditions of the parameters. In the example we shall use the double quote to refer to the previous result.

```
>   Int( 1 / (x * sqrt(( b*x + c*x^2 )^3)), x );
```

$$\int \frac{1}{x\sqrt{(bx+cx^2)^3}}\,dx$$

```
>   value(");
```

$$-\frac{2}{3}\sqrt{x\,(b+cx)}(-4\sqrt{bx+cx^2}\,cxb-5\sqrt{bx+cx^2}\,c^2x^2$$
$$+\sqrt{bx+cx^2}\,b^2-3c^2\sqrt{x\,(b+cx)}\,x^2)\big/(x\sqrt{x^3\,(b+cx)^3}\,b^3)$$

```
>   factor(");
```

$$\frac{2}{3}\frac{(b+cx)\,(4cxb+8c^2x^2-b^2)}{\sqrt{x^3\,(b+cx)^3}\,b^3}$$

Assume that all variables are positive and simplify the above result under this condition.

```
>   simplify( ", assume=positive );
```

$$\frac{2}{3}\frac{4cxb+8c^2x^2-b^2}{x^{3/2}\sqrt{b+cx}\,b^3}$$

It is a bit more work to get a look-alike of the tabulated result.

```
>   subs( b+c*x = y/x, " );
```

$$\frac{2}{3}\frac{4\,cx\,b+8\,c^2\,x^2-b^2}{x^{3/2}\sqrt{\dfrac{y}{x}}\,b^3}$$

```
>   simplify( ", assume=positive );
```

$$\frac{2}{3}\frac{4\,cx\,b+8\,c^2\,x^2-b^2}{x\,\sqrt{y}\,b^3}$$

```
>   expand(");
```

$$\frac{8}{3}\frac{c}{\sqrt{y}\,b^2}+\frac{16}{3}\frac{x\,c^2}{\sqrt{y}\,b^3}-\frac{2}{3}\frac{1}{x\,\sqrt{y}\,b}$$

```
>   collect( 3/2*", sqrt(y) );
```

$$\frac{4\dfrac{c}{b^2}+8\dfrac{x\,c^2}{b^3}-\dfrac{1}{x\,b}}{\sqrt{y}}$$

```
>   subs( y = b*x+c*x^2, 2/3*" );
```

$$\frac{2}{3}\frac{4\dfrac{c}{b^2}+8\dfrac{x\,c^2}{b^3}-\dfrac{1}{x\,b}}{\sqrt{b\,x+c\,x^2}}$$

The mistake in the tabulated result is an incorrect minus sign. In the fourth edition of Gradshteyn and Ryzhik [84] in 1980 this has been corrected. Anyway, the result in an integral table you can only believe or not; in Maple you can verify the result by differentiation.

```
>   simplify( diff(",x) - 1 / (x * sqrt(( b*x + c*x^2 )^3)),
>     assume=positive );
```

$$0$$

The second example is more intriguing: the tabulated result is wrong and Maple finds a more general answer.

```
>   Int( sin(a*x)^2 * sin(b*x)^2 *sin(2*c*x) / x,
>       x=0..infinity );
```

$$\int_0^\infty \frac{\sin(a\,x)^2\,\sin(b\,x)^2\,\sin(2\,c\,x)}{x}\,dx$$

```
>   value(");
```

$$\frac{1}{8}\operatorname{signum}(c)\,\pi+\frac{1}{32}\operatorname{signum}(2\,b+2\,c-2\,a)\,\pi$$

$$-\frac{1}{16}\operatorname{signum}(2\,c+2\,b)\,\pi+\frac{1}{32}\operatorname{signum}(-2\,b+2\,c-2\,a)\,\pi$$

$$-\frac{1}{16}\,\mathrm{signum}(\,2\,c-2\,b\,)\,\pi-\frac{1}{16}\,\mathrm{signum}(\,2\,c+2\,a\,)\,\pi$$

$$-\frac{1}{16}\,\mathrm{signum}(\,2\,c-2\,a\,)\,\pi+\frac{1}{32}\,\mathrm{signum}(\,2\,b+2\,c+2\,a\,)\,\pi$$

$$+\frac{1}{32}\,\mathrm{signum}(-2\,b+2\,c+2\,a\,)\,\pi$$

Here, Maple gives the solution for general a, b, and c. You can specialize to the case of positive variables, which is the only case tabulated in [84].

> simplify(", assume=positive); # all variables > 0

$$\frac{1}{32}\,\pi+\frac{1}{32}\,\mathrm{signum}(\,2\,b+2\,c-2\,a\,)\,\pi+\frac{1}{32}\,\mathrm{signum}(-2\,b+2\,c-2\,a\,)\,\pi$$

$$-\frac{1}{16}\,\mathrm{signum}(\,2\,c-2\,b\,)\,\pi-\frac{1}{16}\,\mathrm{signum}(\,2\,c-2\,a\,)\,\pi$$

$$+\frac{1}{32}\,\mathrm{signum}(-2\,b+2\,c+2\,a\,)\,\pi$$

Let us get rid of the 2's in the signs and factorize.

> factor(subs(signum = (signum @ primpart), "));

$$-\frac{1}{32}\,\pi(-1-\mathrm{signum}(\,b+c-a\,)-\mathrm{signum}(-b+c-a\,)+2\,\mathrm{signum}(\,c-b\,)$$

$$+2\,\mathrm{signum}(\,c-a\,)-\mathrm{signum}(-b+c+a\,))$$

So, a constant was wrong and a term was missing in the tabulated result.

In many cases of integration, conditions on parameters are important to obtain an exact result. Below is the example of the definite integral

$$\int_0^\infty \frac{t^{1/3}\ln(at)}{(b+2t^2)^2}\,dx,\quad a,b>0.$$

> # assume that a and b are positive numbers
> assume(a>0, b>0):
> normal(integrate(t^(1/3) * ln(a*t) / (b + 2*t^2)^2,
>   t = 0..infinity));

$$\frac{1}{36}\,\frac{\pi\,2^{1/3}\,(\,2\ln(\,a^{\tilde{}}\,)\sqrt{3}+\pi-3\sqrt{3}-\sqrt{3}\ln(\,2\,)+\sqrt{3}\ln(\,b^{\tilde{}}\,))}{b^{\tilde{}-4/3}}$$

The tildes after a and b in the above result indicate that these variables have certain assumed properties. Maple can inform its user about these properties.

> about(a);

```
Originally a, renamed a~:
  is assumed to be: RealRange(Open(0),infinity)
```

Integration is also a good illustration of another advantage of computer algebra: it provides easy access to advanced mathematical techniques and algorithms. When input in Maple, the following two integrals

$$\int x^2 \exp(x^3)\, dx \quad \text{and} \quad \int x \exp(x^3)\, dx$$

give different kinds of response:

$$\frac{1}{3} \exp(x^3) \quad \text{and} \quad \int x \exp(x^3)\, dx.$$

This means more than just the system's incompetence to deal with the latter integral. Maple can decide, via the Risch algorithm [76], that for this integral no closed form in terms of elementary functions exists. This contrasts with the heuristic methods usually applied when one tries to find an answer in closed form. In the heuristic approach one is never sure whether indeed no closed form exists or that it is just one's mathematical incompetence. The Risch algorithm, however, is a complicated algorithm that is based on rather deep mathematical results and algorithms and that involves many steps that cannot be done so easily by pencil and paper. Computer algebra enables its user to apply such advanced mathematical results and methods without knowing all details.

Using a computer algebra system, one can concentrate on the analysis of a mathematical problem, leaving the computational details to the computer. Computer algebra systems also invite one to do "mathematical experiments." They make it easy to test mathematical conjectures and to propose new ones on the basis of calculations (q.v., [15, 130]). As an example of such a mathematical experiment, we shall conjecture a formula for the determinant of the $n \times n$ matrix A_n defined by

$$A_n(i, j) := x^{\gcd(i,j)}.$$

The first thing to do is to compute a few determinants, and look and see.

```
>   numex := 8:    # number of experiments
>   dets := array( 1..numex ):
>   for n to numex do
>     A[n] := array( 1..n, 1..n, symmetric ):
>     for i to n do
>       for j to i do
>         A[n][i,j] := x^igcd(i,j)
>     od od:
>     dets[n] := factor( linalg[det]( A[n] ) ):
>     print( dets[n] )
>   od:
```

$$x$$
$$x^2 \, (\, x - 1 \,)$$
$$x^3 \, (\, x + 1 \,) \, (\, x - 1 \,)^2$$
$$x^5 \, (\, x + 1 \,)^2 \, (\, x - 1 \,)^3$$
$$x^6 \, (\, x^2 + 1 \,) \, (\, x + 1 \,)^3 \, (\, x - 1 \,)^4$$
$$x^7 \, (\, x^2 + 1 \,) \, (\, x^3 + x - 1 \,) \, (\, x + 1 \,)^4 \, (\, x - 1 \,)^5$$
$$x^8 \, (\, x^2 + x + 1 \,) \, (\, x^2 - x + 1 \,) \, (\, x^2 + 1 \,) \, (\, x^3 + x - 1 \,) \, (\, x + 1 \,)^5 \, (\, x - 1 \,)^6$$
$$x^{12} \, (\, x^2 + x + 1 \,) \, (\, x^2 - x + 1 \,) \, (\, x^3 + x - 1 \,) \, (\, x^2 + 1 \,)^2 \, (\, x + 1 \,)^6 \, (\, x - 1 \,)^7$$

At first sight, it has not been a success. But, look at the quotients of successive determinants.

```
>   for i from 2 to numex do
>     quo( dets[i], dets[i-1], x )
>   od;
```

$$x^2 - x$$
$$x^3 - x$$
$$x^4 - x^2$$
$$x^5 - x$$
$$x^6 - x^3 - x^2 + x$$
$$x^7 - x$$
$$x^8 - x^4$$

In the nth polynomial only powers of x appear that have divisors of n as exponents. Thinking of Möbius-like formulae and playing a little more with Maple, the following conjecture comes readily to mind.

Conjecture. $\det A_n = \displaystyle\prod_{j=1}^{n} \phi_j(x)$, where the polynomials $\phi_j(x)$ are defined by $x^n = \displaystyle\sum_{d|n} \phi_d(x)$.

Some Properties.

(i) If p is a prime number, then

$$\phi_p(x) = x^p - x,$$

and for any natural number r,

$$\phi_{p^r}(x) = \phi_p(x^{p^{r-1}}).$$

(ii) If p is a prime number, not dividing n, then

$$\phi_{pn}(x) = \phi_n(x^p) - \phi_n(x).$$

(iii) Let $n = p_1^{r_1} \ldots p_s^{r_s}$ be a natural number with its prime factorization, then

$$\phi_n(x) = \phi_{p_1 \ldots p_s}(x^{p_1^{r_1-1} \cdots p_s^{r_s-1}}).$$

(iv) We have

$$\phi_n(x) = \sum_{d|n} \mu\left(\frac{n}{d}\right) x^d = \sum_{d|n} \mu(d) x^{\left(\frac{n}{d}\right)},$$

where μ is the Möbius function such that $\mu(1) = 1$, $\mu(p_1 \ldots p_s) = (-1)^s$ if $p_1, \ldots, p_s$ are distinct primes, and $\mu(m) = 0$ if m is divisible by the square of some prime number.

For the interested reader: $\frac{1}{d}\phi_d(q)$ is equal to the number of monic irreducible polynomials of degree d in one variable and with coefficients in a finite field with q elements [138].

However much mathematical knowledge has been included in a computer algebra system, it is still important that an experienced user can enhance the system by writing procedures for personal interest. The author implemented in Maple several algorithms for inversion of polynomial mappings according to the methods developed in [59]. With these programs it is possible to determine whether a polynomial mapping has an inverse that is itself a polynomial mapping, and if so, to compute the inverse. We show an example of an invertible mapping in three unknowns.

```
>   read `invpol.m`; # load user-defined package
>   P := [ x^4 + 2*(y+z)*x^3 + (y+z)^2*x^2 + (y+1)*x
>       + y^2 + y*z, x^3 + (y+z)*x^2 + y, x + y + z ];
```

$$P := [x^4 + 2\,(y+z)\,x^3 + (y+z)^2\,x^2 + (y+1)\,x + y^2 + y\,z,$$
$$x^3 + (y+z)\,x^2 + y, x + y + z]$$

```
>   settime := time(): # start timing
>   invpol( P, [x,y,z] ); # compute inverse mapping
```

$$[x - y\,z, y - x^2\,z + 2\,z^2\,y\,x - z^3\,y^2, -x - y + z + y\,z + x^2\,z - 2\,z^2\,y\,x + z^3\,y^2]$$

```
>   cpu_time = (time()-settime) * seconds; # computing time
```

$$cpu\_time = .833\ seconds$$

Computing the inverse of a polynomial mapping with pencil and paper is almost impossible; one needs a computer algebra system for the symbol crunching. However, one cannot expect designers of computer algebra systems to anticipate all of the needs of their users. One can expect them to provide users with good programming facilities to implement new algorithms.

1.5   Limitations of Computer Algebra

What has been said about computer algebra systems so far may have given the impression that these systems offer unlimited opportunities, and that they are a universal remedy for solving mathematical problems. But this impression is too rosy. A few warnings beforehand are not out of place.

Computer algebra systems often make great demands on computers because of their tendency to use up much memory space and computing time. The price one pays for exact arithmetic is often the exponential increase in size of expressions and the appearance of huge numbers. This may even happen in cases where the final answer is simply "yes" or "no." For example, it is well known that Euclid's algorithm yields the greatest common divisor (gcd) of two polynomials. However, this "naive" algorithm does not perform very well. Look at the polynomials

```
> f[1]  := 7*x^7 + 2*x^6 - 3*x^5 - 3*x^3 + x + 5;
```
$$f_1 := 7\,x^7 + 2\,x^6 - 3\,x^5 - 3\,x^3 + x + 5$$

```
> f[2]  := 9*x^5 - 3*x^4 - 4*x^2 + 7*x + 7;
```
$$f_2 := 9\,x^5 - 3\,x^4 - 4\,x^2 + 7\,x + 7$$

We want to compute the gcd(f_1, f_2) over the rational number by Euclid's algorithm. In the first division step we construct polynomials q_2 and f_3, such that $f_1 = q_2 f_2 + f_3$, where degree$(f_3) <$ degree(f_2) or $f_3 = 0$. This is done by long division.

```
> f[3]  := sort( rem( f[1], f[2], x, q[2] ) );
```
$$f_3 := \frac{70}{27}x^4 - \frac{176}{27}x^3 - \frac{770}{81}x^2 - \frac{94}{81}x + \frac{503}{81}$$

```
> q[2];
```
$$\frac{7}{9}x^2 + \frac{13}{27}x - \frac{14}{81}$$

Next, polynomial q_3 and f_4 are computed such that $f_2 = q_3 f_3 + f_4$, where degree$(f_4) <$ degree(f_3) or $f_3 = 0$, etc. until $f_n = 0$; then gcd$(f_1, f_2) = f_{n-1}$. The following Maple program computes the polynomial remainder sequence.

```
> Euclid_gcd := proc( f::polynom, g::polynom, x::name )
>    local r:
>    if g = 0 then   sort( f )
>    else
>       r := sort( rem( f, g, x ) );
>       if r <> 0 then print( r ) fi;
>          Euclid_gcd( g, r, x )
>    fi
> end:
> Euclid_gcd( f[1], f[2], x ):
```
$$\frac{70}{27}x^4 - \frac{176}{27}x^3 - \frac{770}{81}x^2 - \frac{94}{81}x + \frac{503}{81}$$

$$\frac{100881}{1225}x^3 + 72\,x^2 - \frac{14139}{2450}x - \frac{98037}{2450}$$

$$-\frac{16726864175}{10176976161}x^2 - \frac{5255280625}{10176976161}x + \frac{19754564375}{10176976161}$$

$$\frac{35171085032244648729}{456796710414528050}x + \frac{6605604895087335357}{456796710414528050}$$

$$\frac{240681431042721245661011901925}{121549387831506345564025862481}$$

The conclusion is that the polynomials f_1 and f_2 are relatively prime, because their greatest common divisor is a unit. But look at the tremendous growth in the size of the coefficients from 1-digit integers to rational numbers with 30 digits (even though the rational coefficients are always simplified). In [76, 117] one can read about more sophisticated algorithms for gcd computations that avoid blowup of coefficients as much as possible.

The phenomenon of tremendous growth of expressions in intermediate calculations turns up frequently in computer algebra calculations and is known as *intermediate expression swell*. Although it is usually difficult to estimate the computer time and memory space required for a computation, one should always do one's very best to optimize calculations, both by using good mathematical models and by efficient programming. It is worth the effort. For example, Maple computes the inverse of the 8×8 matrix with (i, j)-entry equal to $(iu + x + y + z)^j$ in 1,125 seconds requiring 3,900 Kbytes of memory space on a SUN SPARCstation 20 M71. The obvious substitution $x + y + z \to v$ reduces the computer time to 6 seconds and the memory requirements to 750 Kbytes.

A second problem in using a computer algebra system is psychological: how many lines of computer output can one grasp? And when one is faced with large expressions, how can one get enough insight to simplify them? For example, merely watching the computer screen it would be difficult to recover the polynomial composition

$$f(x, y) = g\big(u(x, y),\ v(x, y)\big),$$

where

$$\begin{aligned}
g(u, v) &= u^3 v + u v^2 + u v + 5, \\
u(x, y) &= x^3 y + x y^2 + x^2 + y + 1, \\
v(x, y) &= y^3 + x^2 y + x,
\end{aligned}$$

from its expanded form.

While it is true that one can do numerical computations with a computer algebra system in any precision one likes, there is also a negative side of this feature. Because one uses software floating-point arithmetic instead of hardware arithmetic, numerical computation with a computer algebra system is 100 to 1,000 times slower than numerical computation in a programming language like FORTRAN. Hence, for numerical problems, one must always ask oneself, "Is exact arithmetic with rational numbers or high-precision floating-point arithmetic really needed, or is a numerical programming language preferable?"

In an enthusiastic mood we characterized computer algebra systems as mathematical expert systems. How impressive the amount of built-in mathematical knowledge may be, it is only a small fraction of mathematics known today. There are many mathematical areas where computer algebra is not of much help yet, and where more research is required: partial differential equations, indefinite and definite integration involving nonelementary functions like Bessel functions, contour integration, surface integration, calculus of special functions, and noncommutative algebra are just a few examples.

Another serious problem, and perhaps the trickiest, is the wish to specify at an abstract level the number domain in which one wants to calculate. For example, there are an infinite number of fields, and one may want to write algorithms in a computer algebra system using the arithmetic operations of a field, without the need to say what particular field you work with. Moreover, one may want to define one's own mathematical structures. Scratchpad II/AXIOM [54, 55, 108, 109, 179] is the first computer algebra system making steps in this direction. In Maple V, the Gauss package allows its user to create domains in a similar way as AXIOM does.

As far as the syntax and the semantics are concerned, the use of a computer algebra system as a programming language is more complicated than programming in a numerical language like FORTRAN. In a computer algebra system one is faced with many built-in functions that may lead to unexpected results. One must have an idea of how the system works, how data are represented, how to keep data of manageable size, and so on. Efficiency of algorithms, with respect to both computing time and memory space, requires a thorough analysis of mathematical problems and a careful implementation of algorithms. For example, if we had forgotten to expand intermediate results in the procedure for calculating Bessel polynomials as defined in §1.3, it would have resulted in unnecessarily large expressions. The rather unsuccessful implementation of $\mathbf{Y}$ would compute $Y_5(z)$ as follows

```
> Y := proc( n::nonnegint, x::name )
>    if n=0 then 1
>    elif n = 1 then x+1
>    else Y(n,x) := (2*n-1)*x*Y(n-1,x) + Y(n-2,x)
>    fi
> end:
> Y(5,z);
```

$$9 z (7 z (5 z (3 z (z + 1) + 1) + z + 1) + 3 z (z + 1) + 1)$$
$$+ 5 z (3 z (z + 1) + 1) + z + 1$$

Familiarity with the basic features of a computer algebra system, such as elementary data structures and built-in facilities, makes it easier to program efficiently and to foresee some of the many pitfalls in symbolical computation. A good understanding of the computer algebra systems that one has at one's disposal is also prerequisite to making the right choice for the system to use when studying a particular problem. For example, the formula manipulation system FORM [184] is better suited than Maple for doing computations in most noncommutative algebras because, in this system, noncommutative objects are of basic type and pattern matching is an amply supported basic operation. See [46] for a comparison of Maple and FORM in computing with quaternions.

Finally, we mention the technical difficulties in using computer algebra systems. Sometimes input and output formats and the reuse of expressions are confusing and too far removed from standard mathematical notation. In comparison to global manipulations, local manipulations in formulae are often difficult to carry out. Interfaces with other programming languages are frequently absent or inadequate. And last but not least, bugs are a major issue. See [175] for an entertaining discussion on this issue. It is hoped that some of these remarks will soon be outdated. But systems like Maple will always surprise you, for the good or the bad. We end this section with two surprising results in Maple calculations where you have to assist the system a bit.

The first example: an easy integral that can be done without using a computer algebra system.

```
>   Int( 2*x*(x^2+1)^24, x );
```

$$\int 2 x (x^2 + 1)^{24} \, dx$$

The answer is clear, but what does Maple give?

```
>   value(");
```

$$12 x^4 + x^2 + 506 x^8 + 92 x^6 + 7084 x^{12} + 81719 x^{18} + 19228 x^{14}$$
$$+ \frac{653752}{5} x^{20} + 43263 x^{16} + \frac{10626}{5} x^{10} + 92 x^{44} + 12 x^{46}$$
$$+ \frac{10626}{5} x^{40} + 19228 x^{36} + \frac{1}{25} x^{50} + 81719 x^{32} + 43263 x^{34} + x^{48}$$
$$+ 506 x^{42} + \frac{653752}{5} x^{30} + 178296 x^{28} + 208012 x^{26} + 7084 x^{38}$$
$$+ 208012 x^{24} + 178296 x^{22}$$

Surprise! You may think that factorization helps.

```
>   factor(");
```

$$\frac{1}{25}x^2 \left(x^8 + 5x^6 + 10x^4 + 10x^2 + 5 \right)\left(x^{40} + 20x^{38} + 190x^{36} + 1140x^{34} \right.$$
$$+ 4845x^{32} + 15505x^{30} + 38775x^{28} + 77625x^{26} + 126425x^{24}$$
$$+ 169325x^{22} + 187760x^{20} + 172975x^{18} + 132450x^{16} + 84075x^{14}$$
$$\left. + 43975x^{12} + 18760x^{10} + 6425x^8 + 1725x^6 + 350x^4 + 50x^2 + 5 \right)$$

The problem is, as you may have guessed, in the choice of the integration constant.

```
>   factor( " + 1/25 );
```

$$\frac{1}{25} \left(x^2 + 1 \right)^{25}$$

You are expecting too much if you think that such problems can always be avoided.

The second example comes from a study in optics [14] and is about integrating expressions consisting only of terms

$$x^n \sin^i x \cos^j x \cosh^k x \sinh^l x,$$

where $i, j, k, l, n \in \mathbb{N}$. It can easily be shown that any such integral can be expressed completely in the same kind of terms. An example of what Maple does:

```
>   Int( x * sin(x)^2 * cos(x) * sinh(x)^2 * cosh(x), x );
```

$$\int x \sin(x)^2 \cos(x) \sinh(x)^2 \cosh(x) \, dx$$

```
>   value(");
```

$$\frac{1}{32}\left(\frac{3}{10}x - \frac{2}{25} \right) e^{(3x)} \cos(x) - \frac{1}{32}\left(-\frac{1}{10}x + \frac{3}{50} \right) e^{(3x)} \sin(x)$$

$$-\frac{1}{192}x\,e^{(3x)} \cos(3x) + \frac{1}{32}\left(-\frac{1}{6}x + \frac{1}{18} \right) e^{(3x)} \sin(3x)$$

$$-\frac{1}{64}x\,e^{x} \cos(x) + \frac{1}{32}\left(-\frac{1}{2}x + \frac{1}{2} \right) e^{x} \sin(x)$$

$$+\frac{1}{32}\left(\frac{1}{10}x + \frac{2}{25} \right) e^{x} \cos(3x) - \frac{1}{32}\left(-\frac{3}{10}x + \frac{3}{50} \right) e^{x} \sin(3x)$$

$$+\frac{1}{64}x\,e^{(-x)} \cos(x) + \frac{1}{32}\left(-\frac{1}{2}x - \frac{1}{2} \right) e^{(-x)} \sin(x)$$

$$+\frac{1}{32}\left(-\frac{1}{10}x + \frac{2}{25} \right) e^{(-x)} \cos(3x)$$

$$-\frac{1}{32}\left(-\frac{3}{10}x - \frac{3}{50} \right) e^{(-x)} \sin(3x)$$

$$+ \frac{1}{32} \left(-\frac{3}{10} x - \frac{2}{25} \right) e^{(-3x)} \cos(x)$$

$$- \frac{1}{32} \left(-\frac{1}{10} x - \frac{3}{50} \right) e^{(-3x)} \sin(x) + \frac{1}{192} x\, e^{(-3x)} \cos(3x)$$

$$+ \frac{1}{32} \left(-\frac{1}{6} x - \frac{1}{18} \right) e^{(-3x)} \sin(3x)$$

To get the formula in the requested form you have to write the exponentials in terms of hyperbolic sines and cosines and work out the intermediate expression.

```
>   convert( ", ´trig´ ):  # exp -> trigonometric function
>   expand(");
```

$$\frac{1}{15} x \sinh(x) \cos(x)^3 - \frac{1}{10} \cos(x) x \sinh(x) - \frac{1}{50} \cos(x) \cosh(x)^3$$

$$+ \frac{1}{5} \cos(x) x \sinh(x) \cosh(x)^2 + \frac{1}{15} \sin(x) x \cosh(x)^3$$

$$- \frac{1}{10} \sin(x) x \cosh(x) - \frac{13}{450} \sinh(x) \sin(x) \cos(x)^2$$

$$- \frac{13}{450} \sin(x) \sinh(x) \cosh(x)^2 - \frac{1}{6} x \sinh(x) \cosh(x)^2 \cos(x)^3$$

$$+ \frac{1}{50} \cosh(x) \cos(x)^3 - \frac{1}{6} x \cosh(x)^3 \sin(x) \cos(x)^2$$

$$+ \frac{1}{5} x \cosh(x) \sin(x) \cos(x)^2 + \frac{1}{18} \sinh(x) \cosh(x)^2 \sin(x) \cos(x)^2$$

$$+ \frac{19}{450} \sin(x) \sinh(x)$$

The final step might be to combine the command into a procedure for further usage

```
>   trigint := proc()
>       int(args);
>       convert(", ´trig´);
>       expand(")
>   end:
>   trigint( x*sin(x)^2*cos(x)^3, x );
```

$$\frac{1}{15} x \sin(x) \cos(x)^2 + \frac{2}{15} x \sin(x) + \frac{1}{45} \cos(x)^3 + \frac{2}{15} \cos(x)$$

$$- \frac{1}{5} x \cos(x)^4 \sin(x) - \frac{1}{25} \cos(x)^5$$

```
>   trigint( x*sin(x)*cos(x)^2, x=0..Pi );
```

$$\frac{1}{3} \pi$$

This kind of adapting Maple to one's needs happens fairly often. Therefore, this book contains many examples of how to assist the system. Some of them are of a rather sophisticated level. They have been added because merely explaining Maple commands and showing elementary examples does not make you proficient enough at the system for when it comes to real work.

1.6   Design of Maple

The name Maple is not an acronym of **ma**thematical **ple**asure — great fun as it is to use a computer algebra system — but was chosen to draw attention to its Canadian origin. Since November 1980 a lot of work has gone into the development of the Maple system by the Symbolic Computation Group of the University of Waterloo and at ETH Zürich. Since 1992 it has been further developed and marketed by Waterloo Maple Software (since October 1995, Waterloo Maple Inc.) in collaboration with the original developers.

Maple is a computer algebra system open to the public and fit to run on a variety of computers, from a supercomputer like the Cray Y/MP down to desktop computers like Macintosh and IBM PCs or compatibles. The user accessibility shows up best on a mainframe with a time-sharing operating system, where several users of Maple can work simultaneously without being a nuisance to each other or other software users, and without excessive load put on the computer. This is possible because of the modular design of Maple. It consists of four parts: the user interface called the *Iris*, the basic algebraic engine or *kernel*, the external *library*, and the so-called *share library* with contributions of Maple users.

The Iris and the kernel form the smaller part of the system, which has been written in the programming language C; they are loaded when a Maple session is started. The Iris handles input of mathematical expressions (parsing and notification of errors), display of expressions ("prettyprinting"), plotting of functions, and support of other user communication with the system. There are special interfaces called *worksheets* for the X Window System (under Motif), VMS, Amiga, Macintosh, NeXT, and MS-Windows.

In a Maple worksheet you can combine Maple input and output, graphics, and text in one document. See Figure 1.3 (taken from a Maple brochure) for a typical example. Further features of the Maple worksheet interface are that it provides hypertext facilities inside and between documents, allows embedding of multimedia objects (on some platforms), and uses typeset mathematics, and subexpressions of mathematical output can be selected for further processing. A Maple worksheet consists of a hierarchy of regions. Regions can be grouped into sections and subsections. Sections and subsections can be "closed" to hide regions inside. A Maple worksheet can be exported in text or LaTeX format. You are referred to the Maple documentation [187, 188] for precise details about the worksheet interface.

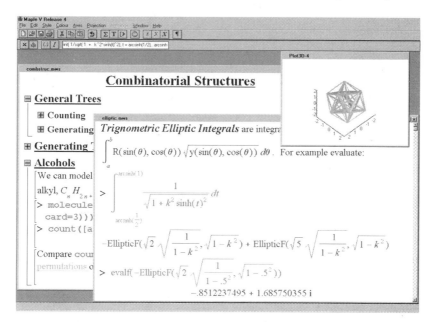

FIGURE 1.3. Example of Maple window with multiple worksheets.

The Maple kernel interprets the user input and carries out the basic algebraic operations such as rational arithmetic and elementary polynomial arithmetic. It also contains certain algebraic routines that are so often used that they must be present in the lower-level systems language, for efficiency reasons. To the latter category belong routines for manipulation of polynomials like **degree**, **coeff**, and **expand**. The kernel also deals with storage management. A very important feature of Maple is that the system keeps only one copy of each expression or subexpression within an entire session. In this way testing for equality of expressions is an extremely inexpensive operation, viz., one machine instruction. Subexpressions are reused instead of being recomputed over and over again.

Most of the mathematical knowledge of Maple has been coded in the Maple programming language and resides as functions in the external library. When a user needs a library function, Maple is in most cases smart enough to load the routine itself. Only infrequently used Maple procedures must be loaded explicitly by the user. Maple must also be informed about the use of separate packages like the linear algebra, number theory, and statistics packages, to name a few. This makes Maple a compact, easy-to-use system. But what is more important, in this setting Maple uses memory space only for essential things and not for facilities in which a user is not interested. This is why many people can use Maple on one computer simultaneously, and why Maple runs on computers with little memory.

Table 1.1 summarizes the design of the Maple system as just described.

Part	Function
Iris	parser display of expressions ("prettyprinting") graphics special user interfaces: worksheet version for X11 (Motif), Macintosh, NeXT, MS-Windows, etc.
Kernel	interpreter memory management basic & time-critical procedures for computations in $\mathbb{Z}$, $\mathbb{Q}$, $\mathbb{R}$, $\mathbb{C}$, $\mathbb{Z}_n$, $\mathbb{Q}[x]$, etc.
Library	library functions application packages on-line help
Share Library	contributions of Maple users

TABLE 1.1. Components of the Maple system.

The Maple language is a well-structured, comprehensible, high-level programming language. It supports a large collection of data structures: functions, sequences, sets, lists, arrays, tables, etc. There are also plenty of easy-to-use operations on these data structures like type-testing, selection and composition of data structures, and so on. These are the ingredients of the programming language in which almost all mathematical algorithms of Maple are implemented, and which is the same language users will employ in interactive calculator mode. Furthermore, anyone who is interested in the algorithms that Maple uses and in the way these algorithms are implemented can look at the Maple code in the library; the procedures are available in readable form or can be reproduced as such inside a Maple session. If desired, a user can enlarge the library with self-written programs and packages. The Maple share library, which can be accessed at the WWW server of Waterloo Maple Inc. (URL: http://www.maplesoft.com) among other locations, contains many user contributions, sample worksheets, documentation, and bug fixes for older versions of Maple. Maple also provides its users with facilities to keep track of the execution of programs, whether self-made or not.

The last advantage of Maple we shall mention is its user-friendly design. Many computer algebra systems require a long apprenticeship or knowledge of a low-level systems language if one really wants to understand what is going on in computations. In many systems one has to leaf through the manual to find the right settings of programming flags and keywords. Nothing of the kind in Maple. First, there is the help facility, which is basically the on-line manual for Maple procedures. Second, the secret to why Maple is so easy to use is the hybrid algorithmic structure of the computer algebra system, where the system itself can decide which algorithm is favorable. As an example we look at some invocations of the Maple procedure **simplify**, which does what its name suggests.

```
>   trig_formula := cos(x)^6 + sin(x)^6
>     + 3*sin(x)^2*cos(x)^2:
>   exp_ln_formula := exp( a +1/2*ln(b) ):
>   radical_formula := (x-2)^(3/2) / (x^2-4*x+4)^(1/4):
>   trig_formula = simplify( trig_formula );
```
$$\cos(x)^6 + \sin(x)^6 + 3 \sin(x)^2 \cos(x)^2 = 1$$

```
>   exp_ln_formula = simplify( exp_ln_formula );
```
$$e^{(a+1/2 \ln(b))} = e^a \sqrt{b}$$

```
>   radical_formula = simplify( radical_formula );
```
$$\frac{(x - 2)^{3/2}}{(x^2 - 4 x + 4)^{1/4}} = \frac{(x - 2)^{3/2}}{((x - 2)^2)^{1/4}}$$

Here, Maple does not assume that $x \geq 2$ and cannot simplify the square root. The generic simplification of the square root can be forced by adding the keyword **symbolic**.

```
>   radical_formula = simplify( radical_formula, symbolic );
```
$$\frac{(x - 2)^{3/2}}{(x^2 - 4 x + 4)^{1/4}} = x - 2$$

But the key point is that just one procedure, viz., **simplify**, carries out distinct types of simplifications: trigonometric simplification, simplification of logarithms and exponential functions, and simplification of powers with rational exponentials. On the other hand, the concept of pattern matching and transformation rules (rewrite rules) is currently underdeveloped in Maple. It is difficult in Maple to program mathematical transformations that can be applied globally.

At many places Maple makes decisions about which way to go; we mention four examples. Computation of the determinant of a matrix is done by the method of minor expansion for a small matrix, otherwise Gaussian elimination is used. Maple has essentially three numerical methods at its disposal to compute definite integrals over a finite interval: the default integration method is Clenshaw-Curtis quadrature, but when convergence is slow (due to nearby singularities) the system tries to remove the singularities or switches to an adaptive double-exponential quadrature method. An adaptive Newton-Cotes method is available when low precision (e.g., Digits $\leq$ 15) suffices. By the way, generalized series expansions and variable transformations are two of the techniques used in the Maple procedure

evalf/int to deal with singularities in an analytic integrand. The interested reader is referred to [71, 75]. At present, there are six algorithms coded into the Maple procedure **fsolve**: Newton, Secant, Dichotomic, inverse parabolic interpolation, a method based on approximating the Jacobian (for systems), and a method of partial substitutions (for systems again). As a user of Maple you normally do not need to know about or act on these details; the system finds its own way. This approach turns Maple into an easy-to-learn and easy-to-use system for mathematical computations on computers.

2

The First Steps: Calculus on Numbers

This chapter covers some of the basics needed to start using Maple, to access the on-line help, and to compute with numbers. A discussion at length of how to interact with Maple will follow in Chapter 4. During the overview of the number fields that are supported by Maple, we shall also introduce you gently to the way Maple stores data internally.

We assume that Maple V Release 4 is used in combination with the worksheet interface under the X Window System. Henceforth, all computations will be done on a SUN SPARCstation 20 M71 running SunOS 4.1.3, with a 75-Mhz Super SPARC II processor, and having 64-MB main memory plus 128-MB swap space. Most of this book applies equally well to other computers and/or operating systems, but there may be implementation differences in areas like starting, interrupting, and quitting Maple, reading and writing of files, and plotting. For system specific aspects you should read the documentation that came with your software. We also assume that you know how to log onto the computer and are using a workstation or X terminal.

2.1 Getting Started

To start Maple with the worksheet interface, type **xmaple** from a Unix shell. Look for local assistance and documentation if this does not work. When Maple has been launched successfully with the worksheet interface, the Maple window appears and the system indicates with a *prompt*, such as the greater-than symbol, ">", in a worksheet document that it is waiting for a command. A series of commands may already have been executed automatically from an initialization file, e.g., from the file .mapleinit in your home directory and/or from the file init in the src subdirectory of the Maple library. Now you can use Maple as an ordinary pocket calculator.

```
>   2 + 100 / 5^2 * 3 ;
```

$$14$$

```
>   5! / 21 ;
```

$$\frac{40}{7}$$

All arithmetic operations that you are familiar with are present: addition (+), multiplication (∗), division (/), exponentiation (^ or ∗∗), **factorial** (!), and double factorial (!!). The usual precedence rules apply, and in doubtful cases, or just for the sake of clarity, you may use parentheses. But there are a few differences in the input mode when using Maple as a pocket calculator:

- Each command must be terminated by a semicolon or a colon. Don't forget these punctuation marks, otherwise the system will sit waiting for more input. Termination by a semicolon informs Maple that input is complete, causes the instruction to be carried out by the system, and displays the result. A colon can be used instead of a semicolon if the output on the screen can be suppressed. This is convenient when you are interested in computing an intermediate result but do not need to look at it. The process of carrying out an instruction is called *evaluation*.

- Maple only deals with an input line when the *newline* character, which is either the carriage return or the *line feed* character, is sent by pressing the RETURN or ENTER key, respectively. After the evaluation of the command Maple prints a prompt at the beginning of a new line, again indicating that it is waiting for input.

The Maple input mode and particularly the roles of the semicolon and the colon are exemplified below.

```
>   2*5;  2^5:  100/4;   100
>                          /6
>   ;
```

$$10$$

$$25$$

$$50$$
$$\frac{50}{3}$$

```
>   12345\
>   6789;
```

$$123456789$$

As you see, more than one instruction may be entered in one line. Maple deals with them one by one, as if they were given separately. To enhance readability you may stretch a command across several lines and you may insert spaces. But be careful, this is not allowed everywhere. For example, you cannot type the number 1000000 as 1 000 000; but you may group the digits into groups of three by typing 1\000\000. The *backslash* is used in Maple as the *continuation* character, which is ignored. When you stretch a command across two or more lines, Maple warns you that it got an incomplete statement or that a semicolon is missing. Maple splits the parts of the command by newline characters, unless you end a line with the backslash; in this case both backslash and newline character are ignored in the final result.

If Maple does not understand your input because of syntactical errors, it will tell you so.

```
>   this is a line Maple does not understand;
syntax error, missing operator or `;`
```

In the worksheet interface, the cursor will blink at the token that was being read when the error occurred. Maple does not say anything more. You must find out yourself what went wrong; Maple just waits for a correction of the input. In the worksheet interface, you can correct or extend input by placing the cursor on the input line and then making all necessary changes and/or additions. The text interface of Maple, which is launched by entering **maple** from a Unix shell, has both a vi- and emacs-like command line editor available that allows you to edit up to 100 previously entered input lines.

You quit Maple by successively clicking on the File and Exit menu items; the system will ask you to confirm this action. Alternatively, you press the corresponding acceleration keys. You can immediately leave Maple by entering the command **quit**, **stop**, or **done**, followed by the newline character.

You can interrupt a lengthy Maple calculation that is in progress by clicking on the Stop button in the tool bar of the Maple window so that the system receives the *interrupt* character (usually CONTROL-C). It is not always possible to stop computation instantly, but after the interrupt is recognized you may enter another command.

Inside Maple you can always start afresh by entering **restart**.

```
>   restart;
```

This statement will clear Maple's internal memory and reread the initialization file(s) so that it acts as if you had started Maple from scratch. Only the current setting of the interface variables is maintained.

2.2   Getting Help

When you click on the [Help] button of a Maple worksheet, you get a menu of available help facilities. A good starting point is the index of help descriptions. You select it by clicking on [Contents] or by entering a C. Figure 2.1 is a screen dump of the index of help descriptions. By clicking on <u>function</u> you follow the hyperlink to the index of descriptions for standard library functions.

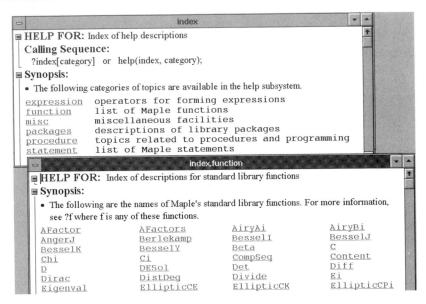

FIGURE 2.1. The index of help descriptions together with the index of descriptions for standard library functions.

You can click on any function for further information, for example, about the dilogarithm. The help window with the actual information on how to use this function is shown in Figure 2.2 on the next page. The same help window appears when you enter

>   ?dilog

The advantage of the index of descriptions for standard functions is that it allows you to explore or to find your way through Maple without browsing through the Maple Handbook [160]. The ?<*topic*> command-line syntax is a faster way of getting information when you know what command you are looking for and only want to refresh your knowledge or look at an example.

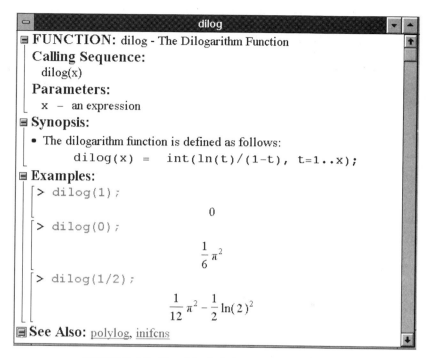

FIGURE 2.2. The Maple help window for `dilog`.

As a more concrete example of available on-line help, let us ask for help about integer factorization.

```
>   ?ifactor
```

The corresponding help message is a clear illustration of the general format of Maple's descriptions of syntax, data types, and functions. Below, we have split the contents of the help window accordingly and at the same time demonstrate how to extract these parts from the help page in a Maple session.

```
>   info( ifactor );

FUNCTION: ifactor - integer factorization

CALLING SEQUENCE:
    ifactor(n)
    ifactor(n, method)

PARAMETERS:
    n        - integer or a rational
    method - (optional) name of base method for factoring
```

The procedure **ifactor** is explained first: what it is meant for and how you can use it. Obviously, you can factorize an integer with it, but the help text informs you that **ifactor** can also be used to factorize a rational number.

If you desire a particular factorization method, then you can specify this with an extra argument in the procedure call. Hereafter, the procedure and its options are described in more detail in the help file. However, there is no built-in procedure to extract the so-called SYNOPSIS part. But as you can see below, it is easy to extend the software by mimicking a comparable procedure.

```
> interface( verboseproc = 3 ): # enable printing of code
> print( usage ); # show example code
```

proc($x::\{indexed, string\}$)
    local $topic$;
    option '*Copyright 1995 by Waterloo Maple Software*';
    if type($x, string$) **then** $topic := x$
    else $topic := $ traperror(convert($x, string$))
    fi;
    print(INTERFACE_HELP('$display$', '$topic$' $= topic$, '$section$' $= $ '$usage$'))
end

In the same spirit we define the **synopsis** procedure and apply it to **ifactor**.

```
> synopsis := proc( x::{indexed,string} )
>    local topic;
>    if type(x,string) then topic := x
>    else topic := traperror( convert(x,string) )
>    fi;
>    print( INTERFACE_HELP(
>       'display', 'topic'=topic, 'section'='synopsis' ) )
> end:
> synopsis( ifactor );

SYNOPSIS:
- ifactor returns the complete integer factorization of n.

- The answer is in the form:
  u * ``(f1)^e1 * ... * ``(fn)^en such that
  n = u * f1^e1 * ... * fn^en where u equals
  sign(n), f1, ..., fn are the distinct prime factors of n,
  and e1, ..., en are their multiplicities (negative in
  the case of the denominator of a rational).

- The expand function may be applied to cause the factors
  to be multiplied together again.

- If a second parameter is specified, the named method
  will be used when the front-end code fails to achieve
  the factorization.  By default, the Morrison-Brillhart
  algorithm is used as the base method.  Currently
  accepted names are:
```

  `squfof`   – D. Shanks' undocumented square-free
             factorization;
  `pollard`   – J.M. Pollard's rho method;
  `lenstra`   – Lenstra's elliptic curve method; and
  `easy`   – which does no further work.

- If the `easy` option is chosen, the result of the
  ifactor call will be a product of the factors that
  were easy to compute, and a name _c.m indicating
  an m-digit composite number that was not factored.

- The pollard base method accepts an additional optional
  integer: ifactor(n,pollard,k), which increases the
  efficiency of the method when one of the factors is of
  the form k*m+1.

What follows in a help page are a few examples. In many cases you can
immediately learn from these examples how to do your work in Maple.

  >   example(ifactor);

EXAMPLES:
> ifactor(61);

                              (61)
> ifactor(60);

                               2
                            (2) (3) (5)
> ifactor(-144);

                               4   2
                          - (2) (3)
> expand(");

                            -144
> ifactor(60, easy);

                               2
                            (2) (3) (5)
> ifactor(4/11);

                               2
                            (2)
                            ----
                            (11)
> n := 8012940887713968000041:
> ifactor(n, easy);

                       (13) (457) _c19
> ifactor(n);

               (13) (457) (473638939) (2847639359)

Finally, Maple refers to related matters.

  >   related(ifactor);

SEE ALSO: ifactors, isprime, factor, type[facint]

By the way, instead of **info**(<*topic*>) and **example**(<*topic*>) you can use
the shortcuts ??<*topic*> and ???<*topic*>, respectively.

You can search by topic in the help system. Figure 2.3 shows the dialog box that appears when you choose ⌐Topic Search⌐ from the ⌐Help⌐ menu. We use the word `updates` to find help topics whose names start with this string.

FIGURE 2.3. Searching by topic.

Searching for help topics whose contents contain specific words is possible as well. Figure 2.4 shows the dialog box that appears when you choose ⌐Full-Text Search⌐ from the ⌐Help⌐ menu. We use the word `fit` to find help topics whose contents contain this string.

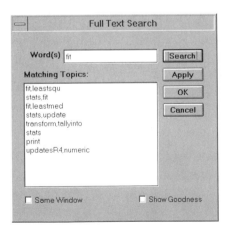

FIGURE 2.4. Full-text searching.

So you see that you can get plenty of help on standard library functions directly from the system. Table 2.1 summarizes how to access the on-line Maple help system.

Type of Help Request	Maple Command
explain on-line help system	**?help**
explain a specific topic	**?**<*topic*>
explain a specific topic in a context	**?**<*context*>, <*topic*>
	?<*context*> [<*topic*>]
list all help categories	**?index**
list operators for forming expressions	**?index,expression**
list standard library functions	**?index,function**
list miscellaneous facilities	**?index,misc**
list all packages	**?index,packages**
list information about procedures	**?index,procedure**
summarize structured data types	**?type,structured**
list basic Maple data types	**?type,surface**
summarize new features	**?update**

TABLE 2.1. The on-line Maple help system.

When you do not use the Help menu, you can get a list of help categories when you enter **?index**. The categories *function, misc,* and *packages* are listed among others. When you enter **?index,function** you get a list of all standard library functions present in Maple. After the command **?index,misc** you will see more rarely used facilities. Entering the command **?index,packages** will provide you with a list of all packages present in Maple. If you want to know what procedures are available in the linear algebra package, for example, just enter **?linalg**. Or if you want to know more about the trace function in the linear algebra package, enter **?linalg,trace** or **?linalg[trace]**. If you omit the first part and simply enter **?trace**, then you will get information about the debugging tool **trace** in Maple, which resides in the standard library. In cases of no ambiguity, e.g., **det** for computing the determinant of a matrix, you may use the abbreviation **?det** instead of **?linalg,det**. Once a package is loaded, you can use abbreviations when you ask for help about a procedure in that package.

Good advice:

> *Familiarize yourself with the help system because it will be your best assistant in learning and using Maple.*

Now we are ready for our tour through Maple, which will be in the form of short Maple sessions interleaved with explanatory remarks. Unless explicitly stated, we assume that in each example all history of previous examples has been forgotten by Maple, as if a new session has been started. Have a close look at the examples, try them yourself with Maple, and change the examples as you like. Only through direct confrontation with the computer algebra system you can acquire the right skills and experience the applicability and limitations of computer algebra personally. For the same reason we have added a set of exercises at the end of each session. Work through these exercises to become more and more proficient at Maple.

2.3   Integers and Rational Numbers

Being a true computer algebra system, Maple is averse to approximations in arithmetic computations. In contrast to pocket calculators, Maple never changes spontaneously arithmetic expression into decimal numbers.

The quotient of two integers with nonzero denominator is only simplified. More precisely, the greatest common divisor is removed automatically from the numerator and the denominator of a rational number. For exact arithmetic on rational numbers, Maple must be able to deal with very large integers.

```
>   5 / 81491528324789773434561
>    -  101 / 10198346916138403856439;
```

$$\frac{-90885029180256389973 4274}{9234209739805835267132808979235203517833 2031}$$

```
>   number := 4^(4^4);
```

$number :=$ 13407807929942597099574024998205846127479365820\
59239337772356144372176403000735469768018742981669034 27\
69003185818648605085375388281194656994643364900608409 6

```
>   length( number );   # number of digits
```

155

Note that Maple spontaneously uses a backslash to indicate that output continues on the next line.

Of course, there is a maximum integer that can be represented by Maple, but it has a much higher value than in most other programming languages; the number of digits is limited to $2^{19} - 9 = 524279$ on a 32-bit machine. See [83] for how to overcome the size limitation. The secret of Maple's capability of computing with large numbers up to 10^{524279} lies in the internal representation of integers. Most programming languages make use of the hardware facilities for calculus on so-called *single-precision integers*. This limits the range of values for integers to those numbers that can be represented in one computer word. Maple has implemented *multiple-precision integer arithmetic* by using several consecutive computer words for the internal representation of an integer [39, 75]. We call such a linear list a *dynamic data vector* and define the *length* of the data vector as the number of computer words used. The internal data structure in Maple representing an integer has the format shown in Figure 2.5 below.

intpos	integer i_0	integer i_1	....	integer i_n

FIGURE 2.5. Internal representation of a positive integer.

The first word in this vector encodes all the information about the data structure: it indicates that the vector represents a positive integer and that the vector length is equal to $n + 2$. The next $n + 1$ words contain single-precision nonnegative integers i_0, i_1, i_2, ..., i_n. Let B be the base of the number system used inside the computer, then the above vector represents the integer

$$i_0 + i_1 B + i_2 B^2 + i_3 B^3 + \cdots + i_n B^n .$$

Maple uses as base B the largest power of 10 such that B^2 can be represented in the single-precision integer arithmetic of the computer ($B = 10^4$ on a 32-bit machine). Because the length of the vector may be chosen dynamically, instead of being of a predefined fixed length, very large integers can be represented in Maple. The only restriction is that the number of computer words necessary for representation of an integer must be specifiable in the first word of the dynamic data vector. Maple uses 17 bits for specification of the vector length, and this explains the "magic number" $2^{19} - 9 = 4\big((2^{17} - 1) - 1\big) - 1$. Maple is clever enough to decide beforehand whether an integer can be represented or not.

```
>   123456789 ^ 987654321;
```

Error, object too large

In Maple there are several procedures for doing calculus on integers. A few examples:

```
>   number := 10^29 - 10^14 - 1;
```

$$number := 99999999999999899999999999999$$

```
>   isprime( number );   # check whether the number is prime
```

false

The quality of Maple's primality test is described in [200].

```
>   settime := time():   # start timing
>   ifactor( number );   # factorize the integer
```

$$(61)(223)(13166701)(97660768252549)(5717)$$

```
>   cpu_time := (time()-settime) * seconds; # computing time
```

$$cpu\_time := 3.583 \ seconds$$

```
>   nextprime( number );   # determine the next largest prime
```

$$9999999999999990000000000000157$$

```
>  # integer approximation to the square root
>  isqrt( number );
```

$$316227766016838$$

Integer factorization is a time-consuming operation, and you may want to know the computing time. As you have seen before, this can be done with the help of the Maple procedure **time**, which gives back the computing time (in seconds) since the start of the Maple session. Enter the command **time()** immediately before and after a computation. By taking the differences of these two numbers, you get the computing time of that particular computation.

Alternatively, you can use the command **time(<*expression*>)** to compute the time to evaluate the given *expression*. For example,

```
>  time( assign( factored_number, ifactor(3!!!) ) );
```

$$1.850$$

computes the prime factorization of $3!!! = 6!! = 720!$ and assigns the result to the variable `factored_number` for later referencing. You cannot use the assignment operator `:=` here because the argument of **time** must be a Maple expression and may not be, for example, an assignment statement.

In all the above procedures, integer division (with remainder) and determination of greatest common divisor play a crucial role.

```
>  a := 1234:   b := 56:
>  q := iquo(a,b);   # quotient of integer division
```

$$q := 22$$

```
>  r := irem(a,b);   # remainder of integer division
```

$$r := 2$$

```
>  testeq( a = q*b + r );   # check identity
```

$$true$$

```
>  igcd(a,b);   # greatest common divisor of integers
```

$$2$$

By use of the procedure **igcdex** Maple can compute the **ex**tended greatest common divisor of integers; for any two integers a and b, two integers, say s and t, are computed such that $a\,s + b\,t = \gcd(a, b)$.

```
>  igcdex( a, b, 's', 't' );
```

$$2$$

```
>  's' = s, 't' = t, 'a*s + b*t' = a*s + b*t;
```

$$s = 1, \ t = -22, \ a\,s + b\,t = 2$$

The quotes around s, t, and $a\,s + b\,t$ in the above examples are used to suppress evaluation of variables. This will be explained in more detail in the next chapter.

Modular arithmetic plays an important role in integer factorization and primality tests [117]. The operator **mod** gives, in modular arithmetic with respect to a nonzero integer n, an answer in the sequence $0, 1, 2, \ldots, |n| - 1$. If you prefer an answer in the sequence

$$- \left\lfloor \frac{|n| - 1}{2} \right\rfloor, \ \ldots, -1, 0, 1, \ \ldots, \ \left\lfloor \frac{|n|}{2} - 1 \right\rfloor, \ \left\lfloor \frac{|n|}{2} \right\rfloor,$$

i.e., symmetrically around zero, then you can specify this beforehand.

```
>   1/2345 mod 6;
```
$$5$$

```
>   `mod` := mods:   1/2345 mod 6;
```
$$-1$$

A drawback of Maple's modular arithmetic is that you cannot specify in one step that all computations are to be done modulo some fixed integer. In each separate command you need to call the **mod** routine.

As we have noted before, Maple simplifies a rational number spontaneously into a unique standard form. The system automatically removes the greatest common divisor from the numerator and the denominator of the rational number, and it guarantees that the denominator is a positive number. If you represent a rational number as a pair of integers (*numerator, denominator*) with positive denominator, this standard form, referred to as *canonical form*, is the most compact one. You would not like to represent $\frac{1}{3}$ as

$$\frac{-41152263041152263041152263041152263041152263}{-123456789123456789123456789123456789123456789}\ .$$

Now, you might think that Maple represents a rational number internally as a data vector consisting of three components, the first component specifying the nature of the data vector, the second component representing the numerator, and the third component representing the positive denominator. However, because the developers of Maple wanted to make Maple as memory-efficient as possible, they have chosen a different design, based on the following rule [36]:

Every (sub)expression in Maple appears internally only once.

Therefore, in a data vector representing a rational number, the last two components do not consist of the multiple-precision integers representing the numerator and denominator themselves, but only contain reference pointers to these integers. In this way, any integer that occurs in several rational numbers appears internally only once. For example, the rational numbers $-\frac{1}{2}$, $\frac{2}{3}$, and $\frac{3}{5}$, when used in the same Maple session, are internally represented as in Figure 2.6 below.

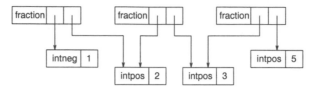

FIGURE 2.6. Internal representation of the fractions $-\frac{1}{2}$, $\frac{2}{3}$, and $\frac{3}{5}$.

2.4   Irrational Numbers and Floating-Point Numbers

In the previous section you have seen that Maple simplifies rational numbers automatically. In general, Maple only carries out computations when it is specifically ordered to do so.

```
>  25^(1/6);
```
$$25^{1/6}$$

```
>  simplify(");
```
$$5^{1/3}$$

```
>  evalf("");
```
$$1.709975947$$

```
>  convert( """, float );
```
$$1.709975947$$

Here, the procedures **simplify** and **evalf** put Maple to work. With the double quote in the command **simplify(")** you refer to the previously evaluated expression, in this case $25^{1/6}$. Two double quotes return the second last expression evaluated; more than three double quotes for referring to previously evaluated expressions are not allowed. Double quotes that are used in the above sense are called *ditto operators*.

You might have expected in the above example that Maple would immediately yield an approximate result for the cube root, but this is against the principle of exact arithmetic. You may want to compute the third power of this cube root and expect the exact result. In approximate floating-point arithmetic you would get a different result.

```
>  25.0^(1/6);
```
$$1.709975947$$

```
>   "^6;
```

$$25.00000003$$

Any number containing a dot is interpreted as a floating-point number, and henceforth Maple computes with it as such. In this case, Maple will also take care of automatic type conversions such as from integers to floating-point numbers.

```
>   90005*0.15;
```

$$13500.75$$

Furthermore, floating-point numbers are contagious in Maple, so `exp(1.)` automatically evaluates to `2.71828....`.

Other Maple notations for a floating-point number, say 0.000001, are $0.1 * 10^{-5}$, `1E-6`, and `Float(10,-6)`. The latter notation is of the form `Float(`*mantissa, exponent*`)` and resembles Maple's internal representation of floating-point number: a data vector consisting of the header `Float`, and pointers to the multiple-precision integers *mantissa* and *exponent*. This vector represents the number *mantissa* $\times 10^{exponent}$. In other words, the significant digits of a floating-point number are stored in the *mantissa* and the overall magnitude is given by the *exponent*. As a consequence of the internal representation of floating-point numbers, the limit of the floating-point precision coincides with the maximum number of digits that an integer can have in Maple. However, the internal addition and multiplication routines that compute the integer values of the exponent are written in C. This means that exponent arithmetic is restricted to C's integer arithmetic.

The precision of floating-point arithmetic can be defined by setting different values to the Maple variable `Digits`, whose default value is equal to 10. There are several functions that make Maple compute in floating-point arithmetic, the most important being **evalf** (**eval**uate using floating-point arithmetic).

```
>   evalf( sqrt(2) );
```

$$1.414213562$$

```
>   Digits;
```

$$10$$

```
>   Digits := 20:    evalf( sqrt(2) );
```

$$1.4142135623730950488$$

```
>   evalf( Pi, 150 );
```

$$3.14159265358979323846264338327950288419716939937510580 \backslash$$
$$20974944592307816406286208998628034825342117067982148 \backslash$$
$$08651328230664709384460955058223172535940813$$

The procedure **evalf** approximates its first argument; the number of digits used is equal to the value of its second argument. If there is no second argument to **evalf**, then Maple takes the value of `Digits` as the number of digits to be used in floating-point arithmetic. For a detailed description of Maple's software floating-point model and its consequences we refer to [188].

Maple knows, of course, some mathematical constants, like Euler-Mascheroni's constant γ and the number π. See Table 2.2 for a list of constants known to Maple.

Mathematical Constant	Maple Name	Value (approx.)
π, the area of a unit circle	Pi	3.141592654
Catalan's number C $$= \sum_{n=0}^{\infty} \frac{(-1)^n}{(2n+1)^2}$$	Catalan	0.9159655942
Euler-Mascheroni's constant γ $$= \lim_{n \to \infty} \left((\sum_{k=1}^{n} \frac{1}{k}) - \ln n \right)$$	gamma	0.5772156649
Boolean values *true, untrue, fail*	true, false, FAIL	
∞	infinity	

TABLE 2.2. Mathematical constants in Maple.

Names of mathematical constants are protected in Maple so that you cannot assign values by accident.

```
> Pi := 3.14;
```

Error, attempting to assign to `Pi` which is protected

You may add your own symbolic constants with name protection.

```
> electron_rest_mass := 9.109558 * 10^(-31) * kg;
```
$$electron\_rest\_mass := .9109558000\,10^{-30}\,kg$$

```
> protect( 'electron_rest_mass' ):
> electron_rest_mass := 5.48593 * 10^(-4)
>    * atomic_mass_units;
```

Error, attempting to assign to `electron_rest_mass` which is protected

You first have to **unprotect** the name before you can assign a new variable.

```
> unprotect( 'electron_rest_mass' ):
> electron_rest_mass := 5.48593 * 10^(-4)
>    * atomic_mass_units;
```
$$electron\_rest\_mass := .0005485930000\,atomic\_mass\_units$$

```
>  protect( ´electron_rest_mass´ ):
```

Alternatively, you can associate the value 9.109558×10^{-31}kg with the protected name electron_rest_mass by use of the procedure **macro**. In this way, electron_rest_mass is just an abbreviation of a specific value, which cannot be assigned a value by accident.

```
>  macro( electron_rest_mass = 9.109558 * 10^(-31) * kg ):
>  electron_rest_mass;
```

$$.9109558000 \; 10^{-30} \; kg$$

The latter mechanism may be used to work conveniently with the base e of the natural logarithm. In Maple this number is denoted by exp(1). But it is cumbersome to type exp(1) each time you want to use the base e of the natural logarithm; you do not only want to see it displayed in the worksheet interface as the character e, but also want to use this short notation. So, to achieve this you can do the following.

```
>  protect( ´e´ ):
>  macro( e = exp(1) ):
>  ln(e);
```

$$1$$

With a scientific pocket calculator you can compute with mathematical functions like the exponential function, the natural logarithm, and trigonometric functions. In Maple, these functions are also present, but the system contains many more. In Table 2.3 we list commonly used mathematical functions and their names in Maple. A more complete list can be obtained by the command **?inifcns** (help about **initially** known **functions**).

Recall the definitions of

the Gamma function $\qquad \Gamma(z) = \displaystyle\int_0^\infty t^{z-1} e^{-t} \, dt, \quad \Re(z) > 0,$

the Riemann zeta function $\quad \zeta(z) = \displaystyle\sum_{n=1}^\infty \frac{1}{n^z},$

the dilogarithm function $\qquad \mathrm{dilog}(x) = \displaystyle\int_1^x \frac{\ln t}{(1-t)} \, dt,$

and the error function $\qquad \mathrm{erf}(x) = \dfrac{2}{\sqrt{\pi}} \displaystyle\int_0^x e^{-t^2} \, dt.$

Maple knows exact values of many of these functions. Trigonometric functions applied to multiples of $\frac{\pi}{8}$, $\frac{\pi}{10}$, and $\frac{\pi}{12}$ yield exact numerical results. The Riemann zeta function yields exact numbers when applied to even, natural numbers less than 50; for larger arguments, you must explicitly **expand** it. $\lim\limits_{x \to \infty} \mathrm{erf}(x)$ is known to be equal to 1. And so on.

Mathematical Function	Maple Name
exponential function	exp
natural logarithm	ln, log
logarithm with base 10	log10
square root function	sqrt
absolute value	abs
trigonometric functions	sin, cos, tan, csc, sec, cot
inverse trigonometric functions	arcsin, arccos, arctan, arccsc, arcsec, arccot
hyperbolic functions	sinh, cosh, tanh, csch, sech, coth
inverse hyperbolic functions	arcsinh, arccosh, arctanh, arccsch arcsech, arccoth
hypergeometric function	hypergeom
Bessel functions	BesselI, BesselJ, BesselK, BesselY
gamma function	GAMMA
binomial coefficient	binomial
polygamma function	Psi
Riemann zeta function	Zeta
dilogarithm	dilog
error function	erf

TABLE 2.3. Commonly used mathematical functions known to Maple.

```
>   sin(Pi/10), Zeta(2), limit( erf(x), x=infinity );
```
$$\frac{1}{4}\sqrt{5} - \frac{1}{4}, \frac{1}{6}\pi^2, 1$$

```
>   Zeta(50) = expand( Zeta(50) );
```

$$\text{Zeta}(50) = \frac{39604576419286371856998202}{285258771457546764463363635252374414183254365234375}\pi^{50}$$

Numerical approximations can be obtained with **evalf**.

```
>   Zeta(3); evalf(");
```

$$\text{Zeta}(3)$$
$$1.2020569031595942854$$

The next examples give more food for thought about exact arithmetic versus floating-point arithmetic.

```
>   sin(4) - 2*sin(2)*cos(2); combine(",`trig`); evalf("");
```

$$\sin(4) - 2\sin(2)\cos(2)$$
$$0$$
$$.1\,10^{-19}$$

```
>   (1+sqrt(2))^2-2*(1+sqrt(2))-1; simplify(""); evalf("");
```

$$(\sqrt{2}+1)^2 - 3 - 2\sqrt{2}$$

$$0$$

$$0$$

You may wonder how the Maple procedure **evalf** distinguishes all these mathematical functions. Maple shows its secrets when you set a higher value to the Maple variable `printlevel`, whose default value is equal to 1.

```
>   printlevel := 5: evalf( sin(1)+ln(2) ); printlevel := 1:
```

```
{--> enter sin, args = 1
<-- exit sin (now at top level) = sin(1)}
{--> enter evalf/sin, args = 1
```

$$x := 1.$$

```
<-- exit evalf/sin (now at top level) = .841470984807896507}
{--> enter evalf/ln, args = 2
```

$$x := 2.$$

```
<-- exit evalf/ln (now at top level) = .6931471805599453094}
```

$$1.53461816536778418161$$

This example indicates that there exists in the Maple library a procedure called **evalf/func** for each mathematical function *func* for which numerical values can be computed. Whenever you apply the procedure **evalf** on a Maple expression, the system finds out what functions are present and automatically applies the appropriate **evalf/func** procedures. In this way, it is only necessary for you to recall the name of *one* procedure for numerical approximation, instead of remembering several distinct procedures. We shall see that similar techniques are used in other areas, such as, integration, differentiation, and simplification.

Maple also has the procedure **evalhf** (**eval**uate using **h**ardware **f**loating-point arithmetic) for the purpose of gaining speed in numerical computations (e.g., in plotting graphs of functions) or for users who want hardware floating-point arithmetic. This procedure converts all its arguments to hardware floating-point numbers, computes the answer in double precision (which is equivalent to a setting of `Digits` around 15), and converts it to a Maple floating-point result. We illustrate the use of **evalhf** with the calculation of the values of the function *g* defined by

```
>   f := x -> arctan( (2*x^2-1)/(2*x^2+1) ):
>   g := (x,y) -> f(x) * f(y):
>   g(x,y);
```

$$\arctan(\frac{2\,x^2-1}{2\,x^2+1})\arctan(\frac{2\,y^2-1}{2\,y^2+1})$$

on a two-dimensional rectangular 50 by 50 grid at equally spaced points in
the ranges $[-3, 3]$ and $[-3, 3]$, respectively.

```
>  settime := time(): # start timing
>  for i to 50 do
>     for j to 50 do
>        evalf( g( -3 + 6*i/50, -3 + 6*j/50 ) )
>  od od:
>  cpu_time := (time()-settime) * seconds; # computing time
```

$$cpu\_time := 7.000\ seconds$$

```
>  settime := time():
>  for i to 50 do
>     for j to 50 do
>        evalhf( g( -3 + 6*i/50, -3 + 6*j/50 ) )
>  od od:
>  cpu_time := (time()-settime) * seconds; # computing time
```

$$cpu\_time := .750\ seconds$$

```
>  evalf( g(1,1) ),  evalhf( g(1,1) );
```

$$.1035234193, .1035234192545466$$

Hardware floating-point arithmetic is used by Maple in plot routines, e.g.,
in **plot3d**, with which you can graph the function g (as shown in Figure
2.7).

```
>  plot3d( g, -3..3, -3..3,
>     grid=[50,50], style=patchnogrid );
```

FIGURE 2.7. Graph of $(x, y) \mapsto \arctan\left(\frac{2x^2-1}{2x^2+1}\right) \cdot \arctan\left(\frac{2y^2-1}{2y^2+1}\right)$.

2.5   Algebraic Numbers

We have already seen examples of radical numbers such as square roots
and cube roots of integers. Maple has little problems in computing with
them.

```
>  ( 1/2 + 1/2*sqrt(5) )^2;
```

$$(\frac{1}{2} + \frac{1}{2}\sqrt{5})^2$$

```
>  expand(");
```

$$\frac{3}{2} + \frac{1}{2}\sqrt{5}$$

```
>  1/";
```

$$\frac{1}{\dfrac{3}{2} + \dfrac{1}{2}\sqrt{5}}$$

```
>  simplify(");
```

$$\frac{2}{3 + \sqrt{5}}$$

```
>  readlib( rationalize ): # load library function
>  rationalize("");
```

$$\frac{3}{2} - \frac{1}{2}\sqrt{5}$$

```
>  (-1-3*Pi-3*Pi^2-Pi^3)^(1/3);
```

$$(-1 - 3\pi - 3\pi^2 - \pi^3)^{1/3}$$

```
>  simplify(");
```

$$\frac{1}{2}(\pi + 1)(1 + I\sqrt{3})$$

In the last example, Maple uses the principal branch of the complex, cube root function. The real-valued root can be found in the following tricky way.

```
>  readlib( surd ): # load library function
>  surd( op(1,"""), 1/op(2,""") );
```

$$-(1 + 3\pi + 3\pi^2 + \pi^3)^{1/3}$$

```
>  simplify(");
```

$$-\pi - 1$$

Nested square roots of the form $\sqrt{r_1 + r_2\sqrt{n}}$, where $n \in \mathbb{N}$ and $r_1, r_2 \in \mathbb{Q}$, are denested where possible by the **sqrt** and **simplify** commands.

```
>  sqrt( 4 + 2*sqrt(3) );
```

$$\sqrt{3} + 1$$

```
>  ( 4 + 2*3^(1/2) )^(1/2);
```

$$\sqrt{4 + 2\sqrt{3}}$$

```
>  simplify(");
```

$$\sqrt{3} + 1$$

You can simplify more complicated nested radicals by **radnormal**.

```
>  readlib( radnormal ): # load library function
>  sqrt(25+5*sqrt(5)) - sqrt(5+sqrt(5)) - 2*sqrt(5-sqrt(5));
```

$$\sqrt{25 + 5\sqrt{5}} - \sqrt{5 + \sqrt{5}} - 2\sqrt{5 - \sqrt{5}}$$

```
>  radnormal(");
```

$$0$$

Radical numbers are instances of so-called algebraic numbers. In general, an *algebraic number* is a root of a univariate polynomial over the rational numbers: $\sqrt{2}$ is a root α of the polynomial $x^2 - 2$, $\sqrt{2} + \sqrt{3} + \sqrt{5}$ is a root α of the polynomial $x^8 - 40x^6 + 352x^4 - 960x^2 + 576$, the nested radical $\sqrt{1 + \sqrt{2}}$ is a root α of the polynomial $x^4 - 2x - 1$. A root α of the polynomial $x^5 + x + 1$ cannot be expressed in terms of radicals (see [170] for a characterization of solvable quintics). Note that in these examples the symbol α can be *any* of the roots of the polynomial, just as the square root of two can be approximately 1.4142 or -1.4142.

Computing with algebraic numbers is complicated and time-consuming [169] and this is no exception in Maple. An algebraic number is represented in the system by means of the procedure **RootOf**, which plays the role of a placeholder. For example,

```
>  alpha := RootOf( z^2 - 2, z );
```

$$\alpha := \text{RootOf}(\_Z^2 - 2)$$

represents any root of 2; in radical notation $\sqrt{2}$ or $-\sqrt{2}$. Here, Maple reveals that it will use the underscore name _Z internally. The procedure **simplify** makes use of the fact that $\alpha^2 = 2$ to simplify expressions containing α.

```
>  simplify( alpha^2 );
```

$$2$$

```
>  simplify( 1/(1+alpha) );
```

$$\text{RootOf}(\_Z^2 - 2) - 1$$

These calculations become much clearer when an **alias** is used for the square root.

```
>  alias( beta = RootOf( z^2 - 2, z ) ):
>  1/(1+beta) + 1/(beta-1);  simplify(");
```

$$\frac{1}{1 + \beta} + \frac{1}{\beta - 1}$$

$$2\beta$$

You can easily convert the representation of an algebraic number from radical into RootOf, and vice versa where possible.

```
>   convert( (-8)^(1/3), RootOf );
```
$$\mathrm{RootOf}(\_Z^3 + 8)$$

```
>   convert( ", radical );
```
$$(-8)^{1/3}$$

Actually, in the above example, α and β can be any of the square roots of two, and the procedure **allvalues** does its very best to show them all.

```
>   allvalues( beta );
```
$$\sqrt{2}, -\sqrt{2}$$

By default, **allvalues** treats all occurrences of the same **RootOf** expression as is if they represent the same root. But you can request independent evaluation of **RootOfs** in an expression.

```
>   beta + 1/beta;
```
$$\beta + \frac{1}{\beta}$$

```
>   allvalues(");
```
$$\frac{3}{2}\sqrt{2}, -\frac{3}{2}\sqrt{2}$$

```
>   allvalues( "", `independent` );
```
$$\frac{3}{2}\sqrt{2}, \frac{1}{2}\sqrt{2}, -\frac{1}{2}\sqrt{2}, -\frac{3}{2}\sqrt{2}$$

In Maple you can do polynomial calculus over algebraic number fields. Below, we shall use this facility to check that $\zeta = \sqrt{2} + \sqrt{3} + \sqrt{5}$ is a root of the polynomial $x^8 - 40x^6 + 352x^4 - 960x^2 + 576$ and that in this case $\sqrt{2} - \frac{1}{576}\zeta^7 - \frac{7}{144}\zeta^5 - \frac{7}{72}\zeta^3 + \frac{5}{3}\zeta$. First, we use resultants to compute the defining polynomial for ζ (q.v., [132]).

```
>   polynomial := resultant(
>     resultant( x^2-5, (x-y)^2-3, x ),  (y-z)^2-2, y );
```
$$polynomial := -960\,z^2 + 352\,z^4 - 40\,z^6 + z^8 + 576$$

```
>   expand( subs( z=sqrt(2)+sqrt(3)+sqrt(5), polynomial ) );
```
$$0$$

So, $\sqrt{2} + \sqrt{3} + \sqrt{5}$ is indeed a root. Introduce the algebraic number ζ and factorize $x^2 - 2$ over $\mathbb{Q}(\zeta)$.

```
>   alias( zeta = RootOf( polynomial, z ) ):
>   factor( x^2-2, zeta );
```

$$\frac{1}{331776}\left(576\,x + 960\,\zeta - 56\,\zeta^3 - 28\,\zeta^5 + \zeta^7\right)$$
$$\left(576\,x - 960\,\zeta + 56\,\zeta^3 + 28\,\zeta^5 - \zeta^7\right)$$

You can also find the two roots of $x^2 - 2$ over $\mathbb{Q}(\zeta)$ by **roots**.

> roots(x^2-2, zeta);

$$[[-\frac{5}{3}\zeta + \frac{7}{72}\zeta^3 + \frac{7}{144}\zeta^5 - \frac{1}{576}\zeta^7, 1],$$
$$[\frac{5}{3}\zeta - \frac{7}{72}\zeta^3 - \frac{7}{144}\zeta^5 + \frac{1}{576}\zeta^7, 1]]$$

The procedure **roots** computes the roots of the polynomial with multiplicities. In this case, $\frac{1}{567}\zeta^7 + \frac{5}{3}\zeta - \frac{7}{72}\zeta^3 - \frac{7}{144}\zeta^5$ is a root of 2 in the field $\mathbb{Q}(\zeta)$ with multiplicity 1, where ζ satisfies $\zeta^8 - 40\zeta^6 + 352\zeta^4 - 960\zeta^2 + 576 = 0$.

The above description of **RootOf** applies for manipulation of any root of a polynomial without specifying which root one actually has in mind. However, there is a selection mechanism for roots. A few examples.

> RootOf(x^2 + 9/10, x);

$$\text{RootOf}(10\_Z^2 + 9)$$

> evalf(");

$$-.9486832981\, I$$

> RootOf(x^2 + 9/10, x, 1.0*I);

$$\text{RootOf}(10\_Z^2 + 9, 1.0\, I)$$

> evalf(");

$$.9486832981\, I$$

> RootOf(x^2 + 9/10, x, -1.0*I .. 1.0*I);

$$\text{RootOf}(10\_Z^2 + 9, -1.0\, I..1.0\, I)$$

> evalf(");

$$-.9486832981\, I$$

The semantics of the two selectors in **RootOf** are given in Table 2.4.

Selector	Selected Root
a + b*I	closest in absolute value to a + b*I
a + b*I .. c + d*I	first root in the given range from the fsolve order

TABLE 2.4. Selectors on **RootOf**.

2.6 Complex Numbers

In contrast to algebraic numbers, complex numbers are of basic type. The complex number i (with $i^2 = -1$) is represented in Maple by I. Numeric complex number arithmetic is automatic.

```
>   ( 2 + 3*I ) * ( 4 + 5*I );
```
$$-7 + 22\,I$$

```
>   Re("), Im("), conjugate("), abs("), argument(");
```
$$-7, 22, -7 - 22\,I, \sqrt{533}, -\arctan(\frac{22}{7}) + \pi$$

```
>   1/"";
```
$$-\frac{7}{533} - \frac{22}{533}\,I$$

In Maple, many mathematical functions are regarded as complex functions. In case of multiple-valued complex functions Maple uses the principal branch.

```
>   cos(I), ln(I), arccoth(0), sqrt(-8);
```
$$\cosh(1), \frac{1}{2}\,I\,\pi, \frac{1}{2}\,I\,\pi, 2\,I\,\sqrt{2}$$

```
>   sqrt( (1.0+I)^2 - 1.0 );
```
$$.7861513778 + 1.272019650\,I$$

```
>   Zeta( 0.5 + I ), GAMMA( 0.5 + I );
```
$$.1439364271 - .7220997435\,I, .3006946173 - .4249678794\,I$$

Two pictures of absolute values of complex functions are shown below.

```
>   plot3d( abs( GAMMA(x+y*I) ), x=-Pi..Pi, y=-Pi..Pi,
>      view=0..5, grid=[30,30], orientation=[-120,45],
>      axes=framed, style=patchcontour );
```

The surface plot of the absolute value of the gamma function in the complex plane is shown in Figure 2.8.

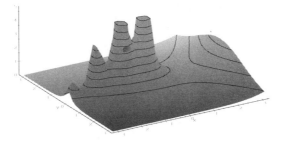

FIGURE 2.8. Plot of the absolute value of the gamma function.

In the above **plot3d** command, we have specified all options necessary to generate this picture. Many of these options can be manually changed after the surface has been drawn. For more details you are referred to Chapter 15, in which graphics is discussed in great detail.

The plot of the absolute value of the Riemann zeta function on the critical line $\Re(z) = \frac{1}{2}$ is shown in Figure 2.9. It shows the first few zeros of the Riemann function on the critical line. The famous Riemann hypothesis [107] states that all the complex zeros lie on the critical line. Many times the Riemann hypothesis has been numerically investigated; see [133, 147] for recent results.

```
> plot( abs( Zeta(1/2+y*I) ), y=0..36, numpoints=1000 );
```

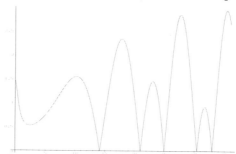

FIGURE 2.9. Plot of the absolute value of the Riemann zeta function on the critical line.

To activate Maple's knowledge about complex numbers in *symbolic* expressions you must use the procedure **evalc** (**eval**uate using **c**omplex number arithmetic). **evalc** assumes that all variables in an expression represent real-valued quantities and puts a complex number in its canonical form $a + b\,\mathrm{I}$, where a and b are real numbers.

```
> 1 / (2 + p - q*I);
```

$$\frac{1}{2 + p - I\,q}$$

```
> evalc(");
```

$$\frac{2 + p}{(2 + p)^2 + q^2} + \frac{I\,q}{(2 + p)^2 + q^2}$$

```
> abs("");
```

$$\frac{1}{|2 + p - I\,q|}$$

```
> evalc(");
```

$$\frac{1}{\sqrt{4 + 4\,p + p^2 + q^2}}$$

In the next example we shall see in the end how assumptions are helpful in obtaining simpler results.

>   sqrt(p + q*I);

$$\sqrt{p + I\,q}$$

>   evalc(");

$$\frac{1}{2}\sqrt{2\sqrt{p^2+q^2}+2\,p} + \frac{1}{2}\,I\,\mathrm{csgn}(\,q - I\,p\,)\,\sqrt{2\sqrt{p^2+q^2}-2\,p}$$

The complex sign function **csgn** is defined by

$$\mathrm{csgn}(z) = \begin{cases} 1 & \text{if } \Re(z) > 0 \text{ or } (\Re(z) = 0 \text{ and } \Im(z) > 0); \\ \texttt{\_Envsignum0} & \text{if } z = 0 \text{ and } \texttt{\_Envsignum0} \text{ is assigned;} \\ 0 & \text{if } z = 0 \text{ and } \texttt{\_Envsignum0} \text{ is not assigned;} \\ -1 & \text{elsewhere.} \end{cases}$$

Here, the value of csgn(0) is determined by the environment variable _Envsignum0 as the following examples show.

>   _Envsignum0 := 13: csgn(0);

$$13$$

>   _Envsignum0 := 1: csgn(0);

$$1$$

>   _Envsignum0 := ´_Envsignum0´: csgn(0);

$$0$$

Why is this special variable introduced? And why is it called _Envsignum0? The latter question is easily answered: the so-called *environment variable* controls the value of signum(0). Of course, **signum** is used for the sign function of a real or expression, defined as

$$\mathrm{signum}(z) = \begin{cases} z\,/\,\mathrm{abs}(z) & \text{if } z \neq 0; \\ \texttt{\_Envsignum0} & \text{if } z = 0 \text{ and } \texttt{\_Envsignum0} \text{ is assigned;} \\ 0 & \text{if } z = 0 \text{ and } \texttt{\_Envsignum0} \text{ is not assigned.} \end{cases}$$

The validity of simplification of expressions may depend on the value at 0. For example, the transformation

$$\mathrm{signum}\big(\mathrm{abs}(x)\big) \to 1$$

is wrong at $x = 0$ if signum(0)=0. Similarly, for real x and y, the transformation

$$\mathrm{signum}(x\,y) \to \mathrm{signum}(x)\,\mathrm{signum}(y)$$

is wrong for $x < 0$ and $y = 0$ if signum(0)=1. Maple should not do the simplification in this case; and indeed it does not simplify automatically.

>   _Envsignum0 := 1: signum(0);

$$1$$

> signum(x*y);

$$\text{signum}(x\,y)$$

The value of _Envsignum0 determines which transformations and simplifications can be applied as follows:

- _Envsignum0 *is not assigned a value.*
  In this case, any transformations that are valid everywhere except possibly at 0 can be applied.

- _Envsignum0 *is assigned a value.*
  In this case, only transformations that are valid everywhere, taking into consideration the assigned value of signum(0), can be applied.

Automatic simplification is a subtle matter, but you see that you as a user have some control over it.

Let us continue with the sqrt example. When you make assumptions, then Maple may be able to simplify further.

> assume(p>0, q>0):
> evalc(sqrt(p + q*I));

$$\frac{1}{2}\sqrt{2\sqrt{p^{\tilde{}2}+q^{\tilde{}2}}+2p^{\tilde{}}}+\frac{1}{2}I\sqrt{2\sqrt{p^{\tilde{}2}+q^{\tilde{}2}}-2p^{\tilde{}}}$$

The tildes after p and q indicate that assumptions hold for these variables. Maple can inform you about the properties via the command **about**. For a more detailed description of **assume** we refer to Chapter 13.

> about(p);

```
Originally p, renamed p~:
  is assumed to be: RealRange(Open(0),infinity)
```

Let us finish with the notation of the square root of -1. Electrical engineers prefer j or J to denote this root so that the capital letter I is free to denote current in an electric circuit. This can be achieved in Maple as follows. Because I is just an **alias** for sqrt(-1), we first unalias I.

> alias(I = I):

and then choose J instead.

> alias(J = sqrt(-1)):

Henceforth, complex numbers have standard notation $a + b\,J$.

> J^2;

$$-1$$

> 1/(1+J);

$$\frac{1}{2}-\frac{1}{2}J$$

```
>   1/(x+y*J);
```

$$\frac{1}{x + J\,y}$$

```
>   evalc(");
```

$$\frac{x}{x^2 + y^2} - \frac{J\,y}{x^2 + y^2}$$

```
>   solve( x^4 = 1, x );
```

$$1, -1, J, -J$$

The two commands `alias( I = I )` and `alias( J = sqrt(-1) )` can be combined to one statement, viz., `alias( I = I, J = sqrt(-1) )`. If you place this command in your Maple initialization file, you can always use the J notation from scratch.

2.7   Exercises

1. Consider the following Maple session.

   ```
   > 3^2:
   ```

   ```
   > 4^2;
   ```
   $$16$$
   ```
   > " + "";
   ```

   Does the last instruction make sense? If so, what is the result? If not, why?

2. Explain the different results of the following Maple commands.

   (a) **x:y;**

   (b) **x/y;**

   (c) **x\y;**

3. In this exercise you can practice your skills in using the help system of Maple.

   (a) Suppose that you want to select from an equation, e.g., $1 = \cos^2 x + \sin^2 x$, only the left or right side. How can you easily do this in Maple?

   (b) Suppose that you want to compute the continued fraction approximation of the exponential function; can Maple do this for you? If yes, carry out the computation.

   (c) Suppose that you want to factor the polynomial $x^8 + x^6 + 10x^4 + 10x^3 + 8x^2 + 2x + 8$ modulo 13. Can Maple do this? If yes, carry out this factorization.

   (d) Suppose that you want to determine all subsets of the set $\{1, 2, 3, 4, 5\}$. How can you do this in Maple?

4. Load the `numtheory` package by entering `with(numtheory);` You may recognize some functions from number theory; some of the routines in this package are useful in answering the following questions.

   (a) Build a list of all integers that divide 9876543210123456789.

   (b) Find the prime number that is closest to 9876543210123456789.

   (c) What is the prime factorization of $5^{5^{5^5}}$?

   (d) Expand the base E of the natural logarithm as a continued fraction up to 10 levels deep.

5. In Maple, what is the difference between $1/3 + 1/3 + 1/3$ and $1.0/3.0 + 1.0/3.0 + 1.0/3.0$?

6. Find the floating-point approximation of $e^{\frac{1}{3}\pi\sqrt{163}}$ using a precision of 10, 20, and 30 digits, respectively.

7. Calculate $\pi^{(\pi^\pi)}$ to nine decimal places.

8. Compute this exercise in a floating-point precision of eight decimal places. What is the result of
$$310.0 \times 320.0 \times 330.0$$
$$- \sqrt{310.0 \times 320.0} \times \sqrt{320.0 \times 330.0} \times \sqrt{330.0 \times 310.0}$$

9. Do you remember which of the numbers $\frac{19}{6}$, $\frac{22}{7}$, and $\frac{25}{8}$ is a fairly good rational approximation of π? Use Maple to find the best of these three numbers. Find the best rational approximation a/b of π, where a and b are natural numbers less than 1,000. (Hint: look at the continued fraction expansion of π.)

10. Check that $\sqrt{2\sqrt{19549} + 286}$ is equal to $\sqrt{113} + \sqrt{173}$.

11. In Maple, transform $\dfrac{1}{\sqrt{3} + 1}$ into an expression of the form $a + b\sqrt{3}$, with rational numbers a and b.

12. Let θ be a root of the polynomial $\theta^3 - \theta - 1$ and consider the extension of the field of rational numbers with θ. So, we consider expressions of the form $a + b\theta + c\theta^2$, where $a, b, c \in \mathbb{Q}$, and in calculations with these expressions, we apply the identity $\theta^3 = \theta + 1$. Transform with Maple $\dfrac{1}{\theta^2 + 1}$ into an expression of the form $a + b\theta + c\theta^2$, where $a, b, c \in \mathbb{Q}$.

13. Let $\alpha = \sqrt{2}$, $\beta = \sqrt{3}$, and $\gamma = \sqrt{5}$. Use the procedure **Primfield** to compute a primitive element ζ for the field extension $\mathbb{Q}(\alpha, \beta, \gamma)$, and compare the result with the last example of §2.5.

14. Show that Maple knows that the exponential power of a complex number can be written in terms of cosine and sine of the real and imaginary parts of that number. Also calculate $e^{\pi i/12}$ in that form.

15. Show with Maple that
$$\tanh(z/2) = \frac{\sinh x + i\sinh y}{\cosh x + \cos y},$$
for any complex number $z = x + yi$ with $x, y \in \mathbb{R}$.

3
Variables and Names

A Maple session usually consists of a series of statements in which values are computed, assigned names, and used in further computations. This chapter discusses what are valid names in Maple, how to assign a name to a value, how to unassign a variable, how to protect or unprotect a variable, and how to associate an attribute or a property to a variable. Unlike in programming languages such as FORTRAN, Algol, and C, there is in Maple no need to declare the types of variables. Maple figures out the type of an expression on the basis of how it is internally represented and how it is used. In this chapter, we shall have a look at the basic data types. Moreover, we shall describe the way symbolic expressions are normally evaluated, viz., by full evaluation.

3.1   Assignment and Unassignment

The secret behind the success of computer algebra systems in scientific computation is that you can manipulate formulae and solve mathematical problems where unknowns and parameters are involved. As an example of the use of such variables, we ask Maple about the general formulae for the solutions of a quadratic equation. Solving equations is usually done in Maple with **solve**.

```
>   solve( a*x^2 + b*x + c = 0, x );
```

$$\frac{1}{2}\frac{-b+\sqrt{b^2-4\,a\,c}}{a}, \frac{1}{2}\frac{-b-\sqrt{b^2-4\,a\,c}}{a}$$

The variables a, b, and c are parameters and x is an unknown; they are used as symbols, neither more nor less. This use of *free* or *unbound variables*, which do not point to any value except their own name, is characteristic of computer algebra systems.

On the other hand, a variable can be bound to, or assigned, a value. The use of *assigned variables* is twofold: you often want to label a calculated result or some complicated expression for further reference, and when you use Maple as a programming language, you want to specify data in an algorithm by name instead of using the data themselves. When data only have some fixed value, we speak of *symbolic constants*. We have seen in §2.4 what symbolic constants Maple initially has available and how new constants can be introduced or removed. In Maple, when you want to use assigned variables, the two-character symbol := is the assignment operator, which is commonly used. The alternative **assign** will be described later in this section.

```
>   polynomial := 9*x^3 - 37*x^2 + 47*x - 19;
```
$$polynomial := 9\,x^3 - 37\,x^2 + 47\,x - 19$$

```
>   # compute roots of the polynomial with multiplicities
>   roots( polynomial );
```
$$[[1,2],[\frac{19}{9},1]]$$

```
>   # substitute x for the root 19/9 into the polynomial
>   subs( x=19/9, polynomial );
```
$$0$$

```
>   polynomial, x;
```
$$9\,x^3 - 37\,x^2 + 47\,x - 19, x$$

In the above example, the effect of the first statement is that the variable **polynomial** is bound to 9*x^3 - 37*x^2 + 47*x - 19. Each time Maple encounters this variable, it takes its value; this is called *evaluation*. So, the instruction

```
                roots( polynomial )
```

is read by Maple as

```
        roots( 9*x^3 - 37*x^2 + 47*x - 19 )
```

In the meantime, the variable x has no value, except its own name. Through the instruction

```
        subs( x=19/9, polynomial )
```

x in the expression labeled by **polynomial**, i.e., in 9*x^3 - 37*x^2 + 47*x - 19 is replaced by 19/9: a *substitution*. But x itself remains unchanged and still points to itself. The same holds for the polynomial; `polynomial` has not been assigned a value through the substitution. You can also check the root 19/9 by assignment of x.

```
>   x := 19/9;
```

$$x := \frac{19}{9}$$

```
>   polynomial;
```

$$0$$

The way Maple carries out the last instruction can be understood as follows:

- Maple sees the variable `polynomial` and evaluates it first to
  9*x^3 - 37*x^2 + 47*x - 19,

- then it evaluates each x in this expression to 19/9,

- and finally simplifies the result to 0, i.e., does the arithmetic.

The disadvantage of checking a root by assignment instead of substitution is that x now points to some number. If you want x to point to something else, you can achieve this by a new assignment.

```
>   x := unknown:
>   polynomial;
```

$$9\,unknown^3 - 37\,unknown^2 + 47\,unknown - 19$$

When you assign a value, say 7, to the variable `unknown`

```
>   unknown := 7;
```

$$unknown := 7$$

then x evaluates to `unknown`, and this for its part evaluates to 7.

```
>   x;
```

$$7$$

You see that Maple evaluates as far as possible, using the values of variables as they are assigned at the state of computing. We refer to this general rule as *full evaluation*.

```
>   polynomial;
```

$$1584$$

We shall come back to full evaluation of expressions in §3.2.

```
>   x := `x`;
```

$$x := x$$

The last instruction gives x back its own name as its value. So, you can use *apostrophes* (also referred to as *forward quotes*, *right quotes*, and *acute accents*) to unassign variables. Whenever apostrophes surround an expression, Maple does not apply evaluation to the enclosed expression. In this particular case, evaluation of x is avoided.

Let us linger over assignment and unassignment of indexed names and concatenated names.

```
>   i := 1;    A[i] := 2;    A[i] := 3;    B[i] := 4;
```

$$i := 1$$

$$A_1 := 2$$

$$A_1 := 3$$

$$B_1 := 4$$

You see that the expression to the left of the assignment operator := is evaluated to a name. The index of an indexed name is evaluated, but the indexed name is then not further evaluated: in the third assignment, the left-hand side A[i] is evaluated to A[1], but A[1] is not further evaluated to 2.

The unassignment method using apostrophes does not work for indexed names and concatenated names.

```
>   A[i] := 'A[i]';    # no unassignment of A[i]
```

$$A_1 := A_i$$

```
>   A[i];    # but infinite recursion occurs
```

Error, too many levels of recursion

Under Unix, when Maple enters an infinite recursion, it will give up at some point, sending the above message; on other platforms or interfaces, the Maple program may even stop executing.

Sometimes, Maple warns you for recursive definitions of names. Suppose that x is still a free variable, then the next instruction gives it the new value x+1.

```
>   x := x+1;
```

Warning, recursive definition of name

```
>   x;    # infinite recursion occurs
```

Error, too many levels of recursion

In the last instruction, Maple is asked to evaluate the expression

$$x \rightarrow x + 1 \rightarrow (x + 1) + 1 \rightarrow ((x + 1) + 1) + 1 \rightarrow \ldots$$

Due to full evaluation, Maple reevaluates x over and over again until a recursion limit is exceeded.

Unassignment of indexed names and concatenated names can be achieved by the procedure **evaln** (**eval**uate to a **n**ame).

```
> A[i] := evaln( A[i] );  A[i];  # unassignment of A[i]
```

$$A_1 := A_1$$
$$A_1$$

The evaluation of the argument of **evaln** is again special: it only evaluates the index and produces a name, which is not further evaluated. Of course, the procedure **evaln** can also be used for variables with "ordinary" names like x, y, and z. It is a kind of sure way to unassign variables.

Because it is hardly possible to recall which variables have been assigned values and which not, the computer algebra system provides for this purpose with a few utility functions; they are tabulated in Table 3.1.

Procedure	Effect
anames	shows assigned names, i.e., the names of bound variables
unames	shows all unassigned names, i.e., the names of all free variables
assigned	checks whether a variable is bound to a value different from its name or not

TABLE 3.1. Utility functions for usage of names.

The next sample session illustrates the use of these Maple procedures.

```
> unames();
```

Embed, identical, equation, anyfunc, endcolon, Factors, Subres, radical,
. . . .,
operator, Rem, terminal, unknown, anything, Irreduc, Berlekamp, Sprem,
Limit, Coeff, prompt, Discrim, indentamount

```
> nops( {"} );  # number of unassigned names
```

219

We have omitted most of the output of **unames**, but from the few names shown and from the number of names it is already clear that the procedure is of little use because it gives too many details. Not only the user-defined names are listed, but also the unassigned names generated and used by Maple itself. Below is the **selec**tion of all initially known, unassigned three-character names.

```
>    select( s -> length(s)=3, { unames() } );
```

$$\{ all, row, not, and, set, Add, Det, Gcd, Int, Lcm, One, Quo, Rem, Sum, Svd \}$$

For a description of the use of the anonymous function `s -> length(s)=3` in the selection process, you are referred to §8.8. Another example is the selection of all unassigned names that contain the substring `con` except the name `con` itself.

```
>    select( s -> SearchText(con,s)>0, { unames() } )
>       minus {con};
```

$$\{ constant, Ratrecon \}$$

Let us look more closely at the procedure **anames** (in a fresh Maple session).

```
>    restart;
>    p := q;   r := q*s;
```

$$p := q$$
$$r := q\,s$$

```
>    anames();
```

$$p, r$$

The procedure **anames** returns a sequence of names that are currently assigned values other than their own name. Here, they are user-defined variables. But when you ask for names that are assigned values of specific type, you will also get names of variables that are assigned initial values in Maple.

```
>    anames( `*` ); # variables whose value is a product
```

$$r$$

```
>    anames( name ); # variables whose value are a name
```

$$libname, p, sysinit, integrate, mod$$

```
>    anames( integer ); # variables with integer value
```

$$Digits, printlevel, Order$$

The meaning of the left quotes and data types will be explained in §3.3 and §3.4.

With the procedure **assigned** you can get the status of individual variables.

```
>  assigned( q ),  assigned( r );
```

$$false, true$$

Meanwhile, you have seen four exceptions of the general rule of full evaluation:

- expressions that are enclosed by apostrophes are not evaluated.

- the expression to the left of the assignment operator := is only evaluated to a corresponding name.

- the argument of the procedure **evaln** is only evaluated to a corresponding name.

- the argument of the procedure **assigned** is only evaluated to a corresponding name.

We end this section with an application of the two Maple procedures **assign** and **unassign**. Their names suggest their functionality, but there are some differences from what we have previously learned about assignments and unassignments.

$$\textbf{assign}(\texttt{name, expression})$$

has the same effect as

$$\texttt{name := expression}$$

except that the first argument of the procedure **assign** is fully evaluated, whereas this general rule is not applied to the left operand of the assignment operator :=. What makes the procedure **assign** worthwhile is, for example, that it can be applied to sets of equations returned by the **solve** function when it is desired to assign the solution values to the variables.

```
>  eqns := { x + y = a,  b*x - 1/3*y = c }:
>  vars := { x, y }:
>  sols := solve( eqns, vars );
```

$$sols := \{ y = -3\,\frac{-b\,a+c}{3\,b+1}, x = \frac{3\,c+a}{3\,b+1} \}$$

```
>  x, y;
```

$$x, y$$

```
> assign( sols );
> x, y;
```

$$\frac{3c+a}{3b+1}, -3\frac{-ba+c}{3b+1}$$

As you will see in §3.6, the command **assign** is also convenient, if not indispensable, in assigning values to names that have been associated certain properties.

unassign can be used to unassign several variables in one statement or to unassign a variable without throwing away its associated properties.

```
> readlib( unassign ):  # load library function
> unassign( `x`, `y` ):  x, y;
```

$$x, y$$

You may be tempted to use it in combination with **anames** in order to clear all your assigned values, but look what a drastic effect this can have on the behavior of Maple.

```
> # compute some integral
> integral := integrate( 1/(x^2+1), x );
```

$$integral := \arctan(x)$$

```
> unassign( anames() ):  # unassign variables
> integrate( 1/(x^2+1), x );  # recompute the integral
```

```
Error, (in int) type `intargs` does not exist
```

The reason for Maple's malfunctioning is that we removed values of not only user-defined variables like `integral` but also system-defined variables like `int/type`. You had better use the **restart** statement to clear internal memory and start Maple afresh without leaving the system.

Table 3.2 summarizes the various styles of assignment and unassignment in Maple.

Template	Left-Hand Side	Right-Hand Side
x := y	to the name	normal
assign(x = y)	normal	normal
x := evaln(y)	to the name	to the name
x := 'y'	to the name	one step
assign(x = evaln(y))	normal	to the name
assign(x = 'y')	normal	one step
unassign(x)	normal	—

TABLE 3.2. Evaluation for assignment and unassignment.

3.2 Evaluation

In general, when Maple encounters a name in an instruction, it searches for the object to which the name points; we say that Maple *evaluates* the name. When a name points to another name, the system will search again for the object to which that name points, and so on, until it arrives at an object that is not a name or that points to itself. The last object is now used as if it were substituted in the instruction. So, the normal process is for every expression to be *fully evaluated*. This explains the next sample session.

```
> a := b;  b := c;  c:= 3;
```

$$a := b$$
$$b := c$$
$$c := 3$$

```
> a;  # evaluation of a
```

$$3$$

To get a better understanding of full evaluation, we look at the effect of assignments in terms of internal data structures. In Maple, a variable is internally represented by a data vector with three components, viz., a first component indicating that the vector represents a variable, a second component pointing to the current value of the variable, and a third component to name the variable. When we assign a value to a variable, we simply set a pointer from the named data vector to the assigned value. In the above example, this results in the internal representation shown in Figure 3.1.

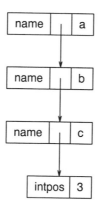

FIGURE 3.1. Internal representation after certain assignments.

The second component of the data vector representing the variable a points to the value of a: so, the value of a is equal to b. Similarly, the value of b is equal to c. We can check this internal representation by use of the **eval** procedure.

```
>  eval(a,1);   # value of a
```
$$b$$

```
>  eval(b,1);   # value of b
```
$$c$$

```
>  eval(c,1);   # value of c
```
$$3$$

```
>  eval(a,2);   # two-level evaluation of a
```
$$c$$

```
>  eval(a,3);   # three-level evaluation of a
```
$$3$$

When we fully evaluate a, we walk down all pointers, starting at the data vector representing a and ending at the object of type "positive integer" and value 3. We say "a evaluates to 3." When the variable c is now assigned a new value, say 5, then the variable a evaluates to 5. However, the value of a remains b; it can only be changed by an assignment.

```
>  c := 5:
>  a;   # a now evaluates to 5
```
$$5$$

```
>  eval(a,1);   # but the value of a remains the same
```
$$b$$

```
>  a := 4:
>  a, eval(a,1);
```
$$4, 4$$

```
>  # the value of a and its full evaluation are both 4
```

In the process of full evaluation of expressions, variables are substituted by the values that they received in their most recent assignments. The next example illustrates this.

```
>  x := y:  y := 7:
:·  # the value of x is y, but x evaluates to 7
·,  eval(x,1), x;
```
$$y, 7$$

```
>  x := x;
```
$$x := 7$$

```
>  # now, the value of x is 7 and x also evaluates to 7
>  y := 9:
>  x;  # the value and evaluation of x remain unchanged
```
$$7$$

The instruction **x := x** suggests that **x** points to its own name again. This is not the case as you have seen before! If you want to achieve this, you should have entered the command **x := evaln(x)** or **x := ´x´**. Here, the apostrophes prevent the full evaluation of **x**.

The easiest way to make sure that a name is passed through as an argument to a Maple procedure is to use *apostrophes* to suppress evaluation. For example, the fourth parameter of the procedure **rem**, which is used for storage of the quotient, must be a name.

```
>  # suppose that quotient has been assigned some value
>  quotient := 0:
>  rem( x^3 + x + 1, x^2 + x + 1, x, ´quotient´ );
```
$$2 + x$$

```
>  quotient; # value has been set in previous command
```
$$x - 1$$

If you really want to go safely, then you should reset the value of a variable first to its own name with the command *variable* := **evaln(***variable***)**.

But what if you forget the apostrophes in the above example?

```
>  quotient := 0:
>  rom( x^3 + x + 1, x^2 + x + 1, x, quotient );
```

```
Error, (in rem) Illegal use of a formal parameter
```

What went wrong? Through the first instruction, the variable quotient gets the value 0. When the second instruction is carried out, Maple first evaluates its arguments, which leads to rem(x^3+x+1, x^2+x+1, x, 0). Maple gives an error because it expects a name to which the computed quotient can be assigned as its fourth argument. If the variable quotient points to x, then an infinitely recursive structure would appear!

```
>  quotient := x:
>  rem( x^3 + x + 1, x^2 + x + 1, x, quotient );
```
$$2 + x$$

```
>  eval(quotient,1), eval(quotient,2);
```
$$x, x - 1$$

So, internally an assignment x := x - 1 is carried out, and this will cause an error when you later refer to x.

In other instances, you also want to or actually need to suppress full evaluation of expressions or of parts of expressions. Let us, for example, compute the sum of the first five prime numbers with the procedure **sum**.

```
>  i := 0: # assume i has been assigned some value
>  sum( ithprime(i), i=1..5 );
```

Error, (in ithprime) argument must be a positive integer

When Maple evaluates the argument ithprime(i) in the above function call it notices that it has gotten an invalid argument, viz., i instead of a natural number. In our next try we use apostrophes to suppress premature evaluation.

```
>  sum( 'ithprime(i)', i=1..5 );
```

Error, (in sum) summation variable previously assigned,
               second argument evaluates to, 0 = 1 .. 5

It still does not work but the error message explains the problem. So, you must also ensure that the summation index evaluates to a name.

```
>  sum( 'ithprime(i)', 'i'=1..5 );
```
$$28$$

Good advice:

> *In commands like* **sum**, *always use quotation marks around the summand and the summation index unless you are sure that they can be omitted.*

The result of evaluation of an expression enclosed by apostrophes can be best described as peeling off a pair of quotes.

```
>  x := 1: # in this example x always has the value 1
>  x+1;
```
$$2$$

```
>  'x'+1;
```
$$x + 1$$

```
>  'x+1';
```
$$x + 1$$

```
>  '''x'+1'';
```
$$''x' + 1'$$

```
>  ";
```
$$'x' + 1$$

```
>  ";
```
$$x + 1$$

```
>  ";
```
$$2$$

3.3 Names of Variables

In Maple, the simplest kind of names of variables and constants are *strings*, i.e., sequences of letters, digits, and underscores, the first of which must be a letter or underscore. The internal representation of strings is similar to that of integers: a dynamic data vector in which the first computer word encodes all the information including the string indicator and the vector length, and in which the other computer words contain the characters (maximum four characters per word on a 32-bit machine). The same size limitation for strings holds: a maximum length of $2^{19} - 9$ characters (q.v., §2.3). A few examples of valid names:

```
> restart:  # make sure that a fresh start is made
> x, a_long_name_containing_underscores, H2O;
```

$$x, a\_long\_name\_containing\_underscores, H2O$$

```
> unknown, UNKNOWN, UnKnOwN;
```

$$unknown, ?, UnKnOwN$$

Note that Maple uses both upper- and lower-case letters and displays UNKNOWN as a question mark in the worksheet interface. Keep this in mind when using Maple names for mathematical constants: π is denoted in Maple by Pi, but the system does not associate the name pi with this constant.

```
> evalf([ Pi, pi ] );
```

$$[3.141592654, \pi]$$

Display of Greek characters in the worksheet interface and in the conversion to LaTeX format have some traps to fall into.

```
> [ Pi, pi ];
```

$$[\pi, \pi]$$

```
> latex( [ Pi, pi ] );
```

[\pi ,\pi]

You may have expected $[\Pi, \pi]$ and $[\backslash Pi, \backslash pi]$, respectively.

```
> [ Zeta, zeta ] ;
```

$$[\zeta, \zeta]$$

$[Z, \zeta]$ would have been a better notation, but probably the notation is inspired by Maple's notation of the Riemann ζ-function.

Also be careful with the Maple name for the complex square root of -1: not i, but I. Another confusing notation is used by Maple for the base of the natural logarithm: not e or E, but exp(1). The next example shows how careful you must be.

```
> [ e^x, exp(x) ] ;
```

$$[e^x, e^x]$$

In the worksheet interface, the output only differs in the font choice. When this expression is converted into LaTeX code, the generated items are the same.

```
> latex(");
```

$[\{e\}^{\wedge}\{x\}, \{e\}^{\wedge}\{x\}]$

But Maple distinguishes the two expressions really as the power of x with the name e (i.e., not with the base of the natural logarithm), and the exponential mapping applied to x. This distinction comes immediately to the surface when you substitute a floating-point number and evaluate the list.

```
> eval(subs( x=0.5, " ));
```

$$[e^{.5}, 1.648721271]$$

Names starting with an underscore are used by Maple itself (recall the result of **RootOf** in §2.5). There are also reserved words that Maple does not accept right away as valid names because they have a special meaning in the Maple programming language. Table 3.3 can be obtained by entering **?reserved**.

and	by	do	done	elif
else	end	fi	for	from
if	in	intersect	local	minus
mod	not	od	option	options
or	proc	quit	read	save
stop	then	to	union	while

TABLE 3.3. Reserved words in Maple.

Furthermore, there are names that already have a meaning in Maple, e.g., names of mathematical functions like **sin**, **cos**, **exp**, **sqrt**, ..., names of Maple procedures like **copy**, **indices**, **lhs**, **rhs**, **type**, **coeff**, **degree**, **order**, ..., and names of data types in Maple like **set**, **list**, **matrix**, ... Most of these names are protected in Maple so that you cannot assign them values by accident. Use the procedures **protect** and **unprotect** if you want to add your own protected words or want to redefine names that are already protected.

An example: you can extend the built-in procedure **unames** so that the output is a sorted list of names.

```
> unprotect(unames):
> unames := subs( old_unames=eval(unames),
>     proc() sort( [old_unames()] ) end ):
> protect(unames):
```

```
>  whattype( unames() ); # check whether it is a list
```

$$list$$

Indexed names are a bit special when you want to protect them. When you assign an indexed name a value, you create a table (see §12.5) with the header of the indexed name as the name of the table. To prevent such an assignment, you must therefore protect the header instead of the indexed name.

```
>  protect(A):   A[1]  := 2;
```

```
Error,
attempting to assign to array/table `A` which is protected
```

A third category of names that cannot be assigned any arbitrary value are the so-called *environment variables*. Entering the help request **?environment** gives you the following list of built-in environment variables.

```
Digits, Normalizer, Testzero, mod, printlevel, ", "", """
```

For example, the environment variable `printlevel` allows you to control and customize the amount of information displayed on the screen during a computation. Its default value is 1, but you cannot make it half as verbose by the following assignment.

```
>  printlevel := 1/2;
```

```
Error, printlevel must be a word size integer
```

An environment variable is Maple's analogue of a *fluid variable* in MuPAD, Reduce, and Lisp: such a variable is globally known inside a procedure and automatically reset to its old value after a procedure has been executed. An example makes this clearer: we define a procedure that does numerical evaluation in 30 digits.

```
>  Digits; # the current value
```

$$10$$

```
>  evalf30 := proc(expr)
>    Digits := 30; # Digits temporarily set to 30
>    evalf( expr )
>  end:
>  evalf30( Pi ); # Pi in 30 digits
```

$$3.141592653589793238462643383328$$

```
>  Digits; # Digits is bound to old value
```

$$10$$

Other environment variables in Maple have names that start with _Env, such as _EnvExplicit for notation of algebraic numbers and functions in the result of **solve**, or _Envsignum0 for definition of signum(0). You can also define your own environment variable: simply choose a name that starts with _Env. But be careful, names starting with an underscore are used by Maple itself at several places. Good advice:

> *Avoid using names that start with an underscore if they are not absolutely necessary.*

Otherwise, you may get puzzled by results of Maple like the one shown below.

```
>  _Z:=sqrt(2):
>  RootOf(x^2-x,x);
```

Error, (in RootOf) expression independent of 2^(1/2)

If you want to use spaces in a name for reasons of readability, or if you want to use special characters such as dots, colons, or slashes, then you must surround the name with *left quotes* (also referred to as *back quotes, grave accents*, and *reversed apostrophes*). These left quotes themselves are not part of the name and disappear when the string is displayed; they only mark the boundaries of the name. Two consecutive left quotes in a string are parsed as an enclosed left quote character. Below are few more examples of valid Maple names.

```
>  `exercise 1`, `/usr/local/lib/maple/lib/C.m`;
```

$$exercise\ 1, /usr/local/lib/maple/lib/C.m$$

```
>   `Answer:`; # the colon is part of the name
```

$$Answer:$$

```
>  ``; # the null string or empty name
```

```
>  ```/usr/local/lib/maple/lib/C.m```;
```

$$`/usr/local/lib/maple/lib/C.m`$$

Don't associate Maple names enclosed by left quotes with *strings* in conventional programming languages like FORTRAN. The following example shows you this.

```
>  miscellanea := `apparent_text`;
```

$$miscellanea := apparent\_text$$

```
>  apparent_text := cos(Pi);
```

$$apparent\_text := -1$$

> miscellanea, `miscellanea`;

$$-1, -1$$

As you see, these left quotes have no influence here. Occasionally, rather strange things happen with these quotes.

> `Here starts a name which is

Warning, string contains newline character. Close strings with ` quote.

> concatenated` := 0;

$$Here\ starts\ a\ name\ which\ is\backslash$$
$$concatenated := 0$$

If you happen to type an opening left quote but forget about the closing one, Maple does not seem to accept input anymore. To get you out of this deadlock, follow Maple's advice: enter a closing left quote followed by a semicolon and everything should work fine again.

Now and then, but mostly when using Maple as a programming language, concatenation of names is handy. A few examples of the use of the procedure **cat** and the concatenation operator (.) follow.

> libnamo, cat(libname,`/C.m`);

$$/usr/local/lib/maple/lib,$$
$$/usr/local/lib/maple/lib/C.m$$

> # alternative way of concatenation
> `` . `/usr/local/lib/maple/lib` . `/` . `C.m` ;

$$/usr/local/lib/maple/lib/C.m$$

> X.Y, X.1;

$$XY, X1$$

> X . (Y, 1);

$$XY, X1$$

> X . (1..8);

$$X1, X2, X3, X4, X5, X6, X7, X8$$

> `` . (X, Y) . (1 .. 4);

$$X1, X2, X3, X4, Y1, Y2, Y3, Y4$$

> i:=4: X.i, i.X;

$$X4, iX$$

The last example shows that when using the concatenation operator, the first name does not get evaluated. The obvious design choice has been that, for example, x.1 should always evaluate to x1, regardless of whether x has been assigned a value or not. This explains why we have used in some of the above examples the empty name as first argument in concatenation.

Don't confuse the use of quotation marks in Maple; we summarize their effects in Table 3.4.

Quote	Purpose
` `	markers for a name with special characters
´ ´	delay of evaluation
"	reference to previously evaluated expression
" "	reference to the second last expression evaluated
" " "	reference to the third last expression evaluated

TABLE 3.4. Quotation marks.

3.4   Basic Data Types

Values of data are divided into classes — the *data types*. The data type fixes, among other things, what values can be taken or what operations are allowed on the data. The usual elementary data types like *integer, floating-point number*, and *string* are present in Maple, but there are many more. Maple can show you the basic type of data with the command **whattype**.

```
>  whattype( 5.0 );
```
$$float$$

```
>  whattype( `an example of a long name` );
```
$$string$$

```
>  whattype( { 1, 2, 3 } );
```
$$set$$

```
>  whattype( 1, 2, 3 );
```
$$exprseq$$

The result of **whattype** is a description of the header of the data vector. These data types that only require the header of the data vector are also called *surface data types*. In Table 3.5 we list the most common surface data types available in Maple. You get a more complete list with **?surface**.

Data	Type	Example
Numbers and Strings:		
integer	`integer`	`1`
fraction	`fraction`	`1/2`
floating-point number	`float`	`0.33333`
alphanumeric text	`string`	`xvalue`
Arithmetic Expressions:		
sum	`` `+` ``	`x + y`
product	`` `*` ``	`x * y`
power	`` `^` `` or `` `**` ``	`x ^ y`
Relational Expressions:		
equation	`` `=` ``, `equation`	`x+1 = 1+x`
inequality	`` `<>` ``	`Pi <> pi`
less-than-relation	`` `<` ``	`2 < 3`
less-than-or-equal relation	`` `<=` ``	`E <= Pi`
Logical Expressions:		
and-expression	`` `and` ``	`P and Q`
or-expression	`` `or` ``	`P or Q`
negation	`` `not` ``	`not P`
Composite Expressions:		
expression sequence	`exprseq`	`a,b,c`
set	`set`	`{a,b,c}`
list	`list`	`[a,b,c]`
table	`table`	`table([a,b,c])`
indexed name	`indexed`	`X[1]`
function call	`function`	`f(x)`, where `f` is not defined
Miscellanea:		
unevaluated concatenation	`` `.` ``	`a.(1..n)`, where `n` has no value
range	`` `..` ``, `range`	`1 .. 3`
generalized power series	`series`	x^{-1} - gamma + O(x)
procedure definition	`procedure`	`proc(x) x^3 end`
unevaluated expression	`uneval`	`` ``x + y`` ``

TABLE 3.5. Commonly used surface data types.

Maple provides three other tools for type testing, viz., **type**, **hastype**, and **typematch**.

```
>  type( x + 1, `+` );
```
$$true$$

```
>  hastype( x + 1, `+` );
```
$$true$$

```
>  typematch( x + 1, (a::string) &+ (b::integer) );
```
$$true$$

```
>  a, b;
```
$$x, 1$$

```
>  hastype( x + 1/2 * y, 'fraction' );
```
$$true$$

```
>  hastype( x + 2 * y, 'fraction' );
```
$$false$$

These three type testing functions not only test for surface data types, but also test more general types of expressions. They traverse expression trees and test for so-called *nested data types*. Furthermore, they can be used to test for so-called *structured data types*. These are expressions different from names that can be interpreted as data types. Some meaningful nested and structured data types:

```
>  type( x^2 + x + 1, polynom );
```
$$true$$

```
>  type( { x^2 + x + 1, x^2 - x }, set(polynom) );
```
$$true$$

```
>  type( x^2 + x + Pi, polynom(integer,x) );
```
$$false$$

```
>  type( x^2 + x + 1, 'quadratic'( x ) );
```
$$true$$

The apostrophes in the second argument of the last procedure call are used to prevent evaluation of this argument, just for the (unlikely) case that quadratic has already a value different from its name. It is not a bad habit to always add quotes in the second argument of **type**. After all, not all names used inside Maple are protected. With structured types, however, this can be cumbersome.

Command	Tested Type
whattype	surface data type
type	nested or structured data type
hastype	existence of subexpression(s) of certain type
typematch	testing and matching a structured type

TABLE 3.6. Tests for types.

In Table 3.6 we have summarized how to test types in Maple. **typematch** is the most powerful command: when it succeeds in matching a structured type, all the pattern variables are assigned values according to this successful match. For example,

```
> typematch( exp(x), a::exp(b::name) );
```

$$true$$

```
> a, b;
```

$$e^x, x$$

Note the use of the double colon (::) in the second part of the **typematch** command. It is not two command separators but an operator that pairs a symbol to a data type. We summarize the usage of names and operators that contain a colon, semicolon, or equal sign in Table 3.7.

Operator	Purpose
:	command separator
;	command separator
=	equation or relation
::	association of type or property
:=	assignment

TABLE 3.7. Combinations of colon, semicolon, and equal sign.

In a conventional programming language like FORTRAN you have to specify the type of a variable and it cannot be changed within a program. Nothing of the kind in Maple: a variable has no fixed type. Otherwise, your interactive work would be overloaded with type declarations, which are almost always superfluous because of the mathematical context, and type conversions would become cumbersome. A few illustrative examples:

```
> number := 1:  whattype( number );
```

$$integer$$

```
> number := 0.75:    whattype( number );
```
$$float$$

```
> number := convert( number, fraction );
```
$$number := \frac{3}{4}$$

```
> convert( number, ´binary´ );
```

Error, (in convert/binary) invalid argument for convert

The last statement illustrates that not all type changes are allowed in Maple; type changes must make sense to the system. For example, the rational number $\frac{3}{4}$ can be written as the **con**tinued **frac**tion

$$0 + \cfrac{1}{1 + \cfrac{1}{3}}$$

```
> convert( number, ´confrac´ );
```
$$[0, 1, 3]$$

Again, if present, the apostrophes around the second argument of the procedure **convert** are used to prevent evaluation. confrac is not a protected name in Maple! You can find out whether a word is protected or not by the command **type**(<*name*>, **protected**). More readable, two-dimensional output of a continued fraction is obtained by the procedure **numtheory[cfrac]** from the numtheory package for number theory.

```
> # load the function cfrac from the numtheory package
> with( numtheory, cfrac ):
> cfrac( number );
```
$$\cfrac{1}{1 + \cfrac{1}{3}}$$

Maple also has the **padic** package to compute with *p-adic numbers*. Let us, for example, write the fraction $\frac{3}{4}$ as a 3-adic number.

```
> with( padic ):  # load the p-adic number package
> # write the number as a 3-adic number in standard size
> evalp( number, 3 );
```
$$3 + 2\,3^2 + 2\,3^4 + 2\,3^6 + 2\,3^8 + O(3^{10})$$

3.5   Attributes

The data structures in Maple that have constant length such as *name, list, set, procedure, function,* and *float* are allowed to have an extra field of information called the *attribute*. Any valid Maple expression is allowed as an attribute. The attribute cannot be seen or modified by any Maple function, except for the two functions **setattribute** and **attributes**. The procedure **setattribute** creates a new data structure with an attribute, and **attributes** returns the attributes of a structure. The Maple kernel recognizes certain attributes such as `protected` for names. Some examples:

```
> setattribute( A, `capital A` );
```
$$A$$

```
> attributes(A);
```
$$capital\ A$$

```
> attributes( diff );
```
$$protected$$

```
> setattribute( differentiate, protected );
```
$$differentiate$$

```
> differentiate := diff;
```

```
Error,
attempting to assign to `differentiate` which is protected
```

```
> S := setattribute( {2,3,5,7,11}, `first 5 primes` );
```
$$S := \{2,3,7,11,5\}$$

```
> attributes( S );
```
$$first\ 5\ primes$$

```
> S := setattribute( algebraicset(
>    [ x*y*z^2 - 4, x^2 +y^2 +z^2 - 1, x - y - 1 ],
>    [ x, y, z ] ), dimension = 0, groebnerbasis =
>    [ x - y - 1, 2*y^2 + z^2 + 2*y, 8 + z^4 ] );
```
$$S := algebraicset([\,x\,y\,z^2 - 4, x^2 + y^2 + z^2 - 1, x - y - 1], [x, y, z])$$

```
> attributes( S );
```
$$dimension = 0, groebnerbasis = [\,x - y - 1, 2\,y^2 + z^2 + 2\,y, 8 + z^4\,]$$

3.6 Properties

You can associate properties to variables by the procedures **assume** and **additionally**. Maple tries to use the properties during calculations and does its best to deduce properties of expressions from given properties. Here we only give some introductory examples and describe some technicalities

with respect to display and assignment. A deeper discussion of assumptions
will follow in Chapter 13.

```
>    (-1)^(m^2+n); # no assumptions
```

$$(-1)^{(m^2+n)}$$

```
>    assume( m, odd ):
>    assume( n, odd ):
>    [ (-1)^m, (-1)^(m+n), cos(m*Pi)];
```

$$[(-1)^{m^\sim}, (-1)^{(m^\sim+n^\sim)}, -1]$$

```
>    simplify(");
```

$$[-1, 1, -1]$$

Here, Maple "understands" all by itself that the cosine of an odd multiple
of π is equal to 1. With **simplify**, Maple also uses the knowledge that the
square of an odd number is odd again, and that the sum of two odd integers
is even, from which it can draw correct conclusions about the powers with
base -1.

The associated property of a variable can be investigated with the procedure **about**.

```
>    about( m );
```

```
Originally m, renamed m~:
   is assumed to be: LinearProp(2,integer,1)
```

So, variables that have associated properties are renamed by adding a tilde.
Let's check this for m and add another property to it by the procedure
additionally.

```
>    m;
```

$$m^\sim$$

```
>    additionally( m>0 ):
>    about( m );
```

```
Originally m, renamed m~: is assumed to be:
AndProp(LinearProp(2,integer,1),
        RealRange(Open(0),infinity))
```

So, indeed the knowledge of $m > 0$ is added in the form of membership of
the open interval $(0, \infty)$. But what about the name: is this the same as the
previous one? The proof is in the eating of the pudding.

```
>    m - ";
```

$$m^\sim - m^\sim$$

Surprise! The secret behind it is that Maple generates a local name at each assumption. This has some consequences with respect to assignments.

```
>  m := 3:
>  about( m );
```

3:
   All numeric values are properties as well as objects.
   Their location in the property lattice is obvious,
   in this case integer.

```
>  m := odd_number:
>  about( m );
```

odd_number:
   nothing known about this object

So, assigning a variable removes all properties known about the variable.

```
>  assume( n, integer );
>  expr := cos(n*Pi);
```

$$expr := (-1)^{n^{\sim}}$$

```
>  n := 2:
>  expr;
```

$$(-1)^{n^{\sim}}$$

What happened? n is assigned the value 2, which is indeed an integer. This assignment removes the previous association with the variable n. However, in the expression expr we still refer to the old variable, which was renamed n˜. One solution: use **assign** as this will evaluate its arguments. If necessary, use **eval** to control the depth of evaluation. An example:

```
>  assume( N, integer );
>  expr := N;
```

$$expr := N^{\sim}$$

```
>  assign( N = 2 ):
>  expr;
```

$$2$$

```
>  assign( eval(N,1), 3 );
>  expr;
```

$$3$$

We end this session with three tricks to remove the tilde in the output of a variable with associated properties on the screen. The first trick uses the **alias** procedure.

```
>  assume( p>0 ):
>  p;
```

$$p^{\sim}$$

```
>   alias( `p` = p ):
>   p;
```

$$p$$

```
>   about( p );
```

Originally p, renamed p~:
  is assumed to be: RealRange(Open(0),infinity)

It is only an optical illusion. For example, the **latex** command will still print the tilde.

```
>   latex( p );
```

\mbox {{\tt `p~`}}

A better way of getting rid of the tilde is provided in Maple V Release 4 through the interface variable showassumed. It may have the values 0, 1, or 2: a setting of 0 hides the display of assumptions; a setting of 1 causes variables with assumptions to be displayed with a trailing tilde (this is the default setting); and a setting of 2 causes a list of assumed variables to be displayed at the end of the expressions.

```
>   interface( showassumed = 0 );
>   assume( q>0 );
>   q;
```

$$q$$

```
>   about( q );
```

Originally q, renamed q~:
  is assumed to be: RealRange(Open(0),infinity)

```
>   latex( q );
```

\mbox {{\tt `q~~`}}

```
>   interface( showassumed = 2 );
>   assume( r>0 );
>   r;
```

$$r$$

with assumptions on r

```
>   about( r );
```

Originally r, renamed r~:
  is assumed to be: RealRange(Open(0),infinity)

```
>   latex( r );
```

\mbox {{\tt `r~~`}}

An even better way of getting rid of the tilde is to overrule Maple. First
we look at the code of Maple that is responsible for the tilde.

```
>   readlib( assume ): # load assume from library
>   interface( verboseproc = 3 ): # make Maple communicative
>   print( `property/Rename` );  # print responsible routine

proc(nm)
local nam;
global _AName;
options `Copyright 1992 Gaston Gonnet,\
Wissenschaftliches Rechnen, ETH Zurich`;
    if assigned(`property/OrigName`[nm]) then
        nam := eval(`property/OrigName`[nm],1)
    else nam := nm
    fi;
    subs(`DUMMY2` = ``.nam.`~`,
        proc(nam)
        local DUMMY2;
        global `property/OrigName`;
            `property/OrigName`[DUMMY2] := nam; nam := DUMMY2
        end );
    nm = "(nam)
end
```

Now it is easy to adapt the code so that the tilde does not appear.

```
>   `property/Rename` := proc(nm)
>     local nam;
>     global _AName;
>     if assigned(`property/OrigName`[nm]) then
>         nam := eval(`property/OrigName`[nm],1)
>     else nam := nm
>     fi;
>     subs(`DUMMY2` = ``.nam,
>       proc(nam)
>         local DUMMY2;
>         global `property/OrigName`;
>         `property/OrigName`[DUMMY2] := nam;
>         nam := DUMMY2
>       end
>     );
>     nm = "(nam)
>   end:
>   assume( s>0 ):  s; # no tilde!
                            s
```

```
>   about( s );

Originally s, renamed s:
  is assumed to be: RealRange(Open(0),infinity)
```

```
>   latex( s );

\mbox {{\tt `s`}}
```

3.7 Exercises

1. What is the difference in the use of the variables a and b in

   ```
   >  a := ´a´;   b:= ´b´;   a := b;   b := 10;
   ```
   and

   ```
   >  a := ´a´;   b := ´b´;   b := 10;   a := b;
   ```
   Can you add one extra assignment at the end of the sentence below, so that the total effect of carrying out the instructions on this line is the same as the result of entering the first of the above sentences?

   ```
   >  a := ´a´;  b := ´b´;  b:= 10;
   ```

2. Explain in detail what happens when you enter the following commands in sequence.

   ```
   >  p := ´p´ ; q := ´q´ ;
   >  7 * 5 ;
   >  p = 10 ;
   >  q : 3 ;
   >  """" ; """" ; """" ;
   >  p ; q ;
   ```

3. Explain the different result of the following Maple commands:

   x*y;, x.y;, and x\y;.

4. Describe in detail the difference between the two Maple sessions below (e.g., by drawing pictures of the internal data structures).

   ```
   >  a := b;
   >  b := 3;
   >  a;
   >  b := 4;
   >  a;
   ```
   and

   ```
   >  b := 3;
   >  a := b;
   >  a;
   >  b := 4;
   >  a;
   ```

5. Predict the results of entering the following commands and check your answers with Maple.

   ```
   >  X1 := 5;   j := 1;
   >  X . j;
   >  ´X . j´;
   >  ´X´ . j;
   >  `X . j`;
   ```

6. Suppose that the variables **v1**, **v2**, and **v3** are bound. Why can't you unassign these variables by the following repetition statement (or do-loop)?

   ```
   >  for i to 3 do   v.i := 'v.i' od:
   ```

   Find two ways for having the intended unassignment done in a loop?

7. Explain what goes wrong when you enter the following commands.

   ```
   >  gcd( x^2 - 1, x - 1, x );
   >  x;
   ```

8. Carry out the following instructions, predict the Maple results and compare these with the actual answers of the system.

   ```
   >  i := 3:   x := 4:
   >  sum( x^i, i = 1..5 );
   >  sum( x^i, 'i' = 1..5 );
   >  sum( 'x^i', 'i' = 1..5 );
   >  sum( 'x'^i, 'i' = 1..5 );
   >  sum( x^'i', 'i' = 1..5 );
   >  sum( 'x'^'i`, 'i' = 1..5 );
   >  sum( `x^i`, 'i' = 1..5 );
   >  'sum( x^i, i = 1..5 )';
   ```

9. Successively transform the expression $a + b + c$ into $a * b * c$, and $[a, b, c]$.

10. Use Maple to find the continued fraction expansion of $\sqrt{2}$, c 1, and the golden ratio $\dfrac{1 + \sqrt{5}}{2}$, respectively.

9. Successively transform the expression $a + b + c$ into $a * b * c$, and $[a, b, c]$.

10. Use Maple to find the continued fraction expansion of $\sqrt{2}$, $e - 1$, and the golden ratio $\dfrac{1 + \sqrt{5}}{2}$, respectively.

4

Getting Around with Maple

This chapter describes in detail how to get around with Maple: how Maple handles input and output, how to change Maple to your own taste (prompt, width of printout, labeling, etc.), how to edit inputs, how to read and write files, how to get more information about usage of computer resources, how to trace computations, and how to get user information about chosen techniques or algorithms. Formatted I/O and code generation are examples of interaction between Maple and programming or typesetting languages. Moreover, the setup of the Maple library (standard library, miscellaneous library, packages, and share library) is explained.

Some of the topics in this chapter depend on the user interface and/or operating system; we shall assume that the worksheet interface is used on a Unix-compatible machine. Occasionally we shall describe how things work in the text-based user interface or non-Unix platforms.

4.1 Maple Input and Output

Maple can react in several ways when you enter an instruction:

- The system understands the command and returns either

    ▷ the result in one or more lines followed by a new prompt,

  or

    ▷ a new prompt at once, indicating that Maple is waiting for another instruction.

In the former case the previous input line was closed by a semicolon; the latter reaction occurs when the input line was closed by a colon. When a colon is used Maple performs the calculation quietly. Later in this section we shall encounter some exceptions to this general rule.

- Your instruction is not finished yet, e.g., because you simply forgot to enter a semicolon or a colon to separate commands. In this case too, Maple is short in its response and only returns a new prompt. You may still finish your instruction.

```
>   Digits := 25:    evalf(
>     log(cos(Pi/12)) )
>   ;
```

$$-.03466823209753695510470884$$

- You entered an instruction that Maple does not understand and you are punished with a *syntax error* message. In the text-based interface, Maple points with the *caret* (^) to the place where the syntax error appeared. In a worksheet, a blinking cursor appears at the location where the syntax error was recognized by Maple. The only thing that you can do is to correct the instruction line and reenter what you hope is a correct instruction.

```
>   x*
>     *3;
```

```
Syntax error, `*` unexpected:
```

```
>   x**
>     3;
```

$$x^3$$

When you use the worksheet interface, you can place the cursor at any place to correct input (in most cases, to add brackets, to insert mathematical operators like *, etc.) and reexecute it. When the *replace mode* option has been turned on, the newly generated output replaces the previous one. The text-based user interface of Maple has a command line editor built in that allows you to edit 100 previous input lines.

- Although the command is syntactically correct, Maple refuses to carry out the instruction.

```
>   read a_non_existing_file;
```

```
Error, unable to read `a_non_existing_file`
```

```
>   123456789 ^ 987654321;
```

```
Error, object too large
```

After an error message, Maple is usually ready for new input; and it certainly is after you have entered an empty statement in the form of a single semicolon. This does not apply if you have started a name with a left quote and forgotten about the closing left quote. In this case you must first finish the name with a left quote before Maple listens to you again.

```
>   `This is a long name;
```

Warning, string contains newline character. Close strings with ` quote.

```
>   2+3; @%!
```

Warning, string contains newline character. Close strings with ` quote.

```
>   that contains funny characters`;
```

$$This\ is\ a\ long\ name;\ \backslash$$
$$2+3;\ @\%!\backslash$$
$$that\ contains\ funny\ characters$$

Here, the backslash is used as continuation character.

- By using the *sharp symbol*, #, you entered a comment. Maple does not echo the text after the sharp symbol.

```
>   # this is a comment
>   a := 2  # a := two ;
>   # semicolon on previous line is part of a comment!
>   ;
```

$$a := 2$$

```
>   a;
```

$$2$$

- Although you change conditions under which a computation is carried out, Maple does not take this into account but merely picks up a previous result from a lookup table. An example:

```
>   eqns := { seq( x[i]^2 = x[i], i=1..7 ) };
```

$$eqns := \left\{ x_1{}^2 = x_1, x_2{}^2 = x_2, x_3{}^2 = x_3, x_4{}^2 = x_4, x_5{}^2 = x_5, \right.$$
$$\left. x_6{}^2 = x_6, x_7{}^2 = x_7 \right\}$$

```
>   nops( { isolve(eqns) } );
```

$$100$$

Actually, there should be $2^7 = 128$ integral solutions. The maximum number of solutions sought for can be controlled by the variable _MaxSols. But if you set it at a higher value and call **isolve** again, Maple just takes the previous result of 100 solutions.

```
>  _MaxSols := 500:
>  nops( { isolve(eqns) } );
```

$$100$$

You must explicitly **forget** previous results to get work done.

```
>  readlib( forget ): # load library function
>  forget( isolve ):  # forget previous results of isolve
>  nops( { isolve(eqns) } ); # all solutions found
```

$$128$$

So, Maple's reaction to your input depends upon the way you finish your command and upon the history of the session. You have more influence on the output. First, there is the variable `printlevel` whose default value is equal to 1. When you assign a negative value to this variable, then no results are shown irrespective of whether a command is finished with a semicolon or colon. On the other hand, when you set a higher value to `printlevel` Maple tells you more of what it is doing. Values in the range from 2 to 4 are for information such as explanatory remarks about the chosen algorithm or information about parameters, local variables, and the precise statement being executed if a run-time error occurs. The higher the value of `printlevel`, the more information you get. High values of `printlevel`, say in the hundreds or thousands, are not unusual when you want to debug a Maple program, even though Maple contains a debugger (enter **?debugger** for more information). If you only want to see what technique or algorithm is chosen, then you should use the **userinfo** facility, which can be invoked by the assignment `infolevel[`*function*`]` := *level* for the requested *function* or by the assignment `infolevel[all]` := *level* for all functions. User information is available at several levels as shown in Table 4.1.

Level	Purpose
1	all necessary information
2, 3	general information, including technique or algorithm being used
4, 5	detailed information about how the problem is being solved

TABLE 4.1. **userinfo** facility.

Two examples clarify the use of `printlevel` and `infolevel`.

```
>  printlevel := 2:  # set printlevel a higher value
>  lhs( x + y );
```

```
Error, (in lhs) invalid arguments
 executing statement: ERROR(`invalid arguments`)
 lhs called with arguments: x+y
```

When `printlevel` has been assigned the value 2, Maple is not much more communicative than usual, except when an error occurs; in that case it will inform you about what function is called and what values arguments and local variables have. These data may give you some insight in why things do not go as expected.

```
>  printlevel := 1:  # reset printlevel
>  infolevel[ integrate ] := 1:  # raise infolevel
>  integrate( 1/(x^3+x+1),   x = 0 .. infinity );
```

```
int/indef:    first-stage indefinite integration
int/ratpoly:   rational function integration
int/rischnorm:    enter Risch-Norman integrator
int/risch:    enter Risch integration
int/risch:    exit Risch integration
```

$$-\left(\sum_{\_R=\%1} \_R \ln(-\frac{62}{9}\_R^2 + \frac{31}{9}\_R + \frac{4}{9}) \right)$$

$$\%1 := \text{RootOf}(31 \_Z^3 - 3 \_Z - 1)$$

If you still want to see a result on the terminal screen while `printlevel` has been assigned a negative value, then you must say so. Use either one of the procedures **print** or **lprint**. The difference is in the display of results: **print** yields a so-called two-dimensional layout, which resembles common mathematical notation as much as possible. **lprint** ("linear print") displays results in one-dimensional, left-adjusted format. An example:

```
>  printlevel := -1:  # Maple becomes silent
>  sols := solve( a*x^2 + b*x + c = 0, x );
>  print( sols );  # 2-dimensional output
```

$$-\frac{1}{4}b + \frac{1}{4}\sqrt{b^2 - 8c}, -\frac{1}{4}b - \frac{1}{4}\sqrt{b^2 - 8c}$$

```
>  lprint( sols );   # left-adjusted, 1-dimensional output
```

```
-1/4*b+1/4*(b^2-8*c)^(1/2)    -1/4*b-1/4*(b^2-8*c)^(1/2)
```

```
>  printlevel := 10: # Maple gives more details
>  integrate( 1/ ( x^5 + 1 ), x = 0 .. infinity );
```

```
{--> enter int, args = 1/(x^5+1), x = 0 .. infinity
```

$$\_Envsignum0 := \_Envsignum0$$
$$x := x$$
$$ra := 0$$
$$rb := \infty$$
$$indef := false$$
$$\_EnvIndefinite := false$$
$$g := \frac{1}{x^5 + 1}$$
$$surds := false$$
$$r := \frac{1}{25} \pi \sqrt{5} \sqrt{2} \sqrt{5 + \sqrt{5}}$$

```
<-- exit int (now at top level) = 1/25*Pi*5^(1/2)*2^(1/2)*(
5+5^(1/2))^(1/2)}
```

$$\frac{1}{25} \pi \sqrt{5} \sqrt{2} \sqrt{5 + \sqrt{5}}$$

```
{--> enter int, args = 1/(x^5+1), x = 0 .. infinity
```

```
<-- exit int (now at top level) =
    1/25*Pi*5^(1/2)*2^(1/2)*(5+5^(1/2))^(1/2)}
```

```
>  printlevel := 1: # reset printlevel to default.
```

By the way, you cannot refer to the result of the procedures **print** and **lprint** by the ditto operators or in any other way, because both procedures work via side effect as display of formulae but in reality evaluate to the special name NULL. This special name is used in Maple to indicate an empty sequence of expressions or an empty statement. When you use the ditto operator to refer to a previous result, NULL is skipped. So, note the differences in the following commands.

```
>  Example := 11/12, evalf(exp(-10)), NULL, (1-x)/(1+x):
>  `some text`;
```

some text

```
>  lprint( Example ); # display of some expressions
```

```
11/12    .4539992976248485153559152e-4    (1-x)/(1+x)
```

```
>  ";
```

some text

```
>  Example: # evaluation to a sequence of expressions
>  ";
```

$$\frac{11}{12}, .0000453999297624848515355915 2, \frac{1 - x}{1 + x}$$

```
>   interface( prettyprint = 0 );
>   ";
```

11/12, .4539992976248485153559152e-4, (1-x)/(1+x)

The last two instructions show that you can set the value of the interface variable **prettyprint** to 0 so that henceforth Maple output is left-adjusted and in one-dimensional format. In §4.7 we shall see what other interface options you have in Maple to change the system to your own taste.

4.2   The Maple Library

The Maple library consists of four parts:

- the *standard library*,

- the *miscellaneous library*,

- *packages*, and

- the *share library*.

The size of the Maple library, the share library exclusive, is more than 10 megabytes, but the system loads only those functions into main memory that it actually needs.

Whenever you enter an instruction that uses a procedure from the *standard library* that has not been used before in the Maple session, the system is smart enough to load the requested procedure from the external memory into main memory itself and to carry out the computation.

The *miscellaneous library* contains less frequently used procedures. These functions must be explicitly loaded from the external memory into main memory by the command **readlib**.

```
>   f := exp(a*z) / ( 1 + exp(z) );   # some formula
```

$$f := \frac{e^{(a z)}}{1 + e^z}$$

```
>   residue( f, z=Pi*I );
```

$$\mathrm{residue}(\frac{e^{(a z)}}{1 + e^z}, z = I\pi)$$

The procedure **residue** for computing the residue of a complex function at a pole resides in the *miscellaneous library* and has not yet been loaded into main memory. Maple leaves it this way and waits for the moment that you define the function, i.e., load it from the library.

```
>   readlib( residue );   # load library function
```

$$\mathrm{proc}(f, a) \ldots \mathrm{end}$$

```
>   residue( f, z=Pi*I );
```

$$-e^{(I \, a \, \pi)}$$

```
>   residue( 1 / ( z^2 + a^2 ), z=a*I );
```

$$-\frac{1}{2}\frac{I}{a}$$

There are also packages for more specialized purposes in Maple, e.g., the orthopoly package for orthogonal polynomials (among others, Hermite, Legendre, Laguerre, and Chebyshev polynomials). To use a function from this package you have to mention the name of the package as well. For example, to compute a Chebyshev polynomial you enter

```
>   orthopoly[T](4,x);
```

$$8 \, x^4 - 8 \, x^2 + 1$$

There are four ways to avoid having to use such long names:

- Use the procedure **alias** to define a synonym.
  ```
  >   alias( T = orthopoly[T] ):
  >   T(5,x);
  ```
  $$16 \, x^5 - 20 \, x^3 + 5 \, x$$

  To remove the alias definition of T enter
  ```
  >   alias( T = T ):
  ```

- Use the procedure **macro** to define an abbreviation.
  ```
  >   macro( T = orthopoly[T] ):
  >   T(6,x);
  ```
  $$32 \, x^6 - 48 \, x^4 + 18 \, x^2 - 1$$

  The difference between macro and **alias** is that the macro facility is a simple abbreviation mechanism working on the input side,
  ```
  >   'T(6,x)';
  ```
  $$orthopoly_T(\, 6, x \,)$$

  whereas the alias facility affects both input and output (see also the examples in §2.5). To remove the macro definition of T enter
  ```
  >   macro( T = T ):
  ```

- Explicitly load the Chebyshev function **T** from the orthopoly package.
  ```
  >   with( orthopoly, T );
  ```
  $$[T]$$

```
>  T(7,y);
```

$$64\,y^7 - 112\,y^5 + 56\,y^3 - 7\,y$$

- Tell Maple that you want to use the complete package.

```
>  with( orthopoly );
```

$$[\,G, H, L, P, T, U\,]$$

The result of invoking **with(orthopoly)** is that a group of names (such as **T** or **U**) is defined to point to the same procedure as their corresponding package style names (**orthopoly[T]** or **orthopoly[U]**). The complete code of all procedures is *not* loaded from the library.

```
>  T(8,z);
```

$$128\,z^8 - 256\,z^6 + 160\,z^4 - 32\,z^2 + 1$$

Only at this point is the code for the procedure **orthopoly[T]** loaded and executed for the given arguments.

Enter **?index,packages** to get a complete list of packages that are available in the Maple library. Packages can contain subpackages: the `stats` package is an example of this setup; all package functions are grouped in the seven subpackages listed in Table 4.2.

Subpackage	Purpose
anova	Analysis of variance
describe	Data analysis functions
fit	Linear regression
transform	Data manipulation functions
random	Random number generators
statevalf	Numerical evaluation of distributions
statplots	Statistical plotting functions

TABLE 4.2. Subpackages of `stats` package.

For example, computing the mean value of a list of numerical values can be done with the **mean** procedure from the subpackage **describe**. This procedure can be activated in several ways.

```
>  data := [ seq(i,i=1..6) ];
```

$$data := [\,1, 2, 3, 4, 5, 6\,]$$

```
>  stats[describe,mean](data);   # direct call
```

$$\frac{7}{2}$$

```
>  with( stats ):  # load stats package
>  describe[mean]( data );  # semidirect call
```

$$\frac{7}{2}$$

```
>  with( describe ):  # load subpackage
>  mean( data );  # call after loading subpackage
```

$$\frac{7}{2}$$

Finally, there is the *share library* containing user-developed Maple procedures and packages. Enter **?share,address** to see where to get updates of the share library from, and enter **?share,contrib** to see how you can contribute yourself to the share library. When Maple is properly installed, you can access the code in the share library by entering

```
>  with( share ):
```

Hereafter you can read each procedure and load each package from the share library as if it were a regular Maple procedure or package. For example, you can load Dongming Wang's implementation of Ritt-Wu's characteristic sets method [186] and use it to solve a system of polynomial equations.

```
>  readshare( charsets, algebra ):
>  with( charsets );
```

$[cfactor, charser, charset, csolve, ecs, eics, ics, iniset, ivd, mcharset,$
$\quad mcs, mecs, qics, remset, triser]$

```
>  polys := [x^2 - 2*x*z + 5, x*y^2 + y*z^3,
>     3*y^2 - 8*z^3 ];
```

$$polys := [\, x^2 - 2\,x\,z + 5, x\,y^2 + y\,z^3, 3\,y^2 - 8\,z^3 \,]$$

```
>  vars := [ x, y, z ]:
>  sols := csolve( polys, vars );
```

$$sols := \{\, y = 0, x = I\,\sqrt{5}, z = 0 \,\}, \{\, y = 0, x = -I\,\sqrt{5}, z = 0 \,\},$$
$$\{\, x = \%1, y = -\frac{8}{3}\,\%1, z = \frac{1}{2}\,\frac{\%1^2 + 5}{\%1} \,\}$$
$$\%1 := \mathrm{RootOf}(\, 3\,\_Z^6 - 64\,\_Z^5 + 45\,\_Z^4 + 225\,\_Z^2 + 375 \,)$$

4.3   Reading and Writing Files

First of all we distinguish between

- worksheet files;

- files containing Maple code in a format that can only be understood by the computer algebra system;

- files containing Maple code in a user-readable and user-understandable format, i.e., code that has been written in the Maple programming language itself;

- files containing results of Maple calculations, which for their part cannot be used as input for further computations, and

- files containing formatted input/output, which are created by or can be read by other applications.

The latter category of files will be dealt with in the next sections. Here, we shall concentrate on only the first four types of files.

Let us first look at worksheet files, which often have the extension `.mws` (Maple WorkSheet). These are ASCII files that contain the input, output, graphics, and text cells of worksheets together with style information. They can be loaded in a new Maple session and commands can be recomputed.

Next, we look at the fourth category of files, i.e., files used for display or storage of computational results. Normally, the result of a Maple command that has been terminated by a semicolon is embedded in the worksheet or shown on the terminal screen. However, you can also transfer the output to a file so that you can read through the results at your leisure or print the results on paper. For example, to transfer all results in a Maple session to the file `outputfile` it suffices to enter

```
>  writeto( outputfile ):
```

Henceforth, all Maple output is redirected to the file instead of to the worksheet or terminal screen. However, there is a difference between the worksheet and text-based user interface. When you use the text-based interface, then also the prompt ">", the given instructions, and the run-time messages are written into the file. The reason for this is that, when the text-based interface is used, Maple cannot write simultaneously to a file and the terminal screen. The instructions that you enter are carried out in a row. Suppose that you enter the commands

```
>  number := 90;
>  polynomial := x^2 + 81;
>  subs( x = number, polynomial );
>  writeto( terminal );
```

Everything from the last command is shown on the terminal screen again.

```
>    ";
```

$$8181$$

```
>    quit
```

The file `outputfile` looks as follows (in case you use the text-based interface, you must turn off printing of input statements and bytes-used message via **interface(echo=0)**).

$$number \; := \; 90$$

$$
\begin{array}{c}
2 \\
polynomial \; := \; x \; + \; 81
\end{array}
$$

$$8181$$

Keep in mind that **writeto** overwrites an existing file. If you want to avoid this and just want to append output, then you should use the procedure **appendto**. As was remarked before, you cannot do very much else with the output file but reading and printing. You cannot use it as input for a new Maple session without further processing.

With the procedure **save** you can indeed save results of Maple calculations in such a way that they can be used again in a Maple session. You read data from such a file back into memory with the Maple procedure **read**. The data transfer into an output file can be done in two ways:

- in an internal format that can only be understood by Maple (when the filename ends with ".m") or otherwise

- in a human-readable format or plain text format.

Let us look at an example.

```
>    restart; # ensure a fresh start of maple
>    polynomial := x^2 + 2*x +1; `number four` := 4;
```

$$polynomial := x^2 + 2\,x + 1$$
$$number\;four := 4$$

```
>    save datafile;
>    save `datafile.m`;
>    quit
```

Do not forget to use the back quotes around the name `datafile.m`, otherwise Maple concatenates it to `datafilem` and consequently transfers results in user-readable format instead of internal Maple format. Note that you will also need the back quotes when you want to make use of a subdirectory and need the Unix-separator /, otherwise this symbol is used as a division operator. If you work under Unix, you cannot use abbreviations like ~ (tilde) for your home directory, but must use full pathnames instead. Otherwise, reading and writing is always done relative to the directory from which you started the Maple session.

The files `datafile` and `datafile.m` both contain all the knowledge of Maple just before the data transfer. This can be the starting point for a new Maple session; you can read (and if desired change) the file `datafile` with an editor or look at it with the Unix command **cat** or **more**. Inside Maple you can supply such a command via **ssystem**. This command returns a list of two values: the first is an integer, the return code of the system, and the second is a Maple name with all the output. We shall only look at the second value.

```
>  ssystem( `cat datafile` )[2];
```

```
                `number four`  := 4;
                polynomial := x^2+2*x+1;
```

You see that readability leaves a lot to be desired because of the one-dimensional layout chosen by Maple. But let us read the file in a new Maple session.

```
>  read datafile;
```

$$polynomial := x^2 + 2\,x + 1$$
$$number\ four := 4$$

```
>  `number four` * polynomial;
```

$$4\,x^2 + 8\,x + 4$$

```
>  quit
```

You see that the instructions in the file `datafile` are dealt with as if they were entered directly from the keyboard. Therefore, you can prepare in your favorite editor a file suitable for **read** by writing down Maple instructions one after another.

When you start Maple, the system always looks first for an initialization file that can be read in the above way. For example, under the Unix operating system, Maple searches first for a system-wide initialization file called `init` in the `src` subdirectory of the Maple library, and second for an initialization file `.mapleinit` in your home directory. Using this file you can automatically load library packages that you always want to use, reset interface variables (see the last section), and so on.

When all data have been read from a file by the Maple procedure **read**, Maple resumes the handling of instructions entered from the previous input stream; this may be from the Maple worksheet, the terminal screen, or from another file.

You see that all incoming data from the **read** instruction are redisplayed on the terminal screen. In some cases this is a handy reminder, but at others it is just too much information. You could have suppressed display of data by prepending to the user-readable file two lines in which you save the current value of **printlevel** and give it the new value -1, and by appending a line in which **printlevel** gets back its old value. But this is extra work. As you will see in the session below, echoing of input from a file does not happen when the file is in internal Maple format, i.e., a file with the name extension ".m." However, the most important advantage of using internal Maple format is that reading and writing is done more efficiently than in user-readable format. The file datafile.m used below is not user-readable, but in internal Maple format. However, the file is in ASCII characters so that it can be transferred by email.

```
> read `datafile.m`;
> polynomial := factor( polynomial );
```

$$polynomial := (x + 1)^2$$

```
> squarenumber := subs( x=`number four`, polynomial );
```

$$squarenumber := 25$$

You do not have to save all variables; you may choose. As a continuation of the above session we write the variable **number four** and the expression $(x + 1)^2$ to the user-readable file **output**.

```
> save `number four`, polynomial, output;
```

The file **output** will have the following contents.

```
`number four` := 4;
polynomial := (x+1)^2;
```

Speed and silence while reading files that are in internal Maple format becomes more important when you load procedures from the Maple library. You don't want to see messages about use or definitions of library functions each time they are loaded.

But why another Maple procedure, viz., **readlib**, for reading library functions? Why not use the **read** command? The answer lies in the hierarchical file structure that Maple presumes. Reading from and writing to a file always takes place with respect to the position where you were in the file structure when you launched Maple, unless you specify a full pathname. You can ask for the full pathname of the Maple library by asking the value of the variable **libname** within a Maple session. The answer will look like

```
> libname;
```

$$/usr/local/lib/maple/lib$$

From there you can read, for instance, the file mtaylor.m by

```
>  read `/usr/local/lib/maple/lib/mtaylor.m`:
```

or

```
>  read `` . libname . `/mtaylor.m`:
```

Of course it is cumbersome and error-prone to type such long names whenever you need something from the Maple library. An abbreviation is more convenient.

```
>  readlib( mtaylor ):
```

Maple seems to interpret the command as

```
>  read `` . libname . `/` . mtaylor . `.m`:
```

Actually, Maple does more: it checks whether a procedure with the name **mtaylor** is indeed defined as a result of this read instruction or not, and it returns the value read as the value of the **readlib** command. Hence, you can immediately specify the arguments and compute a multivariate taylor series.

```
>  readlib( mtaylor )( sin(x+y), [x,y] );
```

$$x + y - \frac{1}{6}\,x^3 \quad \frac{1}{2}\,y\,x^2 - \frac{1}{2}\,y^2\,x - \frac{1}{6}\,y^3 + \frac{1}{120}\,x^5 + \frac{1}{24}\,y\,x^4 + \frac{1}{12}\,y^2\,x^3$$
$$+ \frac{1}{12}\,y^3\,x^2 + \frac{1}{24}\,y^4\,x + \frac{1}{120}\,y^5$$

```
>  sort( simplify( ", {z=x+y}, [x,y,z] ) );
```

$$\frac{1}{120}\,z^5 - \frac{1}{6}\,z^3 + z$$

```
>  subs( z=x+y, " );
```

$$\frac{1}{120}\,(x+y)^5 - \frac{1}{6}\,(x+y)^3 + x + y$$

Fortunately, most of the Maple procedures are loaded automatically from the library when invoked. An example of such a *readlib-defined function* is **gcd**, which is initially defined by gcd := 'readlib('gcd')'.

```
>  eval( gcd, 1 ); # value of gcd
```

$$\text{readlib}('gcd')$$

```
>  gcd( x^3-1, x^2-1 );
```

$$x - 1$$

As you have seen above, readlib-defined functions will be automatically loaded when invoked. So, you actually need not know the distinction between them and functions in the kernel.

In Maple you can use more than one library. For example, when the *share library* has been loaded, the variable **sharename** contains the location of the share library, and the variable `libname` is a sequence of names of two libraries that are searched in order.

> `with( share ):`

> `sharename;`

$$/usr/local/lib/share$$

> `libname;`

$$/usr/local/lib/maple/lib,\ /usr/local/lib/maple/share$$

The support of multiple libraries also allows users to override the Maple library and to have private libraries. By the assignment

> `libname := `/ufs/heck/private_maplelib`, libname:`

you instruct Maple to look first in the private library and, if this does not lead to a result, in the standard library, whenever you call the **readlib** procedure or a readlib-defined procedure.

Table 4.3 summarizes the commands for reading and writing of Maple files.

Command	Meaning
read(*file* **)**	read Maple input from readable *file*
read(`*file.m*` **)**	read Maple input from internally formatted `*file.m*`
readlib(*command* **)**	read *command* from corresponding library file
save(*file* **)**	save all assigned variables to readable *file*
save(`*file.m*` **)**	save all assigned variables to internally formatted `*file.m*`
save(*varseq, filename* **)**	save variables from the sequence *varseq* to the file called *filename*
appendto(*file* **)**	append all subsequent results to readable *file*
writeto(*file* **)**	write all subsequent results to readable *file*
writeto(*terminal* **)**	write all subsequent results to the screen

TABLE 4.3. Reading and writing of Maple files.

4.4   Importing and Exporting Numerical Data

Importing Numerical Data

The procedures **readline** and **readdata** are utilities in Maple to read raw data from a file or terminal screen. **readline** reads in one line from the specified file or terminal. **readdata** reads in numerical data arranged in columns from a file or terminal screen.

Consider a data file, say numericaldata, in the current directory and three
lines long with the following information:

```
1        .84        .54
2        .91       -.42
3        .14       -.99
```

Below are a few examples of how this file or part of it can be read.
```
>  readlib( readdata ):  # load the library function
>  readdata( numericaldata, 3 ); # read 3 columns of floats
```
$$[[1., .84, .54], [2., .91, -.42], [3., .14, -.99]]$$

```
>  readdata( numericaldata, 2 ); # read 2 columns of floats
```
$$[[1., .84], [2., .91], [3., .14]]$$

```
>  readdata( numericaldata );    # read 1st column of floats
```
$$[1., 2., 3.]$$

For **readdata**, the data must consist of integers or floats arranged in
columns separated by white space. You can explicitly ask for reading integers.
```
>  readdata( numericaldata, integer );
```
$$[1, 2, 3]$$

```
>  readdata( numericaldata, [integer,float,float] );
```
$$[[1, .84, .54], [2, .91, -.42], [3, .14, -.99]]$$

```
>  readline( numericaldata ); # read first line
```
$$1\ 0.84\ .54$$

```
>  readline( numericaldata ); # read second line
```
$$2\ 0.91 - .42$$

The last two expressions are of type *string*.
```
>  whattype(""), whattype(");
```
$$string,\ string$$

Data files frequently contain both numbers and text. These more
sophisticated data files can be read only as formatted input, e.g., via the
procedures **readline** and **fscanf**. We shall come back to this in the next
section. Here, we only show how the last string can be decoded into a list
of an integer and two floating-point numbers via **sscanf**.
```
>  sscanf( "", `%d%f%f` );
```
$$[2, .91, -.42]$$

Exporting Numerical Data

The procedures **writeline** and **writedata** are utilities in Maple to write
raw data to a file or terminal screen. **writeline** writes the specified Maple
expressions to the specified file, separated by newlines, and followed by a
newline. **writedata** writes numerical data to a file or terminal screen.

Suppose we have a matrix containing the following data.

```
>   data := matrix( 3, 3, [ [1, 0.84,   0.54],
>                           [2, 0.91, -0.42],
>                           [3, 0.14, -0.99] ] );
```

$$ data := \begin{bmatrix} 1 & .84 & .54 \\ 2 & .91 & -.42 \\ 3 & .14 & -.99 \end{bmatrix} $$

The following command writes these numerical data as floating-point
numbers on the terminal screen.

```
>   writedata( terminal, data, float );
```

```
1 .84 .54
2 .91 -.42
3 .14 -.99
```

You can also write the numerical data to a file, say `outputfile`.

```
>   writedata( outputfile, data, float );
```

The file contents can be displayed as follows:

```
>   ssystem( `cat outputfile` )[2];
```

```
                1 .84 .54
                2 .91 -.42
                3 .14 -.99
```

You can also be more specific about the format of the data.

```
>   writedata( terminal, data, [integer,float,float] );
```

```
1          .84        .54
2          .91       -.42
3          .14       -.99
```

writedata can also handle nonnumeric data values, i.e., data items that are
not integers, rationals, or floats. You can actually specify a Maple procedure
that prints a nonnumeric data value in a format that you choose yourself.
A typical example is to print an asterisk if a data value is not numeric.

```
>   for i to 3 do data[i,1] := evaln( data[i,1] ) od:
>   print(data);
```

$$ \begin{bmatrix} data_{1,1} & .84 & .54 \\ data_{2,1} & .91 & -.42 \\ data_{3,1} & .14 & -.99 \end{bmatrix} $$

```
>  writedata( terminal, data, float,
>    proc(x) printf(`*`,x) end );
```

```
*  .84  .54
*  .91  -.42
*  .14  -.99
```

4.5   Low-Level I/O

Maple allows you to read and write to general objects called *streams*. A stream is a source of input or output. Files, Unix pipes, and the terminal screen are examples of streams.

The basic low-level scheme for writing output to a stream is as follows. First, you open the stream for output, i.e., you inform Maple that you want to write output to a particular file or pipe. Having opened a stream you can write to it. Finally, you close the output stream.

Table 4.4 lists the kind of streams Maple distinguishes and the commands to open and close them.

Stream type	Meaning	Open/Close
STREAM	a buffered file	**fopen, fclose**
RAW	an unbuffered file	**open, close**
PIPE	a double-ended Unix pipe	**pipe, close**
PROCESS	a Unix pipe with one end attached to another process	**popen, pclose**
DIRECT	direct access to current (default) stream or top-level (terminal) I/O stream	not applicable

TABLE 4.4. Maple streams: opening and closing.

When you open a stream, you must inform Maple how you intend to use it: READ, WRITE, or APPEND. Maple distinguishes between text and binary files: the types are TEXT for a stream of characters, and BINARY for streams of bytes.

A simple example:

```
>  fd := fopen( outputfile, WRITE, TEXT );
```

$$fd := 0$$

fd is the file descriptor, outputfile is the file name, WRITE is the file mode, and TEXT is the file type. Let us write two lines to the file and close it hereafter.

```
> writeline( fd, `this is some text` );
                          18

> writeline( fd, `this is some more text` );
                          23

> fclose(fd):
```

The output of **writeline** is the number of characters written to the file in the statement. The file outputfile indeed consists of two lines.

```
> ssystem( `cat outputfile` )[2];
```

```
                this is some text
                this is some more text
```

You can append a third line to this file in the following way.

```
> fd := fopen( outputfile, APPEND, TEXT ):
> writeline( fd, `third line` );
                          11

> fclose(fd);  :
> ssystem( `cat outputfile` )[2];
```

```
                this is some text
                this is some more text
                third line
```

An example of a two-sided Unix pipe:

```
> with( process );
```

$$[\, block, exec, fork, kill, pclose, pipe, popen, wait\,]$$

When you want to use Unix pipes, you first have to load the **process** package for the utility functions. Let us open a two-sided pipe.

```
> pds := pipe(); # pipe descriptors
```

$$pds := [\,0, 1\,]$$

A list of two file descriptors is returned, the first of which is open for reading, and the second of which is open for writing. Pipes are opened with type **BINARY**. Let us write some text in binary format via the procedure **writebytes**.

```
> writebytes( pds[2], `This is a` );
                          9

> convert( ` test`, ´bytes´ );
```

$$[\,32, 116, 101, 115, 116\,]$$

```
> writebytes( pds[2], " );
                          5
```

You can read the text from the other end in binary format and convert it to an ASCII character string.

```
>   readbytes( pds[1], 14 );
```

$$[\,84, 104, 105, 115, 32, 105, 115, 32, 97, 32, 116, 101, 115, 116\,]$$

```
>   convert( ", ´bytes´ );
```

This is a test

Finally, the pipe is closed.

```
>   close( pds[1] ):
>   close( pds[2] ):
```

Of course you can have more than one stream open at a time. The status of all open files can be asked for by entering **iostatus()**.

```
>   restart:
>   open( testFile, WRITE );
```

$$0$$

```
>   fopen( anotherFile, APPEND, TEXT );
```

$$1$$

```
>   process[popen]( rev, WRITE );
```

$$2$$

```
>   iostatus();
```

$$[3, 0, 7, [\,0, testFile, RAW, FD = 5, WRITE, BINARY\,],$$
$$[\,1, anotherFile, STREAM, FP = 728220, READ, TEXT\,],$$
$$[\,2, rev, PROCESS, FP = 728240, WRITE, TEXT\,]]$$

The first three elements of the above list are the number of streams opened by the I/O library, the number of currently active nested read commands, and the the upper bound on the sum of both numbers. The additional elements describe the status of open streams.

Maple supports formatted input and output. This allows you to read data created by other applications and to write data for use in other applications in any way you want. The I/O procedures **printf, fprintf, sprintf, scanf, fscanf,** and **sscanf** resemble their C equivalents. Their meanings are summarized in Table 4.5.

Command	Meaning
fprintf(*stream, format, args*)	print the arguments *args* to *stream* based on the *format*
printf(*format, args*)	print the arguments *args* to default output stream based on the *format*
sprintf(*format, args*)	write the arguments *args* into a Maple string based on the *format*
fscanf(*stream, format*)	read from *stream* based on the *format*
scanf(*format*)	read from current input stream based on the *format*
sscanf(*string, format*)	decode *string* based on the *format*

TABLE 4.5. Low-level formatted I/O routines.

So, the output procedure

$$\textbf{printf}(\textit{format}, \textit{arg}_1, \textit{arg}_2, \ldots)$$

prints the arguments $arg_1, arg_2, \ldots$, under control of the conversion specification *format* to the default output stream. For example, to print the numerical approximation of $\frac{5}{3}$ as a 15-digit number with 8 digits after the decimal point and 0 for the pad character you enter

```
>   printf( `%015.8f`, 5/3 );
```

    000001.66666666

In general, the format specification is of the form

$$\%[\text{flags}][\text{width}][.\text{precision}][\text{code}]$$

The conversion specifications elements and their meanings are shown in Tables 4.6 and 4.7.

Flag	Meaning
−	left adjustment within the field
0	use 0 as the pad character instead of a space (if padding is to the left of the converted value)
+	the result of a signed conversion will always start with a sign
space	a signed numeric value is output with either a leading − or a leading blank
#	if a number-sign flag is present, then an alternative output format is used

TABLE 4.6. Flags in **printf**.

Code	Printed as
a	Maple's lprint format
c	single character
d	signed decimal number
e, E	signed decimal floating-point number in scientific notation
f	signed decimal floating-point number
g, G	signed decimal floating-point number in d, e, or f format, or in E format if G was specified, depending on the value to be printed
%	single percent symbol (no conversion)
m	internal Maple format
o	unsigned octal number
p	machine address in human-readable format
s	string
u	unsigned decimal number
x, X	unsigned hexadecimal number, using a,b,c,d,e,f, or A,B,C,D,E,F for 10, 11, ..., 15

TABLE 4.7. Conversion codes in **printf**.

The main differences with C's **printf** is that %a (for algebraic) will include any algebraic expression (with no line breaks) as printed by **lprint**, and that * for field lengths are not handled. Below are some examples, in which the **lprint()** instruction has been added to get each prompt on a new line.

```
>   printf( `x=%d        y=%4.2f`, 12, 34.3 );  lprint():

x=12       y=34.30

>   printf( `%a`, 1/(x^2+1) );  lprint():

1/(x^2+1)

>   printf( `%c, %s`, a, abc );  lprint():

a, abc

>   printf( `%g, %g`, 1/2, 1/2^16 );  lprint():

.5, 1.525878e-05

>   printf( `%f`, 10.^10 );  lprint():

10000000000

>   printf( `%a`, 10.^10 );  lprint():

.1000000000e11
```

Escape characters are also convenient when using the text-based user interface of Maple V Release 4. For example, they allow you to add newline characters so that you don't need to use the **lprint()** command as in the above examples. The complete list of character escape codes is listed in Table 4.8; precede them by a backslash when you use them.

Escape Code	Meaning
b	backspace
f	formfeed
n	newline
r	carriage return
t	horizontal tabulate
v	vertical tabulate
\	backslash
'	single quote
"	double quote
?	question mark

TABLE 4.8. Character escape codes.

A few examples:

```
>   printf( `\n%s\n`,
>   `string enclosed by newlines\nand a newline inside` );
```

```
string enclosed by newlines
and a newline inside
```

```
>   printf(`\n%s\n`, `backspacing\b\b\b\b\b\b\b\bxxxxx`);
```

```
bacxxxxxing
```

```
>   printf(`\n%s\n%s\n`, `x\ty\nz`,`w`);
```

```
x        y
z
w
```

The procedure **sscanf(** *string, format* **)** is the inverse of **sprintf** and decodes the *string* according to the *format* into a list of Maple objects. The only difference to C's **sscanf** is that the Maple version returns a list of the scanned objects. Two examples:

```
>   sscanf( `x = 123.45, y = 6.7E-8, 9.10`,
>     `x = %f, y = %g, %d.%d` );
```

$$[123.45, .67\,10^{-7}, 9, 10]$$

```
>   sscanf( `f = x/(1+x^2)`, `f = %a` );
```

$$\left[\frac{x}{x^2 + 1}\right]$$

In general, the format specification is of the form

$$\%[*][\text{width}][\text{code}]$$

The optional * indicates that the object is to be scanned, but not returned as part of the result (i.e., it is discarded).

```
>   sscanf(`0-123`,`%*d%d`);
```

$$[-123]$$

```
>   sscanf(`0-123`,`%d%d`);
```

$$[0, -123]$$

The width indicates the maximum number of characters to scan for this object. This can be used to scan one larger object as two or more smaller objects.

```
>   sscanf( `date = 16121992`, `date = %2d%2d%4d` );
```

$$[16, 12, 1992]$$

The conversion specification elements and their meanings are given in Table 4.9.

Code	Converted into
a	unevaluated Maple expression
c	character
d, D	signed decimal number
e, f, g	signed decimal floating-point number
m	a Maple expression in internal format
n	number of characters read so far
s	string
o, O	unsigned octal number
p	a pointer value of a computer memory address
u, U	unsigned decimal number
x, X	unsigned hexadecimal number, using abcdef or ABCDEF for 10, 11, ...
%	single percent symbol
[...]	longest non-empty string of input characters from the set between brackets
[^...]	longest non-empty string of input characters *not* from the set between brackets

TABLE 4.9. Conversion codes in **sscanf**.

The **parse** command parses a string as a Maple statement. The option
`statement` determines whether the full evaluation should take place or not.

```
>  x := 1:
>  parse( `x + 1` );
```

$$x + 1$$

```
>  ";
```

$$2$$

```
>  parse( `x + 1`, statement );
```

$$2$$

Together with the routines **filepos**, **feof**, **fflush**, and **fremove** for file
information and control, the above low-level formatted I/O routines can be
used as building blocks for input and output of data. A few examples will
give you an idea of possibilities.

Formatted Numerical Data

The first example is about exporting and importing numerical data in
a specified format. Suppose that we have a matrix filled with randomly
generated floating-point numbers in the range (-3,3) and that we want to
write the matrix entries row-by-row into a file as 3-digit numbers with 2
digits after the decimal point (in scientific notation) separated by horizontal
tabulates.

```
>  data := matrix( 4,3,
>    (i,j) -> stats[random,uniform[-3,3]]() );
```

$$data := \begin{bmatrix} -.435481985 & -1.073335840 & -.938201558 \\ -.154463138 & .350752314 & 1.480522983 \\ -2.807626668 & 1.337844731 & .625833683 \\ 1.473480224 & -1.441128284 & -1.139547077 \end{bmatrix}$$

```
>  data := convert( data, 'listlist' );
>  fd := fopen( datafile, WRITE, TEXT ):
>  for row in data do
>    for item in row do
>      fprintf( fd, `%3.2e\t`, item )
>    od:
>    fprintf( fd,`\n` ):
>  od:
>  fclose( fd ):
```

The contents of `datafile` are now:

```
>  ssystem(`cat datafile`)[2];
```

```
        -4.35e-01  -1.07e+00  -9.38e-01
        -1.54e-01   3.50e-01   1.48e+00
        -2.80e+00   1.33e+00   6.25e-01
         1.47e+00  -1.44e+00  -1.13e+00
```

Let us import these data again but as two new lists of lists: the first list of lists contains the first two columns; the second list contains the last column of the original data.

```
>   fd := fopen( datafile, READ, TEXT ):
>   line := table(): nline := 0:
>   while not feof( fd )
>   do
>     nline := nline + 1:
>     line[nline] := fscanf( fd, `%e\t%e\t%*e` )
>   od:
>   newdata1 := [ seq( line[k], k=1..nline-1 ) ];
```

$$newdata1 :=$$
$$[[-.435, -1.07], [-.154, .350], [-2.80, 1.33], [1.47, -1.44]]$$

Or in matrix notation:

```
>   setattribute( newdata1, matrix );
```

$$\begin{bmatrix} -.435 & -1.07 \\ -.154 & .350 \\ -2.80 & 1.33 \\ 1.47 & -1.44 \end{bmatrix}$$

Next, we return to the starting point of `datafile` and read the third column.

```
>   filepos( fd, 0 ):  # rewind file
>   line := table():  nline := 0:
>   while not feof( fd )
>   do
>     nline := nline + 1:
>     line[nline] := fscanf(fd,`%*e\t%*e\t%e`)
>   od:
>   newdata2 := [ seq( line[k], k=1..nline-1 ) ];
```

$$newdata2 := [[-.938], [1.48], [.625], [-1.13]]$$

```
>   fclose( fd ):
```

Mixed Numerical and Textual Data

An alternative way of importing data from a file is via **readline**. We illustrate this on data that are of both numerical and textual nature. First we generate the data and export them to a file.

```
>   data := [ seq( [ d.i, stats[random,uniform[0,1]]() ],
>     i=1..5 ) ]:
>   writedata( datafile, data, [string,float] );
>   ssystem(`cat datafile`)[2];
```

```
d1 .797179
d2 .039169
d3 .088430
d4 .960498
d5 .812920
```

Next, we import the above data again.

```
> filepos( datafile, 0 ): # ensure starting point
> lines := table(): nline := 0:
> line := readline( datafile ):
> while line <> 0
> do
>   nline := nline + 1:
>   lines[nline] := sscanf( line, `%s%f` ):
>   line := readline( datafile ):
> od:
> newdata := [ seq( lines[k], k=1..nline ) ]:
```

Nonuniform Data

Our final example of formatted I/O will be about importing nonuniform data. Many data files contain, besides numerical data, also headers that describe the file's contents, creation time, author, and so on. Furthermore, data may not have the same format throughout the entire data set. The data set **agriculture** is extracted from a dataset about agriculture in the Netherlands obtained from Statistics Netherlands (URL: http://www.cbs.nl). Its contents are

```
Title   Livestock in Holland in Recent Years.
Origin  Statistics Netherlands (http://www.cbs.nl).
```

Livestock	unit	1985	1990	1993	1994
Cattle	mln	5.2	4.9	4.8	4.7
Pigs	mln	12.4	13.9	15.0	14.6
Sheep	mln	0.8	1.7	1.9	1.8
Chickens	mln	90	93	96	92
Horses	1000	62	70	92	97
Goats	1000	12	61	57	64

We import these data and process them.

```
> fd := fopen( agriculture, READ, TEXT ):
> readline( fd ); # read title
```

$$Title\ Livestock\ in\ Holland\ in\ Recent\ Years.$$

```
> title := substring( ", 7..length(") );
```

$$title := Livestock\ in\ Holland\ in\ Recent\ Years.$$

```
> readline( fd ); # read origin
```
$$Origin\ Statistics\ Netherlands\ (http://www.cbs.nl)$$

```
> origin := substring( ", 8..length(") );
```
$$origin := Statistics\ Netherlands\ (http://www.cbs.nl)$$

```
> readline( fd ): # read empty line
> fscanf( fd, `%s%s%d%d%d%d` );
```
$$[\,Livestock, unit, 1985, 1990, 1993, 1994\,]$$

```
> header := ":
> readline( fd ): # read empty line
> livestock := table():
> while not feof( fd )
> do
>    line := fscanf(fd,`%s%a%f%f%f%f`):
>    if line <> 0 then
>      line := subs( mln=10^6, line ):
>      fctr := line[2]:
>      livestock[line[1]] := map( z -> fctr*z, line[3..6] )
>    fi
> od:
> livestock[Horses], livestock[Sheep]; # two examples
```
$$[\,62000., 70000., 92000., 97000.\,],$$
$$[\,800000.0, .17000000\,10^7, .19000000\,10^7, .18000000\,10^7\,]$$

4.6   Code Generation

You can find the roots of a third-degree polynomial with **solve**, Maple's general equation solver.

```
> polyeqn := x^3 - a*x = 1;
```
$$polyeqn := x^3 - a\,x = 1$$

```
> sols := solve( polyeqn, x );
```
$$sols := \frac{1}{6}\,\%1^{1/3} + 2\,\frac{a}{\%1^{1/3}},$$
$$-\frac{1}{12}\,\%1^{1/3} - \frac{a}{\%1^{1/3}} + \frac{1}{2}\,I\,\sqrt{3}\,(\,\frac{1}{6}\,\%1^{1/3} - 2\,\frac{a}{\%1^{1/3}}\,),$$

$$-\frac{1}{12}\,\%1^{1/3}-\frac{a}{\%1^{1/3}}-\frac{1}{2}\,I\,\sqrt{3}\,\Big(\frac{1}{6}\,\%1^{1/3}-2\,\frac{a}{\%1^{1/3}}\Big)$$
$$\%1:=108+12\,\sqrt{-12\,a^3+81}$$

If you want to use such analytical Maple results in a FORTRAN program you can have Maple translate the formulae via the procedure **fortran**. You cannot do this for all the solutions in the sequence simultaneously because the expression sequence data type does not exist in FORTRAN; you must translate each solution separately, or put the solutions in a vector or list.

```
>  sol1 := sols[1];  # take 1st solution
```

$$sol1:=\frac{1}{6}\,(\,108+12\,\sqrt{-12\,a^3+81}\,)^{1/3}+2\,\frac{a}{(\,108+12\,\sqrt{-12\,a^3+81}\,)^{1/3}}$$

When you add the keyword **optimized** in a call of the Maple procedure **fortran** (reasonably) optimized FORTRAN code is generated. When you want double precision FORTRAN code set the options **precision** and **mode** to **double**. The **precision** option takes care of the translation of floating-point numbers, whereas the **mode** option handles the translation of mathematical functions.

```
>  fortran( sol1, 'optimized',
>    precision=double, mode=double );

      t1 = a**2
      t6 = (108.D0+12.D0*dsqrt(-12.D0*t1*a+81.D0))**(1.D0/3.D0)
      t9 = t6/6.D0+2.D0*a/t6
```

How well or how badly the code has been optimized can be checked with the procedure **cost**.

```
>  readlib( cost )( sol1 );
```

$$5\,additions+15\,multiplications+8\,functions$$

```
>  cost( optimize(sol1) );
```

$$3\,additions+8\,multiplications+divisions+4\,functions+4\,assignments$$

Note that Maple only searches for common powers and products in terms of the internal representation. For example, the obvious code optimization for sums

$$(a+b+c)(b+c)\quad\longrightarrow\quad t\overset{\text{def}}{=}b+c;\quad(a+t)\,t$$

is not found by Maple.

```
>  optimize( (a+b+c)*(b+c) );
```

$$t3=(\,a+b+c\,)\,(\,b+c\,)$$

The Maple procedure **C** generates C language code. An additional argument of the form `filename = `*file.c*` ` can be used to direct the output to the file *file.c*. By the way, the previously discussed **fortran** routine also provides this storage facility.

```
>   readlib( C ): # load the C routine
>   C( sol1, filename = `file.c` ): # generate code
```

You can store more than one formula in a file.

```
>   C( sol1, `optimized`, filename = `file.c` ):
```

The optimized C code for the first solution is appended to the end of the file as you can see from the contents below (Remark: we split the first line of this file in two places so that it can be displayed in the current text width).

```
        t0 = pow(108.0+12.0*sqrt(-12.0*a*a*a+
81.0),1.0/3.0)/6+2.0*a/pow(108.0+
12.0*sqrt(-12.0*a*a*a+81.0),1.0/3.0);
        t1 = a*a;
        t4 = sqrt(-12.0*t1*a+81.0);
        t6 = pow(108.0+12.0*t4,1.0/3.0);
        t9 = t6/6+2.0*a/t6;
```

The **fortran** and **C** routines can also be applied to named arrays, lists of equations, and complete Maple procedures. The few examples below also demonstrate other options that can be used in the code generation routines.

```
>   fortran( [ x=Pi*ln(t), y=x^2-sqrt(gamma) ],
>     precision=single, mode=complex );

    x = 0.3141593E1*clog(t)
    y = x**2-csqrt(0.5772157E0)
>   fortran( [ p=x, q=x^2, r=p+q ], `optimized` );

    p = x
    q = x**2
    r = x+q
```

The latter can be understood as part of the FORTRAN routine generated from the following Maple procedure.

```
>   f := proc(x) global p,q,r:
>     p := x: q := x^2: r := p+q end:
>   fortran( f, `optimized` );

    real function f(x)
    real x

    common/global/p,q,r
    real p
```

```
real q
real r

  p = x
  q = x**2
  r = x+q
return
end
```

But there is more flexibility about the nature of variables. For example, you can specify p as a local variable in the computation sequence.

```
> fortran( [ p=x, q=x^2, r=p+q ], ´optimized´,
>   locals=[p] );

  q = x**2
  r = x+q
```

In the following more spectacular example of FORTRAN code generation from a Maple procedure we illustrate handling of arrays, printing of output, and error handling.

```
> trigvalues := proc(x)
>   local i,trigs: global Digits:
>   if not type( x, numeric ) then
>       ERROR( `non-numeric input` )
>   elif Digits < 15 then
>       Digits := 15
>   fi:
>   trigs := array( 1..4, sparse,
>     [ (1)=sin(x), (2)=cos(x), (3)=tan(x) ] ):
>   for i to 4 do print( trigs[i] ) od:
>   trigs
> end:
> fortran( trigvalues, precision=single );

  subroutine trigvalues(x,crea_par)
  real x
  real crea_par(4)

  integer i
  real trigs(4)

  common/global/Digits
  integer Digits

    if ( .not. type(x,numeric)) then
      write(6,*) 'non-numeric input'
      call exit(0)
    else
```

```
          if (Digits .lt. 15) then
            Digits = 15
          endif
        endif
        trigs(1) = sin(x)
        trigs(2) = cos(x)
        trigs(3) = tan(x)
        trigs(4) = 0
        do 1000 i = 1,4,1
          write(6,*) trigs(i)
1000      continue
        crea_par(1) = trigs(1)
        crea_par(2) = trigs(2)
        crea_par(3) = trigs(3)
        crea_par(4) = trigs(4)
        return
      return
      end
```

Tables 4.10 and 4.11 list the options to the **fortran** and **C** procedure, respectively.

Option	Meaning	Default
digits = n	use precision n for truncating constants	7, 16 decimal digits
filename = *file*	append output to *file*	terminal output
globals = g	specify globals g in computation sequence	all global
locals = l	specify locals l in computation sequence	none
mode = *type*	convert functions according to *type* (single, double, generic, or complex)	single
optimized	optimize code	no optimization
parameters = p	specify parameters p in computation sequence	non–left-hand sides
precision = p	specify precision p (single, double)	single

TABLE 4.10. Options of **fortran**.

Option	Meaning	Default
ansi	ansi C compatible code	"Kernighan and Ritchie" cc compiler
digits $= n$	use precision n for truncating constants	7, 16 decimal digits
filename $= file$	append output to $file$	terminal output
globals $= g$	specify globals g in computation sequence	all global
locals $= l$	specify locals l in computation sequence	none
optimized	optimize code	no optimization
parameters $= p$	specify parameters p in computation sequence	non–left-hand sides
precision $= p$	specify precision p (single, double)	single

TABLE 4.11. Options of **C**.

Maple provides the procedure **latex** to generate L&AT&EX code. When you want to generate L&AT&EX code for several formulae one after another and store them in one file use the function **appendto**. In the example below, we generate the L&AT&EX code for two of the above solutions. Here, we also show how the **latex** procedure can be adjusted to one's needs — we add the possibility of specifying L&AT&EX's math mode. We assume that the text-based user interface of Maple is used.

```
>  # ensure that all remember tables are present
>  readlib( latex ):
>  `latex/special_names`[`beginmath`] :=
>    `\\begin{displaymath}`:
>  `latex/special_names`[`endmath`] :=
>    `\\end{displaymath}`:
>  # suppress messages, prompts, etc.
>  interface( quiet=true ):
>  appendto( `file.tex` ):
>  latex(beginmath); latex(sol1); latex(endmath);
>  writeto(terminal); interface( quiet=false );
>  quit
```

If the interface variable **screenwidth** equals the default value 80, then the file **file.tex** will look like

```
\begin{displaymath}
1/6\,\sqrt[3]{108+12\,\sqrt{-12\,{a}^{3}+81}}+2\,{\frac {a}{\sqrt[3
]{108+12\,\sqrt{-12\,{a}^{3}+81}}}}
\end{displaymath}
```

In typeset format, the formula looks like

$$1/6 \sqrt[3]{108 + 12\sqrt{-12\,a^3 + 81}} + 2\,\frac{a}{\sqrt[3]{108 + 12\sqrt{-12\,a^3 + 81}}}.$$

When it bothers you to add the statements latex(beginmath) and latex(endmath) each time, you can write a small program like

```
mylatex := proc(x)
  global 'latex/special_names';
  readlib(latex):
  'latex/special_names'['beginmath'] :=
    '\\begin{displaymath}':
  'latex/special_names'['endmath'] :=
    '\\end{displaymath}':
  latex(beginmath); latex(x); latex(endmath);
end:
```

and call the procedure **mylatex** instead of the regular **latex**. After the statement

```
>  macro( latex=mylatex ):
```

you could even use the name **latex** instead of **mylatex** during the session. When formulae are too large to fit on one line, you have to edit the LaTeX file and insert breaks yourself. The worksheet interface allows you to have this breaking apart done automatically.

A complete Maple worksheet can be saved in LaTeX format, which typesets well under the style files delivered together with the software (and available by anonymous ftp at ftp.maplesoft.com). This is even more convenient for large formulae as it will take care of splitting formulae into parts according to the text width, which can be set interactively.

4.7   Changing Maple to Your Own Taste

In the text-based user interface, Maple will print during lengthy Maple computations *bytes-used* messages about the use of computer memory and computing time. These messages inform you about memory usage and computing time since the start of the session. The *bytes-used* message is of the following form:

$$bytes\ used = <x>, \quad alloc = <y>, \quad time = <z>$$

Here $<x>$ is equal to the total computer memory used throughout the Maple session, whereas $<y>$ measures the currently allocated amount of memory, both measured in bytes. $<z>$ tells you the computing time since the beginning of the Maple session, measured in seconds. An example of *bytes-used* messages sent during numerical integration:

```
>   evalf( Int( ln(x)*ln(1-x), x=0..1 ) );
```

```
bytes used=1003520, alloc=851812, time=0.62
bytes used=2006136, alloc=1572576, time=1.58
bytes used=3006436, alloc=1834672, time=2.78
bytes used=4006776, alloc=1965720, time=3.98
```

$$.3550659332$$

You can control the frequency of the *bytes-used* messages in the text-based interface with the procedure **kernelopts**.

```
>   oldprintbytes := kernelopts( printbytes = false );
```

$$oldprintbytes := true$$

Hereafter no *bytes-used* messages appear. In the worksheet interface you yourself decide via menu selection whether the message regions at the bottom of the worksheet are present or not. In the above statement we set the new value of the kernel option **printbytes** and store the old value at the same time. This format is convenient for restoring the old value.

```
>   kernelopts( printbytes =  oldprintbytes ):
```

Whereas the total number of computer words used steadily grows during a Maple session, this does not mean that the actual memory requirements grow as fast; reuse of memory takes place, and this cleaning up of memory is called *garbage collection*. Whenever this occurs Maple shows a *bytes-used* message (unless suppressed). You can explicitly request garbage collection with the procedure **gc**.

```
>   gc():
```

With the kernel option **gcfreq** you can control the frequency of the garbage collection. When you enter

```
>   oldfreq := kernelopts( gcfreq = 10^6 );
```

$$oldfreq := 250000$$

garbage collection takes place whenever one million extra computer words have been used during a Maple session; the default is, as you see, 250,000 words (1 word = 4 or 8 bytes; you can ask for the word size of your machine via **kernelopts(wordsize)**).

If you mind these Maple messages in the text-based interface, then you can silence the computer algebra system in two ways.

```
>   kernelopts( printbytes = false ):
```

This is the method you already learned. You can always find the status of the system with respect to the memory usage and computing time through the kernel options `bytesused`, `bytesalloc`, and `cputime` (enter **?kernelopts** to find out what other kernel options are available).

```
>   kernelopts( bytesused , bytesalloc, cputime );
```
$$7155008, 1965720, 7.233$$

Another, more drastic way of making Maple less verbose is to enter

```
>   interface( quiet = true ):
```

A side effect is that the Maple prompt disappears and that, if you try to write results to a file with **writeto**, the input lines are not written to the file anymore. To Maple, silence means absolute silence!

With the same procedure **interface** you can arrange the output to appear in different ways. If desired you can change the prompt, stop Maple's automatic use of labels for common subexpressions, or force the Maple output into left-adjusted, one-dimensional format. A few examples:

```
>   interface( prompt = `---> ` ); # an arrow as a prompt
---> solve(x^3+x+1,x); # labels for common subexpressions
```

$$-\frac{1}{6}\%2 + 2\%1, \frac{1}{12}\%2 - \%1 + \frac{1}{2}I\sqrt{3}\left(-\frac{1}{6}\%2 - 2\%1\right),$$

$$\frac{1}{12}\%2 - \%1 - \frac{1}{2}I\sqrt{3}\left(-\frac{1}{6}\%2 - 2\%1\right)$$

$$\%1 := \frac{1}{\left(108 + 12\sqrt{93}\right)^{1/3}}$$

$$\%2 := \left(108 + 12\sqrt{93}\right)^{1/3}$$

```
---> interface( labeling = false ); # no labels anymore
---> solve(x^3+x+1,x);
```

$$-\frac{1}{6}\left(108 + 12\sqrt{93}\right)^{1/3} + 2\frac{1}{\left(108 + 12\sqrt{93}\right)^{1/3}}, \frac{1}{12}\left(108 + 12\sqrt{93}\right)^{1/3}$$

$$-\frac{1}{\left(108 + 12\sqrt{93}\right)^{1/3}}$$

$$+\frac{1}{2}I\sqrt{3}\left(-\frac{1}{6}\left(108 + 12\sqrt{93}\right)^{1/3} - 2\frac{1}{\left(108 + 12\sqrt{93}\right)^{1/3}}\right),$$

$$\frac{1}{12}\left(108 + 12\sqrt{93}\right)^{1/3} - \frac{1}{\left(108 + 12\sqrt{93}\right)^{1/3}}$$

$$-\frac{1}{2}I\sqrt{3}\left(-\frac{1}{6}\left(108 + 12\sqrt{93}\right)^{1/3} - 2\frac{1}{\left(108 + 12\sqrt{93}\right)^{1/3}}\right)$$

```
---> Example := (1-x)/(1+x):

---> Example; # 2-dimensional layout
```

$$\frac{1-x}{1+x}$$

```
---> interface( prettyprint = 0 );

---> Example; # 1-dimensional layout

(1-x)/(1+x)

---> # reset prettyprint to high resolution

---> interface( prettyprint = 2 ):

---> interface( verboseproc = 2 ): # make Maple verbose

---> readlib( unassign ); # procedure body is printed
proc()
local i,j,n;
global assign;
options 'Copyright 1990 by the University of Waterloo';
    i := false;
    for n in args do
        if n = 'assign' then i := true
        elif type(n,indexed) then 'unassign/indexed'(n)
        else assign(n,n)
        fi
    od;
    if i then assign := evaln(assign) fi;
    NULL
end

---> interface( verboseproc = 3 ): # make Maple more verbose

---> readlib( ln ); # procedure body + remember table

proc(x)
options 'Copyright 1992 by the University of Waterloo';
    if nargs <> 1 then
        ERROR('expecting 1 argument, got '.nargs)
    elif type(x,'complex(float)') then evalf('ln'(x))
    elif x = 0 then ERROR('singularity encountered')
    elif type(x,'function') and op(0,x) = exp and
        Im(op(1,x)) = 0 then
        op(1,x)
    elif type(x,'rational') and numer(x) = 1 and 0 < x then
        -ln(denom(x))
    elif type(x,'constant^numeric') and signum(op(1,x)) = 1
```

```
          then
        op(2,x)*ln(op(1,x))
      elif type(x,'`^`') and
          (type(op(2,x),'integer') or is(op(2,x),'integer'))
           and (signum(0,Re(op(1,x)),1) = 1 or
          member(signum(0,Im(op(1,x)),0),{-1,1})) then
          op(2,x)*ln(op(1,x))
      else ln(x) := 'ln'(x)
      fi
end
# (-1) = (-1)^(1/2)*Pi
# (1) = 0
# (infinity) = infinity
# ((-1)^(1/2)) = 1/2*(-1)^(1/2)*Pi
# (-(-1)^(1/2)) = -1/2*(-1)^(1/2)*Pi
```

The last two examples show that you can view the source code of library functions together with stored values in the remember tables. Only the C code of kernel functions is not viewable.

A handy interface variable is **errorbreak**. It determines what should happen when you read from a corrupted input file. Possible values are listed in Table 4.12.

Value	Purpose
0	report error and continue reading
1	stop reading after syntax error
2	stop reading after any error

TABLE 4.12. Values of **errorbreak**.

Enter **?interface** to get a list of all interface variables, their possible values, and their purposes.

4.8   Exercises

1. Find out where the Maple library resides on your computer and read the file `isolate.m` from the library in two ways.

   (a) by **read**.

   (b) by **readlib** after you have set the interface variable **verboseproc** to two.

2. Study the interface variable `echo`.

   – First, create the file `readfile` in your home directory and let the file contain the single Maple command

   ```
   b := 2;
   ```

   – Second, create the file `testfile` in your home directory and let the file contain the following command lines.

   ```
   interface( echo = X );
   a := 1;
   read readfile;
   quit
   ```

   – Third, if your platform allows this, launch Maple from your home directory by

   ```
   maple < testfile
   ```

   so that all commands come from the particular file, while changing X in the first line of `testfile` into 0, 1, 2, 3, and 4, respectively.

   – Finally, read the `testfile` in a Maple session with the procedure **read**, while changing X in the first line of `testfile` into 0, 1, 2, 3, and 4, respectively.

3. Create a file with the following contents

   ```
   I := 1;   # syntactically correct, but run-time error
   x := 2;   # correct input line
   wrong name := 3;   # syntax error
   y := 4;   # correct input line
   ```

   For each possible value of the interface variable `errorbreak`, find out what happens when you read the file in a Maple session.

4. Consider a data file, three lines long with the following information

   ```
   1    2
   3    4
   5    6
   ```

   Read this file, convert the data into a matrix, transpose the matrix, and then printout the data in the format

   ```
   1    2    3
   4    5    6
   ```

5. Compute the second derivative of the expression x^{x^x} and translate the result into FORTRAN. Check the effect of code optimization.

5

Polynomials and Rational Functions

Maple's favorite mathematical structures are polynomials and rational functions. This chapter is an introduction to univariate and multivariate polynomials, rational functions, and conversions between distinct forms. Keywords are greatest common divisor (gcd), factorization, expansion, sorting in lexicographic or degree ordering, normalization of rational functions, and partial fraction decomposition.

5.1   Univariate Polynomials

Polynomials and rational functions (i.e., quotients of polynomials) are Maple's favorite data type. The computer algebra system manipulates them in full generality and at a high speed. For simplicity we start with polynomials in one indeterminate, say x; these are symbolic expressions that are from mathematical point of view equivalent to

$$a_n x^n + a_{n-1} x^{n-1} + \cdots + a_2 x^2 + a_1 x + a_0 \ .$$

This representation is called the *expanded canonical form* with coefficients a_0, a_1, ..., a_{n-1}, and a_n. If $a_n \neq 0$, then we call a_n the *leading coefficient* and the natural number n the *degree* of the polynomial. Later you will see that the coefficients of a polynomial are not subject to many restrictions, but for the moment we shall restrict ourselves to "ordinary" numbers like integers, rational numbers, real numbers, or complex numbers. We say that a polynomial in x is in *collected form*, when all the coefficients with the same power of x have been collected together. The only distinction from the expanded canonical form is that in a polynomial in collected form all terms are not necessarily sorted in descending order with respect to the degree. An example:

```
>  p1 := -3*x + 7*x^2 - 3*x^3 + 7*x^4; # collected form
```
$$p1 := -3\,x + 7\,x^2 - 3\,x^3 + 7\,x^4$$

```
>  type( p1, polynom );
```
$$true$$

```
>  leading_coefficient = lcoeff(p1);
```
$$leading\_coefficient = 7$$

```
>  degree = degree(p1);
```
$$degree = 4$$

```
>  # p2 is in expanded canonical form
>  p2 := 5*x^5 + 3*x^3 + x^2 - 2*x + 1;
```
$$p2 := 5\,x^5 + 3\,x^3 + x^2 - 2\,x + 1$$

```
>  2*p1 - 3*p2 + 3;
```
$$11\,x^2 - 15\,x^3 + 14\,x^4 - 15\,x^5$$

```
>  p1 * p2;
```
$$(-3\,x + 7\,x^2 - 3\,x^3 + 7\,x^4)\,(5\,x^5 + 3\,x^3 + x^2 - 2\,x + 1)$$

```
>  expand(");
```
$$-17\,x^6 + 11\,x^4 - 20\,x^3 + 13\,x^2 - 3\,x + 56\,x^7 + 4\,x^5 - 15\,x^8 + 35\,x^9$$

Contrary to multiplication of numbers, the product of polynomials is not worked out automatically by Maple; you must give a separate command, viz., **expand**. This looks like a handicap, but really it is not. It is better to leave a factored form like $(3x + 5)^{10}$ intact as long as possible in computations. This is clearer than the expanded form

$$59049x^{10} + 984150x^9 + 7381125x^8 + \cdots + 58593750x + 9765625.$$

Although Maple computes the product of two polynomials correctly, the terms in the answer are mixed up and not in ascending or descending order with respect to the degree. This often leads to sloppy expressions that are difficult to read. Terms in polynomials are not sorted into some standard ordering for efficiency reasons (both with respect to computing time and memory storage). If you really want to rearrange terms of a polynomial in descending order with respect to the degree, then you should apply the procedure **sort**.

```
>  sort(");
```
$$35\,x^9 - 15\,x^8 + 56\,x^7 - 17\,x^6 + 4\,x^5 + 11\,x^4 - 20\,x^3 + 13\,x^2 - 3\,x$$

Actually, **sort** will change the internal data structure. This is necessary because Maple stores only one copy for each expression or subexpression in memory, or more precisely in its *simplification table*. For any new expression Maple checks by "internal algebra" whether the expression can be simplified by elementary operations to an expression that has been used before and stored in the simplification table. If this is the case, then Maple skips the new expression and uses the old expression from the simplification table instead. Otherwise the expression, together with its subexpressions, is stored in the simplification table. Changing terms in a sum or factors in a product are examples of elementary simplifications that are used to test mathematical equivalence of expressions.

```
>   p := 1+x+x^3+x^2; # random order
```
$$p := 1 + x + x^3 + x^2$$

```
>   x^3+x^2+x+1; # no rearrangement, so still random order
```
$$1 + x + x^3 + x^2$$

```
>   q := (x-1)*(x^3+x^2+x+1); # the same for subexpressions
```
$$q := (x - 1)(1 + x + x^3 + x^2)$$

```
>   sort( p ); # rearrange w.r.t. descending degree order
```
$$x^3 + x^2 + x + 1$$

```
>   q; # subexpression of q has also changed
```
$$(x - 1)(x^3 + x^2 + x + 1)$$

Maple offers many procedures to manipulate polynomials; we shall have a look at some of them. Until further notice, p1 and p2 are equal to the previously defined polynomials.

```
>   `p1` = p1, `p2` = p2;
```
$$p1 = -3x + 7x^2 - 3x^3 + 7x^4, p2 = 5x^5 + 3x^3 + x^2 - 2x + 1$$

The **coefficient** of a power or monomial can be determined with the procedure **coeff**.

```
>   coeff( p2, x^3 ), coeff( p2, x, 2 );
```
$$3, 1$$

The leading and trailing **coefficients** can be found with **lcoeff** and **tcoeff**, respectively.

```
>   lcoeff( p2, x ), tcoeff( p2, x );
```
$$5, 1$$

You get a sequence of all **coeff**icients and the corresponding powers with the procedure **coeffs**.

```
>   coeffs( p2, x, `powers` );
```
$$1, 3, 1, -2, 5$$

```
>   powers; # assigned in the previous command
```
$$1, x^3, x^2, x, x^5$$

Maple expects that polynomials be in collected form before you use **lcoeff**, **tcoeff**, **coeffs**, and **degree**.

```
>   lcoeff( x^2 - x*(x-1), x );
```
$$0$$

```
>   coeffs( (x^2-1) * (x^2+1), x );
```

```
Error, invalid arguments to coeffs
```

```
>   coeffs( collect((x^2-1)*(x^2+1),x), x );
```
$$-1, 1$$

```
>   degree( x^2 - x*(x-1), x );
```
$$2$$

One of the most fundamental operations with polynomials is *division with remainder*. Maple has two procedures, viz., **quo** and **rem** — **quo**tient and **rem**ainder — to do this.

```
>   q := quo( p2, p1, x, `r` );
```
$$q := \frac{5}{7} x + \frac{15}{49}$$

The fourth argument in the call of **quo** is optional, but when used it is assigned the remainder of the polynomial division.

```
>   r;
```
$$1 - \frac{53}{49} x^3 + x^2 - \frac{53}{49} x$$

```
>   testeq( p2 = expand(q*p1+r) ); # test equality
```
$$true$$

```
>   rem( p2, p1, x, `q` );
```
$$1 - \frac{53}{49} x^3 + x^2 - \frac{53}{49} x$$

```
>   q; # quotient has been set in previous command
```
$$\frac{5}{7} x + \frac{15}{49}$$

Mind the use of apostrophes around the fourth argument of these procedures to suppress unintended evaluation of this argument.

Another important function is **gcd** to compute greatest common
divisors of polynomials over the rational numbers.

> gcd(p1, p2);

$$x^2 + 1$$

The computation of greatest common divisors is so important for so many
mathematical calculations that developers of computer algebra systems
(q.v., [37, 76, 117]) have put great effort into the design and implementation
of efficient GCD algorithms.

An even more complicated algorithm is factorization of polynomials; the
interested reader is referred to [112, 114, 115]. The procedure **factor** writes
polynomials with rational coefficients as a product of irreducible (over $\mathbb{Q}$)
polynomials.

> polynomial := expand(p1*p2);

polynomial :=
$$-17\,x^6 + 11\,x^4 - 20\,x^3 + 13\,x^2 - 3\,x + 56\,x^7 + 4\,x^5 - 15\,x^8 + 35\,x^9$$

> factor(polynomial);
$$x\,(7\,x - 3)\,(5\,x^3 - 2\,x + 1)\,(x^2 + 1)^2$$

Computations with polynomials over domains differing from the integers
or rational numbers are possible, e.g., over finite fields or over algebraic
number and function fields. Examples of factorizations of the above polynomial over such domains are

- Factorization over $\mathbb{Z}[i]$, the ring of Gaussian integers.
    > factor(polynomial, I);
    $$(5\,x^3 - 2\,x + 1)\,(7\,x - 3)\,x\,(x + I)^2\,(x - I)^2$$

- Factorization over $\mathbb{Z}_2$, the field of two elements, 0 and 1.
    > sort(polynomial mod 2); # polynomial over {0,1}
    $$x^9 + x^8 + x^6 + x^4 + x^2 + x$$

    > Factor(polynomial) mod 2;
    $$(x^2 + x + 1)\,x\,(x + 1)^6$$

    > expand(") mod 2;
    $$x^9 + x^8 + x^6 + x^4 + x^2 + x$$

Note the use of the upper-case character in **Factor**. The purpose of this is to suppress factorization over the integers; **Factor**$(\ldots)$ is just a placeholder for representing the factorization of the polynomial and the **mod** operator actually gets the computation going. Otherwise, the polynomial is first factored over the rational numbers, and then modulo arithmetic is applied.

```
> factor( polynomial) mod 2;
```
$$x\,(\,x+1\,)\,(\,x^3+1\,)\,(\,x^2+1\,)^2$$

- Factorization over the Galois field GF(4), in particular the algebraic extension of $\mathbb{Z}_2$ with respect to the irreducible polynomial z^2+z+1.

```
> alias( alpha = RootOf( z^2 + z + 1, z ) ):
> Factor( polynomial, alpha ) mod 2;
```
$$x\,(\,x+1\,)^6\,(\,x+\alpha+1\,)\,(\,x+\alpha\,)$$

The mechanism of placeholders for manipulations of polynomials is used for other procedures like **Gcd**, **Divide**, **Expand**, and so on. A few examples:

```
> Gcd(p1,p2) mod 2;
```
$$x^3+x^2+x+1$$

```
> Expand( p1 * p2 ) mod 2;
```
$$x^9+x^8+x^6+x^4+x^2+x$$

```
> q := Quo( p2, p1, x, 'r' ) mod 2;
```
$$q := x+1$$

```
> r;
```
$$x^3+x^2+x+1$$

```
> Expand( p2 - q*p1 - r ) mod 2;
```
$$0$$

5.2   Multivariate Polynomials

Multivariate polynomials are polynomials in more than one unknown. An example of a polynomial in two indeterminates x and y is

```
> polynomial := 6*x*y^5 + 12*y^4 + 14*y^3*x^3
>    - 15*x^2*y^3 + 9*x^3*y^2 - 30*x*y^2 - 35*x^4*y
>    + 18*y*x^2 + 21*x^5;
```

$$polynomial := 6\,x\,y^5 + 12\,y^4 + 14\,y^3\,x^3 - 15\,x^2\,y^3 + 9\,x^3\,y^2 - 30\,x\,y^2$$
$$- 35\,x^4\,y + 18\,y\,x^2 + 21\,x^5$$

You see that Maple has no personal feelings about term orderings or orderings of indeterminates within monomials; it just takes the ordering that it encounters first. Again, you can do something about it with the procedure **sort**.

```
>  sort( polynomial, [x,y], `plex` );
```

$$21\,x^5 - 35\,x^4\,y + 14\,x^3\,y^3 + 9\,x^3\,y^2 - 15\,x^2\,y^3 + 18\,x^2\,y + 6\,x\,y^5$$
$$- 30\,x\,y^2 + 12\,y^4$$

Here, the terms are ordered in a **p**ure **lex**icographic ordering defined by

$$x^i y^j \prec x^{i'} y^{j'} \iff i < i' \text{ or } (i = i' \text{ and } j < j').$$

So,

$$1 \prec y \prec y^2 \prec \ldots \prec x \prec xy \prec x^2 \ldots .$$

You can also use the **t**otal **deg**ree ordering defined by

$$x^i y^j \prec x^{i'} y^{j'} \iff i + j < i' + j' \text{ or } (i + j = i' + j' \text{ and } i < i').$$

So,

$$1 \prec y \prec x \prec y^2 \prec xy \prec x^2 \prec y^3 \prec xy^2 \prec x^2 y \prec x^3 \prec \ldots .$$

In this term ordering, which is the default ordering used by **sort**, we get

```
>  sort( polynomial );
```

$$14\,x^3\,y^3 + 6\,x\,y^5 + 21\,x^5 - 35\,x^4\,y + 9\,x^3\,y^2 - 15\,x^2\,y^3 + 12\,y^4 + 18\,x^2\,y$$
$$- 30\,x\,y^2$$

The above polynomial can also be considered as a polynomial in the indeterminate **x**, with polynomials in **y** as coefficients. You can bring the polynomial into this form with the procedure **collect**.

```
>  collect( polynomial, x );
```

$$21\,x^5 - 35\,x^4\,y + (\,14\,y^3 + 9\,y^2\,)\,x^3 + (\,18\,y - 15\,y^3\,)\,x^2$$
$$+ (\,-30\,y^2 + 6\,y^5\,)\,x + 12\,y^4$$

Alternatively, you can consider `polynomial` as a polynomial in the main variable **y**.

```
>  collect( polynomial, y );
```

$$6\,x\,y^5 + 12\,y^4 + (\,-15\,x^2 + 14\,x^3\,)\,y^3 + (\,9\,x^3 - 30\,x\,)\,y^2$$
$$+ (\,-35\,x^4 + 18\,x^2\,)\,y + 21\,x^5$$

Many of the Maple procedures for manipulation of univariate polynomials work as well for polynomials in more than one unknown. We only show a few examples, and invite you to experiment with multivariate polynomials yourself.

```
>   coeff( polynomial, x^3 ),   coeff( polynomial, x, 3 );
```
$$14\,y^3 + 9\,y^2, 14\,y^3 + 9\,y^2$$

```
>   coeffs( polynomial, x, `powers` );    powers;
```
$$12\,y^4, 14\,y^3 + 9\,y^2, 18\,y - 15\,y^3, -30\,y^2 + 6\,y^5, -35\,y, 21$$
$$1, x^3, x^2, x, x^4, x^5$$

```
>   coeff( coeff( polynomial, x^3 ), y^2 );
```
$$9$$

```
>   settime := time(): # start timing
>   factor( polynomial );
```
$$(3\,x^2 - 5\,x\,y + 2\,y^3)(7\,x^3 + 6\,y + 3\,x\,y^2)$$

```
>   Factor( polynomial ) mod 7;
```
$$2\,y\,(2 + x\,y)(3\,y^3 + 3\,x\,y + x^2)$$

```
>   cpu_time := (time()-settime) * seconds;
```
$$cpu\_time := 1.083\ seconds$$

No human can come near in speed to such factorizations; just ask your mathematical friends and colleagues to do such factorizations with pencil and paper! There is a lot of mathematical knowledge and complicated programming behind the procedures **factor** and **Factor**.

5.3   Rational Functions

A rational function in the unknown x is an expression that can be written in the the form f/g, where f and g are polynomials in x, and g is not equal to 0. For example,

```
>   f := x^2 + 3*x + 2:   g := x^2 + 5*x + 6:   f/g;
```
$$\frac{x^2 + 3\,x + 2}{x^2 + 5\,x + 6}$$

You can select the **numer**ator and the **denom**inator of a rational expression with the procedure **numer** and **denom**, respectively.

```
>   numer("), denom(");
```
$$x^2 + 3\,x + 2, x^2 + 5\,x + 6$$

Note that contrary to calculations with rational numbers, Maple does not simplify rational expressions into a form where numerator and denominator are relatively prime by itself. Simplifications are carried out automatically only when Maple immediately recognizes common factors.

```
>  ff := (x-1)*f; gg := (x-1)^2*g;
```

$$ff := (x-1)(x^2+3x+2)$$
$$gg := (x-1)^2(x^2+5x+6)$$

```
>  ff/gg;
```

$$\frac{x^2+3x+2}{(x-1)(x^2+5x+6)}$$

If you want to bring a rational expression into such form, then you should apply the procedure **normal**. This procedure leaves factors in the numerator and denominator in factored form as much as possible for efficiency reasons.

```
>  normal( f/g );
```

$$\frac{x+1}{x+3}$$

```
>  normal( ff/gg );
```

$$\frac{x+1}{(x+3)(x-1)}$$

There are three reasons for not doing **normal**ization of rational expressions automatically:

▷ it does not always give simpler results, e.g., $(x^{10000}-1)/(x-1)$ is more compact than its normalization, which is a polynomial with 10,000 terms;

▷ it is too time-consuming to do normalization for every rational expression that appears in a Maple computation;

▷ a user may want other manipulations, e.g., partial fraction decompositions.

We end this section with an example of a rational expression in more than one unknown, in which we divide out a common factor in numerator and denominator (check this yourself by factoring these subexpressions).

```
>  f  := 161*y^3 + 333*x*y^2 + 184*y^2 + 162*x^2*y
>       + 144*x*y + 77*y + 99*x + 88:
>  g  := 49*y^2 + 28*x^2*y + 63*x*y + 147*y + 36*x^3
>       + 32*x^2 + 117*x + 104:
>  ratexpr := f/g;
```

$ratexpr :=$

$$\frac{161\,y^3+333\,x\,y^2+184\,y^2+162\,x^2\,y+144\,x\,y+77\,y+99\,x+88}{49\,y^2+28\,x^2\,y+63\,x\,y+147\,y+36\,x^3+32\,x^2+117\,x+104}$$

```
> normal( ratexpr );
```

$$\frac{18\,x\,y + 23\,y^2 + 11}{4\,x^2 + 7\,y + 13}$$

5.4   Conversions

The *Horner form* of a polynomial is most suitable for numerical processing because in this representation the number of arithmetical operations
is minimal. We illustrate this with the previously defined polynomial p1.
The number of additions and multiplications can be tabulated with the
procedure **cost**.

```
> p1;
```

$$-3\,x + 7\,x^2 - 3\,x^3 + 7\,x^4$$

```
> readlib(cost)( p1 );
```

$3\ additions + 10\ multiplications$

```
> convert( p1, `horner` );
```

$$(-3 + (7 + (-3 + 7\,x)\,x)\,x)\,x$$

```
> cost(");
```

$3\ additions + 4\ multiplications$

Conversion of rational expressions to their **con**tinued **frac**tion forms can
also speed up numerical computations.

```
> q := (x^3 + x^2 - x + 1) / p1;
```

$$q := \frac{x^3 + x^2 - x + 1}{-3\,x + 7\,x^2 - 3\,x^3 + 7\,x^4}$$

```
> cost( q );
```

$6\ additions + 13\ multiplications + divisions$

```
> convert( q, `confrac`, x );
```

$$\cfrac{1}{7}\cfrac{1}{x - \cfrac{10}{7} + \cfrac{24}{7}\cfrac{1}{x + \cfrac{11}{6} + \cfrac{1}{9}\cfrac{1}{x - \cfrac{71}{24} + \cfrac{429}{64}\cfrac{1}{x + \cfrac{17}{8}}}}}$$

```
> cost(");
```

$7\ additions + 4\ divisions$

The conversion to Horner form and to continued fraction form are also available in the package numapprox for numerical approximation as the procedures **hornerform** and **confracform**, respectively. See §11.2 for more details about this Maple package.

Partial fraction decomposition — **convert** to **part**ial **frac**tion form — can easily be done in Maple.

```
> convert( q , 'parfrac', x );
```

$$\frac{143}{87}\frac{1}{-3+7x} - \frac{1}{3}\frac{1}{x} + \frac{1}{29}\frac{3+7x}{x^2+1}$$

From the partial fraction decomposition you can almost immediately tell the indefinite integral of this rational expression.

```
> integrate( q, x );
```

$$-\frac{1}{3}\ln(x) + \frac{143}{609}\ln(-3+7x) + \frac{7}{58}\ln(x^2+1) + \frac{3}{29}\arctan(x)$$

Note that in the above example Maple assumes that the field of definition is the rational number field. You can specify that you want floating-point real or floating-point complex partial fractions by adding a fourth keyword, real or complex.

```
> convert( q , 'parfrac', x, real );
```

$$\frac{.2348111659}{x-.4285714286} - \frac{.3333333334}{x}$$
$$+ .1428571429\frac{.7241379320+1.689655174\,x}{x^2+1.}$$

```
> convert( q , 'parfrac', x, complex );
```

$$\frac{.1206896552+.05172413794\,I}{x+I} + \frac{.1206896552-.05172413794\,I}{x-1.I}$$
$$+ \frac{.2348111659+.1542341075\,10^{-10}\,I}{x-.4285714286} - \frac{.3333333334}{x}$$

You can also do partial fraction decomposition over the algebraic closure of the field of definition so that you get all linear factors of the denominator. A detailed description of the algorithm can be found in [23]. This full partial fraction decomposition — **convert** to **full part**ial **frac**tion form — can be done in the following way.

```
> convert( q , 'fullparfrac', x );
```

$$-\frac{1}{3}\frac{1}{x} + \left(\sum_{\_\alpha=\%1} \frac{\frac{595}{2523} - \frac{3}{58}\_\alpha + \frac{581}{5046}\_\alpha^2}{x-\_\alpha} \right)$$

$$\%1 := \text{RootOf}(\,7\_Z^3 - 3\_Z^2 + 7\_Z - 3\,)$$

You can have the roots of the third-degree polynomial in radical form and
the summation carried out.

```
>  convert( ", radical );
```

$$-\frac{1}{3}\frac{1}{x}+\frac{143}{609}\frac{1}{x-\dfrac{3}{7}}+\frac{\dfrac{7}{58}-\dfrac{3}{58}I}{x-I}+\frac{\dfrac{7}{58}+\dfrac{3}{58}I}{x+I}$$

Of course it is not forbidden to help Maple when you know or guess a
suitable extension of the field of definition; simply add the extension(s) as
a fourth argument.

```
>  1 / ( x^4 - 5*x^2 + 6);
```

$$\frac{1}{x^4-5x^2+6}$$

```
>  convert( ", ´parfrac´, x, sqrt(2) );
```

$$\frac{1}{x^2-3}+\frac{1}{4}\frac{\sqrt{2}}{x+\sqrt{2}}-\frac{1}{4}\frac{\sqrt{2}}{x-\sqrt{2}}$$

```
>  convert( "", ´parfrac´, x, {sqrt(2),sqrt(3)} );
```

$$\frac{1}{6}\frac{\sqrt{3}}{x-\sqrt{3}}-\frac{1}{6}\frac{\sqrt{3}}{x+\sqrt{3}}+\frac{1}{4}\frac{\sqrt{2}}{x+\sqrt{2}}-\frac{1}{4}\frac{\sqrt{2}}{x-\sqrt{2}}$$

A final example of partial fraction decomposition of a rational expression
in more than one indeterminate follows.

```
>  ratfun := (x-a)/(x^5+b*x^4-c*x^2-b*c*x);
```

$$ratfun := \frac{x-a}{x^5+bx^4-cx^2-bcx}$$

```
>  convert( ratfun, ´parfrac´, x );
```

$$\frac{a}{bcx}-\frac{b+a}{b(b^3+c)(x+b)}-\frac{-b^2c-bca+bcx+cxa+x^2ab^2-cx^2}{c(b^3+c)(x^3-c)}$$

```
>  # write numerators as polynomials in x
>  map( collect, ", x );
```

$$\frac{a}{bcx}-\frac{b+a}{b(b^3+c)(x+b)}-\frac{(ab^2-c)x^2+(bc+ca)x-b^2c-bca}{c(b^3+c)(x^3-c)}$$

```
>  convert( ratfun, ´parfrac´, x, true );
```

$$\frac{a}{bcx}-\frac{-bc-ca+ax^2b+ax^3}{bc(x^4+bx^3-cx-bc)}$$

In the last command, we add the extra argument **true** to indicate that
no application of the procedure **normal** on **ratfun** is needed and that the
denominator can be considered to be already in the desired factored form.

5.5   Exercises

1. Consider the rational expression $\dfrac{x^4 + x^3 - 4x^2 - 4x}{x^4 + x^3 - x^2 - x}$. Transform the expression into:

   (a) $\dfrac{(x+2)(x+1)(x-2)}{x^3 + x^2 - x - 1}$

   (b) $\dfrac{x^4 + x^3 - 4x^2 - 4x}{x(x-1)(x+1)^2}$

   (c) $\dfrac{(x+2)(x-2)}{(x-1)(x+1)}$

   (d) $\dfrac{x^2}{(x-1)(x+1)} - 4\dfrac{1}{(x-1)(x+1)}$

2. Consider the same rational expression as in the previous exercise.

   (a) Write it as a continued fraction.

   (b) Compute a partial fraction decomposition.

3. Let f be the polynomial $x^7 + x^5 + 2x^3 + 2x^2 + 3x + 2$.

   (a) Factor f over $\mathbb{Z}_5$, and over $\mathbb{Z}_7$.

   (b) How can you conclude from the former factorizations that f is irreducible over the ring over integers (Hint: look at the degrees of the factors). Check with Maple that f is indeed irreducible over $\mathbb{Z}$.

4. Some factorizations modulo a prime number:

   (a) Factor $x^2 - 2$ over $\mathbb{Z}_2$.

   (b) Factor $x^3 - 3$ over $\mathbb{Z}_3$.

   (c) Factor $x^5 - 5$ over $\mathbb{Z}_5$.

   (d) Factor $x^{23} - 23$ over $\mathbb{Z}_{23}$.

   (e) By now you may have an idea how $x^p - x$ factors for any prime number p; check your conjecture for some prime number distinct from previous choices. Do you understand the result?

5. Let $f = 2x^4 - 3x^2 + x + 4$ and $g = 2x^5 - 6x^4 - 4x^3 + x^2 - 3x - 2$. Consider them as polynomials over $\mathbb{Z}_7$ and compute the greatest common divisor of f and g. Determine also polynomials s and t over $\mathbb{Z}_7$ such that $sf + tg = \gcd(f, g)$ (gcd with respect to $\mathbb{Z}_7$, of course).

6. If you ask Maple to factor $x^{2458} + x^{1229} + 1$ over $\mathbb{Z}$, then the system will complain about insufficient memory, or after several hours it will still not have found an answer. So, let us have a closer look at this problem and see if we can assist Maple. First, we note that 1229 is a prime number (e.g., with **isprime**). So, the polynomial is of the form $x^{2p} + x^p + 1$, where p is a prime number. Determine with Maple the factorization of this polynomial for low prime values of p and propose a conjecture about the form of the factored polynomial for the general case.

An experienced mathematician can tell you that the polynomial $x^n - 1$, where n is a natural number, can be factored over $\mathbb{Z}$ in the *cyclotomic polynomials* $\phi_k(x)$.

$$x^n - 1 = \prod_{k|n} \phi_k(x)$$

These cyclotomic polynomials are irreducible over $\mathbb{Z}$. With this knowledge and under the assumption that your conjecture is correct, it should not be too difficult to prove the result.

6
Internal Data Representation and Substitution

This chapter describes in detail the internal representation of polynomials and rational functions. This topic is not only of theoretical interest; it is also important to know about data representation when you want to fully understand conversion between distinct data structures and substitution.

We shall generalize the concept of rational expressions, and explain how the procedures defined for polynomial and rational functions extend to more general mathematical structures.

Maple's procedures for type checking and selection of parts of formulae will also be treated. These routines support you when studying or manipulating data structures.

Finally, we shall discuss sequential and simultaneous substitution, and how this can be used in the process of simplifying expressions.

6.1 Internal Representation of Polynomials

In the previous chapter, we have already seen some Maple procedures that transform polynomials from one shape into another. To get a better understanding of these manipulations and others to come, we dot the i's and cross the t's and have a closer look at the internal data representation of polynomials in Maple.

We take the polynomial $x^4 + x^3 - x^2 - x$ as our example. The expanded canonical form is represented internally by the set of data vectors shown in Figure 6.1, which is, in graph-theoretical terms, a *directed acyclic graph (DAG)*.

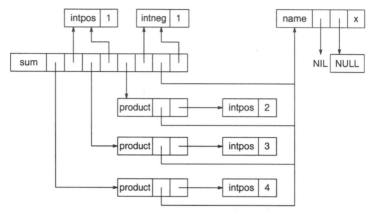

FIGURE 6.1. The internal representation of $x^4 + x^3 - x^2 - x$.

Here, you must interpret the data vector of Figure 6.2 as if it consists of pairs of expressions and their numerical coefficients: it represents the sum

$$\text{coeff}_1 \times \text{expr}_1 + \text{coeff}_2 \times \text{expr}_2 + \cdots.$$

sum	expr1	coeff1	expr2	coeff2	....

FIGURE 6.2. The internal representation of a sum.

Similarly, Figure 6.3 shows the data vector that represents the product

$$\text{expr}_1^{\text{expon}_1} \times \text{expr}_2^{\text{expon}_2} \times \cdots.$$

product	expr1	expon1	expr2	expon2	....

FIGURE 6.3. The internal representation of a product.

The NIL pointer in Figure 6.1 is used to indicate that the variable x is unbound. The pointer to the Maple expression NULL, which stands for an empty expression sequence, means that no attributes are associated with x.

At the first level, the internal representation of $x^4 + x^3 - x^2 - x$ reflects the way Maple considers it, viz., as a sum of four terms, x^4, x^3, x^2, and x, with coefficients 1, 1, -1, and -1, respectively. These components are internally represented by data vectors. But, surprise, the term x^4 is internally represented by a data vector consisting of the header product, a pointer to the unknown x, and a pointer to the exponent 4. You might have expected a data vector as in Figure 6.4.

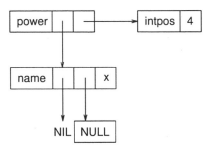

FIGURE 6.4. False internal representation of x^4.

This type of DAG indeed exists in Maple, but if the exponent is a numerical constant, it is changed to the **product** structure by Maple's simplifier.

Maple only recognizes x^4, x^3, x^2, $-x^2$, x, and $-x$ as subexpressions of the polynomial $x^4 + x^3 - x^2 - x$; as far as Maple is concerned, $x^4 + x^3$ and $x^4 - x$ are not subexpressions of $x^4 + x^3 - x^2 - x$. The fact that Maple does not recognize every mathematical subexpression plays an important role in substitution. Only this can explain substitutions like

```
>   subs( 1 = 7, x^4 + x^3 - x^2 - x );
```
$$7x^4 + 7x^3 - x^2 - x$$

```
>   subs( 1 = 3, Pi*x + x + 1 );
```
$$3\pi^3 x^3 + 3x + 9$$

Let us have a closer look at the last example. $\pi x + x + 1$ is represented internally as in Figure 6.5.

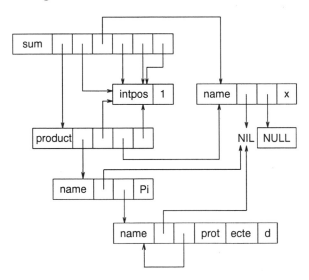

FIGURE 6.5. Internal representation of $\pi x + x + 1$.

The above directed acyclic graph clearly reflects that Pi has the attribute protected. This attribute is a valid Maple expression, viz., a name. The characters of a name are stored on a 32-bit machine in groups of at most four characters. The data structure protected has its own name as attribute; so, this name is protected in Maple as well.

If you replace the data vector that represents 1 by a vector representing 3, then you will understand the result of the substitution of 3 for 1.

The two examples above show you that the internal representation can differ significantly from the external representation, which looks more familiar and is actually what you see on the screen. For Maple, however, it is only the internal representation that counts; two expressions are identical if and only if they have the same DAG, and simplification is for the system nothing more than a transformation from one DAG into another.

Before we continue, let us think about the reasons that the designers of Maple may have had for their choice of representing sums and powers. Let us consider the representation of the monomial $x^2y^3z^4$. Maple's internal representation is shown in Figure 6.6.

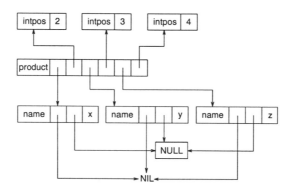

FIGURE 6.6. Internal representation of $x^2y^3z^4$.

An alternative could be to consider $x^2y^3z^4$ as a product of the three powers x^2, y^3, and z^4, with the internal representation as shown in Figure 6.7. In this picture, you see that more memory storage is needed in the latter representation. But what is more important, suppose that during a computation $x^2y^3z^4$ is multiplied by like factors, say x^5z^6. Then Maple's simplifier should recognize the like factors as quickly as possible, add their exponents and build the new data structure. In the data representation chosen by Maple, this can be done easily compared to the alternative representation. Similarly, the internal representation of sums allows easy identification of like terms and addition of their coefficients. In short, Maple's internal data representation has been optimized to make polynomial arithmetic fast.

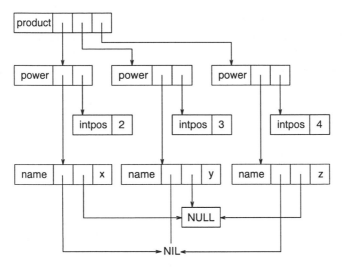

FIGURE 6.7. False internal representation of $x^2y^3z^4$.

Let us forget for the moment that Maple stores (sub)expressions only once. Then the directed acyclic graph has the graph theoretical structure of a *tree*. The *representation tree* for our example is shown in Figure 6.8.

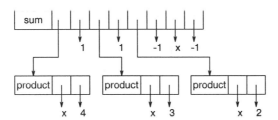

FIGURE 6.8. Representation tree of $x^4 + x^3 - x^2 - x$.

Here we have omitted the data vectors of the building blocks 1, -1, and x; they are considered as atomic elements in the formula. The representation tree of $x^4 + x^3 - x^2 - x$ also indicates that the polynomial consists of x^4, x^3, $-x^2$, and $-x$, and that x^2 is a subexpression. The main advantage of the representation tree is that it is not as messy as the directed acyclic graph. An essential difference between the directed acyclic graph and the representation tree is that in the directed acyclic graph one node is used for identical subexpressions whereas in the representation tree they are represented by separate subtrees. If one keeps this in mind, then the representation tree is an adequate and easy-to-understand description of the internal structure of a Maple expression.

Perhaps your brain is reeling from all those data vectors, directed acyclic graphs, and representation trees. Are you wondering uneasily whether you will always be able to grasp the internal structure of a Maple expression? Well, let it be a relief to you that in most cases your intuition will not fail and that in doubtful cases the system itself can assist you in the determination of the internal data structure. The surface data type of an expression can be determined by the procedure **whattype**.

>   p1 := x^4 + x^3 - x^2 - x;   # expanded canonical form

$$p1 := x^4 + x^3 - x^2 - x$$

>   whattype(p1);

$$+$$

By the symbol "+", the computer algebra system denotes that the expression is a **sum**. The procedure **nops** (**n**umber **of** **op**erands) gives you the number of summands.

>   nops(p1);

$$4$$

You get the sequence of components of a symbolic expression with the procedure **op** (extract **op**erands).

>   op(p1);

$$x^4, x^3, -x^2, -x$$

You can unravel each subexpression separately. For example, the first term is a power of x with exponent 4.

>   `first term` := op(1,p1);

$$\textit{first term} := x^4$$

>   whattype(");

$$\char`\^$$

>   op("");

$$x, 4$$

Here, the symbol "^" is used as an indication for the data type power.

The third term, $-x^2$, is the product of -1 and the power x^2. Maple denotes the **product** data type as "*".

>   `third term` := op(3,p1);

$$\textit{third term} := -x^2$$

>   whattype(");

$$*$$

>   op(`third term`);

$$-1, x^2$$

```
> op( [3,2], p1 ); # 2nd operand of 3rd operand of p1
```
$$x^2$$

In the same manner, you can unravel any Maple expression, not just polynomials. The only thing that you must keep in mind is that identical subexpressions are stored in Maple only once. In the above example, the character x occurs at four places, but internally it is only one Maple object. If you substitute y for x in the polynomial $x^4 + x^3 - x^2 - x$, you get the polynomial $y^4 + y^3 - y^2 - y$.

If you really want to dive into Maple and consider the direct acyclic graph instead of the representation tree, Maple can show you the details via the **dismantle** procedure. It displays the structure of a Maple expression, showing each subexpression and its length.

```
> readlib( dismantle ): # load library function
> dismantle( x^4+x^3-x^2-x );

SUM(9)
   PROD(3)
      NAME(4): x
      INTPOS(2): 4
   INTPOS(2): 1
   PROD(3)
      NAME(4): x
      INTPOS(2): 3
   INTPOS(2): 1
   PROD(3)
      NAME(4): x
      INTPOS(2): 2
   INTNEG(2): -1
   NAME(4): x
   INTNEG(2): -1
```

6.2   Generalized Rational Expressions

The following Maple session reveals the internal representation of a rational function.

```
> r := (y^2-1) / (y-1);
```
$$r := \frac{y^2 - 1}{y - 1}$$

```
> type( r, ratpoly ); # check if rational expression
```
$$true$$

```
> whattype( r );
```

$$*$$

```
>  op(r);
```

$$y^2 - 1, \frac{1}{y - 1}$$

```
>  op(2,r);
```

$$\frac{1}{y - 1}$$

```
>  whattype("");
```

$$\hat{}$$

```
>  op("");
```

$$y - 1, -1$$

```
>  normal( r ); # normal form
```

$$y + 1$$

Here, you see again that the internal data structure may differ from the external form shown on the worksheet or terminal screen: the rational expression is a product of the numerator and the denominator raised to the power -1. If we consider the expression as an element of the field $\mathbb{R}(y)$, then it can be normalized to the polynomial $y + 1$. Considered as real functions, $\frac{y^2 - 1}{y - 1}$ and $y + 1$ are different. In other words: in the generic case $(y \neq 0)$ you can convert $\frac{y^2 - 1}{y - 1}$ into $y + 1$.

Let us now look at the following expression:

```
>  r := (sin(x)^2-1)/(sin(x)-1);
```

$$r := \frac{\sin(x)^2 - 1}{\sin(x) - 1}$$

```
>  type( r, ratpoly );
```

false

Maple agrees that this is not a rational function. But if you replace $\sin x$ by y, then you get back the previous rational function. This is also revealed when you inspect the internal data structure of $\frac{\sin^2 x - 1}{\sin x - 1}$ with the procedures **op**, **nops**, and **whattype**. Compare the two expression trees in Figure 6.9.

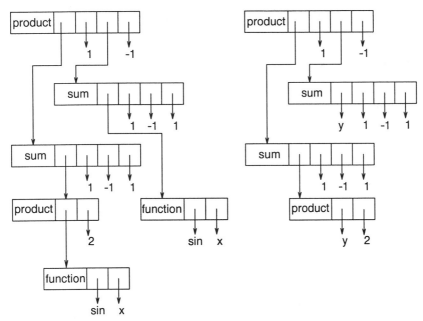

FIGURE 6.9. The representation trees of $\dfrac{\sin^2 x - 1}{\sin x - 1}$ and $\dfrac{y^2 - 1}{y - 1}$.

So, we may say that $\dfrac{\sin^2 x - 1}{\sin x - 1}$ is a rational expression in $\sin x$ with integer coefficients. Maple agrees.

```
>  type( r, ratpoly( integer, sin(x) ) );
```
$$true$$

It explains the following result.

```
>  normal( r );
```
$$\sin(x) + 1$$

Maple considers $\dfrac{\sin^2 x - 1}{\sin x - 1}$ as a *generalized rational expression*. When it applies the procedure **normal**, several things happen. First, the argument of every function call to an elementary transcendental function (trigonometric function, logarithm, exponential function, square root function, etc.) is recursively normalized before it is "frozen" to a unique name. Next, **normal** is applied to the rational expression. Finally, the frozen expressions are "thawed" again. This freezing and thawing of subexpressions is done automatically in Maple for the procedures **normal** and **factor**. Sometimes you have to help Maple in the process of considering a general expression as a rational expression via the procedure **frontend**.

```
>  num := numer(r);   den := denom(r);
```
$$num := \sin(x)^2 - 1$$

$$den := \sin(x) - 1$$

```
>  gcd( num, den );
```

```
Error, (in gcd)
arguments must be polynomials over the rationals
```

```
>  frontend( gcd, [num,den] );
```

$$\sin(x) - 1$$

The procedure **gcd** expects polynomials over the rational numbers. **frontend** is employed to "temporarily freeze" `sin(x)` in `num` and `den` to a unique name. On the intermediate results we can apply the procedure **gcd**. Finally, the frozen names are thawed. In the next section, we shall get acquainted with another method of freezing subexpressions.

6.3   Substitution

An important tool to manipulate expressions is *substitution*. Huge expressions, which are difficult to read, can be simplified by replacement of large subexpressions by smaller ones. For example, the matrix

$$\begin{pmatrix} a & b & e & f & a & b \\ c & d & g & h & c & d \\ -e & -f & a & c & e & f \\ -g & -h & b & d & g & h \\ -a & -b & -e & -f & e & g \\ -c & -d & -g & -h & f & h \end{pmatrix},$$

can be rewritten in block form as

$$\begin{pmatrix} X & Y & X \\ -Y & X^T & Y \\ -X & -Y & Y^T \end{pmatrix},$$

where

$$X = \begin{pmatrix} a & b \\ c & d \end{pmatrix} \quad \text{and} \quad Y = \begin{pmatrix} e & f \\ g & h \end{pmatrix}.$$

On many occasions it will be more convenient to use the block matrix instead of the original matrix.

Maple introduces abbreviations in the printing of large formulae by labeling large subexpressions as %1, %2, and so on.

As a rule, you use the procedure **subs** for **subs**titution. The simplest form of a substitution command is

$$\textbf{subs}(\ var = replacement,\ expression\ ).$$

The effect is that *replacement* is substituted for all occurrences of the variable *var* in the *expression*. An example:

```
>   kinetic_energy := momentum^2 / (2*mass);
```

$$kinetic\_energy := \frac{1}{2}\frac{momentum^2}{mass}$$

```
>   subs( momentum = mass * velocity, kinetic_energy );
```

$$\frac{1}{2}\,mass\,velocity^2$$

```
>   kinetic_energy;
```

$$\frac{1}{2}\frac{momentum^2}{mass}$$

Note that the variable kinetic_energy keeps its value after substitution. It can only be changed by an assignment.

```
>   kinetic_energy := subs( momentum = mass * velocity,
>      kinetic_energy ):
>   kinetic_energy;
```

$$\frac{1}{2}\,mass\,velocity^2$$

The next two examples show that the result of a substitution is simplified but not evaluated. You have to take care of this yourself.

```
>   # substitution, but no evaluation
>   subs( x-0, cos(x) * ( sin(x) + x^2 + 1 ) );
```

$$\cos(0)\,(\sin(0)+1\,)$$

```
>   eval("); # extra evaluation
```

$$1$$

```
>   sum( 1 / binomial(n,k), k=1..n );
```

$$\sum_{k=1}^{n}\frac{1}{\text{binomial}(\,n,k\,)}$$

```
>   subs(n=3,") = eval( subs(n=3,") );
```

$$\sum_{k=1}^{3}\frac{1}{\text{binomial}(\,3,k\,)}=\frac{5}{3}$$

If you want evaluation to be performed automatically after substitution, then one way of achieving this is to enter the following command (or to put it in your initialization file).

```
>   macro( subs = eval @ subs ):
```

See also §8.7.

As an example of multiple substitution, we consider a double substitution, which is specified in Maple as

> subs(*var1* = *replacement1*, *var2* = *replacement2*, *expression*).

The effect of this double substitution is that first *replacement1* is substituted for all occurrences of *var1* in the *expression*, and then *var2* is replaced in the intermediate result by *replacement2*. More generally, in multiple substitutions the specified replacements are applied to intermediate expressions from left to right. We call this form of multiple substitution *sequential substitution*. Two examples:

```
>   kinetic_energy := momentum^2 / (2*mass);
```

$$kinetic\_energy := \frac{1}{2}\frac{momentum^2}{mass}$$

```
>   subs( momentum = mass * velocity,
>     velocity = acceleration * time, kinetic_energy );
```

$$\frac{1}{2}\,mass\,acceleration^2\,time^2$$

```
>   expression := 1 + tan(x)^2;
```

$$expression := 1 + \tan(\,x\,)^2$$

```
>   subs( tan(x) = sin(x)/cos(x), sin(x)^2 = 1 - cos(x)^2,
>     expression );
```

$$1 + \frac{1 - \cos(\,x\,)^2}{\cos(\,x\,)^2}$$

```
>   normal(");
```

$$\frac{1}{\cos(\,x\,)^2}$$

Instead of sequential substitution you can also carry out so-called *simultaneous substitution*, simply by grouping the substitution equations together in a set or a list.

> subs({ *var1* = *replacement1*, *var2* = *replacement2* }, *expression*)

In simultaneous substitution, the replacements in the expression take place all at once. Better stated, Maple traverses the representation tree, inspects each subexpression, and going from left to right through the set of substitution equations, checks whether there is a match between the left-hand side of a substitution equation and the particular subexpression; if so, the replacement is carried out in the original expression and not in intermediate results. The following examples show you better the difference between sequential and simultaneous substitution.

```
>   subs( x=y, y=z , x*y^2 );      # sequential substitution
```

$$z^3$$

```
>  subs( { x=y, y=z }, x*y^2 );  # simultaneous substitution
```
$$y\,z^2$$

```
>  subs( a=b, b=c, c=a, a + 2*b + 3*c );
```
$$6\,a$$

```
>  subs( { a=b, b=c, c=a }, a + 2*b + 3*c );
```
$$b + 2\,c + 3\,a$$

```
>  subs({ p=q, q=p }, f(p,q) );  # interchange p and q
```
$$f(q,p)$$

```
>  [a+b=d,a=b^2,b=c^2];
```
$$[\,a + b = d, a = b^2, b = c^2\,]$$

```
>  subs( ", (a+b)^2*b*a );
```
$$d^2\,c^2\,b^2$$

Not only variables can be replaced in a symbolic expression by the procedure **subs**, but also larger subexpressions. In this case, substitution is limited to subexpressions that are recognized as such by Maple. This means that only subexpressions that can be reached by (several applications of) the procedure **op** are allowed to play a role in substitution. For example,

```
>  expr1 := x*y + z;   expr2 := x*y*z;   cxpr3 := (x*y)^2;
```
$$expr1 := x\,y + z$$
$$expr2 := x\,y\,z$$
$$expr3 := x^2\,y^2$$

```
>  subs( x*y = w, expr1 );
```
$$w + z$$

```
>  subs( x*y = w, expr2 );
```
$$x\,y\,z$$

```
>  subs( x*y = w, expr3 );
```
$$x^2\,y^2$$

```
>  op( expr1 );
```
$$x\,y, z$$

```
>  op( expr2 );
```
$$x, y, z$$

```
> op( expr3 );
```

$$x^2, y^2$$

Because the product x*y in the second and third expression is not recognized by Maple as a subexpression, the product cannot be easily replaced. If such a substitution is desired, you will just have to make do with solutions like

```
> subs( x = w / y, expr2 );
```

$$w\,z$$

```
> subs( {x = w, y = 1}, expr2 );
```

$$w\,z$$

```
> subs( x*y*z = product*z, expr2 );
```

$$product\,z$$

The last substitution only makes sense when expr2 is part of a larger formula that contains x, and other terms involving x should stay intact. In the same manner:

```
> expression := a + b + c;
```

$$expression := a + b + c$$

```
> subs( a + b = d, expression );
```

$$a + b + c$$

```
> subs( a = d - b, expression );
```

$$d + c$$

```
> subs( {a = d, b = 0}, expression );
```

$$d + c$$

```
> subs( a + b + c = d + c, expression );
```

$$d + c$$

Maple also contains a procedure, viz., **algsubs** (**alg**ebraic **subs**titution), that is designed to carry out "mathematical" substitutions, and does not rely solely on syntactic substitutions as is the case with **subs**. Applied to the above example, you get:

```
> algsubs( a + b = d, expression );
```

$$d + c$$

Algebraic substitution can be ambiguous. For example, what should the result of

$$\text{algsubs}(a + b = d, a + 2 * b + 3 * c)$$

be?

$$b + d + 3 * c$$

or

$$-a + 2 * c + 2 * d?$$

And if both answers should be possible, how can you arrange this? This problem is partly solved in **algsubs** by the optional arguments in which you can specify

- the ordering of the variables

- one of the options `exact` and `remainder`

The variable ordering allows you to inform Maple which variables you prefer to see in the answer. In `remainder` mode (the default mode) a generalized polynomial division with remainder is used to find the occurrences of a pattern. In `exact` mode, if the pattern is a sum of terms, say $f_1 + f_2$, then replacement is only made in a subexpression, say $t_1 + t_2$, if and only if $f_1 + f_2 = c \times (t_1 + t_2)$ for some coefficient c. Notice that we speak of polynomial division: **algsubs** only works for patterns and expressions that consist of monomials with integral exponents. Thus, a pattern or an expression like $x^{\frac{1}{2}}$ is not taken into account by **algsubs**. Examples make things clearer.

```
>    algsubs( a + b = d, a + 2*b + 3*c );
```
$$d + b + 3c$$

```
>    algsubs( a + b = d, a + 2*b + 3*c, `exact` );
```
$$a + 2b + 3c$$

```
>    algsubs( a + b = d, a + 2*b + 3*c, [a,b] );   # a<b
```
$$d + b + 3c$$

```
>    algsubs( a + b = d, a + 2*b + 3*c, [b,a] );   # b<a
```
$$-a + 2d + 3c$$

```
>    algsubs( a^2 + 1 = d, (a^2+1)^4 + a^3 + 2*a^2 + 1 );
```
$$d^4 + (-1 + d)a - 1 + 2d$$

```
>    algsubs( a^2 + 1 = d, (a^2+1)^4 + a^3 + 2*a^2 + 1,
>      `exact` );
```
$$d^4 + a^3 + 2a^2 + 1$$

Note the difference with

```
>  subs( a^2 = d - 1, (a^2+1)^4 + a^3 + 2*a^2 + 1 );
```

$$d^4 + a^3 - 1 + 2\,d$$

Truncating powers is an important application of **algsubs**.

```
>  sum( x^k, k=-5..5 );
```

$$\frac{1}{x^5} + \frac{1}{x^4} + \frac{1}{x^3} + \frac{1}{x^2} + \frac{1}{x} + 1 + x + x^2 + x^3 + x^4 + x^5$$

```
>  algsubs( x^3 = 0, " );
```

$$\frac{1}{x^5} + \frac{1}{x^4} + \frac{1}{x^3} + \frac{1}{x^2} + \frac{1}{x} + 1 + x + x^2$$

```
>  algsubs( 1/x^3 = 0, " );
```

$$1 + \frac{1}{x^2} + \frac{1}{x} + x + x^2$$

algsubs also works for generalized rational expressions.

```
>  algsubs( sin(x)^2 + cos(x)^2 = 1,
>     sin(x)^2 / ( sin(x)^3 + cos(x)^3 ) );
```

$$\frac{-\cos(x)^2 + 1}{\sin(x) - \cos(x)^2\sin(x) + \cos(x)^3}$$

```
>  algsubs( sin(x)^2 + cos(x)^2 = 1,
>     sin(x)^2 / ( sin(x)^3 + cos(x)^3 ), [cos(x),sin(x)] );
```

$$\frac{\sin(x)^2}{\cos(x) - \sin(x)^2\cos(x) + \sin(x)^3}$$

algsubs differs in some technical terms from **subs**:

- no sequential or simultaneous substitution in one command;

- automatic evaluation after substitution;

- no action on procedure names or indices

Let us end with an example from polynomial calculus.

```
>  algsubs( x*y^2 = s, x^3*y^4 );
```

$$s^2\,x$$

```
>  algsubs( x*y^2 = x*y, x^3*y^4 );
```

$$x^3\,y^2$$

The last example shows that the replacement may contain variables that
are part of the pattern. In our example, the expression x^3y^4 can be considered as $x(xy^2)^2$, which explains the result of substitution. You could also
make implicit use of the Gröbner basis package **grobner** by applying the
procedure **simplify** with respect to side relations.

```
>  simplify( x^3*y^2, {x*y=s}, [y,x,s] );
```
$$s^2\,x$$

```
>  simplify( x^3*y^4, {x*y^2=x*y}, [y,x,s] );
```
$$x^3\,y$$

The last example shows that the side relation as a whole is taken into
account, i.e., the right-hand side is part of the rule that is applied. We
shall come back to simplification with respect to side relations in §14.7.

When Maple checks whether a certain expression occurs as a subexpression of a given symbolic expression, the computer algebra system traverses
the entire representation tree. Substitution is of a global nature in Maple:
every occurrence of the subexpression in the original symbolic expression
or intermediate results is substituted.

```
>  expression := (x+y)^2 + x;
```
$$expression := (\,x+y\,)^2 + x$$

```
>  op( expression );
```
$$(\,x+y\,)^2,\,x$$

```
>  op( op( 1, (x+y)^2 ) );
```
$$x,\,y$$

```
>  subs( x = z, expression );
```
$$(\,z+y\,)^2 + z$$

So, in case of substitution, it is important to know how a Maple expression
is built up and which subexpressions are recognized by the system.

Keep in mind that Maple stores common subexpressions only once.
During substitution with **subs** all occurrences of a subexpression are substituted. There is another possibility: by **subsop** you can substitute one
or more operands of a Maple expression. For example, the effect of the
command

subsop($num1$ = $replacement1$, $num2$ = $replacement2$, $expression$)

is that the subexpressions **op**($num1$, $expression$) and **op**($num2$, $expression$)
of the given $expression$ are simultaneously replaced by $replacement1$ and
$replacement2$, respectively. The effect of the substitution

subsop($[\,i,\,j\,]$ = $replacement$, $expression$)

is that the jth operand of the ith operand in the internal representation of the given expression is replaced. A few examples show how it works.

```
>  expression := x^2 + x + 1/x;
```
$$expression := x^2 + x + \frac{1}{x}$$

```
>  subsop( 3 = y, expression );   # replace 3rd operand
```
$$x^2 + x + y$$

```
>  subsop( 3 = 0, expression );   # replace 3rd operand
```
$$x^2 + x$$

```
>  # replace 1st and 2nd operand
>  subsop( 1 = z, 2 = y, expression );
```
$$z + y + \frac{1}{x}$$

```
>  # replace 1st operand of 3rd operand
>  subsop( [3,1] = y,  expression );
```
$$x^2 + x + \frac{1}{y}$$

```
>  1 + 1/(1+cos(x^2+1/x^2));
```
$$1 + \cfrac{1}{1 + \cos(x^2 + \cfrac{1}{x^2})}$$

```
>  # replace several levels deep
>  subsop( [2,1,2,1,2] = y, " );
```
$$1 + \cfrac{1}{1 + \cos(x^2 + y)}$$

```
>  subsop( 0 = J, BesselJ(1,x) );
```
$$J(1, x)$$

These examples show you the local nature of the procedure **subsop**. Only specified parts of an expression are replaced, and all other operands are left alone. This is opposite to the global nature of **subs**, with which you can replace one or more subexpressions, irrespective of where these subexpressions occur in the given symbolic expression. If you only have to manipulate part of a symbolic expression, you can exploit the local nature of **subsop**. Another advantage of the procedure **subsop** is that you do not have to retype the perhaps very large subexpression that you want to replace. Two examples:

```
>  poly:= ( x^2 + y^2 + 2*x*y ) * ( (x+y)^2 + 1);
```
$$poly := (x^2 + y^2 + 2xy)((x+y)^2 + 1)$$

```
> factor( poly );
```
$$(x+y)^2\,(x^2+y^2+2\,x\,y+1)$$

```
> subsop( 1 = factor( op(1, poly) ), poly );
```
$$(x+y)^2\,((x+y)^2+1)$$

```
> expression := (x^2 + 2*x + 1)^2 + (x^2 - 2*x +1)^2;
```
$$expression := (x^2+2\,x+1)^2+(x^2-2\,x+1)^2$$

```
> factor( expression );
```
$$2\,x^4+12\,x^2+2$$

```
> subsop( 1 = factor( op(1,expression) ),
>    2 = factor( op(2,expression) ), expression );
```
$$(x+1)^4+(x-1)^4$$

Because such mathematical operations on operands of expressions are often needed, there are two library procedures that make life easier, viz., **applyop** and **map**. Let us illustrate them via the same examples:

```
> applyop( factor, 1, poly );
```
$$(x+y)^2\,((x+y)^2+1)$$

Indeed,
$$\textbf{applyop}(\ func,\ index,\ expression\ )$$

is the same as

$$\textbf{subsop}(\ index = func\ (\textbf{op}(\ index,\ expression\ )\ ),\ expression\ )$$

In the second example you want to apply a function to all operands at level one of the expression. The procedure **map** is fit for this purpose.

```
> map( factor, expression );
```
$$(x+1)^4+(x-1)^4$$

The command **map**(*procedure, expression*) has the following effect: apply the *procedure* to all operands of the *expression* separately, combine the results into an expression of the original data type, and carry out automatic simplification (which may change the type of the expression). In §8.8 we shall come back to the procedure **map**.

Let us note that the substitution in the first of the above two examples could also have been carried out as follows.

```
> subs( x+y = z, poly );
```
$$(x^2+y^2+2\,x\,y)\,(z^2+1)$$

```
>  factor(");
```
$$(x+y)^2(z^2+1)$$

```
>  subs( z=x+y, " );
```
$$(x+y)^2((x+y)^2+1)$$

This technique of temporary replacement of a subexpression by an unknown, manipulation of the intermediate result, and back substitution of the "frozen" subexpression, is a frequently used simplification strategy. What follows is another illustration of this method.

```
>  expression := (x+y)^2 + 1/(x+y)^2;
```
$$expression := (x+y)^2 + \frac{1}{(x+y)^2}$$

We want to change this expression into one of the form $\dfrac{numerator}{denominator}$ without expansion of the powers $(x+y)^2$. The procedure **normal** does not quite do what we want.

```
>  normal( expression );
```
$$\frac{x^4 + 6x^2y^2 + 4x^3y + 4xy^3 + y^4 + 1}{(x+y)^2}$$

If we temporarily replace the subexpression $x+y$ in the powers by a new unknown, say z, normalize the intermediate rational function, and finally substitute back $x+y$ for z, then we get the desired result.

```
>  subs( x + y = z, expression );
```
$$z^2 + \frac{1}{z^2}$$

```
>  normal(");
```
$$\frac{z^4+1}{z^2}$$

```
>  subs( z = x + y, " );
```
$$\frac{(x+y)^4+1}{(x+y)^2}$$

Because it is not always easy in a long Maple session to recall which variables are already in use and which substitutions have already been applied, the Maple system offers you the procedures **freeze** and **thaw** as utility functions. When you use them, Maple itself chooses new names for subexpressions and keeps track of them. The above example would look like

```
>  readlib( freeze ): # load the library function
>  subs( x+y=freeze(x+y), expression );
```
$$freeze/R0^2 + \frac{1}{freeze/R0^2}$$

```
>  normal(");
```

$$\frac{freeze/R0^4 + 1}{freeze/R0^2}$$

```
>  thaw(");
```

$$\frac{(x + y)^4 + 1}{(x + y)^2}$$

We end this section with some simple examples that illustrate the problem of specialization.

```
>  integrate( 1/(x-a)^2, x = 0..2 );
```

$$\frac{1}{-2 + a} - \frac{1}{a}$$

Maple has successfully solved a generic problem (a is an indeterminate with no value associated). When you specialize a, or in other words, take the analytical approach, you get trapped in strange results. For example, substituting $a = 1$ in this integral gives a negative result of integration of a positive integrand.

```
>  subs( a = 1, " );
```

$$-2$$

Maple would have gotten the correct answer if you had immediately asked for the $\int_0^2 \frac{1}{(x-1)^2}\, dx$.

```
>  integrate( 1/(x-1)^2, x = 0..2 );
```

$$\infty$$

Unfortunately, making the assumption in Maple that a is between 0 and 2 does not help (yet).

Consider the following equation, which depends on the parameter a.

```
>  eq := (a^2-1) * x^2 + (2*a^2+a-3) * x + 2*a - 2 = 0;
```

$$eq := (a^2 - 1)x^2 + (2a^2 + a - 3)x + 2a - 2 = 0$$

For a = 1 the equation is trivial.

```
>  subs( a = 1, " );
```

$$0 = 0$$

However, solving the generic case and substituting a =1 afterward gives only two solutions.

```
>  solve( eq, x );
```

$$-\frac{1}{a+1}, -2$$

> subs(a = 1, {"});

$$\{-2, \frac{-1}{2}\}$$

Consider the matrix $M = \begin{pmatrix} 1 & a \\ 0 & 1 \end{pmatrix}$ and compute the Jordan form.

> with(linalg):

Warning, new definition for norm
Warning, new definition for trace

> A := matrix([[1,a],[0,1]]);

$$A := \begin{bmatrix} 1 & a \\ 0 & 1 \end{bmatrix}$$

> jordan(");

$$\begin{bmatrix} 1 & 1 \\ 0 & 1 \end{bmatrix}$$

Obviously, this result does not hold for a = 0.

> B := matrix([[a,1],[0,1]]);

$$B := \begin{bmatrix} a & 1 \\ 0 & 1 \end{bmatrix}$$

> jordan(");

$$\begin{bmatrix} 1 & 0 \\ 0 & a \end{bmatrix}$$

This previous result is not valid for a = 1.

6.4   Exercises

1. Describe in detail the internal representation in Maple of the polynomial $2x(y^2 + 1)^2$. Draw the corresponding directed acyclic graph (DAG) and the representation tree. Write down all subexpressions that are recognized as such by Maple. Enlarge your trust in your answer by use of the procedures **whattype**, **nops**, and **op**. By use of the procedures **dismantle**, **addressof**, **pointto**, **disassemble**, and **assemble** you can completely check your answer.

2. Transform $(x + y)^2 + \dfrac{1}{x + y}$ into $\dfrac{(x + y)^3 + 1}{x + y}$ and vice versa.

3. Transform
$$x^2 + 2x + 1 + \frac{1}{x^2 + 2x + 1}$$
into
$$\frac{(x+1)^4 + 1}{(x+1)^2}$$
and vice versa.

4. Explain the result of the following substitution:
> x^2-x+1/x-1/x^2;
$$x^2 - x + \frac{1}{x} - \frac{1}{x^2}$$

> subs(-1=1,");
$$x^2 + 2\,x + \frac{1}{x^2}$$

5. Transform
$$\frac{(x+1)^{10} - 2y}{(x+y)^{10}} + \frac{1}{(x+y)^9} - \frac{x}{(x+y)^{10}}$$
into
$$\frac{(x+1)^{10} - y}{(x+y)^{10}}.$$

7

Manipulation of Polynomials and Rational Expressions

This chapter systematically discusses manipulations of polynomials and rational expressions. The following manipulations are reviewed: expansion, factorization, normalization, collection, and sorting of polynomials and rational expressions. We shall consider manipulation of expressions that are defined over the rational numbers as well as manipulation of expressions that are defined over other domains, like finite fields, algebraic numbers, and algebraic function fields. Furthermore, we shall give a short, theoretical introduction to canonical and normal form simplification.

7.1 Expansion

Suppose that you want to transform $(x^2 - x)(x^2 + 2x + 1)$ from this factored form into the expanded canonical form $x^4 + x^3 - x^2 - x$. Then you can use the procedure **expand**, and if necessary **sort** the result. In **expand**, first the factors are multiplied out, and second, similar terms are collected. In our example, the first step leads to $x^4 + 2x^3 + x^2 - x^3 - 2x^2 - x$, and then Maple simplifies this to $x^4 + x^3 - x^2 - x$ (or eventually to a different ordering if the polynomial was already in memory in a different form; in this case you need the procedure **sort** to rearrange terms).

```
> partially_factored_form:= (x^2-x) * (x^2+2*x+1);
```

$$partially\_factored\_form := (x^2 - x)(x^2 + 2x + 1)$$

```
>  expanded_form := expand(  partially_factored_form );
```
$$expanded\_form := x^4 + x^3 - x^2 - x$$

The way in which Maple distributes products over sums can be illustrated best by an easier example.

```
>  factored_form := (a+b) * (c+d);
```
$$factored\_form := (a+b)(c+d)$$

```
>  expanded_form := expand( factored_form );
```
$$expanded\_form := ac + ad + bc + bd$$

With the Maple procedure **expand** all products are distributed over sums and like terms are automatically collected by Maple's simplifier. The terminology *full expansion* is more appropriate. For example, in our last example, the expansion of the factored form can be described as a two-step mechanism: first, the factored form is transformed to the expression $a(c+d)+b(c+d)$, and after that the intermediate expression is transformed to the final form $ac + ad + bc + bd$. If you want to avoid this second step, then you must specify in the call of the procedure **expand** that you want to keep the subexpression $c + d$ intact.

```
>  partially_expanded_form := expand( factored_form, c+d );
```
$$partially\_expanded\_form := (c+d)a + (c+d)b$$

The procedure **expand** also distributes powers with positive integer exponents over sums, simply by considering these powers as repeated products and by distributing them over sums.

```
>  power := (x+1)^3;
```
$$power := (x+1)^3$$

```
>  expand(");
```
$$x^3 + 3x^2 + 3x + 1$$

Negative powers are left untouched by **expand**.

```
>  power := (x+1)^(-2);
```
$$power := \frac{1}{(x+1)^2}$$

```
>  whattype(");
```

^

```
>  op( power );
```
$$x+1, -2$$

```
> expand( power );
```

$$\frac{1}{(x+1)^2}$$

If you consider this expression as a rational one of which the denominator is equal to $(x+1)^2$, then you can expand the denominator separately.

```
> 1 / expand( denom(") );
```

$$\frac{1}{x^2 + 2x + 1}$$

Maple does not expand powers with noninteger exponents.

```
> power := (x+1)^(3/2);
```

$$power := (x+1)^{3/2}$$

```
> expand(");
```

$$(x+1)^{3/2}$$

The only effect of **expand** on rational expressions is that sums in the numerator are expanded.

```
> (x+1)^2 / ((x^2+x)*x);
```

$$\frac{(x+1)^2}{(x^2+x)x}$$

```
> expand(");
```

$$\frac{x}{x^2+x} + 2\frac{1}{x^2+x} + \frac{1}{(x^2+x)x}$$

So far, we have looked at only expansion of polynomials and rational functions defined over the integers. When you manipulate polynomials that are defined over a finite ring, over algebraic numbers, or over algebraic function fields, then you must use the inert form of expansion, namely **Expand**, if necessary in combination with **evala** (**eval**uate in a context of algebraic numbers or function fields). A few examples will do.

- Expansion over $\mathbb{Z}_8$.
  ```
  > Expand( (x+1)^8 ) mod 8;
  ```
  $$x^8 + 4x^6 + 6x^4 + 4x^2 + 1$$

- Expansion over $\mathbb{Q}(\alpha)$, where α is a root of the polynomial $z^5 + z + 1$.
  ```
  > alias( alpha = RootOf( z^5 + z + 1, z ) ):
  > (x+alpha)^5;
  ```
  $$(x+\alpha)^5$$

```
>  evala( Expand(") );
```
$$x^5 + 5\,\alpha\,x^4 + 10\,\alpha^2\,x^3 + 10\,\alpha^3\,x^2 + 5\,\alpha^4\,x - \alpha - 1$$

- Expansion over $\mathbb{Z}_5(\alpha)$, where α is a root of the polynomial $z^5 + z + 1$.

```
>  Expand("") mod 5;
```
$$x^5 + 4\,\alpha + 4$$

- Expansion over the algebraic function field $\mathbb{Q}\big(\sqrt{1+y}\,\big)$.

  Recall that an algebraic function over $\mathbb{Q}$ is a function that annihilates a univariate polynomial with coefficients in a rational function field. In our example, $\sqrt{1+y}$ is defined as a root of the polynomial $z^2 - 1 - y$ with coefficients in the rational function field $\mathbb{Q}(y)$.

```
>  alias( beta = RootOf( z^2 - 1 - y, z ) ):
>  (x+beta)^2;
```
$$(x + \beta)^2$$

```
>  evala( Expand(") );
```
$$x^2 + 2\,\beta\,x + 1 + y$$

7.2   Factorization

The Maple procedure **factor** is **expand**'s big brother. It computes the factorization of a polynomial over the rationals in irreducible factors. The result is unique up to ordering of factors; we speak of a *factored normal form*. The procedure also works fine for rational expressions, in that common factors in numerator and denominator are first canceled before they are factored.

In §5.1 we have already seen that Maple can factor polynomials over various domains. Below are some more examples. In case of polynomials over finite fields and algebraic function fields, you may have to use the inert form **Factor**. The algorithms implemented in Maple are Cantor and Zassenhaus [33] and Berlekamp [16] for univariate polynomials over finite fields, Hensel lifting for multivariate polynomials [113, 202], and Lenstra [129] and Kronecker-Trager [182] for polynomials over algebraic number and function fields.

- Factorization over $\mathbb{Q}\big(\sqrt{6}\,\big)$.

```
>  factor( 8*x^3 - 12*x, sqrt(6) );
```
$$2\,(\,2\,x - \sqrt{6}\,)\,(\,2\,x + \sqrt{6}\,)\,x$$

- Factorization over finite fields $\mathbb{Z}_2$, $\mathbb{Z}_3$, and $\mathbb{Z}_5$.

```
>   x^4 + 1;
```

$$x^4 + 1$$

```
>   Factor(") mod 2;
```

$$(x+1)^4$$

```
>   Factor("") mod 3;
```

$$(x^2 + x + 2)(x^2 + 2x + 2)$$

```
>   Factor(""") mod 5;
```

$$(x^2 + 2)(x^2 + 3)$$

- Factorization over $\mathbb{Z}_7(\alpha)$, where α is a root of the polynomial $z^7 + z^3 + 1$.

```
>   alias( alpha = RootOf( z^7 + z^3 + 1, z ) ):
>   x^7 + 6*alpha^3 + 6;
```

$$x^7 + 6\alpha^3 + 6$$

```
>   Factor(") mod 7;
```

$$(x+\alpha)^7$$

- Factorization over the algebraic function field $\mathbb{Q}(\sqrt{1+y})$.

```
>   alias( beta = RootOf( z^2 - 1 - y, z ) ):
>   x^2 + 2*beta*x + 1 + y;
```

$$x^2 + 2\beta x + 1 + y$$

```
>   factor( x^2 + 2*beta*x + 1 + y, beta );
```

$$(x+\beta)^2$$

The extension of the field of rational numbers with the square root of six appeared more or less out of nothing to yield the complete factorization of $8x^3 - 12x$. But Maple itself can compute the splitting field of a univariate polynomial with the procedure **split**.

```
>   readlib( split ):   # load the library function
>   split( 8*x^3 - 12*x, x );
```

$$8\left(x - \frac{1}{2}\text{RootOf}(\_Z^2 - 6)\right)\left(x + \frac{1}{2}\text{RootOf}(\_Z^2 - 6)\right)x$$

```
>   convert( ", radical );
```

$$8\left(x - \frac{1}{2}\sqrt{6}\right)\left(x + \frac{1}{2}\sqrt{6}\right)x$$

An example of a multivariate polynomial that is irreducible over $\mathbb{Q}$:

```
>  p := x^4 + 2*y^4;
```

$$p := x^4 + 2\,y^4$$

- Factorization over extension with $\sqrt{2}$ and I.

```
>  factor( p, { sqrt(2), I } );
```

$$(x^2 + I\,y^2\,\sqrt{2})\,(x^2 - I\,y^2\,\sqrt{2})$$

- Factorization over $\mathbb{Z}_3$.

```
>  Factor( p ) mod 3;
```

$$2\,(2\,x + y)\,(x^2 + y^2)\,(x + y)$$

- Factorization over Galois field GF(9), in particular the algebraic extension of $\mathbb{Z}_3$ with respect to the irreducible polynomial $x^2 - 2$.

```
>  alias( alpha = RootOf( z^2 - 2, z ) ):
>  Factor( p, alpha ) mod 3;
```

$$2\,(x + y)\,(x + 2\,y)\,(x + \mathrm{RootOf}(\_Z^2 + 1)\,y)$$
$$(x + 2\,\mathrm{RootOf}(\_Z^2 + 1)\,y)$$

```
>  convert( ", radical );
```

$$2\,(x + y)\,(x + 2\,y)\,(x + I\,y)\,(x + 2\,I\,y)$$

AFactor does absolute factorization of multivariate polynomials over the complex numbers.

```
>  evala( AFactor( x^3 + y^3 ) );
```

$$(x + y)\,(x + (-1 + \frac{1}{5}\,\mathrm{RootOf}(\_Z^2 - 5\,\_Z + 25))\,y)$$
$$(x - \frac{1}{5}\,\mathrm{RootOf}(\_Z^2 - 5\,\_Z + 25)\,y)$$

```
>  convert( ", radical ); # go to radical notation
```

$$(x + y)\,(x + (-\frac{1}{2} - \frac{1}{2}\,I\,\sqrt{3})\,y)\,(x - \frac{1}{5}\,(\frac{5}{2} - \frac{5}{2}\,I\,\sqrt{3})\,y)$$

One of the first steps in the factorization of a polynomial by **factor** is the *square-free factorization* of the polynomial. The square-free factorization of a nonconstant polynomial is defined as a decomposition of the form $c\,p_1\,p_2^2\,p_3^3 \ldots$, where c is a rational constant and the polynomials p_1, p_2, p_3, ... are relatively prime and have no multiple factors. In Maple you can compute the square-free factorization by explicit conversion or by calling the procedure **sqrfree**.

```
>  x^4 + x^3 - x^2 - x;
```

$$x^4 + x^3 - x^2 - x$$

```
>  convert( ", sqrfree );
```
$$(x-1)x(x+1)^2$$

```
>  sqrfree("");
```
$$[1,[[x-1,1],[x,1],[x+1,2]]]$$

When you compute over the field $\mathbb{Z}_2$ with two elements, the latter polynomial has a square-free factorization equal to $x(x+1)^3$; in Maple computed as

```
>  Sqrfree(""") mod 2;
```
$$[1,[[x,1],[x+1,3]]]$$

7.3   Canonical Form and Normal Form

So far the terms *canonical form* and *normal form* have appeared several times in the context of simplification or manipulation of expressions. It is worthwhile to linger a bit longer on them, even though it is a more theoretical intermezzo. A detailed survey can be found in [26].

The main problem with simplification is that a mathematical expression can be written in several equivalent forms whereas it is not always easy to recognize equivalence. For example, the third Hermite polynomial is equal to $8x^2 - 12x$, but you can easily write down four equivalent formulae:

$$x(8x^2 - 12),$$
$$4x(2x^2 - 3),$$
$$2x(2x - \sqrt{6})(2x + \sqrt{6}),$$
$$(2x)^3 - 6\cdot(2x).$$

What is the simplest form? If you want to stress the fact that it is a polynomial in $2x$, then $2x(2x - \sqrt{6})(2x + \sqrt{6})$ and $(2x)^3 - 6\cdot(2x)$ are good candidates. If you use the number of terms as criterion, then $8x^3 - 12x$ and $(2x)^3 - 6\cdot(2x)$ would be your favorites.

A more clearly specified problem is the so-called *zero equivalence* problem, i.e., to recognize whether an expression is equal to zero. But even this may turn out to be a hard problem as in

$$\ln\tan(\frac{1}{2}x + \frac{1}{4}\pi) - \text{arcsinh}\tan x = 0.$$

Verification of this equality is nontrivial.

In general the simplification problem can be treated as follows. Let $\mathcal{E}$ be a class of symbolic expressions (e.g., univariate polynomials over the integers) and let $\sim$ be an equivalence relation defined on $\mathcal{E}$. The problem of finding an equivalent but simpler expression can be characterized as finding a computable transformation $\mathcal{S}: \mathcal{E} \longrightarrow \mathcal{E}$ such that for any expression t in $\mathcal{E}$ we have

$$\mathcal{S}(t) \sim t \text{ and } \mathcal{S}(t) \preceq t.$$

Here, $\preceq$ denotes some simplification concept: $s \prec t$ is our notation for "expression s is simpler in $\mathcal{E}$ than expression t," and this means, for example, "expression s has less terms than t," "s uses less memory than t," or "s is more readable than t." We say that expressions s and t are identical and denote this by $s \equiv t$, when s and t are built up in the same way from basic elements, or more precisely when they have the same directed acyclic graph (see, e.g., the previous chapter for a description of Maple's internal data representation).

A *canonical simplifier* $\mathcal{S}$ on $\mathcal{E}$ is a computable procedure such that for all s and t in $\mathcal{E}$ we have

$$\mathcal{S}(t) \sim t \text{ and}$$
$$s \sim t \implies \mathcal{S}(s) \equiv \mathcal{S}(t).$$

A canonical simplifier chooses a unique representative in each equivalence class, the *canonical form*.

For univariate polynomials, the expanded canonical form can be obtained as follows:

(i) recursively distribute all products over sums,

(ii) collect terms of the same degree, and

(iii) remove superfluous terms and reorder the remaining terms in descending order of their degrees.

The requirements for canonical simplification are high and cannot always be met. A weaker form of simplification is *normal form simplification*. Suppose that there is a distinguished element, say 0, in $\mathcal{E}$. A *normal simplifier* $\mathcal{S}$ on $\mathcal{E}$ is a computable procedure such that for all s and t in $\mathcal{E}$ holds

$$\mathcal{S}(t) \sim t \text{ and}$$
$$t \sim 0 \implies \mathcal{S}(t) \equiv \mathcal{S}(0).$$

An expression t is called a *normal form* in $\mathcal{E}$ when $\mathcal{S}(t) \equiv t$. So, the normal form need not be unique in each equivalence class except for the class to which 0 belongs in $\mathcal{E}$.

For univariate polynomials, the expanded normal form, which we called collected form, can be obtained as follows:

(i) recursively distribute all products over sums,

(ii) collect terms of the same degree, and

(iii) remove superfluous terms.

Normal simplification is usually easier than canonical simplification. Other examples of normal forms of polynomials are the square-free form and the Horner form, which is a nested form often used for efficiency reasons.

```
>   poly := expand( (x+y+z)^2*(x+y+1) );
```

$$poly := x^3 + 3\,x^2\,y + x^2 + 3\,x\,y^2 + 2\,x\,y + 2\,x^2\,z + 4\,x\,z\,y + 2\,x\,z + y^3 + y^2 + 2\,y^2\,z + 2\,y\,z + z^2\,x + z^2\,y + z^2$$

```
>   readlib(cost)( poly);
```
$$14\ additions + 32\ multiplications$$

```
>   horner_form := convert( poly, `horner`, [x,y,z] );
```

$$horner\_form := z^2 + (\,(\,2+z\,)\,z + (\,2\,z+1+y\,)\,y\,)\,y + (\,(\,2+z\,)\,z + (\,2+4\,z+3\,y\,)\,y + (\,2\,z+1+3\,y+x\,)\,x\,)\,x$$

```
>   cost( horner_form );
```
$$14\ additions + 13\ multiplications$$

Partial fraction decomposition of rational functions is an example of a normal simplifier of rational expressions.

7.4 Normalization

The procedure **normal** provides the normal simplification for rational functions over $\mathbb{Q}$ in Maple. A rational function is converted into the so-called *factored normal form*. This is the form *numerator / denominator*, where the numerator and denominator are relatively prime polynomials with integer coefficients; the numerator and denominator are both products of expanded polynomials and during the simplification to normal form common factors are kept intact as much as possible.

```
>   (x-1)*(x+2)/((x+1)*x) + (x-1)/(1+x)^2;
```
$$\frac{(\,x-1\,)(\,x+2\,)}{(\,x+1\,)\,x} + \frac{x-1}{(\,x+1\,)^2}$$

```
>   normal(");
```
$$\frac{(\,x-1\,)(\,x^2+4\,x+2\,)}{(\,x+1\,)^2\,x}$$

```
>   (x^2+x-2)/((x+1)*x)+(x-1)/(1+x)^2;
```

$$\frac{x^2+x-2}{(x+1)x} + \frac{x-1}{(x+1)^2}$$

```
>   normal(");
```

$$\frac{x^3+3x^2-2x-2}{(x+1)^2 x}$$

```
>   normal( """, ´expanded´ );
```

$$\frac{x^3+3x^2-2x-2}{x^3+2x^2+x}$$

You specify with the keyword **expanded** that you want both numerator and denominator in expanded normal form.

There exist several normal forms for rational expressions and you can produce some of them by application of the procedures **normal**, **expand** and **factor** upon numerator and denominator separately. Alternatives are

```
>   ratfunc := (x^4+x^3-4*x^2-4*x) / (x^3+x^2-x-1);
```

$$ratfunc := \frac{x^4+x^3-4x^2-4x}{x^3+x^2-x-1}$$

- $\dfrac{factored\ normal\ form}{factored\ normal\ form}$

```
>   factor( ratfunc );
```

$$\frac{(x-2)(x+2)x}{(x-1)(x+1)}$$

- $\dfrac{factored\ normal\ form}{expanded\ canonical\ form}$

```
>   factor(numer(ratfunc)) / sort(expand(denom(ratfunc)));
```

$$\frac{x(x-2)(x+2)(x+1)}{x^3+x^2-x-1}$$

- $\dfrac{expanded\ canonical\ form}{factored\ normal\ form}$

```
>   sort(expand(numer(ratfunc))) / factor(denom(ratfunc));
```

$$\frac{x^4+x^3-4x^2-4x}{(x-1)(x+1)^2}$$

- $\dfrac{expanded\ canonical\ form}{expanded\ canonical\ form}$

```
>   sort( normal( ratfunc, ´expanded´ ));
```

$$\frac{x^3-4x}{x^2-1}$$

Above, we have applied **normal** on a rational function, but, as was already explained in §6.2, you can also normalize a *generalized* rational expression with this procedure. We confine ourselves to one example, which explains the recursive character of **normal**.

```
>  sin(x+1/x) + 1/sin(x+1/x);
```

$$\sin\left(x + \frac{1}{x}\right) + \frac{1}{\sin\left(x + \dfrac{1}{x}\right)}$$

```
>  normal(");
```

$$\frac{\sin\left(\dfrac{x^2+1}{x}\right)^2 + 1}{\sin\left(\dfrac{x^2+1}{x}\right)}$$

The procedure **normal** has a twin brother called **Normal**. This procedure is a normal simplification for various coefficient domains. We give two examples.

```
>  Normal( ratfunc ) mod 3;
```

$$x$$

```
>  ( x^2 - a ) / ( x - sqrt(a) );
```

$$\frac{x^2 - a}{x - \sqrt{a}}$$

```
>  convert( ", RootOf );
```

$$\frac{x^2 - a}{x - \mathrm{RootOf}(\,\_Z^2 - a\,)}$$

```
>  evala( Normal(") );
```

$$x + \mathrm{RootOf}(\,\_Z^2 - a\,)$$

```
>  convert( ", radical );
```

$$x + \sqrt{a}$$

7.5 Collection

The procedure **collect** is used to group coefficients of like terms in a polynomial. The various ways of collecting terms are best shown by examples.

```
>  poly := expand( (x+y+z)^2 * (x+y+1) );
```

$$poly := x^3 + 3\,x^2\,y + x^2 + 3\,x\,y^2 + 2\,x\,y + 2\,x^2\,z + 4\,x\,z\,y + 2\,x\,z + y^3$$
$$+ y^2 + 2\,y^2\,z + 2\,y\,z + z^2\,x + z^2\,y + z^2$$

This is an example of the *distributed* or *expanded form* of a polynomial in
Maple. We use the notation $\mathbb{Z}[x, y, z]$ to denote the set of distributed multivariate polynomials in the unknowns x, y, and z, with integer coefficients.

Consider poly as a polynomial in z whose coefficients are distributed
polynomials in x and y, i.e., consider poly as an element in $\mathbb{Z}[x, y][z]$.

```
> collect( poly, z );
```

$$(x + y + 1) z^2 + (4xy + 2x + 2x^2 + 2y^2 + 2y) z + x^3 + 3x^2 y + x^2$$
$$+ 3xy^2 + 2xy + y^2 + y^3$$

Now consider poly as a polynomial in z whose coefficients are polynomials
in y whose coefficients are polynomials in x with integer coefficients, i.e.,
consider poly as an element of $\mathbb{Z}[x][y][z]$.

```
> collect( poly, [z,y], 'recursive' );
```

$$(x + y + 1) z^2 + (2y^2 + (4x + 2) y + 2x + 2x^2) z + y^3 + (3x + 1) y^2$$
$$+ (3x^2 + 2x) y + x^3 + x^2$$

Loosely speaking, we have considered here poly as a polynomial in z and
y with preference for the indeterminate z.

Of course you can also consider poly as a polynomial in z and y without
giving preference to any of the two unknowns, i.e., you can consider the
poly as an element of $\mathbb{Z}[x][y, z]$.

```
> collect( poly, [z,y], 'distributed' );
```

$$x^3 + x^2 + (2x + 2x^2) z + (3x^2 + 2x) y + (x + 1) z^2 + y^3 + (3x + 1) y^2$$
$$+ (4x + 2) y z + 2y^2 z + z^2 y$$

Finally, you can add as an argument to **collect** the name of a procedure
that has to be applied to each coefficient separately.

```
> collect( poly, z, factor ); # recursive order by default
```
$$(x + y + 1) z^2 + 2(x + y + 1)(y + x) z + (x + y + 1)(y + x)^2$$

```
> collect( poly , [z,y], 'distributed', factor );
```

$$x^2 (x + 1) + 2(x + 1) x z + x(3x + 2) y + (x + 1) z^2 + y^3$$
$$+ (3x + 1) y^2 + (4x + 2) y z + 2y^2 z + z^2 y$$

The main reasons for using collected forms of multivariate polynomials in
Maple are readability and efficiency with respect to memory and computing
time. If a polynomial is dense in some variable, it is advantageous to collect
with respect to this variable because this will reduce representation space
compared to the expanded form. Collecting terms is a way to overcome

the length limitation of internal Maple objects. In Maple, a sum with more than $65,535\ (=2^{16}-1)$ terms cannot be represented, and the system will print

System Error, object too large

By maintaining the expression collected in some of the indeterminates, you may be able to reduce the maximum size of the sums in the expression. In our example above, the expanded form of poly has 15 terms, whereas the collected form in $\mathbb{Z}[x,y][z]$ with all coefficients in factored form has only three terms.

Like **normal**, the procedure **collect** can be applied to generalized rational expressions.

```
>   ln(x)^3/a + ln(x)^2*x/(a^2+a) + a^2*ln(x)^2*x/(a^2+a)
>       + 2*x^2/(1+a)+a*x^2/(1+a) + a^3*ln(x)/(a^2+a)
>       + 2*ln(x)*a/(a^2+a) + ln(x)/(a^2+a) + a/(a^2+a);
```

$$\frac{\ln(x)^3}{a} + \frac{\ln(x)^2 x}{a^2+a} + \frac{a^2\ln(x)^2 x}{a^2+a} + 2\frac{x^2}{1+a} + \frac{a x^2}{1+a} + \frac{a^3\ln(x)}{a^2+a}$$
$$+ 2\frac{\ln(x)a}{a^2+a} + \frac{\ln(x)}{a^2+a} + \frac{a}{a^2+a}$$

```
>   collect( ", [x,ln(x)], 'distributed', normal );
```

$$\frac{1}{1+a} + \frac{(2+a)x^2}{1+a} + \frac{(a^3+2a+1)\ln(x)}{a(1+a)} + \frac{(1+a^2)x\ln(x)^2}{a(1+a)}$$
$$+ \frac{\ln(x)^3}{a}$$

Note that you can collect only with respect to names and function calls, but not with respect to polynomial expressions. If the first few terms of

```
>   x^5 - 5*x^4*y^2 + 10*x^3*y^4 - 10*x^2*y^6 + 5*x*y^8
>       - y^10 - 2;
```

$$x^5 - 5x^4 y^2 + 10 x^3 y^4 - 10 x^2 y^6 + 5 x y^8 - y^{10} - 2$$

remind you of $(x-y^2)^5$, then you cannot simply collect with respect to $x-y^2$.

```
>   collect( ", x - y^2 );
```

Error, (in collect) cannot collect, x-y^2

Instead, you can simplify with respect to the side relation $x-y^2=z$.

```
>   siderel := {z = x - y^2};
```

$$siderel := \{\, z = x - y^2 \,\}$$

```
>   simplify( "", siderel, [x,y,z] );
```

$$-2 + z^5$$

```
>  subs( siderel, " " );
```

$$-2 + (x - y^2)^5$$

See §14.7 for more examples of such polynomial simplifications.

7.6   Sorting

The procedure **sort** is used to sort polynomials in some suitable ordering. We have already described this in §5.2. Here, we only give an example of a generalized rational function whose numerator and denominator are sorted.

```
>  r := sort( (cos(x) - sin(x)) / (cos(x) + sin(x)),
>     [cos(x),sin(x)], 'plex' );
```

$$r := \frac{\cos(x) - \sin(x)}{\cos(x) + \sin(x)}$$

```
>  sort( r,  [sin(x),cos(x)], 'plex' );
```

$$\frac{-\sin(x) + \cos(x)}{\sin(x) + \cos(x)}$$

7.7   Exercises

Remark: in your answers to the exercises below, the ordering of factors may differ.

1. Describe a canonical simplification of univariate rational functions with rational coefficients.

2. Consider the following rational expression.

$$\frac{x^4 + x^3 - 4x^2 - 4x}{x^4 + x^3 - x^2 - x}$$

Transform this expression with Maple into:

(a) $\dfrac{x^2 - 4}{x^2 - 1}$

(b) $\dfrac{(x - 2)(x + 2)}{x^2 - 1}$

3. Consider the following rational expression.

$$2\frac{x^3 - yx^2 - yx + y^2}{x^3 - yx^2 - x + y}$$

Transform this expression with Maple into:

(a) $2\dfrac{x^2 - y}{x^2 - 1}$

(b) $2\dfrac{x^2 - y}{(x - 1)(x + 1)}$

(c) $2 - \dfrac{y - 1}{x - 1} + \dfrac{y - 1}{x + 1}$

(d) $2 - 2\dfrac{y - 1}{x^2 - 1}$

4. Consider the polynomial $(2x^2 - x)(2x^2 + x)$.
   Transform this polynomial with Maple into:

   (a) $(-1 + 4x^2)x^2$

   (b) $x^2(2x - 1)(2x + 1)$

   (c) $(2x^3 + x^2)(2x - 1)$

5. Consider the polynomial $(x^2 + xy + x + y)(x + y)$.
   Transform this polynomial with Maple into:

   (a) $x^3 + 2x^2y + xy^2 + x^2 + 2xy + y^2$

   (b) $(x + 1)(x + y)^2$

   (c) $y^2 + (2y + y^2)x + (1 + 2y)x^2 + x^3$

   (d) $x^3 + x^2 + (2x^2 + 2x)y + (x + 1)y^2$

8

Functions

In Maple, a functional relationship can be specified in three ways: as a formula, as an arrow operator (similar to common mathematical notation), and as a procedure. This chapter discusses all methods in detail. Special attention is paid to recursively defined procedures and functions. The role of the `remember` `option` in defining efficient, recursive functions is treated in detail.

This chapter is not about programming; we discuss only how mathematical functions can be defined in Maple. We focus on practical issues like "how to define a function," "how to transform a formula into a function," and "when to use anonymous functions."

8.1   Mathematical Functions

In previous chapters we have already seen some commonly used mathematical functions that are available in Maple. You can get a complete list with the instruction **?inifcns** (help about **initially** known **functions**). This list also contains names of less known functions such as *Lambert's W function.* This function has been introduced as the solution of the following equation in [66].

```
>   f(x) * exp(f(x)) = x;
```

$$\mathrm{f}(\,x\,)\,e^{\mathrm{f}(\,x\,)} = x$$

> `solve( ", f(x) );`

$$\mathrm{LambertW}(x)$$

A more detailed description of Lambert's W function can be found in [48]. It is a multivalued complex function. The best plot of the two real branches of this function together in one picture can be obtained in Maple as a parametric plot. The graph is shown in Figure 8.1.

> `plot( [ y*exp(y), y, y = -5..0.75 ] );`

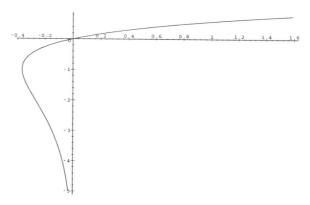

FIGURE 8.1. Graph of two real branches of Lambert's W function.

The ranges of the branches of the complex multiple-valued function W can be shown with the procedure **branches**; see Figure 8.2. Presently, this procedure also "knows" about the inverse trigonometric functions and the natural logarithm.

> `readlib( branches ): # load the library function`
> `branches( LambertW, thick );`

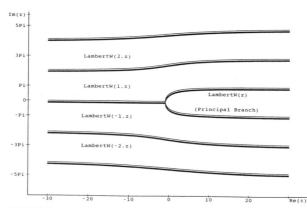

FIGURE 8.2. Ranges of branches of Lambert's W function.

Below are two examples of computations in which Lambert's W function plays a role.

```
>  a*x + b^x =c;
```

$$a\,x + b^x = c$$

```
>  solve(",x);
```

$$-\frac{\mathrm{LambertW}\left(\dfrac{\ln(b)\,e^{\left(\frac{\ln(b)c}{a}\right)}}{a}\right)a - \ln(b)\,c}{a\ln(b)}$$

```
>  f(x) = solve( f(x) = x^f(x), f(x) );
```

$$f(x) = -\frac{\mathrm{LambertW}(-\ln(x))}{\ln(x)}$$

The latter result is nothing more than saying that the function

$$f:x \longmapsto x^{x^{x^{\cdot^{\cdot^{\cdot}}}}}$$

is equal to

$$f:x \longmapsto -\frac{\mathrm{LambertW}(-\ln x)}{\ln x}$$

for $x \in (0,1)$. The graph of the function is show in Figure 8.3.

```
>  plot(rhs("), x=0..1 );
```

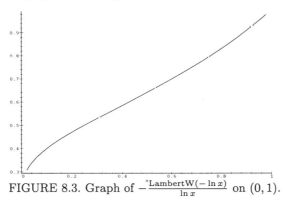

FIGURE 8.3. Graph of $-\dfrac{^x\mathrm{LambertW}(-\ln x)}{\ln x}$ on $(0,1)$.

In Maple, you can specify functional relationship in three ways:

- **As a formula.**

  The dependency of a quantity on variables can be specified in a formula. For example, if the temperature of a body decreases exponentially in time, then the following formula can be entered in Maple.

  ```
  >   T := T0 * exp(-c*t);
  ```

  $$T := T\!0\,e^{(-c\,t)}$$

To get the value of the temperature at a particular time you can replace t by some value.

```
>   subs( t=1/c, T );
```

$$T0\, e^{(-1)}$$

- **As a function.**

You can introduce functions in a more mathematical way.

```
>    T := t -> T0 * exp(-c*t);
```

$$T := t \rightarrow T0\, e^{(-ct)}$$

```
>   T(2/c), T(time), T(0);
```

$$T0\, e^{(-2)}, T0\, e^{(-c\,time)}, T0$$

The so-called *arrow operator* will be discussed in more detail in the next section.

- **As a procedure.**

The above mathematical function can be defined as Maple procedure.

```
>    T := proc(t) T0 * exp(-c*t) end;
```

$$T := \mathrm{proc}(t)\, T0 \exp(-ct)\, \mathrm{end}$$

```
>   T(2/c), T(time), T(0);
```

$$T0\, e^{(-2)}, T0\, e^{(-c\,time)}, T0$$

In fact, the arrow operator is a special case of a procedure definition. There will be ample discussion of procedures in §8.4 and §8.5.

Mathematical functions often come in handy, and you should be careful to distinguish in Maple between a variable that points to an expression in other unknowns and a variable whose value is a function. Referring to the above function definition of T:

```
>   T;   # evaluation to the name of the function
```

$$T$$

```
>   T(t);   # evaluation of function value at t
```

$$T0\, e^{(-ct)}$$

```
>   solve( T = 100, t );
>
```

Maple does not show a result after the last instruction, as a sign that no solution is found. If `infolevel[solve]` has a value greater than zero, then the system notifies that no solution is found.

```
>   infolevel[solve] := 1:
>   solve( T = 100, t );
```

```
solve:    Warning: no solutions found
```

Indeed, there is no value for t such that the *function* T is equal to the number 100. This was of course not what we intended to do; when we ask the correct question, Maple finds the answer.

```
>  solve(T(t) = 100, t );
```

$$-\frac{\ln(\dfrac{100}{T0})}{c}$$

8.2 Arrow Operators

In the previous section, you have seen one way of defining functions in Maple, viz., the *arrow operator* definition, which mimics the syntax for functions often used in mathematics:

$$function\_name := parameter(s) -> expression.$$

You may be tempted to define functions as follows:

```
>  T(t) := T0 * exp(-c*t);
```

$$T(t) := T0\, e^{(-ct)}$$

Maple accepts the instruction. It looks promising, but it does not really do what you think it means, as illustrated below.

```
>  T(t), T(1/c), T(0);
```

$$T0\, e^{(-ct)}, T(\frac{1}{c}), T(0)$$

What happened? You created a function without a function description.

```
>  print(T);
```

$$\text{proc() option } remember; \ 'procname(\,args\,)'\, end$$

Instead, you stored in the *remember table* of the procedure T the value of the function at t. When you ask for the function value at 1/c, then Maple has no value in the remember table nor a function description. Therefore, the system can do nothing more than printing the function call; perhaps you will want to assign a function description to T later in the session.

You have already seen the case of a function in one variable. Functions with more than one variable are defined similarly.

```
>  f := (x,y) -> x^3 - 3*x*y^2;
```

$$f := (x,y) \to x^3 - 3\,x\,y^2$$

```
>  f(3,2);
```

$$-9$$

```
>  plot3d( f, -1..1, -1..1,
>    numpoints=2500, style=patchcontour, axes=framed );
```

This graph is shown in Figure 8.4.

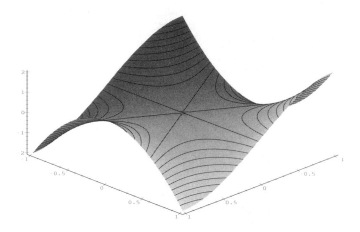

FIGURE 8.4. Surface plot of $x^3 - 3xy^2$ on $[0,1] \times [0,1]$.

Mind the brackets around the function parameters in the definition; otherwise Maple will interpret it as

```
>   f := x, ( y -> x^3 - 3*x*y^2);
```

$$f := x, y \rightarrow x^3 - 3\,x\,y^2$$

i.e., you have created the expression sequence f consisting of the variable x and the anonymous function $y \longrightarrow x^3 - 3xy^2$. Functions with zero parameters can be defined as well.

```
>   goldenratio := () -> (1+sqrt(5))/2;   # constant function
```

$$goldenratio := (\ ) \rightarrow \frac{1}{2} + \frac{1}{2}\sqrt{5}$$

```
>   goldenratio();
```

$$\frac{1}{2} + \frac{1}{2}\sqrt{5}$$

```
>   goldenratio( x ); # no check on number of arguments
```

$$\frac{1}{2} + \frac{1}{2}\sqrt{5}$$

Be careful with the use of variables that are not parameters in the function definition. There might be side effects. Sometimes you get a warning that Maple declares a variable in the expression as a local one.

```
>   duplicate := (x,n) -> seq(x, j = 1..n);
```

```
Warning, `j` in call to `seq` is not local
```

$$duplicate := (\,x, n\,) \rightarrow seq(\,x, j = 1..n\,)$$

But in this case it is false alarm (due to the implementation of the sequence operator **seq**). Sometimes Maple remains silent, but then there is interference with global variables. An example:

```
>   ERF := x -> 2/Pi^(1/2) * int( exp(-t^2), t = 0..x );
```

$$ERF := x \rightarrow 2 \frac{\int_0^x e^{(-t^2)}\, dt}{\sqrt{\pi}}$$

```
>   ERF(1);   # indeed, ERF is nothing but the error function
```

$$\mathrm{erf}(\,1\,)$$

```
>   t := 0:   # let t be assigned a value!
>   ERF(1);   # all goes wrong
```

Error, (in int) wrong number (or type) of arguments

The only solution to this problem is to declare t as a local variable. Because the arrow-definition only allows one expression, one conditional statement, or one procedure definition, you have to use the long format of defining procedures.

```
>   ERF := proc(x)
>       options operator, arrow;
>       local t;
>       2/Pi^(1/2) * int( exp(-t^2), t = 0..x );
>   end;
```

$$ERF := x \rightarrow \mathbf{local}\, t;\; 2 \frac{\mathrm{int}(e^{(\ -t^2\ )}, t = 0..x)}{\sqrt{\pi}}$$

Now there are no side effects anymore.

```
>   ERF(1);   # indeed, ERF is nothing but the error function
```

$$\mathrm{erf}(\,1\,)$$

In §8.4 we shall have a close look at the general format of defining a procedure.

8.3   Piecewise Defined Functions

Piecewise defined functions can easily be introduced with the arrow operator notation. There are two ways of defining such functions, the second of which is the best.

- **As a case-statement.**

  Use a conditional statement to distinguish the cases. The general format is as follows:

parameter(s) ->

```
            if 1st condition then
                1st value
            elif 2nd condition then
                2nd value
                . . . . . .
            elif Nth condition then
                Nth value
            else
                default value
            fi
```

- **Via the procedure piecewise.**

    Mathematical knowledge for piecewise defined functions is available
    in Maple when using the procedure **piecewise**. The general format
    is as follows:

    parameter(s) -> **piecewise(**

             1st condition, 1st value,

             2nd condition, 2nd value,

             . . . . . .

             Nth condition, Nth value,

             default value

)

We shall look at both ways of defining piecewise defined functions. To
start, let us consider a step function whose values are -1 for real numbers
less than 1, 0 at 1, and 1 otherwise.

```
>   step := x -> if x<1 then -1 elif x=1 then 0 else 1 fi;
```

$$step := \text{proc}(x)$$
$$\text{option } operator, arrow;$$
$$\quad \text{if } x < 1 \text{ then } -1 \text{ elif } x = 1 \text{ then } 0 \text{ else } 1 \text{ fi}$$
$$\text{end}$$

```
>   step(3/2), step(1), step(1/2);
```

$$1, 0, -1$$

```
>   plot( step, -1..Pi,
>   title=`graph of step function`, style=line );
```

In Figure 8.5 you see the Maple plot of this piecewise defined function.

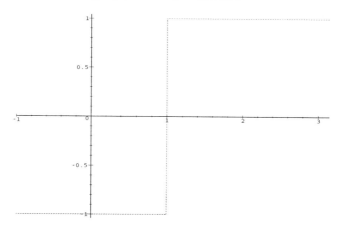

FIGURE 8.5. Graph of step function.

That such a function definition is already more delicate than at first sight becomes clear in the following instruction.

```
>   printlevel := 2:   # make Maple more communicative
>   step(P1);
```

```
Error, (in step) cannot evaluate boolean
  executing statement:
if x < 1 then `...` elif x = 1 then `...` else `...` fi
  step called with arguments: Pi
```

The problem here is that when Maple executes the condition

$$\text{if } 1 < \text{Pi then } \ldots$$

it cannot do it. Maple can compare only numbers of type *numeric*, i.e., integers, fractions, and floating-point numbers. Of course we know that 1 < Pi. This inability to evaluate an expression in a Boolean context is also the reason why we plotted the step function in functional notation and did not enter the command

```
>   plot( step(x), x = -1 .. 3.14 );
```

```
Error, (in step) cannot evaluate boolean
  executing statement:
if x < 1 then `...` elif x = 1 then `...` else `...` fi
  step called with arguments: x
```

Computing the sign of a real number can be seen as a membership test of the open interval $(0, \infty)$. You can use the **assume** facility for this purpose, and particularly call the procedure **is**. Then you do not have problems with evaluation and moreover you can work with indeterminates that have properties associated with them. The improved definition of the step function below relies on interval arithmetic in the current precision and on computing with properties in the assume facility.

```
>   step := x -> if is( x<1 ) then
>                   -1
>                elif is( x=1 ) then
>                   0
>                elif is( x>1 ) then
>                   1
>                else # nothing known or all fails
>                   ´procname´(x)
>                fi;
```

$$step := \operatorname{proc}(x)$$
$$\text{option } operator, arrow;$$
$$\quad \text{if is}(x < 1) \text{ then } -1$$
$$\quad \text{elif is}(x = 1) \text{ then } 0$$
$$\quad \text{elif is}(1 < x) \text{ then } 1$$
$$\quad \text{else } 'procname'(x)$$
$$\quad \text{fi}$$
$$\text{end}$$

Within the procedure, we use the special name **procname** to refer to the name with which the procedure is invoked (in this case **step**). Let us see how the function works.

```
>   step(Pi), step( 1 + sqrt(2)*sqrt(3) - sqrt(6) );
```
$$1, 0$$

```
>   step( exp(Pi/3*sqrt(163)) - 640319 );
```
$$1$$

```
>   assume( s > sqrt(2) ):
>   step(s);
```
$$1$$

```
>   step(u);
```
$$\operatorname{step}(u)$$

In the case-statement, the Boolean tests are evaluated from left to right, and as soon as a condition is fulfilled, the corresponding value is returned. Therefore, it is perfectly valid to define the following function and apply it to 0.

```
>   f := x -> if x<=0 then x else 1/x fi:
>   f(0);
```
$$0$$

But a big disadvantage of the definition of a piecewise defined function by a conditional statement is that you cannot do much mathematics with it. Nothing of the following kind:

```
>  diff( step(u), u );
```

$$\frac{\partial}{\partial u} \text{step}(u)$$

```
>  solve( step(u)=0, u );
```

$$\text{RootOf}(\text{step}(\_Z))$$

```
>  diff( g(u), u ) = step(u);
```

$$\frac{\partial}{\partial u} \text{g}(u) = \text{step}(u)$$

```
>  # try to solve the differential equation
>  dsolve( ", g(u) );
```

$$\text{g}(u) = \int \text{step}(u)\, du + \_C1$$

Many of the drawbacks of defining piecewise defined function as case statements are overcome with the Maple procedure **piecewise**. Let us first look at the same example as before.

```
>    STEP := x -> piecewise( x<1, -1,
>                            x=1, 0,
>                            x>1, 1,
>                            'procname'(x) # default
>                          );
```

$$STEP := x \rightarrow \text{piecewise}(x < 1, -1, x = 1, 0, 1 < x, 1, '\text{procname}'(x))$$

```
>    STEP(3/2), STEP(1), STEP(1/2), STEP(Pi);
```

$$1, 0, -1, 1$$

It works fine. You can also use unknowns.

```
>    STEP(u);
```

$$\begin{cases} -1 & u < 1 \\ 0 & u = 1 \\ 1 & 1 < u \\ STEP(u) & \text{otherwise} \end{cases}$$

What you get is a description of the function call which can be used for further processing.

```
>    dsolve( diff(g(u),u) = STEP(u), g(u) );
```

$$\begin{cases} -u + \_C1 & u \le 1 \\ u - 2 + \_C1 & 1 < u \end{cases}$$

The procedure **piecewise** also cascades the Boolean tests. However, in a call of **piecewise**, all arguments are evaluated and substituted into the procedure body before a branch decision is made. That is why the following function definition cannot be applied to 0.

```
>  f := x -> piecewise( x<=0, x, x>0, 1/x );
```

$$f := x \rightarrow \text{piecewise}(\, x \le 0, x, 0 < x, \frac{1}{x}\,)$$

```
>  f(0);
```

```
Error, (in f) division by zero
  executing statement: piecewise(x <= 0,x,0 < x,1/x)
  f called with arguments: 0
```

The advantage of **piecewise** is that Maple has mathematical knowledge built in to work with these objects. You can differentiate and integrate such piecewise defined functions, solve equations and differential equations that contain such functions, compute Taylor series, and so on. Moreover, well-known mathematical functions like the absolute value function, the maximum and minimum function, and the Heaviside step function can be converted into `piecewise`-format for further processing. One example will do here; more examples you will encounter in chapters on differentiation and integration, series expansion, limits, and solving differential equations.

```
>  f := min( x - 1, x^2 - 4 );
```

$$f := \min(\, x - 1, x^2 - 4\,)$$

```
>  plot( f, x = -2..3 );
```

The graph is below in Figure 8.6

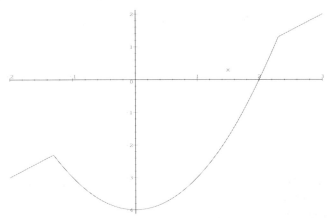

FIGURE 8.6. Graph of $\min(\, x - 1, x^2 - 4\,)$ on interval $(-2, 3)$.

Conversion to piecewise definition:

```
> F := convert( f, piecewise );
```

$$F := \begin{cases} x - 1 & x < \frac{1}{2} - \frac{1}{2}\sqrt{13} \\ x^2 - 4 & x \le \frac{1}{2} + \frac{1}{2}\sqrt{13} \\ x - 1 & \frac{1}{2} + \frac{1}{2}\sqrt{13} < x \end{cases}$$

Now you can differentiate F with respect to x, solve equations, or compute a Taylor series around some expansion point.

```
> diff( F, x );
```

$$\begin{cases} 1 & x < \frac{1}{2} - \frac{1}{2}\sqrt{13} \\ \textit{undefined} & x = \frac{1}{2} - \frac{1}{2}\sqrt{13} \\ 2x & x < \frac{1}{2} + \frac{1}{2}\sqrt{13} \\ \textit{undefined} & x = \frac{1}{2} + \frac{1}{2}\sqrt{13} \\ 1 & \frac{1}{2} + \frac{1}{2}\sqrt{13} < x \end{cases}$$

```
> integrate( F, x );
```

$$\begin{cases} -x + \frac{1}{2}x^2 & x \le \frac{1}{2} - \frac{1}{2}\sqrt{13} \\ -4x + \frac{19}{12} + \frac{1}{3}x^3 - \frac{13}{12}\sqrt{13} & x \le \frac{1}{2} + \frac{1}{2}\sqrt{13} \\ -x + \frac{1}{2}x^2 - \frac{13}{6}\sqrt{13} & \frac{1}{2} + \frac{1}{2}\sqrt{13} < x \end{cases}$$

```
> plot( ", x = -2..5 );
```

The graph is below in Figure 8.7

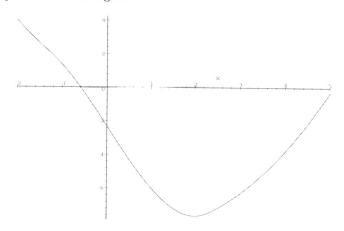

FIGURE 8.7. Graph of $\int \min(x - 1, x^2 - 4)\, dx$ on interval $(-2, 5)$.

```
> solve( F=-3, x );
```

$$-2, 1, -1$$

```
>   series( F, x=1, 3 );
```
$$-3 + 2(x-1) + (x-1)^2$$

```
>   convert( ", polynom );
```
$$-5 + 2x + (x-1)^2$$

```
>   expand( " );
```
$$x^2 - 4$$

8.4   Maple Procedures

Look again at the output of the arrow operator definition of the step function of the previous section: it is a *procedure*. In general, the definition of a Maple procedure has the following syntax:

> **proc(** *parameter_sequence* **)**
> [**local** *name_sequence;*]
> [**global** *name_sequence;*]
> [**options** *name_sequence;*]
>   *statements*
> **end**

where *name_sequence* is a sequence of Maple names separated by commas. The *parameter_sequence* is in many cases a sequence of Maple names, too, but when the dynamic type checking facility is used, each name may be followed by its data type (separated by the double colon ::).

```
>   sgn := proc( n::integer ) (-1)^n end:
>   sgn(Pi);
```

```
Error, sgn expects its 1st argument, n, to be of type
integer, but received Pi
```

```
>   sgn(-2);
```
$$1$$

The procedure **sgn** has one parameter. When it is called, Maple checks whether the given argument is of type *integer*. If not, or when no argument is supplied, the system returns an error message. Otherwise, it computes the power.

In general, the value returned by a procedure is the last value computed unless there is an explicit return via **RETURN**. An example:

```
> MEMBER := proc( x::anything, L::list, pos::name )
>    local i;
>    for i to nops(L) do
>      if L[i] = x then pos := i; RETURN(true) fi
>    od:
>    false
> end:
> MEMBER( 2, [2,1,3,2], 'position' );
```

$$true$$

```
> position;
```

$$1$$

```
> MEMBER( 4, [2,1,3,2] );
```

$$false$$

When a variable inside a function definition is assigned a value and nothing about local or global definition of the variable has been stated, then Maple will automatically assume that it is a local variable. The next example illustrates this.

```
> f := proc(x)
>   y := 1 + sin(x);
>   y^2 + y + 1/y + 1/y^2
> end;
```

```
Warning, `y` is implicitly declared local
```

$$f := \mathrm{proc}(x)\,\mathrm{local}\,y;\; y := 1 + \sin(x);\; y^2 + y + 1/(y) + 1/y^2 \;\mathrm{end}$$

```
> y := unspecified:  f(Pi);
```

$$4$$

It goes without saying that you better specify the scope of the variables used in a procedure definition via `local` and `global` declarations. The declarations may be placed in any order, but each one may appear only once.

Maple has a *subscripted function* calling facility. For example, it is used for the logarithm with different bases. **log[b]** is used to specify the logarithm with base b. Here, we give only one example. It should give you an idea about the definition of subscripted functions. We extend Maple's implementation of Euler's beta function to the incomplete beta function, which is defined as

$$B_x(p,q) = \int_0^x t^{p-1}(1-t)^{q-1}\,dt\,.$$

$B_1(p,q)$ becomes the regular (complete) beta function. In Maple, a rudimentary, but not foolproof implementation of $B_x(p,q)$ can be as follows.

```
> BETA := proc(p,q)
>   local x:
>   if type( procname, indexed ) then
>     x := op( procname );
>     int( t^(p-1)*(1-t)^(q-1), t=0..x )
>   else
>     Beta(p,q)
>   fi
>   end:
> BETA[1](2,3), Beta(2,3);
```

$$\frac{1}{12}, \frac{1}{12}$$

```
> BETA(3/2,5/2);
```

$$\frac{1}{16}\pi$$

When the procedure **BETA** is called, Maple will first have a closer look at the actual procedure name. It checks whether the variable procname inside the procedure is an indexed name of the form **BETA**[x] or not. If not, it is assumed that **BETA** is equal to the regular (complete) beta function. If an indexed name is used, the local variable x is assigned the value of the index, and the integral that defines the incomplete beta function is computed.

8.5   Recursive Procedure Definitions

Recursive definition of a function or procedure is possible in Maple. We shall illustrate this with the computation of Lucas numbers L_n, which are defined by the linear recurrence

$$L_1 = 1, \; L_2 = 3, \; \text{and} \; L_n = L_{n-1} + L_{n-2}, \; \text{for} \; n > 2.$$

In the arrow operator notation, it can be coded directly by

```
> L := n ->
>   if not type( n, posint )
>   then ERROR( `wrong type of arguments` )
>   elif n=1 then 1
>   elif n=2 then 3
>   else L(n-1) + L(n-2)
>   fi;
```

$L := \text{proc}(n)$
option *operator, arrow*;
      if not type($n, posint$) then ERROR('*wrong type of arguments*')
      elif $n = 1$ then 1
      elif $n = 2$ then 3

$$\text{else}\,L(\,n-1\,)+L(\,n-2\,)$$
$$\text{fi}$$
end

Here, we have used the procedure **ERROR** to generate an error message from within the function when the given argument is not a **positive integer**. The standard way of defining Maple procedures is slightly more convenient.

```
>   L := proc( n::posint )
>     if n = 1 then 1
>     elif n = 2 then 3
>     else L(n-1) + L(n-2)
>     fi
>     end:
>   L(6);
```

$$18$$

However, this is not an efficient way to compute the Lucas numbers. Let us have Maple count the number of procedure calls with **exprofile** (see the help system for a detailed description).

```
>   readlib( exprofile ):  # load the library function
>   kernelopts( profile = true ):  # enable profiling
>   writeto( ´output´ );  # redirect output to file
```

While in this mode, no prompt will appear at the terminal.

```
L(6):
kernelopts( profile = false ): # disable profiling
writeto( ´terminal´ ); # redirect output to screen
```

```
>   exprofile( ´output´ );
```

name	#calls
====	======
Main_Routine	1
type/posint	15
L	15

Here, we have omitted information about computing time and memory usage. The information shown becomes clear when you realize how Maple computes the Lucas numbers. To compute L(6), it is necessary to compute L(5) and L(4). For each of these Lucas numbers two more function calls are needed, and this goes on until all needed Lucas numbers have been calculated. Figure 8.8 is the graph of function calls when computing L(6).

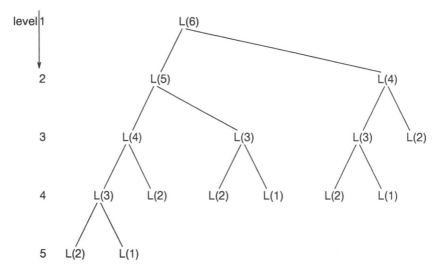

FIGURE 8.8. Recursive computation of L(6) without option remember.

The graph is in agreement with the result of **exprofile** and shows clearly that, for example, L(2) is computed five times. So, with the above procedure definition of **L**, it takes exponential time (2^n) to compute the nth Lucas number, and it shall take almost forever to compute L(100). But we can do better. It is clear that we should remember the function values as they are computed so that they can be used when they are needed. Maple provides the option remember for this purpose.

```
>   L := proc( n::posint ) Lucas( n ) end:
>   Lucas := proc(n)
>     option remember;
>     if n = 1 then 1
>     elif n = 2 then 3
>     else Lucas(n-1) + Lucas(n-2)
>   fi
>   end:
>   kernelopts( profile = true ):
>   writeto( ´output´ ):

L(6):
kernelopts( profile = false ): # disable profiling
writeto( ´terminal´ ); # redirect output to screen

>   exprofile( ´output´ );
```

name	#calls
====	======
Main_Routine	1
Lucas	6
type/posint	1
L	1

With the new definition of **L**, time-complexity is linear ($2n$). What happens when **L** is called is the following: the type of the argument is checked, and if valid, the recursive procedure **Lucas** is called. In this manner, we check only once the type of the argument and not over and over again during the recursive computation that follows. Each Maple procedure has an associated *remember table*. In many cases it is nonexistent in the sense that the pointer to the remember table is the special name NULL. But Maple's remember mechanism becomes activated when you add the **option remember** to the procedure definition. The entries of the remember table will be function values indexed by the arguments of the corresponding function calls. When, in our example, the procedure **Lucas** is called with some argument n, Maple will first look up the remember table of **Lucas** to see if the value Lucas(n) has been computed before. If it has, it returns the result from the remember table. Otherwise, it executes the code present in the procedure body of **Lucas**, and automatically stores the pair (n,Lucas(n)) in the remember table of **Lucas**. In this way, each Lucas number is computed only once. In terms of the above graph of function calls, it can be understood as "follow the depth-first strategy of traversing the graph, compute function values only once, store the results, and use them when needed."

The remember table of a procedure is printed along with the procedure body when the interface variable **verboseproc** has been set to the value 3. In our case.

```
>   interface( verboseproc = 3 ):
>   print( Lucas );
```

proc(n)
option *remember*;
      if $n = 1$ then 1 elif $n = 2$ then 3 else Lucas($n - 1$) + Lucas($n - 2$) fi
end
♯ (2) = 3 ♯ (3) = 4 ♯ (1) = 1 ♯ (4) = 7 ♯ (5) = 11 ♯ (6) = 18

The remember table of a procedure is accessible as the fourth operand of the procedure structure.

```
>   op( 4, eval(Lucas) );   # remember table of Lucas
```

$$\text{table}([$$
$$2 = 3$$
$$3 = 4$$
$$1 = 1$$
$$4 = 7$$
$$5 = 11$$
$$6 = 18$$
$$])$$

The remember table of a procedure can be explicitly updated by a function assignment of the form *procedure(argument) := value*. We illustrate this possibility of explicitly saving values in a remember table by using the so-called *functional assignment*. We start a new Maple session.

```
>  restart:
>  Lucas := proc(n) Lucas(n) := Lucas(n-1) + Lucas(n-2) end:
>  Lucas(1) := 1:   Lucas(2) := 3:
>  op( 4, eval(Lucas) );  # initial remember table
```

$$
\text{table}([
$$
$$
2 = 3
$$
$$
1 = 1
$$
$$
])
$$

```
>  Lucas(4): op( 4, eval(Lucas) ); # updated remember table
```

$$
\text{table}([
$$
$$
2 = 3
$$
$$
3 = 4
$$
$$
1 = 1
$$
$$
4 = 7
$$
$$
])
$$

Maple provides the utility function **forget** to remove one or all entries from a remember table.

```
>  readlib( forget ):   # load the utility function
>  forget( Lucas, 3):   # forget the result of Lucas(3);
>  op( 4, eval(Lucas) );   # updated remember table
```

$$
\text{table}([
$$
$$
2 = 3
$$
$$
1 = 1
$$
$$
4 = 7
$$
$$
])
$$

To empty the remember table of **Lucas** and of all procedures whose name start with Lucas/, enter

```
>  forget( Lucas ):
>  op( 4, eval(Lucas) );  # clear remember table
```

$$
\text{table}([
$$
$$
])
$$

To remove the remember table of **Lucas** and the remember tables of procedure whose name start with Lucas/ completely, enter

```
> Lucas := subsop( 4 = NULL, eval(Lucas) ):
> op( 4, eval(Lucas) );  # NULL pointer to remember table
>
```

You may wonder why **forget**(<*name*>) not only clears the remember table of the procedure *name*, but also the remember tables of procedures that start with *name/*. The reason is that, in this way, you can remove all tables for routines like **int** or **evalc** without knowing precisely which subfunctions starting with **int/** or **evalc/** make use of remember tables. Thus, **forget** really gives you a fresh start. For details about customizing the behavior of **forget** in this sense you are referred to the on-line help system.

8.6 **unapply**

There is a third way of making new functions, a way that is especially convenient when you encounter, in the midst of a Maple session, a symbolic expression that you want to use as a description of a function. This is done by **unapply**. As the name implies, it is the opposite of applying a function to symbolic parameters.

```
> formula := ( b^2*x^2*sin(b*x) - 2*sin(b*x)
>     + 2*b*x*cos(b*x)*a*t ) / b^3;
```

$$formula := \frac{b^2 x^2 \sin(bx) - 2\sin(bx) + 2bx\cos(bx)at}{b^3}$$

```
> F := unapply( formula, x, t );
```

$$F := (x,t) \rightarrow \frac{b^2 x^2 \sin(bx) - 2\sin(bx) + 2bx\cos(bx)at}{b^3}$$

```
> F(0,1), F(Pi/b,5);
```

$$0, -10\frac{\pi a}{b^3}$$

In a definition of an arrow function, you may be tempted to refer to a previous formula by the ditto operator, but this does not work.

```
> formula := ( b^2*x^2*sin(b*x) -2*sin(b*x)
>     + 2*b*x*cos(b*x)*a*t ) / b^3:
> F := (x,t) -> ";
```

$$F := (x,t) \rightarrow "$$

```
> F(u,v);
>
```

The problem is that the ditto operator actually is an *environment variable*, which works locally inside the procedure **F**, but does not refer to anything outside. The external value has been placed on the stack when the procedure was called and is restored when the procedure call is left.

```
>  G := (x,t) -> formula;
```

$$G := (x,t) \rightarrow formula$$

```
>  G(1,2);
```

$$\frac{b^2 x^2 \sin(bx) - 2\sin(bx) + 2bx\cos(bx)at}{b^3}$$

In this case, you get what you ask for: for any argument of **G**, the value is the evaluation of **formula**. So, you really have to type the function description in *parameter* -> *description* form. The only alternative is to substitute the expression into the function description via a global variable, say, body.

```
>  H := subs( body = formula, (x,t) -> body );
```

$$H := (x,t) \rightarrow \frac{b^2 x^2 \sin(bx) - 2\sin(bx) + 2bx\cos(bx)at}{b^3}$$

```
>  H(u,v);
```

$$\frac{b^2 u^2 \sin(bu) - 2\sin(bu) + 2bu\cos(bu)av}{b^3}$$

8.7   Operations on Functions

Elementary operations on functions like addition, multiplication, and composition are easily done in Maple. A few examples:

```
>  f := x -> ln(x) + 1:  g := y -> exp(y) - 1:
>  h := f + g:  h(z);
```

$$\ln(z) + e^z$$

```
>  h := f * g:  h(z);
```

$$(\ln(z) + 1)(e^z - 1)$$

```
>  h := f @ g:  h(z);
```

$$\ln(e^z - 1) + 1$$

```
>  h := g @ f:  h(z);
```

$$e^{(\ln(z)+1)} - 1$$

```
>  simplify(");
```

$$z e - 1$$

```
>  (f@@4)(z);  # equivalent to f(f(f(f(z))))
```

$$\ln(\ln(\ln(\ln(z) + 1) + 1) + 1) + 1$$

The use of the @ operator in combination with the **macro** facility can be a powerful mechanism to introduce abbreviations in Maple. An example: substitution. Recall from §6.3 that **subs** only does substitution and no evaluation at the end.

```
>   subs( n=2, Zeta(n) ); # substitution
```
$$\zeta(2)$$

```
>   "; # evaluation
```
$$\frac{1}{6}\pi^2$$

Suppose that we always want to apply evaluation on the result of substitution, then we can do the following:

```
>   macro( subs = eval @ subs ):  # new version of subs
>   subs( n=2, Zeta(n) );  # with new version of subs
```
$$\frac{1}{6}\pi^2$$

8.8 Anonymous Functions

You are not obliged to name a function. Such *anonymous functions* come in handy when you want to perform an operation only once and do not want to waste a name on it. Anonymous functions are used mostly in conjunction with procedures like **map**, **select**, **remove**, **zip**, and **collect**. Some examples:

```
>   map( x -> x + 2, [1,2,3] );  # add 2 to list elements
```
$$[3, 4, 5]$$

```
>   map( x -> x^2, a + b + c );  # square summands
```
$$a^2 + b^2 + c^2$$

```
>   data := [[1,1.0], [2,3.8], [3,5.1] ]:
>   # take the logarithm of the 2nd element of each entry
>   map( x-> applyop(ln,2,x), data );
```
$$[[1,0],[2,1.335001067],[3,1.629240540]]$$

```
>   # compute sums of derivative and antiderivative
>   map( (f,x) -> diff(f,x) + int(f,x),
>      [cos(z), sin(z), exp(z), ln(z) ], z );
```
$$[0, 0, 2e^z, \frac{1}{z} + z\ln(z) - z]$$

```
>   sum( 'x^i', 'i' = 0..6 );
```
$$1 + x + x^2 + x^3 + x^4 + x^5 + x^6$$

```
> # select low and high order terms in polynomial
> select( t -> degree(t)<3, " " );
```
$$1 + x + x^2$$

```
> remove( t -> degree(t)<3, "" );
```
$$x^3 + x^4 + x^5 + x^6$$

```
> # combine two lists of data
> zip( (x,y) -> [x,ln(y)], [1,2,3], [1.0,3.8,5.1] );
```
$$[[1,0],[2,1.335001067],[3,1.629240540]]$$

```
> # collect a polynomial in x and square coefficients
> collect( x^2 + y*x^2 + 2*x +y, x, z -> z^2 );
```
$$(1+y)^2 x^2 + 4x + y^2$$

8.9 Exercises

1. Consider $x^3 - (a-1)x^2 + a^2 x - a^3 = 0$ as an equation in x. Solve it, make a function out of the first solution, and compute the solution for $a = 0$ and for $a = 1$. Give an approximate result for $a = 2$.

2. Define a function in Maple that is 1 on the segment $[-1, 1]$, and 0 otherwise. Also plot the graph of your function.

3. Define the function $f\colon t \longmapsto \sum_{n=1}^{8} (-1)^{n+1} \frac{2}{n} \sin(nt)$. Compute $f(\frac{\pi}{10})$ and $f(\frac{\pi}{6})$. Plot the graph of your function.

4. After the following assignments,

   ```
   > x := 1:
   > f := proc(x) 2 end:
   > f(x) := 3:
   ```

   what will be `f(1)`, `f(4)`, and `f()`?

5. Write a Maple procedure that computes the Legendre polynomials $L_n(x)$. These polynomials satisfy the recurrence relation $L_0(x) = 1$, $L_1(x) = x$, and $L_n(x) = \frac{n-1}{n} (x L_{n-1}(x) - L_{n-2}(x)) + x L_{n-1}(x)$, for $n > 1$. Compute $L_7(x)$, and check your answer with the Maple procedure **orthopoly[P]**. Can your procedure compute $L_{50}(x)$?

6. Write an anonymous function that selects from a set of integers those values that are between 0 and 10. Use the procedure **rand** to generate a set of 100 integers and apply your anonymous function to this set.

7. Write an anonymous function to drop from a polynomial in two unknowns (which can be created by the procedure **randpoly**) all terms with negative coefficients.

9

Differentiation

This chapter explains the procedures **diff** and **D** for computing derivatives symbolically, gives examples of implicit differentiation, and briefly discusses Maple's automatic differentiation facility.

9.1 Symbolic Differentiation

With the Maple procedure **diff** you can differentiate a formula.
```
>   ´diff( exp(-x^2), x)´;
```
$$\frac{\partial}{\partial x} e^{(-x^2)}$$

```
>   ";
```
$$-2\, x\, e^{(-x^2)}$$

The apostrophes around the first command are to postpone computation of the derivative and will print the input in two-dimensional layout. For this purpose we could have also used the inert **Diff** command, which simply returns unevaluated, and explicitly ask for its value afterward.
```
>   Diff( ln(x/(x^2+1)), x ):   " = value(");
```
$$\frac{\partial}{\partial x} \ln(\frac{x}{x^2+1}) = \frac{(\frac{1}{x^2+1} - 2\frac{x^2}{(x^2+1)^2})(x^2+1)}{x}$$

```
> normal(");
```

$$\frac{\partial}{\partial x} \ln(\frac{x}{x^2+1}) = -\frac{x^2-1}{x(x^2+1)}$$

In a real Maple session, you will probably first use the inert procedure **Diff** to check whether the formula entered is the one you had in mind. Next, if the formula is really the one you want to differentiate, you can use worksheet facilities (or, in Maple's text-based user interface, the built-in command line editor) to change **Diff** into the "active" procedure **diff** to compute the derivative or ask explicitly for its **value**. In the examples below, we shall use **Diff** to make results clearer and better understandable.

```
> Diff( x^(x^x), x ):   " = value(");
```

$$\frac{\partial}{\partial x} x^{(x^x)} = x^{(x^x)}(x^x(\ln(x)+1)\ln(x) + \frac{x^x}{x})$$

```
> collect( ", ln(x), simplify );
```

$$\frac{\partial}{\partial x} x^{(x^x)} = x^{(x^x+x)}\ln(x)^2 + x^{(x^x+x)}\ln(x) + x^{(x^x+x-1)}$$

Rigorous application of differentiation rules without simplification quickly leads to incomprehensible results. Taking account of this expression swell, higher derivatives can be computed without any difficulty.

```
> Diff( x^(x^x), x, x ): " = value("):
> collect( ", ln(x), simplify );
```

$$\frac{\partial^2}{\partial x^2} x^{(x^x)} = x^{(x^x)}(x^2)^x\ln(x)^4 + (x^{(x^x+x)} + 2x^{(x^x)}(x^2)^x)\ln(x)^3$$
$$+ (2x^{(x^x+x)} + 2x^{(x^x-1)}(x^2)^x + x^{(x^x)}(x^2)^x)\ln(x)^2$$
$$+ (3x^{(x^x+x-1)} + x^{(x^x+x)} + 2x^{(x^x-1)}(x^2)^x)\ln(x) + x^{(x^x-2)}(x^2)^x$$
$$+ 2x^{(x^x+x-1)} - x^{(x^x+x-2)}$$

```
> Diff( exp(-x^2), x$5 ):   " = value(");
```

$$\frac{\partial^5}{\partial x^5} e^{(-x^2)} = -120\,x\,e^{(-x^2)} + 160\,x^3\,e^{(-x^2)} - 32\,x^5\,e^{(-x^2)}$$

Here, we have used the sequence operator **$** to shorten input.

$$\text{diff(exp(-x^2), x$5)}$$

is equivalent to

$$\text{diff(exp(-x^2), x,x,x,x,x).}$$

Remark: **diff**(*expression*, [*var$n*]) is an alternative notation for higher derivatives. It has been added to Maple to allow the empty list as notation for the 0th derivative, i.e., nothing else than the original expression.

```
>  for i from 0 to 8 by 4 do
>    `.i.`th derivative` = diff( x^8 / 1680, [x$i] )
>  od;
```

$$Oth\ derivative = \frac{1}{1680}\ x^8$$

$$4th\ derivative = x^4$$

$$8th\ derivative = 24$$

Differentiation of a function y of x that is implicitly defined by an equation can be done in the following elegant way.

```
>  alias( y = y(x) ):   # consider y as a function of x
>  eq := x^2 + y^2 = c; # equation defining y; c is constant
```

$$eq := x^2 + y^2 = c$$

```
>  diff(eq,x);
```

$$2\,x + 2\,y\,(\frac{\partial}{\partial x}\,y) = 0$$

```
>  dydx := solve( ", diff(y,x) ); # 1st derivative
```

$$dydx := -\frac{x}{y}$$

```
>  diff(eq,x$2);
```

$$2 + 2\,(\frac{\partial}{\partial x}\,y)^2 + 2\,y\,(\frac{\partial^2}{\partial x^2}\,y) = 0$$

```
>  solve( ", diff(y,x$2) ); # 2nd derivative
```

$$-\frac{1 + (\frac{\partial}{\partial x}\,y)^2}{y}$$

```
>  d2ydx2 := normal( subs( diff(y,x) = dydx, " ) );
```

$$d2ydx2 := -\frac{x^2 + y^2}{y^3}$$

You can simplify further with respect to the original equation as a side relation.

```
>  d2ydx2 := simplify( ", {eq}, [x,y,c] );
```

$$d2ydx2 := -\frac{c}{y^3}$$

```
>  d3ydx3 := diff(",x);
```

$$d3ydx3 := 3\,\frac{c\,(\frac{\partial}{\partial x}\,y)}{y^4}$$

```
>  d3ydx3 := normal( subs( diff(y,x) = dydx, " ) );
```

$$d3ydx3 := -3\,\frac{c\,x}{y^5}$$

Higher derivatives can be computed in the same style. At the end of this section we shall describe the library procedure **implicitdiff** for implicit differentiation.

```
>  alias( y = y ): # unalias y for further usage
```

Partial derivatives cause no extra problems for **diff**. Two examples of functions in two unknowns:

```
>  Diff(exp(a*x*y^2), x, y$2 ):   " = factor( value(") );
```

$$\frac{\partial^3}{\partial y^2\,\partial x}\,e^{(a\,x\,y^2)} = 2\,a\,e^{(a\,x\,y^2)}\,(1 + 5\,a\,x\,y^2 + 2\,a^2\,y^4\,x^2)$$

```
>  Diff( sin(x+y)/y^4, x$5, y$2 ):   " = value(");
```

$$\frac{\partial^7}{\partial y^2\,\partial x^5}\,\frac{\sin(x+y)}{y^4} = -\frac{\cos(x+y)}{y^4} + 8\,\frac{\sin(x+y)}{y^5} + 20\,\frac{\cos(x+y)}{y^6}$$

```
>  collect( ", cos(x+y), normal );
```

$$\frac{\partial^7}{\partial y^2\,\partial x^5}\,\frac{\sin(x+y)}{y^4} = -\frac{(y^2-20)\cos(x+y)}{y^6} + 8\,\frac{\sin(x+y)}{y^5}$$

If you want to differentiate a function instead of a formula, then you can use the **D** operator. **D** works on a function and computes the derivative as a function again. This is convenient when you want to compute or specify the derivative of a function at some point.

```
>  g := x -> x^n * exp(sin(x)); # the function
```

$$g := x \rightarrow x^n\,e^{\sin(x)}$$

```
>  D(g); # the derivative
```

$$x \rightarrow \frac{x^n\,n\,e^{\sin(x)}}{x} + x^n\,\cos(x)\,e^{\sin(x)}$$

```
>  D(g)(Pi/6); # the derivative at Pi/6
```

$$6\,\frac{(\frac{1}{6}\,\pi)^n\,n\,e^{(1/2)}}{\pi} + \frac{1}{2}\,(\frac{1}{6}\,\pi)^n\,\sqrt{3}\,e^{(1/2)}$$

Basically, D(f) is equivalent to **unapply(diff(f(x),x), x)**.

It is essential to make a clear distinction between **diff** and **D**; **diff** differentiates a *formula* and returns a formula, whereas **D** differentiates a *mapping* and returns a mapping. A few examples:

```
>  diff( cos(t), t );   # derivative of a formula
```

$$-\sin(t)$$

```
> D(cos);  # derivative of a function
```
$$-sin$$

```
> (D@@2)(cos);  # 2nd derivative of a function
```
$$-cos$$

```
> D(cos)(t);  # derivative of a function at some point
```
$$-\sin(t)$$

```
> D( cos(t) );
```
$$D(\cos(t))$$

In the last command, Maple does not consider `cos(t)` as the cosine function, nor as the composition of the cosine function and some function `t`. For the latter purpose you must follow Maple's syntax and semantics closely and use the composition operator `@`.

```
> D( cos @ t );
```
$$(-sin)@t\, D(t)$$

However, if we assume that `t` is a constant, then Maple is indeed willing to consider `cos(t)` as a function, viz., as a constant function.

```
> assume( t, constant ):  D( cos(t) );
```
$$0$$

It is easier to understand this for a familiar constant number.

```
> D( cos(1) );
```
$$0$$

`cos(1)` is a number and can be considered as a constant function whose derivative is equal to the zero function.

```
> t := 't': # unassign t, i.e., forget assumption
> diff( cos, t );
```
$$0$$

In the last example, Maple considered `cos` as an expression in which `t` did not occur.

If you want to differentiate an implicitly defined function, it is convenient to manipulate the mapping as if it is an expression, and let **D** do the differentiation. The same example as was treated before with **diff** will be as follows in the new formalism.

```
> eq := x^2 + y^2 = c:   D( eq );
```
$$2\,D(x)\,x + 2\,D(y)\,y = D(c)$$

We specify that x is an independent variable and that c is a constant.

```
>  D(x) := 1:   D(c) := 0:   dydx := solve( """, D(y) );
```

$$dydx := -\frac{x}{y}$$

```
>  (D@@2)( eq );
```

$$2 + 2\,D^{(2)}(y)\,y + 2\,D(y)^2 = 0$$

```
>  solve( ", (D@@2)(y) );
```

$$-\frac{1 + D(y)^2}{y}$$

```
>  d2ydx2 := normal( subs( D(y)=dydx, " ) );
```

$$d2ydx2 := -\frac{x^2 + y^2}{y^3}$$

And so on.

Use of the **D** operator is not restricted to univariate functions. An indexed function call to **D** will enable you to compute partial derivatives.

```
>  h := (x,y,z) -> 1/(x^2+y^2+z^2)^(1/2);
```

$$h := (x, y, z) \rightarrow \frac{1}{\sqrt{x^2 + y^2 + z^2}}$$

```
>  # partial derivative w.r.t. x
>  `D[1](h)` = D[1](h);
```

$$D_1(h) = ((x, y, z) \rightarrow -\frac{x}{(x^2 + y^2 + z^2)^{3/2}})$$

Here, D[1](h) means the partial derivative of h with respect to the first argument. D[1](h) is equivalent to unapply(diff(h(x,y,z),x), x,y,z), but simplification differences may be present.

```
>  # partial derivative w.r.t. x and y
>  `D[1,2](h)` = D[1,2](h);
```

$$D_{1,2}(h) = ((x, y, z) \rightarrow 3\frac{y\,x}{(x^2 + y^2 + z^2)^{5/2}})$$

Here, D[1,2](h) is equivalent to D[1](D[2](h)).

```
>  # 2nd partial derivative w.r.t. x
>  `D[1,1](h)` = D[1,1](h);
```

$$D_{1,1}(h) = ((x, y, z) \rightarrow 3\frac{x^2}{(x^2 + y^2 + z^2)^{5/2}} - \frac{1}{(x^2 + y^2 + z^2)^{3/2}})$$

If we compute the Laplacian $\left(\dfrac{\partial^2}{\partial x^2} + \dfrac{\partial^2}{\partial y^2} + \dfrac{\partial^2}{\partial z^2} \right) h$, limitations of the operator method, due to lack of simplification of intermediate results, emerge.

```
>   L[h] := ( D[1,1] + D[2,2] + D[3,3] )(h);
```

$$L_h := ((x, y, z) \rightarrow 3\, \frac{x^2}{(x^2 + y^2 + z^2)^{5/2}} - \frac{1}{(x^2 + y^2 + z^2)^{3/2}})$$
$$+ ((x, y, z) \rightarrow 3\, \frac{y^2}{(x^2 + y^2 + z^2)^{5/2}} - \frac{1}{(x^2 + y^2 + z^2)^{3/2}})$$
$$+ ((x, y, z) \rightarrow 3\, \frac{z^2}{(x^2 + y^2 + z^2)^{5/2}} - \frac{1}{(x^2 + y^2 + z^2)^{3/2}})$$

```
>   normal( L[h](x,y,z) );
```

$$0$$

All roads lead to Rome. We have used **diff** and **D** to perform implicit differentiation. But the Maple library itself also contains the **implicitdiff** routine for this purpose. It is intended to make life easy for the user of the software. We shall apply this procedure for the same example as was treated with MACSYMA in section 1.5.4 of [53]. Let $g(x, y)$ be an implicit form, where y is a function of x. Below, we shall determine formulae for the first, second, and third derivative of y with respect to x, in terms of partial derivatives of g.

```
>   dydx := implicitdiff( g(x,y), y(x),  x );
```

$$dydx := -\frac{D_1(g)(x, y)}{D_2(g)(x, y)}$$

Perhaps you are more familiar with the following notation.

```
>   convert( dydx, diff );
```

$$-\frac{\frac{\partial}{\partial x} g(x, y)}{\frac{\partial}{\partial y} g(x, y)}$$

Let us go on with computing higher derivatives of y.

```
>   d2ydx2 := implicitdiff( g(x,y), y(x), x$2 );
```

$$d2ydx2 := (-D_{1,1}(g)(x, y)\, D_2(g)(x, y)^2$$
$$+ 2\, D_{1,2}(g)(x, y)\, D_1(g)(x, y)\, D_2(g)(x, y)$$
$$- D_{2,2}(g)(x, y)\, D_1(g)(x, y)^2) \Big/ D_2(g)(x, y)^3$$

```
>   convert( ", diff );
```

$$(-(\frac{\partial^2}{\partial x^2} g(x, y)) (\frac{\partial}{\partial y} g(x, y))^2$$

$$+ 2 \left(\frac{\partial^2}{\partial y \, \partial x} g(x,y) \right) \left(\frac{\partial}{\partial x} g(x,y) \right) \left(\frac{\partial}{\partial y} g(x,y) \right)$$

$$- \left(\frac{\partial^2}{\partial y^2} g(x,y) \right) \left(\frac{\partial}{\partial x} g(x,y) \right)^2 \right) \Big/ \left(\frac{\partial}{\partial y} g(x,y) \right)^3$$

The computation of the third derivative of y clearly shows the advantage of computer algebra usage over pencil and paper calculation.

```
>   d3ydx3 := convert( implicitdiff( g(x,y), y(x), x$3 ),
>      diff );
```

$$d3ydx3 := -\left(\left(\frac{\partial^3}{\partial x^3} g(x,y) \right) \left(\frac{\partial}{\partial y} g(x,y) \right)^4 \right.$$

$$+ 3 \left(\frac{\partial}{\partial x} g(x,y) \right)^2 \left(\frac{\partial}{\partial y} g(x,y) \right)^2 \left(\frac{\partial^3}{\partial y^2 \, \partial x} g(x,y) \right)$$

$$- 3 \, \%2 \left(\frac{\partial}{\partial y} g(x,y) \right)^3 \%3 + 6 \, \%2^2 \left(\frac{\partial}{\partial y} g(x,y) \right)^2 \left(\frac{\partial}{\partial x} g(x,y) \right)$$

$$- 3 \left(\frac{\partial^3}{\partial y \, \partial x^2} g(x,y) \right) \left(\frac{\partial}{\partial x} g(x,y) \right) \left(\frac{\partial}{\partial y} g(x,y) \right)^3$$

$$- \left(\frac{\partial}{\partial x} g(x,y) \right)^3 \left(\frac{\partial}{\partial y} g(x,y) \right) \left(\frac{\partial^3}{\partial y^3} g(x,y) \right)$$

$$+ 3 \left(\frac{\partial}{\partial x} g(x,y) \right) \%1 \, \%3 \left(\frac{\partial}{\partial y} g(x,y) \right)^2 + 3 \, \%1^2 \left(\frac{\partial}{\partial x} g(x,y) \right)^3$$

$$- 9 \, \%2 \left(\frac{\partial}{\partial y} g(x,y) \right) \%1 \left(\frac{\partial}{\partial x} g(x,y) \right)^2 \right) \Big/ \left(\frac{\partial}{\partial y} g(x,y) \right)^5$$

$$\%1 := \frac{\partial^2}{\partial y^2} g(x,y)$$

$$\%2 := \frac{\partial^2}{\partial y \, \partial x} g(x,y)$$

$$\%3 := \frac{\partial^2}{\partial x^2} g(x,y)$$

Finally, we compute derivatives for g equal to the function $\exp(x^2 + y^2)$.

```
>   g := (x,y) -> exp( x^2 + y^2 );
```

$$g := (x,y) \to e^{(x^2 + y^2)}$$

```
>   dydx;
```

$$- \frac{x}{y}$$

```
>   normal( d2ydx2 );
```

$$- \frac{x^2 + y^2}{y^3}$$

> `normal( d3ydx3 );`

$$-3\,\frac{x\,(\,x^2+y^2\,)}{y^5}$$

The formulae are in agreement with the results obtained earlier for the function y that was implicitly defined by $x^2+y^2=c$.

9.2   Automatic Differentiation

The **D** operator also addresses the problem of *automatic differentiation*, i.e., to differentiate Maple procedures. Let us start with an example of a piecewise defined function that is presented as a case statement.

> `F := x -> if x>0 then sin(x) else arctan(x) fi;`

$F :=$
   $\mathrm{proc}(x)$ option *operator*, *arrow*; if $0 < x$ then $\sin(x)$ else $\arctan(x)$ fi end

> `Fp := D(F); # 1st derivative`

$Fp := \mathrm{proc}(x)$
       option *operator*, *arrow*;
       if $0 < x$ then $\cos(x)$ else $1/(\,1+x^2\,)$ fi
       end

Plot F and its first derivative.

> `plot( { F, Fp }, -3*Pi..3*Pi );`

The graphs of the function F and its derivative are shown in Figure 9.1.

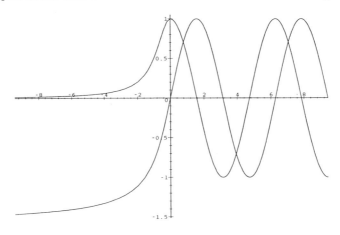

FIGURE 9.1. Graph of piecewise defined function and its derivative.

Maple can differentiate procedures that consist of more than one statement.
A simple example:

```
>  f := proc(x)
>     local s,t;
>     s := ln(x);
>     t := x^2;
>     s*t + 3*t
>  end:
>  fp := D(f);
```

$$fp := \mathrm{proc}(x)$$
$$\mathrm{local}\ s, sx, tx, t;$$
$$sx := 1/(x)\,;\ s := \ln(x)\,;\ tx := 2\,x\,;\ t := x^2\,;\ sx\,t + s\,tx + 3\,tx$$
$$\mathrm{end}$$

Does the procedure **fp** really compute f'? In this case, we can prove
that it does by executing the procedure on symbolic parameters, in effect
converting the function represented by the procedure into a formula.

```
>  diff(f(x),x) - fp(x);
```

$$0$$

Such a check is *not* possible for procedures that contain a conditional statement involving a formal parameter (like is the case in the above function
F). By the way, this is also one of the reasons for introducing automatic
differentiation: not every function can be (conveniently) described by a
formula.

How is the procedure **fp** constructed? Comparison of the source codes of
f and **fp** gives a clue to the following general method of automatic differentiation:

> For each assignment statement $v := f(v_1, \ldots, v_n)$ that appears
> in the procedure, where the v_i are local variables or formal pa-
> rameters, precede it by $v_x := fp(v_1, \ldots, v_n)$ where $fp(v_1, \ldots, v_n)$
> is obtained by differentiating $f(v_1, \ldots, v_n)$ formally. Replace the
> last statement (or any RETURN value) by its derivative.

This method is called *forward automatic differentiation*; the function and
its derivative are constructed in one sweep through the procedure. This is
the method implemented in Maple. There are restrictions to what is allowed
inside the procedure body: no recursive procedures, no option remember,
no assignments to global variables, and only constant loop variables, are a
few of the restrictions.

There exists another method, called *reverse automatic differentiation*, in
which there is a forward sweep in the procedure to compute the function
and a backward sweep to compute the derivative. The reverse mode of

automatic differentiation is not (yet) implemented in Maple. For a gentle introduction to automatic differentiation we refer to [87, 88]. A good reference, in which many algorithms, implementations, and applications are described, is [89].

We end this section by illustrating another reason to use automatic differentiation: cost-effectiveness with respect to computing time and memory space. Suppose we are interested in the iterated powers f_n recursively defined by

$$f_1 = x, \; f_n = x^{f_{n-1}} \text{ for } n > 1,$$

and their derivatives. As we have seen in §9.1, the formulae for the derivatives become already quite large for small values of n. On the other hand, the derivative procedure obtained by automatic differentiation is very compact. We shall use the following iterative definition of f_n.

```
>   f := proc(x,n)
>       local i,t;
>       t := 1;
>       for i to n do t := x^t od;
>       t
>   end;
```

$$f := \mathrm{proc}(x, n) \, \mathrm{local} \, i, t; \, t := 1; \, \mathrm{for} \, i \, \mathrm{to} \, n \, \mathrm{do} \, t := x^t \, \mathrm{od}; \, t \, \mathrm{end}$$

```
>   fp := D[1](f); # 1st derivative of f w.r.t. x
```

$$fp := \mathrm{proc}(x, n)$$
$$\quad \mathrm{local} \, tx, t, i;$$
$$\quad tx := 0; \, t := 1; \, \mathrm{for} \, i \, \mathrm{to} \, n \, \mathrm{do} \, tx := x^t \, (\, tx \ln(\, x\,) + (\,t\,)\,/(\,x\,)\,); \, t := x^t \, \mathrm{od};$$
$$\quad tx$$
$$\quad \mathrm{end}$$

We shall compute the third derivative of f_{22} in two ways: by automatic differentiation, and by symbolic differentiation. There will be big differences in computing time and memory usage.

- *automatic differentiation*

```
>   fppp := D[1$3](f): # 3rd derivative of f w.r.t. x
>   # register memory usage
>   setbytes := kernelopts( bytesused ):
>   # start timing
>   settime := time():
>   fppp( 1.1, 22 );
```

$$18.23670379$$

```
>   cpu_time := (time()-settime) * seconds; # computing time
```

$$cpu\_time := .567 \; seconds$$

```
>  memory_used := evalf(
>    ( kernelopts( bytesused ) - setbytes ) /
>    1024 * kbytes, 5);
```

$$memory\_used := 402.70 \; kbytes$$

- *symbolic differentiation*

```
>  f22 := unapply( f(x,22), x );
```

$$f22 \; := \; x \rightarrow x^{x^{x^{x^{x^{x^{x^{x^{x^{x^{x^{x^{x^{x^{x^{x^{x^{x^{x^{x^{x^{(x^x)}}}}}}}}}}}}}}}}}}}}}$$

```
>  setbytes := kernelopts( bytesused ):
>  settime := time():
>  (D@@3)(f22)(1.1);
```

$$18.23670379$$

```
>  cpu_time := (time()-settime) * seconds; # computing time
```

$$cpu\_time := 113.067 \; seconds$$

```
>  memory_used := evalf(
>    ( kernelopts( bytesused ) - setbytes ) /
>    1024 * kbytes, 5);
```

$$memory\_used := 40935. \; kbytes$$

9.3   Exercises

1. Let f, g, and h be the following multivariate real functions.

$$f(x,y) \quad := \quad \frac{\ln\left(1 + x^4 + y^4\right)}{\sqrt{x^2 + y^2}}$$

$$g(x,y,z) \quad := \quad \frac{1}{\sqrt{(x-a)^2 + (y-b)^2 + (z-c)^2}}$$

$$h(x,y,z) \quad := \quad \frac{z}{x^2 + y^2 + z^2}$$

(a) Determine all partial derivatives of f of order 2.

(b) Check that g is a solution of the Laplace differential equation, i.e.,

$$\left(\frac{\partial^2}{\partial x^2} + \frac{\partial^2}{\partial y^2} + \frac{\partial^2}{\partial z^2}\right) g = 0.$$

(c) Check that h is a solution of the differential equation

$$\frac{\partial^2 h}{\partial x \partial y} + \left(\frac{4x}{x^2 + y^2 + z^2}\right)\frac{\partial h}{\partial y} = 0.$$

2. Compare the results of the following Maple commands:

```
> diff( f(x), x);
> convert( ", D );
> unapply( ", x );
```

3. Compute the derivative of the function $f(x) := \max(x^3, x)$.

4. Let the function $y(x)$ be implicitly defined by $\sqrt{x} + \sqrt{y} = 1$. Compute the derivative y' and the second derivative y''.

5. Let the bivariate function $z(x, y)$ be implicitly defined by $h(x, y, z) = 0$, for some trivariate function h. Determine formulae for $\dfrac{\partial z}{\partial x}$ and $\dfrac{\partial^2 z}{\partial x \partial y}$. What are the results for $h = \sqrt{x} + \sqrt{y} + \sqrt{z} - 1$?

6. Consider the function f_n recursively defined by

$$f_0 = 0, \quad f_1 = x, \quad f_n = f_{n-1} + \sin(f_{n-2}) \text{ for } n > 1.$$

Determine (by automatic differentiation) a procedure to compute the first derivative of f_n.

10

Integration and Summation

Integration (both definite and indefinite), is one of the highlights in computer algebra. Maple uses nonclassical algorithms such as the Risch algorithm for integrating elementary functions, instead of heuristic integration methods, which are described in most mathematics textbooks. We shall briefly discuss Maple's strategy to compute integrals and give many examples so that you can get an idea of Maple's capabilities and of ways to assist the system. Examples of integral transformations like Laplace, Fourier, Mellin, Hilbert, and Hankel transforms will also be given. Their application in the field of differential equations will be treated in Chapter 17.

Summation, which can be seen as the discrete analogue of integration, is another important topic in calculus for which Maple uses advanced methods. A few examples will illustrate this.

10.1 Indefinite Integration

Maple has several powerful built-in algorithms for integration of functions. First, it tries traditional techniques taught at school and university: lookup tables and pattern matching, integration by parts, change of variables, application of the chain rule, and so on. When these heuristic methods fail, then the system proceeds to deterministic methods, and in particular to the so-called Risch algorithm [163].

Let us first look at an example of indefinite integration performed by the procedure **int**.

```
>   Int( x/(x^3+1), x ) =   int( x/(x^3+1), x );
```

$$\int \frac{x}{x^3+1}\, dx =$$

$$-\frac{1}{3}\ln(x+1) + \frac{1}{6}\ln(x^2 - x + 1) + \frac{1}{3}\sqrt{3}\arctan(\frac{1}{3}(2x-1)\sqrt{3})$$

Note that Maple leaves out the constant of integration; the reason is that this is more convenient in the manipulation of the results. There is no harm in some common distrust; so let us check the answer.

```
>   diff( rhs("), x );
```

$$-\frac{1}{3}\frac{1}{x+1} + \frac{1}{6}\frac{2x-1}{x^2-x+1} + \frac{2}{3}\frac{1}{1+\frac{1}{3}(2x-1)^2}$$

```
>   normal( ", `expanded` );
```

$$\frac{x}{x^3+1}$$

Later on in this chapter, you will see examples where such checks of integration results are not so easily done.

In the above example, we used the inert form procedure **Int** for display reasons. Henceforth we shall use **Int** to show the integrand and integration limits, and we shall use the procedure **value** to actually compute the integral.

One of the most handsome tricks you learn at school for integration of rational functions is partial fraction decomposition. It works well for the integral above. However, it becomes a more tedious and error-prone trick when you have to use it in cases like the following.

```
>   Int( x/(x^5+1), x ): " = value(");
```

$$\int \frac{x}{x^5+1}\, dx = -\frac{1}{5}\ln(1+x) + \frac{1}{20}\ln(2x^2 - x - \sqrt{5}x + 2)$$

$$-\frac{1}{20}\ln(2x^2 - x - \sqrt{5}x + 2)\sqrt{5} + \frac{2}{5}\frac{\arctan(\frac{4x-1-\sqrt{5}}{\sqrt{10-2\sqrt{5}}})\sqrt{5}}{\sqrt{10-2\sqrt{5}}}$$

$$+\frac{1}{20}\ln(2x^2 - x + \sqrt{5}x + 2) + \frac{1}{20}\ln(2x^2 - x + \sqrt{5}x + 2)\sqrt{5}$$

$$-\frac{2}{5}\frac{\arctan(\frac{4x-1+\sqrt{5}}{\sqrt{10+2\sqrt{5}}})\sqrt{5}}{\sqrt{10+2\sqrt{5}}}$$

```
>  normal( diff(rhs("),x), `expanded` ); # check the answer
```

$$\frac{x}{x^5 + 1}$$

And the trick of partial fraction decomposition does not work any more
when the integrand is only changed a little bit.

```
>  infolevel[int] := 2:  # make Maple more communicative
>  Int( x/(x^5+2*x+1), x ):   " = value(");
```

```
int/indef:    first-stage indefinite integration
int/ratpoly:    rational function integration
int/rischnorm:    enter Risch-Norman integrator
int/risch:    enter Risch integration
int/risch:    the field extensions are
```

$$[\_X]$$

```
unknown:    integrand is
```

$$\frac{\_X}{\_X^5 + 2\_X + 1}$$

```
int/risch/ratpoly:    integrating
```

$$\frac{\_X}{\_X^5 + 2\_X + 1}$$

```
int/risch/ratpoly:    Horowitz' method yields
```

$$\int \frac{\_X}{\_X^5 + 2\_X + 1} d\_X$$

```
int/risch/ratpoly:
starting computing subresultants at time    3.433
int/risch/ratpoly:
end of subresultants computation at time    3.466
int/risch/ratpoly:
Rothstein's method - factored resultant is
```

$$[[z^5 - \frac{500}{11317}z^3 + \frac{4}{11317}z + \frac{1}{11317}, 1]]$$

```
int/risch/ratpoly:    result is
```

$$\sum_{\_R=\%1} \_R\ln(\_X + \frac{65376045600}{64828679}\_R^4 - \frac{4270752875}{64828679}\_R^3$$

$$- \frac{625000000}{64828679}\_R^2 + \frac{447235682}{64828679}\_R - \frac{21514240}{64828679})$$

$$\%1 := RootOf(11317\_Z^5 - 500\_Z^3 + 4\_Z + 1)$$

`int/risch:    exit Risch integration`

$$\int \frac{x}{x^5 + 2\,x + 1}\,dx = \sum_{\_R=\%1} \_R\ln(x + \frac{65376045600}{64828679}\,\_R^4 - \frac{4270752875}{64828679}\,\_R^3$$
$$- \frac{625000000}{64828679}\,\_R^2 + \frac{447235682}{64828679}\,\_R - \frac{21514240}{64828679})$$
$$\%1 := RootOf(\,11317\,\_Z^5 - 500\,\_Z^3 + 4\,\_Z + 1\,)$$

```
> normal( diff(rhs("),x), 'expanded' ); # check the answer
```

$$\frac{x}{x^5 + 2\,x + 1}$$

```
> infolevel[int] := 0: # back to default information level
```

In the above example, we have assigned `infolevel[int]` the value 2, so that we see what method Maple actually uses. Maple's general approach for integration of rational functions is as follows.

- In the "first-stage indefinite integration," Maple tries simple methods such as table lookups and selects on the basis of the integrand what method should be tried further on.

- If simple methods fail, Maple enters "the second-stage indefinite integration." Maple tries now heuristic methods like "derivative-divides" (integrand of the form $\frac{p}{q}$ where q' divides p), substitutions, integration by parts, and partial fraction decomposition (for denominators of degree less than seven). Furthermore, Maple treats special forms such as $f(ux + v)\frac{p(x)}{q(x)}$ and $Bessel(x) \cdot p(x)$, where f is either exp, ln, sin, cos, sinh, or cosh, and p and q are polynomials.

- If the heuristic methods of the second-stage indefinite integration fail, Maple enters the Risch algorithm. This goes as follows for rational functions.

  (i) Horowitz-Ostrogradsky reduction [105] is applied to express the integral in the form $\frac{c}{d} + \int \frac{a}{b}$, where a, b, c, and D are polynomials, b is square-free, and degree(a) < degree(b). In this form, $\frac{c}{d}$ is called the rational part because the remaining integral can be expressed only by introducing logarithms. Thus, $\int \frac{a}{b}$ is called the logarithmic part.

  (ii) The Rothstein/Trager method [164, 182] is used to express the logarithmic part in the form $\sum_i c_i \log v_i$, where c_i are nonzero constants and v_i are monic, square-free, relatively prime polynomials of positive degree. Actually, the Lazard/Rioboo/Trager improvement [125], in which algebraic extensions and factorizations are avoided in the computation of the logarithmic part, has been implemented.

Of course, you may doubt the usefulness of the answer of the above example because it contains roots of a fifth-degree polynomial that cannot be computed analytically. But the same algorithm is applied in cases like the following one taken from [181].

```
>    Int( (7*x^13+10*x^8+4*x^7-7*x^6-4*x^3-4*x^2+3*x+3) /
>       (x^14-2*x^8-2*x^7-2*x^4-4*x^3-x^2+2*x+1), x ):
>    " = value(");
```

$$\int \frac{7\,x^{13} + 10\,x^8 + 4\,x^7 - 7\,x^6 - 4\,x^3 - 4\,x^2 + 3\,x + 3}{x^{14} - 2\,x^8 - 2\,x^7 - 2\,x^4 - 4\,x^3 - x^2 + 2\,x + 1}\, dx =$$

$$\frac{1}{2}\ln(x^7 - \sqrt{2}\,x^2 + (-\sqrt{2} - 1)\,x - 1)\sqrt{2}$$

$$+ \frac{1}{2}\ln(x^7 - \sqrt{2}\,x^2 + (-\sqrt{2} - 1)\,x - 1)$$

$$+ \frac{1}{2}\ln(x^7 + \sqrt{2}\,x^2 + (\sqrt{2} - 1)\,x - 1)$$

$$- \frac{1}{2}\ln(x^7 + \sqrt{2}\,x^2 + (\sqrt{2} - 1)\,x - 1)\sqrt{2}$$

```
>    normal( diff(rhs("),x), `expanded` ); # check the answer
```

$$\frac{7\,x^{13} + 10\,x^8 + 4\,x^7 - 7\,x^6 - 4\,x^3 - 4\,x^2 + 3\,x + 3}{x^{14} - 2\,x^8 - 2\,x^7 - 2\,x^4 - 4\,x^3 - x^2 + 2\,x + 1}$$

The strength of the Risch algorithm [163] comes into prominence when you apply it to a larger class of functions, viz., the class of *elementary functions*. Elementary functions of x can be roughly described as follows.

- Start with a set of constants, e.g., $\mathbb{Q}$, $\mathbb{R}$, or $\mathbb{C}$.

- Make polynomials $p(x)$ with constant coefficients.

- Make rational functions $\dfrac{p(x)}{q(x)}$.

- Add exponentials of these (this will include the trigonometric and hyperbolic functions, and their inverses if the complex number i is one of the constants).

- Add logarithms of these (if we just go this far we have the *elementary transcendental functions*).

- Add algebraic functions, i.e., solutions of polynomial equations whose coefficients are functions of the types already introduced (e.g., add $\sqrt{x^2 + 1}$, which solves the equation $y^2 - x^2 - 1 = 0$).

It is assumed in the construction that every step (except the choice of constants) can be iterated, so we can form a rational function of polynomials of logarithms and so on.

Risch [163] described an algorithm that, given an elementary transcendental function, decides whether its integral can be expressed as an elementary function, and if so, computes the integral. It is based on:

Liouville's Principle *If an elementary function $f(x)$ has an elementary integral, then it has one of the form*

$$\int f(x)\,dx = v(x) + \sum_{i=1}^{n} c_i \log(u_i(x))$$

where the c_i's are constants, and v and the u_i's involve no quantity not already in f and the c_i's.

Liouville's theorem bounds, so to speak, the search space for elementary integrals. A further generalization would be to take *Liouvillian functions*, defined as elementary functions together with anything of the form $\int f(x)\,dx$ for any function $f(x)$ already in the class considered; again the constructions can be iterated. This class includes, for example, the error function erf and the exponential integral function Ei, defined by

$$\mathrm{erf}(x) = \frac{2}{\sqrt{\pi}} \int_0^x \exp(-t^2)\,dt \text{ and } \mathrm{Ei}(x) = \int_x^\infty \frac{\exp(-t)}{t}\,dt, \text{ respectively.}$$

For details about the Risch algorithm, the interested reader is referred to [20, 21, 52, 53, 74, 76, 143, 163]. Here, we only sketch Maple's general approach to integration of an elementary function:

- If the heuristic methods have failed, Maple applies first the "Risch-Norman front end" [74] to avoid introduction of complex exponentials and logarithms for integrands in which trigonometric and hyperbolic functions are involved.

- If still no answer is found, the Risch algorithm is entered.

In the final step, the most difficult part is the integration of algebraic functions. Trager's method [183] for algebraic functions in **RootOf** notation has been implemented. But there are some restrictions in the current implementation.

- In the case where the coefficient field is not an algebraic number field, the transcendental part of the integral is not computed. In practice this means that when the integrand contains parameters, Maple may fail to find an answer even though it exists.

- The algorithm is slow due to the complexity.

- The integrand must contain a single **RootOf** involving the integration variable. The **evala@Primfield** procedure may be used to achieve this condition.

- Integration methods for nested **RootOf**s are not available.

Let us look at some examples to get a better idea of Maple's integration capabilities.

```
>  Int( ln(x-1)`3, x ):   " = value(");
```

$$\int \ln(x-1)^3 \, dx = \ln(x-1)^3 (x-1) - 3(x-1)\ln(x-1)^2$$
$$+ 6(x-1)\ln(x-1) - 6x + 6$$

```
>  diff( rhs("), x ); # check the answer
```

$$\ln(x-1)^3$$

```
>  int( ln(x-1)^2/x, x );
```

$$\int \frac{\ln(x-1)^2}{x} \, dx$$

The first of these integrals is computed by a table-driven integration by parts in the integrator's front end. The Risch algorithm decides that the second integral cannot be expressed in closed form, i.e., in elementary functions. In such cases, Maple simply returns the input command or introduces a new function, i.e., extends the class of admissible functions (with functions such as the error function, exponential integral, sine integral, and so on).

```
>  Int( exp(-x^2), x ):   " = value(");
```

$$\int e^{(-x^2)} \, dx = \frac{1}{2} \sqrt{\pi} \, \mathrm{erf}(x)$$

```
>  Int( exp(-x)/x, x ):   " = value(");
```

$$\int \frac{e^{(-x)}}{x} \, dx = -\mathrm{Ei}(1, x)$$

In addition to heuristic methods, Maple uses for integrands consisting of logarithms alone.

```
>  Int( ln(1-b*x/(a+c*x^2))/x, x ):   " = value(");
```

$$\int \frac{\ln\left(1 - \frac{bx}{a+cx^2}\right)}{x} \, dx = \ln(x)\ln\left(1 - \frac{bx}{a+cx^2}\right)$$
$$- \ln\left(\frac{1}{2} \frac{b+\sqrt{b^2-4ca}}{c}\right)\ln\left(-\frac{-2cx+b+\sqrt{b^2-4ca}}{b+\sqrt{b^2-4ca}}\right)$$
$$- \ln\left(\frac{1}{2} \frac{b-\sqrt{b^2-4ca}}{c}\right)\ln\left(-\frac{-2cx+b-\sqrt{b^2-4ca}}{b-\sqrt{b^2-4ca}}\right)$$
$$+ \mathrm{dilog}\left(2 \frac{cx}{b+\sqrt{b^2-4ca}}\right) + \mathrm{dilog}\left(2 \frac{cx}{b-\sqrt{b^2-4ca}}\right)$$

$$+ \ln(\frac{\sqrt{-ca}}{c}) \ln(\frac{cx - \sqrt{-ca}}{\sqrt{-ca}}) + \ln(-\frac{\sqrt{-ca}}{c}) \ln(-\frac{cx + \sqrt{-ca}}{\sqrt{-ca}})$$
$$- \operatorname{dilog}(\frac{cx}{\sqrt{-ca}}) - \operatorname{dilog}(-\frac{cx}{\sqrt{-ca}})$$

```
>  Int( sin(x) / ( x^3 + x + 1 ), x ):  " = value(");
```

$$\int \frac{\sin(x)}{x^3 + x + 1} \, dx = \sum_{\_R1 = \%1} \frac{\operatorname{Si}(x - \_R1)\cos(\_R1) + \operatorname{Ci}(x - \_R1)\sin(\_R1)}{3\_R1^2 + 1}$$

$$\%1 := \operatorname{RootOf}(\_Z^3 + \_Z + 1)$$

Above, Maple noticed that the integrand involves a sine function and applied Hermite reduction for expressions consisting of trigonometric functions alone.

```
>  Int( 1 / ( x * (x^2+1)^(1/3) ), x ):  " = value(");
```

$$\int \frac{1}{x\,(x^2 + 1)^{1/3}} \, dx = \int \frac{1}{x\,(x^2 + 1)^{1/3}} \, dx$$

In this case, Maple insists on the use of radicals in **RootOf** notation. So, let us introduce α as a cube root of $x^2 + 1$. From the result it will be clear that it is also convenient to introduce a root β of the polynomial $z^2 + z + 1$.

```
>  alias( alpha = RootOf( z^3 - x^2 - 1, z ),
>            beta = RootOf( z^2 + z + 1, z ) ):
>  convert( "", RootOf ):
```

In this notation, Maple can compute the integral.

```
>  settime := time(): # start timing
>  "";  # evaluation
```

$$\int \frac{1}{x\,\alpha} \, dx = \frac{1}{2} \ln(-(5 - 19\,\beta - 4\,\beta^2 - 9\,x^2\,\beta + 4\,\beta^2\,x^2 + 2\,x^2 - 24\,\alpha$$
$$- 9\,\alpha\,\beta + 24\,\beta\,\alpha^2 + 15\,\alpha^2) / x^2) + \frac{1}{2}\beta \ln((17\,\beta - 4 - 4\,\beta^2$$
$$+ 4\,\beta^2\,x^2 + 11\,x^2\,\beta - 3\,x^2 + 21\,\alpha - 21\,\alpha^2 - 21\,\beta\,\alpha^2) / x^2)$$

```
>  # check the answer
>  evala( Normal( diff(rhs("),x) - 1/(x*alpha) ) );
```

$$0$$

```
>  cpu_time := (time()-settime) * seconds; # computing time
```

$$cpu\_time := 156.000 \; seconds$$

In [52], the Chebyshev integral [41]

$$\int \frac{2x^6 + 4x^5 + 7x^4 - 3x^3 - x^2 - 8x - 8}{(2x^2 - 1)^2 \sqrt{x^4 + 4x^3 + 2x^2 + 1}}$$

was computed with REDUCE. In Maple, the computation and the result are as follows.

```
>   alias( beta =
>     RootOf( z^2 - x^4 - 4*x^3 - 2*x^2 - 1, z ) ):
>   settime := time():
>   Int( ( 2*x^6 + 4*x^5 + 7*x^4 - 3*x^3 - x^2 - 8*x - 8) /
>     ( (2*x^2-1)^2 * beta ), x):   " = value(");
```

$$\int \frac{2\,x^6 + 4\,x^5 + 7\,x^4 - 3\,x^3 - x^2 - 8\,x - 8}{(\,2\,x^2 - 1\,)^2\,\beta}\,dx = \frac{1}{2}\,\frac{(\,2\,x + 1\,)\,\beta}{2\,x^2 - 1} + \frac{1}{2}\ln\,((\,$$

$$1025\,x^{10} + 6138\,x^9 + 12307\,x^8 + 10188\,x^7 + 4503\,x^6 + 3134\,x^5$$
$$+\, 1589\,x^4 + 140\,x^3 + 176\,x^2 + 2 - 4104\,\beta\,x^7 - 2182\,\beta\,x^5$$
$$-\, 5084\,\beta\,x^6 - 805\,\beta\,x^4 - 624\,\beta\,x^3 - 28\,\beta\,x - 10\,\beta\,x^2$$
$$-\, 1023\,\beta\,x^8\,)/(\,2\,x^2 - 1\,)^5\,)$$

```
>   # check the answer
>   evala( Normal( diff(rhs("),x) - op(1,lhs(")) ) );
```

$$0$$

```
>   cpu_time := (time()-settime) * seconds; # computing time
```

$$cpu\_time := 34.500\ seconds$$

The most time-consuming part is the computation of the transcendental part.

Algebraic functions appear in the following two integrals.

```
>   Int( x/(x^3 + x + a), x ):   " = value(");
```

$$\int \frac{x}{x^3 + x + a}\,dx =$$

$$\sum_{\_R=\%1} \_R\ln(\,x + 9\,\frac{a\,(\,4 + 27\,a^2\,)\,\_R^2}{2 + 27\,a^2} + \frac{(\,4 + 27\,a^2\,)\,\_R}{2 + 27\,a^2} + 6\,\frac{a}{2 + 27\,a^2}\,)$$

$$\%1 := \mathrm{RootOf}(\,(\,4 + 27\,a^2\,)\,\_Z^3 + \_Z + a\,)$$

```
>   Int( 1/(x^16 + a), x ):   " = value(");
```

$$\int \frac{1}{x^{16} + a}\,dx = \sum_{\_R=\%1} \_R\ln(\,x + 16\,a\,\_R\,)$$

$$\%1 := \mathrm{RootOf}(\,18446744073709551616\,a^{15}\,\_Z^{16} + 1\,)$$

The next example, which is a parametrization of one of the previous integrals, shows that the current implementation of integration of algebraic functions is limited to cases where the coefficient field is an algebraic number field. Below, we capitalize the message that says so.

```
>  alias( gamma = RootOf( z^3 - x^2 - a, z ) ):
>  infolevel[int] := 1: # set higher information level
>  int( 1/(x*gamma), x );
```

```
int/indef:    first-stage indefinite integration
int/indef2:   second-stage indefinite integration
int/rischnorm:   enter Risch-Norman integrator
int/risch:    enter Risch integration
int/algrisch/int:
Risch/Trager´s algorithm for algebraic function
int/algrisch/int:
computation of the algebraic part: start time    204.450
int/algrisch/int:
computation of the algebraic part: end time    204.483
int/algrisch/int:
computation of the transcendental part: start time 204.516
int/algrisch/transcpar:    PARAMETRIC CASE NOT HANDLED YET
int/algrisch/int:
computation of the transcendental part: end time    204.516
int/algrisch/int:
could not find an elementary antiderivative
```

$$\int \frac{1}{x\,\gamma}\,dx$$

```
>  infolevel[int] := 0:  # back to default value
```

10.2   Definite Integration

Definite integration is also performed in Maple by **int** (and by the alias
integrate). Again, for display reasons we shall use the inert form **Int** in
combination with the procedure **value**.

```
>  Int( x/(x^3+1), x = 1..a ):  " = value(");
```

$$\int_{1}^{a} \frac{x}{x^3+1}\,dx = -\frac{1}{3}\ln(1+a) + \frac{1}{6}\ln(a^2 - a + 1)$$
$$+ \frac{1}{3}\sqrt{3}\arctan(\frac{1}{3}\sqrt{3}(2\,a - 1)) + \frac{1}{3}\ln((2)) - \frac{1}{18}\sqrt{3}\,\pi$$

```
>  Int( ln(t)/(1-t), t = 0..x ):  " = value(");
```

$$\int_{0}^{x} \frac{\ln(t)}{1-t}\,dt = \mathrm{dilog}(x) - \frac{1}{6}\pi^2$$

```
>  Int( 1/((1+x^2)*(1+2*x^2)), x = 0..1 ):
>  " = value(");
```

$$\int_{0}^{1} \frac{1}{(1+x^2)(1+2\,x^2)}\,dx = -\frac{1}{4}\pi + \sqrt{2}\arctan(\sqrt{2})$$

Definite integration does not always compute the corresponding indefinite integral and substitute in the limits of integration as the next example, in which $\int_{-1}^{1} \frac{1}{x^2}\, dx$ is computed, illustrates.

```
> Int( 1/x^2, x ): " = value(");
```

$$\int \frac{1}{x^2}\, dx = -\frac{1}{x}$$

```
> subs( x=1, rhs(") ) - subs( x=-1, rhs(") );
```

$$-2$$

The problem here is that the analytic conditions for application of the fundamental theorem of analysis are not fulfilled: there is a nonremovable singularity at $x = 0$ in the integrand within the interval $(-1, 1)$. Maple checks continuity of the integrand over the given interval and, in case of possible errors in the answer, simply returns the command. By the way, you can force continuity of the integrand over the interval by adding the keyword continuous. In the example chosen, Maple itself can prove that the definite integral diverges.

```
> Int( 1/x^2, x = -1..1 ): " = value(");
```

$$\int_{-1}^{1} \frac{1}{x^2}\, dx = \infty$$

A more difficult example is

$$\int_{0}^{2\pi} \frac{1}{1 + 3\sin^2 t}\, dt$$

```
> Int( 1/(1+3*sin(t)^2), t = 0..2*Pi ):   " = value(");
```

$$\int_{0}^{2\pi} \frac{1}{1 + 3\sin(t)^2}\, dt = \pi$$

The answer is correct. But again, it is not a result of computing the indefinite integral and substituting the limits. The indefinite integral computed by Maple itself is even discontinuous over the interval of definite integration (see Figure 10.1) although there exists a continuous antiderivative, viz.,

$$\frac{t - \arctan\left(\dfrac{\sin(2t)}{\cos(2t) - 3}\right)}{2}$$

```
>  Int( 1/(1+3*sin(t)^2), t ):   " = value(");
```

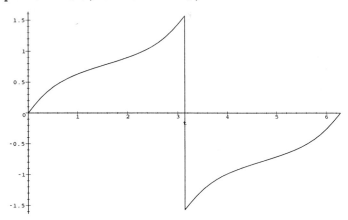

```
>  plot( rhs("), t = 0..2*Pi );
```

FIGURE 10.1. Graph of discontinuous antiderivative of $\frac{1}{1+3\sin^2 t}$.

In many cases Maple uses lookup tables and pattern matching [73, 167], and differentiation of special functions with respect to a parameter to compute definite integrals.

```
>  Int( exp(-sqrt(t)) / ( t^(1/4) * (1-exp(-sqrt(t))) ),
>     t = 0..infinity ):   " = value(");
```

$$\int_0^\infty \frac{e^{(-\sqrt{t})}}{t^{1/4}\left(1-e^{(-\sqrt{t})}\right)}\,dt = \sqrt{\pi}\,\zeta(\frac{3}{2})$$

```
>  evalf( rhs(") );
```

$$4.630314748$$

```
>  Int( t^4 * ln(t)^2 / (1+3*t^2)^3, t = 0..infinity ):
>  " = value(");
```

$$\int_0^\infty \frac{t^4 \ln(t)^2}{(1+3t^2)^3}\, dt =$$

$$\frac{1}{216}\sqrt{3}\,\pi + \frac{1}{576}\pi^3\sqrt{3} - \frac{1}{108}\pi\sqrt{3}\ln(3) + \frac{1}{576}\pi\sqrt{3}\ln(3)^2$$

These are examples of integrals of the general form

$$\int_0^\infty \frac{\exp(-u_1 t^{s_1} - u_2 t^{s_2})t^w \ln(b\, t^{d_l})^m \left\{ {\cos \atop \sin} \right\}(c\, t^r)}{(a_0 + a_1 f^d)^p}\, dt,$$

where

$$f = t \text{ or } \exp(t^s),$$

p and m are nonnegative integers,

$\mathrm{signum}(a_0/a_1) > 0,$

s_1 and s_2 are nonzero real numbers,

d and d_l are any real numbers,

b, u_1, and u_2 are positive real numbers,

w is a complex number such that $\Re\left(\dfrac{w+1}{s}\right) > 0,$ and

$r = 0$ or $r = s$ or $r = 2s$ or $s = 2r.$

Other types of definite integrals that are computed by pattern matching are

$$\int_0^\infty \exp(-u\, t^s)t^w \ln(b\, t^{d_l})^m \left\{ {\mathrm{erf} \atop \mathrm{erfc}} \right\}\left(f\, t^v + g\right) dt,$$

$$\int_0^\infty \exp(-u\, t^s)t^w \mathrm{BesselJ}(b, c\, t^{s_p})^{k_J}\, \mathrm{BesselY}(\pm b, c\, t^{s_p})^{k_Y}\, dt,$$

and

$$\int_{t_0}^{t_1} \left\{ {\sin \atop \cos} \right\}\left(z\left\{ {\sin \atop \cos} \right\}(a\, t)\right)\left\{ {\sin \atop \cos} \right\}(b\, t)\, dt.$$

Two more examples:

```
>   Int( t * exp(-t^2) * erf(2*t+1), t = 0..infinity ):
>   " = value(");
```

$$\int_0^\infty t\, e^{(-t^2)} \mathrm{erf}(2\,t+1)\, dt =$$

$$\frac{1}{2}\mathrm{erf}(1) + \frac{1}{5}\sqrt{5}\, e^{(-1/5)} - \frac{1}{5}\sqrt{5}\, e^{(-1/5)} \mathrm{erf}\left(\frac{2}{5}\sqrt{5}\right)$$

```
>   Int( x * exp(-x^2) * BesselJ(0,x) * BesselY(0,x),
>     x = 0..infinity ):  " = value(");
```

$$\int_0^\infty x\, e^{(-x^2)} \operatorname{BesselJ}(0,x)\operatorname{BesselY}(0,x)\,dx = -\frac{1}{2}\frac{e^{(-1/2)}\operatorname{BesselK}\!\left(0,\frac{1}{2}\right)}{\pi}$$

```
>   Int( sin(z*sin(x)) * sin(3*x), x = 0..Pi):
>   " = value(");
```

$$\int_0^\pi \sin(z\sin(x))\sin(3x)\,dx =$$

$$8\frac{\pi\operatorname{BesselJ}(1,z)}{z^2} - 4\frac{\pi\operatorname{BesselJ}(0,z)}{z} - \pi\operatorname{BesselJ}(1,z)$$

Elliptic integrals of the first, second, and third kind are available both in algebraic form (Jacobi's notation) and in Legendre's form. Two notations exist: one that follows the Handbook of Elliptic Integrals by Byrd and Friedman [29] and one that follows the Handbook of Mathematical Functions [1]. See Table 10.1.

Description	Definition	Maple Function
incomplete elliptic integral of the 1st kind	$\int_0^x \frac{1}{\sqrt{(1-t^2)(1-k^2t^2)}}\,dt$	LegendreF(x,k) EllipticF(x,k)
incomplete elliptic integral of the 2nd kind	$\int_0^x \frac{\sqrt{1-k^2t^2}}{\sqrt{1-t^2}}\,dt$	LegendreE(x,k) EllipticE(x,k)
incomplete elliptic integral of the 3rd kind	$\int_0^x \frac{1}{(1-at^2)\sqrt{(1-t^2)(1-k^2t^2)}}\,dt$	LegendrePi(x,a,k) EllipticPi(x,a,k)
complete elliptic integral of the 1st kind	$\int_0^1 \frac{1}{\sqrt{(1-t^2)(1-k^2t^2)}}\,dt$	LegendreKc(k) EllipticK(k)
complete elliptic integral of the 2nd kind	$\int_0^1 \frac{\sqrt{1-k^2t^2}}{\sqrt{1-t^2}}\,dt$	LegendreEc(k) EllipticE(k)
complete elliptic integral of the 3rd kind	$\int_0^1 \frac{1}{(1-at^2)\sqrt{(1-t^2)(1-k^2t^2)}}\,dt$	LegendrePic(a,k) EllipticPi(a,k)
associated complete elliptic integral of the 1st kind	$\int_0^1 \frac{1}{\sqrt{(1-t^2)(1-c^2t^2)}}\,dt$	LegendreKc1(k) EllipticCK(k)
associated complete elliptic integral of the 2nd kind	$\int_0^1 \frac{\sqrt{1-c^2t^2}}{\sqrt{1-t^2}}\,dt$	LegendreEc1(k) EllipticCE(k)
associated complete elliptic integral of the 3rd kind	$\int_0^1 \frac{1}{(1-at^2)\sqrt{(1-t^2)(1-c^2t^2)}}\,dt$	LegendrePic1(a,k) EllipticCPi(a,k)

TABLE 10.1. Some elliptic integrals in Maple.

Here, $0 < k < 1$, and $c = \sqrt{1-k^2}$.

The notation of the Handbook of Mathematical Functions [1] is the one Maple actually prefers most. A few examples:

```
>   Int( 1/sqrt((t^2-1)*(t^2-2)), t = 2..infinity ):
>   " = value(");
```

$$\int_2^\infty \frac{1}{\sqrt{(t^2-1)(t^2-2)}}\,dt = \frac{1}{2}\sqrt{2}\,\mathrm{EllipticF}(\frac{1}{2}\sqrt{2},\frac{1}{2}\sqrt{2})$$

```
>   readlib( radnormal ):   # load simplification routine
>   Int( 1/sqrt((t-1)*(t-2)*(t-3)*(t-4)),
>     t = 4..infinity ):   " = radnormal( value(") );
```

$$\int_4^\infty \frac{1}{\sqrt{(t-1)(t-2)(t-3)(t-4)}}\,dt =$$
$$2\,(-\mathrm{EllipticK}(-2\,3^{3/4}\sqrt{2}+4\,3^{1/4}\sqrt{2})$$
$$+\mathrm{EllipticF}(\frac{1}{4}\sqrt{2}+\frac{1}{4}\sqrt{3}\sqrt{2},-2\,3^{3/4}\sqrt{2}+4\,3^{1/4}\sqrt{2}))\,(\sqrt{3}-2)$$

```
>   Int( 1 / sqrt(t*(1-t)*(1+t)),
>     t = 0..1 ): " = radnormal( value(") );
```

$$\int_0^1 \frac{1}{\sqrt{t(1-t)(1+t)}}\,dt = -4\frac{\mathrm{EllipticK}(3-2\sqrt{2})(3\sqrt{2}-4)}{-2+\sqrt{2}}$$

```
>   Int( 1 / ( 1 - 1/9*sin(t)^2 )^(5/2),
>     t = 0..Pi/2 ): " = value(");
```

$$\int_0^{1/2\,\pi} \frac{1}{(1-\frac{1}{9}\sin(t)^2)^{5/2}}\,dt = -\frac{3}{8}\mathrm{EllipticK}(\frac{1}{3})+\frac{17}{12}\mathrm{EllipticPi}(\frac{1}{9},\frac{1}{3})$$

10.3 Numerical Integration

A computer algebra system aims at getting exact results, but Maple also has several numerical facilities, e.g., numerical integrators.

```
>   int( exp( arcsin(x) ), x = 0..1 );
```

$$\int_0^1 e^{\arcsin(x)}\,dx$$

```
>   evalf(");
```

$$1.905238690$$

```
>   Int( exp(-2*t) * t * ln(t), t = 0..infinity ):
>   [ ", value(") ];
```

$$[\int_0^\infty e^{(-2t)}\,t\ln(t)\,dt,\ -\frac{1}{4}\ln(2)+\frac{1}{4}-\frac{1}{4}\gamma]$$

```
>  evalf(");
```
$$[-.06759071137, \ -.0675907114]$$

```
>  evalf( "", 20 );
```
$$[-.06759071136536954206, \ -.06759071136536954251]$$

Note that we have used above the inert form **Int** instead of the active **int**. This is to avoid computing of exact results but going straight on to numerical approximation via the composition **evalf@Int** (or more specifically via the procedure **evalf/int**). The default numerical integration method is Clenshaw-Curtis quadrature, but when convergence is slow (due to nearby singularities) the system tries to remove the singularities or switches to an adaptive double-exponential quadrature method. An adaptive Newton-Cotes method is available when low precision (e.g., `Digits <= 15`) suffices. The optional fourth argument indicates the preferred integration method.

```
>   evalf( Int( 1/sqrt(x), x = 0..1, 10, _Dexp ) );
```
$$1.999999983$$

Generalized series expansions and variable transformations are two of the techniques used in the Maple procedure **evalf/int** to deal with singularities in an analytic integrand. The interested reader is referred to [71, 75].

10.4   Integral Transforms

In this section, we shall give examples of integral transformations such as Laplace transforms, Fourier transforms, Mellin transforms, Hilbert transforms, and Hankel transforms. In general, the integral transform $T(f)$ of a function f with respect to the kernel K is defined by

$$T(f)(s) = \int_a^b f(t) \, K(s,t) \, dt,$$

at least when this integral exists. The Fourier, Laplace, and Mellin transforms are the most popular ones, with kernels e^{-ist}, e^{-st}, and t^{s-1}, respectively. In Table 10.2 we list the integral transforms that are available in Maple via the package `inttrans`.

Expressions in the form of sums of rational expressions of polynomials or certain functions like the **Dirac** function, the **Heaviside** function, or Bessel functions can be transformed to their Laplace transform by the Maple procedure **laplace**. The corresponding inverse Laplace transform can be computed with **invlaplace**.

```
>  with( inttrans );
```

$[addtable, fourier, fouriercos, fouriersin, hankel, hilbert, invfourier,$
   $invhilbert, invlaplace, laplace, mellin]$

Transform	Definition	Maple Function
Fourier	$\displaystyle\int_{-\infty}^{\infty} f(t)e^{-ist}\,dt$	fourier($f(t), t, s$)
Fourier-Bessel, Hankel	$\displaystyle\int_{0}^{\infty} f(t)tJ_n(st)\,dt$	hankel($f(t), t, s, n$)
Fourier-Cosine	$\displaystyle\sqrt{\frac{2}{\pi}}\int_{0}^{\infty} f(t)\cos(st)\,dt$	fouriercos($f(t), t, s$)
Fourier-Sine	$\displaystyle\sqrt{\frac{2}{\pi}}\int_{0}^{\infty} f(t)\sin(st)\,dt$	fouriersin($f(t), t, s$)
Hilbert	$\displaystyle\frac{1}{\pi}\int_{-\infty}^{\infty} \frac{f(t)}{t-s}\,dt$	hilbert($f(t), t, s$)
Laplace	$\displaystyle\int_{0}^{\infty} f(t)e^{-st}\,dt$	laplace($f(t), t, s$)
Mellin	$\displaystyle\int_{0}^{\infty} f(t)t^{s-1}\,dt$	mellin($f(t), t, s$)

TABLE 10.2. Integral transforms in Maple.

```
>  t * BesselJ(0,a*t);
```
$$t\,\mathrm{BesselJ}(\,0, a\,t\,)$$

```
>  laplace( ", t, s );
```
$$\frac{s}{(\,s^2 + a^2\,)^{3/2}}$$

```
>  invlaplace( ", s, t );
```
$$t\,\mathrm{BesselJ}(\,0, a\,t\,)$$

```
>  (cosh(3*t) - 3*t*sinh(3*t) - 1) / t^2;
```
$$\frac{\cosh(\,3\,t\,) - 3\,t\sinh(\,3\,t\,) - 1}{t^2}$$

```
>   laplace( ", t, s );
```

$$-\ln(s)s + \frac{1}{2}\ln(s-3)s + \frac{1}{2}\ln(3+s)s$$

```
>   invlaplace( ", s, t );
```

$$-\text{invlaplace}(\ln(s)s, s, t) + \frac{1}{2}\text{invlaplace}(\ln(s-3)s, s, t)$$
$$+ \frac{1}{2}\text{invlaplace}(\ln(3+s)s, s, t)$$

We were too optimistic; Maple is not able to convert the problem to inverse Laplace transforms that are tabulated internally. We have to assist Maple a bit. First, we rewrite the formula and specify that $s > 3$.

```
>   factor( "" );
```

$$\frac{1}{2}s\left(-2\ln(s) + \ln(3+s) + \ln(s-3)\right)$$

```
>   assume( s>3 );
>   combine( ", ln, integer );
```

$$\frac{1}{2}s^{\sim}\ln(\frac{(3+s^{\sim})(s^{\sim}-3)}{s^{\sim 2}})$$

Now, Maple can compute the inverse Laplace transform.

```
>   invlaplace( ", s, t );
```

$$-\frac{3}{2}\frac{e^{(3t)}}{t} + \frac{3}{2}\frac{e^{(-3t)}}{t} - \frac{1}{t^2} + \frac{1}{2}\frac{e^{(3t)}}{t^2} + \frac{1}{2}\frac{e^{(-3t)}}{t^2}$$

We check the answer.

```
>   convert( ", 'trig' );
```

$$-\frac{3}{2}\frac{\cosh(3t)+\sinh(3t)}{t} + \frac{3}{2}\frac{\cosh(3t)-\sinh(3t)}{t} - \frac{1}{t^2}$$
$$+ \frac{1}{2}\frac{\cosh(3t)+\sinh(3t)}{t^2} + \frac{1}{2}\frac{\cosh(3t)-\sinh(3t)}{t^2}$$

```
>   normal(");
```

$$-\frac{-\cosh(3t)+3t\sinh(3t)+1}{t^2}$$

```
>   combine("); # get rid of the minus sign
```

$$\frac{\cosh(3t)-3t\sinh(3t)-1}{t^2}$$

The next example shows that integral transforms can be used to enlarge the class of integration problems that can be solved through Maple.

```
>   integrate( x^5*BesselJ(0,x), x = 0..t );
```

$$\int_0^t x^5 \, \mathrm{BesselJ}(\, 0, x \,) \, dx$$

However, it can be shown that

$$\int_0^t x^m J_n(x) \, dx, \qquad m \ge n \ge 0,$$

is integrable in terms of Bessel functions and powers of t for $m + n$ odd. Let us help Maple by computing the Laplace transform, simplifying the intermediate result, performing the inverse Laplace transform, and checking the integration constant.

```
>   laplace( ", t, s );
```

$$\dfrac{945 \dfrac{s^5}{(\, s^2 + 1\,)^{11/2}} - 1050 \dfrac{s^3}{(\, s^2 + 1\,)^{9/2}} + 225 \dfrac{s}{(\, s^2 + 1\,)^{7/2}}}{s}$$

```
>   normal(");
```

$$15 \dfrac{8\,s^4 - 40\,s^2 + 15}{(\, s^2 + 1\,)^{11/2}}$$

```
>   invlaplace( ", s, t );
```

$$\frac{8}{21} t^3 \, \mathrm{BesselJ}(\, 3, t\,) + \frac{16}{21} t^4 \, \mathrm{BesselJ}(\, 2, t\,) + \frac{8}{63} t^5 \, \mathrm{BesselJ}(\, 1, t\,)$$

$$- \frac{40}{63} t^4 \, \mathrm{BesselJ}(\, 4, t\,) - \frac{40}{63} t^5 \, \mathrm{BesselJ}(\, 3, t\,) \, | \, \frac{5}{21} t^5 \, \mathrm{BesselJ}(\, 5, t\,)$$

```
>   eval( subs( t=0, " ) );
```

$$0$$

Let us check the answer by differentiation.

```
>   expand( diff( "", t ) );
```

$$t^5 \, \mathrm{BesselJ}(\, 0, t\,)$$

Conclusion:

$$\int x^5 J_0(x) \, dx =$$

$$\frac{8}{21} x^3 J_3(x) + \frac{16}{21} x^4 J_2(x) + \frac{8}{63} x^5 J_1(x) - \frac{40}{63} x^4 J_4(x) - \frac{40}{63} x^5 J_3(x) + \frac{5}{21} x^5 J_5(x).$$

Like any integral transform, the main application of Laplace transforms is in the field of differential equations and integral equations. Differential equations will be studied extensively in Chapter 17. Here, we give an example of an integral equation.

```
>   int_eqn := integrate( exp(a*x) * f(t-x), x = 0..t )
>       + b*f(t) = t;
```

$$int\_eqn := \int_0^t e^{(a\,x)} f(t-x)\,dx + b\,f(t) = t$$

```
>   laplace( ", t, s );
```

$$\frac{\text{laplace}(f(t), t, s)}{s-a} + b\,\text{laplace}(f(t), t, s) = \frac{1}{s^2}$$

```
>   readlib(isolate)( ", laplace( f(t), t, s ) );
```

$$\text{laplace}(f(t), t, s) = \frac{1}{s^2\left(\dfrac{1}{s-a} + b\right)}$$

```
>   invlaplace( ", s, t );
```

$$f(t) = \frac{1}{(-1+b\,a)^2} + \frac{a\,t}{-1+b\,a} - \frac{e^{\left(\frac{(-1+b\,a)\,t}{b}\right)}}{(-1+b\,a)^2}$$

```
>   map( factor, " );
```

$$f(t) = \frac{1 - a\,t + a^2\,t\,b - e^{\left(\frac{(-1+b\,a)\,t}{b}\right)}}{(-1+b\,a)^2}$$

Let us check the answer.

```
>    f := unapply( rhs("), t );
```

$$f := t \to \frac{1 - a\,t + a^2\,t\,b - e^{\left(\frac{(-1+b\,a)\,t}{b}\right)}}{(-1+b\,a)^2}$$

```
>   testeq( int_eqn );
```

$$true$$

The Maple procedure **fourier** can transform sums of rational functions of polynomials to their Fourier transforms.

```
>   1/(1+t^3);
```

$$\frac{1}{1+t^3}$$

```
> fourier( ", t, omega );
```

$$\frac{1}{3} I e^{(I\omega)} \pi \left(\text{Heaviside}(-\omega) - \text{Heaviside}(\omega) \right) + e^{(-1/2 I\omega)} \big($$

$$- \frac{1}{3} I \left(1 + I \sqrt{3}\right) e^{(1/2 \sqrt{3}\,\omega)} \pi \, \text{Heaviside}(-\omega)$$

$$- \frac{1}{3} I \left(-1 + I \sqrt{3}\right) e^{(-1/2 \sqrt{3}\,\omega)} \pi \, \text{Heaviside}(\omega) \big)$$

We can check the answer by computing the inverse Fourier transform with **invfourier**.

```
> invfourier( ", omega, t );
```

$$4 \frac{1}{(t+1)\left(-I + \sqrt{3} + 2 I t\right)\left(I + \sqrt{3} - 2 I t\right)}$$

```
> normal( ", ´expanded´ );
```

$$\frac{1}{1 + t^3}$$

Maple can also apply convolution methods, table lookups, and definite integration to handle special functions such as trigonometric functions, the **Dirac** and **Heaviside** functions, the exponential function, and Bessel functions.

```
> fourier( BesselJ(0,t), t, omega );
```

$$-2 \frac{\text{Heaviside}(\omega - 1) - \text{Heaviside}(\omega + 1)}{\sqrt{1 - \omega^2}}$$

```
> fourier( BesselJ( 0, sqrt(t^2+1) ), t, omega );
```

$$2 e^{(I\omega)} \cos\left(-1 + \omega^2\right) \left(\text{Heaviside}(\omega + 1) - \text{Heaviside}(\omega - 1)\right) / \sqrt{1 - \omega^2}$$

You can define Fourier transforms for your own functions with the procedure **addtable**. For example, Maple does not know the Fourier transform of $x/\sinh x$. When you give this function a name, say F, then you can add it to the lookup table of **fourier** in the following way.

```
> addtable(
>    fourier,      # name of integral transform
>    F(t),         # name of user function
>    2/Pi*exp(Pi*w)/(1+exp(Pi*w))^2, # transform
>    t, w          # variables used in transform
> );
> fourier( F(x), x, omega );
```

$$2 \frac{e^{(\pi\omega)}}{\pi \left(1 + e^{(\pi\omega)}\right)^2}$$

```
> fourier( x^2 * F(x), x, omega );
```

$$-2\,\frac{\pi\,e^{(\pi\,\omega)}}{(1+e^{(\pi\,\omega)})^2}+12\,\frac{(e^{(\pi\,\omega)})^2\,\pi}{(1+e^{(\pi\,\omega)})^3}-12\,\frac{(e^{(\pi\,\omega)})^3\,\pi}{(1+e^{(\pi\,\omega)})^4}$$

```
> simplify(");
```

$$2\,\frac{\pi\,(-e^{(\pi\,\omega)}+4\,e^{(2\,\pi\,\omega)}-e^{(3\,\pi\,\omega)})}{(1+e^{(\pi\,\omega)})^4}$$

In the same way you can add with **addtable** an item to the lookup table of any integral transform.

fourier and **invfourier** are procedures for computing symbolic Fourier transforms and their inverses. The procedures FFT and iFFT are meant for numerical **Fast Fourier Transforms** and their inverses. Recall the definition of the Fourier transform $X = [X_0, X_1, \cdots, X_{N-1}]$ for a list of complex numbers $x = [x_0, x_1, \cdots, x_N]$ of length N.

$$X[k] = \sum_{j=0}^{N-1} x_j e^{-2\pi ijk/N},$$

for $0 \le k \le N-1$. For N equal to a power of two, the so-called fast Fourier transform method [47] has been implemented. In the first example below, we take $N = 2^3$, and compute the fast Fourier transform of the sequence of real numbers $[-1, -1, -1, -1, 1, 1, 1, 1]$.

```
> readlib( FFT ): # load the procedure FFT
> x := array([-1,-1,-1,-1,1,1,1,1]):   # real parts of data
> y := array([0,0,0,0,0,0,0,0]): # imaginary parts of data
> FFT(3,x,y): # transform data
> print(x);    # real parts of transformed data
```

$$[\,0, -2.000000001, 0, -1.999999999, 0, -1.999999999, 0, -2.000000001\,]$$

```
> print(y); # imaginary parts of transformed data
```

$$[\,0, 4.828427122, 0, .828427124, 0, -.828427124, 0, -4.828427122\,]$$

The procedure **zip** comes in handy when you want to write the complex numbers in a more conventional way.

```
> # normal complex notation
> zip( (a,b) -> a+b*I, x, y ):  convert( ", list );
```

$$[0, -2.000000001 + 4.828427122\,I, 0, -1.999999999 + .828427124\,I,$$
$$0, -1.999999999 - .828427124\,I, 0, -2.000000001 - 4.828427122\,I]$$

```
> iFFT(3,x,y): # check results
> print(x);
```

$$[\,-1.000000000, -.9999999990, -.9999999995, -.9999999985,$$
$$1.000000000, .9999999990, .9999999995, .9999999985\,]$$

```
> print(y);
```

$$[\ 0, .2500000000\ 10^{-9}, 0, -.2500000000\ 10^{-9}, 0, -.2500000000\ 10^{-9}, 0,$$
$$.25000000001\ 10^{-9}\ ]$$

The procedure **fnormal** comes in handy when you want to normalize small values to zero.

```
> y := map( fnormal, y );
```

$$y := [\ 0, 0, 0, 0, 0, 0, 0, 0\ ]$$

A common and important application of fast Fourier transforms is doing convolutions in data smoothing. Below is a simple, but artificial example. It is presented without comments, but all data types and procedures used will be dealt with later in this book.

First, we load the random number generator for the standard normal distribution from the stats package.

```
> noise := stats[ random, normald ]:
```

Next, we generate data; in particular, we generate the real and imaginary parts of the data separately.

```
> re_data := array( [ seq( sin(0.0625*k) + 0.1*noise(),
>    k=1..2^8) ] ):
> im_data := array( [ seq( 0, k=1..2^8) ] ):
```

To get an idea of what data we have in hand, we plot the data points. By construction it will look like the sine function as can be seen in Figure 10.2.

```
> xcoords := array( [ seq( 0.0625*k, k=1..2^8) ] ):
> plotdata := convert( zip( (a,b) -> [a,b], xcoords,
>    re_data ), list ):
> plot( plotdata, style = POINT );
```

We shall use the kernel function $t \rightarrow \exp(-\frac{100}{256}t^2)$ for smoothing the data.

```
> re_kernel := array( [ seq( exp( -100.0 * (k/2^8)^2 ),
>    k=1..2^8 ) ] ):
> im_kernel := array( [ seq( 0, k=1..2^8) ] ):
```

We compute the fast Fourier transforms of the data and kernel and write them as arrays of complex numbers.

```
> FFT( 8, re_data, im_data ):
> FFT( 8, re_kernel, im_kernel ):
> data := zip( (a,b) -> (a+b*I), re_data, im_data ):
> kernel := zip( (a,b) -> (a+b*I), re_kernel, im_kernel ):
> newdata := zip( (a,b) -> a*b, data, kernel ):
> new_re_data := map( Re, newdata ):
> new_im_data := map( Im, newdata ):
```

Finally, we compute the inverse fast Fourier transform of the product of Fourier transforms of data and kernel. Up to a scalar, this is a smooth version of the original data. The plot 10.3 shows this best.

```
>  iFFT( 8, new_re_data, new_im_data ):
>  plotdata := convert( zip( (a,b) -> [a,b], xcoords,
>    new_re_data), list ):
>  plot( plotdata, style=POINT );
```

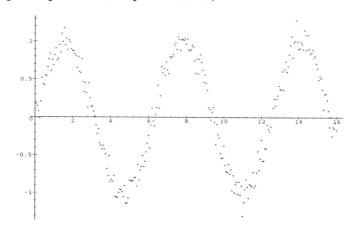

FIGURE 10.2. Sine function with noise.

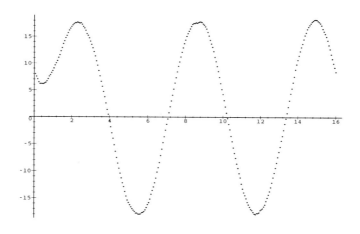

FIGURE 10.3. Data smoothing.

We end this section on integral transforms with some examples of the other integral transforms available in Maple.

- Hankel transform

```
>  with( inttrans ):
>  assume( k, integer, k>0 ):
>  hankel( sqrt(t), t, s, k );
```

$$2 \, \frac{\sqrt{2} \, \Gamma \left(\dfrac{5}{4} + \dfrac{1}{2} k^{\sim} \right)}{s^{5/2} \, \Gamma \left(\dfrac{1}{2} k^{\sim} - \dfrac{1}{4} \right)}$$

- Fourier-Sine and Fourier-Cosine transform

```
>  assume( a>0 ):
>  fouriercos( Heaviside(a-t), t, s );
```

$$\frac{\sqrt{2} \sin(a^{\sim} s)}{\sqrt{\pi} \, s}$$

```
>  fouriercos( ", s, t );
```

$$\frac{1}{2} \, \mathrm{signum}(a^{\sim} - t) + \frac{1}{2}$$

```
>  convert( ", Heaviside );
```

$$\mathrm{Heaviside}(a^{\sim} - t)$$

- Hilbert transform

```
>  assume( k, integer, k>0 ):
>  hilbert( Dirac(x) + sin(k*x)/x, x, y );
```

$$\frac{-1 + \pi \cos(k^{\sim} y) - \pi}{y \, \pi}$$

- Mellin transform

```
>  mellin( 1 / (1+t), t, s );
```

$$\frac{\pi}{\sin(\pi s)}$$

```
>  mellin( ln(1+t), t, s );
```

$$-\frac{\pi}{\sin(\pi (s + 1)) \, s}$$

10.5   Assisting Maple's Integrator

In this section, we shall look at some integration problems where Maple cannot find a solution all by itself, but with some assistance actually can solve the problem. Human assistance is quite often needed when nonelementary functions are involved or when parameters must satisfy certain conditions.

The first integration problem involves a parameter that must satisfy a certain condition in order that the integral can be solved analytically.

```
>   Int( exp(-c*x^2), x = 0..infinity ):   " = value(");
```

$$\int_0^\infty e^{(-c\,x^2)}\,dx = \lim_{x\to\infty}\frac{1}{2}\,\frac{\sqrt{\pi}\,\mathrm{erf}\left(\sqrt{c}\,x\right)}{\sqrt{c}}$$

A common mistake in thought: *you* may think of c as a positive real constant, but *Maple* does not start from this assumption! From the above answer it is clear that Maple at least knows the indefinite integral. If you want to get further with the computation of the definite integral you must **assume** that c is a positive real constant; for nonpositive values the integral diverges.

```
>   assume( c>0 ):
>   Int( exp(-c*x^2), x = 0..infinity ):   " = value(");
```

$$\int_0^\infty e^{(-c^\sim x^2)}\,dx = \frac{1}{2}\,\frac{\sqrt{\pi}}{\sqrt{c^\sim}}$$

Below is another example of an integral where Maple does not work fully automatically because of lack of information.

```
>   int( sqrt( (x^2-a^2) * (b^2-x^2) ), x = a..b );
```

$$\int_a^b \sqrt{(x^2 - a^2)(b^2 - x^2)}\,dx$$

This often happens: you forget to tell Maple about the assumptions on the parameters. Let us fix this.

```
>   assume( a>0, b>0 ):
>   infolevel[int] := 2:
>   int( sqrt( (x^2-a^2) * (b^2-x^2) ), x = a..b );
```

```
int/ellalg/trxlgdre: cannot determine sign: 1/a~^2-1/b~^2
int/indef:   first-stage indefinite integration
int/algebraic:   algebraic integration
int/indef:   first-stage indefinite integration
int/algebraic:   algebraic integration
int/rischnorm:   enter Risch-Norman integrator
int/risch:   enter Risch integration
int/risch:   the field extensions are
```

$$[\_X, \_\mathrm{root}((-\_X^2 + a^{\sim 2})(-b^{\sim 2} + \_X^2), 2)]$$

```
int/risch:     Introduce the namings:
```

$$\{\_th_1 = \_root((-\_X^2 + a^{\sim 2})(-b^{\sim 2} + \_X^2), 2)\}$$

```
unknown:       integrand is
```

$$\frac{(-\_X^2 + a^{\sim 2})(-b^{\sim 2} + \_X^2)}{\_th_1}$$

```
int/risch/alg1:   integrand is
```

$$\frac{(-\_X^2 + a^{\sim 2})(-b^{\sim 2} + \_X^2)}{\_th_1}$$

```
int/risch/alg1:   integral expressed as
```

$$\frac{1}{3} \frac{\_X(-\_X^2 + a^{\sim 2})(-b^{\sim 2} + \_X^2)}{\_th_1}$$

$$+ \int \frac{-\dfrac{2}{3} a^{\sim 2} b^{\sim 2} + \dfrac{1}{3} \_X^2 a^{\sim 2} + \dfrac{1}{3} \_X^2 b^{\sim 2}}{\_th_1} \, d\_X$$

```
int/indef:     first-stage indefinite integration
int/indef2:    second-stage indefinite integration
int/indef2:    trying integration by parts
int/risch:     exit Risch integration
int/def:       definite integration
int/def:       definite integration
int/contour:   contour integration
```

$$\int_{a^{\sim}}^{b^{\sim}} \sqrt{(x^2 - a^{\sim 2})(b^{\sim 2} - x^2)} \, dx$$

```
>   infolevel[int] := 1:
```
Still no answer, but luckily we made Maple more communicative by raising the `infolevel[int]` to 2. A lot of messages appear on the screen telling what Maple is doing, but one of the first messages says

```
int/ellalg/trxlgdre: cannot determine sign: 1/a~^2-1/b~^2
```

This gives us the clue to add the assumption $b > a$, which *we* took for granted, but *Maple* did not.

```
>   additionally( b>a ):
>   int( sqrt( (x^2-a^2) * (b^2-x^2) ), x = a..b );
```

$$-\frac{2}{3} a^{\sim 2} b^{\sim} \text{EllipticK}\left(\sqrt{1 - \frac{a^{\sim 2}}{b^{\sim 2}}}\right)$$

$$+ \frac{a^{\sim 2}\left(\dfrac{1}{3} a^{\sim 2} + \dfrac{1}{3} b^{\sim 2}\right) \text{EllipticPi}\left(1 - \dfrac{a^{\sim 2}}{b^{\sim 2}}, \sqrt{1 - \dfrac{a^{\sim 2}}{b^{\sim 2}}}\right)}{b^{\sim}}$$

One final remark on this example. If for some reason you guess that elliptic integration comes into play, you can also give `infolevel[elliptic]` a higher value in order to be informed about signs of expressions, without the abundant messages of other attempts of Maple.

Choosing the right assumptions that make Maple do an integration job as far as possible is tricky business, and you often have to use all your mathematical knowledge or computational skills. In [141] is described how you can redefine the built-in **signum** function so that Maple asks for sign information during a computation. A drawback of this method is that Maple can ask you information where it is unclear what it has to do with your problem.

Sometimes you must delineate a method, e.g., a change of variables or integration by parts. This is conveniently done through the **student** package in Maple.

```
>  with( student ): # load the student package
>  Int( sqrt( x + sqrt(x) ), x );
```
$$\int \sqrt{x + \sqrt{x}}\, dx$$

```
>  changevar( sqrt(x)=y, ", y );
```
$$\int 2 \sqrt{y^2 + y}\, y\, dy$$

```
>  "" = value(");
```
$$\int \sqrt{x + \sqrt{x}}\, dx =$$
$$\frac{2}{3}\, (y^2 + y)^{3/2} - \frac{1}{4}\, (2\,y + 1)\, \sqrt{y^2 + y} + \frac{1}{8}\, \ln\left(y + \frac{1}{2} + \sqrt{y^2 + y}\right)$$

```
>  subs( y=sqrt(x), " );
```
$$\int \sqrt{x + \sqrt{x}}\, dx = \frac{2}{3}\, (x + \sqrt{x})^{3/2} - \frac{1}{4}\, (2\,\sqrt{x} + 1)\, \sqrt{x + \sqrt{x}}$$
$$+ \frac{1}{8}\, \ln\left(\sqrt{x} + \frac{1}{2} + \sqrt{x + \sqrt{x}}\right)$$

```
>  radnormal( diff(",x) ); # check answer
```
$$\sqrt{x + \sqrt{x}} = \sqrt{x + \sqrt{x}}$$

Another example.
```
>  Int( x*exp(-a^2*x^2)*erf(b*x), x );
```
$$\int x\, e^{(-a^2\, x^2)}\, \mathrm{erf}(\,b\,x\,)\, dx$$

```
> intparts( ", erf(b*x) ):  "" = value(");
```

$$\int x \, e^{(-a^2 x^2)} \operatorname{erf}(bx) \, dx = -\frac{1}{2} \frac{\operatorname{erf}(bx) \, e^{(-a^2 x^2)}}{a^2} + \frac{1}{2} \frac{\operatorname{erf}\left(\sqrt{b^2 + a^2} \, x\right) b}{\sqrt{b^2 + a^2} \, a^2}$$

Sometimes you have to apply the well-known method of contour integration and use Maple as a computational tool. Below, we shall compute in this way

$$\int_{-\infty}^{\infty} \frac{e^{ax}}{1 + e^x} \, dx, \qquad 0 < a < 1.$$

First, we replace the real variable by the complex variable z and integrate around the contour shown in Figure 10.4.

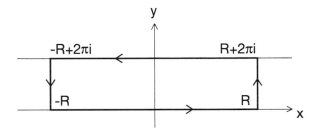

FIGURE 10.4. Contour of integration.

If we take the limit $R \to \infty$, the horizontal sections of the contour lead to our integral and the vertical sections vanish because of the assumptions on a:

$$\oint_C \frac{e^{az}}{1 + e^z} \, dz = (1 - e^{2\pi a}) \lim_{R \to \infty} \int_{-\infty}^{\infty} \frac{e^{ax}}{1 + e^x} \, dx.$$

The answer to the contour integral is $2\pi i \sum$ *residues inside strip*. So, we search for the roots of the denominator that lie in the strip and compute their residues.

```
> exp(a*z) / ( 1 + exp(z) );
```

$$\frac{e^{(az)}}{1 + e^z}$$

```
> solve( denom("), z ); # the solution in the strip
```

$$I \pi$$

```
> readlib( residue )( "", z = " );
```

$$-e^{(I a \pi)}$$

```
> ( 1 - exp(2*Pi*a*I) ) * integral = 2*Pi*I * ";
```

$$\left(1 - e^{(2 I a \pi)}\right) integral = -2 I \pi \, e^{(I a \pi)}$$

```
>   (lhs/rhs)(") = 1;
```

$$\frac{1}{2}\frac{I\left(1-e^{(2\,I\,a\,\pi)}\right) integral}{\pi\,e^{(I\,a\,\pi)}} = 1$$

```
>   simplify( ", exp );
```

$$\frac{integral\,\sin(a\,\pi)}{\pi} = 1$$

```
>   Int( exp(a*x)/(1+exp(x)), x = -infinity..infinity )
>      = solve( ", integral );
```

$$\int_{-\infty}^{\infty}\frac{e^{(a\,x)}}{1+e^{x}}\,dx = \frac{\pi}{\sin(a\,\pi)}$$

Usual tricks such as differentiation with respect to parameters prior to integration are performed easily in Maple. An example:

```
>   assume( a>0 ):
>   int( tanh(a*x/2) / (x*cosh(a*x)) , x = 0..infinity );
```

$$\int_{0}^{\infty}\frac{\tanh\left(\frac{1}{2}\,a\tilde{\ }x\right)}{x\cosh(a\tilde{\ }x)}\,dx$$

```
>   diff( ", a );
```

$$0$$

So, the definite integral does not depend on the positive parameter a.

Last but not least, some good advice: use your brains when using Maple and think twice before computing. An example: Maple cannot determine

$$\int_{-\pi}^{\pi}\frac{\sin t}{1+\sin^{8}t}\,dt.$$

But there is no need to use Maple in this case. You can almost immediately conclude that the integrand is odd and that therefore the integral must be equal to zero.

10.6   Summation

Finite sums of numbers can be easily computed with the procedure **add**.

```
>   Sum( k^7, k = 1..20 ) = add( k^7, k = 1..20 );
```

$$\sum_{k=1}^{20}k^{7} = 3877286700$$

```
>   primes := [11,31,41,71,101,131,181,191,211,241]:
>   Sum( i, i = primes) = add( i, i = primes );
```

$$\sum_{i=\%1} i = 1210$$

$$\%1 := [\, 11, 31, 41, 71, 101, 131, 181, 191, 211, 241 \,]$$

```
>   poly := add( a[i]*x^i, i=0..5 );
```

$$poly := a_0 + a_1\, x + a_2\, x^2 + a_3\, x^3 + a_4\, x^4 + a_5\, x^5$$

"Symbolic summation" is also possible. Let us first consider indefinite summation: given a sequence

$$a_1, a_2, a_3, \ldots$$

or more precisely, an expression generating this sequence, we want to find an expression s_k, in which no summation sign occurs and such that

$$a_k = s_k - s_{k-1}.$$

This is the discrete analogue of indefinite integration. Maple uses the following methods to find s_k.

- Polynomials are summed using a formula based on Bernoulli polynomials:

$$\sum_{k=0}^{n-1} k^m = \frac{1}{m+1} \sum_{k=0}^{m} \binom{m+1}{k} B_k n^{m+1-k},$$

  where the Bernoulli numbers are defined by the implicit recurrence relation

$$B_0 = 1 \quad \text{and} \quad \sum_{k=0}^{m} \binom{m+1}{k} B_k = 0, \quad \text{for all } m \geq 0.$$

- Moenck's method [140] is used for summing rational functions of the summation index. The result is a rational function plus a sum of terms involving the Polygamma function Psi and its derivatives.

- Gosper's decision procedure [82] is the discrete analogue of the Risch algorithm. It deals with the case that s_k is a hypergeometric term, therefore $s_k/s_{k-1} \in \mathbb{Q}(k)$.

- The extended Gosper algorithm [120] deals with the question: given a nonnegative integer m, find the sequence s_k for given a_k satisfying $a_k = s_k - s_{k-m}$ in the particular case that s_k is an m-fold hypergeometric term.

In Maple are also implemented the (extended) Wilf-Zeilberger method for definite summation of hypergeometric terms [193, 194] together with the use of hypergeometric identities. The interested reader is referred to [120, 153, 177] and references therein. The sumtools package in Maple is a collection of routines for handling indefinite and definite sums explicitly. In most cases, the procedure **sum** already does the job automatically.

A few examples:

- Method of Bernoulli polynomials

```
>   Sum( k^7, k = 1..n ):   " = value(");
```

$$\sum_{k=1}^{n} k^7 = \frac{1}{8}(n+1)^8 - \frac{1}{2}(n+1)^7 + \frac{7}{12}(n+1)^6 - \frac{7}{24}(n+1)^4$$
$$+ \frac{1}{12}(n+1)^2$$

```
>   factor(");
```

$$\sum_{k=1}^{n} k^7 = \frac{1}{24} n^2 (3n^4 + 6n^3 - n^2 - 4n + 2)(n+1)^2$$

- Moenck's method

```
>   Sum( 1/(k^2+k)^3, k = 1..n ):   " = value(");
```

$$\sum_{k=1}^{n} \frac{1}{(k^2+k)^3} = -\frac{-2-3n+6(n+1)^2}{(n+1)^3} + 6\,\Psi(1,n+2) + 10 - \pi^2$$

```
>   limit( rhs("), n = infinity );
```

$$10 - \pi^2$$

```
>   Sum( 1/(k^5+2*k+1),k = 0..n ):   " = value(");
```

$$\sum_{k=0}^{n} \frac{1}{k^5+2k+1} = \Big(\sum_{\_\alpha=\%1}$$
$$(\frac{4096}{11317} + \frac{2560}{11317}\_\alpha^4 - \frac{1600}{11317}\_\alpha^3 + \frac{1000}{11317}\_\alpha^2 - \frac{625}{11317}\_\alpha)$$
$$\Psi(n+1-\_\alpha)\Big) - \Big(\sum_{\_\alpha=\%1}$$
$$(\frac{4096}{11317} + \frac{2560}{11317}\_\alpha^4 - \frac{1600}{11317}\_\alpha^3 + \frac{1000}{11317}\_\alpha^2 - \frac{625}{11317}\_\alpha)$$
$$\Psi(-\_\alpha)\Big)$$

$$\%1 := \text{RootOf}(\_Z^5 + 2\_Z + 1)$$

```
> limit( rhs("), n = infinity );
```

$$-\sum_{\_\alpha=\%1}\left(\frac{1}{11317}\right.$$

$$\left(4096 + 2560\,\_\alpha^4 - 1600\,\_\alpha^3 + 1000\,\_\alpha^2 - 625\,\_\alpha\right)\Psi(-\_\alpha)\bigg)$$

$$\%1 := \mathrm{RootOf}(\_Z^5 + 2\_Z + 1)$$

```
> evalf(");
```

$$1.282579632$$

```
> Sum( 1/(k^2 - 4) , k = 3..infinity ):  " = value(");
```

$$\sum_{k=3}^{\infty}\frac{1}{k^2-4} = \frac{25}{48}$$

```
> Sum( 1/(3*k+1)/(3*k+2)/(3*k+3)/(3*k+4),
>      k = 0..infinity ):  " = value(");
```

$$\sum_{k=0}^{\infty}\frac{1}{(3k+1)(3k+2)(3+3k)(3k+4)} = \frac{1}{6} + \frac{1}{36}\pi\sqrt{3} - \frac{1}{4}\ln(3)$$

- Gosper's method

```
> # see (SIAM Review, 1994, Problem 94-2)
> Sum( (-1)^(k+1)*(4*k+1)*(2*k)! /
>      (k!*4^k*(2*k-1)*(k+1)!), k = 1..n ):
> " = value(");
```

$$\sum_{k=1}^{n}\frac{(-1)^{(k+1)}(4k+1)(2k)!}{k!\,4^k\,(2k-1)(k+1)!} =$$

$$-2\frac{(n+2)(-1)^{(n+2)}(2n+2)!}{(n+1)!\,4^{(n+1)}(2n+1)(n+2)!} + 1$$

- Hypergeometric identities

```
> Sum( (-1)^(n-k) * binomial(2*n,k)^2, k = 0..2*n ):
> " = value(");
```

$$\sum_{k=0}^{2n}(-1)^{(n-k)}\mathrm{binomial}(2n,k)^2 = \frac{(-1)^n\sqrt{\pi}}{2^{(-2n)}\Gamma(n+1)\Gamma(\frac{1}{2}-n)}$$

For computing a numerical estimate of an infinite sum, Maple uses Levin's
u-transform [91, 192] to accelerate the convergence of a sum or even to
give values to divergent sums. You better always check the quality of the
answer.

```
> Sum( 1/k^2, k=1..infinity );
```

$$\sum_{k=1}^{\infty} \frac{1}{k^2}$$

```
> evalf(");
```

$$1.644934067$$

```
> value("");    # the exact answer.
```

$$\frac{1}{6}\pi^2$$

```
> evalf( " - "" ); # comparison
```

$$.1\,10^{-8}$$

```
> Sum( 3^(-k), k=1..infinity );
```

$$\sum_{k=1}^{\infty} 3^{(-k)}$$

```
> evalf(");
```

$$.5000000000$$

```
> value("");
```

$$\frac{1}{2}$$

```
> Sum( 3^k, k=1..infinity );
```

$$\sum_{k=1}^{\infty} 3^k$$

```
> evalf(");
```

$$-1.500000000$$

```
> value("");
```

$$\infty$$

```
> Sum( 1/k^3, k=1..infinity );
```

$$\sum_{k=1}^{\infty} \frac{1}{k^3}$$

```
>   evalf(");
```
$$1.202056903$$

```
>   value("");
```
$$\zeta(\,3\,)$$

```
>   evalf(");
```
$$1.202056903$$

```
>   Sum( 1/k^(1/3), k=1..infinity );
```
$$\sum_{k=1}^{\infty} \frac{1}{k^{1/3}}$$

```
>   evalf(");
```
$$-.9733602484$$

```
>   value("");
```
$$\infty$$

In the examples

$$\sum_{k=1}^{\infty} 3^k$$

and

$$\sum_{k=1}^{\infty} \frac{1}{\sqrt[3]{k}}$$

you better check whether the numerical answer matches your definition of summation for the divergent series. The answers of Maple may look strange (negative results for positive summands) but are not really weird. For example, the last result can be justified via analytic continuation of the Riemann ζ-function (approximate $\zeta(1/3)$ in Maple to see this).

10.7   Exercises

1. Compute the following indefinite integrals and check the answers by differentiation and simplification.

   (a) $\displaystyle\int \sqrt{e^x - 1}\, dx$

   (b) $\displaystyle\int \frac{x}{(2ax - x^2)^{3/2}}\, dx$

   (c) $\displaystyle\int \sqrt{x^2 - a^2}\, dx$

(d) $\displaystyle\int \frac{1}{x\sqrt{1+x^2}}\,dx$

(e) $\displaystyle\int \sec^3 x\,dx$

(f) $\displaystyle\int \frac{1}{1+\sin x + \cos x}\,dx$

(g) $\displaystyle\int \frac{\ln x}{x(x^2+1)^2}\,dx$

2. Compute $\displaystyle\int x^n e^x\,dx$ for general integer n and check the result for distinct values of n.

3.   (a) Compute $\displaystyle\int_0^1\left(\int_0^1 \frac{x-y}{(x+y)^3}\,dy\right)dx$.

(b) Compute $\displaystyle\int_0^1\left(\int_0^1 \frac{x-y}{(x+y)^3}\,dx\right)dy$.

(c) Compare the results of (a) and (b). Does Maple make a mistake or is there something else going on?

4. Compute the following definite integrals.

(a) $\displaystyle\int_1^{10} \frac{4x^4 + 4x^3 - 2x^2 - 10x + 6}{x^5 + 7x^4 + 16x^3 + 10x^2}\,dx$

(b) $\displaystyle\int_0^{\pi/2} x^4 \sin x \cos x\,dx$

(c) $\displaystyle\int_{1/7}^{1/5} \frac{1}{x\sqrt{5x^2 - 6x + 1}}\,dx$

(d) $\displaystyle\int_{-2}^{-1} \frac{1}{x}\,dx$

5. Compute the following definite integrals:

(a) $\displaystyle\int_0^1 \frac{1}{\sqrt{1-x^2}}\,dx$

(b) $\displaystyle\int_0^1 x\arctan x\,dx$

(c) $\displaystyle\int_0^\infty e^{-ax}\cos^2(bx)\,dx$, for a positive real number a

(d) $\displaystyle\int_0^\infty \frac{\sin x}{x}\,dx$

(e) $\displaystyle\int_0^\infty e^{-x}\ln x\,dx$

(f) $\displaystyle\int_0^\infty \frac{e^{-ax}\ln x}{\sqrt{x}}\,dx$, for a positive real number a

(g) $\displaystyle\int_0^\infty \frac{e^{-\sqrt{t}}}{t^{1/4}\left(1-e^{-\sqrt{t}}\right)}\,dt$

(h) $\displaystyle\int_1^\infty \frac{1}{\sqrt{x^4-1}}\,dx$

(i) $\displaystyle\int_0^{\frac{\pi}{2}} \sqrt{\cos x}\,dx$

(j) $\displaystyle\int_1^3 \frac{1}{\sqrt{x^4+4x^2+3}}\,dx$

(k) $\displaystyle\int_0^{\frac{\pi}{2}} \sqrt{\tan x}\,dx$

(l) $\displaystyle\int_0^\infty \frac{\sin^2 ax \sin bx}{x}\,dx$

(m) $\displaystyle\int_0^\infty \frac{1}{\cosh ax}\,dx$, for a positive real number a

6. Let F be the function defined by $F(T) := \displaystyle\int_1^T \frac{\exp(-u^2 T)}{u}\,du$.

(a) Define the corresponding Maple function F and determine a numerical approximation of $F(2)$.

(b) Compute the derivative F' (by **D**) and compute $F'(2)$.

7. Let A be the area $\left\{(x,y) \in \mathbb{R}^2 | 1/2 \le xy \le 2, 1 \le x \le 3\right\}$. Compute
$$\iint_A \frac{\exp(\frac{1}{xy})}{y^2(x+1)^2}\,dx\,dy.$$

8. In this exercise, we shall keep track of the Risch algorithm and prove that the integral
$$\int \frac{\ln^2(x-1)}{x}\,dx$$
does not exist in the class of elementary functions. In the first place, Liouville's principle implies the following representation of the integral, when it would exist as an elementary function:
$$B_3(x)\ln^3(x-1) + B_2(x)\ln^2(x-1) + B_1(x)\ln(x-1) + B_0(x),$$
where $B_3(x)$, $B_2(x)$, and $B_1(x)$ are rational functions and only $B_0(x)$ may contain new logarithmic extensions.

(a) Determine the differential equations satisfied by $B_0(x), \ldots, B_3(x)$.

(b) Show that $B_3(x)$ is a rational constant.

(c) Prove that the differential equation for $B_2(x)$ cannot be solved in terms of rational functions. This proves that $\dfrac{\ln^2(x-1)}{x}$ cannot be integrated in terms of elementary functions.

9. Show by the method of residues that

$$\int_0^{2\pi} \frac{1}{a^2 \cos^2 \theta + b^2 \sin^2 \theta} \, d\theta = \frac{2\pi}{ab},$$

for a, b real and nonzero, and $\left|\frac{b-a}{b+a}\right| < 1$. Compare your answer with Maple's answer when entering the integral.

10. Solve the following integral equation by Laplace transforms.

$$\sin t = \int_0^t J_0(t - \theta) f(\theta) \, d\theta$$

11. Solve the integral equation $f(t) = 1 + \int_0^t (t - \theta) f(\theta) \, d\theta$.

12. Compute $\int_0^\infty \frac{x}{1 + x^2} \sin w^2 x \, dx$.

13. Compute $\int_0^{\frac{\pi}{4}} \frac{1}{(1 + k^2 \sin^3 t)^3 \sqrt{1 + k^2 \sin^2 t}} \, dt$.

14. Compute $\int_0^1 \frac{x^a - 1}{\ln x} \, dx$, for nonnegative a.

15. Compute $\int_0^\infty \frac{\ln x}{(x + a)(x - 1)} \, dx$, for positive a.

16. Compute $\int \frac{\ln(x^2 + 1)}{x^2 + 1} \, dx$.

17. Compute $\int \frac{x^2}{\sqrt{x^6 + 1}} \, dx$.

18. Compute $\int \tan\left(\frac{1}{3} \arctan(x)\right) dx$.

19. Compute $\int \arcsin^2(x/a) \, dx$.

20. Compute $\int \frac{1}{\sqrt{a\sqrt{x} + b}} \, dx$.

21. Compute the following infinite sums.

(a) $\sum_{k=0}^\infty \frac{2k + 3}{(k + 1)(k + 2)(k + 3)}$

(b) $\sum_{k=1}^\infty \frac{k^2 + k - 1}{(k + 2)!}$

(c) $\sum_{k=2}^\infty \frac{k}{(k - 1)^2 (k + 1)^2}$

(d) $\dfrac{1}{4} + \displaystyle\sum_{k=1}^{\infty} \dfrac{3n+2}{n^3(n+1)(n+2)}$

(e) $\displaystyle\sum_{k=0}^{\infty} \dfrac{k^3 + 7k^2 + 4k + 6}{k^2(k^2+2)(k^2+2k+3)}$

22. Compute $\displaystyle\sum_{k=0}^{n} \binom{2n}{2k}(-3)^k$.

23. Compute $\displaystyle\sum_{k=0}^{n} \binom{2k}{k}\left(\dfrac{1}{2}\right)^{2k}$.

24. Compute the product of the first 32 prime numbers.

25. Compute the product $\displaystyle\prod_{k=2}^{\infty} 1 - 1/k^2$. (Hint: find a closed formula for the product with k running from 2 to N and then compute with **limit** the limit for N going to infinity.)

26. Compute $\displaystyle\sum_{k=1}^{n}(m\,k - 1)$ and compare the result with Formula 0.122 of Gradshteyn and Ryzhik [84].

27. Compute $\displaystyle\sum_{k=1}^{n-1} k^2 x^2$ and compare the result with Formula 0.114 of Gradshteyn and Ryzhik [84].

11

Series, Approximation, and Limits

Four topics from calculus will be examined in this chapter: truncated series, formal power series, approximation theory, and limits From the examples it will be clear that various truncated series expansions such as Taylor series, Laurent series, Puisseux series, and Chebyshev series are available in Maple. Padé and Chebyshev Padé are part of Maple's numerical approximation package, which is called **numapprox**. When appropriate, series expansions are used in computing limits [72].

11.1 Truncated Series

Taylor series expansions of univariate functions are easily and quickly computed with Maple. For example, in a very short time you can compute the Taylor series of $\sin(\tan x) - \tan(\sin x)$ about $x = 0$ up to order 25.

```
> taylor( sin(tan(x)) - tan(sin(x)), x=0, 25 );
```

$$-\frac{1}{30} x^7 - \frac{29}{756} x^9 - \frac{1913}{75600} x^{11} - \frac{95}{7392} x^{13} - \frac{311148869}{54486432000} x^{15} -$$
$$\frac{10193207}{4358914560} x^{17} - \frac{1664108363}{1905468364800} x^{19} - \frac{2097555460001}{7602818775552000} x^{21}$$
$$-\frac{374694625074883}{6690480522485760000} x^{23} + \mathrm{O}(x^{25})$$

You only have to specify the function, the variable, the expansion point, and the truncation order in the call to the procedure **taylor**. The order symbol $O(x^{25})$ indicates that Maple has a special internal data structure for series expansions.

```
> whattype(");
```

$$series$$

```
> readlib(dismantle)("");
```

```
SERIES(22)
   NAME(4): x
   RATIONAL(3): -1/30
   [7]
   RATIONAL(3): -29/756
   [9]
   RATIONAL(3): -1913/75600
   [11]
   RATIONAL(3): -95/7392
   [13]
   RATIONAL(3): -311148869/54486432000
   [15]
   RATIONAL(3): -10193207/4358914560
   [17]
   RATIONAL(3): -1664108363/1905468364800
   [19]
   RATIONAL(3): -2097555460001/7602818775552000
   [21]
   RATIONAL(3): -374694625074883/6690480522485760000
   [23]
   FUNCTION(3)
      NAME(4): O
      EXPSEQ(2)
         INTPOS(2): 1
   [25]
```

The general format of the **series** data structure is shown in Figure 11.1 below.

FIGURE 11.1. Internal representation of a truncated series.

Here, the first expression **expr** has the general form **x-a**, where **x** denotes the main variable and **a** denotes the expansion point. The remaining entries are pairs of pointers to coefficients and exponents. The coefficient O(1) at the end of the data vector is interpreted by Maple as the "order" term.

The above data type is also the name of a corresponding procedure **series**. This procedure can be used for more general truncated series expansions, e.g., for computing a Laurent series.

```
> series( GAMMA(x), x=0, 2 );
```

$$x^{-1} - \gamma + (\frac{1}{12}\pi^2 + \frac{1}{2}\gamma^2)x + O(x^2)$$

The truncation order to which the Taylor series expansion is computed can be obtained by inspection of the order symbol or by the procedure **order**.

```
> order(");
```

$$2$$

The third argument of the **series** procedure may be left out. Maple then uses the value of the environment variable Order to determine the truncation order. Its default value is equal to six.

```
> Order;
```

$$6$$

```
> Order:= 3: series( f(x), x=a );
```

$$f(a) + D(f)(a)(x - a) + \frac{1}{2}D^{(2)}(f)(a)(x - a)^2 + O((x - a)^3)$$

```
> series( f(x)/(x-a)^2, x=a );
```

$$f(a)(x - a)^{-2} + D(f)(a)(x - a)^{-1} + \frac{1}{2}D^{(2)}(f)(a) + O(x - a)$$

```
> series( 1/(cos(x)-sec(x)), x=0 );
```

$$-x^{-2} + O(x^{-1})$$

The last example illustrates that the "truncation order of a Laurent series" is only the order used by Maple during the series computation; fewer terms may be present in the final answer. It is like losing precision in numerical arithmetic. The opposite can happen as well in series expansions.

```
> series( 1/(1-x^2), x=0, 5 );
```

$$1 + x^2 + x^4 + O(x^6)$$

Although you only ask for the series expansion up to order 5, Maple decides on its own that the fifth order term is equal to zero, and it informs you about this. In most cases, the reason is that through the remember option Maple keeps track of previously computed expansions of larger order. For example, after the command series(cos(x), x=0, 25), the expansion of the cosine function will always be at least up to 25 terms.

If you want to restrict yourself to Laurent series, use the procedure **laurent** from the numapprox package. Otherwise, Maple may yield more general series such as Puiseux series.

```
> 1/(x*(1+sqrt(x)));
```

$$\frac{1}{x(1 + \sqrt{x})}$$

```
>   series(",x);
```

$$\frac{1}{x} - \frac{1}{\sqrt{x}} + 1 - \sqrt{x} + x - x^{3/2} + x^2 - x^{5/2} + x^3 - x^{7/2} + x^4 - x^{9/2} + x^5$$
$$- x^{11/2} + O(x^6)$$

Sometimes Maple chooses coefficients in a series expansion that depend on the main variable.

```
>   series( x^(x^x), x=0, 5 );
```

$$x + \ln(x)^2 x^2 + \left(\frac{1}{2}\ln(x)^3 + \frac{1}{2}\ln(x)^4\right)x^3 +$$
$$\left(\frac{1}{6}\ln(x)^4 + \frac{1}{2}\ln(x)^5 + \frac{1}{6}\ln(x)^6\right)x^4 + O(x^5)$$

```
>   series( dilog(x), x=0, 3 );
```

$$\frac{1}{6}\pi^2 + (\ln(x) - 1)x + \left(\frac{1}{2}\ln(x) - \frac{1}{4}\right)x^2 + O(x^3)$$

The growth of a coefficient in such *generalized series expansions* [72] must be less than the polynomial in x.

A nice feature of Maple is that it can compute a truncated series expansion of a function that is only defined by an integral or differential equation. An example:

```
>   integrate( ln(1+s*t)^2/(1+t^2), t=0..infinity );
```

$$\int_0^\infty \frac{\ln(1+st)^2}{1+t^2}\, dt$$

```
>   series( ", s=0, 5 );
```

$$\frac{1}{3}\pi^2 s - \frac{1}{2}\pi s^2 + \left(-\ln(s) + \frac{7}{6} - \frac{1}{9}\pi^2\right)s^3 + \frac{11}{24}\pi s^4 + O(s^5)$$

The above series expansion is computed in three steps:

- differentiate the integrand with respect to s and integrate it,

- compute the series expansion of the intermediate result at $s = 0$, and

- integrate the terms of the series expansion and determine the correct integration constant.

Another example: the series expansion of the solution of the differential equation describing a two-dimensional pendulum (see Figure 17.3).

```
>   DESol( l*diff(theta(t),[t$2]) = -g*sin(theta(t)),
>       theta(t), {theta(0)=0, D(theta)(0)=v[0]/l} );
```

$$\mathrm{DESol}(\{l\,(\frac{\partial^2}{\partial t^2}\,\theta(t)) + g\sin(\theta(t))\}, \{\theta(t)\},$$
$$\{\mathrm{D}(\theta)(0) = \frac{v_0}{l}, \theta(0) = 0\})$$

```
>   series(",t);
```

$$\frac{v_0}{l}\,t - \frac{1}{6}\,\frac{g\,v_0}{l^2}\,t^3 + \frac{1}{120}\,\frac{g\,v_0\,(g + \frac{v_0{}^2}{l})}{l^3}\,t^5 + \mathrm{O}(t^6)$$

The order symbol vanishes in the case of polynomials, at least when the truncation order of the series expansion is high enough.

```
>   polynomial := a*x^3+b*x^2+c*x+d;
```

$$polynomial := a\,x^3 + b\,x^2 + c\,x + d$$

```
>   taylor_series := series( polynomial, x, 4 );
```

$$taylor\_series := d + c\,x + b\,x^2 + a\,x^3$$

```
>   series( (x+y)^7, x, infinity ); # infinite order
```

$$y^7 + 7\,y^6\,x + 21\,y^5\,x^2 + 35\,y^4\,x^3 + 35\,y^3\,x^4 + 21\,y^2\,x^5 + 7\,y\,x^6 + x^7$$

Although a series expansion looks like a polynomial, certainly in the last examples, the internal data structure is, as you have seen, completely different.

```
>   whattype( polynomial );
```

$$+$$

```
>   op( polynomial );
```

$$a\,x^3, b\,x^2, c\,x, d$$

```
>   whattype( taylor_series );
```

$$series$$

```
>   op( taylor_series );
```

$$d, 0, c, 1, b, 2, a, 3$$

```
>   op( 0, taylor_series );  # the main variable
```

$$x$$

Objects of type *series* are dealt with differently in Maple; many operations allowed for polynomials do not work for series expansions.

```
>   sin_series := series( sin(x), x=0, 6 );
```

$$sin\_series := x - \frac{1}{6}\,x^3 + \frac{1}{120}\,x^5 + \mathrm{O}(x^6)$$

```
>  subs( x=2,  sin_series );
```

Error, invalid substitution in series

```
>  sin_series * sin_series;
```

$$(x - \frac{1}{6} x^3 + \frac{1}{120} x^5 + O(x^6))^2$$

```
>  expand(");
```

$$(x - \frac{1}{6} x^3 + \frac{1}{120} x^5 + O(x^6))^2$$

```
>  series( ", x );
```

$$x^2 - \frac{1}{3} x^4 + O(x^6)$$

Some of these difficulties have been removed with the procedure **mtaylor**, fit for multivariate Taylor series expansions. The reason is that the result type of **mtaylor** is not a series but an ordinary polynomial.

```
>  F := (3*x*y-2*y^2) * (3*x+y) / (6*x^2-6*y);
```

$$F := \frac{(3xy - 2y^2)(3x+y)}{6x^2 - 6y}$$

```
>  readlib( mtaylor ):
>  mtaylor( F, [x=1,y], 5 );
```

$$\frac{3}{2} y + y^2 - \frac{5}{2}(x-1)y^2 + \frac{2}{3}y^3 + 4y^2(x-1)^2 - \frac{23}{6}(x-1)y^3 + \frac{2}{3}y^4$$

```
>  normal(");
```

$$\frac{3}{2} y + \frac{15}{2} y^2 - \frac{21}{2} xy^2 + \frac{9}{2}y^3 + 4y^2 x^2 - \frac{23}{6} xy^3 + \frac{2}{3}y^4$$

```
>  subs( y=1, " );
```

$$\frac{85}{6} - \frac{43}{3} x + 4x^2$$

Coming back to the series representation of univariate functions, you normalize series expansions with **normal** and you extract coefficients with respect to the main variable with **coeff**.

```
>  series( F, x, 4 );
```

$$\frac{1}{3} y^2 + \frac{1}{2} yx - \frac{1}{6} \frac{9y - 2y^2}{y} x^2 + \frac{1}{2} x^3 + O(x^4)$$

```
>  normal(");
```

$$\frac{1}{3} y^2 + \frac{1}{2} yx + (-\frac{3}{2} + \frac{1}{3}y) x^2 + \frac{1}{2} x^3 + O(x^4)$$

```
> coeff( ", x^2 );
```

$$-\frac{3}{2} + \frac{1}{3} y$$

You can only extract coefficients in the main variable.

```
> coeff( "", y^2 );
```

```
Error, unable to compute coeff
```

With the procedure **coeftayl**, you can compute a coefficient in a Taylor series expansion without actually computing the series. Instead,

$$\mathbf{coeftayl}(f, x = x_0, k)$$

computes the coefficient of $(x - x_0)^k$ in the series expansion of f about $x = x_0$ as

$$\lim_{x \to x_0} \frac{\dfrac{d^k f}{d x^k}(x)}{k!}.$$

```
> readlib(coeftayl):
> coeftayl( F, x=0, 20 );
```

$$\frac{1}{3} \frac{1}{y^8} - \frac{3}{2} \frac{1}{y^9}$$

coeftayl can also be used for multivariate series.

```
> coeftayl( F, [x,y]-[1,0], [1,3] );
```

$$\frac{-23}{6}$$

If you are only interested in the leading term of a univariate series expansion you can explicitly ask for it.

```
> series( 1/tan(x), x );
```

$$x^{-1} - \frac{1}{3} x - \frac{1}{45} x^3 + O(x^4)$$

```
> series( leadterm( 1/tan(x) ), x, infinity );
```

$$x^{-1}$$

You can also differentiate and integrate a series.

```
> sin_series;
```

$$x - \frac{1}{6} x^3 + \frac{1}{120} x^5 + O(x^6)$$

```
> diff( sin_series, x );
```

$$1 - \frac{1}{2} x^2 + \frac{1}{24} x^4 + O(x^5)$$

```
>  integrate( sin_series, x );
```

$$\frac{1}{2} x^2 - \frac{1}{24} x^4 + \frac{1}{720} x^6 + O(x^7)$$

Series reversion can be done with the Maple procedure **solve**.

```
>  solve( y = sin_series, x );
```

$$y + \frac{1}{6} y^3 + \frac{3}{40} y^5 + O(y^6)$$

Compare with

```
>  arcsin_series := series( arcsin(y), y );
```

$$arcsin\_series := y + \frac{1}{6} y^3 + \frac{3}{40} y^5 + O(y^6)$$

and with

```
>  series( RootOf( y = sin(x), x ), y );
```

$$y + \frac{1}{6} y^3 + \frac{3}{40} y^5 + O(y^7)$$

A problem in applied mathematics, which can be solved as a problem of series reversion, is the computation of the series expansion of the solution of Kepler's equation

$$E = u + e \sin E .$$

Here, E is the moon's eccentric anomaly and we want to express it in terms of the mean anomaly u and the orbital eccentricity e, which is regarded as a small quantity (q.v., [8]). We shall also write the coefficients in the expansion as linear combinations of trigonometric functions.

```
>  series( E - u - e*sin(E), E=u );
```

$$-e \sin(u) + (1 - e \cos(u)) (E - u) + \frac{1}{2} e \sin(u) (E - u)^2 +$$
$$\frac{1}{6} e \cos(u) (E - u)^3 - \frac{1}{24} e \sin(u) (E - u)^4 - \frac{1}{120} e \cos(u)$$
$$(E - u)^5 + O((E - u)^6)$$

```
>  solve( ", E - u );
```

$$\sin(u) e + \cos(u) \sin(u) e^2 + (\cos(u)^2 \sin(u) - \frac{1}{2} \sin(u)^3) e^3 +$$
$$(\cos(u)^3 \sin(u) - \frac{5}{3} \cos(u) \sin(u)^3) e^4 +$$
$$(\cos(u)^4 \sin(u) - \frac{11}{3} \cos(u)^2 \sin(u)^3 + \frac{13}{24} \sin(u)^5) e^5 + O(e^6),$$
$$-\frac{e}{-1+e} u - \frac{1}{6} \frac{e}{(-1+e)^4} u^3 - \frac{1}{120} \frac{e(9e+1)}{(-1+e)^7} u^5 + O(u^6)$$

We need the first solution and simplify the expansion of E in e.

```
>  u + map( combine, "[1], 'trig' );
```

$$u + (\sin(u)e + \frac{1}{2}\sin(2u)e^2 + (\frac{3}{8}\sin(3u) - \frac{1}{8}\sin(u))e^3 +$$
$$(\frac{1}{3}\sin(4u) - \frac{1}{6}\sin(2u))e^4 +$$
$$(\frac{125}{384}\sin(5u) - \frac{27}{128}\sin(3u) + \frac{1}{192}\sin(u))e^5 + O(e^6))$$

In many computations it is convenient to convert series expansions into polynomials. This is a simple matter.

```
>  sin_series;
```

$$x - \frac{1}{6}x^3 + \frac{1}{120}x^5 + O(x^6)$$

```
>  convert( sin_series, polynom );
```

$$x - \frac{1}{6}x^3 + \frac{1}{120}x^5$$

Padé approximations and continued fraction series expansions, i.e., approximations by rational functions, are also available in Maple. You can use the procedure **convert** or the procedures **pade** and **confracform** from the numapprox package (if you do not want to compute a series expansion first, or if you want a procedure instead of a formula).

```
>  convert( sin_series, ratpoly );
```

$$\frac{-\frac{7}{60}x^3 + x}{1 + \frac{1}{20}x^2}$$

```
>  convert( sin_series, ratpoly, 1, 2);
```

$$\frac{x}{1 + \frac{1}{6}x^2}$$

```
>  convert( sin_series, 'confrac' );
```

$$\frac{x}{1 + \cfrac{x^2}{6 - \frac{7}{10}x^2}}$$

These approximations can be used in conjunction with the so-called Chebyshev series expansion.

```
>  Digits := 5:
>  chebyshev( sin(x), x );  # Chebyshev expansion
```

$$.88010\,T(1,x) - .039127\,T(3,x) + .00049952\,T(5,x)$$
$$- .30152\,10^{-5}\,T(7,x)$$

```
> convert( ", ratpoly );
```

$$\frac{.89083\,T(\,1,x\,) - .027887\,T(\,3,x\,)}{T(\,0,x\,) + .025529\,T(\,2,x\,)}$$

```
> with( orthopoly, T ):   "";
```

$$\frac{.97449\,x - .11155\,x^3}{.97447 + .051058\,x^2}$$

Maple is liberal with respect to conversion to polynomials.

```
> series( sin(x+a)/x^2, x, 4 );
```

$$\sin(\,a\,)\,x^{-2} + \cos(\,a\,)\,x^{-1} - \frac{1}{2}\sin(\,a\,) - \frac{1}{6}\cos(\,a\,)\,x + \mathrm{O}(\,x^2\,)$$

```
> convert( ", polynom );
```

$$\frac{\sin(\,a\,)}{x^2} + \frac{\cos(\,a\,)}{x} - \frac{1}{2}\sin(\,a\,) - \frac{1}{6}\cos(\,a\,)\,x$$

```
> series( sqrt(x*(1-x)) , x=0 , 2 );
```

$$\sqrt{x} - \frac{1}{2}\,x^{3/2} - \frac{1}{8}\,x^{5/2} + \mathrm{O}(\,x^{7/2}\,)$$

```
> convert( ", polynom );
```

$$\sqrt{x} - \frac{1}{2}\,x^{3/2} - \frac{1}{8}\,x^{5/2}$$

```
> (a*x^3+b*x^2)/(x^2+1);
```

$$\frac{a\,x^3 + b\,x^2}{x^2 + 1}$$

```
> series( ", x=infinity, 8 ); # asymptotic expansion
```

$$a\,x + b - \frac{a}{x} - \frac{b}{x^2} + \frac{a}{x^3} + \frac{b}{x^4} - \frac{a}{x^5} - \frac{b}{x^6} + \frac{a}{x^7} + \mathrm{O}(\,\frac{1}{x^8}\,)$$

```
> convert( ", polynom );
```

$$a\,x + b - \frac{a}{x} - \frac{b}{x^2} + \frac{a}{x^3} + \frac{b}{x^4} - \frac{a}{x^5} - \frac{b}{x^6} + \frac{a}{x^7}$$

Stirling's formula is an example of an *asymptotic series expansion* of general type.

```
> asympt( ln(x!), x, 4 );
```

$$(\,\ln(\,x\,) - 1\,)\,x + \frac{1}{2}\ln(\,x\,) + \ln(\,\sqrt{2}\,\sqrt{\pi}\,) + \frac{1}{12}\frac{1}{x} + \mathrm{O}(\,\frac{1}{x^3}\,)$$

Here, we have used the procedure **asympt**, instead of the **series** command, with `infinity` as expansion point.

```
> simplify( ", ln ); # simplification of logarithmic terms
```

$$(\ln(x) - 1) x + \frac{1}{2} \ln(x) + \frac{1}{2} \ln((2)) + \frac{1}{2} \ln(\pi) + \frac{1}{12} \frac{1}{x} + O(\frac{1}{x^3})$$

In [3] it is stated that one of the difficulties in using a computer algebra system is the fact that a system may not be able to use all the mathematical rules it knows in the right places. This is illustrated with the following example.

$$\lim_{\epsilon \to 0} \frac{\epsilon}{\sqrt{1 + \epsilon} \sin^2 \phi + \sqrt{1 - \epsilon} \cos^2 \phi - 1}$$

Maple and most other systems are not able to use the trigonometric simplification rule $\sin^2 \phi + \cos^2 \phi = 1$ in the right places and in this way produce incorrect results.

```
> expr := epsilon / ( sqrt(1+epsilon)*sin(phi)^2 +
>     sqrt(1-epsilon)*cos(phi)^2-1 );
```

$$expr := \frac{\varepsilon}{\sqrt{1 + \varepsilon} \sin(\phi)^2 + \sqrt{1 - \varepsilon} \cos(\phi)^2 - 1}$$

```
> limit( expr, epsilon=0 );
```

$$0$$

This answer is wrong. The problem lies in the following incorrect series expansion.

```
> series( expr, epsilon, 3 );
```

$$\frac{1}{\sin(\phi)^2 + \cos(\phi)^2 - 1} \varepsilon - \frac{\frac{1}{2} \sin(\phi)^2 - \frac{1}{2} \cos(\phi)^2}{(\sin(\phi)^2 + \cos(\phi)^2 - 1)^2} \varepsilon^2 + O(\varepsilon^3)$$

The denominator of the first term simplifies to zero.

Fortunately, you can fine-tune Maple's **series** command with respect to the zero recognition of coefficients. All you have to do is to redefine the environment variables **Testzero**, which is initialized with the relatively trivial test function `proc() evalb(normal(args[1]) = 0) end`. The recommended change is to use the environment variable **Normalizer** instead of **normal** and redefine this procedure so that coefficients are handled better in the **series** command.

```
> Testzero := proc() evalb( Normalizer(args[1]) = 0 ) end:
> Normalizer := proc() normal( simplify(args[1]) ) end:
```

After this adaptation of Maple everything works well.

```
> readlib( forget ):
> forget( series ): # clear the remember table of series
> forget( limit  ): # clear the remember table of limit
> series( expr, epsilon, 3 );
```

$$\frac{1}{\frac{1}{2}\sin(\phi)^2 - \frac{1}{2}\cos(\phi)^2} + 2\frac{-\frac{1}{8}\sin(\phi)^2 - \frac{1}{8}\cos(\phi)^2}{(2\cos(\phi)^2 - 1)(\frac{1}{2}\sin(\phi)^2 - \frac{1}{2}\cos(\phi)^2)}\varepsilon$$
$$+ O(\varepsilon^2)$$

```
> map( combine, ", 'trig' );
```

$$-2\frac{1}{\cos(2\phi)} + \frac{1}{\cos(4\phi)+1}\varepsilon + O(\varepsilon^2)$$

```
> limit( expr, epsilon=0 );
```

$$\frac{2}{\sin(\phi)^2 - \cos(\phi)^2}$$

11.2   Approximation of Functions

To evaluate most mathematical functions, you must first produce easily computable approximations to them. In general, it is more efficient with respect to space and time to have an analytical approximation rather than to store a table and use interpolation. There are various forms of approximation functions: Taylor polynomials, Padé approximants, Chebyshev series, and so on [155]. The numapprox package contains various procedures for developing numerical approximations. In this section we shall have a look at them when trying to find good approximations of the exponential map on the interval (-2,2). The interested reader is referred to [77] for another example.

Our first approximation is a Taylor polynomial of third degree around zero.

```
> with( numapprox ):  # load the numapprox package
> Digits := 4: # set precision for approximation
> taylor( exp(x), x );
```

$$1 + x + \frac{1}{2}x^2 + \frac{1}{6}x^3 + \frac{1}{24}x^4 + \frac{1}{120}x^5 + O(x^6)$$

```
> P[5] := convert( ", polynom );
```

$$P_5 := 1 + x + \frac{1}{2}x^2 + \frac{1}{6}x^3 + \frac{1}{24}x^4 + \frac{1}{120}x^5$$

The polynomial can be converted to Horner (nested multiplication) form.

```
>   hornerform( P[5], x );
```

$$1 + (1 + (\frac{1}{2} + (\frac{1}{6} + (\frac{1}{24} + \frac{1}{120}x)x)x)x)x$$

```
>   taylorapprox := unapply(",x);
```

$$taylorapprox := x \rightarrow 1 + (1 + (\frac{1}{2} + (\frac{1}{6} + (\frac{1}{24} + \frac{1}{120}x)x)x)x)x$$

The Taylor remainder theorem gives an estimation of the error:

$$e^x - P_5(x) = \frac{1}{720}e^\xi x^6,$$

where ξ is between 0 and x. To examine the error carefully, you can use the procedures **maximize** and **minimize**.

```
>   readlib(maximize)( exp(x) - P[5], x, -2..2 );
```

$$e^2 - \frac{109}{15}$$

```
>   evalf(");
```

$$.122$$

```
>   readlib(minimize)( exp(x) - P[5], x, -2..2 );
```

$$e^{\%1} - 1 - \%1 - \frac{1}{2}\%1^2 - \frac{1}{6}\%1^3 - \frac{1}{24}\%1^4 - \frac{1}{120}\%1^5$$
$$\%1 := RootOf(24e^{-\_Z} - 24 - 24\_Z - 12\_Z^2 - 4\_Z^3 - \_Z^4, .013009)$$

```
>   evalf(");
```

$$.00001125$$

Alternatively, you can use the procedure **infnorm** from the numapprox package to compute the error. This procedure computes an estimate of the infinity norm of a continuous real function on the segment $[a, b]$, which is defined as

$$\|f\|_\infty = \max_{a \le x \le b} |f(x)|.$$

```
>   infnorm( exp - taylorapprox, -2..2 );
```

$$.1224$$

So, the maximum error is approximately 0.122. The error is not distributed evenly through the interval (-2,2) as can be seen in Figure 11.2.

```
>   Digits := 10: # reset precision for plotting
>   plot( exp - taylorapprox, -2..2 );
```

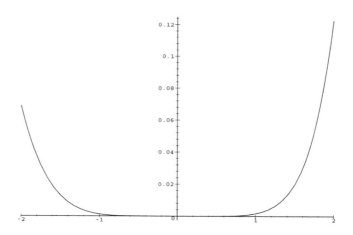

FIGURE 11.2. Error curve of Taylor approximation of exponential map about 0 of 5th degree.

Next, the Padé rational approximation of degree (3,2) is taken under consideration.

```
>   Digits := 4: # set precision for approximation
>   R[3,2] := pade( exp(x), x, [3,2] );
```

$$R_{3,2} := \frac{1 + \dfrac{3}{5} x + \dfrac{3}{20} x^2 + \dfrac{1}{60} x^3}{1 - \dfrac{2}{5} x + \dfrac{1}{20} x^2}$$

To minimize multiplications you can convert to continued fraction form.

```
>   confracform(",x);
```

$$\frac{1}{3} x + \frac{17}{3} + \frac{152}{3} \cfrac{1}{x - \cfrac{117}{19} + \cfrac{3125}{361} \cfrac{1}{x - \cfrac{35}{19}}}$$

```
>   padeapprox := unapply(",x);
```

$$padeapprox := x \rightarrow \frac{1}{3} x + \frac{17}{3} + \frac{152}{3} \cfrac{1}{x - \cfrac{117}{19} + \cfrac{3125}{361} \cfrac{1}{x - \cfrac{35}{19}}}$$

The error is smaller than in the Taylor approximation.

```
>   infnorm( exp - padeapprox, -2..2 );
```

$$.05572$$

So, the maximum error is approximately 0.056. The distribution of the error over the interval (-2,2) is shown in Figure 11.3.

```
>   Digits := 10: # reset precision for plotting
>   plot( exp - padeapprox, -2..2 );
```

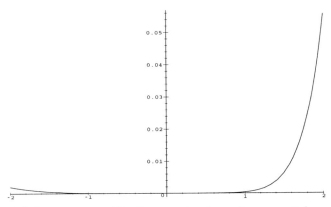

FIGURE 11.3. Error curve of Padé approximation of exponential map about 0 of degree (3,2).

Instead of expansion in monomials x^n on (-2,2), $n >= 0$, you can use orthogonal polynomials to obtain better approximations. In the **numapprox** package you can work with Chebyshev polynomials via **chebyshev** and **chebpade**. Utility functions are: **chebmult**, **chebsort**, and **chebdeg**.

Figures 11.4 and 11.5 show the error curves of the Chebyshev and Chebyshev-Padé approximation of the exponential map, respectively.

```
>   Digits := 4: # set precision for approximation
>   chebP[5] := chebyshev( exp(x), x );
```

$$chebP_5 := 1.266\,T(\,0,x\,) + 1.131\,T(\,1,x\,) + .2715\,T(\,2,x\,)$$
$$+ .04434\,T(\,3,x\,) + .005475\,T(\,4,x\,) + .0005430\,T(\,5,x\,)$$

```
>   chebP[5] := (eval@subs)( T = orthopoly[T], " );
```

$$chebP_5 :=$$
$$1.000 + 1.001\,x + .4992\,x^2 + .1665\,x^3 + .04380\,x^4 + .008688\,x^5$$

```
>   hornerform(",x);
```

$$1.000 + (\,1.001 + (\,.4992 + (\,.1665 + (\,.04380 + .008688\,x\,)\,x\,)\,x\,)\,x\,)\,x$$

```
>   chebapprox := unapply(",x);
```

$$chebapprox := x \to 1.000$$
$$+ (\,1.001 + (\,.4992 + (\,.1665 + (\,.04380 + .008688\,x\,)\,x\,)\,x\,)\,x\,)\,x$$

```
>   infnorm( exp - chebapprox, -2..2 );
```

$$.07944$$

```
>   Digits := 10: # reset precision for plotting
>   plot( exp - chebapprox, -2..2 );
```

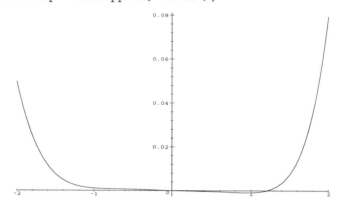

FIGURE 11.4. Error curve of Chebyshev approximation of exponential map about 0 of 5th degree.

```
>   Digits := 4: # set precision for approximation
>   chebR[3,2] := chebpade( exp(x), x=-2..2, [3,2] );
```

$chebR_{3,2} :=$

$$\frac{1.208\,\mathrm{T}(0,\frac{1}{2}\,x) + 1.223\,\mathrm{T}(1,\frac{1}{2}\,x) + .2894\,\mathrm{T}(2,\frac{1}{2}\,x) + .03149\,\mathrm{T}(3,\frac{1}{2}\,x)}{\mathrm{T}(0,\frac{1}{2}\,x) - .7092\,\mathrm{T}(1,\frac{1}{2}\,x) + .08160\,\mathrm{T}(2,\frac{1}{2}\,x)}$$

```
>   chebR[3,2] := eval( subs( T = orthopoly[T], " ) );
```

$$chebR_{3,2} := \frac{.9186 + .5643\,x + .1447\,x^2 + .01575\,x^3}{.9184 - .3546\,x + .04080\,x^2}$$

```
>   Digits := 5: confracform("",x);
```

$$.38603\,x + 6.9017 + \cfrac{65.125}{x - 6.6514 + \cfrac{8.9424}{x - 2.0398}}$$

```
>   chebpadeapprox := unapply(",x):
>   infnorm( exp - chebpadeapprox, -2..2 );
```

$$.0016120$$

```
>   Digits := 10: # reset precision for plotting
>   plot( exp - chebpadeapprox, -2..2 );
```

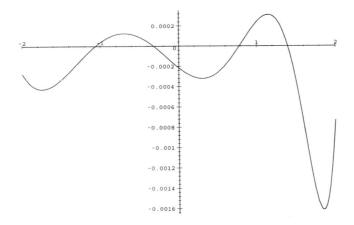

FIGURE 11.5. Error curve of Chebyshev-Padé approximation of exponential map about 0 of 5th degree.

The best uniform approximation to the exponential mapping found above has an error curve that oscillates in sign. It can be improved by "leveling" the error curve. This can be done by the **minimax** procedure, which uses the Remez algorithm [161, 162] to find the best minimax rational approximation of certain degree with respect to a given weight function. Specifically, given a continuous real function f and a positive weight function w on a segment $[a, b]$, **minimax** computes the rational function p/q such that

$$\max_{a \leq x \leq b} w(x)\big|f(x) - p(x)/q(x)\big|$$

is minimized over all rational function p/q with numerator p of degree $\leq m$ and denominator q of degree $\leq n$.

Let us first look at the minimax approximation of the exponential map to a polynomial of fifth degree.

```
>   minimaxP[5] := minimax( exp, -2..2, [5,0], 1,
>      'maxerror' );
```

$$minimaxP_5 := x \rightarrow 1.003137731 + (1.002686427 + (.4860498435$$
$$+ (.1624711328 + (.05072464725 + .01005370283\,x\,)\,x\,)\,x\,)\,x\,)\,x$$

The maximum error in the minimax approximation to a 5th degree polynomial is recorded during the Remez algorithm.

```
>   maxerror;
```
$$.0032642372$$

The error curve is shown in Figure 11.6. The best rational approximation of degree (3,2) and its error curve is computed below.

```
>   plot( exp - minimaxP[5], -2..2 );
```

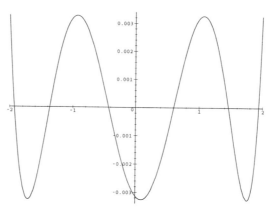

FIGURE 11.6. Error curve of minimax approximation of exponential map to 5th degree polynomial.

Next, we find the minimax approximation of the exponential map to a rational function of degree (3,2). The error curve is shown in Figure 11.7.

```
>   minimaxR[3,2]  := minimax( exp, -2..2, [3,2], 1,
>      'maxerror' );
```

$$minimaxR_{3,2} := x \rightarrow (.9223619725$$
$$+ (.5751247189 + (.1517495888 + .01744849505\,x)\,x)\,x) / ($$
$$.9223699826 + (-.3480389417 + .03881500871\,x)\,x)$$

```
>   maxerror;
```

$$.000294578$$

```
>   plot( exp - minimaxR[3,2], -2..2 );
```

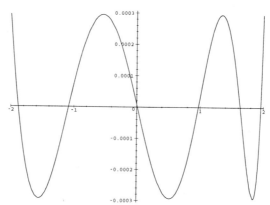

FIGURE 11.7. Error curve of minimax approximation of exponential map to a rational function of degree (3,2).

We end this section with the minimax approximation of the exponential map to a rational function of degree (3,2) with respect to the relative error.

```
>   minimaxapprox32 := minimax( exp, -2..2, [3,2],
>   x -> 1/ exp(x), 'maxerror' );
```

$$minimaxapprox32 := x \rightarrow (.9133842411$$
$$+ (.5504989451 + (.1363414205 + .01407497565\, x)\, x)\, x)\, / ($$
$$.9131465774 + (-.3625452375 + .04342671130\, x)\, x)$$

```
>   maxerror;
```

$$.0002764955323$$

The error curve of this approximation is shown in Figure 11.8, together with the error curve of the previous minimax approximation with respect to absolute error.

```
>   plot( { 1 - minimaxapprox32 / exp,
>     exp - minimaxapprox32 }, -2..2 );
```

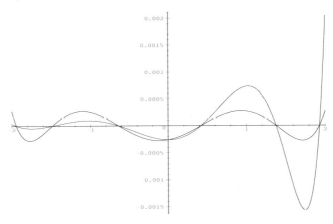

FIGURE 11.8. Error curve of minimax approximations of exponential map to rational functions of degree (3,2).

11.3   Power Series

The powseries package provides facilities for manipulation of formal power series. As with all Maple library packages it must be loaded first with the command

```
>   with( powseries );
```

[compose, evalpow, inverse, multconst, multiply, negative, powadd,

powcos, *powcreate*, *powdiff*, *powexp*, *powint*, *powlog*,
powpoly, *powsin*, *powsolve*, *powsqrt*, *quotient*, *reversion*,
subtract, *tpsform*]

You learn best about this package by examples. Henceforth we shall consider the power series

$$\exp(ax) = \sum_{n=0}^{\infty} \frac{a^n}{n!} x^n \quad \text{and} \quad \ln(1+x) = \sum_{n=1}^{\infty} \frac{(-1)^{n+1}}{n} x^n.$$

First, we define the two power series with the procedure **powcreate**.

```
>   powcreate( f(n)=a^n/n! ):
>   powcreate( g(n)=(-1)^(n+1)/n, g(0)=0 ):
```

We have now specified the rules to compute coefficients in the power series. Let us ask for the first five terms with **tpsform** (truncated power series form).

```
>   f_series := tpsform( f, x, 5 );
```

$$f\_series := 1 + a\,x + \frac{1}{2}\,a^2\,x^2 + \frac{1}{6}\,a^3\,x^3 + \frac{1}{24}\,a^4\,x^4 + O(x^5)$$

```
>   g_series := tpsform( g, x, 5 );
```

$$g\_series := x - \frac{1}{2}\,x^2 + \frac{1}{3}\,x^3 - \frac{1}{4}\,x^4 + O(x^5)$$

Let us do some manipulations with these power series: addition, multiplication, inversion with respect to multiplication, and composition, respectively.

```
>   s := powadd(f,g):    tpsform(s,x,3);
```

$$1 + (a+1)\,x + (\frac{1}{2}\,a^2 - \frac{1}{2})\,x^2 + O(x^3)$$

```
>   p := multiply(f,g): tpsform(p,x,4);
```

$$x + (-\frac{1}{2} + a)\,x^2 + (\frac{1}{3} - \frac{1}{2}\,a + \frac{1}{2}\,a^2)\,x^3 + O(x^4)$$

```
>   i := inverse(f):     tpsform(i,x,5);
```

$$1 - a\,x + \frac{1}{2}\,a^2\,x^2 - \frac{1}{6}\,a^3\,x^3 + \frac{1}{24}\,a^4\,x^4 + O(x^5)$$

```
>   p := multiply(i,f): tpsform(p,x,10);
```

$$1 + O(x^{10})$$

```
>   c := compose(f,g):   tpsform(c,x,4);
```

$$1 + a\,x + (-\frac{1}{2}\,a + \frac{1}{2}\,a^2)\,x^2 + (\frac{1}{3}\,a - \frac{1}{2}\,a^2 + \frac{1}{6}\,a^3)\,x^3 + O(x^4)$$

```
>  a := 1:  # special case, which may take a while
>  c := compose(f,g):   eval( tpsform(c,x,10) );
```

$$1 + x + O(x^{10})$$

The last result could have been obtained much more efficiently by

```
>  c := powexp(g):  tpsform(c,x,10);
```

$$1 + x + O(x^{10})$$

You can also apply the logarithmic function to a power series.

```
>  a := 'a': # reset a to a free variable
>  r := powlog(f):  tpsform(r,x,10);
```

$$a\,x + O(x^{10})$$

Other computations are differentiation and integration.

```
>  d := powdiff(f): tpsform(d,x,4);
```

$$a + a^2\,x + \frac{1}{2}\,a^3\,x^2 + \frac{1}{6}\,a^4\,x^3 + O(x^4)$$

```
>  i := powint(f):   tpsform(i,x,4);
```

$$x + \frac{1}{2}\,a\,x^2 + \frac{1}{6}\,a^2\,x^3 + O(x^4)$$

Reversion of a power series with respect to composition is also easily done in Maple. We shall use the power series expansion of the function $\ln(1 + x)$ as our example; the reverse power series should be of the series expansion of $\exp(x) - 1$.

```
>  r := reversion(g):  tpsform(r,x,5);
```

$$x + \frac{1}{2}\,x^2 + \frac{1}{6}\,x^3 + \frac{1}{24}\,x^4 + O(x^5)$$

```
>  c := compose(g,r):  tpsform(c,x,5);
```

$$x + O(x^5)$$

```
>  c := compose(r,g):  tpsform(c,x,5);
```

$$x + O(x^5)$$

We end this section with the popular example of the computation of the "f and g series," which are used in certain expansions of elliptic motion in celestial mechanics (q.v., [63]). The coefficients of the series expansions are defined by the following recurrences.

$$f_n = -\mu g_{n-1} - \sigma(\mu + 2\epsilon)\frac{\partial f_{n-1}}{\partial \epsilon} + (\epsilon - 2\sigma^2)\frac{\partial f_{n-1}}{\partial \sigma} - 3\mu\sigma\frac{\partial f_{n-1}}{\partial \mu}, \; f_0 = 1,$$

$$g_n = f_{n-1} - \sigma(\mu + 2\epsilon)\frac{\partial g_{n-1}}{\partial \epsilon} + (\epsilon - 2\sigma^2)\frac{\partial g_{n-1}}{\partial \sigma} - 3\mu\sigma\frac{\partial g_{n-1}}{\partial \mu}, \qquad g_0 = 0.$$

First we define the coordinate functions.

```
> mu := (mu,sigma,epsilon) -> mu:
> sigma := (mu,sigma,epsilon) -> sigma:
> epsilon := (mu,sigma,epsilon) -> epsilon:
```

Using the **D** operator, we can define the recurrence relations,

```
> with( powseries ):
> powcreate( f(n) = -mu*g(n-1) - sigma*(mu+2*epsilon)
>     *D[3](f(n-1)) + (epsilon-2*sigma^2)*D[2](f(n-1))
>     - 3*mu*sigma*D[1](f(n-1)), f(0) = 1 ):

> powcreate( g(n) = f(n-1) - sigma*(mu+2*epsilon)
>     *D[3](g(n-1)) + (epsilon-2*sigma^2)*D[2](g(n-1))
>     - 3*mu*sigma*D[1](g(n-1)), g(0) = 0 ):
```

and compute the first terms of the series expansion.

```
> tpsform(f,T,5);
```

$$1 - \mu T^2 + 3\mu\sigma T^3 + (\mu^2 + 3(\varepsilon - 2\sigma^2)\mu - 9\mu\sigma^2)T^4 + O(T^5)$$

There is a drawback. You would probably prefer to expand intermediate results, but when you define the recurrence relations in the **powcreate** command, there is no easy way to specify this. After the computation of the series you can simplify it.

```
> map(factor,");
```

$$1 - \mu T^2 + 3\mu\sigma T^3 + \mu(\mu + 3\varepsilon - 15\sigma^2)T^4 + O(T^5)$$

The only trick to expanding intermediate results is based on the implementation details of the **powseries** package: before computing any truncated series expansion with **tpsform** add the following two statements.

```
> f(_k) := 'expand'( f(_k) ):  g(_k) := 'expand'( g(_k) ):
```

Then the intermediate results are indeed expanded.

11.4   Limits

Internally, Maple often uses generalized series expansion for the computation of limits [72, 80]. For example, from the asymptotic series expansion

```
> ln(x) - ln(x+exp(-x));
```

$$\ln(x) - \ln(x + e^{(-x)})$$

```
> series( ", x=infinity, 2 );
```

$$-\frac{1}{x\,e^x} + \frac{O(\frac{1}{x^2})}{(e^x)^2}$$

it is clear that

```
>  Limit( "", x=infinity ):   " = value(");
```

$$\lim_{x \to \infty} \ln(x) - \ln(x + e^{(-x)}) = 0$$

Here, we have used the **value** procedure to evaluate the call to the inert **Limit** procedure. What you see is that you don't have to worry much about details but only have to use the procedure **limit**.

You may specify some options to **limit**: `left`, `right`, `real`, and `complex`. An example:

```
>  Limit( cos(x)^(1/x^3), x=0 ):   " = value(");
```

$$\lim_{x \to 0} \cos(x)^{\left(\frac{1}{x^3}\right)} = undefined$$

```
>  Limit( cos(x)^(1/x^3), x=0, ´right´ ):   " = value(");
```

$$\lim_{x \to 0+} \cos(x)^{\left(\frac{1}{x^3}\right)} = 0$$

```
>  Limit( cos(x)^(1/x^3), x=0 , ´left´ ):   " = value(");
```

$$\lim_{x \to 0-} \cos(x)^{\left(\frac{1}{x^3}\right)} = \infty$$

If the direction is not specified in **limit**, the limit is the real bidirectional limit (except in the case where the limit point is $+\infty$ or $-\infty$, in which case the limit is from the left or the right, respectively).

In some cases Maple needs more information. For example:

```
>  y := exp(-a*x)*cos(b*x);
```

$$y := e^{(-a\,x)} \cos(b\,x)$$

```
>  limit( y, x = infinity );
```

$$\lim_{x \to \infty} e^{(-a\,x)} \cos(b\,x).$$

Of course Maple did not presume that you had in mind a positive value of a. But you could also have added the assumption

```
>  assume( a>0 ):
```

before the computation of the limit.

```
>  limit( y, x = infinity );
```

$$0$$

As was noted at the beginning of this section, most limits are resolved by computing series. This implies that you may have to increase the value of the environment variable `Order` to avoid problems of cancellation.

```
> expr := ( exp(x) - sum( x^k/k!, k=0..11 ) ) / x^12;
```

$$expr := (e^x - 1 - x - \frac{1}{2} x^2 - \frac{1}{6} x^3 - \frac{1}{24} x^4 - \frac{1}{120} x^5 - \frac{1}{720} x^6$$
$$- \frac{1}{5040} x^7 - \frac{1}{40320} x^8 - \frac{1}{362880} x^9 - \frac{1}{3628800} x^{10}$$
$$- \frac{1}{39916800} x^{11}) / x^{12}$$

```
> limit( expr, x=0 );
```

$$\lim_{x \to 0} (e^x - 1 - x - \frac{1}{2} x^2 - \frac{1}{6} x^3 - \frac{1}{24} x^4 - \frac{1}{120} x^5 - \frac{1}{720} x^6 - \frac{1}{5040} x^7$$
$$- \frac{1}{40320} x^8 - \frac{1}{362880} x^9 - \frac{1}{3628800} x^{10} - \frac{1}{39916800} x^{11}) / x^{12}$$

```
> Order := 13:
> limit( expr, x=0 );
```

$$\frac{1}{479001600}$$

In the first section on truncated series expansion you have seen an example of a series expansion in which you had to adapt the zero test function to get correct results. Here, we give another example of the same kind.

```
> expr := x / ( sin(phi)^2 +(1+x)*cos(phi)^2 - 1 );
```

$$expr := \frac{x}{\sin(\phi)^2 + (1+x)\cos(\phi)^2 - 1}$$

```
> limit( ", x=0 );
```

$$0$$

In fact, the expression does not depend on x but it is certainly not equal to 0.

```
> simplify( expr );
```

$$\frac{1}{\cos(\phi)^2}$$

The reason for the wrong result lies in the incorrect truncated series expansion about zero.

```
> series( expr, x=0, 3 );
```

$$\frac{1}{\sin(\phi)^2 + \cos(\phi)^2 - 1} x - \frac{\cos(\phi)^2}{(\sin(\phi)^2 + \cos(\phi)^2 - 1)^2} x^2 + O(x^3)$$

The denominator of the first term simplifies to zero, but this is not automatically recognized by Maple. Actually, Maple uses two procedures for determining the leading term of a series, viz., **Testzero** and **Normalizer**. The environment variable **Testzero**, which is initialized with the relatively trivial test function `proc() evalb(normal(args[1]) - 0) end`, determines whether a leading coefficient is zero for division. The environment variable **Normalizer** is used in **series** to normalize leading terms of divisors. All you have to do to obtain correct results is to redefine these procedures. The recommended change is to use the environment variable **Normalizer** instead of **normal** in **Testzero** and to redefine this procedure so that coefficients are handled better in the **series** command.

```
>   Testzero := proc() evalb( Normalizer(args[1]) = 0 ) end:
>   Normalizer := proc() normal( simplify(args[1]) ) end:
```

After this adaptation of Maple everything works well.

```
>   readlib( forget ):
>   forget( series ): # clear the remember table of series
>   forget( limit  ): # clear the remember table of limit
>   series( expr, x=0, 3 ),  limit( expr, x=0 );
```

$$\frac{1}{\cos(\phi)^2}, \quad \frac{1}{\cos(\phi)^2}$$

11.5 Exercises

1. Study various numerical approximations of the sine function on the segment $[-\pi, \pi]$.

2. Study various numerical approximations of the function

$$x \longmapsto \frac{1}{x} \int_0^x \frac{\sin(\sin u)}{u} \, du$$

for $|x| < \pi$.

3. Compute the following limits and check the answers.

   (a) $\displaystyle\lim_{x \to 0} \frac{\sin x}{x}$

   (b) $\displaystyle\lim_{x \to 0} (\sin x)^{1/x}$

   (c) $\displaystyle\lim_{x \to 0} \frac{1 - \cos x}{x}$

   (d) $\displaystyle\lim_{x \to \infty} (1 + \frac{\pi}{x})^x$

   (e) $\displaystyle\lim_{x \to 0} x^{\sin x}$

   (f) $\displaystyle\lim_{x \to \infty} (2^x + 3^x)^{1/x}$

4. Compute the following limits.

(a) $\lim\limits_{x\to\infty} \dfrac{\ln x}{x}$

(b) $\lim\limits_{x\to\infty} \dfrac{\ln x}{e^x}$

(c) $\lim\limits_{x\to\infty} \dfrac{x^2 + \sin x}{2x^2 + \cos 4x}$

(d) $\lim\limits_{x\downarrow 0} \dfrac{2}{1 + e^{-1/x}}$

(e) $\lim\limits_{x\to\infty} \sinh(\tanh x) - \tanh(\sinh x)$

5. In a fresh Maple session or after the **restart** command, compute the Taylor series expansion of $x^3 - 1 - 4x^2 + 5x$ about $x = 1$ up to order 10. We do want you to enter the terms in the polynomial in the above ordering. Of what data type is the obtained expression? To what order does Maple think that the series expansion goes?

6. What is the asymptotic expansion of $\binom{2n}{n}$?

7. What is the power series expansion of Lambert's W function?

8. In this exercise the Chebyshev polynomials of the first kind are introduced via their generating function.

   (a) Compute the Taylor series expansion of $\dfrac{1 - t^2}{1 - 2xt + t^2}$ about $x = 0$ and $t = 0$ up to degree 8.

   (b) The Chebyshev polynomials $T_n(x)$ of the first kind are defined by the generating function

   $$\frac{1 - t^2}{1 - 2xt + t^2} = \sum_{n=0}^{\infty} \epsilon_n T_n(x) t^n \,,$$

   where $\epsilon_0 = 1$ and $\epsilon_n = 2$ for $n \geq 1$. Compute $T_2(x)$ and $T_{10}(x)$. Check your answer with the built-in command **orthopoly[T]**.

9. Find the Taylor series expansion up to order 25 of the solution for Kepler's equation $E = u + e \sin E$ by use of the **RootOf** procedure. Compare the efficiency with the method described in the first section of this chapter.

10. Find the series expansion $x = a$ up to order 3 of the function

$$x \longmapsto \frac{x^a - a^x}{x^x - a^a} \,.$$

11. When you study Josephson's junction circuit you may need the series expansion of the function ptan defined as $\mathrm{ptan}(s) = p$, if $p - \tan p = s$. Compute the series expansion of this function.

12. Compare the series solution of Kepler's equation $E = u + e \sin E$, which was computed in the first section of this chapter, with the following exact solution in terms of Bessel functions: $E = u + 2 \sum_{n=1}^{\infty} J_n(n\,e) \sin(n\,u)/n$.

12
Composite Data Types

Active knowledge of Maple data types is quite often needed even when using Maple interactively as a symbolic calculator. Recall the elementary data types *polynom* and *ratpoly*, and the simplification and manipulation of such expressions. This chapter introduces you to *composite data types* like *sequence, set, list, array, table,* and *function call,* which are built from elementary data types and used for grouping objects together.

12.1 Sequence

You have seen objects of type `exprseq` (expression sequence) before. For example, the result of the **op** function is in most cases a sequence of objects separated by commas.

```
>   polynomial := x^3 - 6*x^2 + 11*x - 6;
```
$$polynomial := x^3 - 6\,x^2 + 11\,x - 6$$

```
>   sequence := op( polynomial );
```
$$sequence := x^3, -6\,x^2, 11\,x, -6$$

Sequences are frequently used in Maple. Below, not only the result of the command `solve( polynomial, x )` is a sequence, but also the arguments of the function call form a sequence.

```
>   arguments := polynomial, x;
```
$$arguments := x^3 - 6\,x^2 + 11\,x - 6, x$$

```
> whattype( arguments );
```

$$exprseq$$

```
> solve( arguments );
```

$$1, 2, 3$$

Inside a procedure definition you can refer to the sequence of actual arguments via the variable **args**; the actual number of arguments is available via the variable **nargs**. The following example illustrates this.

```
> procargs := proc()
>     print( `number of arguments` = nargs,
>               `actual arguments` = args )
> end:
> procargs(x);
```

$$number\ of\ arguments = 1, actual\ arguments = (\,x\,)$$

```
> procargs(x,y,z);
```

$$number\ of\ arguments = 3, actual\ arguments = (\,x, y, z\,)$$

Note that a sequence is one object: internally it is represented by one data vector (Figure 12.1).

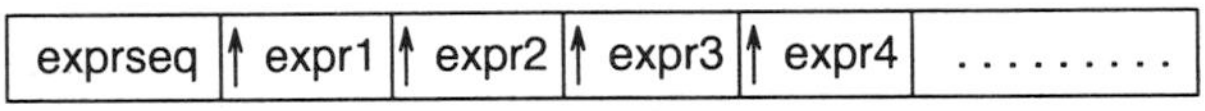

| exprseq ↑ | expr1 ↑ | expr2 ↑ | expr3 ↑ | expr4 | . . . . |

FIGURE 12.1. Internal data structure of a sequence.

Here, the symbols ↑expr1, ↑expr2, ... indicate pointers to the data vectors that correspond to the expressions **expr1**, **expr2**, and so on. The components of an expression sequence are not necessarily of the same type.

```
> seq1 := M, a, p, l, e:
> seq2 := 77, 97, 112, 108, 101: # name in ASCII code
> `concatenated sequence` := seq1, seq2;
```

$$concatenated\ sequence := M, a, p, l, e, 77, 97, 112, 108, 101$$

Maple uses the special name **NULL** to denote the empty sequence.

```
> `empty sequence`:= NULL;
```

$$empty\ sequence :=$$

```
> 1, 2, `empty sequence`, 2, 1;
```

$$1, 2, 2, 1$$

Sequences can also be generated by the **seq** function.

```
> # generate the first nine odd prime numbers
> seq( ithprime(i), i = 2..10 );
```

$$3, 5, 7, 11, 13, 17, 19, 23, 29$$

A function call of the form **seq**($f(i)$, $i = m \ldots n$) generates the sequence $f(m)$, $f(m+1)$, $f(m+2)$, ..., $f(n)$. Alternatively, Maple provides the sequence operator **$**.

```
>   x$4;
```
$$x, x, x, x$$

Except for the above use in combination with a function call of **diff**, the sequence operator **$** is of limited use. It may even be dangerous to use.

```
>   ('[k,l] $ k=1..2') $ l=3..4;
```
$$[1,3],[2,3],[1,4],[2,4]$$

In this example, the quotes are absolutely necessary to prevent premature evaluation, and more quotes would be needed if the sequence indices k and l had been assigned values before. In the worst case, you would have had to enter a horrible command like

```
>   ('['k','l'] $ 'k'=1..2') $ 'l'=3..4:
```
Instead, you would certainly prefer the command

```
>   seq( seq( [i,j], i = 1..2 ), j = 3..4 ):
```
The call **seq**($f(i)$, $i = expression$) generates a sequence by applying f to each operand of the *expression*.

```
>   seq( i^2, i = { 1, 2, 3, 4, 5 } );
```
$$1, 4, 9, 16, 25$$

```
>   seq( i^2, i = x + y + z );
```
$$x^2, y^2, z^2$$

You select an element of a sequence by the selection operator [].

```
>   "[2];   # 2nd element
```
$$y^2$$

```
>   ""[-1]; # last element
```
$$z^2$$

You can also select more than one element of a sequence at the same time.

```
>   sequence := v, w, x, y, z: sequence[ 2..4 ];
```
$$w, x, y$$

You may consider the last command as an abbreviation of

```
>   seq( sequence[i], i = 2..4 );
```
$$w, x, y$$

Such abbreviations also occur at other places, e.g., when you want to generate a sequence of names *p1, p2,...* by concatenation via

```
>   p.( 1..5 );
```
$$p1, p2, p3, p4, p5$$

```
>  seq( p.i, i = 1..5 );
```
$$p1, p2, p3, p4, p5$$

We end this section with a short remark on the subexpression of the form

$$left\_expression \, .. \, right\_expression$$

It is a regular Maple expression of type *range*. You have already seen such expressions being used as range specifications for integration and summation. You may choose any Maple expression as *left_* and *right_expression*, but in most cases it should evaluate to a numerical value. By the way, you may use more than two dots as the range operator; but remember that *one dot* is used as the concatenation operator.

12.2   Set

You use objects of type *set* most frequently when you try to solve systems of equations with the Maple procedure **solve**. The arguments of this procedure are a set of equations and a set of unknowns, and the solution is in general a sequence of objects of type *set*.

Maple uses the common mathematical notation of a set: a sequence between braces. Data do not occur more than once in a set. As a user you have almost no control on the ordering of the elements of a set, because the system uses internal address ordering.

```
>  { 1, 3, 5, 2, 4}; # used earlier in increasing ordering
```
$$\{1, 2, 3, 4, 5\}$$

```
>  { x, x, x*y, x*(x-1), y*x, x^2-x };
```
$$\{x, x(x-1), x^2 - x, x y\}$$

```
>  `empty set` := {};
```
$$empty\ set := \{\,\}$$

Figure 12.2 shows the internal representation of a set.

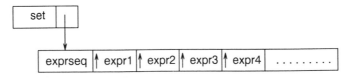

FIGURE 12.2. Internal data structure of a set.

The entries in the expression sequence are sorted in increasing address order. In this way, it can be assured that no duplicates are present.

For objects of type *set* the usual operators are present: **union, minus,** and **intersect.**

```
>   {0,1,2,3} union {0,2,4,6};
```
$$\{0,1,2,3,4,6\}$$

```
>   {0,1,2,3} minus {0,2,4,6};
```
$$\{1,3\}$$

```
>   {0,1,2,3} intersect {0,2,4,6};
```
$$\{0,2\}$$

You can ask whether a certain Maple object is an element of a set, and if so, find its position in the set.

```
>   member( 2, {0,1,2,3}, `position` );
```
$$true$$

```
>   position;
```
$$3$$

You can select an element of a set by the selection operator [] or by the function **op**. The latter selection scheme is less efficient as it will evaluate the whole set.

```
>   # generate all subsets of {1,2,3}
>   collection := combinat[powerset](3);
```

$$collection := \{\,\{\ \},\{1\},\{1,2\},\{1,3\},\{1,2,3\},\{2,3\},\{3\},\{2\}\,\}$$

```
>   nops( collection ); # number of elements in the set
```
$$8$$

```
>   collection[4];   # 4th element in set
```
$$\{1,3\}$$

```
>   collection[-1]; # last element in set
```
$$\{2\}$$

```
>   op( 8, collection );
```
$$\{2\}$$

```
>   collection[6..8]; # returns a subset
```
$$\{\,\{2,3\},\{3\},\{2\}\,\}$$

```
>   collection[3..-3]; # omit first and last 2 elements
```
$$\{\,\{1,2\},\{1,3\},\{1,2,3\},\{2,3\}\,\}$$

```
>  collection[]; # sequence of set elements
```
$$\{\ \},\{1\},\{1,2\},\{1,3\},\{1,2,3\},\{2,3\},\{3\},\{2\}$$

If you want to select elements of a set that meet some criterion, then the Maple function **select** is helpful. The opposite function **remove** also exists. A few examples:

```
>  die := rand(-10..10): numberset := { ´die()´ $ 11 };
```
$$numberset := \{0, -4, -5, -6, 6, 7, -8, 8, 10\}$$

```
>  select( isprime, numberset ); # select prime numbers
```
$$\{7\}$$

```
>  # select nonnegative integers
>  select( type, numberset, ´nonnegint´ );
```
$$\{0, 6, 7, 8, 10\}$$

```
>  remove( x -> x < -3, numberset ); # remove numbers < -3
```
$$\{0, 6, 7, 8, 10\}$$

The general format of selection and removal is

$$\textbf{select}(\ criterion,\ set,\ extra\ arguments\ )$$

and

$$\textbf{remove}(\ criterion,\ set,\ extra\ arguments\ )$$

The criterion should always return a Boolean value *true* or *false*. Extra arguments of the selection/removal criterion are always added after the set from which elements will be selected or removed.

12.3 · List

Whereas sets are sequences enclosed by braces, you can construct an object of type *list* by enclosing a sequence in square brackets. You have already seen such objects being used as arguments in **collect** to specify the ordering of variables in polynomials.

```
>  1 + x + y^2 + z^3 + x^2*y^2 + x^2*z^3 + y^3*z^3;
```
$$1 + x + y^2 + z^3 + x^2 y^2 + x^2 z^3 + y^3 z^3$$

```
>  collect( ", [ x, y, z ] );
```
$$(y^2 + z^3) x^2 + x + 1 + y^2 + z^3 + y^3 z^3$$

```
>  collect( ", [ z, y, x ] );
```
$$(x^2 + 1 + y^3) z^3 + (x^2 + 1) y^2 + x + 1$$

Important differences between objects of type *list* and *set* are that

- in a list the same objects may occur more than once;
- the ordering of the elements of a list is preserved;
- list elements can easily be assigned new values.

The internal structure of a list (Figure 12.3) is however similar to that of a set (Figure 12.2).

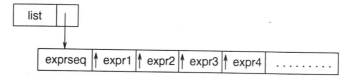

FIGURE 12.3. Internal data structure of a list.

```
>  [ x, x, x*y, x*(x-1), y*x, x^2-x ];
```
$$[x, x, x\,y, x\,(x-1), x\,y, x^2 - x]$$

```
>  sort( ", address' );  # sort by machine address
```
$$[x, x, x\,(x-1), x^2 - x, x\,y, x\,y]$$

```
>  convert( ", set );
```
$$\{x, x\,(x-1), x^2 - x, x\,y\}$$

```
>  [ x$5 ];  # list of five x'ses
```
$$[x, x, x, x, x]$$

```
>  `empty list` := [];
```
$$empty\ list := [\,]$$

Below, the most frequently used operations on lists are listed and examples show how they can be carried out in Maple.

- Find the length of a list.
  ```
  >  cl := [ black, red, green, yellow, blue, white ]:
  >  nops( cl );  # number of colors
  ```
  $$6$$

- Search for an element in a list.
  ```
  >  member( indigo, cl );
  ```
  $$false$$

```
> member( blue, cl, 'position' );
```
$$true$$

```
> position;
```
$$5$$

- Select one or more elements.

```
> cl[5];        # efficient selection
```
$$blue$$

```
> op(5,cl);   # inefficient selection
```
$$blue$$

The efficiency of the selection of a list element by **op** is $O(n)$, where n is the length of the list, because the whole list is evaluated. When the square brackets are used, Maple uses a different evaluation scheme such that the evaluation of the whole list is suppressed and becomes constant time. The following example illustrates this.

```
> L := [ x $ (2^17-2) ]: # x-list of maximal length
> # access-time to "long" list
> time(): L[1]: time(): cpu_time = ("-""") * second;
```
$$cpu\_time = 0$$

```
> time(): op(1,L): time(): cpu_time = ("-""") * second;
```
$$cpu\_time = .133 \ second$$

```
> time(): L[2^17-2]: time():
> cpu_time = ("-""") * second;
```
$$cpu\_time = 0$$

```
> time(): op(2^17-2,L): time():
> cpu_time = ("-""") * second;
```
$$cpu\_time = .117 \ second$$

The selection of list elements is more general. Some examples, involving the preceding list **cl**:

```
> cl[-1];        # first list element from the right
```
$$white$$

```
> cl[3..6];     # return a sublist
```
$$[\,green, yellow, blue, white\,]$$

```
> op(3..6,cl); # return a sequence
```
$$green, yellow, blue, white$$

```
>  cl[-2..-1];  # the sublist of last two elements
```
$$[\,blue, white\,]$$

```
>  cl[];  # sequence of list elements
```
$$black, red, green, yellow, blue, white$$

```
>  # special cases: drop the first or the last element:
>  cl[ 2 .. nops(cl) ];
```
$$[\,red, green, yellow, blue, white\,]$$

```
>  cl[ 2 .. -1 ];
```
$$[\,red, green, yellow, blue, white\,]$$

```
>  subsop( 1 = NULL, cl );
```
$$[\,red, green, yellow, blue, white\,]$$

```
>  cl[ 1 .. nops(cl)-1 ];
```
$$[\,black, red, green, yellow, blue\,]$$

```
>  cl[ 1 .. -2 ];
```
$$[\,black, red, green, yellow, blue\,]$$

```
>  subsop( nops(cl) = NULL, cl );
```
$$[\,black, red, green, yellow, blue\,]$$

- Prepend, append, and insert elements.
```
>  [ crimson, op(cl) ];
```
$$[\,crimson, black, red, green, yellow, blue, white\,]$$

```
>  [ op(cl), crimson ];
```
$$[\,black, red, green, yellow, blue, white, crimson\,]$$

```
>  [ op(cl[1..3]), crimson, op(cl[4..nops(cl)]) ];
```
$$[\,black, red, green, crimson, yellow, blue, white\,]$$

Note that for long lists the creation of a sublist followed by conversion to a sequence is more efficient than direct use of **op** with the requested range as in the latter case the whole list is fully evaluated.

- Concatenate lists.
```
>  cl2 := [ crimson, indigo ]:  [ op(cl), op(cl2) ];
```
$$[\,black, red, green, yellow, blue, white, crimson, indigo\,]$$

- Replace one element in a list.
  ```
  > subsop( 5 = indigo, cl );  # cl unchanged
  ```
  $$[\,black, red, green, yellow, indigo, white\,]$$

  ```
  > cl[5] := purple; cl;  # cl changed
  ```
  $$cl_5 := purple$$
  $$[\,black, red, green, yellow, purple, white\,]$$

  The latter assignment is more efficient than the command
  `cl := subsop( 5 = indigo, cl )`. However, direct assignment of
  a list element is restricted to lists with at most 100 entries.

- Replace all specified elements in a list.
  ```
  > subs( red = crimson, cl );  # replace every color red
  ```
  $$[\,black, crimson, green, yellow, purple, white\,]$$

- Rearrange lists.
  ```
  > # sort the list (in lexicographic ordering)
  > sort( cl, lexorder );  # variable cl is not changed
  ```
  $$[\,black, red, green, purple, white, yellow\,]$$

  ```
  > # reverse the list
  > [ seq( cl[-i], i=1..nops(cl) ) ];
  ```
  $$[\,white, purple, yellow, green, red, black\,]$$

  ```
  > # rotate the list one position to the left or right
  > [ op( 2..nops(cl), cl ), cl[1] ];
  ```
  $$[\,red, green, yellow, purple, white, black\,]$$

  ```
  > # rotate the list one position to the left or right
  > [ op( cl[2..-1] ), cl[1] ];
  ```
  $$[\,red, green, yellow, purple, white, black\,]$$

  ```
  > [ cl[nops(cl)], op( 1..nops(cl)-1, cl ) ];
  ```
  $$[\,white, black, red, green, yellow, purple\,]$$

  ```
  > [ cl[-1], op( cl[1..-2] ) ];
  ```
  $$[\,white, black, red, green, yellow, purple\,]$$

Using a few basic Maple functions and constructs you can carry out most operations on lists so easily that the designers of Maple have chosen not to waste function names for these operations. If you wish, you can easily transcribe the above examples into Maple procedures. For example, the last two operations could be transcribed into procedures in the following way.

```
>  rotateleft := proc(L::list)
>    [ op( L[2..-1] ), L[1] ]
>  end:
>  rotateright := proc(L::list)
>    [ L[-1], op( L[1..-2] ) ]
>  end:
>  rotateleft( cl );
```

$$[\,red, green, yellow, purple, white, black\,]$$

```
>  (rotateright@@3)( cl ); # rotate 3 places to the right
```

$$[\,yellow, purple, white, black, red, green\,]$$

```
>  (rotateleft@rotateright)( cl ); # do nothing
```

$$[\,black, red, green, yellow, purple, white\,]$$

You may have wondered above why we appended an element *elem* to a list L via [op(L),elem] and not by the assignment L[nops(L)+1]:=elem. The example below shows that you can assign value to existing list elements but cannot extend a list in this way.

```
>  L := [a,b,c];
```

$$L := [\,a, b, c\,]$$

```
>  L[3] := [c,c]; # assignment of existing list element
```

$$L_3 := [\,c, c\,]$$

```
>  L;
```

$$[\,a, b, [\,c, c\,]\,]$$

```
>  L[3,2] := d;   # assignment of existing list element
```

$$L_{3,2} := d$$

```
>  L;
```

$$[\,a, b, [\,c, d\,]\,]$$

```
>  L[4] := e;  # no extension of list
```

```
Error, out of bound assignment to a list
```

In Table 12.1 we summarize the selectors for a composite data structure T, which can be of type *sequence*, *set*, or *list*.

Selection	Returned Data Structure
T[]	expression sequence of components
T[i], (i∈ N)	i-th component from the left
T[-i], (i∈ N)	i-th component from the right
T[i..j], (i,j∈ ℤ)	the range between i and j
	as sequence, set, or list
T[i,j,...]	T[i][j,...]
T[i..j,k,...]	seq((T[n])[k,...], k=i..j)
	as a sequence, set, or list

TABLE 12.1. Selection in sequence, set, or list.

12.4 Array

This section is a short introduction to the data type *array*, and related objects like *vectors* and *matrices*. In Chapter 18 we shall describe in more detail how arrays are used in matrix algebra. In this section, we restrict ourselves to the construction of these data structures. Evaluation of arrays will be discussed further on, in §12.6.

Like conventional programming languages, Maple has a data structure for one-, two-, or multidimensional arrays. Below is an example of an object of type *array*.

```
>   array( -1..1, 0..1,
>      [ (-1,0)=a, (-1,1)=b, (0,0)=c, (0,1)=d ] );
```

$$\text{array}(-1..1, 0..1, [$$
$$(-1,0) = a$$
$$(-1,1) = b$$
$$(0,0) = c$$
$$(0,1) = d$$
$$(1,0) = ?_{1,0}$$
$$(1,1) = ?_{1,1}$$
$$])$$

First, the ranges of the indices of the two-dimensional array are specified. Second, some, but not necessarily all, array elements are assigned values. Be careful not to mess up the round and square brackets; this is a little bit confusing, as selection of array elements is done by square brackets.

The data type *array* is actually a special case of the data type *table*, which is frequently used by Maple itself (e.g., remember tables of procedures) and will be discussed in the next section. Characteristic of the data type *array* is the use of a Cartesian product of segments of contiguous integers as the set of allowed indices.

At first sight, the data type *array* is similar to the data type *list*. This is reflected in the way objects of type *array* can be constructed from objects of type *list*. Below, a one-, two- and three-dimensional array are constructed.

```
>  v := array( [1+a,2+b,3+c] );
```

$$v := [1 + a, 2 + b, 3 + c]$$

```
>  type( v, list );
```

false

```
>  type( v, vector );
```

true

```
>  type( v, array );
```

true

```
>  M := array( [ [1-p,2-q], [1-r,2-s] ] );
```

$$M := \left[\begin{array}{cc} 1 - p & 2 - q \\ 1 - r & 2 - s \end{array} \right]$$

```
>  A := array( [ [ [1,2], [3,4] ], [ [5,6], [8,9] ],
>     [ [10,11], [12,13] ] ] );
```

$$A := \text{array}(1..3, 1..2, 1..2, [$$
$$(1, 1, 1) = 1$$
$$(1, 1, 2) = 2$$
$$(1, 2, 1) = 3$$
$$(1, 2, 2) = 4$$
$$(2, 1, 1) = 5$$
$$(2, 1, 2) = 6$$
$$(2, 2, 1) = 8$$
$$(2, 2, 2) = 9$$
$$(3, 1, 1) = 10$$
$$(3, 1, 2) = 11$$
$$(3, 2, 1) = 12$$
$$(3, 2, 2) = 13$$
$$])$$

By entering the array elements through lists (or lists of lists) a lot of typing is avoided. Furthermore, if you leave out the ranges of indices, Maple determines the index ranges from the lengths of the lists, assuming that the ranges start at one. You can see this in the example of a three-dimensional array the index range is explicitly mentioned in the output. One- and two-dimensional arrays whose index ranges start at one are most frequently used as vectors and matrices, respectively. Hence, the typical vector- and matrix-notation is used.

```
>   type( M, matrix );
```

$$true$$

You could also have constructed the above matrix M and vector v in array representation by the commands **matrix** and **vector**.

```
>   M := matrix( [ [ 1-p, 2-q ], [ 1-r, 2-s ] ] );
```

$$M := \left[\begin{array}{cc} 1-p & 2-q \\ 1-r & 2-s \end{array} \right]$$

```
>   v := vector( [ 1+a, 2+b, 3+c ] );
```

$$v := [1+a, 2+b, 3+c]$$

Sometimes you just want to declare a vector without specifying the elements. This is no problem in Maple.

```
>   vec := vector(100);
```

$$vec := \mathrm{array}(\, 1..100, [\,]\,)$$

```
>   vec := array(-1000..1000, [] );
```

$$vec := \mathrm{array}(\, -1000..1000, [\,]\,)$$

Furthermore, matrices can be conveniently constructed with the help of index functions. For example, a 4×4 Hilbert matrix can be made by

```
>   h := (i,j) -> 1/(i+j-x); # index function
```

$$h := (i,j) \rightarrow \frac{1}{i+j-x}$$

```
>   matrix( 4, 4, h );
```

$$\left[\begin{array}{cccc} \dfrac{1}{2-x} & \dfrac{1}{3-x} & \dfrac{1}{4-x} & \dfrac{1}{5-x} \\ \dfrac{1}{3-x} & \dfrac{1}{4-x} & \dfrac{1}{5-x} & \dfrac{1}{6-x} \\ \dfrac{1}{4-x} & \dfrac{1}{5-x} & \dfrac{1}{6-x} & \dfrac{1}{7-x} \\ \dfrac{1}{5-x} & \dfrac{1}{6-x} & \dfrac{1}{7-x} & \dfrac{1}{8-x} \end{array} \right]$$

In this case, you could also have used the built-in function **linalg[hilbert]** from the linalg package. Another example is the construction of a zero matrix.

```
>   matrix( 3, 3, 0 );
```

$$\begin{bmatrix} 0 & 0 & 0 \\ 0 & 0 & 0 \\ 0 & 0 & 0 \end{bmatrix}$$

In this function call, 0 means the zero function.

The procedure **array** has options available for matrices of special form.

```
>   M := array( symmetric, 1..2, 1..2 ):   M[1,2]:=1:
>   print(M);
```

$$\begin{bmatrix} M_{1,1} & 1 \\ 1 & M_{2,2} \end{bmatrix}$$

```
>   v := array( sparse, 1..10 ):   v[1]:=1:   v[5]:=-1:
>   print(v);
```

$$[\,1,0,0,0,-1,0,0,0,0,0\,]$$

```
>   M := array( sparse, symmetric, 1..2, 1..2 ):   M[1,2]:=1:
>   print(M);
```

$$\begin{bmatrix} 0 & 1 \\ 1 & 0 \end{bmatrix}$$

Other options are `antisymmetric`, `identity`, and `diagonal`. The options can only be used in the procedure **array** and as we shall see in the procedure **table**, but not in **matrix** or **vector**. The role of these options is to indicate how matrix entries can be computed so that actual values do not have to be stored in the internal data structure. When more than one option has been specified, they are handled one by one from left to right.

You can create your own indexing functions in Maple. As an example, we shall define the special indexing function `tridiagonal`, or actually the procedure **index/tridiagonal**. When **index/tridiagonal** is called with two arguments it will evaluate an entry; with three arguments it assigns an entry (Table 12.2).

Format	Purpose
`index/tridiagonal `(ind, arr)	for evaluation
`index/tridiagonal `(ind, arr, val)	for assignment

TABLE 12.2. Formats of call of special indexing function.

Here, `ind` is a list containing the indices, `arr` is an array being indexed, and `val` is a list with the value to be assigned. The first argument of

arr is a name sequence, of which the first name of this sequence was
tridiagonal. The first name decides which special indexing function to
use, and is stripped for this call. Hence, the first argument of the table consists of the remaining names, which could be **symmetric** or **antisymmetric**
among others.

When **index/tridiagonal** is called with two arguments, it returns the
value of the entry being selected. When **index/tridiagonal** is called with
three arguments, it is expected that the function will produce the assignment to an array entry. The value returned is used as the value resulting
from the assignment. For this type of call, the indexing function will normally have a side effect, typically altering **arr**.

The actual code of **index/tridiagonal** can be as follows.

```
>   `index/tridiagonal` := proc( ind, arr, val )
>      if nargs = 2 then
>         if outofband( ind )
>         then 0
>         else arr[op(ind)]
>         fi
>      elif nargs = 3 then
>         if outofband( ind )
>            then ERROR(`band width 1 is exceeded`,
>                          `indices` = ind )
>            else arr[op(ind)] := op(val)
>            fi
>      else ERROR(`invalid arguments`)
>      fi
>   end:
```

Here, the following routine tests whether an index is inside or outside the
band of width 1.

```
>   outofband := proc( ind::list )
>      local indset, pairs, p, d:
>      indset := {op(ind)};
>      if nops(indset) <= 1 then RETURN(false) fi;
>      pairs := combinat[choose]( indset, 2 );
>      for p in pairs do
>         d := p[1] - p[2];
>         if type( d, integer ) and abs(d) > 1
>         then RETURN(true)
>         fi
>      od:
>      RETURN(false)
>   end:
```

A few examples:

```
>   A := array( tridiagonal, 1..4, 1..4 );
```

$$A := \text{array}(\, tridiagonal, 1..4, 1..4, [\,]\,)$$

```
>  A[1,2] := x;
```

$$A_{1,2} := x$$

```
>  A[1,4] := y;
```

```
Error, (in index/tridiagonal) band width 1 is exceeded,
indices = [1, 4]
```

```
>  print(A);
```

$$\begin{bmatrix} A_{1,1} & x & 0 & 0 \\ A_{2,1} & A_{2,2} & A_{2,3} & 0 \\ 0 & A_{3,2} & A_{3,3} & A_{3,4} \\ 0 & 0 & A_{4,3} & A_{4,4} \end{bmatrix}$$

```
>  A := array( tridiagonal, antisymmetric, 1..4, 1..4 );
```

$$A := \text{array}(\,tridiagonal, antisymmetric, 1..4, 1..4, [\,]\,)$$

```
>  A[1,2] := x;
```

$$A_{1,2} := x$$

```
>  print(A);
```

$$\begin{bmatrix} 0 & x & 0 & 0 \\ -x & 0 & A_{2,3} & 0 \\ 0 & -A_{2,3} & 0 & A_{3,4} \\ 0 & 0 & -A_{3,4} & 0 \end{bmatrix}$$

Here, the indexing functions tridiagonal and antisymmetric are both used. When using an entry, the following steps are gone through:

1. the first name tridiagonal is used, and **index/tridiagonal** is called first;

2. if the index is outside the band, then the value 0 is returned. Otherwise **index/tridiagonal** will access an entry of an array that is only antisymmetric (the tridiagonal word is dropped);

3. **index/antisymmetric** will access a table entry with the proper indexing order and a value will be returned;

4. **index/tridiagonal** returns this value.

We have defined the indexing function in such a way that it also works for higher-dimensional arrays and when indices contain unknowns.

```
>  A := array( tridiagonal, 1..3, 1..3, 1..3 );
```

$$A := \text{array}(\,tridiagonal, 1..3, 1..3, 1..3, [\,]\,)$$

```
>   `A[1,2,3]` = [1,2,3];
```

$$A_{1,2,3} = [1,2,3]$$

```
>   `A[1,2,k]` = A[1,2,k];
```

$$A_{1,2,k} = A_{1,2,k}$$

```
>   `A[1,3,k]` = A[1,3,k];
```

$$A_{1,3,k} = 0$$

```
>   `A[1,k,k+1]` = A[1,k,k+1];
```

$$A_{1,k,k+1} = A_{1,k,k+1}$$

```
>   `A[1,k,k+2]` = A[1,k,k+2];
```

$$A_{1,k,k+2} = 0$$

Evaluation of variables that point to data of type *array* is different from the usual *full evaluation*, which applies to variables that point to formulae or lists. This special evaluation scheme will also hold for the data structure *table*. In §12.6 evaluation of these data types and the consequences will be explained in full. Here, we only point out this aspect.

```
>   vec := array( [ 1+a, 2+b, 3+c ] );
```

$$vec := [1 + a, 2 + b, 3 + c]$$

```
>   vec;
```

$$vec$$

Evaluation of the variable **vec** does not show the array. You must force full evaluation by **eval**.

```
>   eval( vec );
```

$$[1 + a, 2 + b, 3 + c]$$

Use **op** or **lprint** if you want to see the index range too.

```
>   op( eval(vec) );
```

$$1..3, [1 = 1 + a, 2 = 2 + b, 3 = 3 + c]$$

```
>   lprint( eval(vec) );

array(1 .. 3, [(1)=1+a, (2)=2+b, (3)=3+c])
```

12.5   Table

A table is similar to the record data structure in other programming languages like Pascal, Algol68, or C. Below is an example of an object of type *table*.

```
> color := table(
>    [ red = RGB(1,0,0),
>       turquoise = RGB(0.7,0.9,0.9),
>       white = RGB(1,1,1)
>    ] );
```

$$color := \text{table}([$$
$$turquoise = \text{RGB}(.7,.9,.9)$$
$$white = \text{RGB}(1,1,1)$$
$$red = \text{RGB}(1,0,0)$$
$$])$$

The entries of a table are stored internally in a hash table and are as such not directly available to you; you have no control in what order they are stored internally. The use of hash tables allows constant-time access for all elements instead of access efficiency that depends on the position of an element in a table. But there is no need for internal access to components because you can easily retrieve the indices and entries of a table.

```
> indices( color );
```

$$[\, turquoise\,],[\, white\,],[\, red\,]$$

```
> entries( color );
```

$$[\,\text{RGB}(.7,.9,.9)\,],[\,\text{RGB}(1,1,1)\,],[\,\text{RGB}(1,0,0)\,]$$

You select or change an element of a table by the selection operator [ ].

```
> color[ red ];
```

$$\text{RGB}(1,0,0)$$

```
> color[ red ]  := HUE(0);
```

$$color_{red} := \text{HUE}(0)$$

```
> print( color );
```

$$\text{table}([$$
$$turquoise = \text{RGB}(.7,.9,.9)$$
$$white = \text{RGB}(1,1,1)$$
$$red = \text{HUE}(0)$$
$$])$$

The assignment to an indexed name is also the easiest way to build up a new table structure in Maple. In the following example we create a table called Laplace with only one entry, viz., the Laplace transform of $\text{erf}(\sqrt{t})$.

```
> Laplace[ erf(sqrt(t)) ]  := 1/(s*sqrt(s+1));
```

$$Laplace_{\text{erf}(\sqrt{t})} := \frac{1}{s\sqrt{s+1}}$$

> `print( Laplace );`

$$\text{table([}$$

$$\text{erf}(\sqrt{t}) = \frac{1}{s\sqrt{s+1}}$$

$$])$$

The procedure **index/newtable**, if defined, is used when an assignment of an indexed name is made where the table or array is not defined yet. By default it will then create a table, but it can also be adapted to your own wishes. For example, you cannot assign to a set element or a sequence by assignment of type `S[x] := y` .

```
>   S := {a,b,c}:   Q := a,b,c:
>   S[3] := U;
```

`Error, cannot assign to a set`

```
>   Q[3] := C;
```

`Error, cannot assign to an expression sequence`

However, the following procedure definition will allow this.

```
>   `index/newtable` := proc( ind, tab, val )
>       if not assigned(tab)
>       then tab := table(): tab[op(ind)] := op(val)
>       elif nops( [ eval(tab) ] ) > 1 # expression sequence
>           and type( ind, [integer] ) and ind[1] >= 1 and
>           ind[1] <= nops( [ eval(tab) ] )
>       then tab := op( subsop( ind[1] = op(val),
>                               [ eval(tab) ] ) )
>       elif type( eval(tab), set )   and
>           type( ind, [integer] ) and ind[1] >= 1 and
>           ind[1] <= nops( eval(tab) )
>       then tab := subsop( ind[1]=op(val), eval(tab) )
>       else ERROR(`not a table/array/set/sequence`)
>       fi
>   end:
>   S; S[3] := U; S;
```

$$\{a, b, c\}$$
$$S_3 := U$$
$$\{a, b, U\}$$

```
>   Q; Q[3] := C; Q;
```

$$a, b, c$$
$$Q_3 := C$$
$$a, b, C$$

Let us continue our discussion of tables and explain why we used **print** in previous examples to display tables and why we used so many **eval**'s in the source code of **index/newtable**. The reason is that the evaluation of variables that point to data of type *table* is different from the usual *full evaluation*. In §12.6 evaluation of an object of type *table* will be explained in full. Here, we only point out this aspect.

```
> Laplace;  # evaluation to the table name
```

$$Laplace$$

You can use **op** or **eval** if you want to display the data structure.

```
> op( Laplace );
```

$$\text{table}([$$
$$\text{erf}(\sqrt{t}) = \frac{1}{s\sqrt{s+1}}$$
$$])$$

```
> eval( Laplace );
```

$$\text{table}([$$
$$\text{erf}(\sqrt{t}) - \frac{1}{s\sqrt{s+1}}$$
$$])$$

Removal of a table entry is done by unassignment, either by apostrophes or by **evaln**.

```
> color[ red ] := evaln( color[ red ] );
```

$$color_{red} := color_{red}$$

```
> print( color );
```

$$\text{table}([$$
$$turquoise = \text{RGB}(.7, .9, .9)$$
$$white = \text{RGB}(1, 1, 1)$$
$$])$$

```
> for c in indices( color ) do
>   color[op(c)] := evaln( color[op(c)] )
> od:
> print( color );
```

$$\text{table}([$$
$$])$$

Now you also know how to define an empty table: just enter

```
>   table([]);
```

$$\text{table}([$$
$$])$$

Or even shorter: **table()**.

Just like **array**, the procedure **table** has options available for structures of special form.

```
>   distance := table( symmetric );
```

$$distance := \text{table}(symmetric, [$$
$$])$$

```
>   distance[ Amsterdam, Brussels ]  := 157 * km:
>   distance[ Amsterdam, `Rio de Janeiro` ]  := 9512 * km:
>   print( distance );
```

$$\text{table}(symmetric, [$$
$$(\,Brussels, Amsterdam\,) = 157\,km$$
$$(\,Amsterdam, Rio\ de\ Janeiro\,) = 9512\,km$$
$$])$$

```
>   distance[ Brussels, Amsterdam ];
```

$$157\,km$$

You can define your own special indexing function in the way we explained in the previous section.

For completeness, we show in Figure 12.4 how an array or table is internally represented.

FIGURE 12.4. Internal data structure of a table.

12.6   Last Name Evaluation

Variables that point to data of type *array*, *table*, or *procedure* evaluate differently from the usual *full evaluation*. We shall illustrate this on the following example of a rotation matrix.

```
>  R := array( [ [ cos(alpha), -sin(alpha) ],
>                [ sin(alpha),  cos(alpha) ] ] );
```

$$R := \begin{bmatrix} \cos(\alpha) & -\sin(\alpha) \\ \sin(\alpha) & \cos(\alpha) \end{bmatrix}$$

```
>  R;
```

$$R$$

```
>  whattype( R );
```

$$string$$

```
>  type( R, array );
```

$$true$$

Evaluation of the variable R does not show the array. You must force full evaluation by **eval**.

```
>  eval(R);
```

$$R := \begin{bmatrix} \cos(\alpha) & -\sin(\alpha) \\ \sin(\alpha) & \cos(\alpha) \end{bmatrix}$$

Actually, the individual matrix entries are not evaluated in the last command, as can be seen from the following continuation of the session.

```
>  alpha := 1: eval(R);
```

$$\begin{bmatrix} \cos(\alpha) & -\sin(\alpha) \\ \sin(\alpha) & \cos(\alpha) \end{bmatrix}$$

```
>  R[1,2];
```

$$-\sin(1)$$

```
>  map( eval, R );
```

$$\begin{bmatrix} \cos(1) & -\sin(1) \\ \sin(1) & \cos(1) \end{bmatrix}$$

The evaluation of arrays, tables, and procedures is called *last name evaluation*. This means that the result of evaluation is the last name in the chain of values just before the final object of type *array*, *table*, or *procedure* is reached. So, in the above example, Maple evaluates R just to its own name of type *string*. Full evaluation can be forced by **eval**, or even further by **map**ping **eval**.

The effect of *last name evaluation* of arrays can of course be shown better by an example in which a variable does not evaluate itself to an array but to a name of an array.

```
>  T := S;
```

$$T := S$$

```
>  S := R;
```
$$S := R$$

```
>  eval(T,1); # value of T
```
$$S$$

```
>  eval(T,2); # value of S
```
$$R$$

```
>  eval(T,3); # value of R
```
$$\begin{bmatrix} \cos(\alpha) & -\sin(\alpha) \\ \sin(\alpha) & \cos(\alpha) \end{bmatrix}$$

```
>  map( eval, T ); # evaluation of matrix entries
```
$$\begin{bmatrix} \cos(1) & -\sin(1) \\ \sin(1) & \cos(1) \end{bmatrix}$$

```
>  T; # evaluation of T to last name
```
$$R$$

The internal data structure looks like that in Figure 12.5.

FIGURE 12.5. Internal data structure showing evaluation of arrays.

It is clear that R, S, and T all point to the same array. When you refer to the matrix element R[1,2], you get the same result as when you had chosen S[1,2] or T[1,2].

```
>  alpha := 'alpha':  # reset alpha to its name
>  R[1,2], S[1,2], T[1,2];
```
$$-\sin(\alpha), -\sin(\alpha), -\sin(\alpha)$$

When you change the matrix element S[1,2], all three matrices are simultaneously changed in the same way. The last name evaluation makes it possible to use names as synonyms.

```
>  eval(R);
```
$$\begin{bmatrix} \cos(\alpha) & -\sin(\alpha) \\ \sin(\alpha) & \cos(\alpha) \end{bmatrix}$$

```
>  S[2,1] := 0:
>  eval(R), eval(S), eval(T);
```
$$\begin{bmatrix} \cos(\alpha) & -\sin(\alpha) \\ 0 & \cos(\alpha) \end{bmatrix}, \begin{bmatrix} \cos(\alpha) & -\sin(\alpha) \\ 0 & \cos(\alpha) \end{bmatrix}, \begin{bmatrix} \cos(\alpha) & -\sin(\alpha) \\ 0 & \cos(\alpha) \end{bmatrix}$$

If you want to make a copy of the matrix and then change this copy without disturbing the original matrix, you should use the procedure **copy**.

```
>  S := copy(R):  S[1,2] := 0:
>  eval(R), eval(S);
```

$$
\begin{bmatrix} \cos(\alpha) & -\sin(\alpha) \\ 0 & \cos(\alpha) \end{bmatrix}, \begin{bmatrix} \cos(\alpha) & 0 \\ 0 & \cos(\alpha) \end{bmatrix}
$$

12.7 Function Call

You can use a function call as a record data structure. For example, a complex number in polar coordinates is represented in Maple as a function call of type **polar**(*absolute value, argument*).

```
>  polar(3,Pi/2);
```

$$
\mathrm{polar}(\,3, \frac{1}{2}\pi\,)
$$

Here, `polar(···)` works as a place holder so that other procedures can act upon the data structure.

```
>  evalc(");
```

$$
3\,I
$$

Other examples of the use of function calls as record data structures are **RootOf, DESol**, and **PIECEWISE**.

One of the nice aspects of function calls is that you yourself can define how to print the function call. For our complex number in polar coordinates you could define the following printing routine.

```
>  `print/polar` := proc(r,a) r*e^(I*a) end:
>  polar(5,Pi/3); # pretty display
```

$$
5\,e^{(\,1/3\,I\,\pi\,)}
$$

```
>  whattype(");   # still a function call
```

$$
function
$$

```
>  lprint("");   # internal representation
```

```
polar(5,1/3*Pi)
```

```
>  evalc("");
```

$$
\frac{5}{2} + \frac{5}{2}I\sqrt{3}
$$

```
>  convert(",`polar`);
```

$$
5\,e^{(\,1/3\,I\,\pi\,)}
$$

Selection of a component of a function call is done by **op**.

```
>   op(2,");
```

$$\frac{1}{3}\,\pi$$

With the **macro** facility you can make sensible names for selection operations.

```
>   macro( radius=1, argument=2 ):
>   op( radius, "" ),   op( argument, "" );
```

$$5, \frac{1}{3}\,\pi$$

Of course, you can also define procedures to select components.

```
>   macro( radius = radius ):
>   radius := proc(z)
>       if type( z, polar(anything,anything) )
>       then op(1,z)
>       else `procname(args)`
>       fi
>   end:
>   polar(5,Pi/3);
```

$$5\,e^{(1/3\,I\,\pi)}$$

```
>   radius(");
```

$$5$$

You can change a component of a function call by **subsop**.

```
>   subsop( argument = Pi/6, "" );
```

$$5\,e^{(1/6\,I\,\pi)}$$

For function calls you can easily extend library routines such as **evalf**, **simplify**, **convert**, and so on. For example, you can extend the evaluation of a complex number in floating-point arithmetic as follows.

```
>   `evalf/polar` := proc()
>       local z;
>       z := polar( evalf(args[1]), evalf(args[2]) );
>       if type( z, polar(float,float) )
>       then op(1,z) * exp( op(2,z)*I )
>       fi
>   end:
>   polar(5,Pi/3);
```

$$5\,e^{(1/3\,I\,\pi)}$$

```
>   evalf(");
```

$$2.500000001 + 4.330127019\,I$$

When **evalf** is applied to an expression that contains function calls **polar**($\cdots$), Maple searches for the definition of the procedure **evalf/polar** and, if necessary, loads it from the Maple library or from your private library. In the above session a definition of **evalf/polar** is available and can be applied.

Another example of extending Maple's facilities: conversion from polar to Cartesian coordinates.

```
>   `convert/cartesian` := proc(z)
>      local r,a;
>      if type( z, polar(anything,anything) )
>      then r := op(1,z); a := op(2,z);
>           r*cos(a) + r*I*sin(a)
>      else `procname(args)`
>      fi
>   end:
>   polar(5,Pi/3);
```

$$5\,e^{(1/3\,I\,\pi)}$$

```
>   convert( ", cartesian );
```

$$\frac{5}{2} + \frac{5}{2}\,I\,\sqrt{3}$$

```
>   polar(R,phi): " = convert( ", cartesian );
```

$$R\,e^{(I\,\phi)} = R\cos(\phi) + I\,R\sin(\phi)$$

Whenever **convert(** ..., *type*) is called, Maple searches for the definition of the procedure **convert/type** and, if necessary, loads it from the Maple library or from your private library. In the above session, a definition of **convert/cartesian** is available and can be applied to the expression.

12.8   Conversion Between Composite Data Types

You have already seen how to convert a sequence into a set or list: simply surround the object by braces or square brackets, respectively. Objects of type *set* or *list* can be converted through the function **op**. Maple also provides some explicit conversion routines for sets and lists. Below are a few examples that summarize these conversions.

```
>   mySequence := a, b, b, q;
```

$$mySequence := a, b, b, q$$

```
>   myList := [ mySequence ]; # sequence --> list
```

$$myList := [\,a, b, b, q\,]$$

```
> mySet :=  { mySequence }; # sequence --> set
```
$$mySet := \{q, a, b\}$$

```
> op( myList ); # list --> sequence
```
$$a, b, b, q$$

```
> myList[];     # list --> sequence
```
$$a, b, b, q$$

```
> op( mySet ); # set --> sequence
```
$$q, a, b$$

```
> mySet[];      # set --> sequence
```
$$q, a, b$$

```
> convert( myList, set ); # list --> set
```
$$\{q, a, b\}$$

```
> convert( mySet, list ); # set --> list
```
$$[q, a, b]$$

Such explicit conversion routines can also be used for conversions between sets and lists on the one hand, and arrays and function calls on the other hand.

```
> myArray := array( myList ); # list --> array
```
$$myArray := [a, b, b, q]$$

```
> convert( myList, array ); # list --> array
```
$$[a, b, b, q]$$

```
> convert( myArray, list ); # array --> list
```
$$[a, b, b, q]$$

```
> convert( myArray, set ); # array --> set
```
$$\{q, a, b\}$$

```
> Call := F( mySequence ); # sequence --> function call
```
$$Call := F(a, b, b, q)$$

```
> convert( Call, list );    # function --> list
```
$$[a, b, b, q]$$

```
> convert( Call, set );     # function --> set
```
$$\{q, a, b\}$$

```
> myArray2D := array( [ myList, myList ] );
```

$$myArray2D := \begin{bmatrix} a & b & b & q \\ a & b & b & q \end{bmatrix}$$

```
> convert( myArray2D, listlist ); # array --> list of lists
```

$$[[a, b, b, q], [a, b, b, q]]$$

```
> convert( ", array ); # list of lists --> array
```

$$\begin{bmatrix} a & b & b & q \\ a & b & b & q \end{bmatrix}$$

These conversions also work for higher-dimensional arrays. You can use combinations of above conversions to change the shape of lists.

```
> L := [ 1, 2, 3, 4, 5, 6, 7, 8, 9, 10, 11, 12 ]:
> matrix( 2,6, L ); # array
```

$$\begin{bmatrix} 1 & 2 & 3 & 4 & 5 & 6 \\ 7 & 8 & 9 & 10 & 11 & 12 \end{bmatrix}$$

```
> convert( ", listlist ); # array --> list
```

$$[[1, 2, 3, 4, 5, 6], [7, 8, 9, 10, 11, 12]]$$

```
> convert( matrix( 6,2, L ), listlist ):
> setattribute( ", matrix ); # display in matrix format
```

$$\begin{bmatrix} 1 & 2 \\ 3 & 4 \\ 5 & 6 \\ 7 & 8 \\ 9 & 10 \\ 11 & 12 \end{bmatrix}$$

```
> op(");
```

$$[1, 2], [3, 4], [5, 6], [7, 8], [9, 10], [11, 12]$$

```
> map(op,"");
```

$$[1, 2, 3, 4, 5, 6, 7, 8, 9, 10, 11, 12]$$

In Table 12.3 we summarize main conversions between composite data types.

$S \backslash T$	seq.	set	list	array	call
seq.		{"}	["]	array(["])	f(")
set	op(") "[]		[op(")] convert(",list)	array([op(")])	f(op(")) f("[])
list	op(") "[]	{op(")} convert(",set)		array(") convert(",array)	f(op(")) f("[])
array		convert(",set)	convert(",list)		
call	op(")	convert(",set)	convert(",list)		

TABLE 12.3. Main conversions from composite data type S to T.

12.9   Exercises

1. Let U be the set of the first ten prime numbers. Let V be the set of the first twenty natural numbers of the form $2^n - 1$.

   (a) Generate the sets U and V in Maple.

   (b) Compute $U \cup V$ and $U \cap V$.

2. (a) Generate a list of 100 randomly chosen integers between -10 and 10.

   (b) Remove all duplicate entries from this list.

   (c) Select from the list obtained in (b) all numbers which can be divided by 2 or 3.

   (d) Pick out from the list obtained in (b) all numbers greater than 5.

   (e) For each number in the list obtained in (d) compute the number of occurrences in the original list of random numbers.

3. You know of course how many solutions the equation $x^{50} - x^{20} = 0$ has over the complex numbers. When you use the procedure **solve** to solve equations, so many equations scroll over the terminal screen that it is difficult to count the number of solutions found by Maple. Use the procedures **nops** and **map** for the above-mentioned equation to count the number of solutions and to check the answers by back substitution. (Advice: to use **map** in combination with **subs** you had better consider the equation as a system of one equation in one variable.)

4. How would you double the elements in the list $[a, b, c]$ into $[a, a, b, b, c, c]$? How can you hereafter transform the list $[a, a, b, b, c, c]$ into $[[a, a], [b, b], [c, c]]$? Can you apply your methods also to the list of the first ten thousand natural numbers and get the result in reasonable time?

5. Write a procedure called **maketable** that, given a list containing indices and a list containing entries, constructs a corresponding table. For example, **maketable([red,green], [0,1/3])** should create the table associations **red** $\to 0$ and **green** $\to \frac{1}{3}$.

6. Create the 3×3 matrix M defined by

$$M_{ij} = x^{\gcd(i+1,j+1)} + 1,$$

and write it as a matrix with factored entries.

7. Create the 5×5 matrix M defined by

$$M_{ij} = 10^{-(i^2+j^2)},$$

and use the procedure **fnormal** to normalize small matrix entries into zero.

8. Create the 7×7 lower-triangular matrix M with all nonzero entries equal to one. Convert it into a list of integers using the row major order.

9. Generalize the special indexing function **tridiagonal** from §12.4 such that it can be used for banded matrices of band width ≥ 1.

10. Define a special indexing function for upper triangular matrices.

11. Define a special indexing function, say **polynomial**, which restricts entries of such arrays to polynomial type.

12. Represent the algebraic number of the form $a + b\sqrt{2}$, with a and b rational numbers, as an ordered pair.

   (a) Implement this number in Maple as the list structure [a,b]. Write procedures ADD, MUL, and DIV that add, multiply, and divide two algebraic numbers of the given type, respectively, and that deliver their result in canonical form.

   (b) Implement the above algebraic number as the function call **algnum(a,b)**. Write a procedure **print/algnum** that prints the number in the common mathematical notation $a + b\sqrt{2}$.

   (c) In the implementation of part (b), rewrite the procedures ADD, MUL, and DIV.

13

The Assume Facility

The **assume** facility allows you to specify properties of variables and expressions. This chapter is an introduction to this facility: the reasons behind it, the model, and the Maple implementation. See also [49] for a leisurely introduction to **assume**, and [189, 190, 191] for more thorough discussions of the model on which the facility is based.

13.1 The Need for an Assume Facility

The main motivation for having an **assume** facility in Maple is the following: it allows the incorporation of knowledge about the domain of a variable, hence it allows simplifications to be carried out as far as possible without sacrificing the validity of the transformations. Let us illustrate this with the example of the square root function.

```
>  expr := sqrt(x^2);
```

$$expr := \sqrt{x^2}$$

Maple does not simplify this expression automatically to x or abs(x). Both answers are incorrect in general. **simplify** considers the square root function as a multiple-valued complex function and this has some effect.

```
>  simplify( expr );
```

$$\operatorname{csgn}(x)\,x$$

The expression is transformed into one that contains the complex sign of **x**. When you are more specific on the domain of computation or on the value of **x**, then Maple will be more specific as well.

```
>   assume( x, real ):
>   simplify( expr );
```

$$\mathrm{signum}(\, x^\sim \,)\, x^\sim$$

Or if you prefer the absolute value function.

```
>   convert( ", abs );
```

$$|\, x^\sim \,|$$

```
>   assume( x>0 ):
>   simplify( expr );
```

$$x^\sim$$

```
>   assume( x<0 ):
>   simplify( expr );
```

$$-x^\sim$$

The tilde appended to the variable **x** indicates that an assumption has been made about it.

The following two examples shows that Maple can compute better results when it has more information.

```
>   integral := int( sin(a*x)/x , x=0..infinity );
```

$$integral := \frac{1}{2}\, \mathrm{signum}(\, a\,)\, \pi$$

```
>   assume( a<0 ):
>   integral;
```

$$-\frac{1}{2}\, \pi$$

```
>   integral := integrate( exp(-s*t), t=0..infinity );
```

$$integral := \lim_{t\to\infty}\, -\frac{\mathrm{e}^{(-s\,t)}}{s} + \frac{1}{s}$$

The partial result means that Maple considers the computation of a limit as an easier problem than integration. If you are more specific about **s**, Maple will be able to compute the limit.

```
>   assume( s>0 ):
>   integral;
```

$$\frac{1}{s^\sim}$$

```
>   assume( s<=0 ):
>   integral;
```

$$\infty$$

So, indeed you find with Maple that

$$\int_0^\infty e^{-st}\, dt = \begin{cases} \dfrac{1}{s} & \text{if } s > 0 \\ \infty & \text{otherwise.} \end{cases}$$

Maple actually does more than just checking the sign of a variable during computations. When, for example, the real variable c is introduced and s is assigned the square of c, then Maple can also figure out which branch of the above integral to choose.

```
>   assume( c, real ):
>   s := c^2;
```

$$s := c^{\~2}$$

Look carefully: it is c˜ raised to the power 2 and not c raised to the power -2. Another point: Maple forgets by this assignment all previous assumptions about s.

```
>   integral;
```

$$\frac{1}{c^{\~2}}$$

The above examples also illustrate that you need to make assumptions when Maple returns:

- an unevaluated **limit** for an integral;

- an answer that has not been simplified as expected or requested;

- an unevaluated **csgn**, **signum**, or **abs** function call;

- an unevaluated **Re** or **Im** function call.

A good piece of advice:

> *Specify assumptions as early as possible in a computation.*

In this way you circumvent Maple's first solving a generic problem and afterward specializing under your assumptions to a simpler but erroneous result. An example to support this point of view: in [3] the question is raised whether the following complex function V in cylindrical coordinates

$$V = \frac{1}{8\pi\epsilon_0}\left(\frac{1}{\sqrt{r^2 + (z-i)^2}} + \frac{1}{\sqrt{r^2 + (z+i)^2}}\right)$$

could be considered as an electrostatic potential of a charge density of physical meaning. The charge density σ in the plane $z = 0$ is computed by using

$$\sigma = \epsilon_0 \left(\lim_{x \downarrow 0} \frac{\partial V}{\partial z} - \lim_{x \uparrow 0} \frac{\partial V}{\partial z} \right).$$

It is reported that Maple and other computer algebra systems give the wrong result $\sigma = 0$. The session below illustrates how Maple can indeed find the correct answer by adding assumptions on r.

```
> V := 1/(8*Pi*epsilon[0]) * ( 1/sqrt(r^2+(z-I)^2) +
>    1/sqrt(r^2+(z+I)^2) );
```

$$V := \frac{1}{8} \frac{\dfrac{1}{\sqrt{r^2 + (z - I)^2}} + \dfrac{1}{\sqrt{r^2 + (z + I)^2}}}{\pi \, \varepsilon_0}$$

```
> E[z]  := - diff( V, z );
```

$$E_z := -\frac{1}{8} \frac{-\dfrac{1}{2} \dfrac{2z - 2I}{(r^2 + (z - I)^2)^{3/2}} - \dfrac{1}{2} \dfrac{2z + 2I}{(r^2 + (z + I)^2)^{3/2}}}{\pi \, \varepsilon_0}$$

```
> sigma := epsilon[0] * ( limit(E[z], z=0, right) -
>    limit( E[z], z=0, left) );
```

$$\sigma := 0$$

```
> assume( r>=1 );
> sigma := epsilon[0]*(
> limit( E[z], z=0, right) - limit( E[z], z=0, left) );
```

$$\sigma := 0$$

```
> assume( 0<r, r<1 );
> sigma := epsilon[0] * ( limit(E[z], z=0, right) -
>    limit( E[z], z=0, left) );
```

$$\sigma := -\frac{1}{2} \frac{1}{\pi \, (1 - r^{\sim 2})^{3/2}}$$

Now look what happens when you set r to $1/2$ and evaluate the last expression:

```
> r := 1/2: "";
```

$$-\frac{1}{2} \frac{1}{\pi \, (1 - r^{\sim 2})^{3/2}}$$

Why does the answer still contains $r^\sim$? The reason is as follows: when you entered assume(0<r, r<1), you actually assigned the variable r to be a new variable $r^\sim$ with the property that its range is $(0,1)$. At that point you could refer to the variable $r^\sim$ via r. Next, you computed the charge density in terms of this new variable. But then you assigned r the value $1/2$ instead of assigning r˜ this value. The charge density however still uses r˜. With the assignment r:=1/2 you also destroyed the easy way of referencing to r˜. In §3.6 we have explained this side effect of Maple's implementation of **assume** more thoroughly and we have described how to assign a value to a variable that has associated properties.

13.2   Basics of **assume**

The **assume** facility contains five basic commands and one command to extend Maple's knowledge with a new property; they are listed in Table 13.1 below.

Command	Meaning
assume	specify assumption(s)
additionally	specify additional assumption(s)
about	display current assumption(s)
is	query property
coulditbe	determine the possibility of a property
addproperty	add property to Maple's knowledge base

TABLE 13.1. Commands of **assume** facility

With the procedure **assume** you tell Maple properties about variables and relationships between variables. There are basically two formats:

$$\textbf{assume}(\ <\ inequality\ >\ )$$

and

$$\textbf{assume}(\ <\ variable\ >,\ <\ property\ >\ ).$$

When you make assumptions about an expression, thereafter the variables that are involved in the assumption print with an appended tilde to indicate that they carry assumptions. The procedure **about** displays current assumptions about variables and expressions.

An example: you can specify that r is a real constant with absolute value less than 1 in various ways.

```
>   assume( abs(r)<1 );
>   about( r );
```

```
Originally r, renamed r~:
  Involved in the following expressions with properties
    abs(`r~`) assumed RealRange(-infinity,Open(1))
  also used in the following assumed objects
  [abs(`r~`)] assumed RealRange(-infinity,Open(1))
```

```
>   assume( r, RealRange( Open(-1), Open(1) ) );
>   about( r );
```

```
Originally r, renamed r~:
  is assumed to be: RealRange(Open(-1),Open(1))
```

```
>   assume( -1<r, r<1 ):
>   about( r );
```

```
Originally r, renamed r~:
  is assumed to be: RealRange(Open(-1),Open(1))
```

The results of **about** are included so that you see that the various assumptions are not always treated in the same way.

The second last command shows that you can combine more than one assumption in one call of **assume**. Note the difference with

```
>   assume( -1<r ):
>   assume(  r<1 ):
>   about( r );
```

```
Originally r, renamed r~:
  is assumed to be: RealRange(-infinity,Open(1))
```

Whenever you make an assumption with **assume**, all previous assumptions on variables that are involved in the new assumption are discarded. At least, when the environment variable _Envadditionally has its default value false.

```
>   _Envadditionally := true:
>   assume( -1<r ):
>   about( r );
```

```
Originally r, renamed r~:
  is assumed to be: RealRange(Open(-1),Open(1))
```

Instead of setting the value of _Envadditionally to true, you can also use the procedure **additionally**.

```
>   additionally( arcsin(r),
>     RealRange( Open(-Pi/2), Open(Pi/2) ) );
>   about( r );
```

```
Originally r, renamed r~:
Involved in the following expressions with properties
arcsin(`r~`) assumed RealRange(Open(-1/2*Pi),Open(1/2*Pi))
is assumed to be: RealRange(Open(-1),Open(1))
also used in the following assumed objects
[arcsin(`r~`)] assumed RealRange(Open(-1/2*Pi),Open(1/2*Pi))
```

The following library functions know about assumptions that have been made:

csgn, signum, abs, Re, Im, frac, trunc, round, ceil, floor

For example, with the above assumption about r, Maple can compute all by itself

```
>   abs( r - 1 ), signum( r^5 - 1 );
```
$$1 - r\tilde{\ }, -1$$

You can also ask via the command **coulditbe** whether a property is in conflict with the assumptions already made or not.

```
>   coulditbe( r>-3 );    # no conflict
```
true

```
>   coulditbe( r>1/3 );   # also no conflict
```
true

The query on a property from the known properties is done in the functions listed above via the procedure **is**. You can also use this procedure to test properties yourself. Again with the previously set assumptions about r

```
>   is( r > 1/3 );   # not necessarily true
```
false

```
>   is( (1-r^2)/(1+r^2) <= 1 );
```
true

The result of **is** is either true, false, or FAIL. When **is** returns FAIL it means that it could not determine whether the desired property was true or false. This could be caused by not having sufficient information, by not being able to compute the logical derivation, or by not spending enough computing resources to determine whether the property is true, false, or undecidable. When **is** returns **true** it means that all the possible values of the expression have the desired property. When **is** returns **false** it means that at least one possible value of the expression does not have the desired property.

After the discussion of the algebra of properties and its implementation in Maple in the next two sections you will have an idea of the power of Maple with regards to properties. Here, we only note that **is** works in two modes, determined by the environment variable _EnvTry: normal mode and hard mode.

```
>   _EnvTry := normal:  # the default value
>   assume( a<=b, b<=c, c<=a );
>   is( a = c );  # successful equality test
```
true

```
>   seq( x.i >= x.(i-1), i=1..10 );
```

$$x0 \le x1, x1 \le x2, x2 \le x3, x3 \le x4, x4 \le x5, x5 \le x6, x6 \le x7,$$
$$x7 \le x8, x8 \le x9, x9 \le x10$$

```
> assume( ", x10 <= x0 ):
> is( x0 = x10 );  # test failure
```
$$FAIL$$

```
> _EnvTry := hard: # let Maple do its very best
> is( x1 = x10 );  # successful equality test
```
$$true$$

The above example leads to a discussion of two other technical points.

- **assume** does not work for indexed names, for this would among other things cause problems in commands where indices are substituted or when indices are equal to running loop indices.

- **is** is a procedure with **option remember**. This means that once the result of a test has been FAIL or whatever value, it will henceforth keep that value, no matter whether we set the value of the environment variable _EnvTry to **hard** or not. To see the effect of this variable in the above Maple session, we did not question the equality x0 = x10 for the second time, but queried another equality. You now know why.

An alternative to avoid problems with the second restriction exists; it works in general for any library function with **option remember**.

> *Whenever Maple looks up a previously computed result, whereas you want it to recompute, you can explicitly forget the previous results stored in a remember table.*

So, in the above example we can do the following.

```
> readlib( forget ): # load library function
> forget( is ):      # forget results of "is"
> _EnvTry := normal: # reset assume mode
> is( x1 = x10 );    # unsuccessful equality test
```
$$FAIL$$

13.3   An Algebra of Properties

An example of the property problem is

Given :	m and n are odd integers
Query :	is $m^2 + n$ an odd integer?

or more generally

Given :	$obj_1 \in Prop_1, \ldots, obj_n \in Prop_n$
Query :	is $f(obj_1, \ldots, obj_n) \in Prop_0$?

Such queries can be handled by manipulating the properties of the objects. Take the above example: given odd integers m and n, query "is $m^2 + n$ odd?" The problem can be split into two parts:

1. Transform the properties along with the objects: For example, if m is an odd integer, then m^2 is also an odd integer. So, with the square function is associated a mapping on properties that maps the "odd integer" property into the same property. When we go on to our example $(m, n) \mapsto m^2 + n$, where m and n are odd integers, we get the mappings

$$(m, n) \quad \rightarrow \quad add \circ (sqr,\ id)(m, n)$$

$$(\mathcal{P},\ \mathcal{P}) \quad \rightarrow \quad \overline{add \circ (sqr,\ id)}(\mathcal{P},\ \mathcal{P})$$

Here, add, sqr, and id stand for addition, the square function, and the identity function, respectively, and $\mathcal{P}$ denotes the property "odd integer."

2. Reduce the query to the problem

$$\overline{add \circ (sqr,\ id)}(\mathcal{P},\ \mathcal{P}) = \overline{add} \circ (\overline{sqr},\ \overline{id})(\mathcal{P},\ \mathcal{P}) \subseteq \mathcal{P}\ ?$$

More generally, the two steps are:

1. Transform the properties along with the objects:

$$(obj_1, \ldots, obj_n) \quad \rightarrow \quad f(obj_1, \ldots, obj_n)$$

$$(Prop_1, \ldots, Prop_n) \quad \rightarrow \quad \overline{f}(Prop_1, \ldots, Prop_n)$$

2. Reduce the query to the problem

$$\overline{f}(Prop_1, \ldots, Prop_n) \sqsubseteq Prop_0\ ?$$

where $\sqsubseteq$ is some relation on properties such that

$$obj \in Prop \Rightarrow obj \in Prop' \quad \text{iff} \quad Prop \sqsubseteq Prop'.$$

Because we shall consider a property as a set of objects that satisfy that property, $\sqsubseteq$ will be set inclusion.

Some examples of properties in Maple:

`integer`	set of integers
`odd`	set of odd integers
`RealRange(0, Open(1))`	$[0, 1) = \{x \in \mathbb{R} \mid 0 \le x < 1\}$
`monotonic`	set of monotonic real functions
`InfinitelyDifferentiable`	set of C^∞ functions
`Non(singular)`	set of nonsingular matrices

Properties form hierarchies under set inclusion. For example,

$$\texttt{posint} \subset \texttt{natural} \subset \texttt{integer}.$$

Properties like `integer`, `fraction`, or constants 0, 1 are basic properties. They can be used to build new properties with the induced lattice operators ¬, ∧, ∨:

- ¬ "not", as in "not zero" (in Maple denoted as `Non(0)`).

- ∧ "and", as in "integer and greater than 2" (in Maple denoted as `AndProp( integer, RealRange(2,infinity) )`).

- ∨ "or", as in "unary or binary" (in Maple denoted as `OrProp( unary, binary )`).

Furthermore, the top element ⊤ is introduced to represent the property "existent", i.e., there is no restriction on the object. In Maple, this property is called `TopProp`. Symmetrically, the lattice structure is completed with the bottom element ⊥ which represents the property "nonexisting," i.e., an object with this property does not exist. In Maple, the bottom element is called `BottomProp`.

Queries on composed functions are handled in the following setting. With a given object function f corresponds a property function $\overline{f}$. For example, the addition operator + induces the property operator $\overline{+}$ for which holds

$$
\begin{aligned}
\overline{+}(\texttt{odd}, \texttt{odd}) &= \texttt{even} \\
\overline{+}(\texttt{odd}, \texttt{even}) &= \texttt{odd} \\
\overline{+}(\texttt{even}, \texttt{odd}) &= \texttt{odd} \\
\overline{+}(\texttt{even}, \texttt{even}) &= \texttt{even} \\
\overline{+}(\texttt{prime}, \texttt{composite}) &= \texttt{integer} \\
\overline{+}(\texttt{fraction}, \texttt{fraction}) &= \texttt{rational} \\
\overline{+}(\texttt{irrational}, \texttt{irrational}) &= \texttt{real}
\end{aligned}
$$

And so on. Of course $\overline{f}$ need not be defined for all properties. We add some basic property functions such as $\overline{+}$, $\overline{*}$, $\overline{\ln}$, $\overline{\exp}$ and their inverses to our model and arrive at an algebra of properties that satisfies the classical lattice axioms plus some extra axioms that allow an effective calculus on properties. In fact, properties have the structure of a Boolean algebra.

13.4   Implementation of **assume**

Currently acceptable properties in Maple are

(a) *a property name*. They are categorized as follows:

alias	e.g., `realcons` instead of `AndProp(real,constant)` and instead of `RealRange(0,infinity)`.
numerical	e.g., `imaginary` and `prime`.
matricial	e.g., `SquareMatrix` and `PositiveDefinite`.
functional	e.g., `unary` and `OddMap`.
other	e.g., `TopProp` and `MutuallyExclusive`.

(b) *most types*. e.g., `integer`, `fraction`, and `rational`. This also includes constants such as 0 and 1.

(c) *a numerical range*. e.g., `RealRange(-infinity,Open(0))`.

(d) *an "and" of properties*. e.g., `AndProp( integer, positive )`.

(e) *an "or" of properties*. e.g., `OrProp( positive, negative )`.

(f) *a property range*. e.g., `PropRange(prime,integer)`. If P = $\text{PropRange}(\text{Prop}_1,\text{Prop}_2)$, then all possible objects in Prop_1 have property P, and all possible objects in P have property Prop_2.

(g) *a linear property*. e.g., `LinearProp(3,integer,0)` represents the set of integers divisible by 3.

(h) *a parametric property*. e.g., `Non(0)` and `Non(singular)`.

An exhaustive list of properties that are known to Maple can be obtained via the on-line help system: enter the command **?property**. The help page reflects the principle that the basic properties (of class (a) and (b) above) are arranged in a directed acyclic graph. Figures 13.1, 13.2, and 13.3 at the end of this chapter show the graph of the predefined numerical, matricial, and functional properties, respectively.

The specification of a property includes all parents and children in the `property/ParentTable` and `property/ChildTable`, respectively. You can ask about the place of a basic property in the directed acyclic graph with **about**. For example,

```
>  about( integer );
```

```
integer:
   a known property having {GaussianInteger, rational} as
   immediate parents and {composite, prime, 1} as immediate
   children. mutually exclusive with {irrational, fraction}
```

The procedure **addproperty** can be used to install a new property in the hierarchy of properties. For example,

```
>   alias(   nonnegative = RealRange(0,infinity),
>     nonnegbutlessthan1 = RealRange(0,Open(1)) ):
>   addproperty( nonnegbutlessthan1, {nonnegative}, {0} ):
```

The lattice of numerical properties is updated.

```
>   `property/ParentTable`[0];
```

$$\{\, composite,\ nonnegbutlessthan1 \,\}$$

```
>   `property/ParentTable`[nonnegbutlessthan1];
```

$$\{\, nonnegative \,\}$$

```
>   `property/ChildTable`[nonnegative];
```

$$\{\, \mathrm{RealRange}(\mathrm{Open}(0),\infty),\ nonnegbutlessthan1 \,\}$$

```
>   is( 1/2, nonnegbutlessthan1 );
```

$$true$$

```
>   is( Pi, nonnegbutlessthan1 );
```

$$false$$

Properties themselves are Maple objects that can satisfy other properties. Their hierarchy is shown in Figure 13.4 at the end of this chapter. So, you can ask questions like the following.

```
>   is( prime, property );
```

$$true$$

For an object function f the corresponding property function $\overline{f}$ is implemented as the procedure `property/f`. A lot of the information on the property function is stored in the remember table of the procedure. Let us use the exponential mapping as our example. By setting the interface variable **verboseproc** the value 3, Maple will also print the remember table of a procedure.

```
>   interface( verboseproc=3 ):
>   print( `property/exp` );

proc(a)
local b,c;
options remember, `Copyright 1992 Gaston Gonnet,\
Wissenschaftliches Rechnen, ETH Zurich`;
    if a::RealRange then
        if op(1,a)::{0,Open(0),identical(-infinity)} and
            op(2,a)::{0,Open(0),identical(infinity)} then
            RealRange(procname(op(1,a)),procname(op(2,a)))
        else b := procname(op(1,a)); c := procname(op(2,a));
            RealRange(b,c)
```

```
            fi
      elif a::EvalfableProp then
            PropRange(BottomProp,
                  RealRange(`property/Shake`(exp(a))))
      elif a::Open(EvalfableProp) then
            PropRange(BottomProp,
                  RealRange(`property/Shake`(exp(op(1,a)))))
      else ERROR(FAIL)
      fi
end
#  (complex) = complex
#  (real) = RealRange(Open(0),infinity)
#  (0) = 1
#  (-infinity) = Open(0)
#  (infinity) = infinity
#  (Open(0)) = Open(1)
```

The property function is used to compute with properties, but there is more. For example, what conclusion can Maple make for the exponential mapping when applied to an integer? Maple works as follows. First, it notices that the property function $\overline{\exp}$ does not give any information. So, Maple decides to investigate the direct ancestors of the property integer. But alas, the property function is not defined for GaussianInteger and rational either. So, the system continues looking at the grandparents, and with success.

$$\begin{aligned}
\overline{\exp}(\text{complex}) &= \text{complex} \\
\overline{\exp}(\text{real}) &= \text{RealRange}(\text{Open}(0), \text{infinity})
\end{aligned}$$

Maple comes to the conclusion that

$$\begin{aligned}
\overline{\exp}(\text{integer}) &\subseteq \text{AndProp}(\overline{\exp}(\text{complex}), \overline{\exp}(\text{real})) \\
&= \text{AndProp}(\text{complex}, \text{RealRange}(\text{Open}(0), \text{infinity})) \\
&= \text{RealRange}(\text{Open}(0), \text{infinity}).
\end{aligned}$$

By inspection of children and grandchildren Maple finds

$$\begin{aligned}
\overline{\exp}(\text{integer}) &\supseteq \text{OrProp}(\overline{\exp}(0), \overline{\exp}(1)) \\
&= \text{OrProp}(1, \text{PropRange}(\text{BottomProp}, \\
&\qquad \text{RealRange}(2.71828182574, 2.71828183118))) \\
&\supseteq \{1\}.
\end{aligned}$$

As far as Maple is concerned, it knows for sure that

$$\{1\} \subseteq \overline{\exp}(\text{integer}) \subseteq (0, \infty).$$

The main functions in the assume facility are **assume** and **is**. With the first function you provide Maple with information about an object, i.e., you declare the properties of an object. For example,

```
>  assume( x>0 ):
```
assigns a local variable x˜ to x and generates or updates the entry
`property/object`[x˜]. Let us inspect this table entry and see what
happens to it when we add another assumption.

```
>  `property/object`[x];
```

$$\mathrm{RealRange}(\,\mathrm{Open}(\,0\,),\infty\,)$$

```
>  additionally( x, integer );
>  `property/object`[x];
```

$$\mathrm{AndProp}(\,integer,\mathrm{RealRange}(\,1,\infty\,)\,)$$

So, all properties about an object are stored in the corresponding entry in
the table `property/object`.

To retrieve information about objects you use the procedure **is**. It applies
the rules of the algebra of properties as described in the previous section to
verify a property of an expression. For example, with the above assumptions
about x, Maple can conclude that $e^x > 1$.

```
>  is( exp(x) > 1 );
```

$$true$$

This is done in four steps:

1. Reformulate the query in terms of properties, i.e.,
   `is( exp(x˜), RealRange(Open(1), infinity) )`.

2. Express the object in terms of the known objects you start with,
   i.e., `object = exp(x˜)`.

3. Look up in the `property/object` table which properties about x˜
   exist and compute $\overline{\mathrm{exp}}(\texttt{`property/object`[x˜])}$.

4. Determine whether $\overline{\mathrm{exp}}(\texttt{`property/object`[x˜]})$ is included in the
   property `RealRange(Open(1), infinity)`. The answer is trivially
   "yes" in this case.

All queries with the procedure **is** are treated in this way:

1. Reformulate the query as `is( object, Property )`.

2. Express the object in terms of the known objects:
   `object = f( obj_1, obj_2, ..., obj_n)`.

3. Look up in the `property/object` table which properties about
   `obj_1, obj_2, ..., obj_n` exist and compute
   $\overline{\mathrm{f}}(\texttt{Prop\_1, Prop\_2, ..., Prop\_n})$.

4. Determine whether $\overline{\mathrm{f}}(\texttt{Prop\_1, Prop\_2, ..., Prop\_n})$ is included in
   `Property`.

We end this section with a peculiar consequence of the Maple implementation of the **assume** facility. Since the assumptions about an object are not associated (e.g., in the form of an attribute) to the object itself but are stored in the `property/object` table, all information is lost when you save an object in a file, leave Maple, restart the system, and finally restore the object from the file. A variation on this theme is the following session.

```
>   assume( x>0 ):
>   `property/object`[x]; # check the property about x
```
$$\text{RealRange}(\,\text{Open}(\,0\,),\infty\,)$$

```
>   xtilde := x: # keep a copy of x
>   save x, foo:
>   `property/object`[x]; # check the property about x
```
$$\text{RealRange}(\,\text{Open}(\,0\,),\infty\,)$$

All is well at this point. Next, we read the file `foo`.

```
>   read foo;
```
$$x := x^{\sim}$$

It still looks good, but

```
>   `property/object`[x];
```
$$property/object_x$$

```
>   `property/object`[xtilde];
```
$$\text{RealRange}(\,\text{Open}(\,0\,),\infty\,)$$

One `x`~ is not the other! What was saved in the file `foo` was the statement `x := x`~. Here, `x`~ is a global variable whose name contains a tilde. The object we have made an assumption about is a local variable `x`~, but after reading the file it can only be referred to by the variable `xtilde`. A remedy is that you save not only the variable, but also the property table.

```
>   save xtilde, `property/object`, foo:
>   read foo:
>   `property/object`[xtilde];
```
$$\text{RealRange}(\,\text{Open}(\,0\,),\infty\,)$$

This example shows that the current assume facility in Maple can still be improved considerably and can still be made more complete and robust. Notwithstanding the limitations and peculiarities it is an important step forward to correctness of computational work in Maple.

13.5   Exercises

1. Compute $\cos(n\pi)$ and $\sin(n\frac{\pi}{2})$ under the assumptions that n is

   - an integer.

   - an odd integer.

   - an odd and positive integer less than 3.

2. Add the interval (-1,1) to the hierarchy of numerical properties.

3. A natural number is called perfect when it is one more than the sum of its nontrivial divisors (e.g., $6 = 2 + 3 + 1$ and $28 = 2 + 4 + 7 + 14 + 1$ are perfect). Add the prefect numbers to the hierarchy of numerical properties.

4. An $n \times n$ matrix A is called skew-diagonal if $A_{ij} = 0$ unless $i + j = n + 1$. Add the property **skewdiagonal** to Maple's knowledge base.

13.6   Hierarchy of Properties

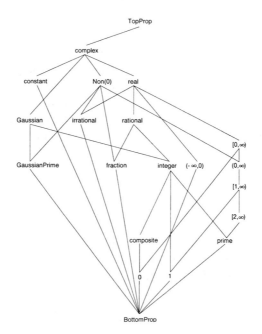

FIGURE 13.1. Hierarchy of numerical properties.

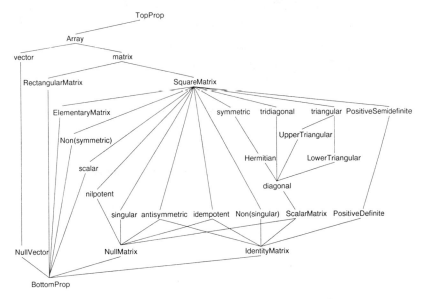

FIGURE 13.2. Hierarchy of properties on matrices.

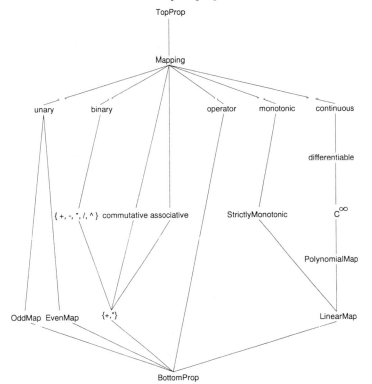

FIGURE 13.3. Hierarchy of functional properties.

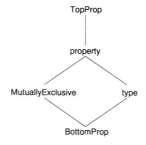

FIGURE 13.4. Hierarchy of miscellaneous properties.

14
Simplification

In Chapter 7 we discussed manipulation of polynomials and rational functions. Manipulations such as normalization, collection, sorting, factorization, and expansion were discussed. Characteristic of these manipulations is that they are carried out on expressions as a whole. However, in computations that involve mathematical functions, you frequently want to apply simplification rules that are known for these mathematical functions. For example, in computations that involve trigonometric functions you often want to apply the equality $\sin^2 + \cos^2 = 1$. This chapter describes how simplifications of expressions containing mathematical functions can be performed, how valid the simplifications offered by Maple are, how simplification can be controlled, and how you can define your own simplification routines or overrule existing Maple routines.

After a short introduction to automatic simplification, the procedures **expand**, **combine**, **simplify**, and **convert** will be described. One of Maple's specialities is that the system itself finds out which mathematical functions are involved and which transformation rules are available. This is another example of Maple's *hybrid algorithmic structure*.

For each simplification procedure we shall look at its effect on trigonometric functions, exponential function and logarithms, powers, radical expressions, and other functions, respectively. In three separate sections, extra attention will be paid to trigonometric simplification, to simplification of expressions with respect to side relations, and to control of the simplification process. We shall also show how to define your own simplification routines and how to overrule Maple's simplification. At the end of this chapter an overview of possible simplifications is given in tabular form.

14.1 Automatic Simplification

Let us first look at some automatic simplifications in Maple.

```
> arcsin(1/2), Zeta(2), GAMMA(1/2), Psi(1/2);
```

$$\frac{1}{6}\,\pi, \frac{1}{6}\,\pi^2, \sqrt{\pi}, -\gamma - 2\ln(2)$$

```
> min( 3, Pi, cos(1)*3 );
```

$$3\cos(1)$$

```
> tan( arctan(x) ),   arctan( tan(x) );
```

$$x, \arctan(\tan(x))$$

```
> sqrt(Pi^2*x^2);
```

$$\pi\sqrt{x^2}$$

```
> ´abs( abs(x) )´ = abs( abs(x) );
```

$$||x|| = |x|$$

```
> ´abs(-Pi*x)´ = abs(-Pi*x);
```

$$|-\pi x| = \pi\,|x|$$

```
> ´sin(-x)´ = sin(-x), ´cos(Pi/2+x)´ = cos(Pi/2+x);
```

$$\sin(-x) = -\sin(x), \cos(\frac{1}{2}\,\pi + x) = -\sin(x)$$

```
> ´exp(3*ln(x))´ = exp(3*ln(x));
```

$$e^{(3\ln(x))} = x^3$$

```
> ln(exp(x)), exp(ln(x));
```

$$\ln(e^x), x$$

```
> assume( x, ´real´ );
> ln( exp(x) );
```

$$x\widetilde{}$$

```
> signum( exp(1)+exp(x));
```

$$1$$

In §1.3 you have already been warned that not all automatic simplifications are valid in full generality; sometimes they only work for the generic case. For example, the automatic simplifications $0 \cdot x \longrightarrow 0$, $(x - x) \longrightarrow 0$, and $x/x \longrightarrow 1$ are desirable (if only for efficiency reasons) but incorrect when x is undefined, a random number, or infinity. The simplification $(x - x) \longrightarrow 0$ has the following side effect in Maple.

```
> limit( exp(1/x), x=0 ) - limit( exp(-1/x), x=0 );
```

$$0$$

The automatic simplification of $0^k \longrightarrow 0$, for all k, has the following side effect in Maple.

```
>   sum( a[k]*x^k, k = 0..n );
```

$$\sum_{k=0}^{n} a_k\, x^k$$

```
>   eval(subs( x=0, " ));
```

$$0$$

The automatic simplification of $\exp\big(\ln(x)\big) \longrightarrow x$ is incorrect for $x \neq 0$ but nevertheless carried out in Maple without scruples.

The above examples show a trade-off between usability and efficiency on the one hand and mathematical correctness on the other hand. Be aware that Maple like most, if not all, computer algebra systems performs automatic simplifications that are not 100% safe.

Automatic simplifications of multiple-valued functions represented by principal values are another source of problems for many systems. The developers have put much effort in correct handling of complex multiple-valued functions in Maple V Release 4. Automatic simplifications are limited to those that are provable correct (with the above exception of $\exp\big(\ln(x)\big) \longrightarrow x$). For example,

```
>   sqrt(Pi^2*x^2);
```

$$\pi \sqrt{x^2}$$

is not further simplified to

```
>   sqrt( Pi^2*x^2, 'symbolic' );
```

$$\pi x$$

For this, you have to make further assumptions or, as we did, use the keyword **symbolic** to do whatever simplification without justification.

But you must keep alert and understand that simplification of multiple-valued functions is still not 100% safe. As you will see in this chapter, Maple allows you to apply simplifications that are valid for the generic case but not valid in all cases. A frightful example:

```
>   ln( exp(x) );  # no automatic simplification
```

$$\ln(\,e^x\,)$$

```
>   simplify( ", ln );    # no harm done
```

$$\ln(\,e^x\,)$$

```
>   simplify( ", exp );   # no harm done
```

$$\ln(\,e^x\,)$$

```
>  simplify( ", {ln,exp} ); # possibly incorrect
```
$$x$$

The latter simplification is only correct when the argument of the complex number x is between $-\pi$ and π (inclusive). You may say that when you push Maple hard, you will get what you asked for, whether it is mathematically correct or not. But such simplifications are often the cause of incorrect results of a computation. If you are not convinced that caution in use of software is needed, you should look at [57, 111, 175], where similar surprising results are described.

14.2   expand

In general, the procedure **expand** does credit to its name and works out an expression. For mathematical functions, this often means that sum rules are applied.

- **Trigonometric and hyperbolic functions**

```
>  cos(2*x):    " = expand(");
```
$$\cos(2x) = 2\cos(x)^2 - 1$$

```
>  cos(5*x):    " = expand(");
```
$$\cos(5x) = 16\cos(x)^5 - 20\cos(x)^3 + 5\cos(x)$$

```
>  cosh(5*x):    " = expand(");
```
$$\cosh(5x) = 16\cosh(x)^5 - 20\cosh(x)^3 + 5\cosh(x)$$

```
>  tan(2*x):    " = expand(");
```
$$\tan(2x) = 2\,\frac{\tan(x)}{1 - \tan(x)^2}$$

```
>  tanh(2*x):    " = expand(");
```
$$\tanh(2x) = 2\,\frac{\sinh(x)\cosh(x)}{2\cosh(x)^2 - 1}$$

```
>  cos(x+y):    " = expand(");
```
$$\cos(x + y) = \cos(x)\cos(y) - \sin(x)\sin(y)$$

```
>  cos(x+2*y):  " = expand(");
```
$$\cos(x + 2y) = 2\cos(x)\cos(y)^2 - \cos(x) - 2\sin(x)\sin(y)\cos(y)$$

```
>  cos(x*(y+z)):    " = expand(");
```
$$\cos(x(y + z)) = \cos(xy)\cos(xz) - \sin(xy)\sin(xz)$$

Two aspects catch the eye in the above example:

(1) The procedure **expand** works out a trigonometric or hyperbolic function over a sum or a multiple. The above examples illustrate again that expansion of trigonometric functions is done as far as possible. A partial expansion like $\cos 5x \longrightarrow \cos x \cos 4x - \sin x \sin 4x$ cannot be done so easily with **expand**. You will have to make do with tricks like

```
>   cos(5*x);
```

$$\cos(5x)$$

```
>   subs( 5*x = x + y, " );
```

$$\cos(x+y)$$

```
>   expand(");
```

$$\cos(x)\cos(y) - \sin(x)\sin(y)$$

```
>   subs( y = 4*x, " );
```

$$\cos(4x)\cos(x) - \sin(x)\sin(4x).$$

Or you must, on the basis of the following source code of **expand/cos**, reprogram the expansion procedure such that the recursive step is taken out of the code.

```
>   interface( verboseproc=2 ):  # make Maple more verbose
>   print( readlib( `expand/cos` ) );  # print source code
```

```
proc(x)
local n,y;
options 'Copyright 1991 by the University of Waterloo';
    y := expand(x);
    if type(y,'+') then
        n := op(1,y); y := y-n; expand(cos(n)*cos(y)-sin(n)*sin(y))
    elif type(y,'*') then
        n := op(1,y);
        if type(n,numeric) and n < 0 then expand(cos(-y))
        elif type(n,integer) and 0 < n and n < 100 then
            y := y/n; expand(2*cos((n-1)*y)*cos(y)-cos((n-2)*y))
        else cos(y)
        fi
    else cos(y)
    fi
end
```

```
>   expand(cos(5*x));  # an example
```

$$16\cos(x)^5 - 20\cos(x)^3 + 5\cos(x)$$

The new code could be as follows:

```
>  `expand/cos` := proc(x)
>  local n,y;
>     y := expand(x);
>     if type(y,`+`) then
>         n := op(1,y);
>         y := y-n;
>         cos(n)*cos(y)-sin(n)*sin(y)
>     elif type(y,`*`) then
>           n := op(1,y);
>           if type(n,numeric) and n < 0 then expand(cos(-y))
>           elif type(n,integer) and 0 < n and n < 100 then
>               y := y/n;
>               2*cos((n-1)*y)*cos(y)-cos((n-2)*y)
>           else cos(y)
>           fi
>     else cos(y)
>     fi
>  end:
```

It will not work immediately as **expand** remembers its previous results, and we already expanded cos(5x) as $16\cos^5 x - 20\cos^3 x + 5\cos x$. Use **forget** with the option `reinitialize=false` to clear the remember table but not re-readlib'ing the original copy of the routines involved.

```
>  readlib(forget)( expand, reinitialize = false ):
>  expand( cos(5*x) );
```

$$16 \cos(x)^5 - 20 \cos(x)^3 + 5 \cos(x)$$

By the way, the remember option of **expand** explains why in the next step in the recursion

```
>  expand(");
```

$$16 \cos(x)^5 - 16 \cos(x)^3 + 3 \cos(x) - 2 \cos(2x) \cos(x)$$

no terms cos(3x) occur anymore. In §14.9 we shall discuss how you can best overrule existing Maple routines.

(2) A tangent (and also a cotangent) is expanded into a rational expression consisting of tangents, but the hyperbolic tangent (and hyperbolic cotangent) is expanded in terms of hyperbolic sines and cosines.

```
>  tan(x+y):   " = expand(");
```

$$\tan(x+y) = \frac{\tan(y) + \tan(x)}{1 - \tan(y)\tan(x)}$$

```
>  tanh(x+y):   " = expand(");
```

$$\tanh(x+y) = \frac{\sinh(x)\cosh(y) + \cosh(x)\sinh(y)}{\cosh(x)\cosh(y) + \sinh(x)\sinh(y)}$$

In §14.9 we shall show how you can redefine the expansion routine of the hyperbolic tangent so that consistency with the corresponding trigonometric function is established.

- **exp, ln**

  > exp(x+y):   " = expand(");
  $$e^{(x+y)} = e^x\, e^y$$

  > ln(x*y):   " = expand(");
  $$\ln(xy) = \ln(x) + \ln(y)$$

  > ln(x^y):   " = expand(");
  $$\ln(x^y) = y\ln(x)$$

  > ln(x/y):   " = expand(");
  $$\ln\left(\frac{x}{y}\right) = \ln(x) - \ln(y)$$

  > exp(x*(y+z)): " = expand(");
  $$e^{(x(y+z))} = e^{(xy)}\, e^{(xz)}$$

The responsibility for whether a transformation rule is valid or not is shifted to the user: e.g., the transformation $\ln(xy) \longrightarrow \ln x + \ln y$ is not valid in general (see what happens when you substitute $x = y = -1$), but the system is always willing to do the transformation when asked to.

- **Powers and radicals**

  > x^(y+z):   " = expand(");
  $$x^{(y+z)} = x^y\, x^z$$

  > (x*y)^z: " = expand(");
  $$(xy)^z = x^z\, y^z$$

  > (-x)^y: " = expand(");
  $$(-x)^y = (-1)^y\, x^y$$

  > (x/y)^z: " = expand(");
  $$\left(\frac{x}{y}\right)^z = x^z\left(\frac{1}{y}\right)^z$$

  > x^(y/3):   " = expand(");
  $$x^{(1/3\,y)} = (x^y)^{1/3}$$

  > (x^(1/2))^(y/2): " = expand(");
  $$(\sqrt{x})^{(1/2\,y)} = x^{(1/4\,y)}$$

We repeat: not all transformations done by **expand** are 100% safe. For example, the transformation $(x\,y)^z \longrightarrow x^z\,y^z$ is not valid in general; substitution of $x = y = -1, z = 1/2$ is a convincing example.

```
>  (x*y)^z:  " = expand(");
```

$$(x\,y)^z = x^z\,y^z$$

```
>  subs( { x=-1, y=-1, z=1/2}, " );
```

$$1 = -1$$

It is the responsibility of the user to verify whether the transformation is valid or not in a particular case. He or she should pay extra attention when a symbolic computation with simplification is carried out and afterward concrete values are substituted in the result; all transformations during the computation were not necessarily valid for the specified values. Such mistakes occur quite often and the phenomenon is known as the *problem of specialization*.

• Other expansions

Other simplifications with **expand** are expansion of factorized natural numbers, expansion of factorials, binomial coefficients and the Gamma function, and simplifications of determinants of products and powers of matrices. Some examples:

```
>  (n+1)!:  " = expand(");
```

$$(n + 1)! = n!\,(n + 1)$$

```
>  binomial(n+1,k+1):  " = expand(");
```

$$\text{binomial}(n + 1, k + 1) = \frac{(n + 1)\,\text{binomial}(n, k)}{k + 1}$$

```
>  binomial(n-1,k-1) + binomial(n-1,k);
```

$$\text{binomial}(n - 1, k - 1) + \text{binomial}(n - 1, k)$$

```
>  expand(");
```

$$\frac{k\,\text{binomial}(n, k)}{n} + \frac{(n - k)\,\text{binomial}(n, k)}{n}$$

```
>  normal(");
```

$$\text{binomial}(n, k)$$

```
>  ifactor(123456789):  " = expand(");
```

$$(3)^2\,(3803)\,(3607) = 123456789$$

```
> BesselJ(5,t):  " = expand(");
```

$$\mathrm{BesselJ}(\,5,t\,) = 384\,\frac{\mathrm{BesselJ}(\,1,t\,)}{t^4} - 192\,\frac{\mathrm{BesselJ}(\,0,t\,)}{t^3}$$

$$- 72\,\frac{\mathrm{BesselJ}(\,1,t\,)}{t^2} + 12\,\frac{\mathrm{BesselJ}(\,0,t\,)}{t} + \mathrm{BesselJ}(\,1,t\,)$$

```
> collect( ", BesselJ );  # group terms
```

$$\mathrm{BesselJ}(\,5,t\,) =$$
$$(\,\frac{384}{t^4} - \frac{72}{t^2} + 1\,)\,\mathrm{BesselJ}(\,1,t\,) + (\,-\frac{192}{t^3} + \frac{12}{t}\,)\,\mathrm{BesselJ}(\,0,t\,)$$

```
> Zeta(50):  " = expand(");
```

$$\zeta(\,50\,) =$$
$$\frac{3960457641928637185699 8202}{28525877145754676446336363 52523744141832543652343 75}\,\pi^{50}$$

```
> dilog(1/x):  " = expand(");
```

$$\mathrm{dilog}(\,\frac{1}{x}\,) = -\mathrm{dilog}(\,x\,) - \frac{1}{2}\ln(\,x\,)^2$$

```
> M := array(1..4,1..4):
> det(M^3):  " = expand(");
```

$$\det(\,M^3\,) = \det(\,M\,)^3$$

```
> det(3*M):  " = expand(");
```

$$\det(\,3\,M\,) = 81\det(\,M\,)$$

What remains to be told is how you can prevent expansions of particular nonrational functions in an expression. This is important because more than one mathematical function may be part of a symbolic expression, but you may not want all functions expanded. For example, suppose that you only want to expand the exponential function in the expression $\sin(x+y) + \exp(x+y)$. When you apply **expand** with the expression as the sole parameter, the effect will be that the expression is fully expanded. Only when you add the keyword **sin** as an extra argument in the function call, is this trigonometric function left intact.

```
> expression := sin(x+y) + exp(x+y);
```

$$\mathit{expression} := \sin(\,x+y\,) + e^{(\,x+y\,)}$$

```
> expand( expression );
```

$$\sin(\,x\,)\cos(\,y\,) + \cos(\,x\,)\sin(\,y\,) + e^x\,e^y$$

```
> expand( expression, sin );
```

$$\sin(x+y) + e^x\,e^y$$

It is the same mechanism described in §7.1: the extra arguments in **expand** specify what should be left untouched.

```
> expand( sin( x^sin(y+z) + w ), x^sin(y+z) );
```

$$\sin(x^{\sin(y+z)})\cos(w) + \cos(x^{\sin(y+z)})\sin(w)$$

```
> expand( ( cos(2*x) + sin(2*y) )^2, cos, sin );
```

$$\cos(2x)^2 + 2\cos(2x)\sin(2y) + \sin(2y)^2$$

If you want to avoid expansion of *all* nonrational functions, then you can use the Maple procedure **frontend**.

```
> frontend( expand, [expression^2] );
```

$$\sin(x+y)^2 + 2\sin(x+y)\,e^{(x+y)} + (e^{(x+y)})^2$$

When you know beforehand that you will not need expansion of certain nonrational functions for some time, then you can inform Maple with the procedure **expandoff**.

```
> expand( expandoff() ):  # enable library function
> expandoff( sin ):  # turn off expansion of sin
> expression := sin(p+q) + exp(p+q);
```

$$expression := \sin(p+q) + e^{(p+q)}$$

```
> expand( expression );
```

$$\sin(p+q) + e^p\,e^q$$

Perhaps you (still) wonder why we have rewritten the previous expression in **x** and **y** in new unknowns **p** and **q**. Well, if we had not done this, Maple would have remembered that the command **expand(expression)** had been entered before, and consequently would have picked up the previous result from the remember table of **expand** instead of recomputing it. See for yourself, using the opposite **expandon** of **expandoff**.

```
> expandon( sin ):  # turn on expansion of sin
> expand( expression );
```

$$\sin(p+q) + e^p\,e^q$$

As shown before in this section, we could have used the library function **forget** to clear the remember table of **expand**.

In §14.8 we shall investigate in more detail how to control the simplification process.

14.3   **combine**

When a computer algebra system provides facilities to expand expressions you may expect the existence of a procedure to do the opposite, i.e., to combine expressions. Be aware of the fact that Maple often leaves it up to the user to verify validity of a combination.

```
>  sqrt(x) * sqrt(y):   " = combine(");
```

$$\sqrt{x}\sqrt{y} = \sqrt{xy}$$

This equality does not hold for all values of x and y.

```
>  subs( {x=-1,y=-1}, " );
```

$$-1 = 1$$

Another example: combination of divergent sums.

```
>  Sum( 1/(2*k), k=1..infinity ) -
>  Sum( 1/(2*k-1), k=1..infinity );
```

$$\left(\sum_{k=1}^{\infty} \left(\frac{1}{2} \frac{1}{k} \right) \right) - \left(\sum_{k=1}^{\infty} \frac{1}{2k-1} \right)$$

```
>  value(");    # correct error message
```

`Error, (in value) invalid cancellation of infinity`

```
>  combine("); # combine sums without checking conditions
```

$$\sum_{k=1}^{\infty} \left(\frac{1}{2} \frac{1}{k} - \frac{1}{2k-1} \right)$$

```
>  value(");
```

$$-\ln(2)$$

• **Trigonometric and hyperbolic functions**

combine transforms a polynomial in sines and cosines into the finite Fourier form by successive application of the rules

$$\sin x \, \sin y \quad \longrightarrow \quad \frac{1}{2} \cos(x-y) - \frac{1}{2} \cos(x+y),$$

$$\sin x \, \cos y \quad \longrightarrow \quad \frac{1}{2} \sin(x-y) + \frac{1}{2} \sin(x+y),$$

$$\cos x \, \cos y \quad \longrightarrow \quad \frac{1}{2} \cos(x-y) + \frac{1}{2} \cos(x+y).$$

```
>  2*sin(x)*cos(x):   " = combine(");
```

$$2\sin(x)\cos(x) = \sin(2x)$$

```
> sin(x)^3:  " = combine(");
```

$$\sin(x)^3 = -\frac{1}{4}\sin(3x) + \frac{3}{4}\sin(x)$$

Similar transformations hold for hyperbolic functions:

$$\sinh x \, \sinh y \quad \longrightarrow \quad \frac{1}{2}\cosh(x+y) - \frac{1}{2}\cosh(x-y),$$

$$\sinh x \, \cosh y \quad \longrightarrow \quad \frac{1}{2}\sinh(x+y) + \frac{1}{2}\sinh(x-y),$$

$$\cosh x \, \cosh y \quad \longrightarrow \quad \frac{1}{2}\cosh(x+y) + \frac{1}{2}\cosh(x-y).$$

```
> cosh(x)^5:  " = combine(");
```

$$\cosh(x)^5 = \frac{1}{16}\cosh(5x) + \frac{5}{16}\cosh(3x) + \frac{5}{8}\cosh(x)$$

When you want to use the Maple procedure **combine**, exclusively for combination of trigonometric functions, then you must say so via the option **trig**. Compare

```
> sqrt(cos(x)^2) * sqrt(sin(x)^2);
```

$$\sqrt{\cos(x)^2}\,\sqrt{\sin(x)^2}$$

```
>  " = combine(");
```

$$\sqrt{\cos(x)^2}\,\sqrt{\sin(x)^2} = \frac{1}{4}\sqrt{2 - 2\cos(4x)}$$

```
>  "" = combine( "", `trig` );
```

$$\sqrt{\cos(x)^2}\,\sqrt{\sin(x)^2} = \frac{1}{4}\sqrt{2\cos(2x) + 2}\,\sqrt{2 - 2\cos(2x)}$$

Strangely enough, you also have to supply the keyword **trig** for hyperbolic functions instead of the keyword **trigh** as you may expect.

```
> sqrt( cosh(x)^2-1) * sqrt(cosh(x)^2+1);
```

$$\sqrt{\cosh(x)^2 - 1}\,\sqrt{\cosh(x)^2 + 1}$$

```
>  " =  combine( ", `trig` );
```

$$\sqrt{\cosh(x)^2 - 1}\,\sqrt{\cosh(x)^2 + 1} = \frac{1}{4}\sqrt{2\cosh(2x) - 2}\,\sqrt{2\cosh(2x) + 6}$$

• **exp, ln**

combine combines expressions in which the exponential function and logarithm occur according to the rules

$$\exp x \exp y \;\longrightarrow\; \exp(x+y),$$
$$\exp(x+n\ln y) \;\longrightarrow\; y^n \exp(x), \text{ for } n \in \mathbb{Z},$$
$$(\exp x)^n \;\longrightarrow\; \exp(n\,x), \text{ for } n \in \mathbb{Z},$$
$$y \ln x \;\longrightarrow\; \ln(x^y), \text{ for } y \in \mathbb{Q}, \text{ and } y\arg(x) = \arg(x^y),$$
$$\ln x + \ln y \;\longrightarrow\; \ln(x\,y), \text{ provided } \arg(x) + \arg(y) = \arg(x\,y).$$

In the logarithmic case, Maple only carries out those combinations that are provable correct.

```
>  exp(x)* exp(y)^(2):   " = combine(");
```
$$e^x \left(e^y\right)^2 = e^{(x+2\,y)}$$

```
>  x*ln(2) + 3*ln(x)+4*ln(5):   " = combine(");
```
$$x\ln(2) + 3\ln(x) + 4\ln(5) = x\ln(2) + 3\ln(x) + \ln(625)$$

```
>  ln(x) + ln(2) + ln(y) - ln(3):   " = combine(");
```
$$\ln(x) + \ln(2) + \ln(y) - \ln(3) = \ln(2\,x) + \ln\left(\frac{1}{3}\,y\right)$$

```
>  exp( x - 2*ln(y) ): " = combine(");
```
$$e^{(x-2\ln(y))} = \frac{e^x}{y^2}$$

Suppose that you really want the combination $\ln x + \ln y \longrightarrow \ln(x\,y)$ to be carried out by Maple. Then you can enforce this by adding the keyword **symbolic** to the function specific call of **combine**.

```
>  expression := ln(x) + 1/2*ln(y) - ln(z);
```
$$expression := \ln(x) + \frac{1}{2}\ln(y) - \ln(z)$$

```
>  combine( expression, ln );   # by default, nothing done
```
$$\ln(x) + \frac{1}{2}\ln(y) - \ln(z)$$

```
>  expression: " = combine( ", ln, 'symbolic' );
```
$$\ln(x) + \frac{1}{2}\ln(y) - \ln(z) = \ln\left(\frac{x\sqrt{y}}{z}\right)$$

Actually, you have more control of the simplification process. For example, you may restrict combination to logarithmic terms with integer coefficients.

```
>  expression: " = combine( ", ln, integer, 'symbolic' );
```
$$\ln(x) + \frac{1}{2}\ln(y) - \ln(z) = \frac{1}{2}\ln(y) + \ln\left(\frac{x}{z}\right)$$

```
>  expression: " = combine( ", ln, 'positive', 'symbolic' );
```

$$\ln(x) + \frac{1}{2}\ln(y) - \ln(z) = -\ln(z) + \ln(x\sqrt{y})$$

The type **anything** is useful in the generic case.

```
>  expression := m*ln(x) + n*ln(y) + 3*ln(z);
```

$$expression := m\ln(x) + n\ln(y) + 3\ln(z)$$

```
>  expression:   " = combine( ", ln, 'symbolic' );
```

$$m\ln(x) + n\ln(y) + 3\ln(z) = m\ln(x) + n\ln(y) + \ln(z^3)$$

```
>  expression:   " = combine( ", ln, string, 'symbolic' );
```

$$m\ln(x) + n\ln(y) + 3\ln(z) = 3\ln(z) + \ln(x^m\, y^n)$$

```
>  expression:   " = combine( ", ln, anything,
>     'symbolic' );
```

$$m\ln(x) + n\ln(y) + 3\ln(z) = \ln(x^m\, y^n\, z^3)$$

Possible ways of having the transformations

$$n\ln y \longrightarrow \ln(y^n)$$

and

$$\exp(x + n\ln y) \longrightarrow y^n\exp(x)$$

carried out via **combine** regardless of the type of n are the following:

```
>  y*ln(x): combine( ", ln, anything, 'symbolic' );
```

$$\ln(x^y)$$

```
>  exp( x+n*ln(y) ):
>  " = map( combine, ", ln, anything, 'symbolic' );
```

$$e^{(x+n\ln(y))} = e^{(x+\ln(y^n))}$$

```
>  combine(");
```

$$e^{(x+n\ln(y))} = y^n\, e^x$$

• **Powers and radicals**

The two most important **combine** rules for powers are

$$x^y\, x^z \quad\longrightarrow\quad x^{y+z},$$
$$(x^y)^z \quad\longrightarrow\quad x^{yz}.$$

The Maple procedure **combine** is not very good in recognizing that powers are involved in an expression. For example,

```
>  combine( x^y * x^z );
```

$$x^y\, x^z$$

has no effect, but

```
> combine( x^y * x^z, `power` );
```
$$x^{(y+z)}$$

does the job. By adding the keyword **symbolic** you can enforce transformations that are not 100% valid.

```
> combine( (x^y)^z, `power` );
```
$$(x^y)^z$$

```
> " = combine( ", `power`, `symbolic` );
```
$$(x^y)^z = x^{(yz)}$$

Another option in this class is for powers with rational exponents: **radical**. It takes care mainly of the transformation $x^{(m/d)} y^{(n/d)} \longrightarrow (x^m y^n)^{(1/d)}$, where x and y are both positive, m, n, and d are integers such that $|m| < d$, $|n| < d$, and $d > 1$. By omitting the keyword, **combine** sometimes does too much radical simplification.

```
> x^(1/4) * y^(1/4);
```
$$x^{1/4} y^{1/4}$$

```
> combine( ", radical ); # no simplification
```
$$x^{1/4} y^{1/4}$$

```
> combine("); # too much simplification
```
$$(xy)^{1/4}$$

Let us look at some more examples of simplification of powers and radicals.

```
> (1/2)^m * (1/2)^n:   " = combine( ", `power` );
```
$$\left(\frac{1}{2}\right)^m \left(\frac{1}{2}\right)^n = 2^{(-m-n)}$$

```
> combine( (x^y)^z, `power` );
```
$$(x^y)^z$$

```
> " = combine( ", `power`, `symbolic` );
```
$$(x^y)^z = x^{(yz)}$$

```
> x^y / x^(2/3):   " = combine( ", `power` );
```
$$\frac{x^y}{x^{2/3}} = x^{(y-2/3)}$$

```
> 2^(1/3) * (x+1)^(1/3):   " = combine( ", radical );
```
$$2^{1/3}(x+1)^{1/3} = (2x+2)^{1/3}$$

• Other combinations

Other applications of **combine** are combinations of expressions involving square roots, arctangents, and polylogarithms, and rearrangements of expressions to get rid of minus signs.

```
>  sqrt(x) * sqrt(y):   " = combine(");
```
$$\sqrt{x}\,\sqrt{y} = \sqrt{x\,y}$$

```
>  arctan(x) + arctan(1/x):   " = combine(");
```
$$\arctan(x) + \arctan(\frac{1}{x}) = \frac{1}{2}\operatorname{signum}(x)\,\pi$$

```
>  arctan(1/2) + arctan(1/3):   " = combine(");
```
$$\arctan(\frac{1}{2}) + \arctan(\frac{1}{3}) = \frac{1}{4}\pi$$

```
>  combine( arctan(x) + arctan(y) );
```
$$\arctan(x) + \arctan(y)$$

```
>  " = combine( ", arctan, ´symbolic´ );
```
$$\arctan(x) + \arctan(y) = \arctan(\frac{x+y}{1-x\,y})$$

```
>  polylog(2,z) + polylog(2,1-z):   " = combine(");
```
$$\operatorname{polylog}(2,z) + \operatorname{polylog}(2,1-z) = \frac{1}{6}\pi^2 - \ln(z)\ln(1-z)$$

```
>  -(-x+1)/x:   " = combine(");
```
$$-\frac{-x+1}{x} = \frac{x-1}{x}$$

14.4   simplify

simplify is Maple's general purpose simplification routine.

• Trigonometric and hyperbolic functions

Rational expressions in which trigonometric functions and hyperbolic functions occur are normalized by **simplify** according to the rules

$$\sin^2 x \longrightarrow 1 - \cos^2 x,$$
$$\sinh^2 x \longrightarrow \cosh^2(x) - 1,$$
$$\tan x \longrightarrow \frac{\sin x}{\cos x},$$
$$\tanh x \longrightarrow \frac{\sinh x}{\cosh x}.$$

More precisely, powers of sines and hyperbolic sines with exponent greater than one are simplified by the above rules as much as possible. The tangent and hyperbolic tangent rule is only applied in the presence of other trigonometric functions.

```
> cosh(x)^2 - sinh(x)^2:  " = simplify(");
```
$$\cosh(x)^2 - \sinh(x)^2 = 1$$

```
> sinh(x)^3:  " = simplify(");
```
$$\sinh(x)^3 = -\sinh(x) + \sinh(x)\cosh(x)^2$$

```
> 2*sin(x) / ( 1 + tan(x)^2 ):  " = simplify(");
```
$$2\,\frac{\sin(x)}{1 + \tan(x)^2} = 2\sin(x)\cos(x)^2$$

If you prefer the rule $\cos^2 x \rightarrow 1 - \sin^2 x$ to the rule $\sin^2 x \rightarrow 1 - \cos^2 x$, then you should simplify with respect to side relations. We shall discuss simplification with respect to side relations in detail in §14.7.

```
> sin(x)^3 + cos(x)^3;
```
$$\sin(x)^3 + \cos(x)^3$$

```
> simplify(");
```
$$\cos(x)^3 + \sin(x) - \sin(x)\cos(x)^2$$

```
> simplify( "", {cos(x)^2+sin(x)^2=1}, [sin(x),cos(x)] );
```
$$\cos(x)^3 + \sin(x) - \sin(x)\cos(x)^2$$

```
> simplify( """, {cos(x)^2+sin(x)^2=1}, [cos(x),sin(x)] );
```
$$\sin(x)^3 + \cos(x) - \cos(x)\sin(x)^2$$

If you want to specify trigonometric simplification only, add the keyword trig.

```
> 4^(1/2) - sin(x)^2 - 1;
```
$$\sqrt{4} - \sin(x)^2 - 1$$

```
> " = simplify( ", `trig` );
```
$$\sqrt{4} - \sin(x)^2 - 1 = \sqrt{4} - 2 + \cos(x)^2$$

```
> "" = simplify("");
```
$$\sqrt{4} - \sin(x)^2 - 1 = \cos(x)^2$$

Also note that normalization is done before trigonometric simplification. The following lines show the consequences.

```
> ( sin(x)^3 - 1) / ( sin(x)^2 - 1 );
```
$$\frac{\sin(x)^3 - 1}{\sin(x)^2 - 1}$$

```
> simplify( ", ´trig´ );
```
$$-\frac{-\sin(x) - 2 + \cos(x)^2}{\sin(x) + 1}$$

```
> normal("");
```
$$\frac{\sin(x)^2 + \sin(x) + 1}{\sin(x) + 1}$$

```
> map( simplify, """, ´trig´ );
```
$$-\frac{-1 + \sin(x) - \sin(x)\cos(x)^2}{\cos(x)^2}$$

• Inverse trigonometric and hyperbolic functions

simplify takes care of the transformation $arctrig(trig(x)) \longrightarrow x$, where $trig = $ sin, cos, tan, sinh, cosh, tanh, etc., when this transformation is valid. Furthermore, **simplify** "knows" some transformations for inverse tangents like **combine** did.

```
> simplify( arcsin( sin(x) ) );
```
$$\arcsin(\sin(x))$$

```
> simplify( ", assume=RealRange(-Pi/2,Pi/2) );
```
$$x$$

```
> simplify( "", ´arctrig´, ´symbolic´ );
```
$$x$$

```
> arctan(x) + arctan(1/x):   " = simplify(");
```
$$\arctan(x) + \arctan\left(\frac{1}{x}\right) = \frac{1}{2}\operatorname{csgn}(x)\pi$$

• exp, ln

For the exponential function, **simplify** does the same as **expand** with two exceptions, viz., $\exp x \exp y \longrightarrow \exp(x+y)$ and $\dfrac{1}{\exp x} \longrightarrow \exp(-x)$.

```
> exp(x) * exp(y):   " = simplify(");
```
$$e^x e^y = e^{(x+y)}$$

```
> expand( rhs(") );
```
$$e^x e^y$$

```
> exp(x)^2:   " = simplify(");
```
$$(e^x)^2 = e^{(2x)}$$

```
>  1/exp(x):   " = simplify(");
```

$$\frac{1}{e^x} = e^{(-x)}$$

For the natural logarithm, **simplify** factors the argument and then applies the following transformation rules.

$$\ln(x^y) \quad \longrightarrow \quad y\ln(x) \text{ for positive } x \text{ and real } y,$$
$$\ln(x^y) \quad \longrightarrow \quad y\ln(-x) \text{ for negative } x \text{ and even integer } y,$$
$$\ln(x^y) \quad \longrightarrow \quad y\ln(x) \text{ for negative } x \text{ and odd integer } y,$$
$$\ln(x^y) \quad \longrightarrow \quad y\ln(x) \text{ for odd integer } x,$$
$$\ln(x^y) \quad \longrightarrow \quad \frac{y}{2}\ln(x^2) \text{ for even integer } x,$$
$$\ln(x\,y) \quad \longrightarrow \quad \ln(x) + \ln(y) \text{ for positive } x,$$
$$\ln(x\,y) \quad \longrightarrow \quad \ln(-x) + \ln(-y) \text{ for negative } x,$$
$$\ln(\exp(x)) \quad \longrightarrow \quad x \text{ for real } x,$$
$$\ln(\text{LambertW}(x)) \quad \longrightarrow \quad \ln(x) + \text{LambertW}(x) \text{ for positive } x.$$

The simplifications $\ln(x\,y) \longrightarrow \ln(x) + \ln(y)$ and $\ln(x^y) \longrightarrow y\ln(x)$ can always be forced by using the keyword **ln** together with the keyword **symbolic** or an extra assumption.

```
>  simplify( ln(x^2), ln );
```

$$\ln(\,x^2\,)$$

```
>  " = simplify( ", ln, `symbolic` );
```

$$\ln(\,x^2\,) = 2\ln(\,x\,)$$

```
>  "" = simplify( "", ln, assume=positive );
```

$$\ln(\,x^2\,) = 2\ln(\,x\,)$$

```
>  """ = simplify( """, ln, assume=negative );
```

$$\ln(\,x^2\,) = 2\ln(\,-x\,)$$

- **Powers and radicals**

simplify does the same as **expand** for most powers, with the important exception $x^y x^z \longrightarrow x^{y+z}$ and, as you will see below, simplification of powers with fractions as exponents. Another important difference with **expand** is that **simplify** takes more care of the validity of a transformation as you will notice in the examples below.

```
>  x^y * x^z:   " = simplify(");
```

$$x^y\,x^z = x^{(y+z)}$$

```
>  expand( rhs(") );
```

$$x^y\,x^z$$

```
>   simplify( (x^y)^z );
```
$$(x^y)^z$$

```
>   " = simplify( ", `power`, `symbolic` );
```
$$(x^y)^z = x^{(y\, z)}$$

```
>   simplify( (x/y)^z );
```
$$\left(\frac{x}{y} \right)^z$$

```
>   " = simplify( ", `power`, `symbolic` );
```
$$\left(\frac{x}{y} \right)^z = x^z\, y^{(-z)}$$

```
>   simplify( (-x)^y );
```
$$(-x)^y$$

```
>   " = simplify( ", `power`, `symbolic` );
```
$$(-x)^y = (-1)^y\, x^y$$

```
>   (x^(1/2))^(y/2):    " = simplify(");
```
$$(\sqrt{x})^{(1/2\, y)} = x^{(1/4\, y)}$$

```
>   simplify( (x*y)^z );
```
$$(x\, y)^z$$

```
>   " = simplify( ", `power`, `symbolic` );
```
$$(x\, y)^z = x^z\, y^z$$

For powers with fractional exponents, the procedure **simplify** differs a lot from **expand**. In this case, **simplify** relies in fact on the procedure **radsimp** (**rad**ical **simp**lification). The procedure **radsimp** is especially designed to simplify expressions in which square roots and powers with other fractional exponents occur. Such simplifications are often difficult and time-consuming. When you mention the keyword `radical` in a call of **simplify** then Maple knows that you want simplification only of this type and nothing else.

```
>   (2/27)^(1/3):    " = simplify(");
```
$$\frac{1}{27}\, 2^{1/3}\, 27^{2/3} = \frac{1}{3}\, 2^{1/3}$$

Note the difference between the following:

```
>   (2/27)^(1/3):    " = simplify( ", `power` );
```
$$\frac{1}{27}\, 2^{1/3}\, 27^{2/3} = \frac{1}{27}\, 2^{1/3}\, 27^{2/3}$$

> (2/27)^(1/3): " = simplify(", radical);

$$\frac{1}{27}\, 2^{1/3}\, 27^{2/3} = \frac{1}{3}\, 2^{1/3}$$

> (1-y^2)^(3/2) - (1-y^2)^(1/2): " = simplify(");

$$(1 - y^2)^{3/2} - \sqrt{1 - y^2} = -\sqrt{1 - y^2}\, y^2$$

> (1-sin(x)^2)^(3/2) - (1-sin(x)^2)^(1/2);

$$(1 - \sin(x)^2)^{3/2} - \sqrt{1 - \sin(x)^2}$$

> simplify(", radical);

$$-\sqrt{1 - \sin(x)^2}\, \sin(x)^2$$

> "" = simplify("");

$$(1 - \sin(x)^2)^{3/2} - \sqrt{1 - \sin(x)^2} =$$
$$-\mathrm{csgn}(\cos(x))\cos(x) + \mathrm{csgn}(\cos(x))\cos(x)^3$$

Radical simplification is carried out by Maple with much care.

> (x^4)^(5/4): " = simplify(");

$$(x^4)^{5/4} = x^4\,(x^4)^{1/4}$$

> (x^4)^(5/4): " = simplify(", radical, assume=positive);

$$(x^4)^{5/4} = x^5$$

• Other simplifications

Maple knows many rules for functions like the gamma function, the Riemann zeta function, the hypergeometric function, and a lot more. Two examples:

> GAMMA(n+1/2)/GAMMA(n-1/2): " = simplify(");

$$\frac{\Gamma(n + \frac{1}{2})}{\Gamma(n - \frac{1}{2})} = n - \frac{1}{2}$$

> readlib(hypergeom):
> hypergeom([-1,-3/2],[1/2],z^2/t^2);

$$\mathrm{hypergeom}([-1, \frac{-3}{2}], [\frac{1}{2}], \frac{z^2}{t^2})$$

> simplify(");

$$\frac{t^2 + 3z^2}{t^2}$$

If you do not want to apply all possible simplifications provided for, then you must explicitly mention, in the call to **simplify**, those mathematical functions for which simplification should be carried out (as in the above example where the keyword radical was added). Note that this is the opposite to the way in which expansion of functions is suppressed.

```
>   exp(x)*exp(y) + cos(x)^2 + sin(x)^2;
```
$$e^x \, e^y + \cos(\,x\,)^2 + \sin(\,x\,)^2$$

```
>   simplify(");
```
$$e^{(\,x+y\,)} + 1$$

```
>   simplify( "", exp );
```
$$e^{(\,x+y\,)} + \cos(\,x\,)^2 + \sin(\,x\,)^2$$

```
>   simplify( """, 'trig' );
```
$$e^x \, e^y + 1$$

14.5   convert

Expressions in which (hyperbolic) trigonometric functions and their inverses occur can be explicitly transformed into different forms with **convert**. Some examples:

• Conversion of (hyperbolic) trigonometric functions into exponential form and the reverse conversion.

```
>   cos(x):  " = convert( ", exp );
```
$$\cos(\,x\,) = \frac{1}{2} \, e^{(\,I\,x\,)} + \frac{1}{2} \, \frac{1}{e^{(\,I\,x\,)}}$$

```
>   map( convert, ", 'trig' );
```
$$\cos(\,x\,) = \frac{1}{2} \, \cos(\,x\,) + \frac{1}{2} \, I \sin(\,x\,) + \frac{1}{2} \, \frac{1}{\cos(\,x\,) + I \sin(\,x\,)}$$

```
>   simplify(");
```
$$\cos(\,x\,) = \cos(\,x\,)$$

```
>   cosh(x):  " = convert( ", exp );
```
$$\cosh(\,x\,) = \frac{1}{2} \, e^x + \frac{1}{2} \, \frac{1}{e^x}$$

```
>   map( convert, ", 'trig' );
```
$$\cosh(\,x\,) = \frac{1}{2} \, \cosh(\,x\,) + \frac{1}{2} \, \sinh(\,x\,) + \frac{1}{2} \, \frac{1}{\cosh(\,x\,) + \sinh(\,x\,)}$$

> simplify(");

$$\cosh(x) = \cosh(x)$$

Note the difference between

> exp(x+I*y): " = convert(", `trig`);

$$e^{(x+Iy)} = (\cosh(x) + \sinh(x))(\cos(y) + I\sin(y))$$

and

> exp(x+I*y): " = evalc(");

$$e^{(x+Iy)} = e^x \cos(y) + I e^x \sin(y)$$

• Conversion of inverse (hyperbolic) trigonometric functions into logarithmic expressions.

> arcsin(x): " = convert(", ln);

$$\arcsin(x) = -I\ln(\sqrt{1 - x^2} + I x)$$

> arcsinh(x): " = convert(", ln);

$$\text{arcsinh}(x) = \ln(x + \sqrt{x^2 + 1})$$

The above conversions of (hyperbolic) trigonometric functions and their inverses can be combined into one conversion by the keyword **expln**.

• Conversions of trigonometric functions into expressions with only tangents.

> sin(x): " = convert(", tan);

$$\sin(x) = 2\,\frac{\tan(\frac{1}{2}x)}{1 + \tan(\frac{1}{2}x)^2}$$

> cos(x): " = convert(", tan);

$$\cos(x) = \frac{1 - \tan(\frac{1}{2}x)^2}{1 + \tan(\frac{1}{2}x)^2}$$

> sin(x)/cos(x): " = convert(", tan);

$$\frac{\sin(x)}{\cos(x)} = \tan(x)$$

• Conversions of (hyperbolic) trigonometric functions into expressions with only (hyperbolic) sines and cosines

> tan(x): " = convert(", `sincos`);

$$\tan(x) = \frac{\sin(x)}{\cos(x)}$$

```
> tanh(x):   " = convert( ", `sincos` );
```

$$\tanh(x) = \frac{\sinh(x)}{\cosh(x)}$$

• Conversions of trigonometric functions into expressions with only sines and cosines, and conversions of hyperbolic functions into expressions with only exponential functions.

```
> tan(x):   " = convert( ", `expsincos` );
```

$$\tan(x) = \frac{\sin(x)}{\cos(x)}$$

```
> tanh(x):   " = convert( ", `expsincos` );
```

$$\tanh(x) = \frac{(e^x)^2 - 1}{(e^x)^2 + 1}$$

• Furthermore, Maple provides conversions of factorials and binomial coefficients into gamma functions and vice versa.

```
> n!:   " = convert( ", GAMMA );
```

$$n! = \Gamma(n+1)$$

```
> rhs(") = convert( rhs("), `factorial` );
```

$$\Gamma(n+1) = \frac{(n+1)!}{n+1}$$

```
> lhs(") = expand( rhs(") );
```

$$\Gamma(n+1) = n!$$

```
> binomial(n,k):   " = convert( ", GAMMA );
```

$$\mathrm{binomial}(n,k) = \frac{\Gamma(n+1)}{\Gamma(k+1)\Gamma(n-k+1)}$$

```
> binomial(n,k):   " = convert( ", factorial );
```

$$\mathrm{binomial}(n,k) = \frac{n!}{k!\,(n-k)!}$$

```
> rhs(") = convert( rhs("), binomial );
```

$$\frac{n!}{k!\,(n-k)!} = \mathrm{binomial}(n,k)$$

```
> multinomial(n,a,b,c,d):   " = convert( ", GAMMA );
```

$$\mathrm{multinomial}(n,a,b,c,d) = \frac{\Gamma(n+1)}{\Gamma(a+1)\Gamma(b+1)\Gamma(c+1)\Gamma(d+1)}$$

14.6 Trigonometric Simplification

Substitution of trigonometric expressions plays a special role in Maple. The computer algebra system provides an extra facility: for simple expressions it can suggest equivalent ones. The Maple procedure is called **trigsubs** and should first be loaded from the library. A few examples:

```
>   readlib(trigsubs):  # load library function
>   trigsubs( sin(2*x) );
```

$$[\sin(2x), \sin(2x), 2\sin(x)\cos(x), \frac{1}{\csc(2x)}, \frac{1}{\csc(2x)}, 2\frac{\tan(x)}{1+\tan(x)^2},$$

$$-\frac{1}{2}I(e^{(2Ix)} - e^{(-2Ix)})]$$

```
>   convert( trigsubs( tan(x)^2 ), 'set' );
```

$$\left\{\tan(x)^2, 4\frac{\tan(\frac{1}{2}x)^2}{(1-\tan(\frac{1}{2}x)^2)^2}, \frac{1}{\cot(x)^2}, 4\frac{\cot(\frac{1}{2}x)^2}{(\cot(\frac{1}{2}x)^2-1)^2},\right.$$

$$\frac{4}{(\cot(\frac{1}{2}x)-\tan(\frac{1}{2}x))^2}, -\frac{(e^{(Ix)}-e^{(-Ix)})^2}{(e^{(Ix)}+e^{(-Ix)})^2}, \sec(x)^2-1,$$

$$\left.\frac{\sin(x)^2}{\cos(x)^2}, \frac{\sin(2x)^2}{(1+\cos(2x))^2}, \frac{(1-\cos(2x))^2}{\sin(2x)^2}\right\}$$

```
>   trigsubs( sin(x) + sin(y) );
```

$$[2\sin(\frac{1}{2}x+\frac{1}{2}y)\cos(\frac{1}{2}x-\frac{1}{2}y)]$$

Do not expect miracles; many trigonometric equivalences are not recognized by Maple via **trigsubs**. In the case where trigonometric substitution is desired, **trigsubs** can also be used as an alternative for the substitution procedure **subs**, with the extra feature that the trigonometric equality in the first argument is verified via the knowledge base.

```
>   trigsubs( cos(2*x) = cos(x)^2 - sin(x)^2,
>      cos(2*x) + sin(x)^2 + 1);
```

$$\cos(x)^2 + 1$$

Trigonometric simplification can be cumbersome, as you may have to convert between different representation during a computation. A simple example: let us start with the expansion of $\tan(3x)$.

```
>    expand( tan(3*x) );
```

$$\frac{3\tan(x) - \tan(x)^3}{1 - 3\tan(x)^2}$$

Try to recover from this result the original expression. You may expect that the following command does the job.

```
>    combine(");
```

$$\frac{-3\tan(x) + \tan(x)^3}{-1 + 3\tan(x)^2}$$

Alas. You first have to write the expression in terms of sines and cosines.

```
>    convert( ", ´sincos´ );
```

$$\frac{-3\dfrac{\sin(x)}{\cos(x)} + \dfrac{\sin(x)^3}{\cos(x)^3}}{-1 + 3\dfrac{\sin(x)^2}{\cos(x)^2}}$$

Do not be too optimistic and immediately apply **combine**.

```
>    combine(");
```

$$\frac{\sin(6x) + 3\sin(2x) + 3\sin(4x)}{3\cos(4x) + 1 + 3\cos(2x) + \cos(6x)}$$

You first have to simplify the rational expression of sines and cosines before you can combine trigonometric terms.

```
>    normal("");
```

$$\frac{\sin(x)\,(-3\cos(x)^2 + \sin(x)^2)}{\cos(x)\,(-\cos(x)^2 + 3\sin(x)^2)}$$

```
>    combine(");
```

$$\frac{\sin(3x)}{\cos(3x)}$$

Finally, convert the expression into a tangent.

```
>    convert( ", tan );
```

$$\tan(3x)$$

Maple V Release 4 takes into account knowledge about properties of variables when doing trigonometric simplification. An example:

```
>    cos( x + n*Pi );
```

$$\cos(x + n\pi)$$

```
>    expand(");
```

$$\cos(x)\cos(n\pi) - \sin(x)\sin(n\pi)$$

```
>  assume( n, integer );
>  ";
```

$$\cos(x)(-1)^{n^{\sim}}$$

We end this section with an example of trigonometric simplification that shows how cumbersome it can be in practical cases. The task is to compute

```
>  Sum( cos( omega*t - alpha - n*beta ), n=-N..N );
```

$$\sum_{n=-N}^{N} \cos(\omega t - \alpha - n\beta)$$

```
>  value("):
```

The lengthy result is not shown; we first simplify it.

```
>  simplify("):
```

This result is not much shorter than before and therefore not displayed. But what we gained is that, in its present form, combination of the trigonometric terms will improve the simplicity of the result.

```
>  combine(");
```

$$\frac{1}{2}(\sin(\beta + N\beta + \omega t - \alpha) - \sin(-\beta - N\beta + \omega t - \alpha)$$
$$+ \sin(-\alpha + N\beta + \omega t) - \sin(-\alpha - N\beta + \omega t))/(\sin(\beta))$$

$\omega t - \alpha$ appears in all terms; let us take this term apart.

```
>  algsubs( omega*t-alpha = zeta, " );
```

$$\frac{1}{2}(\sin(N\beta - \zeta) + \sin(\beta + N\beta - \zeta)$$
$$+ \sin(\beta + N\beta + \zeta) + \sin(N\beta + \zeta))/(\sin(\beta))$$

We expand the expression and simplify the result again.

```
>  simplify( expand(") );
```

$$\cos(\zeta)(\cos(N\beta)\sin(\beta) + \cos(\beta)\sin(N\beta) + \sin(N\beta))/(\sin(\beta))$$

We combine the trigonometric terms again but leave $\cos\zeta$ intact. One way to do this here is the following:

```
>  map( combine, " );
```

$$\frac{\cos(\zeta)(\sin(N\beta) + \sin(\beta + N\beta))}{\sin(\beta)}$$

This formula is not ugly, but let us see whether the formula for sum of sines brings us further. First, we temporarily forget about the term $\cos\zeta$.

```
>  coeff( ", cos(zeta) );
```

$$\frac{\sin(N\beta) + \sin(\beta + N\beta)}{\sin(\beta)}$$

Let us ask **trigsubs** for help.

```
> readlib(trigsubs):
> subs( s=beta+N*beta, trigsubs( subs(
>        beta+N*beta=s, numer("") ) ) );
```

$$[\, 2\sin(\tfrac{1}{2}\beta + N\beta)\cos(-\tfrac{1}{2}\beta)\,]$$

```
> trigsubs( denom(""") );
```

$$\left[\sin(\beta),\sin(\beta),2\sin(\tfrac{1}{2}\beta)\cos(\tfrac{1}{2}\beta),\frac{1}{\csc(\beta)},\frac{1}{\csc(\beta)},\right.$$

$$\left. 2\frac{\tan(\tfrac{1}{2}\beta)}{1+\tan(\tfrac{1}{2}\beta)^2},-\frac{1}{2}I\,(e^{(I\beta)}-e^{(-I\beta)})\right]$$

The third substitution option is most promising as it will lead to most cancellations.

```
> op(1,"") / op(3,");
```

$$\frac{\sin(\tfrac{1}{2}\beta + N\beta)}{\sin(\tfrac{1}{2}\beta)}$$

So, the sum is equal to

```
> subs( zeta=omega*t-alpha, cos(zeta)*" );
```

$$\frac{\cos(\omega t - \alpha)\sin(\tfrac{1}{2}\beta + N\beta)}{\sin(\tfrac{1}{2}\beta)}$$

A nice result, but obtained via a rather lengthy derivation.

14.7 Simplification w.r.t. Side Relations

Let us consider the following problem from the Dutch Mathematics Olympiad of September 6, 1991.

Let a, b, c be real numbers such that

$$a + b + c = 3, \quad a^2 + b^2 + c^2 = 9, \quad a^3 + b^3 + c^3 = 24.$$

Compute $a^4 + b^4 + c^4$.

Maple's solution is the following:

```
> siderels := { a+b+c=3, a^2+b^2+c^2=9, a^3+b^3+c^3=24 };
    siderels := { a + b + c = 3, a³ + b³ + c³ = 24, a² + b² + c² = 9 }
```

```
>  simplify( a^4+b^4+c^4, siderels );
```
$$69$$

To understand how Maple computes this result you must have some notion of what a *Gröbner basis* is and how it is used. In this section, only the idea behind a Gröbner basis is described; for a more mathematically oriented introduction the interested reader is referred to [13, 26, 27, 51].

First, Maple considers the set of polynomials that specify the side relations as pure polynomials rather than equations.

```
>  polys := map( lhs - rhs, siderels );
```
$$polys := \{\, a + b + c - 3, a^2 + b^2 + c^2 - 9, a^3 + b^3 + c^3 - 24 \,\}$$

Next, Maple computes the minimal, monic Gröbner basis with respect to the pure lexicographic ordering. Roughly speaking, a Gröbner basis is a set of polynomials that generates the same ideal as the original set of polynomials, with some extra properties imposed on the basis. The Maple package for computing this basis is called **grobner**. The command in this package that does the work is **gbasis**.

```
>  with( grobner ):  # load the Groebner basis package
```

Warning, new definition for insert

```
>  G :=  gbasis( polys, [a,b,c], `plex` );
```
$$G := [\, a + b + c - 3, b^2 + c^2 - 3b - 3c + bc, 1 - 3c^2 + c^3 \,]$$

The Gröbner basis depends on the ordering of monomials in a, b, and c. Here, the pure lexicographic ordering with $a \succ b \succ c$ is used (q.v., §5.2).

Characterization of Gröbner bases. *A finite set G of polynomials is a Gröbner basis if each element of the ideal generated by G reduces to zero by application of "reductions" with respect to the ordering $\succ$.*

What is meant by "reductions" can best be explained via the example. From the first polynomial comes the reduction with respect to a,

$$a \longrightarrow 3 - b - c.$$

From the second polynomial the "easiest" reduction with respect to pure lexicographic ordering is that the "largest" monomial is eliminated via

$$b^2 \longrightarrow -bc + 3b - c^2 + 3c.$$

(bc is the "largest" monomial occurring on the right-hand side.) From the third polynomial the "easiest" reduction is to eliminate the highest-degree term

$$c^3 \longrightarrow 3c^2 - 1.$$

When these reductions are applied to a polynomial until they can be applied no longer, then a so-called *normal form* of the given polynomial is reached. A Gröbner basis G can also be characterized by the property that zero is the unique normal form of every element of the ideal generated by G. In other words, in a Gröbner basis G it is guaranteed that the result of successive applications of these reductions on a polynomial in the ideal generated by G will be zero.

A Gröbner basis G is a minimal, monic basis when each element g of G has a leading coefficient equal to 1 and is in normal form with respect to $G\backslash\{g\}$. For a minimal, monic Gröbner basis the normal form of any polynomial is unique; it is a "canonical form" in the sense that two polynomials are equivalent when their normal forms are the exact same polynomial.

Maple provides the procedure **normalf** for computing the normal form. Let us determine the normal form of $a^4 + b^4 + c^4$ with respect to the computed Gröbner basis.

```
>  normalf( a^4+b^4+c^4, G, [a,b,c], `plex` );
```
$$69$$

Hence, simplification with respect to polynomial side relations is nothing but the computation of the normal form of a polynomial with respect to the minimal, reduced Gröbner basis of the ideal generated by the side relations in some term ordering. On a rational expression, simplification with respect to polynomial side relations is applied separately to the numerator and denominator of the normalized quotient. If no variables are specified or if indeterminates are specified as a set, then total degree ordering is chosen. If variables are specified as a list, then induced pure lexicographic ordering is chosen. (For the definition of these term orderings we refer to §5.2.) To control the outcome of simplification with respect to side relations, it is often prudent to specify variables in the ordering needed.

```
>  simplify( x^3 + y^3, {x^2 + y^2 = 1}, [x,y] );
```
$$y^3 + x - x\,y^2$$

```
>  simplify( x^3 + y^3, {x^2 + y^2 = 1}, [y,x] );
```
$$x^3 - y\,x^2 + y$$

```
>  simplify( (x^3-y^3) / (x^3+y^3), {x^2 + y^2 = 1} );
```
$$\frac{-y^3 + x - x\,y^2}{y^3 + x - x\,y^2}$$

Compare this simplification with

```
>  siderel := { cos(x)^2 + sin(x)^2 = 1 };
```
$$siderel := \{\, \cos(\,x\,)^2 + \sin(\,x\,)^2 = 1 \,\}$$

```
>  eqn := cos(x)^3 + sin(x)^3;
```
$$eqn := \cos(\,x\,)^3 + \sin(\,x\,)^3$$

```
>  simplify( eqn, siderel, [cos(x),sin(x)] );
```

$$\sin(x)^3 - \cos(x)\sin(x)^2 + \cos(x)$$

```
>  simplify( eqn, siderel, [sin(x),cos(x)] );
```

$$\cos(x)^3 - \sin(x)\cos(x)^2 + \sin(x)$$

From this it should be clear how simplification with side relations works for generalized rational expressions.

Simplification with respect to side relations is a powerful tool. Consider, for example, the simplification of the polynomial f defined as

```
>  f;
```

$$y^3 x^6 - 3 y^3 x^4 + 3 y^2 x^5 + 8 y^2 x^4 + 3 y^3 x^2 - 6 y^2 x^3 + 3 y x^4$$
$$- 16 y^2 x^2 + 16 y x^3 - y^3 + 3 y^2 x + 23 y x^2 + x^3 + 8 y^2$$
$$- 16 y x + 8 x^2 - 26 y + 26 x + 40$$

```
>  simplify( f, { u = x^2*y - y + x + 4 }, {x,y} );
```

$$u^3 - 4 u^2 + 10 u.$$

By pencil and paper such compositions of polynomials are difficult to find and to verify.

In many cases, the procedure **match** may be a good alternative because it uses a polynomial time algorithm of algebraic pattern matching, whereas the time and memory requirements for Gröbner basis calculations can be immense.

```
>  guess := a*u^3 + b*u^2 + c*u + d:
>  u := x^2*y - y + x + 4:
>  match( f=guess, x, ´parms´ );
```

$$true$$

```
>  parms;
```

$$\{ y = y, d = 0, b = -4, c = 10, a = 1 \}$$

```
>  subs( parms, eval(guess,1) );
```

$$u^3 - 4 u^2 + 10 u$$

By the way, Maple provides the procedure **compoly** for finding a composition of polynomials. For the above function f, **compoly** finds the composition

```
>  compoly(f);
```

$$40 + 26 x + 8 x^2 + x^3, x = x^2 y - y + x$$

This must be interpreted as $f = 40 + 26v + 8v^2 + v^3$, where $v = yx^2 - y + x$. As you see, compositions of polynomials are not unique.

As a second example, we consider the univariate polynomial

```
>  f := x^6 + 6*x^4 + x^3 + 9*x^2 + 3*x - 5;
```

$$f := x^6 + 6\,x^4 + x^3 + 9\,x^2 + 3\,x - 5$$

```
>  compoly(f);
```

$$x^2 - 5 + x, x = 3\,x + x^3$$

So, f composes as $g \circ h$, where $g = x^2 + x - 5$ and $h = x^3 + 3x$. Let Maple check its answer.

```
>  subs( "[2], "[1] );
```

$$(3\,x + x^3)^2 - 5 + 3\,x + x^3$$

```
>  expand( " - f );
```

$$0$$

Note that the composition is not unique: f also composes as $g \circ h$, where $g = x^2 - \frac{21}{4}$ and $h = x^3 + 3x + \frac{1}{2}$.

The algorithm used for univariate polynomials is described in [10, 92]. The more general case of composing a rational function in one variable into a composition of rational functions is discussed in [93, 94, 201].

14.8   Control Over Simplification

There are basically three ways to control the simplification process:

- adding assumptions

- omitting validity checks

- restricting the transformations to a class of functions.

Throughout this chapter you have already seen examples of such controls. In this section, we summarize them by giving more examples.

• simplify with assumptions

The command **simplify**(*expression*, **assume** = *property*) will simplify the *expression* assuming that all variables have the given *property*. In this way, you can carry out a simplification that would otherwise have no effect or only a partial effect. An example:

```
>  expr := sqrt((x-1)^2);
```

$$expr := \sqrt{(x-1)^2}$$

```
> simplify( expr );
```
$$\mathrm{csgn}(x - 1)(x - 1)$$

```
> simplify( expr, assume=real );
```
$$\mathrm{signum}(x - 1)(x - 1)$$

```
> simplify( expr, assume=RealRange(1,infinity) );
```
$$x - 1$$

```
> simplify( expr, assume=RealRange(-infinity,1) );
```
$$1 - x$$

Note that the assumption **real** does *not* mean that the domain of computation is the set of real numbers. It *only* means that variables are assumed to be real. This explains why

```
> simplify( (-1)^(1/3), assume=real );
```
$$\frac{1}{2} + \frac{1}{2}I\sqrt{3}$$

still returns a complex value and not the answer -1, which you might have expected.

When assumptions are explicitly made on variables via **assume**, then Maple will (try to) use this information in the simplification process.

```
> ln( exp(x) );
```
$$\ln(e^x)$$

```
> assume( x, real ):
> ln( exp(x) );
```
$$x^{\sim}$$

```
> assume( x>0 ):
> (x^3*y)^(1/3):  " = simplify(");
```
$$(x^{\sim 3}y)^{1/3} = x^{\sim}y^{1/3}$$

```
> assume( y, RealRange(-Pi/2,Pi/2) ):
> arcsin(sin(y)): " = simplify(");
```
$$\arcsin(\sin(y^{\sim})) = y^{\sim}$$

- **omitting validity checks**

The keyword **symbolic** in a call of a simplification procedure indicates that although the validity of a transformation cannot be proven, it is nevertheless carried out. The keyword **delay** has the opposite effect; if you cannot prove validity of a transformation, then return the expression unevaluated. In this case, there is a subtle difference between returning an expression unevaluated and encoding an answer using sign functions. The following example reveals this.

```
>   expr := (x^2)^(1/2); # no automatic simplification
```
$$expr := \sqrt{x^2}$$

```
>   simplify( expr, ´symbolic´ ); # simplify regardless
```
$$x$$

```
>   simplify( expr, ´delay´ ); # valid simplify
```
$$\sqrt{x^2}$$

```
>   simplify( expr );   # simplify with sign functions
```
$$\mathrm{csgn}(\,x\,)\,x$$

● **restricting simplifications**

A Maple teaser:

```
>   (4^x-1)/(2^x-1);
```
$$\frac{4^x - 1}{2^x - 1}$$

```
>   simplify(");
```
$$\frac{4^x - 1}{2^x - 1}$$

```
>   normal(");
```
$$\frac{4^x - 1}{2^x - 1}$$

```
>   combine( ", ´power´ );
```
$$\frac{4^x - 1}{2^x - 1}$$

No simplification procedure seems to recognize 4^x as $(2^x)^2$ so that the expression can be simplified into $2^x + 1$. For this, you first have to convert the expression from powers to exponential mappings and logarithms, and then follow a specific simplification track to get the job done.

```
>   convert( ", exp );
```
$$\frac{e^{(\,x\ln(\,4\,))} - 1}{e^{(\,x\ln(\,2\,))} - 1}$$

```
>   simplify( ", ln );
```
$$\frac{e^{(\,2\,x\ln(\,2\,))} - 1}{e^{(\,x\ln(\,2\,))} - 1}$$

```
>  simplify( ", exp );
```

$$\frac{2^{(2\,x)} - 1}{2^x - 1}$$

```
>  normal( ", 'expanded' );
```

$$2^x + 1$$

In the procedures **combine**, **simplify**, and **convert**, you can add a second argument to restrict the type of simplification to a particular mathematical function or class of expressions. For the procedure **expand** it is the opposite: via extra arguments, you just inform Maple what mathematical functions or expressions should be left untouched during simplification.

```
>  expr := ln(2*x)+sin(2*x);
```

$$expr := \ln(2\,x) + \sin(2\,x)$$

```
>  expand( expr, ln );
```

$$\ln(2\,x) + 2\sin(x)\cos(x)$$

```
>  expand(expr, sin );
```

$$\ln(2) + \ln(x) + \sin(2\,x)$$

```
>  expr .- expr^2,
```

$$expr := (\ln(2\,x) + \sin(2\,x))^2$$

```
>  expand( expr, ln, sin );
```

$$\ln(2\,x)^2 + 2\ln(2\,x)\sin(2\,x) + \sin(2\,x)^2$$

Use **frontend** when it is easier to specify which functions may be expanded than to inform Maple which functions must stay intact.

```
>  frontend( expand, [expr] );
```

$$\ln(2\,x)^2 + 2\ln(2\,x)\sin(2\,x) + \sin(2\,x)^2$$

```
>  frontend( expand, [expr], [{},{sin(2*x)}] );
```

$$\ln(2\,x)^2 + 4\sin(x)\cos(x)\ln(2\,x) + 4\sin(x)^2\cos(x)^2$$

```
>  frontend( expand, [expr], [{`+`,`*`,trig},{}] );
```

$$\ln(2\,x)^2 + 4\sin(x)\cos(x)\ln(2\,x) + 4\sin(x)^2\cos(x)^2$$

frontend has an optional third argument of a list of two sets: first, a set of type names not to be frozen; second, a set of expressions not to be frozen (default is $[\{`+`\},\{`*`\},\{\}]$). So, in the last command we have specified to expand the expression while keeping all functions intact except trigonometric functions. The type names may include types that you yourself define in Maple. For example,

```
>   # sine of 2x
>   `type/t` := z -> evalb( z=sin(2*x) ):
>   expr := sin(2*x) + sin(2*y) + sin(4*x);
```

$$expr := \sin(2\,x) + \sin(2\,y) + \sin(4\,x)$$

```
>   frontend( expand, [expr], [{`+`,`*`,t},{}] );
```

$$2\sin(x)\cos(x) + \sin(2\,y) + \sin(4\,x)$$

```
>   # trigonometric function applied to a sum
>   `type/t` := trig(`+`);
```

$$type/t := \mathrm{trig}(+)$$

```
>   expr := sin(2*x)+sin(3*x)+sin(x+y)+sin(u-v);
```

$$expr := \sin(2\,x) + \sin(3\,x) + \sin(x+y) - \sin(-u+v)$$

```
>   frontend( expand, [expr], [{`+`,t},{sin}] );
```

$$\sin(2\,x) + \sin(3\,x) + \sin(x)\cos(y) + \cos(x)\sin(y) - \sin(-u)\cos(v)$$
$$- \cos(-u)\sin(v)$$

```
>   # trigonometric function applied to a product
>   `type/t` := trig(`*`);
```

$$type/t := \mathrm{trig}(*)$$

```
>   frontend( expand, [expr], [{`*`,t},{sin}] );
```

$$2\sin(x)\cos(x) + 4\sin(x)\cos(x)^2 - \sin(x) + \sin(x+y) - \sin(-u+v)$$

14.9   Defining Your Own Simplification Routines

In the example of partial trigonometric expansion in §14.2 we already touched upon the subject of programming your own expansion rules for functions. For a function, say **F**, you only have to define the procedure **expand/F**. Henceforth, when you apply **expand** to an expression containing **F**, Maple applies to each function call of **F** the expansion as defined in the procedure **expand/F**. An example of an additive function **F**:

```
>   `expand/F` := proc(x)
>      local y,i:
>      y := expand(x):
>      if type(y,`+`) then sum( F(op(i,y)), i=1..nops(y) ) fi
>   end:
>   f(p+q) + F(r+s):   " = expand(");
```

$$f(p+q) + F(r+s) = f(p+q) + F(r) + F(s)$$

```
> F(p*(q+r)):   " = expand(");
```

$$F(p(q+r)) = F(pq) + F(pr)$$

As promised in the section about **expand** we shall illustrate how you can redefine the expansion routine of the hyperbolic tangent so that consistency with the corresponding trigonometric function is established, i.e., we are going to redefine the procedure **expand/tanh** so that it resembles **expand/tan**, and so that the built-in expansion routine is always overruled. It is a prototype of how to add your own procedures in a private library and have them carried out before attempting to use a built-in library routine.

For the implementation of **expand/tanh** we seek inspiration from the source code of the comparable procedure **expand/tan**.

```
> interface( verboseproc=3 ): # make Maple more verbose
> readlib( `expand/tan` ):    # load library routine
> print( `expand/tan` );
```

```
proc(y)
local x,n,t,i,S,c,N,D,T;
    x := expand(y);
    if x <> y then RETURN(expand(tan(x))) fi;
    if type(x,'+') then
        n := nops(x);
        t := [op(x)];
        t := traperror([seq(tan(i),i = t)]);
        if t = 'singularity encountered' then
            RETURN(tan(convert(t,'+')))
        elif t = lasterror then ERROR(lasterror)
        fi;
        t := expand(t);
        for i from 0 to n do
            c := combinat['choose'](t,i);
            S[i] := convert(map(convert,c,'*'),'+');
            if 1 < irem(i,4) then S[i] := -S[i] fi
        od;
        N := convert([seq(S[2*i-1],i = 1 .. iquo(n+1,2))],'+');
        D := convert([seq(S[2*i],i = 0 .. iquo(n,2))],'+');
        N/D
    elif type(x,'*') and type(op(1,x),integer) then
        n := abs(op(1,x));
        t := tan(x/n);
        for i from 0 to n do
            S[i] := binomial(n,i)*t^i;
            if 1 < irem(i,4) then S[i] := -S[i] fi
        od;
        N := convert([seq(S[2*i-1],i = 1 .. iquo(n+1,2))],'+');
        D := convert([seq(S[2*i],i = 0 .. iquo(n,2))],'+');
        N/D
```

```
    else tan(x)
    fi
end
```

Probably, this is a bit overwhelming. By inspection of a few expansions and careful reading of the source code it becomes clear that Maple applies the following rule:

$$\tan(x_1 + x_2 + \cdots + x_n) = \frac{S_1 - S_3 + S_5 - S_7 + \ldots + (-1)^{\lfloor \frac{n-1}{2} \rfloor} S_{2\lfloor \frac{n-1}{2} \rfloor + 1}}{1 - S_2 + S_4 - S_6 - \ldots + (-1)^{\lfloor \frac{n}{2} \rfloor} S_{2\lfloor \frac{n}{2} \rfloor}},$$

where the S_i are the elementary symmetric polynomials in $\tan(x_j)$, which are given by

$$\prod_{i=1}^{n}(t - \tan(x_i)) = \sum_{i=0}^{n}(-1)^i S_i t^{(n-i)}.$$

It is not very difficult to verify that a similar formula holds for the hyperbolic tangent, viz.,

$$\tanh(x_1 + x_2 + \cdots + x_n) = \frac{S_1 + S_3 + S_5 + S_7 + \ldots + S_{2\lfloor \frac{n-1}{2} \rfloor + 1}}{1 + S_2 + S_4 + S_6 + \ldots + S_{2\lfloor \frac{n}{2} \rfloor}},$$

where the S_i are the elementary symmetric polynomials in $\tanh(x_j)$; So, these are given by

$$\prod_{i=1}^{n}(t - \tanh(x_i)) = \sum_{i=0}^{n}(-1)^i S_i t^{(n-i)}.$$

We implement the above expansion formula for the hyperbolic cotangent in the same style as the procedure **expand/tan** and place the code in a Maple file, say tanh. The full contents of the file is as follows:

```
# Expand tanh(f(x)) where f(x) is a sum of products by
# repeatedly applying the following two transformations.
#
#                   tanh(x) + tanh(y)
# tanh(x+y)  =  ---------------------
#                   1 + tanh(x) tanh(y)
#
# and
#
#                   tanh(x)
# tanh(2*x)  = 2 ------------
#                        2
#                   1 + tanh(x)
```

```
#
# Note, the code doesn't apply these two rules recursively
# because that would generate a messy rational expression
# which would then have to be simplified. Instead, the
# following identities are used
#
#                               S[1] + S[3] + S[5] + ...
# tanh(a[1]+a[2]+...+a[n]) = -------------------------- (*)
#                               1 + S[2] + S[4] + ...
#
# where the S[i] are the symmetric polynomials in tanh(a[j]).
#
# The code essentially writes down the formula (*) as a
# rational expression in expand( tanh(a[i]) ).
# The result is not further expanded or normalized.
#
# > expand(tanh(x+y+z));
#
#   tanh(y) + tanh(z) + tanh(x) + tanh(y) tanh(z) tanh(x)
# -------------------------------------------------------------
#  1 + tanh(y) tanh(z) + tanh(y) tanh(x) + tanh(z) tanh(x)
#
# > expand(tanh(2*x+2*y));
#
#        tanh(x)              tanh(y)
#   2 ------------ + 2 ------------
#               2                2
#      1 + tanh(x)       1 + tanh(y)
# -------------------------------
#              tanh(x) tanh(y)
# 1 + 4 ---------------------------
#                2                2
# (1 + tanh(x) ) (1 + tanh(y) )
#
# Author: Andre Heck
# Date:   Aug/95
# Remark: code is copied and adapted from expand/tan

'expand/tanh' := proc(y)
local x, n, t, i, S, c, N, D, T;
x := expand(y);
if x <> y then RETURN( expand(tanh(x)) ) fi;
if type(x,'+') then
  n := nops(x);
  t := [op(x)];
```

```
t := expand([seq(tanh(i),i=t)]);
for i from 0 to n do
  c := combinat['choose'](t,i);
  S[i] := convert( map(convert,c,'*'), '+' );
od;
N := convert( [seq( S[2*i-1], i=1..iquo(n+1,2) )],
  '+' );
D := convert( [seq( S[2*i], i=0..iquo(n,2) )],
  '+' );
N/D # Don't expand the result
elif type(x,'*') and type(op(1,x),integer) then
  n := abs(op(1,x));
  t := tanh(x/n);
  for i from 0 to n do
    S[i] := binomial(n,i)*t^i;
  od;
N := convert( [seq( S[2*i-1], i=1..iquo(n+1,2) )],
  '+' );
D := convert( [seq( S[2*i], i=0..iquo(n,2) )],
  '+' );
N/D # Don't expand the result
else tanh(x)
fi;
end:


savelib( ''expand/tanh'', ''expand/tanh.m''):
quit
```

But where are we going to store the file? For this, we mimic Maple's
library organization. The Maple library is archived into one file, `maple.lib`,
in the library directory, which on Unix platform usually is

```
>  libname;
```

$$/usr/local/lib/maple/lib$$

Let us assume that this is indeed the location of the Maple library. The
names of the Maple procedures reflect their original place in the directory
tree. For example, the procedure **expand/tan** is originally stored in the file
`/usr/local/lib/maple/lib/expand/tan.m`. Let us assume that our private Maple library is kept in the directory `/home/user/private_maplelib`.
In this directory, we define the subdirectory `expand`, which in its turn contains a subdirectory `src`. In `/home/user/private_maplelib/expand/src`
we place the above file `tanh`. We run the following short Maple session from
this directory.

```
>  savelibname := `/home/user/private_maplelib`;
>  read tanh;
```

The file `tanh.m` containing the procedure **expand/tanh** is created in the subdirectory `/home/user/private_maplelib/expand`. Now, everything is ready for use, at least when the private library is first in the list of Maple libraries that **readlib** searches through. The proof of the pudding is, of course, in the eating.

```
>  libname := `/home/user/private_maplelib/`, libname:
>  tanh(x+y+z):  " = expand(");
```

$$\tanh(x+y+z) = \frac{\tanh(x) + \tanh(y) + \tanh(z) + \tanh(x)\tanh(y)\tanh(z)}{1 + \tanh(x)\tanh(y) + \tanh(x)\tanh(z) + \tanh(y)\tanh(z)}$$

```
>  tanh(5*x):  " = expand(");
```

$$\tanh(5\,x) = \frac{5\tanh(x) + 10\tanh(x)^3 + \tanh(x)^5}{1 + 10\tanh(x)^2 + 5\tanh(x)^4}$$

14.10 Exercises

1. Show that $\displaystyle\sum_{k=1}^{\infty} \frac{1}{k^2+1} = \frac{\pi}{2}\coth(\pi) - \frac{1}{2}$.

2. Expand the expression $(\cos(2x)+1)^2$ into $\cos^2(2x) + 2\cos(2x) + 1$, i.e., expand the expression as if it were a polynomial in $\cos(2x)$ and do not expand the trigonometric function.

3. Check how the following pairs of symbolic expressions can be transformed into each other by Maple.

   (a) $x + y + \dfrac{1}{x+y}$ and $\dfrac{(x+y)^2 + 1}{x+y}$

   (b) $\exp(x+y)$ and $\exp(x)\exp(y)$

   (c) $\ln(x/y)$ and $\ln(x) - \ln(y)$

   (d) $x^{(y+z)}$ and $x^y x^z$

   (e) $\sqrt{x^2 - 1}$ and $\sqrt{x-1}\sqrt{x+1}$

4. Simplify the following symbolic expressions.

   (a) $\dfrac{e^x + x}{e^{2x} + 2xe^x + x^2}$

   (b) $\sqrt[3]{x^5 + 40x^4 + 595x^3 + 3905x^2 + 9680x + 1331}$

   (c) $\dfrac{(x-2)^{3/2}}{(x^2 - 4x + 4)^{1/4}}$

   (d) $\dfrac{\sqrt{x} - y}{x - y^2}$

   (e) $\dfrac{1}{2 + 5^{1/3}}$

   (f) $\cos(x+y) + \sin x \sin y + 2^{x+y}$

   (g) $2\cos^2 x - \cos 2x$

5. Solve the following zero-equivalence problems with Maple.

   (a) $(2^{1/3} + 4^{1/3})^3 - 6(2^{1/3} + 4^{1/3}) - 6 = 0$

   (b) $\ln \tan(\frac{1}{2}x + \frac{1}{4}\pi) - \operatorname{arcsinh} \tan x = 0$

6. Use Maple to check the following trigonometric identities.

   (a) $\sin x + \sin y = 2 \sin \frac{1}{2}(x + y) \cos \frac{1}{2}(x - y)$

   (b) $\sin 5x = 5 \sin x - 20\sin^3 x + 16\sin^5 x$

   (c) $\cot^2 x + 1 = \csc^2 x$

   (d) $\tan x + \tan y = \dfrac{\sin(x + y)}{\cos x \cos y}$

   (e) $\cos^6 x + \sin^6 x = 1 - 3\sin^2 x \cos^2 x$

   (f) $\sinh 2x = 2\dfrac{\tanh x}{1 - \tan h^2 x}$

   (g) $\dfrac{\sin 2x + \sin 2y}{\cos 2x + \cos 2y} = \tan(x + y)$

7. Verify with Maple the equality $\pi/4 = 4\arctan(1/5) - \arctan(1/239)$.

8. Compute the following indefinite integrals and check the answers through differentiation and simplification.

   (a) $\displaystyle\int \frac{2}{\sqrt{4 + x^2}}\, dx$

   (b) $\displaystyle\int \sqrt{(1 - cx^2)^3}\, dx$

   (c) $\displaystyle\int \frac{1}{x^4 - 1}\, dx$

   (d) $\displaystyle\int \frac{1}{x^4 - 4}\, dx$

   (e) $\displaystyle\int \sin 3x \cos 2x\, dx$

9. Integrate the real function $x \mapsto \dfrac{1}{(a\,x + b)^2(c\,x + d)^2}$ and bring the result into the following form.

$$\frac{2a\,c \ln\left(\dfrac{c\,x + d}{a\,x + b}\right)}{(a\,d - b\,c)^3} - \frac{2a\,c\,x + a\,d + b\,c}{(a\,d - b\,c)^2(a\,x + b)(c\,x + d)}$$

10. Implement the expansion routine **expand/coth** such that it resembles **expand/cot**, i.e., **expand** should expand hyperbolic cotangents in terms of hyperbolic cotangents instead of hyperbolic sines and cosines. Set things up so that your expansion routine overrules the built-in procedure.

14.11   Simplification Chart

Generic Simplification Chart

procedure	trigonometric functions	exp and log	powers	special functions
expand	$\cos(x+y) \to \cos x \cos y - \sin x \sin y$ $\cos 2x \to 2\cos^2 x - 1$ $\cosh 3x \to 4\cosh^3 x - 3\cosh x$	$\exp(x+y) \to \exp x \exp y$ $\ln(xy) \to \ln x + \ln y$ $\ln(x/y) \to \ln x - \ln y$	$x^{(y+z)} \to x^y x^z$ $(xy)^z \to x^z y^z$ $(x/y)^z \to x^z (1/y)^z$	$(n+1)! \to (n+1)n!$ $\Gamma(n+\frac{3}{2}) \to (n+\frac{1}{2})\Gamma(n+\frac{1}{2})$ $-\mathrm{dilog}(\frac{1}{x}) \to \mathrm{dilog}(x) + \frac{1}{2}\ln^2 x$
combine	$\cos x \cos y - \sin x \sin y \to \cos(x+y)$ $2\sinh x \cosh x \to \sinh 2x$ $4\cos^3 x \to \cos 3x + 3\cos x$	$\exp x \exp y \to \exp(x+y)$ $\ln x + \ln y \to \ln(xy)$ $y \ln x \to \ln(x^y)$	$x^y x^z \to x^{(y+z)}$ $(x^y)^z \to x^{yz}$ $\sqrt{x+1}\sqrt{x} \to \sqrt{x^2+x}$	$\sum_k a_k + \sum_k b_k \to \sum_k (a_k + b_k)$ $\int f + \int g \to \int f + g$
simplify	$\cos^2 x + \sin^2 x \to 1$ $\cosh^2 x - \sinh^2 x \to 1$ $\tan x \to \sin x / \cos x$	$\exp x \exp y \to \exp(x+y)$ $\ln x + \ln y \to \ln(xy)$ $\ln(x^y) \to y \ln x$	$x^y x^z \to x^{(y+z)}$ $(x/y)^z \to x^z y^{-z}$ $\sqrt{x^2 + 2x + 1} \to x + 1$	$\Gamma(n+\frac{1}{2})/\Gamma(n-\frac{1}{2}) \to n - \frac{1}{2}$ ${}_2F_1\left(\frac{1-n}{2}, \frac{-n}{2}, \frac{1}{2}; \frac{z^2}{t^2}\right) \to$ $\left((t+z)^n + (t-z)^n\right)) / 2t^n$
convert	$\cos x \to (e^{ix} + e^{-ix})/2$ $\mathrm{arcsinh}\, x \to \ln(x + \sqrt{x^2+1})$ $\sin 2x \to 2\tan x /(1 + \tan^2 x)$	$e^{ix} \leftrightarrow \cos x + i\sin x$	$\sqrt{a} \leftrightarrow \mathrm{RootOf}(\_Z^2 - a)$	$\binom{n}{k} \to \dfrac{n!}{k!(n-k)!}$ and other type conversions

15
Graphics

Two-dimensional graphics include

- curves defined by functions of a single real variable,

- curves defined by parametric equations,

- implicit curves defined by an equation,

- contour plots and density plots of functions in two real variables and of data,

- plots of vector fields and gradient fields,

- data plots and statistical plots,

- plots of regions defined by linear inequalities,

- geometrical plots (such as polygons, circles, ellipses, etc.), and

- animation of two-dimensional graphics objects.

Maple provides three-dimensional graphics facilities to

- generate surfaces defined by functions of two real variables,

- generate space curves, tubes, and surfaces defined by parametric equations,

- generate implicit surfaces defined by an equation,

- generate surfaces from lists of three-dimensional data points,

- draw geometrical objects such as regular polytopes, cylinders, spheres, and tori, and

- show an animation of three-dimensional graphics objects.

When producing a two- or three-dimensional plot, Maple makes decisions about the number of sample points, positions of axes and tick marks, ranges of values to display, shading or coloring of the graph, and so on. You can modify graphs by using various options, such as choosing another coordinate system (polar, elliptic, logarithmic, spherical, cylindrical, paraboloidal, etc.), or changing the grid size of a surface.

Procedures like **plot** and **plot3d** for plotting functions and surfaces, respectively, can be called in a straightforward way. More graphics capabilities are available via the `plots` package.

We shall assume that the plots package has been loaded in all sample sessions of this chapter.

This is done as follows:

```
> with(plots);  # load graphics package
```

[*animate*, *animate3d*, *changecoords*, *complexplot*, *complexplot3d*,
    conformal, *contourplot*, *contourplot3d*, *coordplot*,
    coordplot3d, *cylinderplot*, *densityplot*, *display*, *display3d*,
    fieldplot, *fieldplot3d*, *gradplot*, *gradplot3d*, *implicitplot*,
    implicitplot3d, *inequal*, *listcontplot*, *listcontplot3d*,
    listdensityplot, *listplot*, *listplot3d*, *loglogplot*, *logplot*,
    matrixplot, *odeplot*, *pareto*, *pointplot*, *pointplot3d*, *polarplot*,
    polygonplot, *polygonplot3d*, *polyhedraplot*, *replot*, *rootlocus*,
    semilogplot, *setoptions*, *setoptions3d*, *spacecurve*,
    sparsematrixplot, *sphereplot*, *surfdata*, *textplot*, *textplot3d*,
    tubeplot]

This list of names may give you an idea of what special two-dimensional and three-dimensional graphics have been made readily available in Maple. The most important command from the `plots` package is **display**. It not only allows you to redraw a plot under different options, but also makes it possible to combine plots.

In this chapter, we shall describe the graphics facilities of Maple V Release 4 under the X Window System. However, most of the graphics examples are also possible when using a different user interface. We shall not treat every possible graphical routine and display option, but put stress on understanding the graphical structure underneath the plotting routines.

In the sample sessions we shall quite often place color informa-
tion in the commands, but the pictures will appear in the text
book in black-and-white.

You will have to redo the examples yourself to see the color rendering.
Anyway, you are invited to experiment with the graphics facilities of Maple.
But please take into account the following:

Some examples in this chapter require quite some computer re-
sources and are time-consuming.

15.1   Some Basic Two-Dimensional Plots

Maple provides the procedure **plot** for graphing a function in one variable.
Maple must of course know what kind of plotting or output device you
are using. If you run Maple on a Macintosh, an MS-DOS computer, or on
a Unix type computer with the worksheet user interface, then the system
selects the display device and display driver automatically. Otherwise, you
must inform Maple and, if necessary, allow it to send special character
sequences for switching from text mode to graphics mode.

For example, if you want to use **plot** in a Tektronix emulation under
MS-KERMIT on an MS-DOS machine you must first enter

```
>  plotsetup( tek, kermit, preplot=[27,12], postplot=[24] ):
```

This command can be understood as follows:

- you inform Maple that you use a Tektronix 4014 terminal or some
  Tektronix emulation,

- the interface variable **preplot** is a list of integers that represent the
  ASCII codes of the characters **escape** and **formfeed**, which are sent
  before a plot to enter graphics mode, and

- the interface variable **postplot** represents the ASCII code of the
  character **cancel**, which is sent after completion of the plot and after
  pressing the Return key to reenter text mode.

In some cases you can make the necessary arrangements swiftly with the
procedure **plotsetup**. Details about available user interfaces can be found
in the Maple Manuals [38, 39, 187, 188].

Henceforth, we shall assume that Maple runs under the X Window System because this display driver will also meet the demands for producing
three-dimensional plots.

Consider the function $f: x \longmapsto e^{-x^2} \sin(\pi x^3)$ on the interval $(-2, 2)$.

```
> f := x -> exp(-x^2) * sin(Pi*x^3);
```

$$f := x \rightarrow e^{(-x^2)} \sin(\pi x^3)$$

The plot of this function is invoked by the command

```
> plot( f, -2..2 );
```

A 2D-plot window may appear containing the graph of the function; the menu allows you to display and manipulate the Maple plot data structure. As shown in the screen dump (Figure 15.1), you can also have the picture in the worksheet (in fact, this is the default behavior).

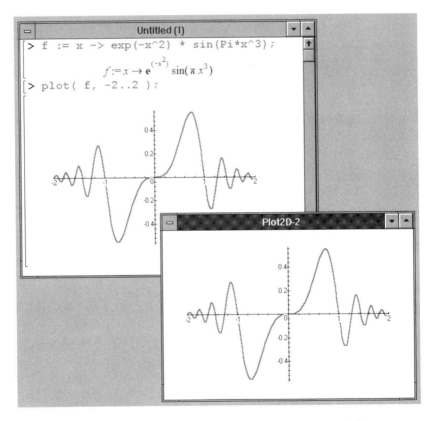

FIGURE 15.1. Screen dump of worksheet and plot window.

The above command is an example of the following general format for drawing a *function f* over the interval (a, b)

$$\mathbf{plot}(\ f,\ a\,..\,b,\ options\ );$$

where *options* describes zero or more options, as will be discussed in the next section.

An alternative way to obtain the graph of a function f defined by the *formula* $f(x)$ is

$$\textbf{plot}(\ f(x),\ x = a \mathbin{..} b, options\ );$$

where $a \mathbin{..} b$ is the horizontal range (of x), and where *options* describes zero or more options. Note the difference in specifying the horizontal range when plotting a *function* and a *formula* — a function only needs a *range*, whereas a formula needs an equation of the form *variable = range*.

So, to plot the formula $e^{-x^2}\sin(\pi x^3)$ for x ranging from -2 to 2, you enter

```
>  plot( f(x), x = -2..2 );
```

The graph differs from Figure 15.1 only in the extra label x for the x-axis.

You can also look at the graph of the function over the entire real line or over a half-line. In Figure 15.2 we display the graph of f over $(0, \infty)$.

```
>  plot( f, 0 .. infinity );
```

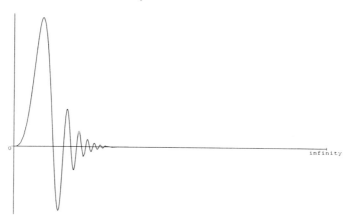

FIGURE 15.2. Infinity plot.

In this case, Maple transforms the entire real line into the interval $(-1, 1)$ by a function that approximates $x \longmapsto \frac{2}{\pi}\arctan(\frac{x}{2\pi})$.

You may plot more than one function at the same time, and on a color display Maple will choose different colors for the graphics objects.

```
>  plot( {f(x), exp(-x^2), -exp(-x^2)}, x=-2..2 );
```

The graph is shown in Figure 15.3 at the top of the next page.

If you want to print a plot or place a plot in PostScript format into some file, you can tell Maple so. You can use the print menu item of the plot window or, if you know beforehand what you want, enter the following command.

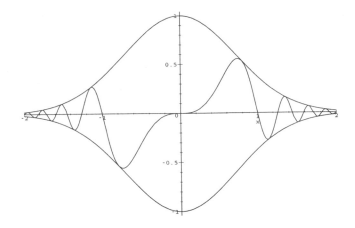

FIGURE 15.3. Graph of $x \mapsto e^{-x^2} \sin(\pi x^3)$, e^{-x^2}, and $-e^{-x^2}$.

```
> plotsetup( PostScript, plotoutput = `plotfile.eps`,
>    plotoptions=`portrait,noborder,height=200,width=600` ):
```

Henceforth, Maple directs the Encapsulated PostScript code, which describes the picture to the file `plotfile.eps` in portrait format, without a plot border, and of size 600×200 (dimensions of width and height are in points, and in this case, the BoundingBox: 0 0 600 200 is generated; 1 inch=72.27 points). You can reset the plotting to the X Windows display with

```
> plotsetup( X11 ):
```

You can simply print this file on a PostScript compatible printer or embed it in a typesetting system such as LaTeX or Framemaker. Without the above `plotoptions`, the graph is printed in landscape mode, with a box around the plot, and the picture is scaled so that it fits maximally on a page of A4 format. Other common plot devices supported by Maple are `win` (for MS-Windows), `hpgl` (for Hewlett-Packard Graphics Library), and `gif` (GIF format). Enter **?plot,device** for more details.

The general format for drawing a two-dimensional plane curve defined in the Cartesian coordinate system by *parametric formulas* $x = f(t)$, $y = g(t)$ is

$$\textbf{plot}(\, [\, f(t), \, g(t), \, t = a \, .. \, b \,], \, \textit{options} \,);$$

where $a \, .. \, b$ is the range of the independent variable t, and where *options* describes zero or more options.

A simple example is shown in Figure 15.4.

```
> plot( [ sin(t), t, t=0..2*Pi ], scaling=constrained );
```

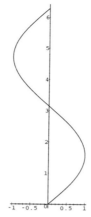

FIGURE 15.4. Parametric plot of curve $t \mapsto (\sin t, t)$.

When a parametric curve is defined by *functions*, the independent variable must be omitted in the **plot** command. A funny example of a function-defined parametric curve is shown in Figure 15.5: a look-alike of a Maple leaf. It is produced as a polar plot.

```
>   S := t -> 100/(100+(t-Pi/2)^8): # for scaling
>   R := t -> S(t)*(2-sin(7*t)-cos(30*t)/2):
>   plot( [ R, t->t, -Pi/2..3/2*Pi ], coords=polar,
>      axes=none, color=green, numpoints=1000 );
```

FIGURE 15.5. Maple leaf created as parametric plot.

15.2 Options of **plot**

When Maple plots a graph, it makes many choices. For example, it chooses the depicted range of the graph, sample points to make a smooth curve, which tick marks to show, and so on. Maple takes care of choosing values for these options that are most convenient in daily use. However, you can customize it to your needs.

Vertical Range

For example, to restrict the vertical range of a graph, you can add the range information to the plot command as a third argument. With the following command you plot the graph of the function defined by the formula $\dfrac{\sin^2 x}{x^2}$ over the interval $(-6, 6)$, where parts of the graph outside the vertical range $[0, 1]$ are not shown (Figure 15.6).

```
>  plot( sin(x^2)/x^2, x=-6..6, 0..1 );
```

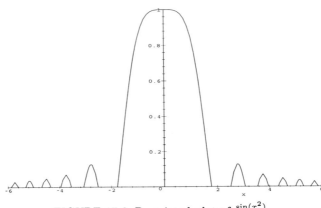

FIGURE 15.6. Restricted plot of $\frac{\sin(x^2)}{x^2}$.

Scaling

Note that Maple chooses the vertical scale that allows the largest display of the plot in A4 size. When you want the same horizontal as vertical scale you can change this interactively or add the option scaling = constrained to the **plot** command (Figure 15.7).

```
>  plot( sin(x^2)/x^2, x=-6..6, scaling=constrained );
```

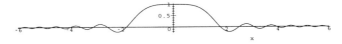

FIGURE 15.7. Restricted plot of $\frac{\sin(x^2)}{x^2}$ with equal scaling.

View

Sometimes, you must restrict the vertical range to get a good picture. In the graph in Figure 15.8, you see that a few function values dominate over all the others so that the behavior of the tangent function over the given domain is not displayed very well. Often the only way to avoid (spurious) spikes in a graph is to specify a "reasonable" vertical range or to increase the number of sample points.

```
>  plot( tan, -Pi..Pi );
```

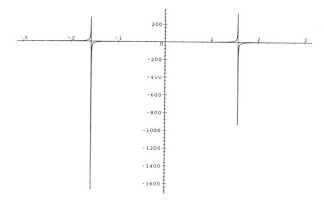

FIGURE 15.8. Bad plot of tangent.

With the following command you replot the graph of the tangent over the interval $(-\pi, \pi)$, where parts of the graph outside the vertical range $[-10, 10]$ are not shown, and the horizontal view has been extended to $[-4, 4]$. However, the graph itself is not computed again; only the rendering is redone (Figure 15.9).

```
> display( ", view=[-4..4,-10..10] );
```

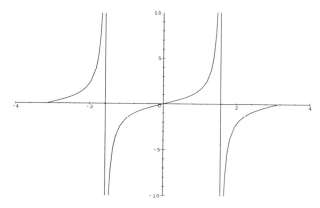

FIGURE 15.9. Improved plot of tangent.

Discontinuities

The vertical asymptotic lines at $x = -\frac{\pi}{2}$ and $x = \frac{\pi}{2}$ are actually present because Maple does not take care of the discontinuities and draws a line between a very high and a very low sample point. You may let Maple try to overcome the discontinuity by adding the option discont = true. But in this case you must work with an expression as Maple needs a variable for locating the discontinuities. Figure 15.10 shows the improved graph of the tangent.

```
> plot( tan(x), x=-Pi..Pi, -10..10, discont=true,
>    xtickmarks=[ -3.14=`-Pi`, -1.57=`-Pi/2`,
>                      1.57=`Pi/2`, 3.14=`Pi` ] );
```

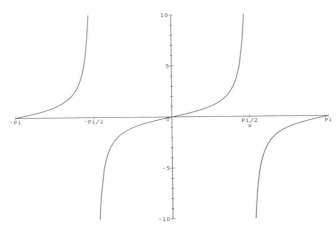

FIGURE 15.10. Best plot of tangent.

Labels, Tick Marks, and a Title

In the above plot, we also gave the horizontal axes more meaningful labels via the option **xtickmarks**. Of course **ytickmarks** exists as well. Instead of explicit labeling, you can just specify the number of tick marks in each direction. You may label a graph and specify the font that you want to use (Figure 15.11).

```
> J := (n,x) -> sqrt(Pi/(2*x)) * BesselJ(n+1/2,x):
> plot( J(0,x), x=0..20, `J(0,x)`=-0.5..1,
>    xtickmarks=8, ytickmarks=4, title=
>    `Spherical Bessel function j(0,x) of the first kind`,
>    titlefont=[HELVETICA,BOLDOBLIQUE,20] );
```

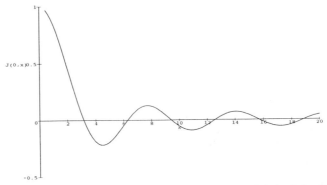

FIGURE 15.11. Plot of spherical Bessel function $J_0(x)$ of the first kind.

When labeling is done in the above way, you cannot do much about the placement of the labels on the axes but make specific changes in the PostScript code of the plot itself. There is an alternative: you may use the commands **textplot** and **display** from the plots package to draw one plot containing text on a specific position, to draw one plot containing the curve and axes, and to display these two plots in one picture (Figure 15.12).

```
>   curve := plot( x->J(0,x), 0..20, -0.5..1,
>      xtickmarks=8, ytickmarks=4, title=
>      `Spherical Bessel function J(0,x) of the first kind`,
>      titlefont=[HELVETICA,BOLDOBLIQUE,20],
>      axesfont=[HELVETICA,BOLD,14] ):

>   text := plots[textplot]( { [2,0.75,`J(0,x)`],
>      [14,-0.1,`x`] }, align={ABOVE,RIGHT},
>      font=[HELVETICA,BOLD,14] ):

>   plots[display]( { curve, text } );
```

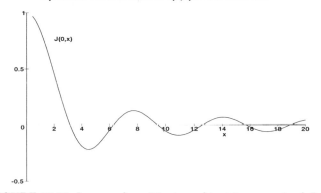

FIGURE 15.12. Improved positioning of text in a graph of $J_0(x)$.

The fonts may be chosen from a small set of families, styles, and sizes.

Sampling

When graphing a function, Maple first computes a number of points of the graph — the number of sample points can be set via the option numpoints or the option sample — and, by default, connects these points by straight lines. As you will see in the next section, Maple will use so-called *adaptive plotting* to make the graphs as smooth as possible; this means that the system increases automatically the number of sample points if necessary to create smooth curves.

Plot Style

Instead of using the default plot style patch, you may select other ones like point or line (only affecting drawings of polygons). If you select the point style, Maple will draw crosses centered around the computed points on a curve and around computed vertices of polygons. You can choose another symbol (Figure 15.13).

```
>   plot( sin, 0..2*Pi, scaling=constrained, style=point,
>     symbol=circle );
```

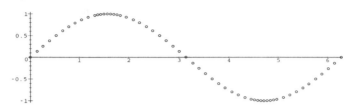

FIGURE 15.13. Point plot of sine function.

Data plots can easily be produced with point plot style; you put the data points in a list and plot the points with the point style. For example, to plot the first nine prime numbers (Figure 15.14) you can do

```
>   plotpoints := [ seq( [ i, ithprime(i) ], i=1..9 ) ]:
>   plot( plotpoints, style=point, symbol=box );
```

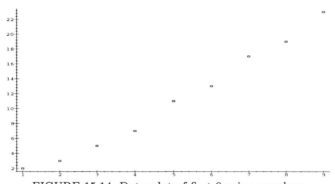

FIGURE 15.14. Data plot of first 9 prime numbers.

In §15.13 we shall look at various built-in procedures for data plotting that extend the above basic plotting.

As an example of the default `line` style we consider a graphical trace of 20 iterations of the cosine function with starting value 1.2. First, we have to generate the list of points.

$$[\,[1.2, 1.2],\ [1.2, \cos(1.2)],\ [\cos(1.2), \cos(1.2)],\ [\cos(1.2), \cos(\cos(1.2))],$$
$$[\cos(\cos(1.2)), \cos(\cos(1.2))],\ [\cos(\cos(1.2)), \cos(\cos(\cos(1.2)))],\ \dots\,]$$

We produce the plot points as pairs of consecutive points starting with

```
>   pair0 := [ [1.2, 1.2], [1.2,cos(1.2)] ]; # starting pair
```
$$pair0 := [\,[\,1.2, 1.2\,], [\,1.2, .3623577545\,]\,]$$

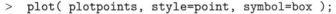

The iteration function to create new pairs of points is

```
>  f := pair -> [ map( cos, pair[1] ),
>                  map( cos, pair[2] ) ]; # iteration
```

$$f := pair \rightarrow [\mathrm{map}\,(\cos, pair_1)\,, \mathrm{map}\,(\cos, pair_2)]$$

To see the effect,

```
>  f( pair0 ); # first new pair
```

$$[[.3623577545, .3623577545], [.3623577545, .9350636470]]$$

which is the numerical evaluation of the pair

$$\Big[[\cos(1.2), \cos(1.2)], [\cos(1.2), \cos(\cos(1.2))]\Big].$$

Now, we can generate all points.

```
>  points := map( op, [ seq( (f@@i)(pair0), i=0..10 ) ] ):
```

Finally, we generate plots of this list of points connected by straight lines, of the identity function, and of the cosine function on the interval $(0, \pi/2)$ and with vertical range $[0, 1]$.

```
>  curveplot := plot( points, x=0..Pi/2, y=0..1,
>     style=line, linestyle=2, color=blue ):
>  identityplot := plot( x, x=0..Pi/2, y=0..1,
>     linestyle=7, color=gray ):
>  cosineplot := plot( cos(x), x=0..Pi/2, y=0..1,
>     thickness=4, color=red ):
```

We show the plots in one picture with the command **display** from the plots package. In the above commands, we chose different colors, line styles (dashing), and drew the cosine function thicker so that the components of the picture can easily be distinguished (Figure 15.15).

```
>  display( { curveplot, identityplot, cosineplot },
>     title=`cobweb-model of iterated cosine` );
```

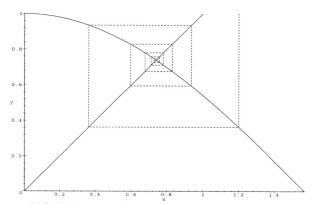

FIGURE 15.15. Cobweb-model of iterated cosine.

Style and Thickness of Lines

Let us investigate what line styles and thicknesses are available. At present, the options `linestyle` and `thickness` can have nonnegative integer values in the ranges [0,7] and [0,15], respectively (modular arithmetic forces the values into the proper range) (Figures 15.16 and 15.17).

```
>   for i from 0 to 15 do
>     thick[i] := plot( i, x=0..1, thickness=i ):
>   od:
>   display( convert( thick, set ),
>     axes=box, tickmarks=[0,15],
>     title=`thickness option: [0,1,..,15]` );
```

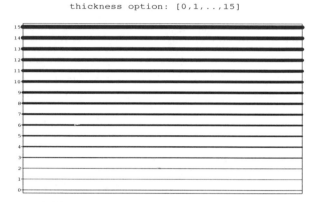

FIGURE 15.16. Thickness of lines in a plot.

```
>   for i from 0 to 7 do
>     line[i] := plot( i, x=0..1, linestyle=i ):
>   od:
>   display( convert( line, set ), axes=box,
>     tickmarks=[0,7], title=`linestyle option: [0,1,..,7]` );
```

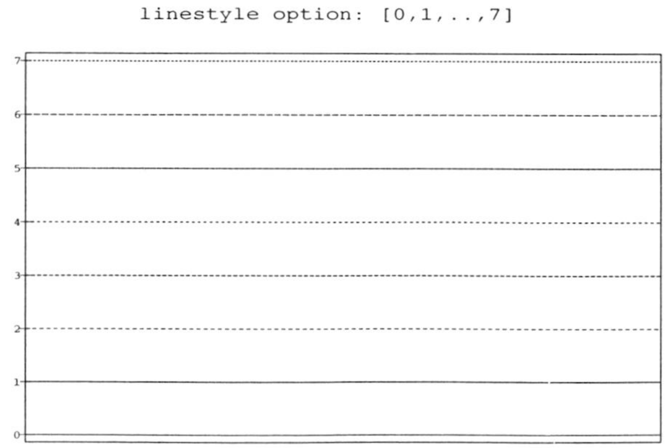

FIGURE 15.17. Line styles in a plot.

Colors

Maple uses two color models: RGB and HSV. In RGB mode, the *red, green,* and *blue* components of a color are set. With the **polygonplot** routine from the plots package you can easily create color charts.

```
> P := seq( seq( polygonplot(
>   [ [i,j], [i+1,j], [i+1,j+1], [i,j+1] ],
>   color=COLOR(RGB,0.1*i, 0.1*j, 0 ) ) ),
>   i=0..10 ), j=0..10 ):
> display( {P}, scaling=constrained,
>   labels=[R,G], title=`RGB color (R, G, 0)`,
>   tickmarks = [ [seq(i+0.5=`.`.i,i=0..9),10.5=`1`],
>   [seq(j+0.5=`.`.j,j=0..9),10.5=`1`] ] );
```

RGB color (R, G, 0)

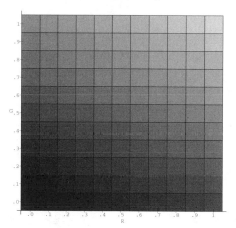

FIGURE 15.18. Projection of a RGB color chart on a gray chart.

Unfortunately, Figure 15.18 only shows the projection of the colors on gray shadings. However, on the screen or on a color printer you should get what you asked for. Figure 15.19 is another picture showing the RGB color model in three dimensions along the edges of a cube.

```
> e1 := seq( seq( seq( display(
>   plottools[cuboid]([i,j,k],[i+1,j+1,k+1]),
>   color=COLOR(RGB,0.1*i, 0.1*j, 0.1*k ), style=patch ),
>   i=0..10 ), j=[0,10] ), k=[0,10] ):
> e2 := seq( seq( seq( display(
>   plottools[cuboid]([i,j,k],[i+1,j+1,k+1]),
>   color=COLOR(RGB,0.1*i, 0.1*j, 0.1*k ), style=patch ),
>   i=[0,10] ), j=0..10), k=[0,10] ):
> e3 := seq( seq( seq( display(
>   plottools[cuboid]([i,j,k],[i+1,j+1,k+1]),
>   color=COLOR(RGB,0.1*i, 0.1*j, 0.1*k ), style=patch ),
>   i=[0,10] ), j=[0,10]), k=0..10 ):
```

```
> display( { e.(1..3) } );
```

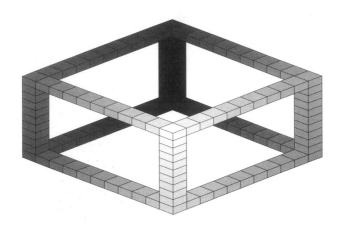

FIGURE 15.19. RGB colors along the edges of a cube.

In HSV mode, the *hue* (or color), *saturation*, and *value* components of a color are set; the last two components indicate the amount of white and black color to add to the color to obtain different shades, tints, and tones. HSV is circular in its argument and provides a cylindrical color space. In Maple, HUE(h) can be used instead of COLOR(HSV, h, 0.9, 1.0). In Figures 15.20 and 15.21 the HUE color chart is displayed in two ways, viz., as a circular band and as a color disk.

```
> plot3d( 1, t=0..2*Pi, z=-2..2, coords=cylindrical,
>   style=patchnogrid, color=t/2/Pi, axes=box,
>   orientation=[45,35], tickmarks=[3,3,0] );
```

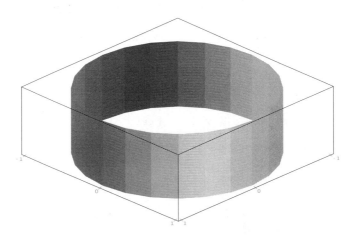

FIGURE 15.20. HUE colors on a circular band.

```
>  P := seq( display( plottools[pieslice](
>     [0,0], 5, Pi*i/10..Pi*(i+1)/10,
>     color=COLOR(HUE,evalf(i/20)) ),
>     scaling=constrained ), i=0..20 ):
>  display( {P}, axes=none );
```

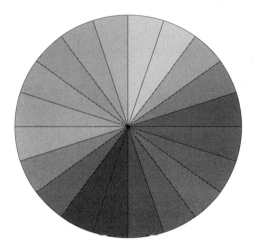

FIGURE 15.21. HUE color disk.

Coordinate Systems

Until now, we have used the Cartesian coordinate system in most plots.
But you have in fact a large choice of coordinate systems in Maple. An
example of a parametric curve in polar coordinates (Figure 15.22):

```
>  plot( [ sin(t), t, t=0..2*Pi ], coords=polar,
>     scaling=constrained );
```

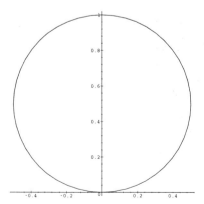

FIGURE 15.22. Parametric curve in polar coordinates.

Compare the graph in Figure 15.22 with our last example in §15.1, where Cartesian
coordinates were used. You can use of the **changecoords** routine from the **plots** package to alter an existing plot structure, which is considered in Cartesian coordinates, to a new coordinate system (Figure 15.23).

```
>  P := ":  # give the previous plot a name
>  changecoords( P, elliptic );
```

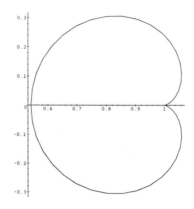

FIGURE 15.23. Plot of curve after change of coordinates.

Notice that this is not the same as

```
>  plot( [ sin(t), t, t=0..2*Pi ], coords=elliptic,
>     scaling=constrained );
```

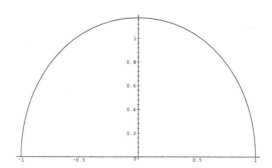

FIGURE 15.24. Plot of curve in elliptic coordinates.

changecoords considers an existing plot as one created in the default coordinate system (usually Cartesian) and transforms the 2D-plot data structure to the new coordinate system. Thus, **changecoords** does not take into account that the 2D-plot data structure may have been created by using a different coordinate system (Figure 15.24).

Default Options

If you want to inspect the default setting of an plot option you can use the
setoptions command from the plots package.

```
>   restart: with(plots):
>   setoptions( numpoints );
```

49

Its main purpose is however to change the default value of an option for
two-dimensional plotting. For example, if you always want to use a frame
instead of normal axes for 2D-plots, and if you always want the same
horizontal and vertical scaling, then you enter

```
>   setoptions( axes = frame, scaling = constrained ):
```

or add this line into your initialization file. You can always overrule the
default by adding the option in a 2D-plot command as the next example
illustrates (Figures 15.25, 15.26, and 15.27).

```
>   plot( ln(x), x = 1/2..2 );
```

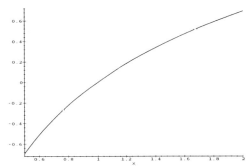

FIGURE 15.25. Plot of natural logarithm on segment $(\frac{1}{2}, 2)$.

```
>   # replot with normal axes
>   display( ", axes=normal );
```

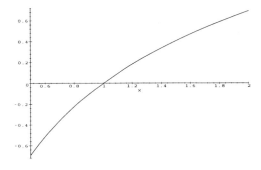

FIGURE 15.26. Plot of logarithm with axes style changed.

```
> # replot with new display area and equal scaling
> display( "", view=[0..2,-2..2], scaling=unconstrained );
```

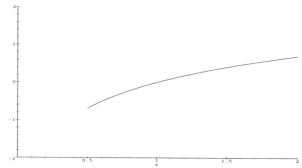

FIGURE 15.27. Plot of logarithm with view frame and scaling changed.

Note that this overruling of options in the **display** command *only* works for those options that do not need recomputation of the graphics object. For example, you cannot expect to change the number of sample points via **numpoints** without recomputing the graphics object.

Many options of two-dimensional plotting routines can be found in the on-line help system via the command **?plot,options**. At the end of this chapter we shall list all plot options that are available. Some of the options in this list have not been discussed yet, but they will be used in examples later in this chapter. The options **linestyle**, **thickness**, **symbol**, **axes**, and **projection** can be changed interactively in the worksheet interface. Others must be adjusted in a plot command.

15.3   The Structure of Two-Dimensional Graphics

To know how reliable the plotting facilities of Maple are, it is important to have a good idea of how plotting is done. The making of a plot proceeds in two phases. In the first phase, the plot points are computed and put in a PLOT object. In the second phase, this object is rendered on the screen. In this section, we shall concentrate on the first phase of plotting.

A two-dimensional graphics object in Maple is a call to the function **PLOT** with arguments describing the axes, function, computed plot points, plot style, and so on. The following object describes a triangle with vertices (1,1), (2,2), and (3,1) (Figure 15.28).

```
> PLOT( CURVES( [ [1,1], [2,2], [3,1], [1,1] ] ),
>   AXESSTYLE(NONE), SCALING(CONSTRAINED) );
```

FIGURE 15.28. A triangle built up from graphics primitives.

The arguments CURVES(...), AXESSTYLE, and SCALING are parts of the arguments of the graphics object obtained by

```
>  P := plot( [ [1,1], [2,2], [3,1], [1,1] ],
>  axes=none, scaling=constrained ):
>  lprint( P ); # print the plot data structure

PLOT(CURVES([[1., 1.], [2., 2.], [3., 1.], [1., 1.]],
     COLOUR(RGB,1.0,0,0)), SCALING(CONSTRAINED),
     AXESSTYLE(NONE))
```

Figure 15.29 is obtained by evaluation of the graphics object

```
>  P;  # plot the graphics object
```

FIGURE 15.29. A triangle drawn via **plot**.

A more general example of a graphics object behind a plot is the plot structure for the graph of the function

$$x \longmapsto \sqrt{2} - \sqrt{2\sqrt{x}},$$

which is shown in Figure 15.30.

```
>  f := x -> sqrt(2) - sqrt(2*sqrt(x)):
>  P := plot( f(x), x=0..1, y=0..sqrt(2),
>   title=`graph of sqrt(2) - sqrt(2*sqrt(x))` ):
>  lprint( P ); # print plot data structure

PLOT(CURVES([[0, 1.414213562373095],
     [.6811610677083333e-3, 1.185744472197018],
     [.1362322135416667e-2, 1.142516494777506],
          . . . . . . . . . . . . . .
     [.9782721018750000, .7745369848915162e-2], [1., 0]],
     COLOUR(RGB,1.0,0,0)),
     TITLE(graph of sqrt(2) - sqrt(2*sqrt(x))),
     AXESLABELS(x,y),
     VIEW(0 .. 1.,0 .. 1.414213562))
```

Maple associates a graphics object with a function in one variable on an interval. This object, which is a regular Maple data structure, will be used for straight line interpolation between computed plot points.

```
>  P;  # display the graph
```

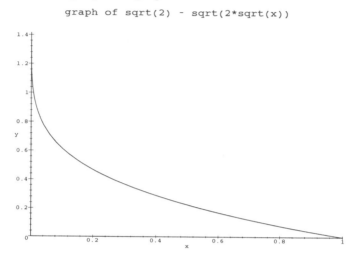

graph of sqrt(2) - sqrt(2*sqrt(x))

FIGURE 15.30. Graph of $2^{1/2}(1 - x^{1/4})$.

First, the argument in the **plot** call that describes the function is evaluated. Hereafter, the function values at the sample points are computed numerically. To increase the speed of plotting, this computing of function values is usually done in hardware floating-point arithmetic.

To obtain nice smooth plots Maple has an algorithm for refining the number of sample points where necessary. First, the function values of 49 equidistant points that span the interval are computed. Jitter is introduced to the sample points so that they are not exactly equidistant anymore. Next, Maple looks at these points as being connected by line segments. If the *kink angle* between two adjacent line segments is too large, then Maple will sample more points around this kink. Maple will not go on forever with subdividing the plot interval: the maximum resolution is controlled by the option **resolution**. The default value of the display resolution is 200. So, by default, the number of sample points is between 49 and 200.

You can zoom in or out by the **display** command in the **plots** package (Figure 15.31).

```
>  display( P, view=[0..0.01, 1..sqrt(2)], title=
>     `zoomed-in graph of sqrt(2) - sqrt(2*sqrt(x))` );
```

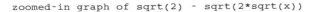

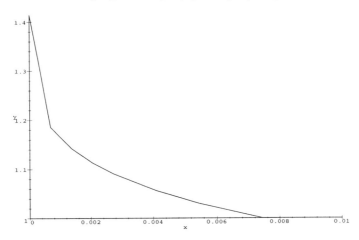

FIGURE 15.31. Zoomed-in graph of $2^{1/2}(1 - x^{1/4})$.

In the above example, Maple already uses the adaptive sampling scheme for small values of x. You are informed about this when you set a higher value to `infolevel[plot]`.

```
>   infolevel[plot] := 2:
>   plot( f(x), x=0..1, y=0..sqrt(2) ):
```

```
plot/adaptive:   evalhf succeeded
plot/adaptive:   produced    59.    output segments
plot/adaptive:   using    59.    function evaluations
```

For comparison, we set the option `adaptive` to `false` below.

```
>   plot( f(x), x=0..1, y=0..sqrt(2), adaptive=false ):
```

```
plot/adaptive:   evalhf succeeded
plot/adaptive:   produced    49.    output segments
plot/adaptive:   using    49.    function evaluations
```

Maple now uses the default number of sample points, i.e., 49. The effect of adaptive sampling becomes more evident when we specify explicitly the initial set of sample points through the plot option `sample`.

```
>   infolevel[plot]:=1: # reset information level
>   plot( x^2, x=0..1, sample = [0,1/2,1], adaptive=true );
>   plot( x^2, x=0..1, sample = [0,1/2,1], adaptive=false );
```

Both pictures are shown for comparison in Figures 15.32 and 15.33.

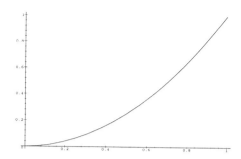

FIGURE 15.32. Graph of $x \mapsto x^2$ with few initial sample points.

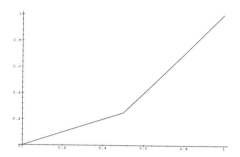

FIGURE 15.33. Graph of $x \mapsto x^2$ with few initial sample points and <u>no</u> adaptive plotting.

Whenever you notice some irregularities in a graph, such as in Figure 15.34 displaying the function defined by $\dfrac{x}{1 - \cos 5x}$ over the interval $(-5, 5)$, you can try to improve the picture and get a nicer, smoother plot by increasing the number of sample points. Just set a higher value to the option numpoints (Figure 15.35).

```
>  plot( x/(1-cos(5*x)), x=-5..5,  -5..5 );
```

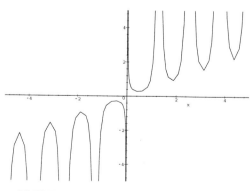

FIGURE 15.34. Sketch of $x \mapsto \frac{x}{1-\cos 5x}$.

```
>  plot( x/(1-cos(5*x)), x=-5..5, -5..5, numpoints=200 );
```

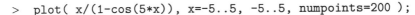

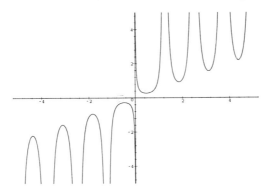

FIGURE 15.35. Smooth graph of $x \mapsto \frac{x}{1-\cos 5x}$.

A plot is a data structure like any other in Maple. You can manipulate it, save it to a file, and read it. An example of a step function:

```
>  step := plot( 2*Heaviside(x-1) - 1, x=-1..2,
>    discont=true, thickness=15 ):
>  step; # display the graph
```

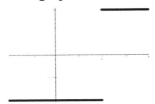

FIGURE 15.36. Graph of the step function $2\,\text{Heaviside}(x - 1) - 1$.

Now we save the variable step in the file graph.m.

```
>  save step, `graph.m`:
```

We replace the variable step by the empty statement to show that after reading the file graph.m., the variable has its old value again.

```
>  step := NULL:    # reassign the variable
>  read `graph.m`: # load the graph
>  step;            # display the graph
```

You can convince yourself that the Figure 15.36 is rendered again. An easy manipulation of the data structure is substitution of the thickness component. Because the thickness information of the curve is inside the CURVES(...) component of the plot data structure and because this component is left untouched by the **plots[display]** command, you have to use substitution for quick changes of overall thickness or rebuild the plot data structure via the **plot** command (Figure 15.37).

```
>  subs( THICKNESS(15)=THICKNESS(1), step );
```

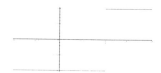

FIGURE 15.37. Replot of the step function $2\,\mathrm{Heaviside}(x-1) - 1$ with different thickness.

15.4   The **plottools** Package

Let us continue with the description of a two-dimensional graphics object. In the previous section you learned about the low-level graphics primitive CURVES(...); a particular example was

$$\mathrm{CURVES}(\,[\,[1.,1.],\ [2.,2.],\ [3.,1.],[1.,1.]\,]\,,\mathrm{COLOUR}(\mathrm{RGB},1.,0,0)\,).$$

Like the entire plot, graphics primitives are implemented in Maple as a function call. The general format is

$$\textit{ObjectName}(\ \textit{ObjectInformation},\ \textit{LocalInformation}\ ).$$

In the above example, CURVES is the object name, the list of points forms the object information, and the color information is local information that specifies the color of the curve. Other object names for 2D-plotting are POINT, POLYGONS, and TEXT. Local information is also implemented as function calls. Typical names are AXESSTYLE, AXESTICKS, COLOUR, FONT, THICKNESS, and VIEW, among others. Enter **?plot,structure** to see all names for local information. These low-level graphics primitives are always in upper-case characters; American spelling is also allowed. They can be used to build up a graphics object. As an example, we construct a blue square without border lines, without axes, and with equal scaling in every direction (Figure 15.38).

```
>   PLOT( POLYGONS( [[0,0], [1,0], [1,1], [0,1]],
>                   COLOR( RGB,0,0,1) ),
>         AXESSTYLE(NONE), STYLE(PATCHNOGRID),
>         SCALING(CONSTRAINED) );
```

FIGURE 15.38. Square without border lines and axes in user-defined color.

Another example is an equilateral triangle with thick, dashed, red border lines with the blue text "equilateral triangle" in Helvetica, 24 point size, oblique font inside the triangle (Figure 15.39).

```
>  PLOT(
>     CURVES( [[0,0],[1,0],[1/2,1/2*sqrt(3)],[0,0]],
>        COLOR( RGB,1,0,0), THICKNESS(15), LINESTYLE(3) ),
>     TEXT( [1/2,1/6*sqrt(3)], `equilateral triangle`,
>        COLOR(RGB,0,0,1), FONT([HELVETICA,BOLDOBLIQUE,24]) ),
>     AXESSTYLE(NONE), SCALING(CONSTRAINED) );
```

Error in iris-plot: Non-numeric vertex definition

We deliberately made a mistake: the above error message explains that the graphics primitives may only contain numerical data, i.e., a floating-point number 0.866 instead of the algebraic number $\frac{1}{2}\sqrt{3}$. The correct input is as follows:

```
>  PLOT(
>     CURVES( [[0,0],[1,0],[1/2,0.866],[0,0]],
>        COLOR(RGB,1,0,0), THICKNESS(15), LINESTYLE(3) ),
>     TEXT( [1/2,0.289], `equilateral triangle`,
>        COLOR(RGB,0,0,1), FONT(HELVETICA,BOLDOBLIQUE,24) ),
>     AXESSTYLE(NONE), SCALING(CONSTRAINED) );
```

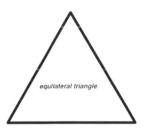

FIGURE 15.39. Equilateral triangle with text inside.

These example illustrate how cumbersome it would be if you had to build up graphics objects from low-level graphics primitives all the time. A collection of commonly used building blocks would very much come in hand, and Maple provides one, viz., the plottools package. In combination with the plots package for specialized graphics, you can create complicated graphics object quite easily. For example, the above pictures can also be obtained in the following way (pictures are omitted because they are as before).

```
>  with(plots): with(plottools): # load packages
>  # blue square
>  display( rectangle( [0,0], [1,1], color=blue ),
>     axes=none, style=patchnogrid, scaling=constrained );
>  # equilateral triangle with text inside
>  lines :=
>     curve( [[0,0],[1,0],[1/2,1/2*sqrt(3)],[0,0]],
>     color=red, thickness=15, linestyle=15 ):
```

```
>  text :=
>    textplot( [1/2,1/6*sqrt(3), `equilateral triangle`],
>    color=blue, font=[HELVETICA,BOLDOBLIQUE,24] ):
>  display( {lines, text}, axes=none, scaling=constrained );
```

If the above examples do not impress you of the usefulness of the `plottools` package, then try to build the happy face of Figure 15.40 from low-level graphics primitives.

```
>  head  := ellipse( [0,0.5], 0.7, 0.9, color=black ):
>  eyes  := disk(  [0.4,0.4],0.1, color=blue ),
>            disk( [-0.4,0.4],0.1, color=blue ):
>  mouth := arc(  [0,0.1], 0.35, 5/4*Pi..7/4*Pi,
>            color=red, thickness=7 ):
>  nose  := line( [0,0.35], [0,-0.1], color=black,
>    thickness=5 ):
>  display( {head, eyes, nose, mouth},
>    scaling=constrained, axes=none ); # happy face
```

FIGURE 15.40. Happy face.

In the `plottools` packages are also present functions that alter an existing graphics object. We list them in Table 15.1. Together with the procedure **changecoords** of the `plots` package, they form the Maple procedures that map one graphics data structure into another.

Procedure	Purpose
rotate	rotate counter-clockwise
scale	scale a plot
stellate	create stellated polygons
transform	generate a function to transform a plot
translate	translate a graphics object

TABLE 15.1. `plottools` functions to alter graphics objects.

Let us use these procedure to produce a spectrum of arrows in different colors, with different sizes, and translated positions so that the arrow points always hit the unit circle. The spectrum is show in Figure 15.43. We start with a horizontal, thick arrow (Figure 15.41).

```
>  a[0] := display( arrow( [0,0], [1,0], 0.1, 0.4, 0.2 ),
>    color=COLOR(HUE,0), axes=none, scaling=constrained ):
>  a[0]; # display the horizontal arrow
```

FIGURE 15.41. Horizontal arrow.

As an example of an alteration of this arrow we rotate it clockwise over $-\frac{\pi}{2}$, scale it with the factor $\frac{1}{4}$ in all directions, and translate it over a distance $\frac{3}{4}$ along the vertical axis in negative direction (Figure 15.42).

```
>  display( a[0],
>    translate( scale(
>      rotate( a[0],-Pi/2 ),
>      1/4, 1/4 ), 0,-3/4 ) );
```

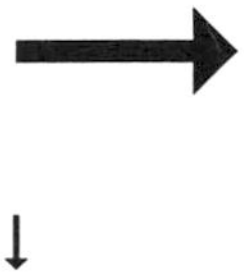

FIGURE 15.42. Original arrow and arrow after rotation, scaling, and translation.

Because the **rotate**, **scale**, **translate**, and **display** do not allow you to change the color of the arrow via an option, we achieve this in the creation of the arrows spectrum below by substitution.

```
>  for i to 15 do
>    a[i] := subs( COLOR(HUE,0) = COLOR(HUE,i/16),
>    translate( scale(
>        rotate( a[0], i*Pi/8 ),
>        (16-i)/16, (16-i)/16 ),
>    i/16*cos(Pi*i/8), i/16*sin(Pi*i/8) ) )
>  od:
>  display( [ seq(a[i],i=0..15) ], scaling=constrained );
```

FIGURE 15.43. Spectrum of arrows in different HUE colors.

The **transform** routine can be used for coordinate transformations (Figure 15.44). As an example, we transform a rectangular grid to a polar grid.

```
>  hpoints := [ seq( [ seq( [i/16,j*Pi/8],
>                     i=0..16) ], j=0..16 )]:
>  hlines := map( curve, hpoints ):
>  vpoints := [ seq( [ seq( [i/16,j*Pi/8],
>                     j=0..16) ], i=0..16 )]:
>  vlines := map( curve, vpoints ):
>  grid := display( hlines,vlines, axes=frame ):
>  f := transform( (r,phi) -> [ r*cos(phi), r*sin(phi) ] ):
>  display( array( [ grid, f(grid) ] ),
>     scaling=constrained );
```

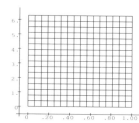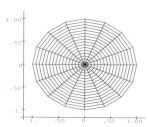

FIGURE 15.44. Transformation of Cartesian to polar coordinates applied to a rectangular grid

Here, we have made use of the ability of the **display** command from the **plots** package to draw plots in a so-called *graphics array*. The grid on the right can be drawn more nicely with the **coordplot** routine from the **plots** package.

15.5   Special Two-Dimensional Plots

Previous examples already illustrated that there is more to graphics than plotting a function in one variable. In this section, we shall list a few more two-dimensional graphics capabilities that are available via the **plots** package. Recall that we assume in this chapter that this package has been loaded in all sample sessions via the command **with(plots)**.

Combining Plots

As an example of combining plots, we draw the sine and cosine function in one graph and color the array between the two functions with red assuming that the background color is white (Figure 15.45).

```
>  sine := plot( sin , 0..4*Pi, color=black, thickness=3 ):
>  s := plot( sin, 0..4*Pi, filled=true, color=red ):
>  cosine :=  plot( cos, 0..4*Pi, color=black,
>     thickness=3 ):
>  c := plot( cos, 0..4*Pi, filled=true, color=red):
```

```
>  f := x -> if cos(x)>0 and sin(x)>0 then
>                   min(cos(x),sin(x))
>                elif cos(x)<0 and sin(x)<0 then
>                   max(cos(x),sin(x))
>                else 0
>                fi:
>  b := plot( f, 0..4*Pi, filled=true, color=white ):
>  display( [ sine, cosine, b, s, c ],
>    scaling = constrained );
```

FIGURE 15.45. Combining plots.

In the above **display** command, the ordering of the graphs in the list is important: graphs are placed behind each other from left to right. So, the background coloring b comes in front of the shading between the sine function and the horizontal axis. Convince yourself of this by using three different shading colors in the above construction.

The procedure **display** can also be used to draw several plots side by side or in a rectangular array in one picture (Figures 15.46 and 15.47). For example,

```
>  ticks := [ [0=`0`, 3.14=`Pi`, 6.28=`2 Pi`],
>             [-0.99=`-1`,0=`0`,0.99=`1`] ]:
>  sine := plot( sin(x), x=0..2*Pi, tickmarks=ticks ):
>  cosine := plot( cos(x), x=0..2*Pi, tickmarks=ticks ):
>  display( array([sine,cosine]) ); # row of plots
```

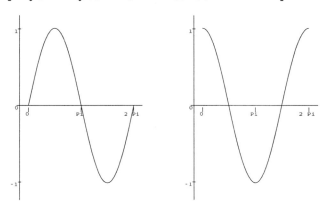

FIGURE 15.46. Graphics array: row vector of plots.

```
>  display( array(1..2,1..1,[[sine],[cosine]]) );
>  # column of plots
```

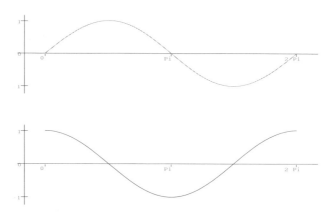

FIGURE 15.47. Graphics array: column vector of plots.

The somewhat strange introduction of tick marks has been done to assure nice tick marks when the plots are combined into one array.

Plots of Plane Algebraic Curves

In the **plots** package resides the procedure **implicitplot** to draw a two-dimensional plane curve defined by an equation (Figure 15.48). An example:

```
>   implicitplot( x^3 + y^3 - 5*x*y + 1/5 = 0,
>      x=-3..3, y=-3..3, grid=[50,50] );
```

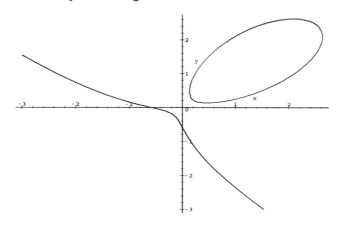

FIGURE 15.48. Implicit plot of $x^3 + y^3 - 5xy + 1/5 = 0$.

In essence, the method used is to consider the equation as a function in three-dimensional space and generate a contour of the equation cutting through the z-plane. Drawbacks of this method are that it generates rough graphs (q.v., the graph obtained without the **grid** option used), and that it does not guarantee correct drawings near singularities and intersections of the curve. Algebraically, this means that Maple may have problems with any point (x, y) on the curve $f(x, y) = 0$ where the partial derivatives $\frac{\partial f}{\partial x}(x, y)$ and $\frac{\partial f}{\partial y}(x, y)$ are both zero. A typical example is the curve

$$2x^4 + y^4 - 3x^2 y - 2y^3 + y^2 = 0,$$

which has has two singular points, (0,0) and (0,1), where the branches intersect [195]. Even when a very fine grid is used, Maple cannot draw the graph correctly with **implicitplot**. For example, the computation of this implicitly defined curve with a 300×300 grid takes 18 minutes and requests about 20 MB main memory on a SPARCstation 20 Model 71, and still does not provide a satisfactory plot around the origin (we omit the picture). In this case, it is better to compute a parametrization of the curve in polar coordinates and graph it with the **polarplot** command (Figure 15.49).

```
>   subs( x=r*cos(phi), y=r*sin(phi),
>     2*x^4 + y^4 - 3*x^2*y - 2*y^3 + y^2 ):
>   factor(");
```

$$r^2(\, 2\, r^2 \cos(\, \phi\,)^4 + r^2 \sin(\, \phi\,)^4 - 3\, r \cos(\, \phi\,)^2 \sin(\, \phi\,) - 2\, r \sin(\, \phi\,)^3$$
$$+ \sin(\phi)^2 \,)$$

```
>   eqn := op(2,"):
>   sols := map( combine, { solve(eqn,r) } );
```

$$sols := \big\{(\, 9 \sin(\, \phi\,) + \sin(\, 3\, \phi\,) + \sin(\, \phi\,)\, \sqrt{30 + 8 \cos(\, 2\, \phi\,) - 22 \cos(\, 4\, \phi\,)} \,)$$
$$\big/ (\, 9 + 3 \cos(\, 4\, \phi\,) + 4 \cos(\, 2\, \phi\,)), (\,$$
$$9 \sin(\, \phi\,) + \sin(\, 3\, \phi\,) - \sin(\, \phi\,)\, \sqrt{30 + 8 \cos(\, 2\, \phi\,) - 22 \cos(\, 4\, \phi\,)} \,) \big/ (\,$$
$$9 + 3 \cos(\, 4\, \phi\,) + 4 \cos(\, 2\, \phi\,))\big\}$$

```
>   sols := map( unapply, sols, phi ):
>   polarplot( sols, 0..2*Pi, view=[-5/2..5/2,0..9/4],
>     scaling=constrained, color=black );
```

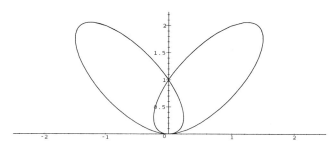

FIGURE 15.49. Parametric plot in polar coordinates.

Logarithmic Plots

Logarithmic plots (Figure 15.50), semi-logarithmic plots (i.e., the horizontal axis is in logarithmic scale), and double-logarithmic plots (Figure 15.51) are available in Maple through the procedures **logplot, semilogplot,** and **loglogplot** in the plots package, respectively.

```
>   # use a random number generator for uniform distribution
>   noise := stats[ random, uniform[0,0.1] ]:
>   # generate data around the function x -> exp(x)
>   plotpoints := [ seq( [ 0.2*i,
>     exp(0.2*i) + noise() ], i=0..20 ) ]:
>   logplot( plotpoints, style=point, symbol=circle );
```

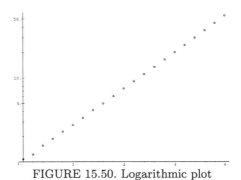

FIGURE 15.50. Logarithmic plot

```
>   loglogplot( x^3 + exp(-x), x=1/10..50, numpoints=200,
>     tickmarks=[3,4], labels=[`x`,`x^3 + exp(-x)`],
>     scaling=constrained, axes=frame );
```

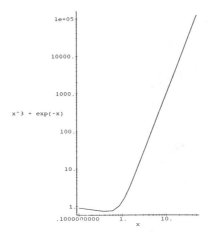

FIGURE 15.51. Double-logarithmic plot.

Check that the option `numpoints` is necessary here for obtaining a "good" plot.

The semi-logarithmic plot that is commonly used in electrical engineering is the Bode plot. Suppose that an electronic circuit has the following response voltage Vout in the frequency domain:

```
>   alias( I=I, J=sqrt(-1) ):
>   Vout := 1/(-12*J*omega^3-2*omega^2+7*J*omega+1);
```

$$Vout := \frac{1}{-12\,J\omega^3 - 2\omega^2 + 7\,J\omega + 1}$$

In the Bode plot the magnitude of the output voltage is taken in Decibel units (defined as $20\,{}^{10}\log x$) and plotted in the semi-logarithmic scaling (Figure 15.52).

```
>   magnitude := 20*log[10]( evalc(abs(Vout)) );
```

$$magnitude := 20\,\frac{\ln\left(\dfrac{1}{\sqrt{-164\,\omega^4 + 45\,\omega^2 + 1 + 144\,\omega^6}}\right)}{\ln(10)}$$

```
>   M := semilogplot( magnitude, omega=0.01..10,
>     labels=[`omega `,`magnitude `] ):
>   M; # display magnitude
```

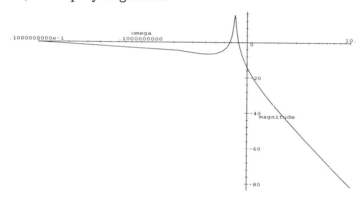

FIGURE 15.52. Magnitude part of Bode plot.

In a Bode plot, the phase or argument of the output voltage is drawn too (Figure 15.53).

```
>   phase := evalc( argument(Vout) );
```

$$phase := \arctan\left(-\frac{-12\,\omega^3 + 7\,\omega}{\left(-2\,\omega^2 + 1\right)^2 + \left(-12\,\omega^3 + 7\,\omega\right)^2},\right.$$
$$\left.\frac{-2\,\omega^2 + 1}{\left(-2\,\omega^2 + 1\right)^2 + \left(-12\,\omega^3 + 7\,\omega\right)^2}\right)$$

```
>   P := semilogplot( 180/Pi*phase, omega = 0.01..10,
>     labels=[`omega `,`phase `] ):
>   P; # display phase
```

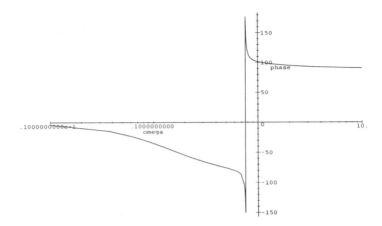

FIGURE 15.53. Phase part of Bode plot.

The Bode plot actually is the combination of the above two plots in column layout (Figure 15.54).

```
>  display( array(1..2,1..1,[[M],[P]]) );
```

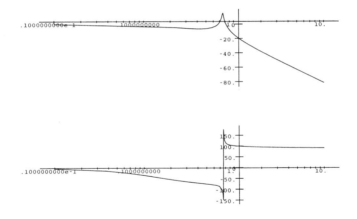

FIGURE 15.54. Bode plot.

You can group the above commands into a procedure. Below, we have defined a procedure **Bodeplot** in such a way that plotting options also are taken care of (Figure 15.55).

```
>  Bodeplot := proc( voltage, domain )
>    local M, P, l, magnitude, omega, opts,
>         phase, r, toption;
>    if not typematch( domain,
>       omega::name = l::algebraic..r::algebraic ) then
```

```
>       ERROR(`invalid input`)
>    elif not type( voltage, ratpoly(anything,omega)) then
>       ERROR(`input must be a rational function in`,omega)
>    fi;
>    opts := [ args[3..nargs] ];
>    if not hasoption( opts, `thickness`, toption, `opts` )
>    then toption:=2  # default thickness
>    fi;
>    l := evalf(l); r := evalf(r);
>    M := plots[semilogplot](
>      20*log[10]( evalc(abs(voltage)) ),
>      omega=l..r, `thickness`=toption,
>      labels=[omega,magnitude], op(opts) );
>    P := plots[semilogplot](
>      180/Pi*evalc(argument(voltage)),
>      omega=l..r, `thickness`=toption,
>      labels=[omega,phase], op(opts) );
>    plots[display]( array(1..2,1..1,[[M],[P]]) );
>  end:

>  Bodeplot( Vout, omega=0.01..10, thickness=5,
>    color=blue, numpoints=200); # greater thickness
```

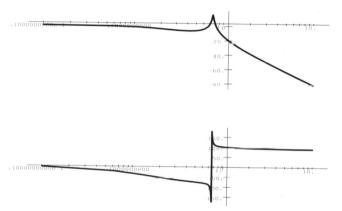

FIGURE 15.55. Bode plot.

A few remarks on this small piece of graphics programming: In the first conditional statement we check whether input is valid or not. Next, we store optional arguments in the variable **opts** and check whether the option **thickness** has been specified. We do this via the procedure **hasoption**. If the plot option **thickness** is present, then **hasoption** takes care of handling it in an appropriate way. If the option has not been specified, then the default value 2 is taken. This is how you pass options and defaults through Maple procedures.

```
>  alias( J=J, I=sqrt(-1) ): #  I = sqrt(-1) again
```

Complex Curves

A complex curve, i.e., a function from $\mathbb{R}$ to $\mathbb{C}$, can be plotted by the procedure **complexplot**. One example will do (recall that $I=\sqrt{-1}$) (Figure 15.56).

```
>  complexplot( sin( Pi/3 + t*I ), t = -1..1 );
```

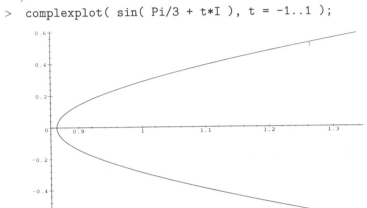

FIGURE 15.56. Complex curve of $t \mapsto \sin(\frac{\pi}{3} + ti)$.

Plots of Conformal Mappings

One example of the procedure **conformal** in the `plots` package will suffice. The complex function $z \longmapsto 1/z$ maps the rectangular grid in Figure 15.57 in the complex plane

```
>  conformal( z, z=-1-I..1+I, grid=[25,25],
>    axes=frame, scaling= constrained );
```

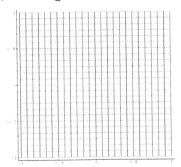

FIGURE 15.57. Square grid in complex plane.

to the grid

```
>  conformal( 1/z, z=-1-I..1+I, grid=[25,25],
>    numxy=[100,100], axes=frame,
>    scaling=constrained, view=[-6..6,-6..6] );
```

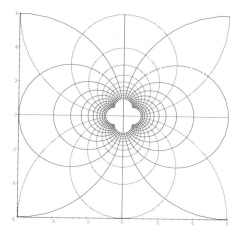

FIGURE 15.58. Conformal plot of complex function $z \mapsto \frac{1}{z}$.

The picture in Figure 15.58 is related to the electric field for the two-dimensional analogue of an electric dipole, i.e., two parallel line charges with opposite polarities, very close together.

Field Plots

Use the procedure **fieldplot** to plot a two-dimensional vector field. An example (Figure 15.59):

```
>  fieldplot( [cos(x),cos(y)], x=-2*Pi..2*Pi, y=-2*Pi..2*Pi,
>     arrows=SLIM, grid=[11,11], axes=box );
```

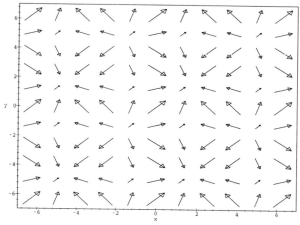

FIGURE 15.59. Field plot of $[\cos x, \cos y]$ on $[-2\pi, 2\pi] \times [-2\pi, 2\pi]$.

As an application of gradient field plotting, we draw the electric field due to two parallel uniform line charges of one unit charge per unit length, of opposite polarities, and at a distance of two unit lengths from each other. Actually, we take line charges infinitely long in the direction perpendicular to the xy-plane, with the negative one going through (-1,0), and the positive line charge going through (1,0). In general, the strength of the electrostatic potential ϕ at position $\vec{P}$ when line charges l_i go through positions $\vec{P_i}$ in the xy-plane is given by

$$\phi = -\frac{1}{2\pi\epsilon_0} \sum_i l_i \, \ln\big(distance(\vec{P}, \vec{P_i})\big).$$

The electric field of the charge distribution is then defined as $\vec{E} = -\nabla\phi$. In our case, when we set the scalar factor $\frac{1}{2\pi\epsilon_0}$ equal to 1:

```
>   phi := ln( sqrt((x+1)^2+y^2) ) - ln( sqrt((x-1)^2+y^2) );
```

$$\phi := \ln(\sqrt{x^2 + 2x + 1 + y^2}) - \ln(\sqrt{x^2 - 2x + 1 + y^2})$$

The two-dimensional gradient vector field can be computed and drawn as follows (Figure 15.60):

```
>   gradplot( -phi, x=-2..2, y=-1..1,
>     arrows=THICK, grid=[11,11], axes=box );
```

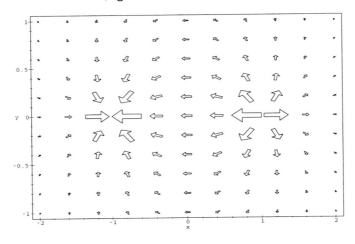

FIGURE 15.60. Electric field of a line charge distribution.

In Chapter 17, when we discuss the DEtools package, we shall come back to this example and compute the field lines. The equipotentials, i.e., the lines of constant electrostatic potential, can be plotted as a contour plot.

Contour Plots and Density Plots

Let us continue the example of an electric field of line charges and draw a contour plot of the electrostatic potential (Figure 15.61)

```
> contourplot( phi, x=-2..2, y=-1..1, color=black,
> numpoints=500, axes=box, contours=10 );
```

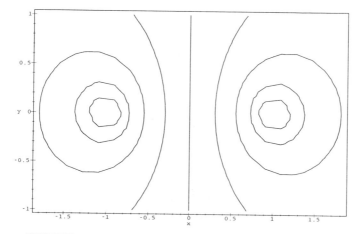

FIGURE 15.61. Equipotentials of an electrostatic potential.

You can also specify explicitly what contour values you want to have in your picture and fill the contour levels with specified coloring; below we choose gray levels (Figure 15.62).

```
> contourplot( phi, x=-2..2, y=-1..1,
> numpoints=500, axes=box, filled=true,
> contours=[seq(i/4,i=-6..6)], coloring=[white,black] );
```

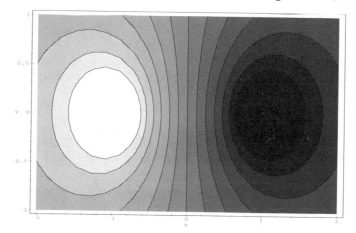

FIGURE 15.62. Equipotentials of an electrostatic potential at specified contour levels.

With some extra work you can create a legend that explains the meaning of the gray levels. Below we show what can be done with modest means (Figure 15.63).

```
>  CP := ":  # store contour plot
>  legendcolors := seq(
>    plottools[rectangle]( [0, i/4], [1,(i+1)/4],
>    color=COLOR( RGB, 1-(i+7)/13, 1-(i+7)/13, 1-(i+7)/13) ),
>    i=-7..6 ):
>  legendtext := seq(
>    textplot( [1.5, i/2, convert(evalf(i/2,2),name)],
>    font=[HELVETICA,BOLD,10] ), i=-3..3 ),
>    textplot( [1.5, 2, Heights], font=[HELVETICA,BOLD,10] ),
>    textplot( [3.5, 2, `        `] ):
>  LP := display( {legendcolors, legendtext},
>    axes=none, scaling=constrained): # store legend
>  display( array([CP,LP]) ); # display in vector layout
```

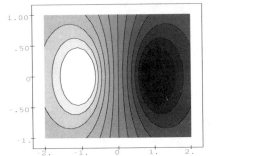

FIGURE 15.63. Contourplot of an electrostatic potential with a plot legend

A density plot of the electrostatic potential ϕ can be generated with **densityplot** (Figure 15.64).

```
>  densityplot( phi, x=-2..2, y=-1..1,
>    grid=[80,80], axes=box, style=patchnogrid,
>    colorstyle=HUE );
```

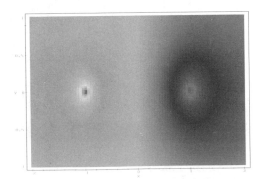

FIGURE 15.64. Density plot of an electrostatic potential with a fine grid.

15.6   Two-Dimensional Geometry

The geometry package provides tools for studying two-dimensional Euclidean geometry. Two examples will do to give you an idea of geometrical and graphical possibilities of the package.

The Circle Theorem of Apollonius. *In any right triangle the circle passing through the midpoints of the edges contains also the feet of the three altitudes.*

Let us see how we can "prove" and graphically illustrate the theorem by means of the geometry package. First, we load the package and define a triangle OAB.

```
>   with(geometry):   # load geometry package
>   assume( x>0, y>0 ):  # assume positive lengths
>   triangle( T,
>     [ point(O,0,0), point(A,x,0), point(B,0,y) ] ):
```

Next, we define the midpoints of the triangle and the circle that passes through these points, i.e., the medial circle.

```
>   midpoint( D, O, A ):
>   midpoint( E, A, B ):
>   midpoint( F, O, B ):
>   circle( C, [ D, E, F ] ):
```

Let G be the foot of the altitude L from O to the edge AB.

```
>   projection( G, O, line('dummy',[A,B]) ):
>   line( L, [O,G] ):   # altitude
```

The power of the geometry package is that you can ask geometrical questions like "Is a point on a line?" and "Are two lines perpendicular?" So, you can verify the theorem by asking Maple whether G is on the medial circle C.

```
>   IsOnCircle( G, C );
```

$$true$$

Now, let us choose a specific triangle T and draw the picture.

```
>   assign(x,2): assign(y,1):
>   draw( [ C(printtext=false), T, D, E, F, G, L ],
>     axes=none, thickness=3, font=[HELVETICA,BOLD,16],
>     color=blue, scaling=constrained );
```

As you see in the above command, the procedure **draw** provides the graphical visualization of objects supported in the geometry package. Both local options for particular objects and global plot options can be applied. In the second example we shall heavily use this feature to improve the geometrical picture; here, we only inform Maple that the center of the Apollonius circle does not need to be drawn (Figure 15.65).

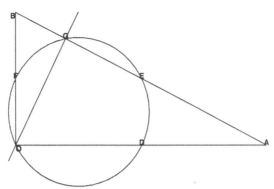

FIGURE 15.65. Illustration of the circle theorem of Apollonius.

For a completely algebraic treatment of the above theorem we refer to example 3 of section 6.4 in [51].

Simson's Theorem. *The pedal points of the perpendiculars drawn from an arbitrary point on a triangle's circumscribed circle to the three edges are collinear.*

Let us see how we can "prove" and graphically illustrate this theorem. First, we define a triangle OAB with its circumscribed circle C.

```
>   triangle( T,
>     [ point(0,0,0), point(A,3,0), point(B,2,2) ] ):
>   circumcircle( C, T ):
```

Next, we define a point D on the circle. For this purpose, we must find a condition for a generic point (u, v) to be on the circle C. In our case:

```
>   point( D, u, v ):
>   IsOnCircle( D, C, ´condition´ );

IsOnCircle:
hint: unable to determine if u^2+v^2-3*u-v is zero
```

$$FAIL$$

```
>   condition;
```

$$u^2 + v^2 - 3u - v = 0$$

So, we assume that this condition is satisfied.

```
>   assume(condition):
```

We can compute the pedal point E, F, G of D on the edges OA, OB, and AB, respectively, in the following way.

```
>   projection( E, D, line( ´dummy´, [O,A] ) ):
>   projection( F, D, line( ´dummy´, [O,B] ) ):
>   projection( G, D, line( ´dummy´, [A,B] ) ):
```

We verify Simson's theorem.

```
>  AreCollinear( E, F, G );
```

$$true$$

So, for the given triangle T, Maple can prove Simson's theorem! Now, let us choose a specific point D on the circle.

```
>  solve( condition );
```

$$\{\, u\tilde{}\ = \frac{3}{2} + \frac{1}{2}\, \sqrt{9 - 4\, v\tilde{}^2 + 4\, v\tilde{}}, v\tilde{}\ = v\tilde{}\,\},$$

$$\{\, u\tilde{}\ = \frac{3}{2} - \frac{1}{2}\, \sqrt{9 - 4\, v\tilde{}^2 + 4\, v\tilde{}}, v\tilde{}\ = v\tilde{}\,\}$$

From this solution, it can easily be seen that $(u, v) = (\frac{3}{2} - \frac{1}{2}\sqrt{6}, 1)$ is a valid point. We choose it and we define the lines from D to the pedal points on the edges, the line L through the pedal points, and an auxiliary line to improve the picture.

```
>  assign( u, 3/2-1/2*sqrt(6) ): assign(v,3/2):
>  line( DE, [D,E] ): line( DF, [D,F] ):
>  line( DG, [D,G] ): line(L,[E,G]):
>  line(H,[B,G]):
```

Everything is ready for drawing the picture that illustrates Simson's theorem (Figure 15.66).

```
>  draw(
>    [ C(filled=false,linestyle=1,printtext=false),
>      T(color=black,filled=false,thickness=5,linestyle=1),
>      DE, DF, DG, H, D, L(color=red,linestyle=1),
>      E, F, G ],
>    axes=none, linestyle=2, thickness=3, color=blue,
>    scaling=constrained, font=[HELVETICA,BOLD,16]
>  );
```

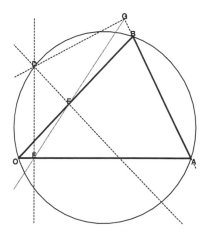

FIGURE 15.66. Illustration of Simson's Theorem.

We leave it as an exercise to prove Simson's theorem, with the help of the **geometry** package, for a general triangle. A completely algebraic treatment of Simson's theorem can be found in [119].

15.7   Plot Aliasing

Adaptive two-dimensional plotting produces, in most cases, reasonable graphs with a minimum of sample points. But you should keep alert for insufficient sampling. As a rather extreme case of plot aliasing, we plot the function $x \longmapsto \frac{1}{10}(x-25)^2 + \cos(2\pi x)$ on the interval $(0, 49)$ (Figure 15.67).

```
>  plot( (x-25)^2/10 + cos(2*Pi*x), x=0..49 );
```

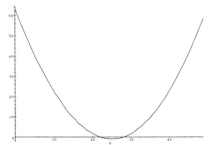

FIGURE 15.67. Plot aliasing for mapping $x \mapsto \frac{1}{10}(x - 25)^2 + \cos(2\pi x)$.

This graph is pretty close to the parabola $y = \frac{1}{10}(x - 25)^2$. This is wrong! The reason is that because of the default choice of 49 almost equidistant sample points, the computed function values tend to be very close to the parabola. Maple has no reason to believe that there is something wrong and it has no reason to sample more points, or to sample other points. You yourself will have to decide to sample more points (by the option **numpoints**) or to choose another plot range (Figure 15.68).

```
>  plot( (x-25)^2/10+cos(2*Pi*x), x=0..49, numpoints=2000 );
```

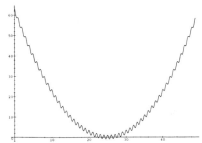

FIGURE 15.68. Improved graph of $x-> \frac{1}{10}(x - 25)^2 + \cos(2\pi x)$.

15.8   A Common Mistake

When you ask Maple to plot a function, say f, as a function of x by
entering a command of the form **plot**($f(x)$, $x = x_{\min}..x_{\max}$), Maple first
evaluates the $f(x)$, presumably getting a symbolic expression in terms of
x, and subsequently evaluates this expression numerically for the sample
points. This may cause you some problems when you try to plot a piecewise
defined function or a numerical function. Below we present one example and
four ways to overcome these problems. Suppose that you have defined the
function f by

```
>  f := t -> if t>0 then exp(-1/t^2) else 0 fi:
```

and want to plot it.

```
>  plot( f(t), t=-1..4 );
```

Error, (in f) cannot evaluate boolean

As you see, you get an error message back instead of a graph. The reason
is that Maple evaluates f(t) and the system gets into trouble because it
cannot pass the test t>0. The trick of the trade is to avoid premature
evaluation by using apostrophes around the first argument (Figure 15.69).

```
>  plot( ´f(t)´, t=-1..4 );
```

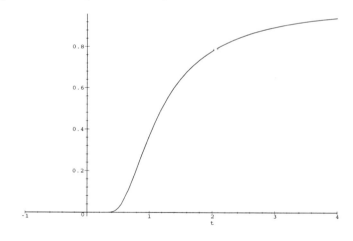

FIGURE 15.69. Graph of piecewise defined function.

Another option is to use the functional notation. For example, the function
f and its derivative f' can be plotted in one picture (Figure 15.70) with

```
>  plot( {f,D(f)}, -1..4 );
```

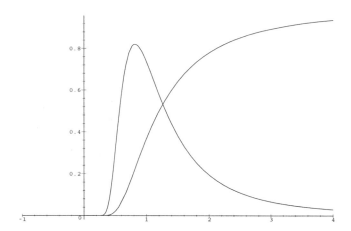

FIGURE 15.70. Graph of piecewise defined function and its derivative.

Two other solutions to the problem are to change the way you define the piecewise defined function. First, Maple has built-in facilities for piecewise defined functions that do not fail, viz., the procedure **piecewise**. If they are present, why not use them?

```
>    f := t -> piecewise( t>0, exp(-1/t^2), 0 ):
>    f(t); # no problem
```

$$\begin{cases} e^{-t^{-2}} & 0 < t \\ 0 & \text{otherwise} \end{cases}$$

Second, as shown in §8.3 you can define the function such that non-numeric arguments are accepted without any further effect. One way of doing this would be

```
>    f := t -> if not type(t,numeric) then
>                    ´procname´(t)
>               elif t>0 then
>                    exp(-1/t^2)
>               else 0
>               fi:
>    f(t); # no problem
```

$$f(t)$$

15.9   Some Basic Three-Dimensional Plots

Plotting a function of two variables is as easy as plotting a function in one variable. Simply use the Maple procedure **plot3d** and specify the ranges of both variables. As an example, let us plot the surface defined by $z = \cos(x\,y)$, where x and y range from -3 to 3 (Figure 15.71).

```
>  plot3d( cos(x*y), x=-3..3, y=-3..3, color=black );
```

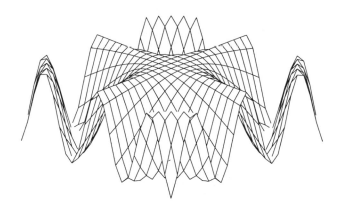

FIGURE 15.71. Surface plot of $z = \cos(x\,y)$ with hidden line removal.

The above command is an example of the following general format for drawing a surface defined by the *formula* $f(x, y)$ of two variables x and y:

plot3d($f(x, y)$, $x = a\,..\,b$, $y = c\,..\,d$, *options*);

where $a\,..\,b$ and $c\,..\,d$ define the range of x and y, and where *options* describes zero or more options, as will be discussed in the next section.

An alternative way of obtaining the graph of a *function* f in two variables is

plot3d(f, $a\,..\,b$, $c\,..\,d$, *options*);

where $a\,..\,b$ and $c\,..\,d$ define the two horizontal ranges, and where *options* describes zero or more options.

Below we draw again the graph of the function $(x, y) \longmapsto \cos(x\,y)$, but now we choose the functional notation and change some of the options. This can be done interactively by selecting proper menu items from the 3D-plot window. But to ensure that you can reproduce the graph, we have added all options in the **plot3d** command (Figure 15.72).

```
>  f := (x,y) -> cos(x*y):
>  plot3d( f, -3..3, -3..3, grid=[50,50], axes=box,
>     scaling=constrained, style=patchcontour,
>     shading=zgrayscale );
```

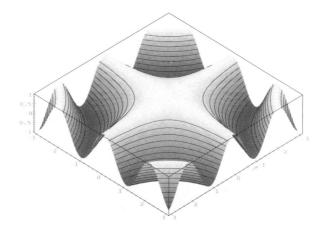

FIGURE 15.72. Graph of $(x, y) \longmapsto \cos(x\,y)$ with gray shading and contour levels.

15.10   Options of **plot3d**

Just as in the two-dimensional case, there are many options to customize a plot. Under the X Window System you can change many options by selecting menu items and/or by mouse actions. We shall discuss some of the options and refer for others to the table of three-dimensional plotting options at the end of this section. In a Maple session, you can always consult the on-line help system by entering **?plot3d,option**.

Style

A surface can be rendered in several ways with the optional argument `style = ` *displaystyle*. The simplest style is `point`, which draws only the computed plot points. Plot points are connected with line segments when the style option `line` is chosen. By the way, the sample points of a surface are in general the grid points of a rectangular uniformly spaced grid. When adjacent plot points are connected by line segments, the result is a picture of style `wireframe` that approximates the shape of the surface. In the first plot of the previous section, the line segments that would be hidden if the surface were opaque are not displayed; this is Maple's default style `hidden`. You can choose the style `patch` if you want to display the surface in full color or gray shading. If you do not want the grid displayed, choose the option `patchnogrid`. With the style option `contour` only the contour lines of the surface are drawn. A combination of two options is the style option `patchcontour`, illustrated in the last picture of the previous section.

Shading

In Maple, a surface can be colored (or gray shaded) in three ways: xyz, xy, and z shading. When you choose the option shading = z, the color/gray shading is according to the z value of the points on the surface. In the xy or xyz shading schemes, each of the axes has its own range of colors and these colors are added together for a point on the surface. The options zhue and zgrayscale produce graphs with color hues and gray levels depending on the z-values. With shading = none, the picture is in one uniform color.

Axes

With the option axes you specify how the axes are to be drawn. There are four choices: none, normal, box, and frame. The names speak for themselves; we only remark that framed axes are drawn along the edges of the surface so that they do not pass through the surface.

Orientation and Projection

Rendering of a three-dimensional graphics object in two dimensions on a screen or on paper is commonly done by projection. The center of projection (or view point) is described in spherical coordinates with respect to the local Cartesian coordinate system at the center of the bounding box (Figure 15.73).

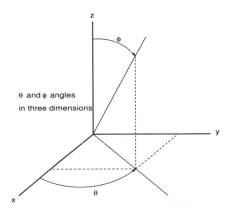

FIGURE 15.73. Orientation in three dimensions: θ and ϕ angles.

The angles θ and ϕ can be set with the option orientation = $[\theta,\phi]$. Increasing the value of rotation angle θ rotates the plot counterclockwise along the z-axis. When this rotation angle is set to zero, you look down on the front and top side of the surface.

ϕ controls the vertical view angle; the value zero means that you look straight down on the surface, ninety degrees means that you look edge on at the xy plane, and more than ninety degrees means that you look up from beneath the surface.

The option projection $= p$, where p is a real constant in the range $[0, 1]$, specifies the distance from the view point to the surface. Value 0 (**fisheye**) means touching; 1 (**orthogonal**) means infinitely far away; **normal** value is $\frac{1}{2}$.

Pictures tell you more than words. Below, plots generated initially by

```
>    plot3d( x^3-3*x*y^2, x=-1..1, y=-1..1,
>       style=patch, axes=box );
```

are shown from different points of view.

theta=45, phi=45

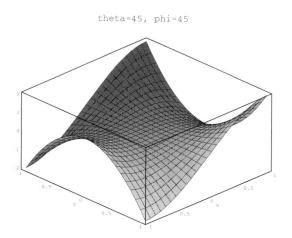

theta=5, phi=45

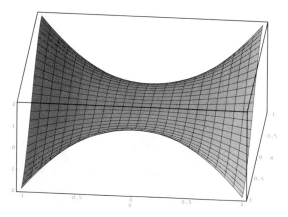

theta=5, phi=80

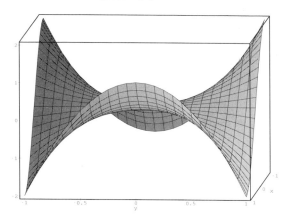

theta=-60, phi=60

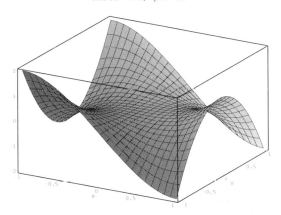

You can create a 3D-graphics array of the above plots, but it is quite some work, especially if you want a decent labeling of the plots like in Figure 15.74. (By trial and error you can find text locations that project nicely in the 3D-graphics array. The obscure way of labeling the plots below is to overcome the programming bug that the 3D-graphics conversion assumes at least one tick mark per axes; the default boxes for tick marks in 3D-graphics arrays is replaced by points, which you do not see on the axes.)

```
>  with( plots, [display,textplot3d] ):
>  angles := [ [45,45], [5,45], [5, 80], [-60,60] ]:
>  ticks := [ [0=` `],[0=` `],[0=` `] ]: # blank tick marks
```

```
> position :=
>    [ [-1,0.25,2], [0,0.1,3], [0,0.1,1.2], [0.8,0.5,2] ]:
> sf := [SYMBOL,10]: # symbol font at point size 10
> for i to 4 do
>    P := plot3d( x^3-3*x*y^2, x=-1..1, y=-1..1,
>       style=patch, tickmarks=ticks,
>       orientation=angles[i] ):
>    T := textplot3d( [ op( position[i] ),
>       cat(`[q,f] = `,convert(angles[i],name)) ],
>       font=sf, color=blue );
>    F[i] := display( {P,T}, axes=frame ):
> od:
> plotarray := matrix( 2, 2,
>    [ seq( F[i], i=1..4) ], array ):
> subs( SYMBOL(BOX)=SYMBOL(POINT),
>    display( plotarray ) ); # draw graphics array
```

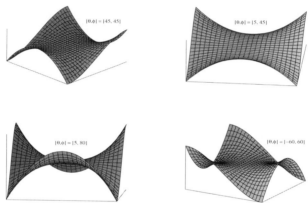

FIGURE 15.74. Plots of $x^3 - 3xy^2$ taken from different view points.

Note that changing the shading or changing the view point does not imply recomputing the graphics object. It is only a matter of rendering the picture on the screen. This does not hold for the next option.

Grid Size

In the three-dimensional case, Maple has no algorithm to refine the grid of sample points. In other words, unlike two-dimensional plotting, **plot3d** uses no adaptive sampling scheme. A default grid with 25 equidistant points in both directions is used. This can be changed by the option grid $= [m,n]$, if you want m points in the x direction and n points in the y direction. So, you must be aware of nasty three-dimensional plot aliasing effects (Figure 15.75) like

```
> plot3d( sin(2*Pi*x), x=0..25, y=0..1,
>    axes=frame, style=patch, shading=zgrayscale );
```

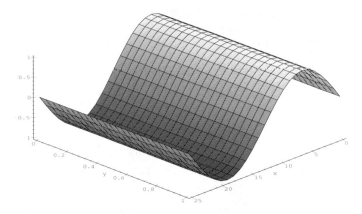

FIGURE 15.75. Extreme case of three-dimensional plot aliasing in plot of $\sin(2\pi x)$.

View Frame

Like in two-dimensional plotting, you may want to restrict the vertical range, or even all three ranges of the surface. This is possible with the option **view**. There are two formats:

$$view = z_{\min}..z_{\max}$$

and

$$view = [\,x_{\min}..x_{\max},\; y_{\min}..y_{\max},\; z_{\min}..z_{\max}\,].$$

Lighting

Maple can simulate lighting for illumination via two options:

- **light** $= [\phi, \theta, r, g, b]$ simulates a light source with given *r*ed, *g*reen, and *b*lue intensities in the RGB color model shining on the graphics object from the direction specified in the spherical coordinates $[\phi, \theta]$.

- **ambientlight** $= [r, g, b]$ gives a nondirectional shading with *r*ed, *g*reen, and *b*lue intensities in the RGB color model.

In the example below, we give the code to look from the top on an octahedron with three light sources (with primary colors) shining on the faces of the polytope.

```
>   display(
>     plottools[octahedron]( [0,0,0], 1 ),
>     style=patch, axes=box,
>     ambientlight=[0.2,0.2,0.2],
>     light=[45,90,1,0,0], light=[135,90,0,1,0],
>     light=[225,90,0,0,1], orientation=[-90,0]);
```

We do not display the picture because the gray shading in this text would not really reveal the effects of the lighting. You have to do the example yourself.

The following example of planes with gray light sources shining on them from directions perpendicular to either one of the planes clearly shows the effect of lighting, too (Figures 15.76 and 15.77).

```
>   plot3d( {x,1-x}, x=0..1, y=0..1, style=patchnogrid,
>     axes=frame, shading=none, orientation=[-45,25],
>     light=[0,0,0.9,0.9,0.9] );
```

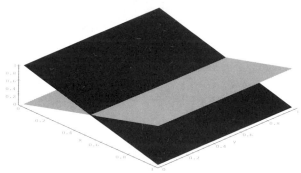

FIGURE 15.76. Effect of lighting on surfaces: light source from direction [0,0].

```
>   plot3d( {x,1-x}, x=0..1,y=0..1, style=patchnogrid,
>     axes=frame, shading=none, orientation=[-45,25],
>     light=[135,0,0.9,0.9,0.9] );
```

FIGURE 15.77. Effect of lighting on surfaces: light source from direction [135,0].

Contours

When you use the 3D-graphics styles `contour` and `patchcontour`, the contour lines of the surface are drawn. The default number of contour lines is 10, but can be reset by the option `contours` (Figures 15.78).

```
>   plot3d( 5.5-y, x=0..1, y=0..5, axes=frame,
>      shading=zgrayscale, thickness=5, style=contour,
>      contours=5 );
```

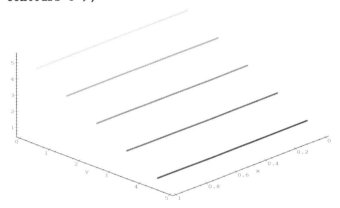

FIGURE 15.78. Contour lines on a surface.

You can also specify explicitly what contour values you want to have in your picture (Figure 15.79).

```
>   plot3d( 5.5-y, x=0..1, y=0..5, axes=frame,
>      shading=zgrayscale, thickness=5, style=contour,
>      contours=[1,2,4] );
```

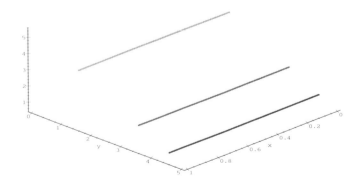

FIGURE 15.79. Contour lines at specified levels on a surface.

You can inspect or reset default options for all subsequent calls of **plot3d** by the procedure **setoptions3d** from the `plots` package.

At the end of this chapter you can find a list of all three-dimensional plot options that are available. Some of them have not been discussed yet, but they will be used in examples later in this chapter. The options style, linestyle, thickness, symbol, gridstyle, shading, light, axes, and projection can be changed interactively in the worksheet interface. Others must be adjusted in a plot command.

15.11   The Structure of Three-Dimensional Graphics

The making of a three-dimensional plot proceeds in two phases, similar to the way two-dimensional plots are generated. In the first phase, the plot points are computed and put in a PLOT3D object. In the second phase, this object is rendered on the screen. In this section, we shall present two examples of three-dimensional graphics objects, which can serve as prototypes for others.

A three-dimensional graphics object in Maple is a call to the function **PLOT3D** with arguments describing the axes, function, computed plot points, plot style, grid size, coloring, and so on.

The following object describes the edges of the tetrahedron with vertices $(1, 1, 1), (-1, -1, 1), (-1, 1, -1)$, and $(1, -1, -1)$ (Figure 15.80).

```
>   PLOT3D( POLYGONS( [ [1,1,1], [-1,-1,1], [-1,1,-1] ],
>     [ [1,1,1], [-1,-1,1], [1,-1,-1] ],
>     [ [-1,1,-1], [1,-1,-1], [-1,-1,1] ],
>     [ [-1,1,-1], [1,-1,-1], [1,1,1] ] ),
>     STYLE(LINE), COLOR(RGB,1,0,0), AXESSTYLE(BOX),
>     ORIENTATION(30,60), SCALING(CONSTRAINED) );
```

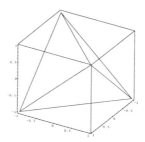

FIGURE 15.80. Tetrahedron built up from graphics primitives.

The arguments POLYGONS(...), STYLE, COLOR, AXESSTYLE, ORIENTATION, and SCALING are parts of the graphics object obtained by

```
>   P := polygonplot3d( [
>     [ [1,1,1], [-1,-1,1], [-1,1,-1] ],
>     [ [1,1,1], [-1,-1,1], [1,-1,-1] ],
```

```
>    [ [-1,1,-1], [1,-1,-1], [-1,-1,1] ],
>    [ [-1,1,-1], [1,-1,-1], [1,1,1] ] ],
>    style=line, color=red, axes=box,
>    orientation=[30,60], scaling=constrained ):
> lprint( P );  # print 3D plot data structure

PLOT3D(POLYGONS([[1., 1., 1.], [-1., -1., 1.],
  [-1., 1., -1.]], [[1., 1., 1.], [-1., -1., 1.],
  [1., -1., -1.]], [[-1., 1., -1.], [1., -1., -1.],
  [-1., -1., 1.]], [[-1., 1., -1.], [1., -1., -1.],
  [1., 1., 1.]]),ORIENTATION(30.,60.),STYLE(LINE),
  SCALING(CONSTRAINED),AXESSTYLE(BOX),
  COLOUR(RGB,1.00000000,0,0))

> P;  # display the graphics object
```

The picture is not shown here because it is the same as Figure 15.80.

A more general example of a graphics object behind a plot is the plot structure for the graph of the function $(x, y) \longmapsto x\, y^2$ (Figure 15.81).

```
> P := plot3d( x*y^2 , x=-1..1, y=-1..1, grid=[5,5],
>    axes=box, orientation=[30,30], style=line,
>    color=red, title=`graph of z=xy^2` ):
> lprint( P );  # print the 3D plot data structure

PLOT3D(GRID(-1. .. 1.,-1. .. 1.,
  [[-1., -.2500000000000000, 0, -.2500000000000000, -1.],
  [-.5000000000000000, -.1250000000000000, 0,
  -.1250000000000000, -.5000000000000000], [0, 0, 0, 0, 0],
  [.5000000000000000, .1250000000000000, 0,
  .1250000000000000, .5000000000000000],
  [1., .2500000000000000, 0, .2500000000000000, 1.]],
  COLOR(RGB,1.00000000,0,0)),ORIENTATION(30.,30.),
  AXESLABELS(x,y,),STYLE(LINE),TITLE(graph of z=xy^2),
  AXESSTYLE(BOX))
```

Maple associates a graphics object with a function in two variables on a rectangular grid. This object, which is a regular Maple object, will be used for straight line interpolation between adjacent plot points.

```
> P;  # display the surface
```

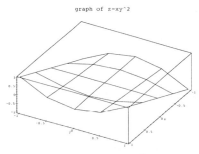

FIGURE 15.81. Surface $z = x\, y^2$ with small grid.

First, the argument in the **plot3d** call that describes the function is evaluated. Hereafter, the function values at the grid points are computed numerically, row by row. To increase the speed of plotting, this computation of function values is usually done in hardware floating-point arithmetic. Unlike two-dimensional plotting, no automatic refinement of the grid takes place when kink angles become large.

We say that inside plotting routines Maple *usually* carries out evaluation of function values through hardware floating-point arithmetic. Of course, when you set Digits to a higher value than is supported by hardware floating-points, Maple has no other choice than omitting the hardware floating-point arithmetic. But you must also watch out for parts in a function that do not allow hardware floating-point arithmetic. For example, use of complex numbers in plotting disables the ability of hardware arithmetic.

```
>  evalhf( 2 + sqrt(3)*I );
```

Error, sqrt of a negative number

This has a tremendous effect on the speed of plotting. Check: plotting the surface $z = \sqrt{x^2 + y^2}$ via the function

```
>  f := proc(x,y) sqrt(x^2+y^2) end:
```

is about 25 times faster than via the function

```
>  g := proc(x,y) z := x+I*y; evalc( abs(z) ) end:
```

If you find this example too artificial, let us consider the plotting of the filled-in Julia set of the complex function $f : z \longmapsto z^2 - 1$, which is the set of those points in the complex plane whose orbits under the function f do not approach infinity. In Figure 15.82, this set is approximated by points that escape to infinity according to the following criteria: a point z_0 escapes to infinity if the orbit of z_0 contains a point with absolute value greater than 3 within the first 25 iterates. In that case we associate a function value $F(z_0) = 1$ with it; otherwise $F(z_0) = 0$. Figure 15.82 is actually the surface plot of this new function F with gray shading based on the function value and viewed from the top. The Maple code

```
>  F := proc(x,y)
>     local z;
>     z :=  evalf( x + y*I ) ;
>     to 25 while abs(z)<=3 do z := z^2 -1 od:
>     if abs(z)>3 then 1 else 0 fi
>  end:
>  plot3d( F, -2..2, -1..1, grid=[200,200],
>     orientation=[-90,0], style=patchnogrid, axes=box,
>     labels=[x,y,` `], shading=zgrayscale );
```

does the job, but is much slower than the "real" version below that benefits from hardware arithmetic.

```
>   F := proc(x, y)
>     local X, Y, XCOPY;
>     X := evalf(x):   Y := evalf(y):
>     to 25 while X^2 + Y^2 <= 9 do
>         XCOPY := X: X := X^2-Y^2-1: Y := 2*XCOPY*Y
>     od:
>     if X^2 + Y^2 > 9 then 1 else 0 fi
>   end:
>   plot3d( F, -2..2, -1..1, grid=[200,200],
>     orientation=[-90,0], style=patchnogrid, axes=box,
>     labels=[x,y,` `], shading=zgrayscale );
```

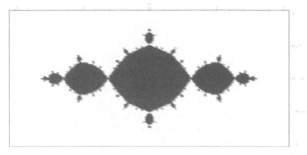

FIGURE 15.82. Filled-in Julia set of complex map $z \longmapsto z^2 - 1$.

The graph of the boundary of the filled-in Julia set, which actually forms the Julia set, can be created by drawing the plane $z = 0$ with the function F as the color function in the HUE color model (Figure 15.83).

```
>   plot3d( 0, -2..2, -1..1, grid=[200,200],
>     orientation=[-90,0], style=patchnogrid,
>     axes=frame, labels=[x,y,` `], color=F );
```

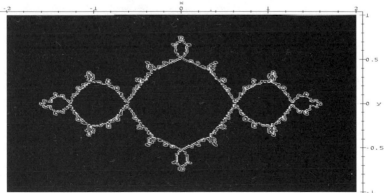

FIGURE 15.83. Julia set of complex map $z \longmapsto z^2 - 1$.

Like in two dimensions, the general format of a three-dimensional graphics primitive is a function call

$$ObjectName(\ ObjectInformation,\ LocalInformation\ ).$$

In the first example of this section, you encountered the object name POLYGONS with the same meaning as in the two-dimensional case. In general, two-dimensional object names like POINT and TEXT can be used in three dimensions as well. The only new object names are GRID and MESH. GRID is the object name that describes a functional grid (in two dimensions) and MESH is a structure that describes a list of lists of three-dimensional points describing a surface. For example, the next function call describes a surface consisting of two triangles (Figure 15.84).

```
>    PLOT3D( MESH([ [ [1,1,1],[0,1,0],[0,0,1] ],
>                   [ [1,1,1],[1,0,0],[0,0,1] ] ] ),
>            STYLE(PATCH),AXES(BOX) );
```

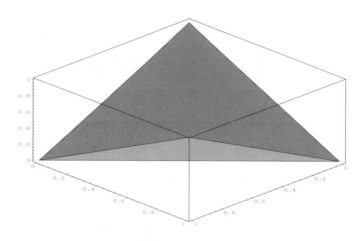

FIGURE 15.84. A three-dimensional mesh of two triangles.

Many of the names for local information in 2D-graphics can also be used in 3D-graphics: AXES, FONT, and SCALING are three names among many. Of course, there are names that only have a meaning in 3D-graphics; AMBIENTLIGHT, GRIDSTYLE, ORIENTATION, and SHADING are some of them. Most names are similar to names of options that are allowed in plotting commands. You can actually see how an option is converted into a graphics primitive.

```
>    convert( [ color=red, orientation=[20,60] ],
>      PLOT3Doptions );
```

$$[\,\mathrm{ORIENTATION}(\,20., 60.\,), \mathrm{COLOUR}(\,RGB, 1.00000000, 0, 0\,)\,]$$

This conversion of plot options into graphics primitives comes in handy sometimes when you want to change a low-level graphics primitive of an existing graphics object.

15.12   Special Three-Dimensional Plots

The Maple packages plots and plottools, which provide utility routines
and building blocks for two- and three-dimensional plotting, respectively,
have been discussed earlier in this chapter for mostly two-dimensional
graphics. Special three-dimensional plots can be generated with procedures
from these packages as well. Therefore, let us load the packages and do some
examples.

```
> with(plots): with(plottools):
```

We start with examples of procedures from the plots package.

Parametric Plots

A three-dimensional space curve can be drawn with **spacecurve** (Figure
15.85).

```
> spacecurve( {
>    [t*cos(2*Pi*t),t*sin(2*Pi*t),2+t],
>    [2+t,t*cos(2*Pi*t),t*sin(2*Pi*t)],
>    [t*cos(2*Pi*t),2+t,t*sin(2*Pi*t)] }, t=0..10,
>    numpoints=400, orientation=[40,70],
>    style=line, thickness=3, axes=box );
```

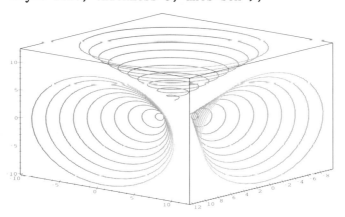

FIGURE 15.85. Three-dimensional space curve.

The general format for drawing a three-dimensional surface defined in the
Cartesian coordinate system by parametric *formulas*

$$x = f(s,t), \ y = g(s,t), \ z = h(s,t)$$

is

plot3d([$f(s,t)$, $g(s,t)$, $h(s,t)$], $s = a \mathbin{..} b$, $t = c \mathbin{..} d$, *options*);

where $a \mathbin{..} b$ and $c \mathbin{..} d$ are the ranges of the independent variables s and t,
and where *options* describes zero or more options.

As an example, we draw the helicoid (Figure 15.86) defined by the parametrization

$$(\phi, z) \longmapsto (r\cos\phi,\ r\sin\phi,\ \phi),$$

where $0 \le r \le 1$ and $0 \le \phi \le 6\pi$.

```
> plot3d( [ r*cos(phi), r*sin(phi), phi ],
>    r=0..1, phi=0..6*Pi, grid=[15,45], style=patch,
>    orientation=[55,70], shading=zhue, axes=box );
```

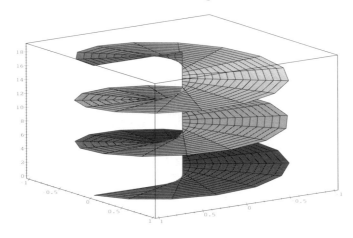

FIGURE 15.86. helicoid.

Coordinate Systems

Spherical (Figure 15.87), cylindrical (Figure 15.88), and many more coordinate systems are also supported by Maple. A few examples, in which we first give the graphics object a name and then render it:

```
> S := plot3d( 1, theta=0..2*Pi, phi=0..Pi, style=patch,
>    coords=spherical, scaling=constrained ):  S;
```

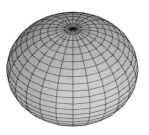

FIGURE 15.87. Sphere.

```
> C := plot3d( 1/2, theta=0..2*Pi, z=-2..2, style=patch,
>    coords=cylindrical, scaling=constrained ):  C;
```

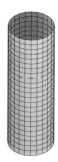

FIGURE 15.88. Cylinder.

```
>   subs( STYLE(PATCH) = STYLE(PATCHCONTOUR),
>      display( {S,C}, axes=box, orientation=[20,70],
>      scaling=constrained ) );
```

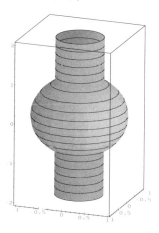

FIGURE 15.89. Combination of a sphere and a cylinder.

You must change the style via the above substitution instead of via the option `style=patchcontour` to obtain Figure 15.89. The reason is that in the procedure **display**, global options like color and style are moved to local ones attached to the corresponding graphical objects.

Tube Plots

The **tubeplot** procedure defines a tube about one or more three-dimensional space curves. Let us draw in this way the torus of type (4,7) (Figure 15.90).

```
>   r := a + b*cos(n*t):   z := c*sin(n*t):
>   curve:=[ r*cos(m*t), r*sin(m*t), z ]:
>   a:=2:  b:=4/5:  c:=1:  m:=4:  n:=7:
>   tubeplot( curve, t=0..2*Pi, radius=1/4, numpoints=200,
>      tubepoints=20, orientation=[45,10], style=patch,
>      shading=xyz );
```

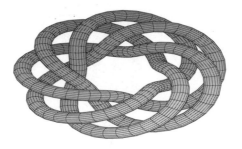

FIGURE 15.90. Torusknot of type (4,7).

Implicit Plot

Nonsingular surfaces defined by an equation in any coordinate system what-
soever can be plotted with **implicitplot3d**. The catenoid is defined in the
Cartesian coordinate system by $\cosh z = \sqrt{x^2 + y^2}$, and can be drawn as
follows (Figure 15.91).

```
>   implicitplot3d( cosh(z)=sqrt(x^2+y^2),
>     x=-3..3, y=-3..3, z=-2.5..2.5, grid=[15,15,20],
>     style=patchcontour, contours=15, axes=box,
>     orientation=[30,70] );
```

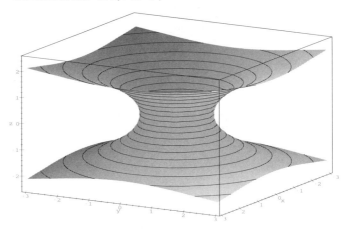

FIGURE 15.91. Implicit plot of the catenoid.

The option `style=patchcontour` ensures that the surface not only is shaded
but also contains contour lines.

A more spectacular implicit plot with contours is the following example
in spherical coordinates (Figure 15.92).

```
>   r * ( 4 + 2*cos(3*theta) - cos(3*theta+2*phi)
>     - cos(-3*theta+2*phi) + 2*cos(2*phi)) = 2;
```

$$r \left(4 + 2\cos(3\,\theta) - \cos(3\,\theta + 2\,\phi) - \cos(3\,\theta - 2\,\phi) + 2\cos(2\,\phi) \right) = 2$$

```
>  implicitplot3d( ", r=0..2, theta=0..2*Pi, phi=0..Pi,
>    coords=spherical, grid=[10,40,40],
>    style=patchcontour, thickness=2, orientation=[35,30] );
```

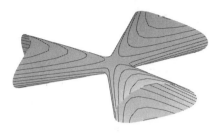

FIGURE 15.92. Implicit plot in spherical coordinates.

Complex plotting

The procedure **complexplot3d** can be used to plot complex functions from $\mathbb{C}$ to $\mathbb{C}$: the height of the surface at position (x, y) is the magnitude of a function value at $x + yi$, and the color at this point is determined by the argument of the function value. An example: the gamma function (Figure 15.93).

```
>  complexplot3d( GAMMA(z), z= -Pi-Pi*I .. Pi+Pi*I,
>    view=0..5, grid=[30,30], orientation=[-120,45],
>    axes=frame, style=patchcontour, thickness=2 );
```

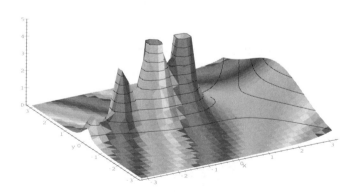

FIGURE 15.93. Plot of complex gamma function.

Compare this picture with Figure 2.8 of §2.6.

Polyhedra

Some popular polyhedra such as the tetrahedron, octahedron, and dodeca-hedron (Figure 15.94) can easily be drawn with **polyhedraplot**. From the help file:

```
>   polyhedraplot( [0,0,0], polytype=dodecahedron,
>   style=patch, scaling=constrained, orientation=[71,66] );
```

FIGURE 15.94. Dodecahedron.

Sierpinsky's Tetrahedron

We shall start the examples that illustrate the features of the **plottools** package with the creation of Sierpinsky's tetrahedron. The example illustrates the commands to scale and to translate an existing 3D-graphics object. It is a small example of graphics programming in Maple (Figure 15.95).

We first create the tetrahedron that will form the starting object in an iteration. We can easily do this with the **tetrahedron** routine:

```
>   base := tetrahedron( [0,0,0], 1 ):
>   display( base,style=patch, scaling=constrained,
>     orientation=[60,50], shading=zgrayscale );
```

FIGURE 15.95. Standard tetrahedron as basic polytope in construction of Sierpinsky's tetrahedron.

Next we scale the tetrahedron by a factor $\frac{1}{2}$ and make four copies of the scaled tetrahedron by translating it in the directions of the four vertices (Figure 15.96).

```
>  vertices := {
>    [ 0, 0, sqrt(3) ],
>    [ 0, 2*sqrt(2)/sqrt(3), -1/sqrt(3) ],
>    [ -sqrt(2), -sqrt(2)/sqrt(3), -1/sqrt(3) ],
>    [  sqrt(2), -sqrt(2)/sqrt(3), -1/sqrt(3) ] }:
>  translations := map( x -> 1/2*x, vertices ):
>  tetrahedra := { seq(
>    translate( scale( base, 1/2, 1/2, 1/2 ), op(t) ),
>    t=translations ) }:
>  display( tetrahedra, style=patch, scaling=constrained,
>    orientation=[60,50], shading=zgrayscale, thickness=2 );
```

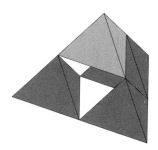

FIGURE 15.96. First step in construction of Sierpinsky's tetrahedron.

This process can be repeated over and over again, thus creating Sierpinsky's tetrahedron. Let us look at the picture after four iterations consisting of 1024 tetrahedra (Figure 15.97).

```
>  translations := map( x -> 1/2*x, vertices ):
>  N := 4: # number of iterations
>  for k from 2 to N do
>    newtranslations  := map( x -> x/2^k, vertices ):
>    translations := { seq( seq( t + tnew,
>      t=translations ), tnew=newtranslations ) }:
>  od:
>  tetrahedra := { seq( translate(
>                     scale( base, 1/2^N, 1/2^N, 1/2^N ),
>                     op(t) ), t=translations ) }:
>  display( tetrahedra, style=patchnogrid, scaling=
>    constrained, orientation=[55,50], shading=zgrayscale );
```

FIGURE 15.97. Sierpinsky's tetrahedron after four iterations.

Canadian Flag

The following fun example of a look-alike of the Canadian flag illustrates transformations from two-dimensional to three-dimensional graphics and other mappings on graphics objects. We start with the Maple logo that we created in §15.1.

```
>   S := t -> 100/(100+(t-Pi/2)^8): # for scaling
>   R := t -> S(t)*(2-sin(7*t)-cos(30*t)/2):
>   mapleleaf := plot( [ R, t->t, -Pi/2..3/2*Pi ],
>       coords=polar, axes=none, color=red, numpoints=1000 ):
```

These commands create a closed curve resembling the Maple leaf. In the Canadian flag, the inner space should be colored red. The easiest way to do this is to replace the CURVES object name by POLYGONS. Moreover, we add two rectangles to get a plane Canadian flag and a border to indicate the white background (we assume that the default background color is white) (Figure 15.98).

```
>   mapleleaf := subs( CURVES=POLYGONS, mapleleaf ):
>   rectangles := rectangle([-5,-1],[-3,4], color=red ),
>                 rectangle([3,-1],[5,4],color=red ):
>   border := plot( {-1,4},-3..3, color=black ):
>   flag2d := display( [ mapleleaf, rectangles, border ],
>     view=[-5..5,-1..4], scaling=constrained ):
>   flag2d;
```

FIGURE 15.98. Look-alike of Canadian flag.

Finally, we use the **transform** procedure from the plottools package with the mapping $(x, y) \longmapsto (x, y, 0)$ to convert the two-dimensional graphics object into a three-dimensional one. Finally, we apply the mapping $(x, y, z) \longmapsto (x, y, 1 + \frac{1}{15} \sin(x))$ to project the plane flag onto the sine surface (Figure 15.99).

```
>   flag3d := transform( (x,y,z) -> [x,y,0] )(flag2d):
>   wavingflag3d :=
>     transform( (x,y) -> [x,y,1+1/15*sin(x)] )(flag3d):
>   display( { flag3d, wavingflag3d },
>     scaling=unconstrained, orientation=[-110,60],axes=none,
>     style=patchnogrid, shading=none );
```

FIGURE 15.99. Flat and waving Canadian flags.

15.13   Data Plotting

When a plot is to be made of some data or numbers instead of functions or expressions then specialized graphics commands must be used. We distinguish *list plotting commands*, whose command names start with **list**, and statistical plotting commands, which reside in the **stats** package.

List Plotting Commands

Some function/expression plotting commands have equivalent list plotting commands in the **plots** package (Table 15.2).

List Plotting	Similar To	Graphics Object
listplot	plot	2D-plot of a list of data
listplot3d	plot3d	3D-plot of a list of data
listcontplot	contourplot	2D contour plot of a data array
listcontplot3d	contourplot3d	3D contour plot of a data array
listdensityplot	densityplot	a density plot of a data array

TABLE 15.2. List plotting.

For some of the following examples, we take a data set about Dutch consumption of beverages in the last few years from Statistics Netherlands (URL: http://www.cbs.nl).

Beverage	Unit	1985	1990	1993	1994
beer	liter	85	91	85	89
soft drink	liter	66	86	89	93
wine	liter	15.0	14.5	16.0	16.0

TABLE 15.3. Dutch consumption of beverages per inhabitant.

The following table beverage contains lists of lists representing the annual consumption of beverages per inhabitant in the last few years.

```
>   beverage[beer] :=
>      [ [1985,85], [1990,91], [1993,85], [1994,89] ] :
>   beverage[soft_drink] :=
>      [ [1985,66], [1990,86], [1993,89], [1994,93] ] :
>   beverage[wine] :=
>      [ [1985,15], [1990,14.5], [1993,16], [1994,16] ] :
```

All data are put in a Maple table called beverage. Let us load the plots package and plot the beer data as points joined with line segments (Fig. 15.100).

```
>   with( plots ):
>   listplot( beverage[beer] );
```

FIGURE 15.100. List plot of annual beer consumption per Dutch inhabitant.

By changing the drawing style you can graph the data points only (Fig. 15.101).

```
>   listplot( beverage[beer], style=point, symbol=circle,
>      color=red );
```

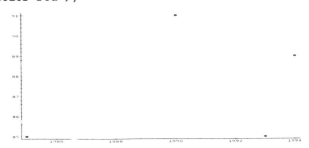

FIGURE 15.101. Point plot of annual beer consumption per Dutch inhabitant.

Both plots can be combined and displayed with a user-defined view frame (Figure 15.102).

```
> display( {"",""}, view=[1984..1995,84..92] );
```

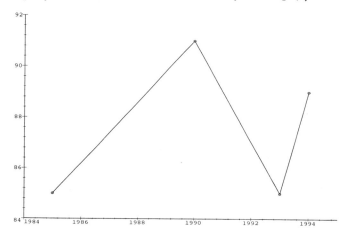

FIGURE 15.102. Annual beer consumption per Dutch inhabitant.

With some effort, two or more beverages can be plotted in one picture with different line and point styles, and a plot legend that explains the meaning of various elements (Figure 15.103).

```
> # Data plot:
> bp := listplot( beverage[beer], style=point,
>    symbol=circle, color=red ):
> bl := listplot( beverage[beer] ):
> sp := listplot( beverage[soft_drink], style=point,
>    symbol=diamond, color=blue ):
> sl := listplot( beverage[soft_drink], linestyle=3 ):

> # Plot legend:
> with( plottools, [line,point] ):
> bL := line( [1990,72], [1992,72] ):
> bP := point( [1991,72], symbol=circle, color=red ):
> bT := textplot( [ 1992.4, 72, beer ], align=RIGHT ):
> sL := line( [1990,70], [1992,70], linestyle=3 ):
> sP := point( [1991,70], symbol=diamond, color=blue ):
> sT := textplot( [ 1992.4, 70, `soft drink` ],
>    align=RIGHT ):

> # Complete picture:
> display( {bp,bl,sp,sl,bL,bP,bT,sL,sP,sT},
>    labels=[year,consumption],
>    title=`annual consumption of beer and soft drink\
>    per inhabitant (in liter)`, view=[1984..1995,65..94] );
```

annual consumption of beer and soft drink per inhabitant (in liter)

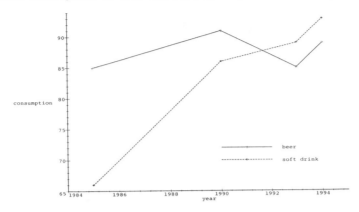

FIGURE 15.103. Annual beer and soft drink consumption per Dutch inhabitant.

Bar charts and pie charts can easily be built from graphics primitives or be generated as special cases of three-dimensional plotting routines. In the next subsection we shall see how the statistical plotting routine **histogram** can be used to generate a bar chart. Here, we show some other representations. We first convert our table of data into a matrix.

```
> M := map( d -> map2(op,2,op(d)), [entries(beverage)] ):
> setattribute( M, matrix );
```

$$\begin{bmatrix} 85 & 91 & 85 & 89 \\ 15 & 14.5 & 16 & 16 \\ 66 & 86 & 89 & 93 \end{bmatrix}$$

The rows in the matrix M describe the following drinks:

```
> indices( beverage );
```

$$[\,beer\,], [\,wine\,], [\,soft\_drink\,]$$

The procedure **matrixplot** from the `plots` package can be used to show these data as a histogram (Figure 15.104).

```
> matrixplot( M, heights=histogram, style=patch,
>   shading=zgrayscale, orientation=[-75,75], axes=box,
>   tickmarks=[[1.5=beer,2.5=wine,3.5=`soft drink`],
>   [1.5=1985,2.5=1990,3.5=1993,4.5=1994],5],
>   labels=[``,``,quantity], font=[HELVETICA,DEFAULT,14]
> );
```

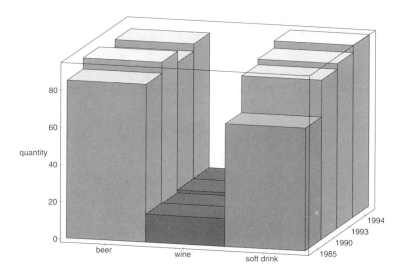

FIGURE 15.104. Histogram of annual consumption of beverages per inhabitant.

The bar chart of beverages consumed in 1994 (Figure 15.105) can be created as follows:

```
>  data94 := linalg[submatrix]( M, 1..3, 4..4 ):
>  matrixplot( data94, heights=histogram, style=patch,
>    shading=zgrayscale, orientation=[-90,90], axes=box,
>    tickmarks=[[1.5=beer,2.5=wine,3.5=`soft drink`],0,5],
>    labels=[`` ,`` ,quantity], font=[HELVETICA,DEFAULT,14],
>    title=`consumption of beverages in 1994` );
```

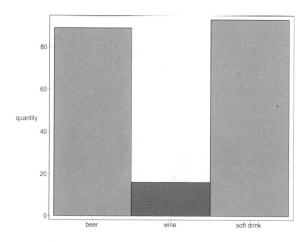

FIGURE 15.105. Bar chart of consumption of beverages in 1994 per Dutch inhabitant.

A circular bar chart (Figure 15.106) can easily be built with the help of the procedure **pieslice** from the `plottools` package. Below we implement a procedure that does the work for lists consisting of pairs [*name of drink*, *quantity*];

```
> circular_bar_chart := proc( d::listlist )
>   local n,i, pies, text, grayshades:
>   n := nops(d):
>   grayshades := map( x->COLOR(RGB,x,x,x),
>     [0.5,0.7,0.9] ):
>   for i to n do
>     pies[i] := plottools[pieslice](
>       [0,0],d[i][2],2*Pi*(i-1)/n..2*Pi*i/n,
>       color=grayshades[eval(1+ (i mod 3))]  ):
>     text[i] := plots[textplot]( [
>       1/2*d[i][2]*cos(Pi*(2*i-1)/n),
>       1/2*d[i][2]*sin(Pi*(2*i-1)/n),
>       convert( d[i][1], name ) ],
>       font=[HELVETICA,BOLD,20] )
>   od:
>   plots[display]( [ seq(pies[i], i=1..n),
>     seq( text[i], i=1..n )], axes=none,
>     scaling=constrained )
> end:
```

Let us apply it to the following data.

```
> data94 := [ seq( [ op(indices(beverage)[i]),
>   data94[i,1]], i=1..3 ) ];
```

$$data94 := [[beer, 89], [wine, 16], [soft\_drink, 93]]$$

```
> circular_bar_chart( data94 );
```

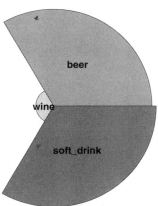

FIGURE 15.106. Circular bar chart of consumption of beverages in 1994.

The above procedure can easily be adapted to produce a pie chart or even an "exploded pie chart," in which pies are separated a bit. This is left as an exercise.

A so-called *Pareto plot* of the 1994 data (Figure 15.107) can be generated by the **pareto** command. A Pareto diagram is a chart with the following elements: a tagged histogram of decreasing frequencies and a curve indicating the cumulative frequencies. Instead of frequencies we shall use percentages by scaling the data.

```
> Values := map( d -> op(2,d), data94 );
```
$$Values := [\,89, 16, 93\,]$$

```
> Percentages := map( (x,s) -> 100*x/s,
>     Values, `+`(op(Values)) );
```
$$Percentages := \left[\frac{4450}{99}, \frac{800}{99}, \frac{1550}{33}\right]$$

```
> Labels := map( d -> op(1,d), data94 );
```
$$Labels := [\,beer, wine, soft\_drink\,]$$

```
> pareto( Percentages, tags=Labels );
```

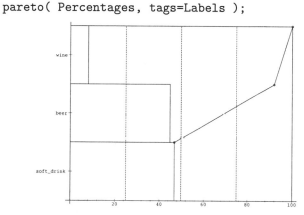

FIGURE 15.107. Pareto plot of consumption of beverages in 1994.

We end this subsection on list plotting commands with an example of **listdensityplot**, viz., a map of the set of Gaussian integers in the complex plane. A square (x, y) is drawn in black if the Gaussian integer $x + y\,i$ is prime, and in white otherwise. For this, we first define a function that takes the value 1 if the corresponding Gaussian integer is prime. Maple has a package called **GaussInt** for arithmetic of Gaussian integers and it is this package that provides the primality test.

```
> isgaussianprime :=
>    (x,y) -> if GaussInt[GIprime](x+I*y) then
>                0
>             else
>                1
>             fi:
```
Next, we generate a 50 × 50 grid and draw the list density plot on this grid

(Figure 15.108).

```
> data := array( [ seq( [ seq( isgaussianprime(i,j),
>    i=-25..25 ) ], j=-25..25 ) ] ):
> ticks := [ 1=-25, 26=0, 51=25 ]:
> display( listdensityplot( data, style=patchnogrid,
>    axes = box, scaling=constrained ),
>    xtickmarks=ticks, ytickmarks=ticks );
```

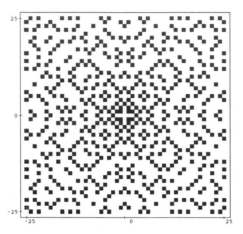

FIGURE 15.108. List density plot of Gaussian primes.

Statistical Plotting

In the statistics package **stats** and more specifically in the subpackage **statplots** reside classical statistical plotting commands as listed in Table 15.4.

Plotting Command	Graphics Object
One-dimensional:	
boxplot	box plot summarizing data
histogram	histogram of data
notchedbox	notched box plot
scatter1d	scatter plot of data
Two-dimensional:	
quantile	plot of observations versus their quantile value
quantile2	quantile-quantile plot
scatter2d	scatter plot of data
symmetry	symmetry plot of data

TABLE 15.4. Statistical plotting commands in **statplots** subpackage.

The utility functions **changecolor**, **xshift**, and **xychange** can be used to adapt the plots. Furthermore, the **fit** subpackage provides a tool for fitting curves to statistical data. Only linear fits are available in Maple.

We shall only show two examples of statistical plots. As promised before, we shall create a bar chart of the 1994 consumption of beverages (Figure 15.109) via the **histogram** procedure. Recall the data.

```
> data94;
```
$$[[\,beer, 89\,], [\,wine, 16\,], [\,soft\_drink, 93\,]\,]$$

Supply these data to the **histogram** procedure as weights.

```
> values94 := [ seq( Weight( i..i+1, data94[i,2] ),
>    i=1..3 ) ]:
```

Load the necessary packages and plot the bar chart.

```
> with( stats ): with( statplots ):
> histogram( values94, color=yellow, tickmarks=
>    [[1.5=beer,2.5=wine,3.5=`soft drink`],default],
>    font=[HELVETICA,DEFAULT,20] );
```

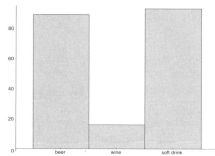

FIGURE 15.109. Bar chart of consumption of beverages in 1994.

The second example is the application of the linear regression method to numerical data and a plot of the least-squares fit. We assume that the numerical data are stored in a file, say `datafile`.

```
> ssystem(`cat datafile`)[2]; # display data
```

```
0     1
0.1   1.1
0.2   1.2
0.3   1.4
0.4   1.6
0.5   1.9
0.6   2.3
0.7   2.8
0.8   3.5
0.9   4.6
1     6.3
```

We decrease numerical precision and import these data. There are several ways of reading in the data; here, we shall use the command **importdata** from the **stats** package.

```
> with( stats): with(statplots):
> Digits := 5:
> data := importdata( datafile, 2 );
```

$$data := [0, .1, .2, .3, .4, .5, .6, .7, .8, .9, 1.],$$
$$[1., 1.1, 1.2, 1.4, 1.6, 1.9, 2.3, 2.8, 3.5, 4.6, 6.3]$$

The data points can be shown in a scatter plot (Figure 15.110):

```
> dataplot := scatter2d( data, symbol=diamond ):
> dataplot; # display the scatter plot
```

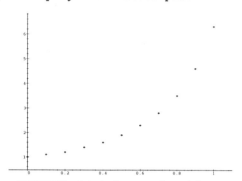

FIGURE 15.110. Scatter plot of data.

Next, we fit these data to the function $x \longmapsto a + b \sin(x) + c \sin(2x)$ via the least squares method, and plot the original data together with the fitted curve (Figure 15.111).

```
> fit[leastsquare[ [x,y], y= a + b*sin(x) + c*sin(2*x),
>    {a,b,c} ]]( [data] );
```

$$y = 1.1563 + 12.770 \sin(x) - 6.5290 \sin(2x)$$

```
> curve := plot( rhs("), x=0..1 ):
> display( { dataplot, curve } );
```

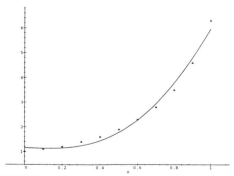

FIGURE 15.111. Least squares fit of data.

15.14 Animation

We end this chapter with some animations. Maple animations are a sequence of pictures ("frames") that are displayed in rapid succession in an animation window (the default number of frames is 8). In Figure 15.112, you see the animation window of a moving sine wave. The individual frames are displayed in Figure 15.113.

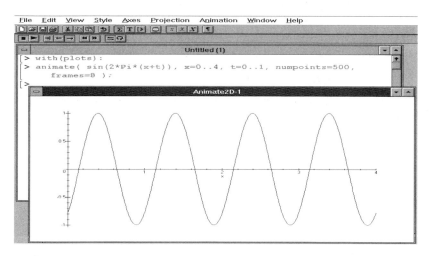

FIGURE 15.112. Screen dump of Maple window and animation window.

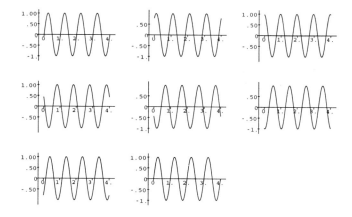

FIGURE 15.113. Eight frames in the animation of a sine wave.

You see that the animation is generated with the procedure **animate** from the **plots** package. The playback mode can be chosen from `forward`, `backward`, and `circular`. The animation can be run in faster or slower mode, or step by step. These options are controlled in the window. But all other plot options can be placed inside the **animate** command and its three-dimensional analogue **animate3d**.

The eight frames in Figure 15.113 are actually displayed in a graphics array by application of the **display** command on the animation data structure.

Animations of three-dimensional surfaces that are generated by a formula or function and surfaces that are represented in parametric form can be made with the **animate3d** command or by combining several plots via **display** with the option insequence = true. Experiment with deformations of your favorite surface.

As an illustration of the option insequence, we produce below an animation of implicitly defined curves, by building up the necessary animation structure. First, we generate a table of implicit plots.

```
>   for i from 0 to 8 do
>     P[i] := implicitplot( x^3 +y^3 - 5*x*y = 1-i/4,
>     x=-3..3, y=-3..3, tickmarks=[2,2] )
>   od:
```

We use the **display** routine from the plots package to display the implicit plots in sequence, i.e., to produce the animation.

```
>   display( [ seq( P[i], i=0..8 ) ], insequence=true );
```

The animation is omitted, but the subsequent frames are shown in Figure 15.114.

```
>   display(");
```

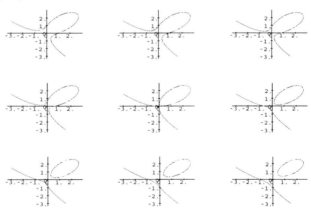

FIGURE 15.114. Frames of the animation of algebraic curves.

We end with the example of a "spin show" around the z-axis of an octahedron, i.e., rotations of the octahedron such that it looks, in an animation, like a spinning object.

```
> with(plots): with(plottools): # load the plots package
> base := display( octahedron([0,0,0],1),
>   color=BLUE, scaling=constrained, axes=none,
>   style=hidden, thickness=3, orientation=[30,60] ):
> N := 16: # number of angles
> angles := [ seq( Pi*k/(2*N), k=0..(N-1) )  ]:
> for phi in angles do
>   P[phi] := rotate( base, 0,0,phi )
> od:
> display( [ seq( P[phi], phi=angles ) ],
>   insequence=true );
```

In circular playback mode the animation looks like a smoothly rotating octahedron.

15.15   List of Plot Options

In this section we list all options of plot routines. They are divided into options that can be used in all plot routines and options specific to the graphics mode. Each table entry consists of the name of the option, its possible values, and its purpose. Note that values of options can be specified in lower-case as well as in upper-case characters (unless we explicitly use upper-case characters in the lists below); both British and American spellings are allowed. Usual defaults of options have been underlined in the tables below. The special names DEFAULT and default are for built-in and platform dependent choices.

Common plot options

axes = *style*

The following axes styles are available.

Axes Style	Meaning
box	plot in a bounding box
DEFAULT	default axes
frame	axes along the edges of the plot
none	no axes
normal	Cartesian axes

axesfont = [*family*, *style*, *size*]

Use the font for labels of tick marks on the axes. See the option font for more details.

color = *colorspec*

Colors can be specified in the following way.

Color Specification	Meaning
COLOR(RGB,r,g,b)	use the RGB color
COLOR(HSV,h,s,v)	use the HSV color
HUE(h)	use this shortcut for COLOR(HSV,h,0.9,1)
color name	use the predefined color name (aquamarine, black, blue, etc.) stored in plot/colortable (enter **readlib(`plot/color`)** before printing the table)

coords = *name*
>   Use the specified coordinate system. Names to think of for two-dimensional graphics are bipolar, cardiod, cartesian, and so on (enter **?plot,coords** to see more allowed names). In three-dimensional graphics, popular coordinate systems are cartesian, cylindrical, spherical, and so on (enter **?plot3d,coords** to see more allowed names).

font = [*family*, *style*, *size*]
>   Specify the font used for text objects. *size* specifies the font size in points. The following combinations of *family* and *style* are available.

Font Family	Font Style
COURIER	BOLD, BOLDOBLIQUE, DEFAULT, OBLIQUE
HELVETICA	BOLD, BOLDOBLIQUE, DEFAULT, OBLIQUE
TIMES	ROMAN, BOLD, ITALIC, BOLDITALIC
SYMBOL	—

labelfont = [*family*, *style*, *size*]
>   Use the font for labels on the axes. See the option **font** for more details.

labels = [string s_x, string s_y (, string s_z)]
>   Add labels to the main axes.

linestyle = nonnegative integer n
>   Draw the curves in the graph using the dash pattern, which is specified by a nonnegative integer between 0 (default) and 7.

numpoints = natural number n
>   Specify the minimum number of sample points used (default: $n = 49$ for 2D plots, $n = 625$ for 3D plots).

scaling = *mode*
>   Three scaling modes are available:

Scaling	Meaning
constrained	use the same scaling of the graph in all directions
DEFAULT	default scaling of the graph
unconstrained	use independent scaling of graph

symbol = *name*

> When the option `style = point` is used, you can specify the following symbols for drawing at each sample point or vertex of a polygon.

Specification	box	circle	cross	DEFAULT	diamond	point
Symbol	□	○	+	usually +	◇	·

thickness = nonnegative integer *n*

> Specify the thickness of lines on the plot by a nonnegative integer and by modular arithmetic bring it to the range [0, 15]. Default value is 0 and a higher value means a thicker line.

tickmarks = [*xspec*, *yspec* (, *zspec*)]

> Specify the number, location, and labeling of the tick marks on the main axes. Each specification may be an integer (i.e., the minimum number of tick marks), a list of numbers (i.e., a list of locations of tick marks), a list of equations (i.e., a list of locations and labels of tick marks), or the special value `default`.

title = string *s*

> Give the graph a title (default: *s*=NULL, i.e., no title).

titlefont = [*family*, *style*, *size*]

> Use the font for a title of the graph. See the option `font` for more details.

view = *v*

> Specify the display region. Each specification *v* may be a range of function values, the special value `default`, or a list of such specifications for the main directions. `default` means a range that allows display of entire curve or surface in that direction. Default value of `view` is `default` along all main axes.

Options specific to plot

adaptive = false/**true**

> Disable/Enable adaptive plotting.

discont = true

> (*Only for expressions*) By default, Maple does not care about discontinuities. But with the option set the value `true`, Maple tries to resolve them.

`filled = true`
> Fill the space between the curve and the horizontal axis.

`resolution = ` natural number n
> Specify the number of pixels across the display device (default: $n = 200$).

`sample = ` list of parameter values
> Specify what parameter values are used for the initial sampling.

`style = ` *name*
> The following drawing styles are available.

Style	Meaning
line	connect sample points by straight line segments and omit the filled interior of polygons
patch	render points as symbols, curves as line segments, and polygons as filled regions with a border
patchnogrid	As patch, but omit the border on polygons
point	display sample points and vertices of polygons only

`xtickmarks = [ ` *xspec* ` ]`
> Specify the tick marks on the horizontal axis. See the option `tickmarks` for more details.

`ytickmarks = [ ` *yspec* ` ]`
> Specify the tick marks on the vertical axis. See the option `tickmarks` for more details.

Options specific to plot3d

`ambientlight = [ ` r, g, b ` ]`
> Use a nondirectional shading with *red*, *green*, and *blue* intensities in the RGB color model.

`color = ` *colorfunc*
> Beside all specifications of colors that were listed in the table of common plot option, you can color a space curve or surface. *colorfunc* can be a *function* or *expression* mapping the resulting values over the plotting domain to the HUE coloring scheme. *colorfunc* can also be a list $[r, g, b]$, where r, g, and b are either functions or expressions that depend only on the plotting domain variables. The resulting values are mapped to the RGB coloring scheme.

`contours = ` *specification*
> You can specify the number n of contours when the drawing `style`

equals `contour` or `patchcontour`. Default: $n = 10$. Moreover, the
specification may be a *list of function values* to be used for contours
when the drawing `style` equals `contour` or `patchcontour`.

`grid = [ natural number` n_x `, natural number` n_y `]`
Specify the dimensions of the grid on which the points will be generated (equally spaced). Default dimensions are $n_x = n_y = 25$.

`gridstyle = rectangular/triangular`
Use a rectangular/triangular grid.

`light = [` ϕ, θ, r, g, b `]`
Simulate a light source with given *red*, *green*, and *blue* intensities
in the RGB color model shining on the graphics object from the
direction specified in the spherical coordinates $[\phi, \theta]$ (in degrees).

`lightmodel =` *name*
In the following table, the predefined lighting models are specified in
terms of the option `ambientlight` and `light`.

Model	Ambient Light	Lights
`light1`	[0.5, 0.5, 0.5]	[90, -45, 0, 0.9, 0], [45, -45, 0, 0, 0.9], [90, 45, 0.9, 0, 0]
`light2`	[0.5, 0.5, 0.5]	[45, 90, 0.9, 0, 0], [45, 45, 0, 0.9, 0], [90, -45, 0, 0, 0.9]
`light3`	[0.5, 0.5, 0.5]	[45, 45, 0, 0., 0.9], [45, 45, 0, 0.9, 0], [0, 135, 0.9, 0, 0]
`light4`	[0.6, 0.6, 0.6]	[85, 60, 0.8, 0.8, 0.8]

`orientation = [` θ, ϕ `]`
Specify the direction from which the plot is viewed; the direction of
the eyepoint is in spherical coordinates: ϕ is the angle with respect
to the z-axis, θ is the angle of the projection of the view point to the
xy-plane (in degrees). See Figure 15.73; default values are $\theta = 45$ and
$\phi = 45$.

`projection =` p
The following perspectives are available.

p	Projection Value	Meaning
`fisheye`	0	wide angle perspective
`normal`	1/2	intermediate perspective
`orthogonal`	1	no perspective
—	real number $p \in [0, 1]$	a user defined perspective

`shading =` *name*
Several shadings are available.

Shading	Meaning
none	no shading scheme used
xyz	shade in color ranges along all axes
xy	shade in color ranges along x and y axes only
z	shade in one color range along the z axis
zgrayscale	shade according to the z-value using only gray tints
zhue	shade according to the z-value in the HUE color model

style = *name*

The following drawing styles are available.

Style	Meaning
contour	draw only the contour lines of the surface
hidden	as wireframe, but with hidden-line removal, i.e., all line segments that are hidden behind other parts of the surface are removed
line	synonym for wireframe
patch	draw the surface with shaded patches on a wireframe grid with hidden-surface removal, i.e., all patches that are hidden behind other parts of the surface are removed
patchcontour	as patch but with contour lines
patchnogrid	as patch but omit the grid
point	display sample points and vertices of polygons only
wireframe	draw a wireframe surface, connecting adjacent sampled points with line segments

Options related to animations

frames = natural number n

n frames are displayed in an animation (default: $n=16$).

framescaling = *name*

The scaling of subsequent frames in an animation can be as follows.

Frame Scaling	Meaning
default	default relationship
nonuniform	scale each frame in an animation individually
uniform	scale all frames in an animation by an equal amount

insequence = true

By default, **display** combines several plots in one picture. With the option set the value true, plots are displayed as separate frames in an animation.

15.16   Exercises

1. Plot the function $x \longmapsto \dfrac{\sin 2x}{\sin x}$ on the interval $(0, 4\pi)$.

2. The sine integral Si is defined as $Si(x) = \displaystyle\int_0^x \dfrac{\sin t}{t}\, dt$. Plot the sinc integral over the interval $(0,100)$, compute $\displaystyle\lim_{x \to \infty} Si(x)$, and compare this with the result that you read off the picture.

3. Plot the factorial function $x \longmapsto x!$ and its derivative over the interval $(-4, 4)$.

4. Enter the command

```
plot( cosh(x)^2 - sinh(x)^2 - 1,   x=0..10 );
```

and explain what you see. Can you improve the result?

5. Plot the function $x \longmapsto x \sin(1/x)$ over an "interesting" domain around zero.

6. Plot the function

$$t \longmapsto \int_{-\infty}^{t} e^{-\theta^4}\, d\theta$$

on the interval $(-2, 2)$.

7. Plot the function $x \longmapsto \displaystyle\int_0^x \sin(\sin \xi)\, d\xi$ on the interval $(0, 2\pi)$.

8. Plot some Lissajous figures, which are defined in parametric form by

$$t \longmapsto \big(\sin(m\,t), \sin(n\,t)\big),$$

for integers m and n. Pay special attention to the case where m and n are consecutive Fibonacci numbers.

9. Draw the Lemniscate of Bernoulli defined by

   (a) the equation $(x^2 + y^2)^2 = (x^2 - y^2)$,

   (b) the polar equation $r^2 = \cos 2\phi$, and

   (c) the parametrization $x = \dfrac{\cos t}{1 + \sin^2 t}$, $y = \dfrac{\cos t \sin t}{1 + \sin^2 t}$, for $-\pi \le t \le \pi$.

10. Draw the following parametric plots.

   (a) $t \longmapsto \left(\dfrac{t^2 - 1}{t^2 + 1}, \dfrac{2t}{t^2 + 1} \right)$, for $t \in (-\infty, \infty)$.

   (b) $t \longmapsto (\frac{4}{9}t^3 - \frac{14}{9}t^2 + \frac{1}{9}t + 1, -\frac{4}{9}t^3 - \frac{1}{9}t^2 + \frac{14}{9}t)$, for $t \in (0, 1)$.

   (c) Draw the previous parametric plot together with the plot of $t \longmapsto \big(\cos(\frac{\pi}{2}t), \sin(\frac{\pi}{2}t)\big)$ for $t \in (0, 1)$.

11. Plot the Heaviside step function H and next draw the graphs of the functions below.

   (a) $H(x - 1) - H(x - 2)$

(b) $\displaystyle\sum_{i=0}^{10}(-1/2)^i H(x-i/2)$

(c) $(1-|x|)\big(H(x+1)-H(x-1)\big)$

12. Draw the parametric plot $t \longmapsto \big(FresnelC(t), FresnelS(t)\big)$ for t in $(0,6)$ and describe the asymptotic behavior of this parametric curve.

13. Plot the Folium, which is defined as a polar plot with radial function $\cos\theta(4\sin^2\theta - 1)$.

14. Plot the function $x \longmapsto x + \cos(\pi x)$ on the interval (-49,49)

    (a) without changing the defaults of **plot**.

    (b) with different options.

15. Plot the function $x \longmapsto e^x + \ln|4 - x|$ on the interval (0,5). What do you think of it?

16. Plot the graph of the function $(x,y) \longmapsto \dfrac{x}{x^2 + y^2}$, for x and y ranging from -1 to 1.

17. Plot the "monkey saddle" defined by the function $(x,y) \longmapsto x(x^2 - 3y^2)$ under various options.

18. Plot the function $(x,y) \longmapsto \sin(2\pi x)\sin(2\pi y)$, for x and y ranging from 0 to 25, without changing the default options. What do you think of it?

19. Plot the surface parametrized by

$$(\phi, \theta) \longmapsto \big(\cos\phi\sin(2\theta),\ \sin\phi\sin(2\theta),\ \sin\theta\big),$$

where ϕ and θ range from 0 to 2π.

20. Draw a contour plot and a density plot of the strength of the potential field of a configuration of unit charges at positions $(-1,0)$ and $(1,0)$.

21. Draw Klein's bottle in Dieudonné's parametrization [56]

$$
\begin{aligned}
x &= \big(2 + \cos(u/2)\sin t - \sin(u/2)\sin(2t)\big)\cos u,\\
y &= \big(2 + \cos(u/2)\sin t - \sin(u/2)\sin(2t)\big)\sin u,\\
z &= \sin(u/2)\sin t + \sin(u/2)\sin(2t),
\end{aligned}
$$

where $0 \le u \le 2\pi$, $0 \le t \le 2\pi$. Compare the result with the first example in the "graphics gallery" in [128].

22. Draw Klein's bottle in Banchoff's parametrization [7]

$$
\begin{aligned}
x &= \Big(\cos(\theta/2)\big(\sqrt{2} + \cos\phi\big) + \sin(\theta/2)\big(\cos\phi\sin\phi\big)\Big)\cos\theta,\\
y &= \Big(\cos(\theta/2)\big(\sqrt{2} + \cos\phi\big) + \sin(\theta/2)\big(\cos\phi\sin\phi\big)\Big)\sin\theta,\\
z &= -\sin(\theta/2)\big(\sqrt{2} + \cos\phi\big) + \cos(\theta/2)\left(\cos\phi\sin\phi\right),
\end{aligned}
$$

where $0 \le \theta \le 4\pi$, $0 \le \phi \le 2\pi$. Compare the result with the color graph in [109].

23. Draw the Möbius strip. (Hint: make a parametrization by rotating a line segment along a circle with varying elevation angle.)

24. Draw the Catenoid defined by the parametrization

$$(\theta, z) \longmapsto (\cos\theta\cosh z,\ \sin\theta\cosh z,\ z),$$

where $0 \le \theta \le 2\pi$ and $-1 \le z \le 1$, directly with this parametrization, and as a cylindrical plot.

25. Draw Enneper's minimal surface defined by the parametrization

$$(u, v) \longmapsto \left(\frac{u}{2} - \frac{u^3}{6} + \frac{uv^2}{2},\ -\frac{v}{2} + \frac{v^3}{6} - \frac{vu^2}{2},\ \frac{u^2}{2} - \frac{v^2}{2}\right).$$

26. Draw Scherk's minimal surface defined by the equation $\exp(z)\cos x = \cos y$.

27. Generate a contour plot and a density plot of the function $(x, y) \longmapsto \sin(xy)$.

28. Plot the two-dimensional gradient vector field of the function $(x, y) \longmapsto \sin x \cos y$.

29. Make an animation of a rotating spiral.

30. Build a picture of a house using graphics primitives only.

31. The RGB specification of a gray shading is given by three equal numbers between 0 and 1. Build up a color chart for gray shadings.

32. Prove and visualize Pascal's theorem with the **geometry** package.

Pascal's Theorem.

Let A, B, C, D, E, and F be six points on a circle. Let P be the intersection of the lines AB and DF, Q be the intersection of the lines BC and FE, and let R be the intersection of the lines CD and EA. Then P, Q, and R are collinear.

33. Prove and visualize the following theorem of Euler.

Euler's Theorem.

In a triangle, the orthocenter (intersection of altitudes), the centroid (intersection of medians), and the circumcenter (center of the circle circumscribing the triangle) lie on a line.

34. Verify and visualize Feuerbach's nine-point circle. Verify with Maple that Feuerbach's nine-point circle is the same as the Euler circle.

Feuerbach's nine-point circle.

Consider a triangle T with vertices A, B, and C. Let A', B', C' be the midpoints of the edges, let D, E, F be the feet of the altitudes, and let X, Y, Z be the midpoints of segments connecting the orthocenter H (intersection of altitudes) to the vertices of T. Then, the points A', B', C', D, E, F, X, Y, and Z lie on a circle whose center N is the midpoint of the segment joining H to the circumcenter O of T, and whose radius is half the circumradius of T.

35. Use the **plottools** package to make an "exploded" version of the pie chart of Figure 15.106 in which pie segments are separated a bit.

16

Solving Equations

This chapter discusses several methods implemented in Maple to solve (systems of) equations and inequalities of various types. Special attention is paid to systems of polynomial equations; the use of the Gröbner basis package is discussed. Recurrence relations are another type of equation, which will be discussed in detail. We shall consider exact methods (over various domains) as well as approximate numerical methods. Examples in this chapter come from application areas such as electronic circuit design, chemical kinetics, neural networks, geodesy, and dimensional analysis.

16.1 Equations in One Unknown

In its simplest form, the Maple procedure **solve** takes an equation in one unknown and tries to solve it analytically.

```
>  eqn := (x-1)*(x^2+x+1) = 0;
```

$$eqn := (x - 1) (x^2 + x + 1) = 0$$

```
>  solve( eqn, x );
```

$$1, -\frac{1}{2} + \frac{1}{2} I \sqrt{3}, -\frac{1}{2} - \frac{1}{2} I \sqrt{3}$$

The equations may contain several unknowns and still you can ask Maple to solve it for one of the unknowns, in terms of the others.

```
>  eqn := x^3 + 2*a*x^2 + a*x = 1;
```

$$eqn := x^3 + 2\,a\,x^2 + a\,x = 1$$

```
>  solve( eqn, x );
```

$$\frac{1}{6}\,\%1^{1/3} - 6\,\%2 - \frac{2}{3}\,a,$$

$$-\frac{1}{12}\,\%1^{1/3} + 3\,\%2 - \frac{2}{3}\,a + \frac{1}{2}\,I\,\sqrt{3}\,\Big(\frac{1}{6}\,\%1^{1/3} + 6\,\%2\Big),$$

$$-\frac{1}{12}\,\%1^{1/3} + 3\,\%2 - \frac{2}{3}\,a - \frac{1}{2}\,I\,\sqrt{3}\,\Big(\frac{1}{6}\,\%1^{1/3} + 6\,\%2\Big)$$

$$\%1 := 72\,a^2 + 108 - 64\,a^3 + 12\,\sqrt{-84\,a^3 - 12\,a^4 + 108\,a^2 + 81}$$

$$\%2 := \frac{\frac{1}{3}\,a - \frac{4}{9}\,a^2}{\%1^{1/3}}$$

Maple finds the three (complex) solutions, which are represented as a
sequence of formulae. From the example, it is clear how Maple represents
complicated expressions; the system looks for common subexpressions and
gives them names like %1, %2, and so on. You can refer to these labels as
long as they are not replaced by other values.

```
>  rationalize( %2^3 );
```

$$-\frac{1}{648}\,a^2 - \frac{1}{432} + \frac{1}{729}\,a^3$$
$$+ \frac{1}{3888}\,\sqrt{-84a^3 - 12a^4 + 1 - a^2 + 81}$$

In practice, only immediate reference is safe; the system itself may reuse
the labels and destroy former information. In the worksheet interface, there
is an alternative way to select the right-hand side of the label: copy the
formula into an input line and give it a name, if you wish.

16.2   Abbreviations in **solve**

Maple expects an equation or a set of equations as the first argument in a
call to **solve**, but the system kindly supplements expressions with "= 0".

```
>  solve( a + ln(x-3) - ln(x), x );
```

$$3\,\frac{e^a}{-1 + e^a}$$

As the second argument, Maple expects a variable or a set of variables.
When this argument is absent, Maple finds all indeterminates in the first
argument with a command similar to

indets(eqns, name) minus { constants }

and uses the result as the second argument of **solve**. This is convenient, but sometimes it has a strange effect.

```
>  solve( a + ln(x-3) - ln(x) );
```

$$\{ a = -\ln(x - 3) + \ln(x),\ x = x \}$$

Maple solved the equation for x and a. The solution $x = x$ means that x can have any value.

You have seen that Maple uses labels to abbreviate large common sub-expressions. The system sometimes uses another kind of abbreviation.

```
>  x^7 - 2*x^6 - 4*x^5 - x^3 + x^2 + 6*x + 4;
```

$$x^7 - 2\,x^6 - 4\,x^5 - x^3 + x^2 + 6\,x + 4$$

```
>  solve(");
```

$$1 + \sqrt{5},\ 1 - \sqrt{5},\ \text{RootOf}(\ \_Z^5 - \_Z - 1\ )$$

In this way, Maple informs you that it has found two real solutions, viz., $1 + \sqrt{5}$ and $1 - \sqrt{5}$, in analytical form, and that the other solutions are roots of the polynomial equation $\_Z^5 - \_Z - 1 = 0$ in $\_Z$.

16.3   Some Difficulties

The main difficulties with **solve** are that no solutions are found in cases where it is known that solutions exist, that not all solutions are found, and that superfluous "solutions" are found. We shall give examples of all cases mentioned and make suggestions to assist Maple.

No solution found, but there exists at least one.

Often it is known that there exist solutions for an equation or system of equations, but no general method for finding the solutions is available. There are cases where, from a mathematical point of view, it is hopeless to find a general solution in analytical form. It is well known from Galois theory that a general formula using radicals only for roots of polynomials of degree five or higher does not exist. From Maple you cannot expect more; it only provides you with a set of reasonably good algorithms for solving equations. Nevertheless, in quite a few mathematical problems general methods fail whereas the user recognizes a way to find a solution. Often this is based on recognizing some pattern within a formula, which the computer algebra system does not see.

When Maple does not find any solution, three things can happen:

1. Maple returns the equation back in the form of a **RootOf** so that you can still process it further.

```
>  solve( cos(x) = x, x );
```

$$\mathrm{RootOf}(\_Z - \cos(\_Z))$$

```
>  evalf(");
```

$$.7390851332$$

2. The system keeps silent because there does not exist a solution.

```
>  solve( x = x + 1, x );
>
```

3. The system keeps silent because it did not find a solution but there might be one, which Maple affirms by setting the variable _SolutionsMayBeLost to true.

```
>  solve( cos(x) = x^2, x );
>
>  _SolutionsMayBeLost;
```

$$true$$

Maple is more communicative when you increase the value of the variable infolevel[solve]. Since **solve** uses option remember to keep track of answers of previous problems, we first **forget** the previous results of **solve**.

```
>  readlib(forget):
>  forget( solve ):  # forget previous results of solve
>  infolevel[solve] := 2: # make Maple more communicative
>  solve( cos(x) = x^2, x );
```

```
solve:   Warning: no solutions found
solve:   Warning: solutions may have been lost
```

It is known that no closed-form solution of this equation exists. So, in this case, you can praise Maple for not having found a solution. However, sometimes results of **solve** are a bit disappointing. For example, computations that require branch selection or that involve radicals, logarithms, or trigonometric functions usually do not come easily to computer algebra systems, and Maple is no exception in this respect.

```
>  infolevel[solve] := 1:  # reset userinfo
>  eqn := x + x^(1/3) = -2;
```

$$eqn := x + x^{1/3} = -2$$

```
>  solve( eqn, x );
```

```
solve:   Warning: no solutions found
```

The real solution $x = -1$ has not been found. In this case, you can help Maple by first transforming the radicals to algebraic numbers in the **RootOf** representation, solve the equation, convert back to radicals, and check for superfluous "solutions."

```
> convert( eqn, RootOf );
```
$$x + \text{RootOf}(\,\_Z^3 - x\,) = -2$$

```
> solve(",x);
```
$$-1, -\frac{5}{2} + \frac{1}{2}I\sqrt{7}, -\frac{5}{2} - \frac{1}{2}I\sqrt{7}$$

All complex roots of the polynomial $(x + 2)^3 + x$ are found.

Another example:

```
> solve( sin(x) = 3*x/Pi, x );
```
$$\text{RootOf}(\,3\,\_Z - \sin(\,\_Z\,)\,\pi\,)$$

```
> evalf(");
```
$$.5235987756$$

From a plot of the sine function and the function $x \longmapsto 3x/\pi$ it is clear that there exist three solutions, and you know them: $\pi/6$, $-\pi/6$, and 0.

But, don't get, from the above examples, a bad impression of Maple's **solve** capacities. A few gems:

```
> (x^6-1)^x = 0; solve(",x);
```
$$(x^6 - 1)^x = 0$$
$$1, \frac{1}{2} - \frac{1}{2}I\sqrt{3}, \frac{1}{2} + \frac{1}{2}I\sqrt{3}$$

```
> x + x^(1/2)+x^(1/3)+x^(1/4) = 4; solve(",x);
```
$$x + \sqrt{x} + x^{1/3} + x^{1/4} = 4$$

$$1$$

```
> x^3*(ln(5)-ln(x))=3; solve(",x);
```
$$x^3\,(\ln(5) - \ln(x)) = 3$$

$$5\,e^{(\,1/3\,\text{LambertW}(\,\frac{-9}{125}\,)\,)},\; 5\,e^{(\,1/3\,\text{LambertW}(-1,\frac{-9}{125}\,)\,)}$$

```
> arccos(3*x) = 2*arcsin(x); solve(",x);
```
$$\arccos(3\,x) = 2\arcsin(x)$$

$$-\frac{3}{4} + \frac{1}{4}\sqrt{17}$$

```
>   arccos(2*x) = arctan(3*x); solve(",x );
```

$$\arccos(2\,x) = \arctan(3\,x)$$

$$\frac{1}{6}\sqrt{-2 + 2\sqrt{10}}$$

```
>   max( x, 2*x-2 ) = min( x^2-1, 5-x ); solve(",x );
```

$$\max(x, 2\,x - 2) = \min(x^2 - 1, 5 - x)$$

$$\frac{1}{2} - \frac{1}{2}\sqrt{5}, \frac{1}{2} + \frac{1}{2}\sqrt{5}, \frac{7}{3}$$

```
>   evalf(["]);
```

$$[-.6180339890, 1.618033989, 2.333333333]$$

Figure 16.1 provides a visual check of this result.

```
>   plot( { max( x, 2*x-2 ), min( x^2-1, 5-x ) },
>       x = -4..4 );
```

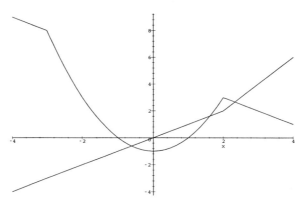

FIGURE 16.1. Graph of $\max(x, 2x - 2)$ and $\min(x^2 - 1, 5 - x)$ on interval $(-4, 4)$.

```
>   abs( x + abs(x+1) ) = 1;   solve(",x );
```

$$|x + |x + 1|| = 1$$

$$0, \mathrm{RealRange}(-\infty, -1)$$

A range of solutions! When using sets, the result will be expressed in set notation as well.

```
>   solve( {""}, {x} );
```

$$\{x = 0\}, \{x \le -1\}$$

Too few solutions.

A classical example of getting too few solutions is the following:
```
>   solve( sin(x) = 1/2, x );
```
$$\frac{1}{6}\,\pi$$

Maple is satisfied with one solution instead of the many solutions $\frac{1}{6}\pi + 2k\pi$ and $\frac{5}{6}\pi + 2k\pi$ for $k \in \mathbb{Z}$. These solutions are only obtained when the environment variable _EnvAllSolutions has been set true.
```
>   readlib(forget):
>   forget( solve ); # forget previous answer

>   _EnvAllSolutions := true:
>   solve( sin(x) = 1/2, x );
```
$$\frac{1}{6}\,\pi + \frac{2}{3}\,\pi\,\_B1\tilde{} + 2\,\pi\,\_Z1\tilde{}$$

The variable _B1~ denotes a binary number (0 or 1) and _Z1~ denotes an arbitrary integer.
```
>   map( about, indets(",name) ):

Pi:
   is assumed to be: Pi

Originally _B1, renamed _B1~:
   is assumed to be: OrProp(0,1)

Originally _Z1, renamed _Z1~:
   is assumed to be: integer
```

Two other examples of this kind:
```
>   solve( exp(x) = 2, x );
```
$$\ln(2) + 2\,I\,\pi\,\_Z\tilde{}$$
```
>   solve( exp(-x) = x, x );
```
$$\mathrm{LambertW}(\_NN1, 1)$$

Here, you get solutions in different branches of the logarithm and Lambert's W function.

Occasionally, you might be confronted with the variable _MaxSols, which limits the number of solutions sought for. Its default value is 100, but if necessary it can be reset.
```
>   eqn := product( x-k, k=1..101 ) = 0:
>   nops( { solve( eqn, x ) } );
```
$$100$$

```
>  _MaxSols := 200:
>  nops( { solve( eqn, x ) } ); # true number of solutions
```

$$101$$

Too many solutions.

A trigonometric equation for which you better assist Maple:

```
>  _EnvAllSolutions := true:
>  eqn := sin(x)^3 -13/2*sin(x)^2 + 11*sin(x) = 4;
```

$$eqn := \sin(x)^3 - \frac{13}{2}\sin(x)^2 + 11\sin(x) = 4$$

```
>  solve( eqn, x );
```

$$\arcsin(2) - 2\arcsin(2)\_B1\tilde{} + 2\pi\_Z1\tilde{} + \pi\_B1\tilde{},$$
$$\frac{1}{6}\pi + \frac{2}{3}\pi\_B1\tilde{} + 2\pi\_Z1\tilde{},$$
$$\arcsin(4) - 2\arcsin(4)\_B1\tilde{} + 2\pi\_Z1\tilde{} + \pi\_B1\tilde{}$$

All complex solutions are found, but most probably you were only searching for the real solutions. Here, more insight is obtained by considering **eqn** as an equation in **sin(x)**.

```
>  solve( eqn, sin(x) );
```

$$2, \frac{1}{2}, 4$$

The three equations $\sin x = 2$, $\sin x = \frac{1}{2}$, and $\sin x = 4$ can now be handled separately.

The next example illustrates that you must be careful with using function calls as names to solve for; Maple does not apply much mathematical knowledge while considering the equation in these names.

```
>  solve( cos(2*x) = cos(x), x );
```

$$\frac{2}{3}\pi - \frac{4}{3}\pi\_B1\tilde{} + 2\pi\_Z1\tilde{}, 2\pi\_Z1\tilde{}$$

```
>  solve( cos(2*x) = cos(x), cos(x) );
```

$$\cos(2x)$$

Be careful, $\cos 2x$ is not considered in the above equation as a polynomial in $\cos x$

```
>  solve( 2*cos(x)^2 - 1 = cos(x), cos(x) );
```

$$\frac{-1}{2}, 1$$

```
> seq( solve( cos(x) = s, x ), s = " );
```

$$\frac{2}{3}\pi - \frac{4}{3}\pi\_B1\tilde{} + 2\pi\_Z1\tilde{}, 2\pi\_Z1\tilde{}$$

We end this section with two more practical issues. The first one is in the preprocessing of an equation. Before trying to find solutions, Maple first tries to simplify the equation without any scruples.

```
> (x-1)^2 / (x^2-1) = 0;
```

$$\frac{(x-1)^2}{x^2-1} = 0$$

```
> solve(");
```

$$1$$

Maple can check itself that its solution is not valid when $\dfrac{(x-1)^2}{x^2-1}$ is considered as a real function.

```
> subs( x=1, "" );
```

```
Error, division by zero
```

But of course, considered as elements from the quotient field $\mathbb{R}(x)$, the expressions $\dfrac{(x-1)^2}{x^2-1}$ and $\dfrac{x-1}{x+1}$ are equivalent. For the analytical continuation it is true that $x = 1$ is a solution.

```
> limit( lhs(""), x=1 );
```

$$0$$

Finally, an example of the problem of not being able to specify criteria for parametrization of solutions of systems of equations.

```
> eqns := { w +x +y + z = 1, w + y = 0,
>    2*w + z = 2, v + z = 0 }:
> vars := indets( eqns );
```

$$vars := \{x, z, v, y, w\}$$

```
> solve( eqns, vars );
```

$$\{y = -w, z = -2w + 2, x = 2w - 1, v = 2w - 2, w = w\}$$

When you solve a system of equations with respect to all unknowns, Maple chooses the parametrization of the solutions on the basis of criteria like "select the equation with the least number of terms" or "select the equation with the simplest coefficients," and so on. But what is there to do if you have different criteria? You can use simplification with respect to side relations to express a variable in terms of the others.

```
> simplify( {v,w}, eqns, [v,w,x,y,z] );
```

$$\left\{ -\frac{1}{2}z + 1, -z \right\}$$

```
> simplify( {v,w}, eqns, [v,w,z,y,x] );
```

$$\left\{ x - 1, \frac{1}{2} x + \frac{1}{2} \right\}$$

But this does not mean that you have solved the original system of equations. This method only works when you know beforehand which variables can be used as parameters. Then you can also leave the parameters out of the set of unknowns.

```
> solve( eqns, {v,w,y,z} );
```

$$\left\{ y = -\frac{1}{2} - \frac{1}{2} x, v = x - 1, w = \frac{1}{2} x + \frac{1}{2}, z = -x + 1 \right\}$$

16.4   Systems of Equations

The last example of the previous section shows that **solve** can be used to solve systems of equations. For **solve**, the equations and unknowns should be presented as sets. Even with a system of equations in one unknown this variable must be presented as a set. In this section, we shall look at some practical examples of how to solve systems of equations.

Linear equations

First we shall look at a system of equations that describes the relations between voltages, currents, and resistors in the electronic circuit of resistors shown in Figure 16.2 (taken from [62]).

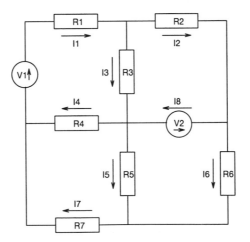

FIGURE 16.2. Electronic circuit of resistors.

Since our example is from electrical engineering, it is convenient to follow the practice of j as notation for $\sqrt{-1}$ instead of i.

```
>  alias( I=I, J=sqrt(-1) ):
```
Applying Kirchhoff's laws you get the following system of equations.
```
>  eqns := { R[1]*I[1]+R[3]*I[3]+R[4]*I[4]-V[1]=0,
>  R[2]*I[2]-V[2]-R[3]*I[3]=0, R[5]*I[5]-R[6]*I[6]-V[2]=0,
>  R[5]*I[5]+R[7]*I[7]-R[4]*T[4]=0, I[1]-I[2]-I[3]-0,
>  I[2]-I[6]-I[8]=0, I[5]+I[6]-I[7]=0, I[4]+I[7]-I[1]=0,
>  I[3]+I[8]-I[4]-I[5]=0 };
```

$$eqns := \{R_1\,I_1 + R_3\,I_3 + R_4\,I_4 - V_1 = 0, I_5 + I_6 - I_7 = 0, I_4 + I_7 - I_1 = 0,$$
$$I_1 - I_2 - I_3 = 0, I_2 - I_6 - I_8 = 0, R_5\,I_5 + R_7\,I_7 - R_4\,I_4 = 0,$$
$$R_5\,I_5 - R_6\,I_6 - V_2 = 0, R_2\,I_2 - V_2 - R_3\,I_3 = 0, I_3 + I_8 - I_4 - I_5 = 0\}$$

Consider it as a linear system of equations in which the resistors and voltages are parameters and the currents actually are the unknowns.
```
>  currents := { seq( I[i], i=1..8 ) }:
>  resistors := { seq( R[i], i=1..7 ) }:
>  voltages := { V[1], V[2] }:
>  sol := solve( eqns, currents ):
```
The solution is not shown. Instead we shall look for a simple formula of current I_5. But first we **assign** the expressions of the currents in the solution, because this is not done automatically by **solve**, and print the formula for I_5 obtained with **solve**.
```
>  assign( sol ):
>  I[5];
```

$$\Big(R_7\,R_2\,R_4\,V_2 + R_4\,V_1\,R_6\,R_3 + R_6\,R_4\,V_1\,R_2 + R_4\,R_3\,R_6\,V_2 + R_4\,R_3\,R_7\,V_2$$
$$+ R_4\,R_3\,R_2\,V_2 + R_4\,R_1\,V_2\,R_3 + R_4\,R_1\,R_2\,V_2 + R_7\,R_3\,R_2\,V_2$$
$$+ R_7\,R_1\,V_2\,R_3 + R_7\,R_1\,R_2\,V_2\Big)\Big/\Big(R_5\,R_7\,R_1\,R_3 + R_5\,R_7\,R_3\,R_2$$
$$+ R_5\,R_4\,R_3\,R_2 + R_5\,R_7\,R_2\,R_4 + R_5\,R_7\,R_3\,R_4 + R_6\,R_4\,R_1\,R_2$$
$$+ R_6\,R_4\,R_1\,R_3 + R_6\,R_4\,R_3\,R_2 + R_6\,R_7\,R_2\,R_4 + R_6\,R_7\,R_3\,R_4$$
$$+ R_5\,R_7\,R_1\,R_2 + R_6\,R_1\,R_3\,R_5 + R_6\,R_3\,R_2\,R_5 + R_6\,R_7\,R_1\,R_2$$
$$+ R_6\,R_7\,R_1\,R_3 + R_6\,R_3\,R_4\,R_5 + R_6\,R_2\,R_4\,R_5 + R_6\,R_1\,R_2\,R_5$$
$$+ R_5\,R_4\,R_1\,R_2 + R_5\,R_4\,R_1\,R_3 + R_6\,R_7\,R_3\,R_2\Big)$$

To simplify this formula we introduce short names for subexpressions and simplify I_5 in terms of the new variables.
```
>  relations := {
>    A = R[1]*R[2]*R[4] + R[1]*R[3]*R[4] + R[2]*R[3]*R[4],
>    B = R[5]*R[6] + R[5]*R[7] + R[6]*R[7], C = R[1]*R[2]
>       + R[1]*R[3] + R[2]*R[3] + R[2]*R[4] + R[3]*R[4],
>    D = R[4]*R[6] }:
>  I[5] := map( simplify, I[5], relations,
>              [op(resistors),A,B,C,D] );
```

$$I_5 := \frac{V_2\,A + V_2\,R_7\,C + V_1\,R_2\,D + (V_1 + V_2)\,R_3\,D}{R_5\,A + R_6\,A + B\,C}$$

```
> I[5] := map( collect, I[5], [V1,V2,D] );
```

$$I_5 := \frac{(\,(V_2 + V_1)\,R_3 + V_1\,R_2\,)\,D + V_2\,A + V_2\,R_7\,C}{R_6\,A + B\,C + R_5\,A}$$

As a second example we consider a system of equations describing the *pseudo steady state* of an enzyme-catalyzed reaction. We shall apply the Michaelis-Menten theory to the dimeric enzymatic reaction shown in Figure 16.3.

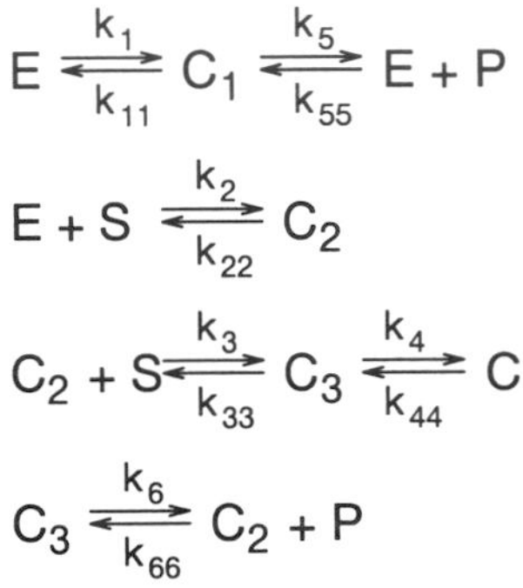

$$E \underset{k_{11}}{\overset{k_1}{\rightleftarrows}} C_1 \underset{k_{55}}{\overset{k_5}{\rightleftarrows}} E + P$$

$$E + S \underset{k_{22}}{\overset{k_2}{\rightleftarrows}} C_2$$

$$C_2 + S \underset{k_{33}}{\overset{k_3}{\rightleftarrows}} C_3 \underset{k_{44}}{\overset{k_4}{\rightleftarrows}} C_1 + S$$

$$C_3 \underset{k_{66}}{\overset{k_6}{\rightleftarrows}} C_2 + P$$

FIGURE 16.3. Dimeric enzymatic reaction.

Here, S, P, E, C_1, C_2, and C_3 are the concentrations of the substrate, product, free enzyme, and the three enzyme substrate complexes, respectively. The deterministic mathematical model that describes the kinetics of this reaction is the following system of differential equations.

$$
\begin{aligned}
S' &= k_{22}C_2 + (k_{33} + k_4)\,C_3 - (k_2 E + k_{44}C_1 + k_3 C_2)\,S \\
P' &= k_5 C_1 + k_6 C_3 - (k_{55}E + k_{66}C_2)\,P \\
E' &= (k_{11} + k_5)\,C_1 + k_{22}C_2 - (k_1 + k_2 S + k_{55}P)\,E \\
C_1' &= (k_1 + k_{55}P)\,E + k_4 C_3 - (k_{11} + k_5 + k_{44}S)\,C_1 \\
C_2' &= k_2 ES + (k_6 + k_{33})C_3 - (k_{22} + k_3 S + k_{66}P)\,C_2 \\
C_3' &= (k_{66}P + k_3 S)\,C_2 + k_{44}C_1 S - (k_{33} + k_4 + k_6)\,C_3
\end{aligned}
$$

Let us concentrate on the first of these equations. For convenience, we introduce with the **alias** and **macro** facility some shortcuts for various names.

```
> alias( S=S(t), P=P(t) ): # s, p as functions of time t
> sequence := seq( k.i = k[i], i=1..6 ),
>             seq( k.i.i = k[i,i], i=1..6 ),
>             seq( C.i = C[i], i=1..6 ):
> (eval@subs)( s=sequence, ´macro(s)´ ):
> RS := k22*C2 + (k33+k4)*C3 - (k2*E+k3*C2+k44*C1)*S;
```

$$RS := k_{2,2}\,C_2 + (k_{3,3} + k_4)\,C_3 - (k_2\,E + k_3\,C_2 + k_{4,4}\,C_1)\,S$$

In the pseudo steady state, it is assumed that the concentrations of the free enzyme and the complexes change very slowly, so that we may even assume them to be constant in time. Thus we get the following system of equations (linear in C_1, C_2, C_3, and E).

```
>  sys :=
>  { 0 = (k11+k5)*C1 + k22*C2 - (k1+k2*S+k55*P)*E,
     0 = (k1+k55*P)*E + k4*C3 - (k11+k5+k44*S)*C1,
     0 = k2*E*S + (k6+k33)*C3 - (k22+k3*S+k66*P)*C2,
     0 = (k66*P+k3*S)*C2 + k44*C1*S - (k33+k4+k6)*C3,
     E0 = C1+C2+C3+E };
```

$$sys := \left\{ 0 = (k_{6,6} P + k_3 S) C_2 + k_{4,4} C_1 S - (k_{3,3} + k_4 + k_6) C_3, \right.$$
$$E0 = C_1 + C_2 + C_3 + E,$$
$$0 = (k_{1,1} + k_5) C_1 + k_{2,2} C_2 - (k_1 + k_2 S + k_{5,5} P) E,$$
$$0 = k_2 E S + (k_6 + k_{3,3}) C_3 - (k_{2,2} + k_3 S + k_{6,6} P) C_2,$$
$$\left. 0 = (k_1 + k_{5,5} P) E + k_4 C_3 - (k_{1,1} + k_5 + k_{4,4} S) C_1 \right\}$$

Maple can solve this system of equations so that the reaction rate S' can be expressed in terms of S, P, E_0, and the rate constants. We do not show the large solution. Instead we shall show the expression when $k_{55} = 0$, $k_{66} = 0$.

```
>  solve( sys, {C1,C2,C3,E} ):
>  assign("):
>  k55 := 0: k66 := 0:
```

The differential equation for substrate concentration becomes

```
>  diff(S,t) = collect( normal(RS), S, factor );
```

$$\frac{\partial}{\partial t} S = E0 S \left(- k_3 S^2 k_{4,4} k_2 k_6 \right.$$
$$- k_3 (k_{1,1} k_4 k_2 + k_{1,1} k_6 k_2 + k_5 k_6 k_2 + k_1 k_{4,4} k_6 + k_5 k_4 k_2) S$$
$$+ k_{4,4} k_1 k_{3,3} k_{2,2} \Big) / \Big(k_2 S^3 k_{4,4} k_3 + \left(k_2 k_{4,4} k_6 + k_5 k_3 k_2 \right.$$
$$+ k_2 k_{4,4} k_{3,3} + k_{1,1} k_3 k_2 + k_2 k_4 k_3 + k_1 k_{4,4} k_3 \Big) S^2 + \Big(k_1 k_4 k_3$$
$$+ k_5 k_4 k_3 + k_5 k_{3,3} k_2 + k_5 k_4 k_2 + k_1 k_{4,4} k_{2,2} + k_{2,2} k_{4,4} k_6$$
$$+ k_{1,1} k_{3,3} k_2 + k_1 k_{4,4} k_{3,3} + k_{2,2} k_{4,4} k_{3,3} + k_{1,1} k_4 k_3 + k_1 k_{4,4} k_6$$
$$+ k_{1,1} k_6 k_2 + k_{1,1} k_4 k_2 + k_5 k_6 k_2 \Big) S$$
$$+ k_{2,2} (k_5 + k_{1,1} + k_1) (k_{3,3} + k_4 + k_6) \Big)$$

Maple can also find the analytical solution of this differential equation with **dsolve**. But more on differential equations in the next chapter.

Nonlinear equations

Enough about systems of linear equations; time and memory are the only computational limitations to solving them. There are two algorithms implemented, viz., a normal Gaussian elimination with a sparse representation and a "primitive" fraction-free algorithm with a sparse representation in case coefficients are integers, radicals, or polynomials, among others. Let us now concentrate on nonlinear systems of equations. Consider the following equations of a circle and a parabola

$$x^2 + y^2 = 25, \quad y = x^2 - 5,$$

and solve this system with Maple.

```
>  eqns := { x^2 + y^2 = 25, y = x^2 - 5 };
```
$$eqns := \{ x^2 + y^2 = 25, y = x^2 - 5 \}$$

```
>  vars := {x,y}:
>  solve( eqns, vars );
```
$$\{ x = 0, y = -5 \}, \{ x = 0, y = -5 \}, \{ x = 3, y = 4 \}, \{ y = 4, x = -3 \}$$

This was simple, but very soon solving nonlinear equations gets more complicated. Consider

$$x^2 + y^2 = 1, \quad \sqrt{x + y} = x^2 - y^2,$$

and solve this system of equations with Maple.

```
>  eqns := { x^2+y^2=1, sqrt(x+y)=x^2-y^2 };
```
$$eqns := \{ x^2 + y^2 = 1, \sqrt{x+y} = x^2 - y^2 \}$$

```
>  vars := {x,y}:
>  sols := solve( eqns, vars );
```

$$sols := \{ y = \mathrm{RootOf}(2\_Z^2 - 1), x = -\mathrm{RootOf}(2\_Z^2 - 1) \},$$
$$\{ y = 0, x = 1 \}, \{ x = 2 + 3\%3 - 4\%3^3 - 2\%3^2, y = \%3 \},$$
$$\{ x = 2 + 3\%2 - 4\%2^3 - 2\%2^2, y = \%2 \}$$
$$\%1 := 4\_Z^4 + 4\_Z^3 - 2\_Z^2 - 4\_Z - 1$$
$$\%2 := \mathrm{RootOf}(\%1, -.3269928304)$$
$$\%3 := \mathrm{RootOf}(\%1, -.8090169944 + .3930756889\,I)$$

Apparently Maple finds four solutions of the given system of equations and represents them as a sequence of sets. Within each set the values of the variables in the particular solution are denoted as equations. This makes substitution of the solution in the original system of equations easy.

```
>  subs( sols[2], eqns );
```
$$\{ 1 = 1 \}$$

```
>  simplify( subs( sols[1], eqns ) );
```
$$\{\, 0 = 0, 1 = 1 \,\}$$

To check a solution, you can also use **testeq**.

```
>  map( testeq, subs( sols[1], eqns ) );
```
$$\{\, true \,\}$$

```
>  convert( ", `and` );
```
$$true$$

The first solution found

```
>  sols[1];
```
$$\{\, y = \mathrm{RootOf}(\, 2\_Z^2 - 1 \,), x = -\mathrm{RootOf}(\, 2\_Z^2 - 1 \,) \,\}$$

is actually a set of two or four solutions. When both **RootOf** expressions correspond with the same complex number, then there are two solutions, which can be obtained by the procedure **allvalues**.

```
>  s1 := allvalues( sols[1], 'dependent' );
```
$$s1 := \left\{\, x = -\frac{1}{2}\,\sqrt{2}, y = \frac{1}{2}\,\sqrt{2} \,\right\}, \left\{\, x = \frac{1}{2}\,\sqrt{2}, y = -\frac{1}{2}\,\sqrt{2} \,\right\}$$

The keyword **dependent** in **allvalues** is used to specify that the **RootOfs** in the first solution represent the same value and should not be evaluated independently of one another. This is Maple's default behavior when applying **allvalues**.

You can also consider the first solution as a set of four candidate solutions and check them separately.

```
>  sols[1];
```
$$\{\, y = \mathrm{RootOf}(\, 2\_Z^2 - 1 \,), x = -\mathrm{RootOf}(\, 2\_Z^2 - 1 \,) \,\}$$

```
>  candidates := allvalues( sols[1], 'independent' );
```
$$candidates := \left\{\, x = -\frac{1}{2}\,\sqrt{2}, y = \frac{1}{2}\,\sqrt{2} \,\right\}, \left\{\, x = \frac{1}{2}\,\sqrt{2}, y = \frac{1}{2}\,\sqrt{2} \,\right\},$$
$$\left\{\, y = -\frac{1}{2}\,\sqrt{2}, x = -\frac{1}{2}\,\sqrt{2} \,\right\}, \left\{\, x = \frac{1}{2}\,\sqrt{2}, y = -\frac{1}{2}\,\sqrt{2} \,\right\}$$

```
>  for c in candidates do
>    simplify( subs( c, eqns ) )
>  od;
```
$$\{\, 0 = 0, 1 = 1 \,\}$$
$$\{\, 2^{1/4} = 0, 1 = 1 \,\}$$
$$\left\{\, \sqrt{-\sqrt{2}} = 0, 1 = 1 \,\right\}$$
$$\{\, 0 = 0, 1 = 1 \,\}$$

You see that only two out of four candidate solutions are valid. You can
select them as follows.

```
>   issol := proc( sol, eqns )
>     convert( map( testeq, subs( sol, eqns ) ),
>       `and` )
>   end: # the selection routine
>   select( issol, {candidates}, eqns );
```

$$\left\{\left\{x = -\frac{1}{2}\sqrt{2}, y = \frac{1}{2}\sqrt{2}\right\}, \left\{x = \frac{1}{2}\sqrt{2}, y = -\frac{1}{2}\sqrt{2}\right\}\right\}$$

The third and fourth solutions show another interesting phenomenon, viz.,
the use of **RootOf**s with an extra argument to select a specific root. You
can convert them into radical notation.

```
>   sols[3];
```

$$\{x = 2 + 3\,\%1 - 4\,\%1^3 - 2\,\%1^2, y = \%1\}$$
$$\%1 := \mathrm{RootOf}(4\_Z^4 + 4\_Z^3 - 2\_Z^2 - 4\_Z - 1,$$
$$-.8090169944 + .3930756889\,I)$$

```
>   convert( ", radical );
```

$$\left\{x = \frac{5}{4} - \frac{3}{4}\sqrt{5} + \frac{3}{4}\sqrt{2 - 2\sqrt{5}} - 4\,\%1^3 - 2\,\%1^2, y = \%1\right\}$$
$$\%1 := -\frac{1}{4} - \frac{1}{4}\sqrt{5} + \frac{1}{4}\sqrt{2 - 2\sqrt{5}}$$

```
>   s3 := simplify(");
```

$$s3 := \left\{y = -\frac{1}{4} - \frac{1}{4}\sqrt{5} + \frac{1}{4}I\sqrt{-2 + 2\sqrt{5}},\right.$$
$$\left. x = -\frac{1}{4} - \frac{1}{4}\sqrt{5} - \frac{1}{4}I\sqrt{-2 + 2\sqrt{5}}\right\}$$

```
>   convert( sols[4], radical );
```

$$\left\{x = \frac{5}{4} + \frac{3}{4}\sqrt{5} - \frac{3}{4}\sqrt{2 + 2\sqrt{5}} - 4\,\%1^3 - 2\,\%1^2, y = \%1\right\}$$
$$\%1 := -\frac{1}{4} + \frac{1}{4}\sqrt{5} - \frac{1}{4}\sqrt{2 + 2\sqrt{5}}$$

```
>   s4 := simplify(");
```

$$s4 := \left\{x = -\frac{1}{4} + \frac{1}{4}\sqrt{5} + \frac{1}{4}\sqrt{2 + 2\sqrt{5}}, y = -\frac{1}{4} + \frac{1}{4}\sqrt{5} - \frac{1}{4}\sqrt{2 + 2\sqrt{5}}\right\}$$

So, Maple found in fact five solutions

```
>  s1, sols[2], s3, s4;
```

$$\left\{x = -\frac{1}{2}\sqrt{2}, y = \frac{1}{2}\sqrt{2}\right\}, \left\{x = \frac{1}{2}\sqrt{2}, y = -\frac{1}{2}\sqrt{2}\right\}, \{y = 0, x = 1\},$$

$$\left\{y = -\frac{1}{4} - \frac{1}{4}\sqrt{5} + \frac{1}{4}I\sqrt{-2+2\sqrt{5}}, x = -\frac{1}{4} - \frac{1}{4}\sqrt{5} - \frac{1}{4}I\sqrt{-2+2\sqrt{5}}\right\},$$

$$\left\{x = -\frac{1}{4} + \frac{1}{4}\sqrt{5} + \frac{1}{4}\sqrt{2+2\sqrt{5}}, y = -\frac{1}{4} + \frac{1}{4}\sqrt{5} - \frac{1}{4}\sqrt{2+2\sqrt{5}}\right\}$$

but by itself used **RootOf**s to specify two or more solutions in one expression. You may be somewhat disappointed that Maple in this example did not come up right away with the solutions in radical notation. After all, the polynomials inside the **RootOf**s are of degree less than five and therefore can be expressed in radical notation. Your wish is Maple's command if you set the environment variable _EnvExplicit to true.

```
>  readlib(forget):
>  forget( solve ):   # forget previous results

>  _EnvExplicit := true:
>  candidates := { solve( eqns ) };
```

$$candidates := \left\{\left\{x = -\frac{1}{2}\sqrt{2}, y = \frac{1}{2}\sqrt{2}\right\},\right.$$

$$\left\{x = \frac{5}{4} + \frac{3}{4}\sqrt{5} + \frac{3}{4}\sqrt{2+2\sqrt{5} - 4\%4^3 - 2\%4^2}, y = \%4\right\},$$

$$\left\{x = \frac{5}{4} + \frac{3}{4}\sqrt{5} - \frac{3}{4}\sqrt{2+2\sqrt{5} - 4\%3^3 - 2\%3^2}, y = \%3\right\},$$

$$\left\{x = \frac{5}{4} - \frac{3}{4}\sqrt{5} + \frac{3}{4}\sqrt{2-2\sqrt{5} - 4\%2^3 - 2\%2^2}, y = \%2\right\},$$

$$\left\{x = \frac{5}{4} - \frac{3}{4}\sqrt{5} - \frac{3}{4}\sqrt{2-2\sqrt{5} - 4\%1^3 - 2\%1^2}, y = \%1\right\},$$

$$\left.\left\{x = \frac{1}{2}\sqrt{2}, y = -\frac{1}{2}\sqrt{2}\right\}, \{y = 0, x = 1\}\right\}$$

$$\%1 := -\frac{1}{4} - \frac{1}{4}\sqrt{5} - \frac{1}{4}\sqrt{2-2\sqrt{5}}$$

$$\%2 := -\frac{1}{4} - \frac{1}{4}\sqrt{5} + \frac{1}{4}\sqrt{2-2\sqrt{5}}$$

$$\%3 := -\frac{1}{4} + \frac{1}{4}\sqrt{5} - \frac{1}{4}\sqrt{2+2\sqrt{5}}$$

$$\%4 := -\frac{1}{4} + \frac{1}{4}\sqrt{5} + \frac{1}{4}\sqrt{2+2\sqrt{5}}$$

```
>  nops(");
```

$$7$$

Too many solutions! The problem is that Maple now does not distinguish which of the four roots of the polynomial $4z^4 + 4z^3 - 2z^2 - 4z - 1$ lead to valid solutions. Now, you yourself have to select the valid solutions. Also, the selection routine **issol**, which we defined before, fails. It depends solely on the power of **testeq** and no precautions are made against failure of this procedure. We adapt it by first bringing all terms to the left, squaring them, and then using **radnormal** for normalization of the expression containing nested radical numbers. The procedure **testeq** can then do the rest. If **testeq** fails, i.e., if it cannot determine whether the candidate solution is a true solution or not, we prefer to be on the safe side and we select the candidate solution.

```
>  issol := proc( sol, eqns )
>     local eqs;
>     eqs := subs( sol, eqns );
>     eqs := map( lhs - rhs, eqs );
>     eqs := map( u -> u^2, eqs );   # <-- square expressions
>     eqs := radnormal( eqs );
>     if not convert( map( testeq, eqs ), `and` )
>     then false
>     else true
>     fi
>  end: # the selection routine
```

In the above selection routine we square intermediate expressions to avoid problems with nested roots as much as possible. Without it, **testeq** may run in problems of not recognizing $1/2\sqrt{2-2\sqrt{5}}+1/2\sqrt{5}\sqrt{2-2\sqrt{5}}$ as a nonzero complex number.

```
>  select( issol, candidates, eqns );
```

$$\left\{ \left\{ x = -\frac{1}{2}\sqrt{2}, y = \frac{1}{2}\sqrt{2} \right\}, \right.$$

$$\left\{ x = \frac{5}{4} + \frac{3}{4}\sqrt{5} - \frac{3}{4}\sqrt{2 + 2\sqrt{5}} - 4\,\%2^3 - 2\,\%2^2, y = \%2 \right\},$$

$$\left\{ x = \frac{5}{4} - \frac{3}{4}\sqrt{5} + \frac{3}{4}\sqrt{2 - 2\sqrt{5}} - 4\,\%1^3 - 2\,\%1^2, y = \%1 \right\},$$

$$\left. \left\{ x = \frac{1}{2}\sqrt{2}, y = -\frac{1}{2}\sqrt{2} \right\}, \{ y = 0, x = 1 \} \right\}$$

$$\%1 := -\frac{1}{4} - \frac{1}{4}\sqrt{5} + \frac{1}{4}\sqrt{2 - 2\sqrt{5}}$$

$$\%2 := -\frac{1}{4} + \frac{1}{4}\sqrt{5} - \frac{1}{4}\sqrt{2 + 2\sqrt{5}}$$

```
> nops(");
```

$$5$$

By taking squares, the original system of equations can be changed into a system of polynomial equations. The newly obtained system can be solved with traditional methods for polynomial equations such as the elimination method.

First, you take squares and write the system of equations as polynomials.

```
> P[1] := ( lhs - rhs )( eqns[1] );
```

$$P_1 := x^2 + y^2 - 1$$

```
> P[2] := ( lhs^2 - rhs^2 )( eqns[2] );
```

$$P_2 := x + y - (x^2 - y^2)^2$$

```
> Peqns := { P[1], P[2] };
```

$$Peqns := \{x + y - (x^2 - y^2)^2, x^2 + y^2 - 1\}$$

Next, you eliminate y by computing the **resultant** with respect to this variable. (For the definition of resultant, check your favorite algebra textbook or [53, 76, 130, 132, 138]).

```
> eqn_x := resultant( P[1], P[2], y ) = 0;
```

$$eqn\_x := -6x^2 - 2x - 8x^5 + 8x^3 + 24x^4 + 16x^8 - 32x^6 = 0$$

```
> eqn_x := factor( eqn_x );
```

$$eqn\_x := 2x(x-1)(2x^2 - 1)(4x^4 + 4x^3 - 2x^2 - 4x - 1) = 0$$

This polynomial equation in x can easily be solved with Maple.

```
> x_roots := solve( eqn_x );
```

$$x\_roots := 0, 1, \frac{1}{2}\sqrt{2}, -\frac{1}{2}\sqrt{2}, -\frac{1}{4} + \frac{1}{4}\sqrt{5} + \frac{1}{4}\sqrt{2 + 2\sqrt{5}},$$

$$-\frac{1}{4} + \frac{1}{4}\sqrt{5} - \frac{1}{4}\sqrt{2 + 2\sqrt{5}}, -\frac{1}{4} - \frac{1}{4}\sqrt{5} + \frac{1}{4}\sqrt{2 - 2\sqrt{5}},$$

$$-\frac{1}{4} - \frac{1}{4}\sqrt{5} - \frac{1}{4}\sqrt{2 - 2\sqrt{5}}$$

Simplification with respect to side relations expresses y in terms of x.

```
> simplify( P[2], { P[1] }, [ y, x ] );
```

$$x + y - 4x^4 + 4x^2 - 1$$

```
> eqn_y := y = solve(",y);
```

$$eqn\_y := y = -x + 4x^4 - 4x^2 + 1$$

The solutions of the new system of equations $\{eqn\_x, eqn\_y\}$ are the same solutions that you would have gotten from **solve** with the environment variable _EnvExplicit set to **true**. The "ghost solutions" have been introduced by taking squares. Anyway, all solutions of the original system of equations have been found.

The elimination process could more easily have been done with the library function **eliminate**.

```
>   readlib( eliminate ):
>   eliminate( {P[1],P[2]}, y );
```

$$[\{y = -x + 4x^4 - 4x^2 + 1\},$$
$$\{x(x-1)(2x^2-1)(4x^4+4x^3-2x^2-4x-1)\}]$$

This routine makes use of pseudo resultants and pseudo subresultants to do the work (q.v., [4, 53, 76, 139]). From the result of **eliminate** you can easily find the solutions.

Let us redo our original example with three variables. First the system of equations is transformed into a system of polynomial equations for which the solution set contains the solutions of the original system of equations. To this end an extra variable, say z, is introduced; it describes the square root.

```
>   eqns := { x^2 + y^2 = 1,   z = x^2 - y^2,   z^2 = x + y };
```

$$eqns := \{z = x^2 - y^2, z^2 = x + y, x^2 + y^2 = 1\}$$

Next consider the set of polynomials that defines the system of equations.

```
>   polys := map( lhs - rhs, eqns );
```

$$polys := \{z - x^2 + y^2, z^2 - x - y, x^2 + y^2 - 1\}$$

Now eliminate y and z:

```
>   eliminate( polys, {y,z} );
```

$$[\{y = -x + 4x^4 - 4x^2 + 1,$$
$$z = 8x^2 + 8x^5 - 8x^3 + 2x - 16x^8 + 32x^6 - 24x^4 - 1\},$$
$$\{x(x-1)(2x^2-1)(4x^4+4x^3-2x^2-4x-1)\}]$$

Basically, we have the same result as was found previously.

In general, analytical solutions of systems of polynomial equations are not always so easily found by the elimination method. A more sophisticated method for solving polynomial equations will be described in the next section.

16.5   The Gröbner Basis Method

The Gröbner basis is an important mathematical notion in the computational theory of polynomials. In §14.7 the Gröbner basis method was applied to simplification with respect to side relations. In this section, its role in the process of finding solutions of systems of polynomial equations will be discussed briefly. More details, e.g., how to test whether a finite set of solutions exists, how to work over rings instead of fields, can be found in [13, 26, 27, 51].

Let us see how the last example of the previous section is treated in the Gröbner basis method.

```
>  polys := { x^2 + y^2 - 1, x^2 - y^2 - z,  x + y - z^2 };
```

$$polys := \{\, x^2 - y^2 - z, x^2 + y^2 - 1, x + y - z^2 \,\}$$

The minimal Gröbner basis with respect to the pure lexicographical ordering of the unknowns x, y, and z, induced by $z \succ y \succ x$ is

```
>  with( grobner ):   # load the Groebner basis package
>  G := gbasis( polys, [z,y,x], `plex` );
```

$$G := [z - 2\,x^2 + 1, x + y - 1 + 4\,x^2 - 4\,x^4,$$
$$-3\,x^2 - x + 4\,x^3 - 4\,x^5 + 12\,x^4 - 16\,x^6 + 8\,x^8]$$

```
>  G := factor( G );
```

$$G := [z - 2\,x^2 + 1, x + y - 1 + 4\,x^2 - 4\,x^4,$$
$$x\,(\,x - 1\,)\,(\,2\,x^2 - 1\,)\,(\,4\,x^4 + 4\,x^3 - 2\,x^2 - 4\,x - 1\,)]$$

The set of common zeros of the Gröbner basis is equivalent to the set of common zeros of the original set of polynomials. However, the Gröbner basis has in this case achieved a complete separation of the variables z and y as polynomials in x and a remaining univariate polynomial in x. The first two polynomials can be trivially solved for y and z.

$$z = 2x^2 - 1, \quad y = -4x^4 - 4x^2 - x + 1$$

The roots of the third polynomial

$$x(x - 1)(2x^2 - 1)(4x^4 + 4x^3 - 2x^2 - 4x - 1)$$

can be found in analytical form. Each root can be plugged into the equations for y and z.

```
>  _EnvExplicit := true:
>  assign( { solve(G[1],{z}), solve(G[2],{y}) } );
>  rootlist := [ solve( G[3] ) ];
```

$$rootlist := \left[0, 1, \frac{1}{2}\,\sqrt{2}, -\frac{1}{2}\,\sqrt{2}, -\frac{1}{4} + \frac{1}{4}\,\sqrt{5} + \frac{1}{4}\,\sqrt{2 + 2\,\sqrt{5}},\right.$$

$$-\frac{1}{4}+\frac{1}{4}\sqrt{5}-\frac{1}{4}\sqrt{2+2\sqrt{5}},\ -\frac{1}{4}-\frac{1}{4}\sqrt{5}+\frac{1}{4}\sqrt{2-2\sqrt{5}},$$

$$\left.-\frac{1}{4}-\frac{1}{4}\sqrt{5}-\frac{1}{4}\sqrt{2-2\sqrt{5}}\right]$$

```
>   for x in rootlist do
>      simplify( [ ´x´=x, ´y´=y, ´z´=z ] );
>      if simplify( subs( ", polys ) ) = {0}
>      then print( `valid solution` )
>      else print( `INvalid solution` )
>      fi
>   od;
```

$$[\,x=0,y=1,z=-1\,]$$
valid solution

$$[\,x=1,y=0,z=1\,]$$
valid solution

$$\left[x=\frac{1}{2}\sqrt{2},y=-\frac{1}{2}\sqrt{2},z=0\right]$$
valid solution

$$\left[x=-\frac{1}{2}\sqrt{2},y=\frac{1}{2}\sqrt{2},z=0\right]$$
valid solution

$$\left[x=-\frac{1}{4}+\frac{1}{4}\sqrt{5}+\frac{1}{4}\sqrt{2+2\sqrt{5}},y=-\frac{1}{4}+\frac{1}{4}\sqrt{5}-\frac{1}{4}\sqrt{2+2\sqrt{5}},\right.$$

$$\left.z=-\frac{1}{4}\sqrt{2+2\sqrt{5}}+\frac{1}{4}\sqrt{5}\sqrt{2+2\sqrt{5}}\right]$$
valid solution

$$\left[x=-\frac{1}{4}+\frac{1}{4}\sqrt{5}-\frac{1}{4}\sqrt{2+2\sqrt{5}},y=-\frac{1}{4}+\frac{1}{4}\sqrt{5}+\frac{1}{4}\sqrt{2+2\sqrt{5}},\right.$$

$$\left.z=\frac{1}{4}\sqrt{2+2\sqrt{5}}-\frac{1}{4}\sqrt{5}\sqrt{2+2\sqrt{5}}\right]$$
valid solution

$$\left[x=-\frac{1}{4}-\frac{1}{4}\sqrt{5}+\frac{1}{4}I\sqrt{-2+2\sqrt{5}},y=-\frac{1}{4}-\frac{1}{4}\sqrt{5}-\frac{1}{4}I\sqrt{-2+2\sqrt{5}},\right.$$

$$\left.z=-\frac{1}{4}I\sqrt{-2+2\sqrt{5}}-\frac{1}{4}I\sqrt{5}\sqrt{-2+2\sqrt{5}}\right]$$
valid solution

$$\left[x=-\frac{1}{4}-\frac{1}{4}\sqrt{5}-\frac{1}{4}I\sqrt{-2+2\sqrt{5}},y=-\frac{1}{4}-\frac{1}{4}\sqrt{5}+\frac{1}{4}I\sqrt{-2+2\sqrt{5}},\right.$$

$$\left.z=\frac{1}{4}I\sqrt{-2+2\sqrt{5}}+\frac{1}{4}I\sqrt{5}\sqrt{-2+2\sqrt{5}}\right]$$
valid solution

The advantage of the Gröbner basis with respect to the elimination method of the previous section is that more insight into the structure of the problem can be gained by experimenting with the term orderings.

The second example is a system of equations that describes the steady state of an ordinary differential equation from a neural network [146]:

$$\{cx + xy^2 + xz^2 = 1, \quad cy + yx^2 + yz^2 = 1, \quad cz + zx^2 + zy^2 = 1\}.$$

We consider it as a system of equations in the unknowns x, y, and z, and with parameter c. The following solution obtained with **solve** contains algebraic functions.

```
>   eqns := { c*x + x*y^2 + x*z^2 = 1,
>       c*y + y*x^2 + y*z^2 = 1, c*z + z*x^2 + z*y^2 = 1 };
```

$$eqns := \{cx + xy^2 + xz^2 = 1, cy + yx^2 + yz^2 = 1, cz + zx^2 + zy^2 = 1\}$$

```
>   _EnvExplicit := false: # stick to RootOfs
>   solve( eqns, {x,y,z} );
```

$$\{z = \mathrm{RootOf}(2\_Z^3 + c\_Z - 1), x = \mathrm{RootOf}(2\_Z^3 + c\_Z - 1),$$
$$y = \mathrm{RootOf}(2\_Z^3 + c\_Z - 1)\},$$

$$\left\{z = \%2, y = -\frac{-1 + 2c\%2 + 2\%2^3}{c}, x = \%2\right\},$$

$$\left\{y = \%2, x = \%2, z = -\frac{-1 + 2c\%2 + 2\%2^3}{c}\right\},$$

$$\left\{x = -\frac{-1 + 2c\%2 + 2\%2^3}{c}, z = \%2, y = \%2\right\}, \left\{z = \%1,\right.$$

$$x = \frac{1}{c + \mathrm{RootOf}(\_Z^2 + \%1\_Z + c + \%1^2)^2 + \%1^2},$$

$$y = \mathrm{RootOf}(\_Z^2 + \%1\_Z + c + \%1^2)\Big\}$$

$$\%1 := \mathrm{RootOf}(1 + \_Z^3 + c\_Z)$$
$$\%2 := \mathrm{RootOf}(2\_Z^4 + 3c\_Z^2 + c^2 - \_Z)$$

This answer does not give you much structural insight. For systems of polynomial equations the procedure **gsolve** in the **grobner** package is quite useful. **gsolve** requires the equations to be expressed as pure polynomials, which are understood to be equal to 0.

```
>   polys := map( lhs - rhs, eqns );
```

$$polys := \{cz + zx^2 + zy^2 - 1, cx + xy^2 + xz^2 - 1, cy + yx^2 + yz^2 - 1\}$$

```
> with( grobner ):  # load Groebner basis package
> settime := time():
> sys := gsolve( polys, {x,y,z} );
```

$$sys := [[\, z - x, y - x, c\,x - 1 + 2\,x^3\,],$$
$$[\, c\,z - 1 + 2\,c\,x + 2\,x^3, y - x, c^2 + 3\,c\,x^2 + 2\,x^4 - x\,],$$
$$[\, z + y + x, y\,x + y^2 + c + x^2, 1 + c\,x + x^3\,],$$
$$[\, 2\,z - c^2 + (\,-c^3 - 2\,)\,x + 4\,c\,x^2 - 2\,c^2\,x^3,$$
$$2\,y - c^2 + (\,-c^3 - 2\,)\,x + 4\,c\,x^2 - 2\,c^2\,x^3,$$
$$c^2\,x^2 + 1 + 2\,c\,x - 2\,x^3 + 2\,c\,x^4\,],$$
$$[\, z - x, c\,y - 1 + 2\,c\,x + 2\,x^3, c^2 + 3\,c\,x^2 + 2\,x^4 - x\,]]$$

```
> cpu_time := (time()-settime) * seconds; # computing time
```

$$cpu\_time := 22.234\ seconds$$

You get a list of new systems of polynomials whose common zeros are the solutions of the original system. Often these new systems of equations are easier to solve. At least, they give you more insight into how the problem can be split into smaller subproblems.

```
> for s in sys do
>      solve( {op(s)}, {x,y,z} )
> od;
```

$$\{z = \mathrm{RootOf}(\,2\,\_Z^3 + c\,\_Z - 1\,), x = \mathrm{RootOf}(\,2\,\_Z^3 + c\,\_Z - 1\,),$$
$$y = \mathrm{RootOf}(\,2\,\_Z^3 + c\,\_Z - 1\,)\}$$

$$\{\, y = \%1, x = \%1, z = -\frac{-1 + 2\,c\,\%1 + 2\,\%1^3}{c}\,\}$$
$$\%1 := \mathrm{RootOf}(\,2\,\_Z^4 + 3\,c\,\_Z^2 + c^2 - \_Z\,)$$

$$\{z = -\mathrm{RootOf}(\,\_Z^2 + \%1\,\_Z + c + \%1^2\,) - \%1,$$
$$y = \mathrm{RootOf}(\,\_Z^2 + \%1\,\_Z + c + \%1^2\,), x = \%1\}$$
$$\%1 := \mathrm{RootOf}(\,1 + \_Z^3 + c\,\_Z\,)$$

$$\{\, x = \%1, y = \frac{1}{2}\,c^2 + \frac{1}{2}\,\%1\,c^3 + \%1 - 2\,c\,\%1^2 + c^2\,\%1^3,$$
$$z = \frac{1}{2}\,c^2 + \frac{1}{2}\,\%1\,c^3 + \%1 - 2\,c\,\%1^2 + c^2\,\%1^3\,\}$$
$$\%1 := \mathrm{RootOf}(\,c^2\,\_Z^2 + 1 + 2\,c\,\_Z - 2\,\_Z^3 + 2\,c\,\_Z^4\,)$$

$$\{\, z = \%1, y = -\frac{-1 + 2\,c\,\%1 + 2\,\%1^3}{c}, x = \%1\,\}$$
$$\%1 := \mathrm{RootOf}(\,2\,\_Z^4 + 3\,c\,\_Z^2 + c^2 - \_Z\,)$$

Let us compare the **gsolve** approach to computing the Gröbner basis of
the original system of polynomials.

```
>   settime := time():
>   G := gbasis( polys, [x,y,z], `plex` ):
>   cpu_time := (time()-settime) * seconds;
```

$$cpu\_time := 670.317 \; seconds$$

```
>   factor( G[-1] );
```

$$(cz - 1 + 2z^3)(cz + 1 + z^3)(c^2 - z + 3cz^2 + 2z^4)$$
$$(z^2 c^2 + 1 + 2cz - 2z^3 + 2z^4 c)$$

In the **gsolve** approach, whenever a polynomial occurs that can be factorized, Maple splits the original problem into subproblems corresponding to
the factors found. The leads to a better efficiency, which is one of the key
issues in applying the Gröbner basis method.

Our third example of a system of polynomial equations attacked by
Gröbner basis methods comes from computational geodesy. Here we shall
only sketch the problem and its solution by Maple; for a detailed account
we refer to [98].

The relationships between the geocentric Cartesian coordinates x, y, and
z of a point P on or near the surface of the earth and the geodetic coordinates h (height), λ (longitude), and ϕ (latitude) of its Helmert's projection
on the geocentric reference ellipsoid are

$$
\begin{aligned}
x &= (N + h)\cos\phi\cos\lambda, \\
y &= (N + h)\cos\phi\sin\lambda, \\
z &= (N(1 - e^2) + h)\sin\phi,
\end{aligned}
$$

where the prime vertical radius of curvature N and the eccentricity e of
the reference ellipsoid are defined by

$$N = \frac{a}{\sqrt{1 - e^2\sin^2\phi}}$$

and

$$e = \sqrt{\frac{a^2 - b^2}{a^2}},$$

a and b being semi-major and semi-minor axes of the reference ellipsoid.
With the above equations, the Cartesian coordinates x, y, and z can be
computed directly from the geodetic coordinates h, λ, and ϕ. The inverse
problem is more difficult: you are asked to solve the above nonlinear system
of equations in the unknowns h, λ, and ϕ for given x, y, and z.

When you ask Maple to solve this system of trigonometric equations, it
returns an answer for the latitude in which roots of an 8th degree polynomials are involved. But you can do better! First, associate with the
system of trigonometric equations a system of polynomial equations by
introducing variables for the trigonometric entities and by adding polynomial equations that originate from well-known trigonometric identities.
Henceforth, we shall use the following variables: $cf = \cos\phi$, $sf = \sin\phi$,
$tf = \tan\phi$, $cl = \cos\lambda$, and $sl = \sin\lambda$. We shall also use the variable S to
deal with the square root $S = \sqrt{1 - e^2\,sf^2}$ and define $d = (N + h)\,cf$. In
this way, we come up with the following system of ten equations:

```
> sys := [ x - (N+h)*cf*cl, y - (N+h)*cf*sl,
>     z - (N*(1-e^2)+h)*sf, cf^2 + sf^2 - 1, cl^2 +sl^2 - 1,
>     tf*cf - sf, N*S - a, S^2 + e^2*sf^2 - 1, (N+h)*cf - d,
>     d^2 - x^2 - y^2 ];
```

$$sys := [x - (N+h)\,cf\,cl, y - (N+h)\,cf\,sl, z - (N(1-e^2)+h)\,sf,$$
$$cf^2 + sf^2 - 1, cl^2 + sl^2 - 1, tf\,cf - sf, N\,S - a, S^2 + e^2\,sf^2 - 1,$$
$$(N+h)\,cf - d, d^2 - x^2 - y^2]$$

We compute the Gröbner basis with respect to the following pure lexicographical ordering of the variables.

$$N > S > x > y > h > cl > sl > cf > sf > tf$$

```
> with( grobner ):  # load Groebner basis package
> vars := [N,S,x,y,h,cl,sl,cf,sf,tf]:
> gsys := gbasis( sys, vars, `plex` ):
```

The complete Gröbner basis is too big to be presented here. Besides, we
are only interested in the univariate polynomial in tf, which is expected to
be the last polynomial in the Gröbner basis.

```
> collect( gsys[-1], tf );  # get the polynomial in tf
```

$$-z^2 + (-d^2 + d^2\,e^2)\,tf^4 + 2\,z\,d\,tf + (-z^2 + e^2\,z^2 - d^2 + a^2\,e^4)\,tf^2$$
$$+ (-2\,d\,z\,e^2 + 2\,z\,d)\,tf^3$$

```
> map( convert, - ", sqrfree ); # rewrite the polynomial
```

$$z^2 - d^2\,tf^4(-1 + e^2) - 2\,z\,d\,tf - (-z^2 + e^2\,z^2 - d^2 + a^2\,e^4)\,tf^2$$
$$+ 2\,d\,tf^3(-1 + e^2)\,z$$

```
> sort( subs( e^2*z^2 = (e^2-1)*z^2 + z^2, " ), tf );
```

$$-d^2(-1 + e^2)\,tf^4 + 2\,d(-1 + e^2)\,z\,tf^3 - ((-1 + e^2)\,z^2 - d^2 + a^2\,e^4)\,tf^2$$
$$- 2\,z\,d\,tf + z^2$$

So, we end up with a 4th degree polynomial in $\tan\phi$, which can be solved analytically (q.v., [150]).

The same answer can be found by the procedure **finduni**.

```
> finduni(tf,sys,vars);
```

$$-z^2 + (-d^2 + d^2 e^2) tf^4 + 2zd\,tf + (-z^2 + e^2 z^2 - d^2 + a^2 e^4) tf^2$$
$$+ (-2dze^2 + 2zd) tf^3$$

This procedure uses the total degree ordering of variables to compute a Gröbner basis and uses this to construct the univariate polynomial (in tf) of least degree in the ideal generated by the polynomials. In this particular case, the computing time is two and a half times longer than the previous one, which uses pure lexicographical ordering.

The examples in this section gave you an idea of the strength of the Gröbner basis method as an alternative to the elimination method or Ritt-Wu's characteristic sets method, which is implemented and contributed by Dongming Wang [186] to the Maple share library. One thing to remember: time and memory complexity of the Gröbner basis algorithm can be a serious drawback.

16.6 Inequalities

The examples below will give you an impression of Maple's capabilities in solving (systems of) inequalities. A necessary condition for success is that the equality points of the inequalities can be properly ordered.

Consider the 3rd degree polynomial function $x \mapsto x^3 + 4x^2 + 2x - 1$, the graph of which is shown in Figure 16.4.

```
> plot( x^3 + 4*x^2 + 2*x - 1, x = -4..1 );
```

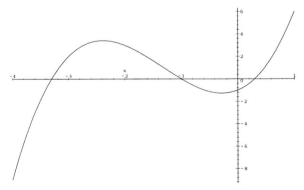

FIGURE 16.4. Graph of $x^3 + 4x^2 + 2x - 1$ on interval $(-4, 1)$.

Determine where the function is positive.
```
>   solve( x^3 + 4*x^2 + 2*x - 1 > 0, x );
```

$$\text{RealRange}(\text{Open}(-\frac{3}{2} - \frac{1}{2}\sqrt{13}), \text{Open}(-1)),$$

$$\text{RealRange}(\text{Open}(-\frac{3}{2} + \frac{1}{2}\sqrt{13}), \infty)$$

As with one equation in one unknown, the solution contains no variable but is expressed in terms of `RealRange`'s. When you specify the problem as a set of equations, you will obtain (as in the case of an equation) solutions containing the unknown.
```
>   solve( { x^3 + 4*x^2 + 2*x - 1 > 0 }, {x} );
```

$$\{-\frac{3}{2} - \frac{1}{2}\sqrt{13} < x, x < -1\}, \{-\frac{3}{2} + \frac{1}{2}\sqrt{13} < x\}$$

You may omit the braces around the inequality and still get solution sets.
```
>   solve( abs(x)*x + exp(x)>=0, {x} );
```

$$\{-2\,\text{LambertW}(\frac{1}{2}) \le x\}$$

```
>   solve( a*x + b >= c, {x} );
```

$$\{-\text{signum}(a)\,x \le \frac{\text{signum}(a)\,(-c + b)}{a}\}$$

solve is not restricted to only one inequality.
```
>   solve( { x^2 - x = 0, x<>0 }, x );   # nonzero solution
```

$$\{x = 1\}$$

```
>   _EnvExplicit := true:
>   solve( {x^4-9, x^2-3<>0} );
```

$$\{x = I\sqrt{3}\}, \{x = -I\sqrt{3}\}$$

```
>   solve( { x<1/3, y<1/2, x^2+y^2=1 }, {x,y} );
```

$$\{y < -\frac{2}{3}\sqrt{2}, x = \sqrt{-y^2 + 1}\}, \{y < -\frac{2}{3}\sqrt{2}, x = -\sqrt{-y^2 + 1}\},$$

$$\{y < \frac{1}{2}, -\frac{2}{3}\sqrt{2} < y, x = \sqrt{-y^2 + 1}\},$$

$$\{y < \frac{1}{2}, -\frac{2}{3}\sqrt{2} < y, x = -\sqrt{-y^2 + 1}\}$$

```
>   evalf(["]);
```

$$[\{x = \sqrt{-1.\,y^2 + 1.}, y < -.9428090414\},$$
$$\{y < -.9428090414, x = -1.\,\sqrt{-1.\,y^2 + 1.}\},$$
$$\{x = \sqrt{-1.\,y^2 + 1.}, -.9428090414 < y, y < .5000000000\},$$
$$\{x = -1.\,\sqrt{-1.\,y^2 + 1.}, -.9428090414 < y, y < .5000000000\}]$$

16.7   Numerical Solvers

For numerical approximations of solutions of equations or systems of equations Maple offers you the procedure **fsolve**. The use of this procedure is similar to the use of **solve**.

```
>   x^7 - 2*x^6 - 4*x^5 - x^3 + x^2 + 6*x + 4;
```
$$x^7 - 2\,x^6 - 4\,x^5 - x^3 + x^2 + 6\,x + 4$$

```
>   fsolve(");
```
$$-1.236067977, 1.167303978, 3.236067977$$

But there are additional options as listed in Table 16.1.

Option	Description
complex	complex-valued root(s)
a..b	search range over the real numbers
maxsols=n	maximum number of solutions
fulldigits	use floating-point number with Digits precision

TABLE 16.1. Options of **fsolve**.

Some examples:

```
>   fsolve( "" , x , complex );
```
$$-1.236067977, -.7648844336 - .3524715460\,I,$$
$$-.7648844336 + .3524715460\,I, .1812324445 - 1.083954101\,I,$$
$$.1812324445 + 1.083954101\,I, 1.167303978, 3.236067977$$

```
>   fsolve( """ , x , 0..2 );
```
$$1.167303978$$

In the latter case, Maple was told to try and find only real solutions between 0 and 2.

For polynomial equations, the procedure **fsolve** returns in general (but not always) all real solutions, and with the option **complex** all complex solutions. For equations of other types, **fsolve** is usually satisfied when one solution has been found.

```
>   eqn := sin(x) = x/2;
```
$$eqn := \sin(x) = \frac{1}{2}\,x$$

```
>   fsolve( eqn, x );
```
$$1.895494267$$

```
>  fsolve( eqn, x, 0.1 .. infinity );
```

$$1.895494267$$

```
>  fsolve( eqn, x, -0.1 .. 0.1 );
```

$$0$$

```
>  fsolve( eqn, x, -infinity .. -0.1 );
```

$$-1.895494267$$

fsolve is based on two methods, the (multidimensional) Newton method and, when this fails, the (multidimensional) secant method [174].

The procedure **realroot** uses Descartes' rule of signs (q.v., [138]) to find a list of isolating intervals for all real roots of a univariate polynomial. The width of the interval is optional.

```
>  readlib( realroot ):
>  x^7 - 2*x^6 - 4*x^5 - x^3 + x^2 + 6*x + 4;
```

$$x^7 - 2x^6 - 4x^5 - x^3 + x^2 + 6x + 4$$

```
>  realroot(");
```

$$[[0,2],[2,4],[-2,-1]]$$

```
>  realroot( "", 1/100 );
```

$$\left[\left[\frac{149}{128}, \frac{75}{64}\right], \left[\frac{207}{64}, \frac{415}{128}\right], \left[\frac{-159}{128}, \frac{-79}{64}\right]\right]$$

The procedure **sturm** allows you to compute the number of real roots of a polynomial in an interval. It is based on Sturm's theorem (q.v., [138]).

```
>  readlib(sturm):
>  x^7 - 2*x^6 - 4*x^5 - x^3 + x^2 + 6*x + 4;
```

$$x^7 - 2x^6 - 4x^5 - x^3 + x^2 + 6x + 4$$

```
>  sturm( ", x, -infinity,infinity ); # three real roots
```

$$3$$

```
>  sturm( "", x, 0, infinity );  # two positive roots
```

$$2$$

```
>  sturm( """, x, 2, 4 );  # one root between 2 and 4
```

$$1$$

16.8   Other Solvers in Maple

isolve

With **isolve** you look for integer solutions of (systems of) equations. The next example is an application in dimensional analysis.

The drag F of a fast-moving object in the air is supposed to depend upon its speed V, diameter d, the air density ρ, the velocity of sound c, and the kinematic viscosity ν. All these quantities have dimensions related to the dimensions mass m, length l, and time t. You can determine dimensional groupings of the quantities F, V, d, ρ, c, and ν in the following way.

```
>   nondimensional := force^f * speed^v * diameter^d
>     * density^r * acoustic_velocity^c
>     * kinematic_viscosity^m;
```

$$nondimensional := force^f\ speed^v\ diameter^d\ density^r\ acoustic\_velocity^c$$
$$kinematic\_viscosity^m$$

```
>   subs( { force = M*L/T^2, speed = L/T, diameter = L,
>     density = M/L^3, acoustic_velocity = L/T,
>     kinematic_viscosity = L^2/T }, nondimensional );
```

$$\left(\frac{ML}{T^2}\right)^f \left(\frac{L}{T}\right)^v L^d \left(\frac{M}{L^3}\right)^r \left(\frac{L}{T}\right)^c \left(\frac{L^2}{T}\right)^m$$

```
>   simplify( ", 'symbolic' );
```

$$M^{(f+r)}\ L^{(f+v+d-3\,r+c+2\,m)}\ T^{(-2\,f-v-c-m)}$$

```
>   eqns := { seq( op(2,i)=0, i= " ) };
```

$$eqns := \{\, f + r = 0, f + v + d - 3\,r + c + 2\,m = 0, -2\,f - v - c - m = 0\,\}$$

```
>   isolve(");  # find all integral solutions
```

$$\{f = -\_N1, v = 2\,\_N1 - \_N2 - \_N3, d = 2\,\_N1 - \_N3, r = \_N1,$$
$$c = \_N2, m = \_N3\}$$

```
>   subs( ", nondimensional );
```

$$force^{(-\_N1)}\ speed^{(2\,\_N1-\_N2-\_N3)}\ diameter^{(2\,\_N1-\_N3)}\ density^{-\_N1}$$
$$acoustic\_velocity^{-\_N2}\ kinematic\_viscosity^{-\_N3}$$

Some tricks enable you to group powers with the same exponent.

```
>   expand( ln(") );
```

$$-\_N1 \ln(force) + 2 \ln(speed)\,\_N1 - \ln(speed)\,\_N2 - \ln(speed)\,\_N3$$
$$+ 2 \ln(diameter)\,\_N1 - \ln(diameter)\,\_N3 + \_N1 \ln(density)$$
$$+ \_N2 \ln(acoustic\_velocity) + \_N3 \ln(kinematic\_viscosity)$$

> `[ coeffs( ", {_N1,_N2,_N3}, ´vars´ ) ];`

$$[-\ln(\,speed\,) + \ln(\,acoustic\_velocity\,),$$
$$-\ln(\,force\,) + 2\ln(\,speed\,) + 2\ln(\,diameter\,) + \ln(\,density\,),$$
$$-\ln(\,diameter\,) - \ln(\,speed\,) + \ln(\,kinematic\_viscosity\,)]$$

> `combine( ", ln, anything, ´symbolic´ );`

$$\left[\ln\left(\frac{acoustic\_velocity}{speed}\right), \ln\left(\frac{speed^2\,diameter^2\,density}{force}\right), \right.$$
$$\left. \ln\left(\frac{kinematic\_viscosity}{diameter\,speed}\right) \right]$$

> `zip( (a,b) -> exp(a)^b, ", [vars] );`

$$\left[\left(\frac{acoustic\_velocity}{speed}\right)^{-N2}, \left(\frac{speed^2\,diameter^2\,density}{force}\right)^{-N1}, \right.$$
$$\left. \left(\frac{kinematic\_viscosity}{diameter\,speed}\right)^{-N3} \right]$$

> `convert( ", `*` );`

$$\left(\frac{acoustic\_velocity}{speed}\right)^{-N2} \left(\frac{speed^2\,diameter^2\,density}{force}\right)^{-N1}$$
$$\left(\frac{kinematic\_viscosity}{diameter\,speed}\right)^{-N3}$$

Here, you have obtained a family of dimensionless variables with three integer parameters. Two combinations are well known in aerodynamics and fluid dynamics.

> `subs( _N1=0, _N2=-1, _N3=0, " );  # the Mach number`

$$\frac{speed}{acoustic\_velocity}$$

> `subs( _N1=0, _N2=1, _N3=-1, "" );  # the Reynold´s number`

$$\frac{acoustic\_velocity\,diameter}{kinematic\_viscosity}$$

msolve

Modular arithmetic is also provided for. One example is a cubic analogue of Pell's equation over $\mathbb{Z}_7$.

```
> msolve( y^2 = x^3 - 28, 7 );
```

$$\{\, x = 4, y = 1 \,\}, \{\, y = 1, x = 2 \,\}, \{\, y = 6, x = 2 \,\}, \{\, x = 4, y = 6 \,\},$$
$$\{\, y = 1, x = 1 \,\}, \{\, y = 6, x = 1 \,\}, \{\, y = 0, x = 0 \,\}$$

rsolve

Maple can also solve recurrence equations. It uses standard techniques like generating functions and z-transforms , and methods based on substitutions and characteristic equations. A few examples:

- Generalized Fibonacci polynomials

```
> rsolve( { f(n+2) = f(n+1) + f(n),
>    f(0)=0, f(1)=1 }, f(n) ); # Fibonacci numbers
```

$$\frac{\left(1 - \frac{1}{5}\sqrt{5}\right)\left(2\dfrac{1}{-1+\sqrt{5}}\right)^{n}}{-1+\sqrt{5}} + \frac{\left(-\frac{1}{5}\sqrt{5}-1\right)\left(-2\dfrac{1}{1+\sqrt{5}}\right)^{n}}{1+\sqrt{5}}$$

```
> rsolve( { f(n+2) = x*f(n+1) + y*f(n),
>    f(0)=0, f(1)=1 }, f(n) );
```

$$-\frac{\left(x^{2} + 4\,y - x\,\sqrt{x^{2}+4\,y}\right)\left(-2\dfrac{y}{x - \sqrt{x^{2}+4\,y}}\right)^{n}}{(x^{2}+4\,y)\left(x - \sqrt{x^{2}+4\,y}\right)}$$

$$-\frac{\left(x\,\sqrt{x^{2}+4\,y} + x^{2} + 4\,y\right)\left(-2\dfrac{y}{x + \sqrt{x^{2}+4\,y}}\right)^{n}}{(x^{2}+4\,y)\left(x + \sqrt{x^{2}+4\,y}\right)}$$

```
> normal( ", `expanded` );
```

$$\frac{(-2)^{n}\,y^{n}\left(\dfrac{1}{x - \sqrt{x^{2}+4\,y}}\right)^{n} - (-2)^{n}\,y^{n}\left(\dfrac{1}{x + \sqrt{x^{2}+4\,y}}\right)^{n}}{\sqrt{x^{2}+4\,y}}$$

```
> # 5th generalized Fibonacci polynomial
> normal( subs( n=5," ), `expanded` );
```

$$x^{4} + 3\,x^{2}\,y + y^{2}$$

By the way, the conjecture that $f(n)$ is irreducible if and only if n is a prime number holds for $n < 100$.

- Complexity of Gauss elimination

```
> rsolve( { T(n) = T(n-1) + n^2, T(1)=0 }, T(n) );
```

$$2\,(n+1)\left(\frac{1}{2}n+1\right)\left(\frac{1}{3}n+1\right) - 3\,(n+1)\left(\frac{1}{2}n+1\right) + n$$

```
>   factor(");
```

$$\frac{1}{6}(n-1)(2n^2+5n+6)$$

- Complexity of merge sort

```
>   rsolve( { T(n) = 2*T(n/2) + n-1, T(1)=0 }, T(n) );
```

$$n\left(2\left(\frac{1}{2}\right)^{\left(\frac{\ln(n)}{\ln(2)}+1\right)}+\frac{\ln(n)}{\ln(2)}-1\right)$$

```
>   simplify(");
```

$$-\frac{-\ln((2))-\ln(n)n+\ln((2))n}{\ln((2))}$$

- Complexity of Karatsuba multiplication

```
>   rsolve( { T(n) = 3*T(n/2) + n, T(1)=1}, T(n) );
```

$$n^{\left(\frac{\ln((3))}{\ln((2))}\right)}+n^{\left(\frac{\ln((3))}{\ln((2))}\right)}\left(-3\left(\frac{2}{3}\right)^{\left(\frac{\ln(n)}{\ln(2)}+1\right)}+2\right)$$

```
>   simplify(");
```

$$3n^{\left(\frac{\ln((3))}{\ln((2))}\right)}-2n$$

Sometimes, only partial solutions of a summation problem are found.

```
>   rsolve( a(n+1) = ln(n+1)*a(n) + 1, a(n) );
```

$$\left\{a(n)=\left(\prod_{\_n1=1}^{n-1}\ln(\_n1+1)\right)\right.$$

$$\left(\left(\sum_{\_n2=1}^{n-1}\frac{1}{\prod_{\_n1=1}^{\_n2}\ln(\_n1+1)}\right)+\ln((2))a(0)+1\right),$$

$$\left.a(0)=a(0)\right\}$$

Even when **rsolve** cannot find a closed formula, it may still give you information on the asymptotic behavior. An example:

```
>   rsolve( u(n+1) = ln( u(n)+1 ), u(n) );
```

$$\text{rsolve}(u(n+1)=\ln(u(n)+1),u(n))$$

```
> asympt( ", n, 4 );
```

$$2\frac{1}{n} + \frac{-C + \frac{2}{3}\ln(n)}{n^2} + O(\frac{1}{n^3})$$

Our final example will be the solution of a problem posed by Knuth [118]. Solve the recurrence

$$x_0 = a, \quad x_1 = b, \quad x_{n+2} = x_{n+1} + x_n/(n+1), \quad \text{for } n = 0, 1, 2, \ldots$$

both analytically (in terms of familiar functions of n) and asymptotically.

```
> infolevel[rsolve] := 5:
> rsolve( { x(n+2) = x(n+1) + x(n)/(n+1),
>   x(0)=a, x(1)=b }, x(n) );
```

$$\_C_1(n+1)$$

We were too optimistic. What Maple has found is in fact the asymptotic formula for the solution. New tools in the LREtools package, which manipulate and solve linear recurrence equations, fail in this example. So let us try to assist Maple and first compute the z-transform of the recurrence equation (written in a different but equivalent way)

```
> readlib( ztrans ):   # load library function
> x(0) := a:   x(1) := b:
> subs( ztrans(x(n),n,z) = F(z),
>   ztrans( (n+1)*x(n+2)=(n+1)*x(n+1)+x(n), n, z ) );
```

$$-z^2 F(z) - z^3 \left(\frac{\partial}{\partial z}F(z)\right) + az^2 = -z^2 \left(\frac{\partial}{\partial z}F(z)\right) + F(z)$$

Next we have to solve the differential equation.

```
> dsolve( ", F(z) );
```

$$F(z) = \frac{z(e^{(\frac{1}{z})}za + \_C1)e^{(-\frac{1}{z})}}{1 - 2z + z^2}$$

The last step of computing the inverse z-transform is the most difficult one.

```
> expand(");
```

$$F(z) = \frac{z^2 a}{z^2 - 2z + 1} + \frac{z\_C1}{(z^2 - 2z + 1)e^{(\frac{1}{z})}}$$

```
> subs( invztrans(F(z),z,n)=x(n), invztrans(",z,n) );
```

$$x(n) = an + a + \_C1 \, \text{invztrans}\left(\frac{z}{e^{(\frac{1}{z})}(z^2 - 2z + 1)}, z, n\right)$$

```
> simplify( factor(") );
```

$$x(n) = a\,n + a + \_C1\ \text{invztrans}\left(\frac{e^{\left(-\frac{1}{z}\right)}z}{(z-1)^2}, z, n\right)$$

```
> f := subs( body = invztrans(exp(-1/z),z,k), k->body );
```

$$f := k \rightarrow \frac{(-1)^k}{k!}$$

```
> g := subs( body = invztrans(z/(z-1)^2,z,k), k->body );
```

$$g := k \rightarrow k$$

So, the inverse z-transform that remains to be computed can be found as
a convolution.

```
> lhs(""") = subsop( 3 = _C1*Sum(f(n-k)*g(k),k=0..n),
>     rhs(""") );
```

$$x(n) = a\,n + a + \_C1\left(\sum_{k=0}^{n}\frac{(-1)^{(n-k)}k}{(n-k)!}\right)$$

```
> (value@subs)( n=1, " );
```

$$b = 2\,a + \_C1$$

```
> solve(",_C1);
```

$$b - 2\,a$$

```
> subs( _C1=", """ );
```

$$x(n) = a\,n + a + (b - 2\,a)\left(\sum_{k=0}^{n}\frac{(-1)^{(n-k)}k}{(n-k)!}\right)$$

Maple can even find a closed formula for the sum.

```
> value(");
```

$$x(n) = a\,n + a + \frac{(b-2\,a)(-1)^{(n-1)}\,\text{hypergeom}([2, -n+1], [\,], 1)}{(n-1)!}$$

The **genfunc** package contains functions for manipulating rational generating functions. It is a convenient tool when you want to apply the method
of generating functions manually to recurrence relations.

match

Currently, Maple has limited facilities for pattern matching. The **match** function puts some computational effort into matching an expression with a pattern in one main variable. A simple example: do there exist a and b such that $x^2 + 2 * x + 3 = (x + a)^2 + b$ for all x? If so, what are these variables equal to?

```
>  match( x^2 + 2*x + 3 = (x+a)^2 + b, x, 'sol' );
```

$$true$$

Maple affirms a true matching. The suitable values for a and b are stored in the third variable `sol`.

```
>  sol;
```

$$\{\, a = 1, b = 2 \,\}$$

Please understand the difference between **match**, which does algebraic pattern matching, and **typematch**, which just matches the form of objects.

```
>  typematch( (x+1)^2 + 2,
>    (a::anything) &+ (b::anything) );
```

$$true$$

```
>  a,b;
```

$$(x+1)^2, 2$$

```
>  typematch( (x+1)^2 + 2,
>  (((u::anything) &+ (v::anything))^2) &+ (w::anything) );
```

$$true$$

```
>  typematch( x^2 + 2*x + 3,
>  (((p::anything) &+ (q::anything))^2) &+ (r::anything) );
```

$$false$$

16.9 Exercises

1. Compute the 6th degree polynomial mapping of which the graph goes through the points $(-5, -120)$, $(-3, 48)$, $(-2, 36)$, $(1, 120)$, $(4, 2400)$, $(10, 220380)$, and $(12, 57408)$.

2. Check whether
$$3x^2 + 3y^2 + 6xy + 6x + 6y + 2$$
can be written in the form
$$a(x + by + c)^n + d$$
for suitable values of a, b, c, d, and n.

3. Consider the stoichiometry of the following two chemical reactions.

   (a) For what values of p, q, r, s, t, u, and v is the reaction equation

   $$p\,\mathrm{KMnO_4} + q\,\mathrm{H_2SO_4} + r\,\mathrm{H_2C_2O_4} \longrightarrow$$

   $$s\,\mathrm{K_2SO_4} + t\,\mathrm{MnSO_4} + u\,\mathrm{H_2O} + v\,\mathrm{CO_2}$$

   balanced?

   (b) For what values of p, q, r, s, and t is the reaction equation

   $$p\,\mathrm{CO} + q\,\mathrm{CO_2} + r\,\mathrm{H_2} \longrightarrow s\,\mathrm{CH_4} + t\,\mathrm{H_2O}$$

   balanced?

4. Solve the following equation in x by **solve** and **fsolve**.

   $$48x^5 + 8x^4 - 6x^3 + 114x^2 - 37x + 18 = 0$$

5. Solve the following equations in x.

   (a) $(x+1)^{(x+a)} = (x+1)^2$

   (b) $x + (1+x)^{(1/2)} + (2+x)^{(1/3)} + (3+x)^{(1/4)} = 5$

   (c) $2\arctan x = \arctan\left(\dfrac{2x}{1-x^2}\right)$

   (d) $2 - \sin(1-x) = 2x$

6. The Cartesian coordinates $(x,\ y,\ z)$ can easily be expressed in spherical coordinates $(r,\ \theta,\ \phi)$:

   $$
   \begin{aligned}
   x &= r\cos\theta\,\sin\phi \\
   y &= r\sin\theta\,\sin\phi \\
   z &= r\cos\phi
   \end{aligned}
   $$

   Express the spherical coordinates in the Cartesian ones.

7. Solve the system $\{x^2 + y^2 = 5,\ xy = y^2 - 2\}$ with **solve** and **fsolve**.

8. Solve the following system of polynomial equations in the unknowns x, y, and z over $\mathbb{R}$ (here, a is a real constant).

   $$
   \begin{aligned}
   \{\,z^2 - x^2 - y^2 + 2ax + 2az - a^2 &= 0, \\
   yz - ay - ax + a^2 &= 0, \\
   -2a + x + y &= 0\,\}
   \end{aligned}
   $$

9. Let f be the homogeneous polynomial $x_0^3 + x_1^3 + x_2^3 + x_3^3$. It defines the Fermat surface in the projective space $\mathbb{P}^3$ as

   $$\{x_0 : x_1 : x_2 : x_3 \in \mathbb{P}^3 \mid f(x_0, x_1, x_2, x_3) = 0\}\,.$$

(a) There are 27 lines on the surface; use Maple to determine these lines. Hint: the line through the two points $x_0:x_1:x_2:x_3$ and $y_0:y_1:y_2:y_3$ is described in so-called Plücker coordinates by

$$p^{ij} := x_i y_j - x_j y_i, \quad \text{with } i,j = 0,1,2,3 \text{ and } i \neq j.$$

In this coordinate system, a line is on the surface iff

$$f(p^{01}u_1 + p^{02}u_2 + p^{03}u_3, \; p^{10}u_0 + p^{12}u_2 + p^{13}u_3,$$

$$p^{20}u_0 + p^{21}u_1 + p^{23}u_3, \; p^{30}u_0 + p^{31}u_1 + p^{32}u_2) = 0$$

for all u_0, u_1, u_2, u_3 in $\mathbb{R}$, and $p^{01}p^{23} + p^{02}p^{31} + p^{03}p^{12} = 0$.

(b) Determine the singular points on the Fermat surface. Recall that a point is singular when the function values and all partial derivatives in this point are equal to zero.

10. Solve the following inequalities in x.

(a) $|x - 3| \cdot |3 - x| > |x|$

(b) $|x^3 - x^2 - x - 1| > \dfrac{1}{|x^2 - 1|}$

11. Solve the recurrence equation $u_{n+1} = (8/5)\, a_n - a_{n-1}$, $a_0 = 0$, $a_1 = 1$.

12. Solve the recurrence equation $a_{n+1} = 3n\, a_n - 2n\,(n-1)\, a_{n-1}$, $a_1 = 5$, $a_2 = 54$.

17
Differential Equations

Maple can solve many ordinary differential equations analytically in explicit and implicit form. Traditional techniques such as the method of Laplace transformations, integrating factors, etc., are available through the ordinary differential equation solver **dsolve**. The procedure **pdesolve** provides classical methods to solve partial differential equations such as the method of characteristics. Lie symmetry methods are also implemented for partial differential equations in the `liesymm` package. They facilitate generating new solutions from a particular solution of a partial differential equation. Approximate methods such as Taylor series and power series methods are also available for ordinary differential equations. And if all fails, one can still use the numerical solver based on the Runge-Kutta method or other numerical methods. The `DEtools` package contains procedures for graphical presentation of solutions of differential equations and for change of variables (dependent as well as independent variables). Moreover, Maple provides all the tools to apply perturbation methods, like the Poincaré-Lindstedt method and the method of multiple scales up to high order. This chapter discusses the tools available in Maple for studying differential equations. Many examples come from applied mathematics.

17.1   First Glance at ODEs

Recall that an *ordinary differential equation* (ODE) is an equation of the form

$$F(y, y', y'', \cdots, y^{(n)}, x) = 0,$$

which holds on a particular interval, where $y', y'', \ldots, y^{(n)}$ are short notations for the derivatives of $y(x)$, and where F is a real function defined over (a subdomain of) $\mathbb{R}^{n+2}$. The ODE is of *order n*, when the function F does depend on the $(n + 1)$th argument. When the function F is linear in its first $n + 1$ arguments, the ODE is called *linear*; it is of the form

$$a_n(x)\, y^{(n)} + a_{n-1}(x)\, y^{(n-1)} + \cdots + a_1(x)\, y' + a_0(x)y + a(x) = 0.$$

When F is a polynomial mapping, then the *degree* of the ODE of order n is defined as the exponent of the $(n + 1)$th argument in F. In short, the order of an ODE is equal to k if the kth derivative is the highest derivative that occurs in the ODE, and the degree is the exponent of this highest derivative. Some examples:

$$
\begin{aligned}
y'' - x^2 y - x^3 &= 0 & \text{a linear ODE of order 2 and degree 1,} \\
y'' - y^3 &= 0 & \text{a nonlinear ODE of order 2 and degree 1,} \\
\left(y''\right)^3 - y &= 0 & \text{a nonlinear ODE of order 2 and degree 3.}
\end{aligned}
$$

Mathematicians have developed a whole range of methods for solving differential equations. The interested reader is referred to [135] for a survey of the use of computer algebra in solving ordinary differential equations. Some of these methods are implemented in Maple. Once again all methods are provided by one procedure, viz., **dsolve** (differential equation **solver**). You can leave it up to the Maple system to choose a method for solving a differential equation or you can select one yourself. For example, when you want to apply the method of Laplace transforms or find a Taylor series solution, then you only have to say so.

To be honest, Maple's capabilities in solving ODEs are impressive but rather limited compared with the vast literature on solving differential equations; in most cases, solutions are only found for ODEs of degree 1 and order less than 3. Limited knowledge about special functions is incorporated in the differential equation solver. Nevertheless, Maple provides valuable facilities for solving ordinary differential equations. In the next sections we shall have a look at these facilities through many examples from applied mathematics.

17.2   Analytic Solutions

Consider the differential equation

$$xy' = y\ln(xy) - y,$$

of order 1 and degree 1. If you have no strong preference for a particular method of solving the ODE, then you call **dsolve** without all the trimmings.

```
>   ODE := x*diff(y(x),x) = y(x)*ln(x*y(x)) - y(x);
```

$$ODE := x\left(\frac{\partial}{\partial x} y(x)\right) = y(x)\ln(x\,y(x)) - y(x)$$

```
>   dsolve( ODE, y(x) );
```

$$x = \_C1\ln(x) + \_C1\ln(y(x))$$

A more natural and convenient notation is provided for by the **alias** construct in Maple. Let us apply it to the same example.

```
>   alias( y=y(x) ):
>   ODE := x*diff(y,x) = y*ln(x*y) - y;
```

$$ODE := x\left(\frac{\partial}{\partial x} y\right) = y\ln(x\,y) - y$$

```
>   dsolve( ODE, y );
```

$$x = \_C1\ln(x) + \_C1\ln(y)$$

You see that Maple chose to find an implicit solution of the differential equation. If you prefer an explicit expression for the function y, you can use the procedure **solve** to this end, but **isolate** is also of help.

```
>   readlib(isolate)(",y);
```

$$y = e^{\left(\frac{x - \_C1\ln(x)}{\_C1}\right)}$$

However, you could have informed Maple about this right from the beginning.

```
>   dsolve( ODE, y, explicit = true );
```

$$y = e^{\left(\frac{x - \_C1\ln(x)}{\_C1}\right)}$$

This is not the simplest expression for the general solution.

```
>   expand(");
```

$$y = \frac{e^{\left(\frac{x}{\_C1}\right)}}{x}$$

```
>   subs( _C1=1/c, " );
```

$$y = \frac{e^{(c\,x)}}{x}$$

This solution of the ODE can easily be checked (and it is good advice to do this as much as you can).

```
>   testeq( subs( ", ODE ) );
```

$$true$$

As a second example, we consider the differential equation

$$y\,y' = \sqrt{y^2 + 2y + 1}.$$

To get more information about what is going on during the computation, we set a higher value to the variable `infolevel[dsolve]`.

```
>   infolevel[dsolve] := 5:
>   alias( y=y ):   # unalias y
```

For a change, we shall introduce the differential equation with the **D** operator instead of with **diff**.

```
>   ODE := ( y * D(y)= sqrt( y^2 - 2*y + 1) )(x);
```

$$ODE := y(x)\,\mathrm{D}(y)(x) = \sqrt{(-1+y(x))^2}$$

dsolve understands this notation.

```
>   dsolve( ODE, y(x) );
```

```
dsolve/diffeq/dsol1:
-> first order, first degree methods:
dsolve/diffeq/dsol1:      trying linear bernoulli
dsolve/diffeq/dsol1:      trying separable
dsolve/diffeq/sepsol:     solving separable d.e.
dsolve/diffeq/dsol1:      separable successful
```

$$\frac{y(x)}{\sqrt{y(x)^2 - 2y(x) + 1}} - \frac{y(x)^2}{\sqrt{y(x)^2 - 2y(x) + 1}} + \frac{\ln(-1 + y(x))}{\sqrt{y(x)^2 - 2y(x) + 1}}$$
$$- \frac{\ln(-1 + y(x))\,y(x)}{\sqrt{y(x)^2 - 2y(x) + 1}} + x = \_C1$$

You can simplify this result into

```
>   simplify(");
```

$$-y(x)\,\mathrm{csgn}(-1 + y(x)) + x - \mathrm{csgn}(-1 + y(x))\ln(-1 + y(x)) = \_C1$$

You see that Maple takes care of what simplifications are valid. This also explains why the explicit method returns two (possible) solutions.

```
>   infolevel[dsolve] := 0: # restore information level
>   dsolve( ODE, y(x), explicit = true );
```

$$y(x) = e^{(-\mathrm{LambertW}(e^{(-1+x-\_C1)}) - 1 + x - \_C1)} + 1,$$
$$y(x) = e^{(-\mathrm{LambertW}(e^{(-1-x+\_C1)}) - 1 - x + \_C1)} + 1$$

A differential equation may contain several variables. For example, look at the differential equation that describes the trajectory of an object that is pulled with a rope of length a by someone who walks along the x-axis to the right.

$$y' = -\frac{y}{\sqrt{a^2 - y^2}}$$

```
>   alias( y=y(x) ):
>   ODE := diff(y,x) = -y / sqrt(a^2-y^2);
```

$$ODE := \frac{\partial}{\partial x}\, y = -\frac{y}{\sqrt{a^2 - y^2}}$$

```
>   solution := dsolve( ODE, y );
```

$$solution := \sqrt{a^2 - y^2} - \frac{a^2 \arctanh(\dfrac{a^2}{\sqrt{a^2}\sqrt{a^2 - y^2}})}{\sqrt{a^2}} + x = \_C1$$

The solution is much simpler when we assume that a is positive.

```
>   solution := simplify( ", assume=positive );
```

$$solution := \sqrt{a^2 - y^2} - a\arctanh(\frac{a}{\sqrt{a^2 - y^2}}) + x = \_C1$$

Note that the constant function 0 is not recognized by Maple as a solution of the differential equation.

When the person starts at the origin and the object is at that time at position $(0, a)$, i.e., when the initial condition is $y(0) = a$, then you can attempt to determine the constant $\_C1$.

```
>   subs( {x=0,y=a}, solution );
```

Error, division by zero

What went wrong? Maple has determined a solution in such an implicit form that it causes problems with the initial condition. When you realize that $\arctanh(1/x)$ and $\arctanh(x)$ differ only in a constant, you may choose the following implicit solution.

```
>   solution := sqrt(a^2-y^2) -
>     a*arctanh( sqrt(a^2-y^2)/a ) + x = C;
```

$$solution := \sqrt{a^2 - y^2} - a\arctanh(\frac{\sqrt{a^2 - y^2}}{a}) + x = C$$

Let us verify this implicit solution:

```
>   diff( solution, x );
```

$$-\frac{y(\frac{\partial}{\partial x}\, y)}{\sqrt{a^2 - y^2}} + \frac{y(\frac{\partial}{\partial x}\, y)}{\sqrt{a^2 - y^2}\,(1 - \dfrac{a^2 - y^2}{a^2})} + 1 = 0$$

```
>  Diff(y,x) = solve( ", diff(y,x) );
```

$$\frac{\partial}{\partial x} y = -\frac{y}{\sqrt{a^2 - y^2}}$$

Now, we can do the substitution without any harm.

```
>  (eval@subs)(  {x=0,y=a}, solution );
```

$$0 = C$$

You might be tempted to substitute as follows.

```
>  subs( x=0, solution );
```

$$\sqrt{a^2 - y(0)^2} - a \operatorname{arctanh}(\frac{\sqrt{a^2 - y(0)^2}}{a}) = C$$

```
>  subs( y(0)=0, " );
```

$$\sqrt{a^2 - y(0)^2} - a \operatorname{arctanh}(\frac{\sqrt{a^2 - y(0)^2}}{a}) = C$$

The reason why this does not work as expected is that y has first been aliased to y(x). After the first substitution x=0 an object y(0) is returned that differs from the one obtained when you enter y(0).

```
>  subs( subs(x=0,y) = a, " );
```

$$-a \operatorname{arctanh}(0) = C$$

```
>  subs( op(0,y)(0) = a, "" );
```

$$-a \operatorname{arctanh}(0) = C$$

These would be tricky solutions compared with the way we have chosen above. We end this example with a description of the curve, which is known as the Tractrix (q.v., [69]).

```
>  Tractrix := subs( C=0, solution );
```

$$Tractrix := \sqrt{a^2 - y^2} - a \operatorname{arctanh}(\frac{\sqrt{a^2 - y^2}}{a}) + x = 0$$

By the way, in Maple you can immediately specify an initial value or boundary value problem. We illustrate this by studying the differential equation

$$u'' + \omega^2 u = 0$$

of the mathematical pendulum (see Figure 17.3, u is the horizontal displacement of the end point). The same problems with aliases as described in the previous example would occur; hence we avoid them.

```
>  ODE := diff(u(t),[t$2]) + omega^2*u(t) = 0;
```

$$ODE := (\frac{\partial^2}{\partial t^2} u(t)) + \omega^2 u(t) = 0$$

```
>   dsolve( { ODE, u(0)=2, D(u)(0)=3 }, u(t) );
```

$$u(t) = 2\cos(\omega t) + 3\,\frac{\sin(\omega t)}{\omega}$$

You specify the first derivative at zero as D(u)(0). Higher derivatives u''(0), u'''(0), ... are given as (D@@2)(u)(0), (D@@3)(u)(0), ...

```
>   dsolve( { ODE, u(0)=1, u(2)=3 }, u(t) );
```

$$u(t) = \cos(\omega t) - \frac{(\cos(\omega)^2 - 2)\,\sin(\omega t)}{\sin(\omega)\cos(\omega)}$$

```
>   combine(");
```

$$u(t) = \frac{-\sin(\omega t - 2\omega) + 3\sin(\omega t)}{\sin(2\omega)}$$

In Maple you can easily use the *method of integral transforms* for solving differential equations. As an example, we will look at the step response of a linear damped oscillator via the method of Laplace transforms. The initial value problem is

```
>   ODE := diff(u(t),[t$2]) + 2*d*omega*diff(u(t),t)
>     + omega^2*u(t) = Heaviside(t);
```

$$ODE := (\frac{\partial^2}{\partial t^2}\,u(t)) + 2\,d\,\omega\,(\frac{\partial}{\partial t}\,u(t)) + \omega^2\,u(t) = \text{Heaviside}(t)$$

```
>   initvals := u(0)=0, D(u)(0)=0:
>   solution := dsolve( { ODE, initvals }, u(t),
>     method = laplace );
```

$$solution := u(t) = \frac{1}{\omega^2} + \frac{e^{(-d\omega t)}\cos\left(\sqrt{-\omega^2\,(d-1)\,(d+1)}\,t\right)}{\omega^2\,(d-1)\,(d+1)}$$
$$-\frac{e^{(-d\omega t)}\,d^2\cos\left(\sqrt{-\omega^2\,(d-1)\,(d+1)}\,t\right)}{\omega^2\,(d-1)\,(d+1)}$$
$$+\frac{e^{(-d\omega t)}\sqrt{\omega^2 - d^2\,\omega^2}\,d\sin\left(\sqrt{-\omega^2\,(d-1)\,(d+1)}\,t\right)}{\omega^3\,(d-1)\,(d+1)}$$

```
>   simplify(");
```

$$u(t) = -\left(\omega - \omega\,d^2 - e^{(-d\omega t)}\cos\left(\sqrt{-\omega^2\,(-1+d^2)}\,t\right)\omega\right.$$
$$+ e^{(-d\omega t)}\,d^2\cos\left(\sqrt{-\omega^2\,(-1+d^2)}\,t\right)\omega$$
$$\left.- e^{(-d\omega t)}\sqrt{-\omega^2\,(-1+d^2)}\,d\sin\left(\sqrt{-\omega^2\,(-1+d^2)}\,t\right)\right)\Big/\Big(\omega^3$$
$$(-1+d^2)\Big)$$

```
> solution := collect( ", {sin,cos}, simplify );
```

$$solution := u(t) = -\frac{e^{(-d\omega t)}\cos\left(\sqrt{-\omega^2\left(-1+d^2\right)}\,t\right)}{\omega^2}$$

$$+\frac{e^{(-d\omega t)}\sqrt{-\omega^2\left(-1+d^2\right)}\,d\sin\left(\sqrt{-\omega^2\left(-1+d^2\right)}\,t\right)}{\omega^3\left(-1+d^2\right)}+\frac{1}{\omega^2}$$

Maple does not distinguish the cases of no damping ($d = 0$), underdamping ($0 < d < 1$), critical damping ($d = 1$), and overdamping ($d > 1$). In most cases, the above formula for the solution is simplified to its most convenient form. This may happen because you make explicit assumptions or because you provide explicit values for the unknowns.

```
> d := 0:
> simplify( solution, assume=positive ); # no damping
```

$$u(t) = -\frac{\cos(\omega t) - 1}{\omega^2}$$

```
> d := 1/6:
> simplify( solution, assume=positive ); # underdamping
```

$$u(t) = -\frac{1}{35}\left(35\,e^{(-1/6\omega t)}\cos(\frac{1}{6}\sqrt{35}\,\omega t)\right.$$

$$\left. + e^{(-1/6\omega t)}\sqrt{35}\sin(\frac{1}{6}\sqrt{35}\,\omega t) - 35\right)\Big/\omega^2$$

You can plot this solution for a range of frequency values (Figure 17.1).

```
> plot3d( rhs("), omega=2/3..4/3, t=0..20,
>    style=hidden, orientation=[-30,45], axes=BOXED );
```

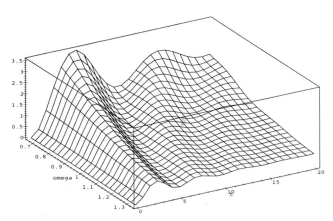

FIGURE 17.1. Step response of an underdamped oscillator for a range of frequencies.

Similarly, you can plot the solutions for a fixed frequency and a range of damping values (Figure 17.2).

```
>  d := 'd': omega := 1:
>  plot3d( rhs(solution), d=1/5..2, t=0..20,
>     style=hidden, orientation=[-10,45], axes=BOXED );
```

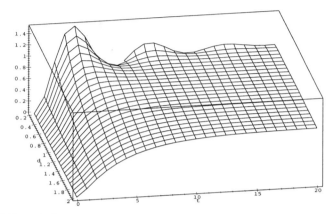

FIGURE 17.2. Step response of an oscillator for a range of damping factors.

From this picture the trade-off between system damping and system response is clear; low damping values result in overshooting while high damping values are slow to respond to input signals.

Other integral transforms such as **fourier**, **fouriersin**, **fouriercos**, **hilbert**, and **hankel** can be applied as well for solving differential equations in Maple. An example:

```
>  diff(u(t),[t$2]) + 3*diff(u(t),t)+ 2*u(t)=exp(-abs(t));
```

$$(\frac{\partial^2}{\partial t^2} u(t)) + 3(\frac{\partial}{\partial t} u(t)) + 2u(t) = e^{(-|t|)}$$

```
>  dsolve( ", u(t), method = fourier );
```

$$u(t) = \frac{2}{3} e^{(-2t)} \text{Heaviside}(t) + \frac{1}{6} e^t \text{Heaviside}(-t)$$
$$+ e^{(-t)} t \text{Heaviside}(t) - \frac{1}{2} e^{(-t)} \text{Heaviside}(t)$$

Systems of linear differential equations can also be solved with **dsolve**.

```
>  ODE := diff(f(t),[t$2]) - 6*diff(g(t),t) = 6*sin(t),
>     6*diff(g(t),[t$2]) + c^2*diff(f(t),t) = 6*cos(t);
```

$$ODE := (\frac{\partial^2}{\partial t^2} f(t)) - 6(\frac{\partial}{\partial t} g(t)) = 6\sin(t),$$

$$6 \left(\frac{\partial^2}{\partial t^2} g(t) \right) + c^2 \left(\frac{\partial}{\partial t} f(t) \right) = 6 \cos(t)$$

```
>  initvals := f(0)= 0, g(0)=1, D(f)(0)=0, D(g)(0)=1:
>  funcs := {f(t),g(t)}:
>  dsolve( { ODE, initvals }, funcs, method = laplace );
```

$$\left\{ f(t) = 12 \frac{\sin(t)}{(c-1)(1+c)} + \frac{6}{c^2} - 12 \frac{\sin(ct)}{(c-1)(1+c)c} \right.$$

$$+ 6 \frac{\cos(ct)}{(c-1)(1+c)c^2} - 6 \frac{\cos(ct)}{(c-1)(1+c)}, g(t) = \frac{\cos(t)}{(c-1)(1+c)}$$

$$+ \frac{\cos(t)c^2}{(c-1)(1+c)} - 2 \frac{\cos(ct)}{(c-1)(1+c)} - \frac{\sin(ct)}{(c-1)(1+c)c}$$

$$\left. + \frac{c\sin(ct)}{(c-1)(1+c)} \right\}$$

```
>  collect( ", {cos(c*t),sin(c*t)}, normal );
```

$$\left\{ f(t) = -6 \frac{\cos(ct)}{c^2} - 12 \frac{\sin(ct)}{(c-1)(1+c)c} + 6 \frac{2\sin(t)c^2 + c^2 - 1}{(c-1)(1+c)c^2}, \right.$$

$$\left. g(t) = -2 \frac{\cos(ct)}{(c-1)(1+c)} + \frac{\sin(ct)}{c} + \frac{(1+c^2)\cos(t)}{(c-1)(1+c)} \right\}$$

Tables 17.1 and 17.2 summarize the kinds of ordinary differential equations that can presently be solved with **dsolve**.

Type of ODE	Shape of ODE
linear	$y' + P(x)y = Q(x)$
exact	$y' = -\dfrac{P(x,y)}{Q(x,y)}$, with $\dfrac{\partial Q}{\partial x} = \dfrac{\partial P}{\partial y}$
inexact	$F(x,y)y' + G(x,y) = 0$, when an integrating factor can be found
separable	$y' = f(x)g(y)$
homogeneous	$y' = F(xy^n)\dfrac{y}{x}$
high degree	$x = F(y, y')$
Bernoulli	$y' + P(x)y = Q(x)y^n$
Clairaut	$y = xy' + F(y')$
Riccati	$y' = P(x)y^2 + Q(x)y' + R(x)$

TABLE 17.1. Solvable first-order ODEs.

Type of ODE	Shape of ODE
linear, constant coeffs.	$ay'' + by' + cy = d(x)$, where $a, b, c \in \mathbb{C}$
Euler	$x^2 y'' + axy' + by = c(x)$
Bessel	$x^2 y'' + (2k+1)xy' + (\alpha^2 x^{2r} + \beta^2)y = 0$, where $k, \alpha, r, \beta \in \mathbb{C}$ and $\alpha r \neq 0$
Bernoulli	$y' + P(x)y = Q(x)y^n$
Hypergeometric	$x(1-x)y'' + \big((c - (a+b+1)x\big)y'$ $-aby = 0$, where $a, b, c \in \mathbb{C}$
Riemann-Papperitz	$y'' + P y' + Q y = 0$, where $P = \frac{1-\alpha_1-\beta_1}{x-a} + \frac{1-\alpha_2-\beta_2}{x-b} + \frac{1-\alpha_3-\beta_3}{x-c}$, $Q = \Big(\frac{\alpha_1\beta_1(a-b)(a-c)}{x-a} + \frac{\alpha_2\beta_2(b-a)(b-c)}{x-b} + \frac{\alpha_3\beta_3(c-a)(c-b)}{x-c} \Big) \times \frac{1}{(x-a)(x-b)(x-c)}$

TABLE 17.2. Solvable second-order ODEs.

Moreover, Kovacic's algorithm [121] has been implemented in Maple; it tries to solve linear homogeneous second-order ODEs of the form

$$P(x)y'' + Q(x)y' + R(x)y = 0,$$

where $P(x)$, $Q(x)$, and $R(x)$ are rational functions. It is a decision procedure like the Risch algorithm; given the linear second-order ODE, Kovacic's algorithm decides whether or not there exists a closed form Liouvillian solution, and if the answer is yes, provides the solution. For higher-order linear differential equations, two important decision procedures have been implemented: Abromov's algorithm RATLODE (RATional Linear ODE, [2]), which determines whether or not a closed-form solution exists in the domain of coefficients of the ODE; and Bronstein's algorithm EXPLODE (EXPonential Linear ODE, [22]), which determines solutions of the form $\exp\big(\int f(x)\,dx\big)$. For a leisurely account on the methods implemented in Maple for linear differential equations we refer to [123]. An example of EXPLODE:

```
>  alias( y=y(x) ):
>  x^2*diff(y,[x$3]) + (x-3*x^2)*diff(y,[x$2]) +
>    (4*x^2-2*x)*diff(y,x) + (x-2*x^2)*y = 0;
```

$$x^2\left(\frac{\partial^3}{\partial x^3}y\right) + (x-3x^2)\left(\frac{\partial^2}{\partial x^2}y\right) + (4x^2-2x)\left(\frac{\partial}{\partial x}y\right) + (x-2x^2)y = 0$$

```
>  dsolve( ", y );
```

$$y = \_C1\, e^x + \_C2\left(-2\,x\,e^x\, \text{BesselJ}(\,0, x\,)\right.$$
$$- x\,e^x\,\pi\,\text{StruveH}(\,0, x\,)\,\text{BesselJ}(\,1, x\,)$$
$$+ x\,e^x\,\pi\,\text{StruveH}(\,1, x\,)\,\text{BesselJ}(\,0, x\,)\Big) + \_C3\left(2\,x\,e^x\,\text{BesselY}(\,0, x\,)\right.$$
$$+ x\,e^x\,\pi\,\text{StruveH}(\,0, x\,)\,\text{BesselY}(\,1, x\,)$$
$$\left.- x\,e^x\,\pi\,\text{StruveH}(\,1, x\,)\,\text{BesselY}(\,0, x\,)\right)$$

An example of a Bessel equation:

```
> alias( y=y(x) ):
> diff(y,[x$2]) + 3*diff(y,x)/x + (x^2-15)/x^2*y - 1/x;
```

$$\left(\frac{\partial^2}{\partial x^2}\,y\right) + 3\,\frac{\frac{\partial}{\partial x}\,y}{x} + \frac{(\,x^2 - 15\,)\,y}{x^2} - \frac{1}{x}$$

```
> dsolve( ", y );
```

$$y = \frac{192 + 16\,x^2 + x^4}{x^5} + \frac{\_C1\,\text{BesselJ}(\,4, x\,)}{x} + \frac{\_C2\,\text{BesselY}(\,4, x\,)}{x}$$

An alternative output form is available in terms of a *solution basis*.

```
> dsolve( "", y, output = basis );
```

$$\left[\left[\frac{\text{BesselJ}(\,4, x\,)}{x}, \frac{\text{BesselY}(\,4, x\,)}{x}\right], \frac{192 + 16\,x^2 + x^4}{x^5}\right]$$

Even if Maple recognizes the type of an ODE it may still need help.

```
> infolevel[dsolve] := 2:
> ODE := diff(y(x),x) + 2*y(x)*exp(x) - y(x)^2
>    - exp(2*x) - exp(x) = 0;
```

$$ODE := \left(\frac{\partial}{\partial x}\,y(\,x\,)\right) + 2\,y(\,x\,)\,e^x - y(\,x\,)^2 - e^{(\,2\,x\,)} - e^x = 0$$

```
> dsolve( ODE, y(x) );

dsolve/diffeq/dsol1:
-> first order, first degree methods:
dsolve:   Warning: no solutions found
```

It is easily checked that e^x is a solution.

```
> subs( y(x) = exp(x), ODE ):   expand(");
```

$$0 = 0$$

Write the required solution $y(x)$ as $z(x) + e^x$, derive the ODE for the function $z(x)$, and try to solve this one.

```
> subs( y(x) = z(x) + exp(x), ODE ):   expand(");
```

$$\left(\frac{\partial}{\partial x}\,z(\,x\,)\right) - z(\,x\,)^2 = 0$$

```
> dsolve( ", z(x), explicit = true );
```

```
dsolve/diffeq/dsol1:
-> first order, first degree methods:
dsolve/diffeq/bernsol:    trying Bernoulli solution
dsolve/diffeq/linearsol: solving 1st order linear d.e.
dsolve/diffeq/dsol1:      linear bernoulli successful
```

$$z(x) = \frac{1}{-x + \_C1}$$

Check the general solution.

```
> solution := exp(x) + rhs(");
```

$$solution := e^x + \frac{1}{-x + \_C1}$$

```
> subs( y(x) = solution, ODE ):  testeq(");
```

$$true$$

Sometimes Maple comes back with a partial solution.

```
> alias( y=y(x) ):
> ODE := diff(y,[x$3]) + (2+2*x)*diff(y,[x$2]) +
>    (4*x+4-1/x)*diff(y,x) + 2*y = 0;
```

$$ODE := (\frac{\partial^3}{\partial x^3} y) + (2 + 2x)(\frac{\partial^2}{\partial x^2} y) + (4x + 4 - \frac{1}{x})(\frac{\partial}{\partial x} y) + 2y = 0$$

```
> dsolve( ODE, y );
```

$$y = \_C1\, e^{(-x^2)} + e^{(-x^2)} \int \mathrm{DESol}\left(\left\{x\,(\frac{\partial^2}{\partial x^2} \_Y(x))\right.\right.$$

$$+ (2x - 4x^2)(\frac{\partial}{\partial x} \_Y(x)) + (-4x^2 - 2x - 1 + 4x^3)\_Y(x)\Big\},$$

$$\Big\{\_Y(x)\}\Big)\, dx$$

This can be considered as the analogue of **RootOf**: **DESol** represents a solution of a differential equation and can be manipulated with **diff**, **series**, **evalf**, and so on. Enter **?DESol** to see examples of this feature. So, we can check the above solution by

```
> simplify( subs(",ODE) );
```

$$0 = 0$$

Table 17.3 summarizes the options of the ordinary differential equation solver **dsolve** when attempting to find an analytical solution (optionally specified as type=exact).

Option	Meaning
method = fourier	Fourier method
method = fouriercos	method of Fourier cosine transform
method = fouriersin	method of Fourier sine transform
method = hankel	method of Hankel transform
method = hilbert	method of Hilbert transform
method = laplace	Laplace method
method = matrixexp	exponential matrix method
output = basis	generate solution basis and particular solution
explicit = true	attempt to find explicit solution
explicit = false	implicit solution

TABLE 17.3. Options of **dsolve**(*ODE*, type=exact).

17.3   Taylor Series Method

When an analytical solution for an ordinary differential equation cannot be found, there is still the possibility of using Maple to find a Taylor series approximation. We shall apply this method to the (large oscillation) pendulum, shown in Figure 17.3 and described by the differential equation

$$l\,\theta'' = -g\sin\theta,$$

where l is the pendulum length, g is the gravitational acceleration, and θ is the angle between the rod and the vertical (Figure 17.3).

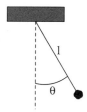

FIGURE 17.3. Pendulum.

```
>   ODE := l*diff(theta(t),[t$2]) = -g*sin(theta(t));
```

$$ODE := l\left(\frac{\partial^2}{\partial t^2}\,\theta(t)\right) = -g\sin(\theta(t))$$

```
>   initvals := theta(0)=0, D(theta)(0)=v[0]/l:
>   Order := 9:
>   solution := dsolve( { ODE, initvals }, theta(t),
>     type = series );
```

$$solution := \theta(t) = \frac{v_0\, t}{l} - \frac{1}{6} \frac{g\, v_0\, t^3}{l^2} + \frac{1}{120} \frac{g\, v_0\, (g\, l + v_0{}^2)\, t^5}{l^4}$$
$$- \frac{1}{5040} \frac{g\, v_0\, (g^2\, l^2 + 11\, g\, l\, v_0{}^2 + v_0{}^4)\, t^7}{l^6}$$

Below, we shall rewrite this solution in dimensionless variables. First, we check dimensions.

```
> subs( { v[0]=L/T, g=L/T^2, l=L }, " );
```

$$\theta(t) = \frac{t}{T} - \frac{1}{6} \frac{t^3}{T^3} + \frac{1}{60} \frac{t^5}{T^5} - \frac{13}{5040} \frac{t^7}{T^7}$$

Next, we determine dimensionless parameters a and b.

```
> nondimensional := v[0]^ev[0] * g^eg * l^el * t^et;
```

$$nondimensional := v_0{}^{evo}\, g^{eg}\, l^{el}\, t^{et}$$

```
> simplify( subs( { v[0]=L/T, g=L/T^2, l=L, t=T },
>    nondimensional ), assume=positive );
```

$$L^{(evo+eg+el)}\, T^{(-evo-2\,eg+et)}$$

```
> isolve( { seq( op(2,i)=0, i=" ) } );
```

$$\{evo = -2\_N1 + \_N2, el = \_N1 - \_N2, eg = \_N1, et = \_N2\}$$

```
> assign("):
> { a = subs( _N1=0,  _N2=1, nondimensional),
>    b = subs( _N1=-1, _N2=0, nondimensional) };
```

$$\left\{ b = \frac{v_0{}^2}{g\, l}, a = \frac{v_0\, t}{l} \right\}$$

We express the gravitation g and length l of the rod in terms of the dimensionless variables, and we substitute these expressions into the solution of the ODE.

```
> solve( ", {g,l} );
```

$$\left\{ l = \frac{v_0\, t}{a}, g = \frac{v_0\, a}{b\, t} \right\}$$

```
> subs( ", convert( rhs(solution), `polynom` ) );
```

$$a - \frac{1}{6} \frac{a^3}{b} + \frac{1}{120} \frac{a^5 \left(\frac{v_0{}^2}{b} + v_0{}^2 \right)}{v_0{}^2\, b} - \frac{1}{5040} \frac{a^7 \left(\frac{v_0{}^4}{b^2} + 11 \frac{v_0{}^4}{b} + v_0{}^4 \right)}{v_0{}^4\, b}$$

```
> map( normal, " );
```

$$a - \frac{1}{6} \frac{a^3}{b} + \frac{1}{120} \frac{a^5\, (1+b)}{b^2} - \frac{1}{5040} \frac{a^7\, (1 + 11\,b + b^2)}{b^3}$$

Compare this with the series expansion of $\sin t$.

```
>  series( sin(t), t, 9 );
```

$$t - \frac{1}{6} t^3 + \frac{1}{120} t^5 - \frac{1}{5040} t^7 + O(t^9)$$

17.4   Power Series Method

Naturally, in a modern computer algebra system like Maple, the method of power series to solve differential equation should not be absent. This facility resides in the **powseries** package. However, note that it only works for linear differential equations with polynomial coefficients. Our first example will be a differential equation of Bessel type.

$$xy'' + y' + 4x^2 y = 0$$

Maple can find the exact solution.

```
>  eqn := x*diff(y(x),[x$2]) + diff(y(x),x) +
>     4*x^2*y(x) = 0;
```

$$eqn := x \left(\frac{\partial^2}{\partial x^2} y(x)\right) + \left(\frac{\partial}{\partial x} y(x)\right) + 4 x^2 y(x) = 0$$

```
>  dsolve( eqn, y(x) );
```

$$y(x) = \_C1 \operatorname{BesselY}\left(0, \frac{4}{3} x^{3/2} \right) + \_C2 \operatorname{BesselJ}\left(0, \frac{4}{3} x^{3/2} \right)$$

Below, we shall compute the power series solution for the initial values $y(0) = 1$, $y'(0) = 0$.

```
>  initvals := y(0)=1, D(y)(0)=0:
>  with( powseries ):   # load the power series package
>  solution := powsolve( { eqn, initvals } );
```

$$solution := \operatorname{proc}(powparm) \ldots \text{end}$$

```
>  tpsform( solution, x, 15 );   # truncated powerseries
```

$$1 - \frac{4}{9} x^3 + \frac{4}{81} x^6 - \frac{16}{6561} x^9 + \frac{4}{59049} x^{12} + O(x^{15})$$

Maple can give you the recurrence relation of the coefficients.

```
>  solution(_k);
```

$$-4 \frac{a(\_k - 3)}{\_k^2}$$

Recall that names starting with an underscore are used by Maple itself and interpret the last result as the relation

$$a_k = -4\frac{a_{k-3}}{k^2}.$$

Our second example is a classical one in quantum mechanics — the solutions of the one-dimensional harmonic oscillator. The Schrödinger equation can be given in dimensionless units as

$$\frac{d^2y(x)}{dx^2} + (\lambda - x^2)\,y(x) = 0.$$

See §17.6 for a derivation of this equation.

```
>  alias( y=y(x), h=h(x) ):
>  eqn := diff(y,[x$2]) + (lambda-x^2)*y = 0;
```

$$eqn := \left(\frac{\partial^2}{\partial x^2}\,y\right) + (\lambda - x^2)\,y = 0$$

Asymptotic analysis suggests the substitution $y(x) = h(x)e^{-x^2/2}$. The differential equation for h is

```
>  subs( y = exp(-x^2/2)*h, " ):
>  collect( ", exp(-x^2/2) ) / exp(-x^2/2);
```

$$-h + x^2\,h - 2\,x\left(\frac{\partial}{\partial x}\,h\right) + \left(\frac{\partial^2}{\partial x^2}\,h\right) + (\lambda - x^2)\,h = 0$$

```
>  eqn := collect( ", [diff(h,[x$2]), diff(h,x), h] );
```

$$eqn := \left(\frac{\partial^2}{\partial x^2}\,h\right) - 2\,x\left(\frac{\partial}{\partial x}\,h\right) + (-1 + \lambda)\,h = 0$$

We solve this differential equation via the power series method.

```
>  with(powseries):
>  H := powsolve(eqn):
>  h := tpsform(H,x,10); # a few terms
```

$$h := C0 + C1\,x - \frac{1}{2}(-1+\lambda)\,C0\,x^2 - \frac{1}{6}(-3+\lambda)\,C1\,x^3 +$$

$$\frac{1}{24}(-5+\lambda)(-1+\lambda)\,C0\,x^4 + \frac{1}{120}(-7+\lambda)(-3+\lambda)\,C1\,x^5 -$$

$$\frac{1}{720}(-9+\lambda)(-5+\lambda)(-1+\lambda)\,C0\,x^6 -$$

$$\frac{1}{5040}(-11+\lambda)(-7+\lambda)(-3+\lambda)\,C1\,x^7 +$$

$$\frac{1}{40320}(-13+\lambda)(-9+\lambda)(-5+\lambda)(-1+\lambda)\,C0\,x^8 +$$

$$\frac{1}{362880}(-15+\lambda)(-11+\lambda)(-7+\lambda)(-3+\lambda)\,C1\,x^9 + O(x^{10})$$

```
> collect( convert( ", 'polynom' ), [C0,C1] );
```

$$\left(1 - \frac{1}{2}(-1+\lambda)x^2 + \frac{1}{24}(-5+\lambda)(-1+\lambda)x^4\right.$$
$$- \frac{1}{720}(-9+\lambda)(-5+\lambda)(-1+\lambda)x^6$$
$$+ \frac{1}{40320}(-13+\lambda)(-9+\lambda)(-5+\lambda)(-1+\lambda)x^8\right) C0$$
$$+ \left(x - \frac{1}{6}(-3+\lambda)x^3 + \frac{1}{120}(-7+\lambda)(-3+\lambda)x^5\right.$$
$$- \frac{1}{5040}(-11+\lambda)(-7+\lambda)(-3+\lambda)x^7$$
$$+ \frac{1}{362880}(-15+\lambda)(-11+\lambda)(-7+\lambda)(-3+\lambda)x^9\right) C1$$

Let us look at the recurrence relation for the coefficients of the series h.

```
> H(_k);
```

$$- \frac{(3+\lambda-2\_k)\,a(\_k-2)}{\_k(\_k-1)}$$

This must be interpreted as

$$a_k = -\frac{(3+\lambda-2k)a_{k-2}}{k(k-1)},$$

or equivalently as

$$(k+1)(k+2)a_{k+2} = (2k+1-\lambda)a_k,$$

for all k. A finite series h is obtained if and only if $\lambda = 2k+1$ for some integer k. This is the famous quantization of the energy levels of the harmonic oscillator. One example of a wave function:

```
> C0 := 1:   C1 := 0:   lambda := 9:
> tpsform(H,x,10): convert(",'polynom');
```

$$1 - 4x^2 + \frac{4}{3}x^4$$

It is a multiple of the fourth Hermite polynomial.

```
> orthopoly[H](4,x) / 12;
```

$$1 - 4x^2 + \frac{4}{3}x^4$$

17.5   Numerical Solutions

You can solve initial value problems numerically in Maple by adding the option type = numeric. By default, the system uses a Fehlberg fourth-fifth order Runge-Kutta method also known as algorithm RKF45 [61], but other numerical methods are available as well. First, we shall apply the Runge-Kutta method to the van der Pol equation

$$y'' - (1 - y^2)y' + y = 0,$$

with initial values $y(0) = 0, y'(0) = -0.1$.

To find a numerical solution of the system of differential equations, call the procedure **dsolve** with the option type = numeric.

```
>  alias( y=y(t), y0=y(0), yp0=D(y)(0) ):
>  eqn := diff(y,[t$2]) - (1-y^2)*diff(y,t) + y = 0;
```

$$eqn := (\frac{\partial^2}{\partial t^2} y) - (1 - y^2)(\frac{\partial}{\partial t} y) + y = 0$$

```
>  initvals := y0=0, yp0=-0.1:
>  F := dsolve( {eqn, initvals}, y, type = numeric );
```

$$F := \mathrm{proc}(rkf45\_x) \ldots \mathrm{end}$$

The numeric solver returns a list consisting of an equation describing the value of the independent variable t, an equation describing the value of the dependent variable y at that point, and an equation describing the value of the derivative y' at that point. Two examples.

```
>  F(0);
```

$$[t = 0, y = 0, \frac{\partial}{\partial t} y = -.1]$$

```
>  F(1);
```

$$[t = 1, y = -.1447686096006437, \frac{\partial}{\partial t} y = -.1781040958088073]$$

You get a better understanding of the solution by plotting it over a domain of interest. Let us first convert the numeric solution into a function. Selection of the right-hand side of the equation of the dependent variable y is easy.

```
>  # The actual numerical solution
>  Y := t -> rhs( op(2,F(t)) );
```

$$Y := t \rightarrow \mathrm{rhs}(\,\mathrm{op}(\,2, \mathrm{F}(\,t\,)\,)\,)$$

Now you can use the **plot** command to draw the graph of the solution (Figure 17.4).

```
>  plot( Y, 0..14, title=
>     `solution of van der Pol´s Equation` );
```

solution of van der Pol's Equation

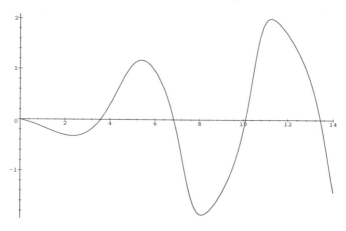

FIGURE 17.4. Graph of solution of the van der Pol equation.

If nonadaptive plotting of the solution is good enough, you could have used
the procedure **odeplot** from the **plots** package (Figure 17.5).

```
>   plots[odeplot]( F, [t,y], 0..30, title=
>     `odeplot of the solution of van der Pol´s  Equation` );
```

odeplot of the solution of van der Pol's Equation

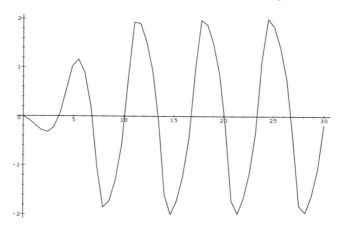

FIGURE 17.5. **odeplot** of solution of the van der Pol equation.

In the second, more lengthy, example we apply the numerical ODE-
solver to the system of differential equations that describe the dynamics
of a frictionless, rigid, two-link robot manipulator without torque (double
pendulum) and we shall use the seventh-eighth order continuous Runge-
Kutta method **dverk78** (Figure 17.6) [58].

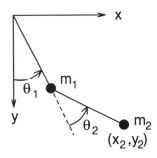

FIGURE 17.6. Double pendulum.

First, we derive the equations of motion via the *Euler-Lagrange* formalism. The interested reader is referred to [122] for the derivation of the equations of motion via the Newton-Euler formalism. Let $\theta = (\theta_1, \theta_2)$ and $\dot{\theta} = (\dot{\theta}_1, \dot{\theta}_2)$, and define the *Lagrangian function* as

$$L(\theta, \dot{\theta}) = T(\theta, \dot{\theta}) - V(\theta),$$

where $T(\theta, \dot{\theta})$ is the kinetic energy and $V(\theta)$ is the potential energy. For the above configuration the kinetic energy is computed as the sum of the kinetic energies T_1 and T_2 of the masses m_1 and m_2, respectively. The kinetic energy of mass m_1 can be written directly as

$$T_1(\dot{\theta}) = \frac{1}{2} m_1 \dot{\theta}_1^2.$$

The Cartesian coordinates (x_2, y_2) of the endpoint are given by

$$
\begin{aligned}
x_2 &= l_1 \sin\theta_1 + l_2 \sin(\theta_1 + \theta_2), \\
y_2 &= l_1 \cos\theta_1 + l_2 \cos(\theta_1 + \theta_2).
\end{aligned}
$$

Hence, the Cartesian components of the velocity are

$$
\begin{aligned}
\dot{x}_2 &= l_1(\cos\theta_1)\dot{\theta}_1 + l_2 \cos(\theta_1 + \theta_2)(\dot{\theta}_1 + \dot{\theta}_2), \\
\dot{y}_2 &= -l_1(\sin\theta_1)\dot{\theta}_1 - l_2 \sin(\theta_1 + \theta_2)(\dot{\theta}_1 + \dot{\theta}_2).
\end{aligned}
$$

Squaring the magnitude of the velocity yields

$$T_2(\theta, \dot{\theta}) = \frac{1}{2} m_2 \left(l_1^2 \dot{\theta}_1^2 + l_2^2 (\dot{\theta}_1 + \dot{\theta}_2)^2 + 2l_1 l_2 (\cos\theta_2) \dot{\theta}_1 (\dot{\theta}_1 + \dot{\theta}_2) \right).$$

The potential energy is determined by the height of the mass.

$$
\begin{aligned}
V_1(\theta) &= -m_1\, g\, l_1 \cos\theta_1, \\
V_2(\theta) &= -m_2\, g\, l_1 \cos\theta_1 - m_2\, g\, l_2 \cos(\theta_1 + \theta_2).
\end{aligned}
$$

All above formulae could have been found with Maple.

```
> alias( theta[1]=theta[1](t), theta[2]=theta[2](t) ):
> macro( m1=m[1], m2=m[2], l1=l[1], l2=l[2],
    x1=x[1], x2=x[2], y1=y[1], y2 = y[2],
    t1=theta[1](t), t2=theta[2](t) ):
> x1 := l1*sin(t1):  y1 := l1*cos(t1):
> x2 := l1*sin(t1) + l2*sin(t1+t2):

> y2 := l1*cos(t1) + l2*cos(t1+t2):
```

The kinetic energy of mass m_1 is computed by

```
> T[1] := simplify( 1/2*m1*(diff(x1,t)^2 + diff(y1,t)^2) );
```

$$T_1 := \frac{1}{2} m_1 l_1^2 \left(\frac{\partial}{\partial t} \theta_1\right)^2$$

The kinetic energy of mass m_2 is obtained in a similar way.

```
> T[2] := expand( 1/2*m2*(diff(x2,t)^2 + diff(y2,t)^2),
    cos(t1+t2), sin(t1+t2) ):
> simplify(");
```

$$m_2 l_1 \cos(\theta_1)\left(\frac{\partial}{\partial t}\theta_1\right)^2 l_2 \cos(\%1)$$

$$+ m_2 l_1 \cos(\theta_1)\left(\frac{\partial}{\partial t}\theta_1\right) l_2 \cos(\%1)\left(\frac{\partial}{\partial t}\theta_2\right) + \frac{1}{2} m_2 l_1^2 \left(\frac{\partial}{\partial t}\theta_1\right)^2$$

$$+ m_2 l_1 \sin(\theta_1)\left(\frac{\partial}{\partial t}\theta_1\right)^2 l_2 \sin(\%1)$$

$$+ m_2 l_1 \sin(\theta_1)\left(\frac{\partial}{\partial t}\theta_1\right) l_2 \sin(\%1)\left(\frac{\partial}{\partial t}\theta_2\right) + \frac{1}{2} m_2 l_2^2 \left(\frac{\partial}{\partial t}\theta_1\right)^2$$

$$+ m_2 l_2^2 \left(\frac{\partial}{\partial t}\theta_1\right)\left(\frac{\partial}{\partial t}\theta_2\right) + \frac{1}{2} m_2 l_2^2 \left(\frac{\partial}{\partial t}\theta_2\right)^2$$

$$\%1 := \theta_1 + \theta_2$$

More simplification is needed, such as computing the finite Fourier series.

```
> map( combine, collect(",diff(t1,t)), `trig` ):
> T[2] := collect( ", [l1,l2,m2,cos(t2)], factor );
```

$$T_2 := \frac{1}{2} m_2 l_1^2 \left(\frac{\partial}{\partial t}\theta_1\right)^2 + \left(\frac{\partial}{\partial t}\theta_1\right)\left(\left(\frac{\partial}{\partial t}\theta_2\right) + \left(\frac{\partial}{\partial t}\theta_1\right)\right)\cos(\theta_2)m_2 l_2 l_1$$

$$+ \frac{1}{2}\left(\left(\frac{\partial}{\partial t}\theta_2\right) + \left(\frac{\partial}{\partial t}\theta_1\right)\right)^2 m_2 l_2^2$$

The Euler-Lagrange equations are

$$\frac{d}{dt}\left(\frac{\partial L}{\partial \dot{\theta}_i}\right) - \frac{\partial L}{\partial \theta_i} = 0,$$

for $i = 1, 2$, which yield in this case the vector equation

$$M(\theta)\ddot{\theta} + C(\theta, \dot{\theta}) + G(\theta) = 0,$$

where $\ddot\theta = (\ddot\theta_1, \ddot\theta_2)$,

$$M(\theta) = \begin{pmatrix} m_1 l_1^2 + m_2 l_1^2 + m_2 l_2^2 + 2m_2 l_1 l_2 \cos\theta_2 & m_2 l_2^2 + m_2 l_1 l_2 \cos\theta_2 \\ m_2 l_2^2 + m_2 l_1 l_2 \cos\theta_2 & m_2 l_2^2 \end{pmatrix},$$

the centripetal or Coriolis term $C(\theta, \dot\theta)$ is defined as

$$\begin{pmatrix} -m_2 l_1 l_2 \sin(\theta_2)\dot\theta_2(2\dot\theta_1 + \dot\theta_2) \\ m_2 l_1 l_2 \sin(\theta_2)\dot\theta_1^2 \end{pmatrix},$$

and the gravitational term $G(\theta)$ is defined as

$$\begin{pmatrix} m_1\, g\, l_1 \sin\theta_1 + m_2\, g\, l_1 \sin\theta_1 + m_2\, g\, l_2 \sin(\theta_1 + \theta_2) \\ m_2\, g\, l_2 \sin(\theta_1 + \theta_2) \end{pmatrix}.$$

Let us see how this can be computed by Maple. First, we compute the potential energy of masses m_1 and m_2, respectively.

```
> V[1] := - m1*g*l1*cos(t1):
> V[2] := - m2*g*l1*cos(t1) - m2*g*l2*cos(t1+t2):
> L := T[1]+T[2]-V[1]-V[2]: # Lagrangian
```

We cannot easily compute the derivatives $\dfrac{\partial L}{\partial\dot\theta_i}$ and $\dfrac{\partial L}{\partial\theta_i}$. We solve this problem by introducing some auxiliary variables.

```
> L := subs( { t1=t_1, t2=t_2, diff(t1,t)=t1p,
>    diff(t2,t)=t2p }, L ):
> dL_dt1p := diff(L,t1p):
> dL_dt2p := diff(L,t2p):
> dL_dt1 := diff(L,t_1):
> dL_dt2 := diff(L,t_2):
> dL_dt1p := subs( { t_1=t1, t_2=t2, t1p=diff(t1,t),
>    t2p=diff(t2,t) }, dL_dt1p ):
> dL_dt2p := subs( { t_1=t1, t_2=t2, t1p=diff(t1,t),
>    t2p=diff(t2,t) }, dL_dt2p ):
> dL_dt1  := subs( { t_1=t1, t_2=t2, t1p=diff(t1,t),
>    t2p=diff(t2,t) }, dL_dt1 ):
> dL_dt2  := subs( { t_1=t1, t_2=t2, t1p=diff(t1,t),
>    t2p=diff(t2,t) }, dL_dt2 ):
```

Now, we are ready to compute the differential equations via the Euler-Lagrange equations.

```
> ode[1] := collect( diff( dL_dt1p, t ) - dL_dt1 = 0,
> [diff(t1,[t$2]),diff(t2,[t$2]),diff(t1,t),diff(t2,t)] );
```

$$ode_1 := (\,m_1\, l_1{}^2 + m_2\, l_1{}^2 + m_2\, l_2{}^2 + 2\cos(\theta_2)\, m_2\, l_2\, l_1\,)\,(\frac{\partial^2}{\partial t^2}\,\theta_1\,)$$

$$+ (m_2 \, l_2{}^2 + \cos(\theta_2) \, m_2 \, l_2 \, l_1) \, (\frac{\partial^2}{\partial t^2} \, \theta_2)$$

$$- 2 \, (\frac{\partial}{\partial t} \, \theta_1) \sin(\theta_2) \, (\frac{\partial}{\partial t} \, \theta_2) \, m_2 \, l_2 \, l_1 - (\frac{\partial}{\partial t} \, \theta_2)^2 \sin(\theta_2) \, m_2 \, l_2 \, l_1$$

$$+ m_2 \, g \, l_2 \sin(\theta_1 + \theta_2) + m_1 \, g \, l_1 \sin(\theta_1) + m_2 \, g \, l_1 \sin(\theta_1) = 0$$

```
>   ode[2] := collect( diff( dL_dt2p, t ) - dL_dt2 = 0,
>   [diff(t1,[t$2]),diff(t2,[t$2]),diff(t1,t),diff(t2,t)] );
```

$$ode_2 := (m_2 \, l_2{}^2 + \cos(\theta_2) \, m_2 \, l_2 \, l_1) \, (\frac{\partial^2}{\partial t^2} \, \theta_1) + (\frac{\partial^2}{\partial t^2} \, \theta_2) \, m_2 \, l_2{}^2$$

$$+ \sin(\theta_2) \, m_2 \, l_2 \, l_1 \, (\frac{\partial}{\partial t} \, \theta_1)^2 + m_2 \, g \, l_2 \sin(\theta_1 + \theta_2) = 0$$

For simplicity, we shall consider the case that both masses and lengths are equal, say $m_1 = m_2 = m$ and $l_1 = l_2 = l$. Then the equations of motion are as follows.

```
>   m1 := m2:    m2 := m:    l1 := l2:    l2 := l:
>   map( x -> x/(m*l^2), lhs(ode[1]) ):
>   ode[1] := map( normal, " ) = 0;
```

$$ode_1 := (3 + 2 \cos(\theta_2)) \, (\frac{\partial^2}{\partial t^2} \, \theta_1) + (1 + \cos(\theta_2)) \, (\frac{\partial^2}{\partial t^2} \, \theta_2)$$

$$- 2 \, (\frac{\partial}{\partial t} \, \theta_1) \sin(\theta_2) \, (\frac{\partial}{\partial t} \, \theta_2) - (\frac{\partial}{\partial t} \, \theta_2)^2 \sin(\theta_2)$$

$$+ \frac{g \sin(\theta_1 + \theta_2)}{l} + 2 \, \frac{g \sin(\theta_1)}{l} = 0$$

```
>   map( x -> x/(m*l^2), lhs(ode[2]) ):
>   ode[2] := map( normal, " ) = 0;
```

$$ode_2 := (1 + \cos(\theta_2)) \, (\frac{\partial^2}{\partial t^2} \, \theta_1) + (\frac{\partial^2}{\partial t^2} \, \theta_2) + \sin(\theta_2) \, (\frac{\partial}{\partial t} \, \theta_1)^2$$

$$+ \frac{g \sin(\theta_1 + \theta_2)}{l} = 0$$

Let us take $l = 1$ and $g = 9.8$. As initial values we choose

$$\theta_1(0) = 0.04, \; \theta_2(0) = 0.04, \; \dot\theta_1(0) = 0, \; \dot\theta_2(0) = 0.$$

Now we are ready to solve the initial value problem numerically.

```
>   l := 1:    g := 9.8:
>   alias( t1_0=theta[1](0), t2_0=theta[2](0),
>     t1p_0=D(theta[1])(0), t2p_0=D(theta[2])(0) ):
```

Once again, all we have to do is to call the procedure **dsolve** with the option **type** = numeric. Here, we choose the method dverk78.

```
>   F := dsolve( {ode[1], ode[2], t1_0=0.04, t2_0=0.04,
>     t1p_0=0, t2p_0=0}, {t1,t2}, type = numeric,
>     method=dverk78 );
```

$$F := \text{proc}(dverk78\_t) \ldots \text{end}$$

```
>   F(0.5);   # an example
```

$$[t = .5, \theta_1 = .02561531652085558, \frac{\partial}{\partial t}\theta_1 = -.09576338917808137,$$

$$\theta_2 = -.01205989941047782, \frac{\partial}{\partial t}\theta_2 = -.07345182765456856]$$

The numeric solver returns a list consisting of an equation describing the value of the independent variable t, two equations describing the value of the dependent variables θ_1 and θ_2 at that point, and two equations describing the value of the derivatives of the dependent variables at that point.

```
>   Theta[1] := t -> rhs( op(2,F(t)) );
```

$$\Theta_1 := t \rightarrow \text{rhs}(\,\text{op}(\,2, F(\,t\,)\,)\,)$$

```
>   Theta[2] := t -> rhs( op(4,F(t)) );
```

$$\Theta_2 := t \rightarrow \text{rhs}(\,\text{op}(\,4, F(\,t\,)\,)\,)$$

We plot the approximations of θ_1 and θ_2 to get an impression of the solution found (Figures 17.7 and 17.8).

```
>   plot( Theta[1], 0..6, title = ' shoulder angle ' );
```

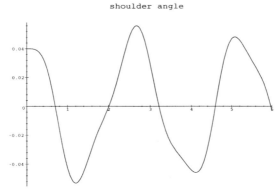

FIGURE 17.7. Graph of shoulder angle of double pendulum.

```
>   plot( Theta[2], 0..6, title = `elbow angle` );
```

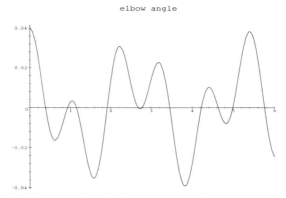

FIGURE 17.8. Graph of elbow angle of double pendulum.

Is this what you expected for the angles? A three-dimensional solution curve for the angles (θ_1, θ_2) can be plotted with the procedure **odeplot** from the **plots** package. By modifying the orientation of the three-dimensional plot, it is possible instead to obtain the above two-dimensional projections of the solution curve. Better insight into the motion of the double pendulum can be obtained from an animation. Below, we give the commands that generate such an animation. Note that this is a continuation of the previous computation. You are invited to mimic the session.

First, we define functions that describe the position of the kink and the tip of the two-link robot arm.

```
>   x1 := t -> sin( Theta[1](t) ):
>   y1 := t -> cos( Theta[1](t) ):
>   x2 := t -> sin( Theta[1](t) ) +
>     sin( Theta[1](t) + Theta[2](t) ):
>   y2 := t -> cos( Theta[1](t) ) +
>     cos( Theta[1](t) + Theta[2](t) ):
```

Second, we generate a sequence of plots that describe the robot-arm at different times in the interval $(0, 6)$.

```
>   for i from 0 to 6 by 1/10 do
>     P[i] := plot( [ [0,0], [x1(i),y1(i)], [x2(i),y2(i)] ],
>       style=line, view=[-0.2..0.2,0..2] )
>   od:  plotsequence := [ seq( P[i/10], i=0..60 ) ]:
```

Third, we display them in sequence with the **display** routine from the **plots** package, i.e., we produce the animation.

```
>   plots[display]( plotsequence, insequence=true );
```

You have encountered by now two Runge-Kutta methods for solving ODEs numerically. But Maple contains many more numerical methods. Table 17.4 summarizes the numerical methods provided by the ordinary differential equation solver **dsolve**. All you have to do is to specify the options **type = numeric, method =** *approach*.

Method	Meaning
classical	forward Euler method (default)
classical[adambash]	Adams-Bashforth ('predictor') method
classical[abmoulton]	Adams-Bashforth-Moulton ('predictor corrector') method
classical[foreuler]	forward Euler method
classical[heunform]	Heun's method
classical[impoly]	improved polygon method (also known as modified Euler method)
classical[rk2]	2nd-order classical Runge-Kutta method
classical[rk3]	3rd-order classical Runge-Kutta method
classical[rk4]	4th-order classical Runge-Kutta method
dverk78	7th-8th-order continuous Runge-Kutta method
gear	Gear single-step extrapolation method
gear[bstoer]	Bulirsch-Stoer rational extrapolation method
gear[polyextr]	polynomial extrapolation method
lsode	Livermore Stiff ODE solver
lsode[adamsband]	implicit Adams method using chord iteration with a banded Jacobian matrix
lsode[adamsdiag]	implicit Adams method using chord iteration with a diagonal Jacobian matrix
lsode[adamsfunc]	implicit Adams method with a functional iteration (default)
lsode[adamsfull]	implicit Adams method using chord iteration with a full Jacobian matrix
lsode[backband]	method of backward differentiation formulae with a banded Jacobian matrix
lsode[backdiag]	method of backward differentiation formulae with a diagonal Jacobian matrix
lsode[backfunc]	method of backward differentiation formulae with a functional iteration
lsode[backfull]	method of backward differentiation formulae with a full Jacobian matrix
mgear	Gear multistep extrapolation method
mgear[adamspc]	Adams predictor-corrector method
mgear[msteppart]	multistep method for stiff systems with evaluation of Jacobian matrix at each step
mgear[mstepnum]	multistep method for stiff systems with numeric differencing of derivatives for the computation of Jacobian matrix (default)
rkf45	Fehlberg 4th-5th-order Runge-Kutta method
taylorseries	numerical Taylor series method

TABLE 17.4. Numerical methods provided by **dsolve**.

A description of the classical numerical approaches can be found in almost any text on numerical solving of ODEs. For the Gear single- and multistep methods we refer to [70]. The code GEAR was further improved to LSODE, Livermore Stiff ODE solver, and is part of a larger program package called ODEPACK (see [102]). The numerical solver for systems of first-order ODEs using a Taylor series method is described in [11].

We refer to the on-line help system for immediate help on how to call the various numerical solvers of ODEs. Here, we only apply the Taylor series method to the following system of ODEs representing an anharmonic oscillator

```
>   ODEs := diff(q(t),t) = p(t),
>      diff(p(t),t) = -q(t) - 4*q(t)^2 - 2*q(t)^3;
```

$$ODEs := \frac{\partial}{\partial t} q(t) = p(t), \frac{\partial}{\partial t} p(t) = -q(t) - 4q(t)^2 - 2q(t)^3$$

with initial conditions

```
>   initvals := q(0)=0, p(0)=1:
>   dsolve( { ODEs, initvals }, {q(t),p(t)},
>      type=numeric, method=taylorseries,
>      output=listprocedure );
```

$$[t = (\,\text{proc}(t) \ldots \text{end}\,), q(t) = (\,\text{proc}(t) \ldots \text{end}\,),$$
$$p(t) = (\,\text{proc}(t) \ldots \text{end}\,)]$$

We have added the option output = listprocedure for numerical solving of ODEs so that the result is a list of equations where the left-hand sides are the names of the independent variable and the dependent functions, and the right-hand sides are procedures. This makes it easy to obtain numerical functions for position (q) and momentum (p):

```
>   Q := subs(",q(t));  # position
```

$$Q := \text{proc}(t) \ldots \text{end}$$

```
>   P := subs("",p(t)): # momentum
```

The plot of position and momentum with respect to time is shown in Figure 17.9. It is computed as follows:

```
>   Qplot := plot( Q, 0..10, linestyle=1 ):
>   Pplot := plot( P, 0..10, linestyle=2 ):
>   plots[display]( {Qplot, Pplot} );
```

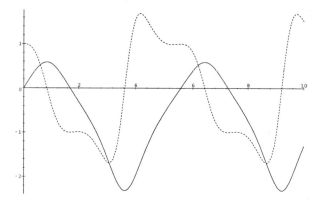

FIGURE 17.9. Graph of position and momentum of an anharmonic oscillator.

A numerical approximation of the period of the anharmonic oscillator can easily be obtained.

```
> fsolve( Q, 5..6 );
```
$$5.583431954$$

Let us verify the position after five oscillations.

```
> Q(5*");
```
$$.1207517867 \ 10^{-7}$$

The oscillator trajectory in phase space (momentum versus position) is shown in Figure 17.10

```
> plot( [ Q, P, 0..5.6 ] ); # phase plot
```

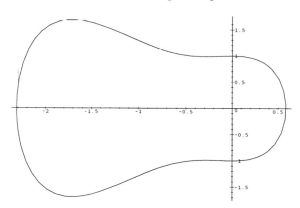

FIGURE 17.10. Phase plot of an anharmonic oscillator.

The kinetic energy versus position looks as follows (Figure 17.11).

```
> plot([ Q, P^2/2, 0..5.6 ] );
```

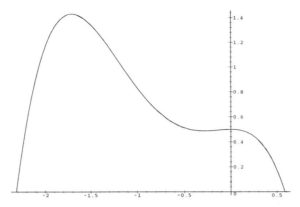

FIGURE 17.11. Kinetic energy versus position for an anharmonic oscillator.

Figure 17.12 illustrates that the corresponding Hamiltonian

$$ H = \frac{1}{2}p^2 + \frac{1}{2}q^2 + \frac{4}{3}q^3 + \frac{1}{2}q^4 $$

is a constant of motion.

```
>   plot( 1/2*P^2 + 1/2*Q^2 + 4/3*Q^3 + 1/2*Q^4,
>      0..5.6, 0.4..0.6, numpoints=25, adaptive=false );
```

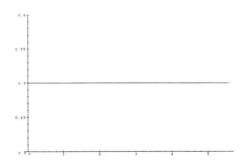

FIGURE 17.12. Hamiltonian as constant of motion.

17.6   DEtools

The DEtools package provides graphical tools to study differential equations numerically. For example, the next command draws the phase portrait with two integral curves of the anharmonic oscillator of the previous section (Figure 17.13).

```
>  with( DEtools ):
>  ODEs := diff(q(t),t) = p(t),
>     diff(p(t),t) = -q(t) - 4*q(t)^2 - 2*q(t)^3;
```

$$ODEs := \frac{\partial}{\partial t}\,q(\,t\,) = p(\,t\,),\, \frac{\partial}{\partial t}\,p(\,t\,) = -q(\,t\,) - 4\,q(\,t\,)^2 - 2\,q(\,t\,)^3$$

```
>  DEplot( {ODEs},[q(t),p(t)], t=0..8,
>     [ [q(0)=0,p(0)=1], [q(0)=1,p(0)=0]],
>     method=dverk78, linecolor=blue );
```

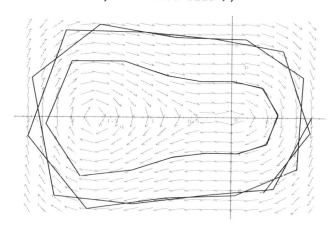

FIGURE 17.13. Phase plot of an anharmonic oscillator

As a second example, we compute field lines of an electric field due to two parallel uniform line charges of one unit charge per unit length, of opposite polarities, and at a distance of two unit lengths of each other. Actually, we consider the same example as in §15.5. The electric field of the charge distribution in the xy-plane is given by $\vec{E} = (E_x, E_y) = -\nabla\phi$, where

$$\phi = \ln\left(\sqrt{(x+1)^2 + y^2}\right) - \ln\left(\sqrt{(x-1)^2 + y^2}\right).$$

A field line can now be thought of as the trajectory of a unit charge under the influence of the electric field. It can be calculated by solving the differential equation $\dfrac{dx}{dt} = E_x, \dfrac{dy}{dt} = Y_y$, where t represents progress down the trajectory.

```
>  phi := ln(sqrt((x+1)^2+y^2)) - ln(sqrt((x-1)^2+y^2));
```

$$\phi := \ln\left(\sqrt{x^2 + 2\,x + 1 + y^2}\right) - \ln\left(\sqrt{x^2 - 2\,x + 1 + y^2}\right)$$

```
>  E := map( normal, linalg[grad]( -phi, [x,y] ) );
```

$$E := \left[\, 2\,\frac{x^2 - 1 - y^2}{(\,x^2 + 2\,x + 1 + y^2\,)\,(\,x^2 - 2\,x + 1 + y^2\,)},\right.$$

$$4\,\frac{y\,x}{(x^2+y^2)},\,4\frac{y\,x}{(x^2+2\,x+1+y^2)\,(x^2-2\,x+1+y^2)}\quad]$$

```
> alias( x=x(t), y=y(t) ):
> ODEs := diff(x,t)=E[1], diff(y,t)=E[2];
```

$$ODEs := \frac{\partial}{\partial t}\,x = -2\,\frac{-x^2+1+y^2}{(x^2+2\,x+1+y^2)\,(x^2-2\,x+1+y^2)},$$

$$\frac{\partial}{\partial t}\,y = 4\,\frac{y\,x}{(x^2+2\,x+1+y^2)\,(x^2-2\,x+1+y^2)}$$

```
> initvals := subs( t=0, [ seq( [x=1+0.05*cos(Pi/20*s),
>    y=.05*sin(Pi/20*s)], s=5..19 ) ] ):
> initvals := evalf( initvals ):
> DEplot( {ODEs}, [x,y], t=0..20, initvals,
>    x=-1.5..1.5, y=0..2.5, stepsize=0.001 );
```

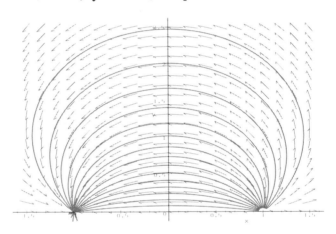

FIGURE 17.14. Electric field plot.

The ranges and step size are set to make the field lines in Figure 17.14 look reasonable near the singular point (-1,0) of the electrostatic potential. Drawbacks of these choices are that the computation of the field lines takes quite a long time and uses much computer memory.

With **PDEplot** you can plot numerical solutions of first-order, quasi-linear partial differential equations of the form

$$P(x,t,u)\frac{\partial u}{\partial x} + Q(x,t,u)\frac{\partial u}{\partial t} = R(x,t,u).$$

As an example, we compute how shock waves develop in fluid systems according to the PDE

$$\frac{\partial u}{\partial t} + u\,\frac{\partial u}{\partial x} = 0,$$

with initial condition

$$u(x,0) = \begin{cases} 1 - x^2, & \text{if } |x| \leq 1; \\ 0, & \text{otherwise.} \end{cases}$$

The propagation of the shock wave is shown in Figures 17.15 and 17.16.

```
>    alias( u=u(x,t) ):
>    PDE := diff(u,t) + u*diff(u,x) = 0:
>    initdata := [s,0,1-s^2]:

>    PDEplot( PDE, u, initdata, s=-1..1, x=-1..3, t=0..2.5,
>      orientation=[-110,60], axes=box, style=hidden,
>      shading=none );
```

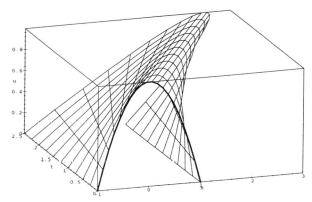

FIGURE 17.15. Propagation of a shock wave.

```
>    plots[display]( ", orientation=[110,60] );
```

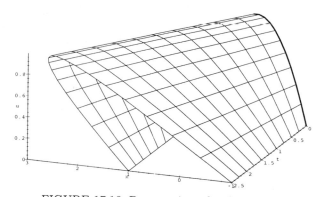

FIGURE 17.16. Propagation of a shock wave.

Another important application of the DEtools package is that it provides tools for performing a change of variables in differential equations. Both

dependent and independent variables can be transformed. The procedures
are **Dchangevar** and **PDEchangecoords**.

As an example of a change of variable in a ODE, we consider the one-
dimensional Schrödinger equation for a particle in a quadratic potential
field:

$$-\frac{\hbar^2}{2m}\frac{d^2\psi}{dx^2} + \frac{1}{2}kx^2\psi = E\psi.$$

```
>   ODE := -h^2/(2*m)*diff(psi(x),[x$2]) +
>     1/2*k*x^2*psi(x) = E*psi(x);
```

$$ODE := -\frac{1}{2}\frac{h^2\left(\frac{\partial^2}{\partial x^2}\psi(x)\right)}{m} + \frac{1}{2}kx^2\psi(x) = E\psi(x)$$

```
>   a := sqrt(h/(m*omega));
```

$$a := \sqrt{\frac{h}{m\omega}}$$

```
>   E := h/2*omega*lambda;
```

$$E := \frac{1}{2}h\omega\lambda$$

```
>   omega := sqrt(k/m); # oscillator frequency
```

$$\omega := \sqrt{\frac{k}{m}}$$

```
>   Dchangevar( { x=a*xi, psi(x)=phi(xi) }, ODE, x, xi );
```

$$-\frac{1}{2}h\sqrt{\frac{k}{m}}\left(\frac{\partial^2}{\partial\xi^2}\phi(\xi)\right) + \frac{1}{2}\frac{kh\xi^2\phi(\xi)}{m\sqrt{\frac{k}{m}}} = \frac{1}{2}h\sqrt{\frac{k}{m}}\lambda\phi(\xi)$$

```
>   simplify( (rhs-lhs)("), assume=positive );
```

$$\frac{1}{2}\frac{h\sqrt{k}\left(\lambda\phi(\xi) + (\frac{\partial^2}{\partial\xi^2}\phi(\xi)) - \xi^2\phi(\xi)\right)}{\sqrt{m}}$$

```
>   select( has, ", phi );
```

$$\lambda\phi(\xi) + \left(\frac{\partial^2}{\partial\xi^2}\phi(\xi)\right) - \xi^2\phi(\xi)$$

```
>   newODE := collect( ", phi );
```

$$newODE := (\lambda - \xi^2)\phi(\xi) + \left(\frac{\partial^2}{\partial\xi^2}\phi(\xi)\right)$$

```
> Dchangevar( phi(xi) = exp(-1/2*xi^2)*y(xi), newODE, xi );
```

$$\left(\lambda - \xi^2 \right) e^{\left(-1/2 \, \xi^2 \right)} y(\xi) - e^{\left(-1/2 \, \xi^2 \right)} y(\xi) + \xi^2 \, e^{\left(-1/2 \, \xi^2 \right)} y(\xi)$$
$$- 2 \, \xi \, e^{\left(-1/2 \, \xi^2 \right)} \left(\frac{\partial}{\partial \xi} y(\xi) \right) + e^{\left(\, 1/2 \, \xi^2 \right)} \left(\frac{\partial^2}{\partial \xi^2} y(\xi) \right)$$

```
> factor(");
```

$$e^{\left(-1/2 \, \xi^2 \right)} \left(y(\xi) \lambda - y(\xi) - 2 \left(\frac{\partial}{\partial \xi} y(\xi) \right) \xi + \left(\frac{\partial^2}{\partial \xi^2} y(\xi) \right) \right)$$

```
> select( has, ", y );
```

$$y(\xi) \lambda - y(\xi) - 2 \left(\frac{\partial}{\partial \xi} y(\xi) \right) \xi + \left(\frac{\partial^2}{\partial \xi^2} y(\xi) \right)$$

```
> HermiteODE := collect( ", y );
```

$$HermiteODE := (\lambda - 1) y(\xi) - 2 \left(\frac{\partial}{\partial \xi} y(\xi) \right) \xi + \left(\frac{\partial^2}{\partial \xi^2} y(\xi) \right)$$

The power series solution of this differential equation has already been computed in §17.4.

A change of coordinates for PDEs can be done with the procedure **PDEchangecoords** in a similar way as you can change coordinate systems for plotting. For example, the two-dimensional Laplace equation can be rewritten in polar coordinates in the following way.

```
> LaplacePDE := diff(F(x,y),[x$2])
>    + diff(F(x,y),[y$2]) = 0;
```

$$LaplacePDE := \left(\frac{\partial^2}{\partial x^2} F(x,y) \right) + \left(\frac{\partial^2}{\partial y^2} F(x,y) \right) = 0$$

```
> PDEchangecoords( LaplacePDE, [x,y], polar, [r,phi] );
```

$$\frac{\left(\frac{\partial}{\partial r} F(r,\phi) \right) r + \left(\frac{\partial^2}{\partial r^2} F(r,\phi) \right) r^2 + \left(\frac{\partial^2}{\partial \phi^2} F(r,\phi) \right)}{r^2} = 0$$

```
> newLaplacePDE := numer(lhs(")) = 0;
```

$$newLaplacePDE :=$$
$$\left(\frac{\partial}{\partial r} F(r,\phi) \right) r + \left(\frac{\partial^2}{\partial r^2} F(r,\phi) \right) r^2 + \left(\frac{\partial^2}{\partial \phi^2} F(r,\phi) \right) = 0$$

You can define your own coordinate transformation via the procedure **addcoords**. We illustrate this by transforming the Fokker-Planck equation

$$\frac{\partial u}{\partial t} = \frac{\partial^2 u}{\partial x^2} + x\,\frac{\partial u}{\partial x} + u$$

into the diffusion equation

$$\frac{\partial v}{\partial \tau} = \frac{\partial^2 v}{\partial \xi^2}.$$

```
>  FokkerPlanckPDE := diff(u(x,t),t) =
>     diff(u(x,t),[x$2]) + x*diff(u(x,t),x) + u(x,t);
```

$$FokkerPlanckPDE := \frac{\partial}{\partial t}\,u(x,t) = (\frac{\partial^2}{\partial x^2}\,u(x,t)) + x\,(\frac{\partial}{\partial x}\,u(x,t)) + u(x,t)$$

The first change of variables is $\xi = xe^t, v = ue^{-t}$.

```
>  readlib( addcoords ):
>  Dchangevar( {u(x,t)=v(xi,t)*exp(t)},
>     FokkerPlanckPDE, x, xi );
```

$$\frac{\partial}{\partial t}\,v(\xi,t)\,e^t = (\frac{\partial^2}{\partial \xi^2}\,v(\xi,t)\,e^t) + \xi\,(\frac{\partial}{\partial \xi}\,v(\xi,t)\,e^t) + v(\xi,t)\,e^t$$

```
>  simplify(");
```

$$(\frac{\partial}{\partial t}\,v(\xi,t))\,e^t + v(\xi,t)\,e^t = (\frac{\partial^2}{\partial \xi^2}\,v(\xi,t))\,e^t + \xi\,(\frac{\partial}{\partial \xi}\,v(\xi,t))\,e^t + v(\xi,t)\,e^t$$

```
>  addcoords( T1, [x,t], [x*exp(-t),t] ):
>  PDEchangecoords( "" , [xi,t], T1 );
```

$$\xi\,(\frac{\partial}{\partial \xi}\,v(\xi,t))\,e^t - \xi\,e^{(-t)}\,(\frac{\partial}{\partial \xi}\,v(\xi,t))\,(e^t)^2 + (\frac{\partial}{\partial t}\,v(\xi,t))\,e^t$$
$$- (e^t)^3\,(\frac{\partial^2}{\partial \xi^2}\,v(\xi,t)) = 0$$

```
>  expand( "/exp(t)^3 );
```

$$\frac{\frac{\partial}{\partial t}\,v(\xi,t)}{(e^t)^2} - (\frac{\partial^2}{\partial \xi^2}\,v(\xi,t)) = 0$$

```
>  combine( ", exp );
```

$$e^{(-2t)}\,(\frac{\partial}{\partial t}\,v(\xi,t)) - (\frac{\partial^2}{\partial \xi^2}\,v(\xi,t)) = 0$$

So, we arrive at the PDE

$$e^{-2t}\frac{\partial v}{\partial t} = \frac{\partial^2 v}{\partial \xi^2}.$$

Next, we introduce a new variable τ by $\tau = \frac{1}{2}e^{2t}$. The PDE is in the new coordinate after simplification in the format known as the diffusion equation.

```
>   addcoords( T2, [x,t], [x,1/2*ln(2*t)] ):
>   PDEchangecoords( "" , [xi,t], T2, [xi,tau] ):
>   diffusionPDE := simplify(");
```

$$diffusionPDE := (\frac{\partial}{\partial \tau}\,v(\xi,\tau)) - (\frac{\partial^2}{\partial \xi^2}\,v(\xi,\tau)) = 0$$

17.7   Perturbation Methods

When you want to apply perturbation methods to find approximate solutions of ODEs, computer algebra systems are most valuable computational tools. In this section, we shall describe two classical methods, viz., the Poincaré-Lindstedt method and the method of multiple scales; and we shall apply them to the van der Pol equation. The interested reader is also referred to [158, 159], which contain many examples of the use of the computer algebra system MACSYMA in perturbation and bifurcation theory. Mathematical background can be found in [144].

Poincaré-Lindstedt Method

The van der Pol equation is

$$y'' - \epsilon\,(1 - y^2)\,y' + y = 0\,.$$

For $\epsilon = 0$ it is the ODE of the mathematical pendulum. We already investigated the case $\epsilon = 1$ numerically in §17.5. For any ϵ, this differential equation possesses an asymptotically stable periodic solution called the *limit cycle*.

We want to compute a good approximation of the limit cycle for small ϵ. Because there are no explicit time-dependent terms in the van der Pol equation we can choose without loss of generality the point that corresponds with $t = 0$; we shall choose the initial value $y(0) = 0$. In the Poincaré-Lindstedt method, time is stretched via the transformation

$$\tau = \omega\,t,$$

where

$$\omega = 1 + \omega_1\epsilon + \omega_2\epsilon^2 + \omega_3\epsilon^3 + \dots$$

Then the van der Pol equation for $y(\tau)$ becomes

$$\omega^2 y'' - \omega\, \epsilon\, (1 - y^2)\, y' + y = 0.$$

Let us verify this with Maple.

```
>   diff( y(t),t$2 ) - epsilon*(1-y(t)^2)*diff(y(t),t)
>      + y(t) = 0;
```

$$\left(\frac{\partial^2}{\partial t^2}\, \mathrm{y}(t) \right) - \varepsilon\, (1 - \mathrm{y}(t)^2)\, \left(\frac{\partial}{\partial t}\, \mathrm{y}(t) \right) + \mathrm{y}(t) = 0$$

```
>   ODE := DEtools[Dchangevar](
>      { t=tau/omega, y(t)=y(tau) }, ", t, tau );
```

$$ODE := \omega^2\, \left(\frac{\partial^2}{\partial \tau^2}\, \mathrm{y}(\tau) \right) - \varepsilon\, (1 - \mathrm{y}(\tau)^2)\, \omega\, \left(\frac{\partial}{\partial \tau}\, \mathrm{y}(\tau) \right) + \mathrm{y}(\tau) = 0$$

We assume that the solution $y(\tau)$ can expanded in a Taylor series in ϵ,

$$y(\tau) = y_0(\tau) + y_1(\tau)\epsilon + y_2(\tau)\epsilon^2 + y_3(\tau)\epsilon^3 + \dots$$

Then we substitute the expansions of $y(\tau)$ and $\omega(\epsilon)$ in the van der Pol equation, collect terms in ϵ, and equate to zero the coefficient of each power of ϵ. The equations for small orders of ϵ are

$$
\begin{aligned}
y_0'' + y_0 &= 0, \\
y_1'' + y_1 &= y_0'\, (1 - y_0^2) - 2\omega_1 y_0'', \\
y_2'' + y_2 &= (1 - y_0^2)\, y_1' - 2 y_0 y_1 y_0' - 2\omega_1 y_1'' \\
&\quad - (2\omega_2 + \omega_1^2)\, y_0'' + \omega_1 (1 - y_0)\, x_0'.
\end{aligned}
$$

The initial value $y(0) = 0$ translates into

$$y_0(0) = 0, \quad y_1(0) = 0, \quad y_2(0) = 0, \quad y_3(0) = 0, \dots$$

Let us check some of the differential equations with Maple, at the same time setting the notation for the rest of the session.

```
>   e_order := 6:
>   macro( e=epsilon, t=tau ):
>   alias( seq( y[i] = eta[i](tau), i=0..e_order ) ):
>   e := () -> e: # introduce e as a constant function
>   for i from 0 to e_order do
>      eta[i] := t -> eta[i](t)
>   od:
>   omega := 1 + sum( `w[i]*e^i`, `i`=1..e_order );
```

$$\omega := 1 + w_1\, \varepsilon + w_2\, \varepsilon^2 + w_3\, \varepsilon^3 + w_4\, \varepsilon^4 + w_5\, \varepsilon^5 + w_6\, \varepsilon^6$$

```
>   y := sum( `eta[i]*e^i`, `i`=0..e_order );
```

$$y := \eta_0 + \eta_1\, \varepsilon + \eta_2\, \varepsilon^2 + \eta_3\, \varepsilon^3 + \eta_4\, \varepsilon^4 + \eta_5\, \varepsilon^5 + \eta_6\, \varepsilon^6$$

```
>   deqn := simplify( collect(ODE,e), {e^(e_order+1)=0} ):
>   for i from 0 to e_order do
>     ode[i] :=coeff( lhs(deqn), e, i ) = 0
>   od:
>   ode[0];
```

$$(\frac{\partial^2}{\partial \tau^2} y_0) + y_0 = 0$$

```
>   ode[1];
```

$$2 w_1 (\frac{\partial^2}{\partial \tau^2} y_0) + (\frac{\partial^2}{\partial \tau^2} y_1) + y_1 + (\frac{\partial}{\partial \tau} y_0) y_0{}^2 - (\frac{\partial}{\partial \tau} y_0) = 0$$

```
>   ode[2];
```

$$2 w_1 (\frac{\partial^2}{\partial \tau^2} y_1) + (\frac{\partial^2}{\partial \tau^2} y_2) + y_2 + (\frac{\partial^2}{\partial \tau^2} y_0) w_1{}^2 + (\frac{\partial}{\partial \tau} y_1) y_0{}^2$$

$$+ 2 (\frac{\partial^2}{\partial \tau^2} y_0) w_2 - (\frac{\partial}{\partial \tau} y_0) w_1 - (\frac{\partial}{\partial \tau} y_1) + (\frac{\partial}{\partial \tau} y_0) w_1 y_0{}^2$$

$$+ 2 (\frac{\partial}{\partial \tau} y_0) y_0 y_1 = 0$$

The initial value problem for $\eta_0(\tau)$ can easily be solved.

```
>   dsolve( { ode[0], eta[0](0)=0, D(eta[0])(0)=C[1] },
>     eta[0](t) );
```

$$y_0 = C_1 \sin(\tau)$$

We assign this function and proceed with the differential equation for $\eta_1(\tau)$.

```
>   eta[0] := unapply( rhs("), t );
```

$$\eta_0 := \tau \to C_1 \sin(\tau)$$

```
>   ode[1];
```

$$(\frac{\partial^2}{\partial \tau^2} y_1) - 2 w_1 C_1 \sin(\tau) - C_1 \cos(\tau) + C_1{}^3 \cos(\tau) \sin(\tau)^2 + y_1 = 0$$

We compute the finite Fourier series with **combine(...,'trig')**.

```
>   map( combine, ode[1], ´trig´ );
```

$$(\frac{\partial^2}{\partial \tau^2} y_1) - 2 w_1 C_1 \sin(\tau) - C_1 \cos(\tau) + \frac{1}{4} C_1{}^3 \cos(\tau)$$

$$- \frac{1}{4} C_1{}^3 \cos(3 \tau) + y_1 = 0$$

```
>   ode[1] := map( collect, ", [sin(t),cos(t)] );
```

$$ode_1 := -2 w_1 C_1 \sin(\tau) + (-C_1 + \frac{1}{4} C_1{}^3) \cos(\tau) + (\frac{\partial^2}{\partial \tau^2} y_1) + y_1$$

$$- \frac{1}{4} C_1{}^3 \cos(3 \tau) = 0$$

The $\sin\tau$ and $\cos\tau$ terms are called the *resonant terms* or *secular terms*; they are responsible for nonperiodic behavior of the approximation — as is clear from the general solution below.

```
>   dsolve( { ode[1], eta[1](0)=0, D(eta[1])(0)=C[2] },
>       eta[1](t), laplace );
```

$$y_1 = -\frac{1}{32} C_1{}^3 \cos(3\tau) + \frac{1}{32} C_1{}^3 \cos(\tau) + C_2 \sin(\tau) + w_1 C_1 \sin(\tau)$$
$$- C_1 \tau w_1 \cos(\tau) + \frac{1}{2} C_1 \tau \sin(\tau) - \frac{1}{8}\tau C_1{}^3 \sin(\tau)$$

```
>   map( collect, ", [sin(t),cos(t),t] );
```

$$y_1 = ((\frac{1}{2} C_1 - \frac{1}{8} C_1{}^3)\tau + C_2 + w_1 C_1)\sin(\tau)$$
$$+ (\frac{1}{32} C_1{}^3 - C_1 \tau w_1)\cos(\tau) - \frac{1}{32} C_1{}^3 \cos(3\tau)$$

So, we choose C_1 and w_1 such that these terms vanish.

```
>   solve( { coeff( lhs(ode[1]), sin(t) ) = 0,
>       coeff( lhs(ode[1]), cos(t) ) = 0 } );
```
$$\{C_1 = 2, w_1 = 0\}, \{C_1 = -2, w_1 = 0\}, \{C_1 = 0, w_1 = w_1\}$$

Because we want to compare it with the numerical method that was discussed in §17.5, we choose a negative amplitude.

```
>   w[1] := 0: C[1] := -2:
>   ode[1];
```

$$(\frac{\partial^2}{\partial\tau^2} y_1) + y_1 + 2\cos(3\tau) = 0$$

We solve the differential equation for $\eta_1(\tau)$ with initial values $\eta_1(0) = 0$, $\eta_1'(0) = C_2$.

```
>   dsolve( { ode[1], eta[1](0)=0, D(eta[1])(0)=C[2] },
>       eta[1](t), laplace );
```

$$y_1 = \frac{1}{4} \cos(3\tau) - \frac{1}{4}\cos(\tau) + C_2 \sin(\tau)$$

```
>   eta[1] := unapply( rhs("), tau );
```

$$\eta_1 := \tau \to \frac{1}{4}\cos(3\tau) - \frac{1}{4}\cos(\tau) + C_2 \sin(\tau)$$

Similarly, we deal with C_2 and $\eta_2(\tau)$. We omit comments.

```
>   map( combine, ode[2], `trig` ):
>   ode[2] := map( collect, ",
>       [ sin(t), sin(3*t), cos(t), cos(3*t) ] );
```

$$ode_2 := (\frac{1}{4} + 4 w_2)\sin(\tau) + (\frac{\partial^2}{\partial\tau^2} y_2) + y_2 - \frac{3}{2}\sin(3\tau)$$
$$+ \frac{5}{4}\sin(5\tau) + 2 C_2 \cos(\tau) - 3 C_2 \cos(3\tau) = 0$$

```
> solve( { coeff( lhs(ode[2]), sin(t) ) = 0,
>    coeff( lhs(ode[2]), cos(t) ) = 0 } );
```

$$\{ w_2 = \frac{-1}{16}, C_2 = 0 \}$$

```
> assign("):
> dsolve( { ode[2], eta[2](0)=0, D(eta[2])(0)=C[3] },
>    eta[2](t), laplace ):
> collect( ", [ sin(t), sin(3*t), sin(5*t),
>    cos(t), cos(3*t), cos(5*t) ] ):
> eta[2] := unapply( rhs("), t );
```

$$\eta_2 := \tau \rightarrow (\frac{29}{96} + C_3) \sin(\tau) + \frac{5}{96} \sin(5\tau) - \frac{3}{16} \sin(3\tau)$$

We assume that you understand the pattern for finding the higher-order terms and compute them repetitively.

```
> for i from 3 to e_order do
>    map( combine, ode[i], `trig` ):
>    ode[i] := map( collect, ",
>      [ seq(sin((2*j+1)*t),j=0..i),
>      seq(cos((2*j+1)*t),j=0..i) ] ):
>    solve( {coeff( lhs(ode[i]), sin(t) ) = 0,
>    coeff( lhs(ode[i]), cos(t) ) = 0} ):
>    assign("):
>    dsolve( { ode[i], eta[i](0)=0, D(eta[i])(0)=C[i+1] },
>      eta[i](t), laplace ):
>    collect( ", [ seq(sin((2*j+1)*t),j=0..i),
>      seq(cos((2*j+1)*t),j=0..i) ] ):
>    eta[i] := unapply( rhs("), t )
> od:
```

Let us look at the final results.

```
> omega;
```

$$1 - \frac{1}{16} \varepsilon^2 + \frac{17}{3072} \varepsilon^4 + \frac{35}{884736} \varepsilon^6$$

```
> y(t);
```

$$-2\sin(\tau) + (\frac{1}{4} \cos(3\tau) - \frac{1}{4} \cos(\tau)) \varepsilon$$

$$+ (\frac{5}{96} \sin(5\tau) - \frac{3}{16} \sin(3\tau)) \varepsilon^2 +$$

$$(- \frac{21}{256} \cos(3\tau) - \frac{7}{576} \cos(7\tau) + \frac{5}{72} \cos(5\tau) + \frac{19}{768} \cos(\tau))$$

$$\varepsilon^3 + \left(- \frac{11}{4096} \sin(\tau) + \frac{29}{768} \sin(3\tau) + \frac{2555}{110592} \sin(7\tau)\right.$$

$$- \frac{61}{20480} \sin(9\tau) - \left.\frac{1385}{27648} \sin(5\tau)\right) \varepsilon^4 + \left(\frac{5533}{7372800} \cos(11\tau)\right.$$

$$+ \frac{4175}{294912} \cos(3\tau) + \frac{153251}{6635520} \cos(7\tau) - \frac{9013}{1228800} \cos(9\tau)$$

$$- \frac{77915}{2654208} \cos(5\tau) - \frac{5807}{4423680} \cos(\tau) \Big) \varepsilon^5 + \Big($$
$$\Big(-\frac{148447039}{55738368000} + C_7 \Big) \sin(\tau) + \frac{715247}{3715891200} \sin(13\tau)$$
$$- \frac{6871193}{398131200} \sin(7\tau) + \frac{690583}{73728000} \sin(9\tau)$$
$$- \frac{143191}{35389440} \sin(3\tau) + \frac{469795}{31850496} \sin(5\tau)$$
$$- \frac{6017803}{2654208000} \sin(11\tau) \Big) \varepsilon^6$$

The constant C_7 would be determined in the next step. We shall only consider $y(\tau)$ up to order 5; results of computations up to order 164 can be
found in [6].

```
>  y := unapply( simplify( y(t), {e^e_order=0} ), t ):
```
Let us plot this function for $\epsilon = 1$ (Figure 17.17).

```
>   e := 1: y(t);
```

$$-\frac{81}{32} \sin(\tau) \cos(\tau)^4 - \frac{1037927}{552960} \sin(\tau) + \frac{13}{256} \sin(\tau) \cos(\tau)^2$$
$$+ \frac{912187}{129600} \cos(\tau)^7 - \frac{799991}{1105920} \cos(\tau) + \frac{5257957}{3317760} \cos(\tau)^3$$
$$- \frac{1212373}{259200} \cos(\tau)^5 - \frac{61}{80} \sin(\tau) \cos(\tau)^8$$
$$+ \frac{1519}{540} \sin(\tau) \cos(\tau)^6 - \frac{114941}{28800} \cos(\tau)^9 + \frac{5533}{7200} \cos(\tau)^{11}$$

```
>  plot( y(t), t=0..14 );
```

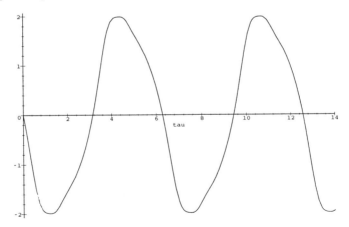

FIGURE 17.17. Solution of the van der Pol equation by the Poincaré-Lindstedt
method.

Compare this with the numerical solution found in §17.5.

Method of Multiple Scales

The Poincaré-Lindstedt method is useful for finding periodic solutions of ODEs, but it does not help to approximate general solutions of ODEs in the neighborhood of a limit cycle. In the method of multiple scales, the solution of an ODE is not viewed as a function of one variable t but as a function of two or more independent variables $t_1, t_2, t_3, \ldots$ defined as

$$t_1 = t, \quad t_2 = \epsilon t, \quad t_3 = \epsilon^2 t, \quad \ldots$$

Then:

$$\frac{d}{dt} = \frac{\partial}{\partial t_1} + \epsilon \frac{\partial}{\partial t_2} + \epsilon^2 \frac{\partial}{\partial t_3} + \cdots,$$

$$\frac{d^2}{dt^2} = \frac{\partial^2}{\partial t_1^2} + 2\epsilon \frac{\partial^2}{\partial t_1 t_2} + \epsilon^2 \left(\frac{\partial}{\partial t_2^2} + 2 \frac{\partial}{\partial t_3} \right) + \cdots.$$

You can verify this with Maple (you can compute higher-order terms by increasing the variable e_order).

```
>   restart;
>   alias( epsilon=e,
>     seq( y[i] = eta[i]( seq(t[j],j=1..3) ), i=0..2 ) ):
>   macro( t1=t[1], t2=t[2], t3=t[3] ):
>   e_order := 2:
>   e := subs( variables = seq( u.j, j=0..e_order),
>     body=e, (variables -> body) ):
>   subs( D = sum( e^(i-1)*D[i], i=1..e_order+1 ),
>     (D@@e_order)(y) ):
>   simplify( collect(",e), {e^(e_order+1)=0} );
```

$$D_{1,1}(y) + 2\varepsilon D_{1,2}(y) + (2 D_{1,3}(y) + D_{2,2}(y))\varepsilon^2$$

In classical notation:

```
>   convert( "(seq( t[j], j=1..e_order+1 )), diff );
```

$$(\frac{\partial^2}{\partial t_1^2} \%1) + 2\varepsilon (\frac{\partial^2}{\partial t_2 \, \partial t_1} \%1) + (2 (\frac{\partial^2}{\partial t_3 \, \partial t_1} \%1) + (\frac{\partial^2}{\partial t_2^2} \%1))\varepsilon^2$$
$$\%1 := y(t_1, t_2, t_3)$$

In the method of multiple scales, the solution y of an ODE is expanded in a power series of ϵ as

$$y = y_0(t_1, t_2, t_3, \ldots) + \epsilon y_1(t_1, t_2, t_3, \ldots) + \epsilon^2 y_2(t_1, t_2, t_3, \ldots) + \cdots.$$

This leads to differential equations for y_0, y_1, y_2, etc.

We shall apply the three variable method to the van der Pol equation

$$y'' - \epsilon(1 - y^2)y' + y = 0,$$

with initial values $y(0) = 0, y'(0) = -1/10$. We shall actually redo work of Noble and Hussain [145].

First, we derive the differential equations for $y_0(t_0, t_1, t_2)$, $y_1(t_0, t_1, t_2)$, and $y_2(t_0, t_1, t_2)$ with Maple.

```
>   ODE := (D@@2)(y) - e*(1-y^2)*D(y) + y=0;
```
$$ODE := D^{(2)}(y) - \varepsilon(1 - y^2)\,D(y) + y = 0$$

```
>   subs( D = sum('e^(i-1)*D[i]', 'i'=1..e_order+1), ODE ):
>   y := sum( 'eta[i]*e^i', 'i'=0..e_order );
```
$$y := \eta_0 + \eta_1\,\varepsilon + \eta_2\,\varepsilon^2$$

```
>   diffeqn := simplify( collect("",e), {e^(e_order+1)=0} ):
>   for i from 0 to e_order do
>        ode[i] := coeff( lhs(diffeqn), e, i ) = 0
>   od;
```
$$ode_0 := D_{1,1}(\eta_0) + \eta_0 = 0$$

$$ode_1 := D_{1,1}(\eta_1) + 2\,D_{1,2}(\eta_0) + \eta_1 - D_1(\eta_0) + D_1(\eta_0)\,\eta_0{}^2 = 0$$

$$ode_2 := -D_1(\eta_1) - D_2(\eta_0) + \eta_0{}^2\,D_1(\eta_1) + \eta_0{}^2\,D_2(\eta_0)$$
$$+ 2\,\eta_0\,\eta_1\,D_1\,\eta_0 + 2\,D_{1,2}(\eta_1) + \eta_2 + D_{2,2}(\eta_0) + D_{1,1}(\eta_2)$$
$$+ 2\,D_{1,3}(\eta_0) = 0$$

So, the required differential equations are:

$$\frac{\partial^2 y_0}{\partial t_1^2} + y_0 = 0,$$

$$\frac{\partial^2 y_0}{\partial t_1^2} + y_1 = -2\frac{\partial^2 y_0}{\partial t_1 t_2} + (1 - y_0^2)\frac{\partial y_0}{\partial t_1},$$

$$\frac{\partial^2 y_2}{\partial t_1^2} + y_2 = -2\frac{\partial^2 y_0}{\partial t_1 t_2} - \frac{\partial^2 y_0}{\partial t_2^2} - 2\frac{\partial^2 y_0}{\partial t_1 t_3} +$$
$$(1 - y_0^2)\left(\frac{\partial y_1}{\partial t_1} + \frac{\partial y_0}{\partial t_2}\right) - 2y_0 y_1\frac{\partial y_0}{\partial t_1}.$$

The first equation has the general solution

$$y_0(t_1, t_2, t_3) := A(t_2, t_3)\sin(t_1 + B(t_2, t_3)).$$

Substituting this in the next equation, we get the following differential equations for $A(t_2, t_3)$ and $B(t_2, t_3)$, if we insist on removal of resonant terms.

$$\frac{\partial B(t_2, t_3)}{\partial t_2} = 0,$$

$$\frac{\partial A(t_2, t_3)}{\partial t_2} = \frac{1}{2}A(t_2, t_3) - \frac{1}{8}A(t_2, t_3)^3.$$

Let us verify this with Maple.

```
>   ode[1] := convert( ode[1](t1,t2,t3), diff );
```

$$ode_1 := (\frac{\partial^2}{\partial t_1{}^2} y_1) + 2(\frac{\partial^2}{\partial t_2 \partial t_1} y_0) + y_1 - (\frac{\partial}{\partial t_1} y_0) + (\frac{\partial}{\partial t_1} y_0)y_0{}^2 = 0$$

```
>   eta[0] := (t1,t2,t3) -> A(t2,t3) * sin(t1 + B(t2,t3));
```

$$\eta_0 := (t1, t2, t3) \rightarrow A(t2, t3)\sin(t1 + B(t2, t3))$$

```
>   combine( ode[1], 'trig' ):
>   ode[1] := collect( ", [ sin(t1+B(t2,t3)),
>     cos(t1+B(t2,t3)) ] );
```

$$ode_1 := -2\,A(t_2, t_3)\sin(t_1 + B(t_2, t_3))(\frac{\partial}{\partial t_2} B(t_2, t_3)) +$$

$$(2(\frac{\partial}{\partial t_2} A(t_2, t_3)) - A(t_2, t_3) + \frac{1}{4} A(t_2, t_3)^3)\cos(t_1 + B(t_2, t_3))$$

$$+ (\frac{\partial^2}{\partial t_1{}^2} y_1) - \frac{1}{4} A(t_2, t_3)^3 \cos(3\,t_1 + 3\,B(t_2, t_3)) + y_1 = 0$$

The resonant terms are

$$\sin(t_1 + B(t_2, t_3)), \quad \cos(t_1 + B(t_2, t_3)).$$

By insisting that coefficients of resonant terms are equal to zero we get the following differential equations.

```
>   restrictions := {
>     coeff( lhs(ode[1]), cos(t1+B(t2,t3)) ) = 0,
>     coeff( lhs(ode[1]), sin(t1+B(t2,t3)) ) = 0 };
```

$$restrictions := \left\{2(\frac{\partial}{\partial t_2} A(t_2, t_3)) - A(t_2, t_3) + \frac{1}{4} A(t_2, t_3)^3 = 0, \right.$$

$$\left. -2\,A(t_2, t_3)(\frac{\partial}{\partial t_2} B(t_2, t_3)) = 0\right\}$$

```
>   2*diff(F(t),t) - F(t) + 1/4*F(t)^3 = 0;
```

$$2(\frac{\partial}{\partial t} F(t)) - F(t) + \frac{1}{4} F(t)^3 = 0$$

```
>   simplify( [dsolve( ", F(t), 'explicit' )], symbolic );
```

$$[F(t) = 2\,\frac{e^{(1/2\,t)}}{\sqrt{e^t + 4\_C1}}, F(t) = -2\,\frac{e^{(1/2\,t)}}{\sqrt{e^t + 4\_C1}}]$$

```
>   simplify( subs( _C1 = 1/4*exp(t)*C, " ), symbolic ):
>   subs( C=C*exp(-t), " );
```

$$[F(t) = 2\,\frac{1}{\sqrt{1 + C\,e^{(-t)}}}, F(t) = -2\,\frac{1}{\sqrt{1 + C\,e^{(-t)}}}]$$

It follows that we can take

$$A(t_2, t_3) = \frac{-2}{\sqrt{1 + C(t_3)e^{-t_2}}}.$$

Moreover, we can take $B(t_2, t_3) = B(t_3)$. Then, the differential equation satisfied by y_1 becomes

```
>    simplify( ode[1], restrictions, convert(
>      [D[1](B)(t2,t3),D[1](A)(t2,t3), A(t2,t3)], diff ) ):
>    combine( ", `trig` );
```

$$(\frac{\partial^2}{\partial t_1{}^2} y_1) + y_1 - \frac{1}{4} A(t_2, t_3)^3 \cos(3 t_1 + 3 B(t_2, t_3)) = 0$$

Now comes a tricky point in the computation: we ignore the solution of the homogeneous differential equation and choose a particular solution y_1 that has a simple form.

```
>    eta[1] := (t1,t2,t3) -> 1/32 * A(t2,t3)^3
>      * sin(3*t1+3*B(t2,t3)+3/2*Pi);
```

$$\eta_1 := (t1, t2, t3) \rightarrow \frac{1}{32} A(t2, t3)^3 \sin(3\, t1 + 3\, B(t2, t3) + \frac{3}{2} \pi)$$

```
>    ""; # verify the solution
```

$$0 = 0$$

We take into account that B does not depend on t_2 and substitute y_1 into the third differential equation:

```
>    eta[1] := `eta[1]`:  eta[0] := `eta[0]`:
>    ode[2] := convert( ode[2](t1,t2,t3), diff ):
>    eta[1]:= (t1,t2,t3)-> 1/32 * A(t2,t3)^3
>        * sin(3*t1+3*B(t3)+3/2*Pi);
```

$$\eta_1 := (t1, t2, t3) \rightarrow \frac{1}{32} A(t2, t3)^3 \sin(3\, t1 + 3\, B(t3) + \frac{3}{2} \pi)$$

```
>    eta[0] := (t1,t2,t3) -> A(t2,t3) * sin(t1 + B(t3));
```

$$\eta_0 := (t1, t2, t3) \rightarrow A(t2, t3) \sin(t1 + B(t3))$$

```
>    combine( ode[2], `trig` ):
>    ode[2] := collect( ", [ sin(t1+B(t3)), cos(t1+B(t3)) ] ):
>    conditions := { coeff( lhs(ode[2]), cos(t1+B(t3)) ) = 0,
>      coeff( lhs(ode[2]), sin(t1+B(t3)) ) = 0 };
```

$$conditions := \Big\{ 2 (\frac{\partial}{\partial t_3} A(t_2, t_3)) = 0, -\frac{1}{128} A(t_2, t_3)^5$$

$$+ (\frac{\partial^2}{\partial t_2{}^2} A(t_2, t_3)) - (\frac{\partial}{\partial t_2} A(t_2, t_3))$$

$$+ \frac{3}{4} A(t_2, t_3)^2 (\frac{\partial}{\partial t_2} A(t_2, t_3)) - 2 A(t_2, t_3) (\frac{\partial}{\partial t_3} B(t_3)) = 0 \Big\}$$

One of the conditions means that $A(t_2, t_3)$ does not depend on t_3 (so, $C(t_3)$ is a constant). From the earlier restrictions, we can derive a necessary condition for $\dfrac{\partial^2 A(t_2, t_3)}{\partial t_2^2}$.

```
>  op( remove( has,restrictions,B) );
```

$$2\left(\frac{\partial}{\partial t_2} A(t_2, t_3)\right) - A(t_2, t_3) + \frac{1}{4} A(t_2, t_3)^3 = 0$$

```
>  diff(",t[2]);
```

$$2\left(\frac{\partial^2}{\partial t_2^2} A(t_2, t_3)\right) - \left(\frac{\partial}{\partial t_2} A(t_2, t_3)\right) + \frac{3}{4} A(t_2, t_3)^2 \left(\frac{\partial}{\partial t_2} A(t_2, t_3)\right) = 0$$

Together with the second last restriction, we can rewrite the above conditions.

```
>  simplify( conditions, { ", "" }, convert(
>     [ D[1,1](A)(t2,t3), D[1](A)(t2,t3),
>     A(t2,t3) ], diff ) );
```

$$\left\{\left(-2\left(\frac{\partial}{\partial t_3} B(t_3)\right) - \frac{1}{4}\right) A(t_2, t_3) + \frac{1}{4} A(t_2, t_3)^3 - \frac{7}{128} A(t_2, t_3)^5 = 0,\right.$$

$$\left. 2\left(\frac{\partial}{\partial t_3} A(t_2, t_3)\right) = 0\right\}$$

```
>  op( select( has, ", B ) );
```

$$\left(-2\left(\frac{\partial}{\partial t_3} B(t_3)\right) - \frac{1}{4}\right) A(t_2, t_3) + \frac{1}{4} A(t_2, t_3)^3 - \frac{7}{128} A(t_2, t_3)^5 = 0$$

```
>  ´diff(B(t3),t3)´ = solve(",diff(B(t3),t3) );
```

$$\frac{\partial}{\partial t_3} B(t_3) = -\frac{1}{8} + \frac{1}{8} A(t_2, t_3)^2 - \frac{7}{256} A(t_2, t_3)^4$$

Because $A(t_2, t_3)$ does not really depend on t_3 we get

$$B(t_3) = -\frac{1}{8}\left(1 - A(t_2, t_3) + \frac{7}{32} A(t_2, t_3)^4\right) t_3 + B_0,$$

where B_0 is a constant. Strictly speaking, the formula for $B(t_3)$ contradicts an earlier restriction, viz., B does not depend on t_2. But A depends on t_2! However, the formula for A shows that it is a slowly varying function of t, and as long as t is not too large we may assume that A is a constant. For a more thorough discussion of how to avoid this contradiction, the interested reader is referred to [145].

Let us see what the approximation is for the initial values $y(0) = 0$, $y'(0) = -0.1$, if we only consider the approximation $y = y_0 + \epsilon y_1$ and set ϵ equal to 1.

```
>   restart: alias( e=epsilon ):
>   y := eta[0] + e*eta[1];
```

$$y := \eta_0 + \epsilon\,\eta_1$$

```
>   eta[0] := t -> A(t)*sin(t+B(t));
```

$$\eta_0 := t \rightarrow A(t)\sin(t + B(t))$$

```
>   eta[1] := t -> -1/32*A(t)^3*cos(3*t+3*B(t));
```

$$\eta_1 := t \rightarrow -\frac{1}{32}\,A(t)^3\cos(3t + 3\,B(t))$$

```
>   B := t-> -1/8*(1-A(t)^2+7/32*A(t)^4)*e^2*t+b;
```

$$B := t \rightarrow -\frac{1}{8}\,(1 - A(t)^2 + \frac{7}{32}\,A(t)^4)\,\epsilon^2\,t + b$$

```
>   A := t-> -2/(1+c*exp(-e*t));
```

$$A := t \rightarrow -2\,\frac{1}{1 + c\,e^{(-\epsilon t)}}$$

```
>   e := 1:    y := unapply( y(t), t ):
>   fsolve( { y(0)=0, D(y)(0)=-0.1 }, {b,c},
>      {b=-0.1..0.1} );
```

$$\{\,b = .0004073638406, c = 16.51715658\,\}$$

```
>   assign(");
```

Let us plot this function (Figure 17.18).

```
>   plot( y(t), t=0..20 );
```

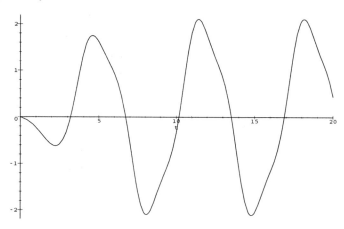

FIGURE 17.18. Solution of the van der Pol equation by the method of multiple scales.

17.8   Partial Differential Equations

For one unknown function u of two independent variables, say x and t, the most general partial differential equation (abbreviated PDE) is an equation of the form

$$F(x, t, u, u_x, u_t, u_{xx}, u_{xt}, u_{tt}, \ldots),$$

where the subscripts are a standard notation for partial differentiation with respect to the indicated variables:

$$u_x = \frac{\partial u}{\partial x}, \ u_{xt} = \frac{\partial^2 u}{\partial x \partial t}, \ u_{tt} = \frac{\partial^2 u}{\partial t^2}, \ \ldots$$

The *order* of the PDE is defined in analogy with that for an ODE as the highest-order derivative appearing in the PDE. So, the most general first-order PDE may be written as a function of x, t, u, u_x, and u_t:

$$F(x, t, u, u_x, u_t) = 0.$$

If F is a polynomial equation of degree r in the highest-order partial derivative, then the PDE is said to be of *degree* r. In particular, if F is linear, then the PDE is also called *linear*. An equation that is of first degree in the highest-order partial derivative but contains other nonlinear terms is called *quasi-linear*. Some famous examples:

$$
\begin{aligned}
u_t - u_{xx} &= 0 \quad \text{heat equation or diffusion equation:} \\
&\qquad \text{a linear PDE of order 2,} \\
u_{tt} - u_{xx} &= 0 \quad \text{wave equation: a linear PDE of order 2,} \\
u_t - u\,u_x + u_{xxx} &= 0 \quad \text{Korteweg–de Vries equation:} \\
&\qquad \text{a quasi-linear PDE of order 3 and degree 1.}
\end{aligned}
$$

We have already seen that PDEs can be solved numerically by the procedure **PDEplot** from the DEtools package. But Maple can also solve some PDEs analytically. The procedure **pdesolve** (**partial differential equation solver**) does the job. Some examples:

```
>   wavePDE := diff(u(x,t),[t$2]) -
>     1/v^2 * diff(u(x,t),[x$2]);
```

$$wavePDE := \left(\frac{\partial^2}{\partial t^2}\, \mathrm{u}(x, t) \right) - \frac{\frac{\partial^2}{\partial x^2}\, \mathrm{u}(x, t)}{v^2}$$

```
>   pdesolve( wavePDE, u(x,t) );
```

$$\mathrm{u}(x, t) = \_F1(-t - v\,x) + \_F2(t - v\,x)$$

Here, _F1 and _F2 are arbitrary functions.

```
>   PDE := a*x*diff(u(x,t),x) + b*t*diff(u(x,t),t) = 0;
```

$$PDE := a\,x \left(\frac{\partial}{\partial x}\, \mathrm{u}(x, t) \right) + b\,t \left(\frac{\partial}{\partial t}\, \mathrm{u}(x, t) \right) = 0$$

```
>   pdesolve( ", u(x,t) );
```

$$u(\,x,t\,) = \_F1(\,\frac{t}{x^{(\frac{b}{a})}}\,)$$

```
>   PDE := a*x^2*diff(u(x,t),x) + b*t^2*diff(u(x,t),t) = 0;
```

$$PDE := a\,x^2\,(\,\frac{\partial}{\partial x}\,\mathrm{u}(\,x,t\,)\,) + b\,t^2\,(\,\frac{\partial}{\partial t}\,\mathrm{u}(\,x,t\,)\,) = 0$$

```
>   pdesolve( PDE, u(x,t) );
```

$$u(\,x,t\,) = \_F1(\,\frac{-b\,t + a\,x}{t\,a\,x}\,)$$

```
>   PDE := diff(u(x,t),x$2) - t^2*diff(u(x,t),t$2)
>      - t*diff(u(x,t),t)=0;
```

$$PDE := (\,\frac{\partial^2}{\partial x^2}\,\mathrm{u}(\,x,t\,)\,) - t^2\,(\,\frac{\partial^2}{\partial t^2}\,\mathrm{u}(\,x,t\,)\,) - t\,(\,\frac{\partial}{\partial t}\,\mathrm{u}(\,x,t\,)\,) = 0$$

```
>   pdesolve( PDE, u(x,t) );
```

$$u(\,x,t\,) = \_F1(\,t\,\mathrm{e}^x\,) + \_F2(\,\frac{t}{\mathrm{e}^x}\,)$$

If Maple does not come back with a straight answer, don't give up too soon. For example, let us have a look at the heat equation $u_t = u_{xx}$.

```
>   heatPDE := diff(u(x,t),t) = diff(u(x,t),[x$2]);
```

$$heatPDE := \frac{\partial}{\partial t}\,\mathrm{u}(\,x,t\,) = \frac{\partial^2}{\partial x^2}\,\mathrm{u}(\,x,t\,)$$

```
>   pdesolve( heatPDE, u(x,t) );
```

$$pdesolve\left(\frac{\partial}{\partial t}\,\mathrm{u}(\,x,t\,) = \frac{\partial^2}{\partial x^2}\,\mathrm{u}(\,x,t\,), \mathrm{u}(\,x,t\,)\right)$$

No solution found. We apply the Fourier transform with respect to the space coordinate.

```
>   with(inttrans):  # load library package
>   diffeqn := fourier( heatPDE, x, w );
```

$$diffeqn := \frac{\partial}{\partial t}\,fourier(\,\mathrm{u}(\,x,t\,),x,w\,) = -w^2\,fourier(\,\mathrm{u}(\,x,t\,),x,w\,)$$

Let us assume an initial condition $u(x,0) = T\delta(x)$, so that the Fourier transform of it is known. We actually have to solve the following ODE.

```
>   ODE := subs( fourier(u(x, t), x, w) = U(t), diffeqn );
```

$$ODE := \frac{\partial}{\partial t}\,\mathrm{U}(\,t\,) = -w^2\,\mathrm{U}(\,t\,)$$

The initial condition is as follows:

```
>   initval := U(0) = fourier( T*Dirac(x), x, w );
```

$$initval := \mathrm{U}(\,0\,) = T$$

Maple has no problem with solving this initial value problem.

```
>  dsolve( { ODE, initval }, U(t) );
```

$$U(t) = e^{(-w^2\,t)}\,T$$

We carry out the back transformation under the assumption $t > 0$.

```
>  assume(t>0):
>  u(x,t) = invfourier( rhs("), w, x );
```

$$\mathrm{u}(x,t\tilde{\;}) = \frac{1}{2}\,\frac{T\,\sqrt{\dfrac{\pi}{t\tilde{\;}}}\,e^{\left(-1/4\frac{x^2}{t\tilde{\;}}\right)}}{\pi}$$

```
>  simplify(");
```

$$\mathrm{u}(x,t\tilde{\;}) = \frac{1}{2}\,\frac{T\,e^{\left(-1/4\frac{x^2}{t\tilde{\;}}\right)}}{\sqrt{t\tilde{\;}}\,\sqrt{\pi}}$$

Thus, assisting Maple, we have found a solution of the initial value problem. The method of separation of variables is another example of how you can obtain solutions of boundary value problems by assisting the computer algebra system.

17.9   Lie Point Symmetries of PDEs

One of the most useful techniques for studying differential equations is the Lie symmetry method. In Maple, the `liesymm` package provides tools to apply Lie symmetry methods in the formalism developed by Harrison and Estabrook [35, 96]. In this section, we shall use the package for finding the Lie symmetries of the Korteweg–de Vries equation

$$u_t + u\,u_x + u_{xxx} = 0,$$

using the abbreviated notation for partial derivatives.

```
>  with(liesymm):  # load library package
>  KdV_eqn := Diff(u(t,x),t) + u(t,x)*Diff(u(t,x),x)
>     + Diff(u(t,x),[x$3])=0;
```

$$KdV\_eqn := \left(\frac{\partial}{\partial t}\,\mathrm{u}(t,x)\right) + \mathrm{u}(t,x)\left(\frac{\partial}{\partial x}\,\mathrm{u}(t,x)\right) + \left(\frac{\partial^3}{\partial x^3}\,\mathrm{u}(t,x)\right) = 0$$

The general idea of Lie symmetry methods for partial differential equations is the following [149, 166, 172]. A *Lie point symmetry* for the PDE

$$\omega(t,x,u,u_t,u_x,u_{tt},u_{tx},u_{xx},\dots) = 0$$

is a mapping

$$t \to \bar{t}(t,x,u), \quad x \to \bar{x}(t,x,u), \quad u \to \bar{u}(t,x,u)$$

such that the new variables obey the original equation. Usually, one considers only one-parameter groups of Lie point symmetries. In this case, the infinitesimal mappings are

$$t \to t + \epsilon\tau, \quad x \to x + \epsilon\xi, \quad u \to u + \epsilon\eta.$$

The PDE is unchanged if

$$X\omega = 0$$

for the operator

$$X = \tau\partial_t + \xi\partial_x + \eta\partial_u + \ldots.$$

This property leads to a system of linear homogeneous PDEs for the functions τ, ξ, and η. This is called the *determining system*. In Maple, you can compute it with the procedure **determine**.

```
>  eqns[1] := determine( KdV_eqn, V, u(t,x), w );
```

$$eqns_1 := \left\{ \frac{\partial^2}{\partial u^2} V2(t, x, u) = 0, \right.$$

$$\frac{\partial}{\partial t} V3(t, x, u) = -u\left(\frac{\partial}{\partial x} V3(t, x, u)\right) - \left(\frac{\partial^3}{\partial x^3} V3(t, x, u)\right),$$

$$\frac{\partial^3}{\partial x^3} V1(t, x, u) = 3\left(\frac{\partial}{\partial x} V2(t, x, u)\right) - \left(\frac{\partial}{\partial t} V1(t, x, u)\right),$$

$$\frac{\partial^3}{\partial x\, \partial u^2} V3(t, x, u) = \frac{\partial^3}{\partial x^2\, \partial u} V2(t, x, u),\ \frac{\partial^2}{\partial u^2} V1(t, x, u) = 0,$$

$$\frac{\partial^3}{\partial u^3} V1(t, x, u) = 0,\ \frac{\partial^2}{\partial x\, \partial u} V1(t, x, u) = 0,$$

$$\frac{\partial^3}{\partial x\, \partial u^2} V1(t, x, u) = 0,\ \frac{\partial^3}{\partial x^2\, \partial u} V1(t, x, u) = 0,\ \frac{\partial^3}{\partial x^3} V2(t, x, u)$$

$$= 2u\left(\frac{\partial}{\partial x} V2(t, x, u)\right) + 3\left(\frac{\partial^3}{\partial x^2\, \partial u} V3(t, x, u)\right) + V3(t, x, u)$$

$$- \left(\frac{\partial}{\partial t} V2(t, x, u)\right),\ \frac{\partial^3}{\partial u^3} V3(t, x, u) = 3\left(\frac{\partial^3}{\partial x\, \partial u^2} V2(t, x, u)\right),$$

$$\frac{\partial^2}{\partial u^2} V3(t, x, u) = 3\left(\frac{\partial^2}{\partial x\, \partial u} V2(t, x, u)\right),\ \frac{\partial}{\partial u} V1(t, x, u) = 0,$$

$$\frac{\partial}{\partial x} V1(t, x, u) = 0,\ \frac{\partial^2}{\partial x^2} V2(t, x, u) = \frac{\partial^2}{\partial x\, \partial u} V3(t, x, u),$$

$$\left. \frac{\partial^3}{\partial u^3} V2(t, x, u) = 0,\ \frac{\partial^2}{\partial x^2} V1(t, x, u) = 0,\ \frac{\partial}{\partial u} V2(t, x, u) = 0 \right\}$$

Here, the following change of notation has been used.

$$V1 = \tau, \quad V2 = \xi, \quad V3 = \eta$$

Maple provides the procedure **autosimp** to simplify the determining system, or if you are lucky, to solve it completely. Let us see what happens in our case.

```
>  eqns[2] := autosimp( eqns[1] );
```

$$eqns_2 := \{\ \}\ \&\text{where}\ \Big\{V3\_2(t,x) = x\,C7 + C5, V3\_5(t) = C5,$$

$$V3\_4(t) = C7, V3\_3(t) \doteq -t\,C7 + C4,$$

$$V3\_1(t,x) = -t\,C7 + C4,$$

$$V3(t,x,u) = u\,(-t\,C7 + C4\,) + x\,C7 + C5,$$

$$V2(t,x,u) = x\,(t\,C7 + C8\,) + t\,C5 + C6,$$

$$V2\_1(t,x) = x\,(t\,C7 + C8\,) + t\,C5 + C6,$$

$$-t\,C7 - 2\,C8 - C4 = 0, V1\_2(t) = C9 + \frac{3}{2}\,t^2\,C7 + 3\,C8\,t,$$

$$V1(t,x,u) = C9 + \frac{3}{2}\,t^2\,C7 + 3\,C8\,t, V2\_2(t) = t\,C7 + C8,$$

$$V2\_3(t) = t\,C5 + C6\Big\}$$

Maple has solved the determining system of equations. But the solution contains the equation $t\,C7 - C4 - 2\,C8 = 0$, which can only be satisfied for all values of t if $C7 = 0$ and $C4 = -2\,C8$. When we do this substitution, we obtain the following expressions for $V1$, $V2$, and $V3$.

```
>  eqns := subs( C7=0,C4=-2*C8, op(2,eqns[2]) ):
>  select( has, eqns, {V1,V2,V3} );
```

$$\{V1(t,x,u) = C9 + 3\,C8\,t, V3(t,x,u) = -2\,u\,C8 + C5,$$

$$V2(t,x,u) = x\,C8 + t\,C5 + C6\}$$

We were lucky and have found the general solution

$$\tau = c_9 + 3c_8 t,$$
$$\xi = c_6 + c_5 t + c_8 x,$$
$$\eta = c_5 - 2c_8 u,$$

where c_5, c_6, c_8, and c_9 are arbitrary constants. So, the four-dimensional symmetry algebra of the Korteweg–de Vries equation (KdV) is spanned by the symmetries tabulated below.

Symmetry	Meaning
∂_t	time translation
∂_x	space translation
$t\partial_x + \partial_u$	Galilean boost
$x\partial_x + 3t\partial_t - 2u\partial_u$	scaling

TABLE 17.5. Lie point symmetries of KdV-equation.

The benefit of the above Lie symmetries is that if $u = f(t, x)$ is a solution of the Korteweg–de Vries equation, so are

$$
\begin{aligned}
u_1 &= f(t - \epsilon, x), \\
u_2 &= f(t, x - \epsilon), \\
u_3 &= f(t, x - \epsilon t) + \epsilon, \\
u_4 &= e^{-2\epsilon} f(e^{-3\epsilon} t, e^{-\epsilon} x),
\end{aligned}
$$

for all real ϵ.

Despite the above success it must be remarked that the current integration capabilities in *liesymm* for solving the determining system automatically are limited. Therefore, quite some work must still be done manually. A very nice overview of other packages for determining symmetries of partial differential equations can be found in [101].

17.10   Exercises

1. Show that
$$
\sqrt{a^2 - y^2} - a \ln(a + \sqrt{a^2 - y^2}) + a \ln y + x = C
$$
is an implicit solution of the differential equation
$$
y' = -\frac{y}{\sqrt{a^2 - y^2}},
$$
which describes the trajectory of an object that is pulled with a rope of length a by someone who walks along the x-axis to the right.

2. Solve the following ODEs with Maple. Try several methods, try to find the solutions in their simplest form, and check if Maple finds all solutions.

    (a) $3y^2 y' + 16x = 12xy^3$.

    (b) $y' = 2\dfrac{y}{x} - \left(\dfrac{y}{x}\right)^2$.

    (c) $xy' - y = x \tan\left(\dfrac{y}{x}\right)$.

3. Some ODEs of degree larger than one can be solved with Maple. Consider the following two examples.

    (a) Solve $y'^2 - y^2 = 0$.

    (b) Solve $y'^2 + xy = y^2 + xy'$.

    Do these two examples give you any clue of how Maple attacks higher degree ODEs?

4. Solve the following ODEs with Maple and check the answers.

    (a) $x^4 y'' - (2x^2 - 1)xy' + y = 0$.

(b) $x^2 y'' + 3xy' + (x^2 - 35)y = x.$

(c) $y' + xy^2 = 1.$

5. Consider the initial value problem

$$y'' - y = 0, \quad y(0) = 1, \quad y'(0) = 0.$$

(a) Find the solutions via the method of Laplace transforms.

(b) Redo (a) after you have given printlevel the value 3.

(c) Repeat (a), but now with printlevel equal to 33.

6. Compute the first 10 terms in a Taylor series solution of the following initial value problem.

$$y' = yz, \quad z' = xz + y, \quad y(0) = 1, \quad z(0) = 0.$$

7. Consider Airy's differential equation,

$$y'' + xy = 0.$$

(a) Find the solution for initial values $y(0) = 1$ and $y'(0) = 0$ via the power series method. Which terms of degree less than 30 occur in the solution?

(b) What recurrence relation holds for the coefficients of the power series found in (a)?

(c) Find the solution for initial values $y(0) = 0$ and $y'(0) = 1$ via the power series method. Which terms of degree less than 30 occur in the solution?

8. Consider Duffing's differential equation,

$$x'' + x + \epsilon x^3 = \epsilon F \cos \omega t.$$

Apply the Poincaré-Lindstedt method to find an approximation of a periodic solution of the ODE that satisfies the initial values

$$x(0) = A \quad \text{and} \quad x'(0) = 0.$$

What are the results when you apply the method of multiple scales and how do both methods compare to a numerical approximation?

9. Compute the determining system for Burgers' equation

$$u_t = u_{xx} + 2u \, u_x = 0,$$

and compute the symmetry algebra.

10. Compute the determining system for the Boltzmann equation,

$$u_{tx} + u_x + u^2 = 0,$$

and try to compute the symmetry algebra. (Hint: you may have to load the procedure **pdint** of the "hidden" package liesymm/difftools.)

18
Linear Algebra: The `linalg` Package

This chapter discusses Maple's basic facilities for computing with matrices, not only elementary matrix operations like addition and multiplication, but also high-level computations like determinants, inverses, eigenvalues, and eigenvectors. We shall give a survey of facilities that the linear algebra package, called `linalg`, provides. For the special evaluation rules for vectors and matrices we refer to §12.6.

18.1 Loading the `linalg` Package

Before you start calculating with vectors and matrices it is wise to load the `linalg` package, which is especially designed for computations in linear algebra.

```
>  with(linalg);

Warning, new definition for norm
Warning, new definition for trace
```

[*BlockDiagonal, GramSchmidt, JordanBlock, LUdecomp, QRdecomp,*
  Wronskian, addcol, addrow, adj, adjoint, angle, augment, backsub, band,
  basis, bezout, blockmatrix, charmat, charpoly, cholesky, col, coldim,
  colspace, colspan, companion, concat, cond, copyinto, crossprod, curl,
  definite, delcols, delrows, det, diag, diverge, dotprod, eigenvals,
  eigenvalues, eigenvectors, eigenvects, entermatrix, equal, exponential,

extend, ffgausselim, fibonacci, forwardsub, frobenius, gausselim,
gaussjord, geneqns, genmatrix, grad, hadamard, hermite, hessian, hilbert,
htranspose, ihermite, indexfunc, innerprod, intbasis, inverse, ismith,
issimilar, iszero, jacobian, jordan, kernel, laplacian, leastsqrs, linsolve,
matadd, matrix, minor, minpoly, mulcol, mulrow, multiply, norm,
normalize, nullspace, orthog, permanent, pivot, potential, randmatrix,
randvector, rank, ratform, row, rowdim, rowspace, rowspan, rref,
scalarmul, singularvals, smith, stack, submatrix, subvector, sumbasis,
swapcol, swaprow, sylvester, toeplitz, trace, transpose, vandermonde,
vecpotent, vectdim, vector, wronskian]

The warnings after loading the package remind you that the functions
norm and **trace** already existed in Maple and that they are replaced by
procedures from the `linalg` package with the same names. You can get
back to the previous definition of a procedure by explicitly reloading it.
For example, to get back the original definition of **norm**, which is for computing the norm of a polynomial, you can enter the following command.

```
>  readlib( norm );
```

$$\mathrm{proc}(p, n, v) \ldots \mathrm{end}$$

Let us undo this and reload the **linalg[norm]** procedure.

```
>  with( linalg, norm );
```

Warning, new definition for norm

$$[\,norm\,]$$

From the above list of available functions, it is clear that most popular matrix operations are available: multiplication and addition of matrices, row
and column operations on matrices, Gaussian elimination and row-reduced
echelon form, determinant, trace, and inverse of a matrix, characteristic
polynomial, characteristic matrix, eigenvectors and eigenvalues, and so on.
Information about individual `linalg` functions can be obtained from the
on-line help system. In this chapter, we shall only present a couple of examples by which the most popular matrix calculations are covered. More
examples can be found in [110]. In the next chapter, we shall look at advanced applications of linear algebra. But practicing yourself will be the
best way to learn about the linear algebra facilities and their usefulness.

> *We assume throughout this chapter that the linalg package has*
> *been loaded.*

18.2   Creating New Vectors and Matrices

Recall from §12.4 that vectors and matrices are implemented in Maple as
arrays. They can be created by calling the procedure **array**. This allows

indexing functions such as *symmetric* and *sparse*. Alternatively, you can use the routines **vector** and **matrix**. This way of creating vectors and matrices is very convenient if you can specify the values of all entries at once through use of an index function. A few examples:

```
>   A := array( 1..2, 1..3, [[a,b,c],[d,e,f]] );
```

$$A := \left[\begin{array}{ccc} a & b & c \\ d & e & f \end{array} \right]$$

```
>   B := array( sparse, antisymmetric, 1..2, 1..2 ):
>   B[1,2] := x:   print(B);
```

$$\left[\begin{array}{cc} 0 & x \\ -x & 0 \end{array} \right]$$

```
>   v := vector( [1,2,3] );
```

$$v := [\, 1, 2, 3 \,]$$

```
>   C := matrix( 4, 4, (i,j) -> i^(j-1) );
```

$$C := \left[\begin{array}{cccc} 1 & 1 & 1 & 1 \\ 1 & 2 & 4 & 8 \\ 1 & 3 & 9 & 27 \\ 1 & 4 & 16 & 64 \end{array} \right]$$

The matrix C is a special case of a Vandermonde matrix; you can convince yourself by using the built-in function **vandermonde**.

```
>   vandermonde( [1,2,3,4] );
```

$$\left[\begin{array}{cccc} 1 & 1 & 1 & 1 \\ 1 & 2 & 4 & 8 \\ 1 & 3 & 9 & 27 \\ 1 & 4 & 16 & 64 \end{array} \right]$$

Maple has more built-in routines for special matrices; Table 18.1 lists them. We refer to the on-line help system for detailed information.

The **entermatrix** procedure prompts you for the values of matrix elements, one by one.

```
>   M := array( antisymmetric, 1..3, 1..3 ):
>   entermatrix( M );

enter element 1,2 > alpha;
enter element 1,3 > beta;
enter element 2,3 > gamma;
```

$$M := \left[\begin{array}{ccc} 0 & \alpha & \beta \\ -\alpha & 0 & \gamma \\ -\beta & -\gamma & 0 \end{array} \right]$$

Procedure	Matrix
JordanBlock	Jordan block matrix
bezout	Bezout matrix of two polynomials
companion	companion matrix associated with a polynomial
fibonacci	Fibonacci matrix
grad	vector gradient of an expression
hessian	Hessian matrix of an expression
hilbert	generalized Hilbert matrix
jacobian	Jacobian matrix of a vector function
sylvester	Sylvester matrix of two polynomials
toeplitz	symmetric Toeplitz matrix corresponding to a list
vandermonde	Vandermonde matrix corresponding to a list
wronskian	Wronskian matrix of a list of functions

TABLE 18.1. Procedures related to special vectors and matrices.

Banded matrices and diagonal matrices can be created with the procedures **band** and **diag**, respectively.

```
>   band( [-1,2,1], 4 );
```

$$
\begin{bmatrix}
2 & 1 & 0 & 0 \\
-1 & 2 & 1 & 0 \\
0 & -1 & 2 & 1 \\
0 & 0 & -1 & 2
\end{bmatrix}
$$

```
>   diag( mu, nu );
```

$$
\begin{bmatrix}
\mu & 0 \\
0 & \nu
\end{bmatrix}
$$

```
>   diag( "", " );
```

$$
\begin{bmatrix}
2 & 1 & 0 & 0 & 0 & 0 \\
-1 & 2 & 1 & 0 & 0 & 0 \\
0 & -1 & 2 & 1 & 0 & 0 \\
0 & 0 & -1 & 2 & 0 & 0 \\
0 & 0 & 0 & 0 & \mu & 0 \\
0 & 0 & 0 & 0 & 0 & \nu
\end{bmatrix}
$$

The last example shows how the procedure **diag** can also be used to create a block matrix out of earlier defined matrices. In §18.5 we shall discuss other `linalg` procedures that allow you to create new vectors and matrices from old ones.

An example of a routine to build up a matrix from another data structure is **genmatrix**; it creates the coefficient matrix associated with a system of linear equations. An example:

```
>   eqns := { (c^2-1)*x + (c-1)*y = (1-c)^2,
>      (c-1)*x + (c^2-1)*y = c-1 };
```

$$eqns := \{\, (c^2 - 1)\, x + (c - 1)\, y = (1 - c)^2, (c - 1)\, x + (c^2 - 1)\, y = c - 1 \}$$

```
>   genmatrix( eqns, [x,y], 'flag' );
```

$$\begin{bmatrix} c^2 - 1 & c - 1 & (1 - c)^2 \\ c - 1 & c^2 - 1 & c - 1 \end{bmatrix}$$

Now you can use matrix algebra to solve the original system of equations. But why would you do this and not simply use **solve**? Look what happens if you apply this procedure to the system of equations.

```
>   solve( eqns, {x,y} );
```

$$\left\{ y = 2\, \frac{1}{c\,(c + 2)}, x = \frac{-2 + c^2}{c\,(c + 2)} \right\}$$

One solution! But if you look more closely at the system of equations, then you see that for $c = 1$ all pairs (x, y) satisfy the equations, and that there does not exist a solution for $c = 0$ and for $c = -2$. However, if you apply linear algebra methods and compute the Hermite normal form (row reduced echelon form over $\mathbb{Q}(c)$), then the special cases become obvious.

```
>   genmatrix( eqns, [x,y], 'flag' );
```

$$\begin{bmatrix} c^2 - 1 & c - 1 & (1 - c)^2 \\ c - 1 & c^2 - 1 & c - 1 \end{bmatrix}$$

```
>   hermite( ", c );
```

$$\begin{bmatrix} c - 1 & c^2 - 1 & c - 1 \\ 0 & -2c + c^3 + c^2 & -2 + 2c \end{bmatrix}$$

```
>   map( factor, " );
```

$$\begin{bmatrix} c - 1 & (c + 1)(c - 1) & c - 1 \\ 0 & c(c + 2)(c - 1) & -2 + 2c \end{bmatrix}$$

Let us continue with the survey of creating vectors and matrices. Random vector and random matrix generators are available through the procedures **randvector** and **randmatrix**, respectively. Options will give you the flexibility to determine the form of the matrix and its entries. The form of the matrix is one of the following: sparse, dense (default), symmetric, antisymmetric, or unimodular (i.e., with determinant 1). If an optional argument takes the form entries = f for a Maple procedure f then f is called to generate an entry. The default function is **rand(-99..99)**, i.e., random two digit integers. One example will do.

```
>   poly := proc() randpoly( x, terms=3, degree=3 ) end:
>   randmatrix( 3, 3, entries=poly, unimodular );
```

$$\begin{bmatrix} 1 & -55\, x^3 - 37\, x - 35 & 50\, x^2 + 79\, x + 56 \\ 0 & 1 & 63\, x^3 + 57\, x - 59 \\ 0 & 0 & 1 \end{bmatrix}$$

Last but not least, you can create a matrix by reading data from a file. Consider a datafile, say `mapledata`, in the current directory and three lines long with the following contents

```
1        2        3
4        5        6
7        8        9
```

With **readdata** you can import the data and then store them in matrix format.

```
>   readlib(readdata):
>   mat := matrix( readdata( matrixdata, 3, integer ) );
```

$$mat := \begin{bmatrix} 1 & 2 & 3 \\ 4 & 5 & 6 \\ 7 & 8 & 9 \end{bmatrix}$$

See §4.4 and §4.5 for more details about importing/exporting data and low level I/O.

18.3   Vector and Matrix Arithmetic

For demonstration purposes we shall use the following matrices:

```
>   A := matrix( 2, 2, [ a, b, c, d ] );
```

$$A := \begin{bmatrix} a & b \\ c & d \end{bmatrix}$$

```
>   B := toeplitz( [ alpha, beta ] );
```

$$B := \begin{bmatrix} \alpha & \beta \\ \beta & \alpha \end{bmatrix}$$

```
>   C := matrix( 3, 2, (i,j) -> i+j-1 );
```

$$C := \begin{bmatrix} 1 & 2 \\ 2 & 3 \\ 3 & 4 \end{bmatrix}$$

Because of the last name evaluation of arrays you cannot add the matrices A and B by

```
>   A + B;
```

$$A + B$$

Instead, you can use **matadd** (**mat**rix **add**ition).

```
>   matadd( A, B );
```

$$\begin{bmatrix} a + \alpha & b + \beta \\ c + \beta & d + \alpha \end{bmatrix}$$

But the most convenient way to calculate with matrices is to use the Maple procedure **evalm** (**eval**uate using **m**atrix arithmetic).

> evalm(A + B);

$$\begin{bmatrix} a + \alpha & b + \beta \\ c + \beta & d + \alpha \end{bmatrix}$$

> evalm(3*A - 2/7*B);

$$\begin{bmatrix} 3a - \dfrac{2}{7}\alpha & 3b - \dfrac{2}{7}\beta \\[2ex] 3c - \dfrac{2}{7}\beta & 3d - \dfrac{2}{7}\alpha \end{bmatrix}$$

Addition of scalars is also possible; the main diagonal is increased by the scalar value.

> evalm(A - 1);

$$\begin{bmatrix} a - 1 & b \\ c & d - 1 \end{bmatrix}$$

> evalm(C + c);

$$\begin{bmatrix} 1 + c & 2 \\ 2 & 3 + c \\ 3 & 4 \end{bmatrix}$$

You cannot use the operator * for matrix multiplication; this operator is reserved in Maple as the *commutative* multiplication operator.

> A*B + 2*B*A;

$$3\,A\,B$$

> A*A + B*C*B;

$$A^2 + B^2\,C$$

As you see, Maple does not take into account the data type of the names A, B, and C when it carries out automatic simplification operations. And, when you want to compute the matrix product with **evalm**, Maple does not always compute what you think it should.

> evalm(B * A);

```
Error, (in evalm/evaluate)
use the &* operator for matrix/vector multiplication
```

You must use the multiplication operator &* or the procedure **multiply** for multiplication of matrices.

> evalm(B &* A);

$$\begin{bmatrix} \alpha a + \beta c & \alpha b + \beta d \\ \beta a + \alpha c & \beta b + \alpha d \end{bmatrix}$$

```
> evalm( A &* B );
```

$$\left[\begin{array}{cc} \alpha a + \beta b & \beta a + \alpha b \\ \alpha c + \beta d & \beta c + \alpha d \end{array}\right]$$

The multiplication operator &* can also be used for multiplication of matrices with vectors. Maple considers vectors as column vectors or row vectors depending on the context.

```
> v := vector( [x,y] );  w := vector([xi,eta]);
```

$$v := [x, y]$$
$$w := [\xi, \eta]$$

```
> evalm( A &* v );   # v used as column vector
```

$$[a x + b y, c x + d y]$$

```
> evalm( v &* A );   # v used as row vector
```

$$[a x + y c, x b + d y]$$

```
> evalm( v &* w );   # mixed situation as inner product
```

$$x \xi + y \eta$$

If you want a column vector be indeed represented in column format, e.g., for educational purposes, then you can use the following trick of the trade. Let us look at the print routine **print/array/vector**, which is actually used to print a vector.

```
> interface( verboseproc=2 ):
> print( `print/array/vector` );

proc(A,aname)
local i,n,lA,v;
options `Copyright 1992 by the University of Waterloo`;
    i := [op(2,A)];
    n := op(2,i[1]);
    lA := A;
    v := `VECTOR`([seq(eval(lA[i],1),i = 1 .. n)]);
    subs(`lA` = aname,v)
end
```

You see that Maple constructs a function call **VECTOR(...)** for display. All we have to do is to mimic the above source code, but produce a list as final result with the attribute column. Henceforth, Maple will print vectors in column format.

```
> `print/array/vector` := proc(A,aname)
>     local i,n,lA,v,column;
>     i := [ op(2,A) ];
>     n := op(2,i[1]);
>     lA := A;
>     v := [ seq( eval(lA[i],1), i=1..n) ];
>     subs( `lA`=aname, v );
```

```
>    setattribute( v, column )
>  end:
>  print( v );
```

$$\begin{bmatrix} x \\ y \end{bmatrix}$$

```
>  evalm( A &* v );
```

$$\begin{bmatrix} a\,x + b\,y \\ c\,x + d\,y \end{bmatrix}$$

Matrix powers can be computed with the usual operator ^.

```
>  evalm( B^3 );
```

$$\begin{bmatrix} (\alpha^2 + \beta^2)\,\alpha + 2\,\alpha\,\beta^2 & (\alpha^2 + \beta^2)\,\beta + 2\,\alpha^2\,\beta \\ (\alpha^2 + \beta^2)\,\beta + 2\,\alpha^2\,\beta & (\alpha^2 + \beta^2)\,\alpha + 2\,\alpha\,\beta^2 \end{bmatrix}$$

With the **map** procedure, you can simplify all matrix entries at the same time.

```
>  map( factor, " );
```

$$\begin{bmatrix} \alpha\,(\alpha^2 + 3\,\beta^2) & \beta\,(3\,\alpha^2 + \beta^2) \\ \beta\,(3\,\alpha^2 + \beta^2) & \alpha\,(\alpha^2 + 3\,\beta^2) \end{bmatrix}$$

Not only natural numbers are accepted by Maple as exponents; negative integral exponents can also be used, provided that the matrix is not singular.

```
>  evalm( B^(-3) );
```

$$\begin{bmatrix} -\dfrac{\%1\,\alpha}{-\alpha^2 + \beta^2} - 2\,\dfrac{\alpha\,\beta^2}{(-\alpha^2 + \beta^2)^3} & \dfrac{\%1\,\beta}{-\alpha^2 + \beta^2} + 2\,\dfrac{\alpha^2\,\beta}{(-\alpha^2 + \beta^2)^3} \\ \dfrac{\%1\,\beta}{-\alpha^2 + \beta^2} + 2\,\dfrac{\alpha^2\,\beta}{(-\alpha^2 + \beta^2)^3} & -\dfrac{\%1\,\alpha}{-\alpha^2 + \beta^2} - 2\,\dfrac{\alpha\,\beta^2}{(-\alpha^2 + \beta^2)^3} \end{bmatrix}$$

$$\%1 := \frac{\alpha^2}{(-\alpha^2 + \beta^2)^2} + \frac{\beta^2}{(-\alpha^2 + \beta^2)^2}$$

```
>  evalm( " &* """ ):
```

Make sure that you enter a space after the **&*** operator; otherwise the operator is not recognized. We have not shown the output because it is rather long. But this matrix simplifies indeed to the identity matrix.

```
>  map( normal, " ); # the expected answer
```

$$\begin{bmatrix} 1 & 0 \\ 0 & 1 \end{bmatrix}$$

Automatic simplification may sometimes surprise you.

```
>  evalm( A^0 );
```

```
>  whattype(");
```

$$integer$$

Furthermore, because the **&*** operator has the same priority as the multiplication and division operators * and /, you should be cautious about precedence of operators. Sometimes you have to use parentheses.

```
>  evalm( A &* 1/A );
```

```
Error, (in evalm/amperstar)
&* is reserved for matrix multiplication
```

```
>  evalm( A &* (1/A) );
```

$$\&*( )$$

Maple uses **&*()** for the identity matrix. With **lprint** you can see what is going on here.

```
>  lprint( A &* 1/A );
```

```
&*(A,1)/A
```

```
>  lprint( A &* (1/A) );
```

```
&*( A, 1/A )
```

18.4   Basic Matrix Functions

The procedures **trace** and **det** compute the trace and the determinant of a matrix, respectively. Let us apply them to the following Toeplitz matrix.

```
>  toeplitz( [1,2,3] );
```

$$\begin{bmatrix} 1 & 2 & 3 \\ 2 & 1 & 2 \\ 3 & 2 & 1 \end{bmatrix}$$

```
>  trace(");
```

$$3$$

```
>  det("");
```

$$8$$

The row and column rank of a matrix, bases for the row and column spaces, and a basis for the kernel of a matrix can be easily computed.

```
>  A := matrix( [ [1,0,0,1], [1,0,1,1], [0,0,1,0] ] );
```

$$A := \begin{bmatrix} 1 & 0 & 0 & 1 \\ 1 & 0 & 1 & 1 \\ 0 & 0 & 1 & 0 \end{bmatrix}$$

```
>  rank(A);
```
$$2$$

```
>  rowspace(A), colspace(A);
```
$$\{[0,0,1,0],[1,0,0,1]\},\{[1,0,-1],[0,1,1]\}$$

```
>  kernel(A);
```
$$\{[0,1,0,0],[-1,0,0,1]\}$$

Computation of the characteristic polynomial, eigenvalues, and eigenvectors is in principle possible; but exact calculus may of course come to the deadlock of an unsolvable characteristic equation.

```
>  A := matrix( [ [-2,2,3], [3,7,-8], [10,-4,-3] ] );
```
$$A := \begin{bmatrix} -2 & 2 & 3 \\ 3 & 7 & -8 \\ 10 & -4 & -3 \end{bmatrix}$$

```
>  cp := charpoly( A, lambda );
```
$$cp := \lambda^3 - 2\lambda^2 - 97\lambda + 282$$

The Cayley-Hamilton theorem states that substitution of the matrix A in its characteristic polynomial yields the zero matrix. Let us check this.

```
>  evalm( subs( lambda=A, cp ) );
```
$$\begin{bmatrix} 0 & 0 & 0 \\ 0 & 0 & 0 \\ 0 & 0 & 0 \end{bmatrix}$$

The characteristic equation must be solved to obtain the eigenvalues of A.

```
>  solve( cp );
```
$$3, -\frac{1}{2} + \frac{1}{2}\sqrt{377}, -\frac{1}{2} - \frac{1}{2}\sqrt{377}$$

The eigenvalues could have been obtained straight away with the procedure **eigenvalues** (or **eigenvals**).

```
>  eigenvalues( A );
```
$$3, -\frac{1}{2} + \frac{1}{2}\sqrt{377}, -\frac{1}{2} - \frac{1}{2}\sqrt{377}$$

Eigenvectors can be computed with **eigenvectors** (or **eigenvects**).

```
>  eigenvectors( A );
```
$$[3, 1, \{\left[\frac{14}{13}, \frac{31}{26}, 1\right]\}], [-\frac{1}{2} + \frac{1}{2}\sqrt{377}, 1, \{\left[\frac{-1}{2}, -\frac{15}{8} - \frac{1}{8}\sqrt{377}, 1\right]\}],$$
$$[-\frac{1}{2} - \frac{1}{2}\sqrt{377}, 1, \{\left[\frac{-1}{2}, -\frac{15}{8} + \frac{1}{8}\sqrt{377}, 1\right]\}]$$

You get a sequence of lists. Each list consists of an eigenvalue, its multiplicity, and a basis of the eigenspace. By default, Maple computes the eigenvalues and eigenvectors using radicals. You can state this explicitly by adding the keyword `radical`. To compute implicitly in terms of **RootOf**s, use the `implicit` notation. Later on, you can compute all values with the procedure **allvalues**. The eigenvalues can also be computed in **RootOf** notation.

```
>   eigenvalues( A, `implicit` );
```
$$3, \text{RootOf}(\_Z^2 + \_Z - 94)$$

```
>   eigenvectors( A, `implicit` );
```

$$[3, 1, \{ \left[\frac{14}{13}, \frac{31}{26}, 1 \right] \}],$$

$$[\text{RootOf}(\_Z^2 + \_Z - 94), 1, \{ \left[\frac{-1}{2}, -\frac{1}{4} \text{RootOf}(\_Z^2 + \_Z - 94) - 2, 1 \right] \}]$$

```
>   map( allvalues, ["], `dependent` );
```

$$[[3, 1, \{ \left[\frac{14}{13}, \frac{31}{26}, 1 \right] \}], [-\frac{1}{2} + \frac{1}{2} \sqrt{377}, 1, \{ \left[\frac{-1}{2}, -\frac{15}{8} - \frac{1}{8} \sqrt{377}, 1 \right] \}],$$

$$[-\frac{1}{2} - \frac{1}{2} \sqrt{377}, 1, \{ \left[\frac{-1}{2}, -\frac{15}{8} + \frac{1}{8} \sqrt{377}, 1 \right] \}]]$$

Until now, most of our matrices had rational coefficients. In fact, all procedures in the `linalg` package work for matrices over the ring of polynomials with rational coefficients. But for many procedures, coefficients may come from a wider class; complex numbers, algebraic numbers, and algebraic functions are allowed in many cases. Below is one example of a Toeplitz matrix.

```
>   A := toeplitz( [ sqrt(2), alpha, beta ] );
```

$$A := \begin{bmatrix} \sqrt{2} & \alpha & \beta \\ \alpha & \sqrt{2} & \alpha \\ \beta & \alpha & \sqrt{2} \end{bmatrix}$$

```
>   factor( det(A), sqrt(2) );
```
$$-\sqrt{2} \, (\beta + \sqrt{2} - \sqrt{2} \, \alpha^2) \, (-\sqrt{2} + \beta)$$

```
>   charpoly( A, lambda );
```
$$\lambda^3 - 3 \lambda^2 \sqrt{2} + 6 \lambda - 2 \lambda \alpha^2 - 2 \sqrt{2} + 2 \sqrt{2} \, \alpha^2 - 2 \beta \alpha^2 - \beta^2 \lambda + \beta^2 \sqrt{2}$$

```
>   factor( ", sqrt(2) );
```
$$-(-2 + 2 \alpha^2 + 2 \lambda \sqrt{2} - \lambda^2 + \beta \lambda - \beta \sqrt{2}) \, (-\sqrt{2} + \beta + \lambda)$$

> eigenvalues(A);

$$\sqrt{2} + \frac{1}{2}\beta + \frac{1}{2}\sqrt{\beta^2 + 8\alpha^2}, \ \sqrt{2} + \frac{1}{2}\beta - \frac{1}{2}\sqrt{\beta^2 + 8\alpha^2}, \ -\beta + \sqrt{2}$$

> eigenvectors(A);

$$[\sqrt{2} + \frac{1}{2}\beta + \frac{1}{2}\%1, 1, \{[1, -\frac{\frac{1}{2}\beta - \frac{1}{2}\%1}{\alpha}, 1]\}],$$

$$[\sqrt{2} + \frac{1}{2}\beta - \frac{1}{2}\%1, 1, \{[1, -\frac{\frac{1}{2}\beta + \frac{1}{2}\%1}{\alpha}, 1]\}],$$

$$[-\beta + \sqrt{2}, 1, \{[-1, 0, 1]\}]$$

$$\%1 := \sqrt{\beta^2 + 8\alpha^2}$$

However, some functions do not allow both floating-point numbers and symbolic expressions.

> A := map(evalf, A);

$$A := \begin{bmatrix} 1.414213562 & \alpha & \beta \\ \alpha & 1.414213562 & \alpha \\ \beta & \alpha & 1.414213562 \end{bmatrix}$$

> eigenvectors(A);

Error, (in linalg/evalf)
matrix entries must all evaluate to float

The error message suggests that in this example Maple wants to switch to a numerical eigenvector routine, but it cannot do this as the matrix contains the symbols α and β. A trick that works in such cases is to convert the floating-point numbers to rational numbers, do the requested computation, and evaluate the intermediate result numerically.

> Digits := 4: # low precision for display reasons
> A := map(convert, A, rational);

$$A := \begin{bmatrix} \frac{41}{29} & \alpha & \beta \\ \alpha & \frac{41}{29} & \alpha \\ \beta & \alpha & \frac{41}{29} \end{bmatrix}$$

> eigenvectors(A);

$$[\frac{41}{29} + \frac{1}{2}\beta + \frac{1}{2}\%1, 1, \{[1, -\frac{1}{29}\frac{\frac{29}{2}\beta - \frac{29}{2}\%1}{\alpha}, 1]\}],$$

$$[\frac{41}{29} + \frac{1}{2}\beta - \frac{1}{2}\%1, 1, \{[1, -\frac{1}{29}\frac{\frac{29}{2}\beta + \frac{29}{2}\%1}{\alpha}, 1]\}],$$

$$[\frac{41}{29} - \beta, 1, \{[-1, 0, 1]\}]$$

$$\%1 := \sqrt{\beta^2 + 8\alpha^2}$$

```
> map( evalf, ["] );
```

$$[[1.414 + .5000\,\beta + .5000\,\%1, 1.,$$

$$\{[1., -.03448\frac{14.50\,\beta - 14.50\,\%1}{\alpha}, 1.]\}],$$

$$[1.414 + .5000\,\beta - .5000\,\%1, 1.,$$

$$\{[1., -.03448\frac{14.50\,\beta + 14.50\,\%1}{\alpha}, 1.]\}],$$

$$[1.414 - 1.\,\beta, 1., \{[-1., 0, 1.]\}]]$$

$$\%1 := \sqrt{\beta^2 + 8.\,\alpha^2}$$

Table 18.2 surveys the basic functions that are available in the linalg package.

Procedure	Computed Object
adj, adjoint	adjoint of a matrix
charmat	characteristic matrix
charpoly	characteristic polynomial
cond	condition number of a matrix
det	determinant of a matrix
eigenvalues, eigenvals	eigenvalues of a matrix
eigenvectors, eigenvects	eigenvectors of a matrix
hadamard	Hadamard bound
htranspose	Hermitian transpose of a matrix,
inverse	inverse of a matrix
kernel	kernel of a matrix
minor	minor of a matrix
minpoly	minimum polynomial of a matrix
permanent	permanent of a matrix
rank	rank of a matrix
singularvals	singular values of a matrix
trace	trace of a matrix
transpose	transpose of a matrix

TABLE 18.2. Basic functions in linalg package.

18.5   Structural Operations

Maple provides many functions for structural operations of matrices; we list them in Table 18.3.

Procedure	Purpose
addcol	form a linear combination of two matrix columns
addrow	form a linear combination of two matrix rows
augment, concat	join matrices together horizontally
blockmatrix	create a block matrix
col	extract column(s) from a matrix as vector(s)
coldim	determine column dimension of a matrix
copyinto	move entries from one matrix into another
delcols	delete columns of a matrix
delrows	delete rows of a matrix
extend	enlarge a matrix
mulcol	multiply a column of a matrix by an expression
mulrow	multiply a row of a matrix by an expression
row	extract row(s) from a matrix as vector(s)
rowdim	determine row dimension of a matrix
scalarmul	multiply a vector or matrix by an expression
stack	join vectors or matrices together vertically
submatrix	extract a submatrix from a matrix
subvector	extract a subvector from a matrix
swapcol	swap two columns in a matrix
swaprow	swap two rows in a matrix

TABLE 18.3. Structural operators.

The `linalg` package also contains functions to verify whether a matrix belongs to a certain class or is related to another matrix; see Table 18.4 below.

Procedure	Test for
definite	positive (or negative) definite matrix
equal	equality of matrices
issimilar	similarity of matrices
iszero	zero matrix
orthog	orthogonal matrix

TABLE 18.4. Test functions for matrices.

Two examples will do. We start with a Jordan block and an identity matrix of the same dimension.

```
>  J := JordanBlock(2,4);
```

$$J := \begin{bmatrix} 2 & 1 & 0 & 0 \\ 0 & 2 & 1 & 0 \\ 0 & 0 & 2 & 1 \\ 0 & 0 & 0 & 2 \end{bmatrix}$$

```
>  Id := band([1],4);
```

$$Id := \begin{bmatrix} 1 & 0 & 0 & 0 \\ 0 & 1 & 0 & 0 \\ 0 & 0 & 1 & 0 \\ 0 & 0 & 0 & 1 \end{bmatrix}$$

We join these matrices horizontally.

```
>  augment( J, Id );
```

$$\begin{bmatrix} 2 & 1 & 0 & 0 & 1 & 0 & 0 & 0 \\ 0 & 2 & 1 & 0 & 0 & 1 & 0 & 0 \\ 0 & 0 & 2 & 1 & 0 & 0 & 1 & 0 \\ 0 & 0 & 0 & 2 & 0 & 0 & 0 & 1 \end{bmatrix}$$

We reduce this matrix to reduced row echelon form using **gaussjord**.

```
>  gaussjord(");
```

$$\begin{bmatrix} 1 & 0 & 0 & 0 & \frac{1}{2} & \frac{-1}{4} & \frac{1}{8} & \frac{-1}{16} \\ 0 & 1 & 0 & 0 & 0 & \frac{1}{2} & \frac{-1}{4} & \frac{1}{8} \\ 0 & 0 & 1 & 0 & 0 & 0 & \frac{1}{2} & \frac{-1}{4} \\ 0 & 0 & 0 & 1 & 0 & 0 & 0 & \frac{1}{2} \end{bmatrix}$$

The 4×4 submatrix on the right should be the inverse of the original Jordan block matrix.

```
>  Jinv := submatrix( ", 1..4, 5..8 );
```

$$Jinv := \begin{bmatrix} \frac{1}{2} & \frac{-1}{4} & \frac{1}{8} & \frac{-1}{16} \\ 0 & \frac{1}{2} & \frac{-1}{4} & \frac{1}{8} \\ 0 & 0 & \frac{1}{2} & \frac{-1}{4} \\ 0 & 0 & 0 & \frac{1}{2} \end{bmatrix}$$

```
>  equal( Jinv, inverse(J) );
```

$$true$$

The second example will demonstrate the matrix test functions. Consider the following two matrices.

```
>  A := matrix( [ [ (sqrt(5)+sqrt(2)*sqrt(5-sqrt(5))+1)/4,
>       -sqrt(2)*sqrt(5-sqrt(5))/2 ],
>    [ sqrt(2)*sqrt(5-sqrt(5))/4,
>       (sqrt(5)-sqrt(2)*sqrt(5-sqrt(5))+1)/4 ] ] );
```

$$A := \begin{bmatrix} \frac{1}{4}\sqrt{5} + \frac{1}{4}\%1 + \frac{1}{4} & -\frac{1}{2}\%1 \\ \frac{1}{4}\%1 & \frac{1}{4}\sqrt{5} - \frac{1}{4}\%1 + \frac{1}{4} \end{bmatrix}$$

$$\%1 := \sqrt{2}\sqrt{5 - \sqrt{5}}$$

```
>  B := matrix( [
>    [ (sqrt(5)+1)/4, -sqrt(2)*sqrt(5-sqrt(5))/4],
>    [ sqrt(2)*sqrt(5-sqrt(5))/4, (sqrt(5)+1)/4 ] ] );
```

$$B := \begin{bmatrix} \frac{1}{4}\sqrt{5} + \frac{1}{4} & -\frac{1}{4}\sqrt{2}\sqrt{5 - \sqrt{5}} \\ \frac{1}{4}\sqrt{2}\sqrt{5 - \sqrt{5}} & \frac{1}{4}\sqrt{5} + \frac{1}{4} \end{bmatrix}$$

We verify that they are similar, i.e., that there exists a nonsingular matrix T such that $B = T A T^{-1}$.

```
>  issimilar( A, B, 'T' );
```

$$true$$

```
>  T := map( simplify, T );
```

$$T := \begin{bmatrix} 1 & 0 \\ -1 & 2 \end{bmatrix}$$

```
>  equal( B,
>    map( simplify, evalm( T &* A &* inverse(T) ) ) );
```

$$true$$

B is indeed an orthogonal matrix.

```
>  orthog( B );
```

$$true$$

The matrix represents the counterclockwise rotation over the angle $\frac{\pi}{5}$.

18.6 Vector Operations

The following vector operations are available. We refer to §19.4 for examples from vector analysis.

Procedure	Computed Object
GramSchmidt	Gram-Schmidt orthogonalization of vectors
angle	angle between two vectors
basis	basis for a vector space
colspace	basis for the column space of a matrix
colspan	spanning vectors for column space of a matrix
crossprod	cross product (outer product) of two vectors
curl	curl of a vector
diverge	divergence of a vector function
dotprod, innerprod	dot product (inner product) of two vectors
intbasis	basis for the intersection of vector spaces
laplacian	Laplacian of an expression
norm	norm of a vector or matrix
normalize	normalized vector
nullspace	basis for the null space
potential	potential of a vector field
rowspace	basis for the row space of a matrix
rowspan	spanning vectors for row space of a matrix
sumbasis	basis for the sum of vector spaces
vecpotent	vector potential
vectdim	dimension of a vector

TABLE 18.5. Vector operations.

18.7 Standard Forms of Matrices

Maple provides facilities for various standard forms of matrices. They are listed in Table 18.6. Examples will give you a better idea of the power of the facilities.

Our first example will be the computation of the LU decomposition of the matrix
$$A = \begin{pmatrix} 0 & -1 & -3 \\ 4 & 5 & 1 \\ 1 & 4 & -1 \end{pmatrix}.$$

We search for a lower-triangular matrix L and an upper-triangular matrix U such that $A = PLU$ for some permutation matrix P.

Procedure	Standard Form
LUdecomp	LU decomposition
QRdecomp	QR decomposition
cholesky	Cholesky decomposition
exponential	matrix exponential
ffgausselim	fraction-free Gaussian elimination
frobenius, ratform	Frobenius form (rational canonical form)
gausselim	Gaussian elimination
gaussjord, rref	Gauss-Jordan form (row reduced echelon form)
hermite	Hermite normal form over univariate polynomials
ihermite	Hermite normal form over integers
ismith	Smith normal form over integers
jordan	Jordan form
smith	Smith normal form over univariate polynomials

TABLE 18.6. Test functions for matrices.

Frobenius, Gausselim, Gaussjord, Hermite, and **Smith** are equivalent but inert functions; you use them when you calculate over a finite field or over an algebraic (function) field.

```
>  A := matrix( [[0,-1,-3], [4,5,1], [1,4,-1] ] );
```

$$A := \begin{bmatrix} 0 & -1 & -3 \\ 4 & 5 & 1 \\ 1 & 4 & -1 \end{bmatrix}$$

```
>  LUdecomp( A,  L=´l´, U=´u´, P=´p´ ):
>  P = eval(p);
```

$$P = \begin{bmatrix} 0 & 1 & 0 \\ 1 & 0 & 0 \\ 0 & 0 & 1 \end{bmatrix}$$

```
>  L = eval(l);
```

$$L = \begin{bmatrix} 1 & 0 & 0 \\ 0 & 1 & 0 \\ \dfrac{1}{4} & -\dfrac{11}{4} & 1 \end{bmatrix}$$

```
>  U = eval(u);
```

$$U = \begin{bmatrix} 4 & 5 & 1 \\ 0 & -1 & -3 \\ 0 & 0 & -\dfrac{19}{2} \end{bmatrix}$$

```
> equal( evalm( p &* l &* u ), A );
```

$$true$$

The Cholesky decomposition of a positive-definite symmetric matrix A is a lower-triangular matrix L such that $A = L L^t$. We let Maple compute this decomposition for the matrix

```
> A := matrix( [ [5,-2,2], [-2,5,1], [2,1,2] ] );
```

$$A := \begin{bmatrix} 5 & -2 & 2 \\ -2 & 5 & 1 \\ 2 & 1 & 2 \end{bmatrix}$$

```
> L := cholesky( A );
```

$$L := \begin{bmatrix} \sqrt{5} & 0 & 0 \\ -\frac{2}{5}\sqrt{5} & \frac{1}{5}\sqrt{105} & 0 \\ \frac{2}{5}\sqrt{5} & \frac{3}{35}\sqrt{105} & \frac{1}{7}\sqrt{21} \end{bmatrix}$$

```
> equal( L &* transpose(L), A );
```

$$true$$

Let $A(x)$ be a matrix of polynomials over a field. Then there exist invertible matrices P and Q over this field, such that

$$A = P \, \mathrm{diag}(a_1(x), a_2(x), \ldots, a_k(x), 0, 0, \ldots, 0) \, Q,$$

where a_i's are polynomials for which a_i divides a_{i+1}. The a_i's are called invariant factors; they are unique up to multiplication by nonzero elements in the field, and k is fixed by A. The diagonal matrix is called the Smith normal form of $A(x)$. Let us consider the following matrix over $\mathbb{Q}[x]$.

```
> A := matrix( [ [1,0,-1,1], [-1,x+1,-x,-x-2],
>     [-1,x+1, 2*x^3+2*x^2-3*x-2, 2*x^3+2*x^2-3*x-4],
>     [0,-x-1,2*x^3+2*x^2-x-1,2*x^3+2*x^2-x-1] ] );
```

$$A := \begin{bmatrix} 1 & 0 & -1 & 1 \\ -1 & x+1 & -x & -x-2 \\ -1 & x+1 & 2x^3+2x^2-3x-2 & 2x^3+2x^2-3x-4 \\ 0 & -x-1 & 2x^3+2x^2-x-1 & 2x^3+2x^2-x-1 \end{bmatrix}$$

The Smith normal form can be computed in Maple by

```
> S := smith( A, x, 'U', 'V' );
```

$$S := \begin{bmatrix} 1 & 0 & 0 & 0 \\ 0 & x+1 & 0 & 0 \\ 0 & 0 & x^3+x^2-x-1 & 0 \\ 0 & 0 & 0 & 0 \end{bmatrix}$$

Let us verify the result.

```
>   P := inverse( U );
```

$$P := \begin{bmatrix} 1 & -3 + 4x^2 & 4 & -\dfrac{1}{2} \\[2mm] -1 & 2 - 2x^2 & -2 & \dfrac{1}{2} \\[2mm] -1 & 0 & 0 & 0 \\[1mm] 0 & -1 & 0 & 0 \end{bmatrix}$$

```
>   Q := inverse( V );
```

$$Q := \begin{bmatrix} 1 & -x - 1 & -2x^3 - 2x^2 + 3x + 2 & -2x^3 - 2x^2 + 3x + 4 \\ 0 & 1 & -2x^2 + 1 & -2x^2 + 1 \\ 0 & -1 & 2x^2 & 2x^2 \\ 0 & 0 & 0 & 1 \end{bmatrix}$$

```
>   equal( map( expand, evalm( P &* S &* Q ) ), A );
```

$$true$$

Now, we consider the matrix A over $\mathbb{F}_2[x]$, i.e., we compute modulo 2.

```
>   A := map( `mod`, A, 2 );
```

$$A := \begin{bmatrix} 1 & 0 & 1 & 1 \\ 1 & x+1 & x & x \\ 1 & x+1 & x & x \\ 0 & x+1 & x+1 & x+1 \end{bmatrix}$$

```
>   Smith( A, x ) mod 2;
```

$$\begin{bmatrix} 1 & 0 & 0 & 0 \\ 0 & x+1 & 0 & 0 \\ 0 & 0 & 0 & 0 \\ 0 & 0 & 0 & 0 \end{bmatrix}$$

Note that this is different from computing the Smith normal form over $\mathbb{Q}[x]$ and afterward doing modular arithmetic.

```
>   map( `mod`, smith( A, x ), 2 );
```

$$\begin{bmatrix} 1 & 0 & 0 & 0 \\ 0 & 1 & 0 & 0 \\ 0 & 0 & x+1 & 0 \\ 0 & 0 & 0 & 0 \end{bmatrix}$$

The same phenomenon holds for the other standard form reductions. Let us compute some of them using the last matrix A.

```
>   A = eval(A);
```

$$A = \begin{bmatrix} 1 & 0 & 1 & 1 \\ 1 & x+1 & x & x \\ 1 & x+1 & x & x \\ 0 & x+1 & x+1 & x+1 \end{bmatrix}$$

> F := frobenius(A, 'P'); # over Q(x)

$$F := \begin{bmatrix} 0 & 0 & 0 & 0 \\ 1 & 0 & 0 & 2\,x+2 \\ 0 & 1 & 0 & -4\,x-2 \\ 0 & 0 & 1 & 3\,x+3 \end{bmatrix}$$

> equal(map(normal, evalm(P &* F &* P^(-1)))), A);

$$true$$

> F := Frobenius(A, 'P') mod 2; # over F_2[x]

$$F := \begin{bmatrix} 0 & 0 & 0 & 0 \\ 1 & 0 & 0 & 0 \\ 0 & 1 & x+1 & 0 \\ 0 & 0 & 0 & 0 \end{bmatrix}$$

We verify the result.

> map(Normal, evalm(P &* F &* (Inverse(P) mod 2)))):
> equal(map('mod',",2), A);

$$true$$

> H := map(expand, hermite(A, x, 'T'));   # over Q[x]

$$\begin{bmatrix} 1 & 0 & 0 & 0 \\ 0 & x+1 & 0 & 0 \\ 0 & 0 & 1 & 1 \\ 0 & 0 & 0 & 0 \end{bmatrix}$$

> equal(map(expand, evalm(T &* A)), H);

$$true$$

> H := Hermite(A, x, 'T') mod 2; # over F_2[x]

$$H := \begin{bmatrix} 1 & 0 & 1 & 1 \\ 0 & x+1 & x+1 & x+1 \\ 0 & 0 & 0 & 0 \\ 0 & 0 & 0 & 0 \end{bmatrix}$$

> equal(map('mod', evalm(T &* A), 2), H);

$$true$$

> gausselim(A);   # Gaussian elimination over Z(x)

$$\begin{bmatrix} 1 & 0 & 1 & 1 \\ 0 & x+1 & x-1 & x-1 \\ 0 & 0 & 2 & 2 \\ 0 & 0 & 0 & 0 \end{bmatrix}$$

> ffgausselim(A); # fraction-free Gaussian elimination

$$
\begin{bmatrix}
1 & 0 & 1 & 1 \\
0 & x+1 & x-1 & x-1 \\
0 & 0 & 2x+2 & 2x+2 \\
0 & 0 & 0 & 0
\end{bmatrix}
$$

> Gausselim(A) mod 2; # Gaussian elimination over F_2[x]

$$
\begin{bmatrix}
1 & 0 & 1 & 1 \\
0 & x+1 & x+1 & x+1 \\
0 & 0 & 0 & 0 \\
0 & 0 & 0 & 0
\end{bmatrix}
$$

> gaussjord(A);   # Gauss-Jordan form over Q(x)

$$
\begin{bmatrix}
1 & 0 & 0 & 0 \\
0 & 1 & 0 & 0 \\
0 & 0 & 1 & 1 \\
0 & 0 & 0 & 0
\end{bmatrix}
$$

> Gaussjord(A) mod 2; # Gauss-Jordan form over F_2(x)

$$
\begin{bmatrix}
1 & 0 & 1 & 1 \\
0 & 1 & 1 & 1 \\
0 & 0 & 0 & 0 \\
0 & 0 & 0 & 0
\end{bmatrix}
$$

18.8   Exercises

1. Consider the following matrices.

$$
A = \begin{pmatrix} 1 & 0 & 2 \\ 2 & -1 & 3 \\ 4 & 1 & 8 \end{pmatrix}, \quad
B = \begin{pmatrix} -3 & 2 \\ 0 & 1 \\ 7 & 4 \end{pmatrix}
$$

Compute:

(a) A^{-1}

(b) AA^t

(c) $B^t AB$

(d) $\left(2A + BB^t\right) A^t$

2. Compute the Wronskian of the following list of functions: $[\cos x, \sin x, e^x]$. Compute the determinant of this matrix. Do the same computation for the list $[\cosh x, \sinh x, e^x]$.

3. Create a 5×5 matrix with entries randomly chosen as univariate polynomials with integral coefficients, three terms, and degree less than 5. Compute the characteristic polynomial and verify the Cayley-Hamilton theorem by substitution of the matrix in the characteristic polynomial when it is collected in the main variable. Also compute the Horner form of the characteristic polynomial and verify the Cayley-Hamilton theorem by substitution of the matrix in the polynomial in Horner form. Compare timings.

4. Consider the matrices

$$A = \begin{pmatrix} -4 & -7 & 0 \\ 0 & 4 & 2 \\ -5 & -7 & 1 \end{pmatrix}$$

and

$$B = \begin{pmatrix} -2 & -1 & -2 \\ 2 & 2 & -2 \\ 0 & 0 & 1 \end{pmatrix}.$$

Show that A and B are similar and compute the corresponding transformation matrix.

5. Let $a, b \in \mathbb{R}$ with $0 \le a \le 1$, $b^2 = 2a(1-a)$, and

$$A = \begin{pmatrix} a & a-1 & b \\ a-1 & a & b \\ -b & -b & 2a-1 \end{pmatrix}.$$

(a) Check with Maple that A is an orthogonal matrix with determinant equal to one.

(b) From (a) follows that A is a matrix that describes a rotation in the standard basis of $\mathbb{R}^3$. Determine the rotation axis.

6. Let $a, b \in \mathbb{R}$ and

$$A = \begin{pmatrix} 0 & a & 1 & 0 & b \\ 1 & 0 & 0 & b & 0 \\ 0 & 1 & b & 0 & 1 \\ b & 0 & 0 & 1 & 0 \\ 0 & b & 1 & 0 & b \end{pmatrix}.$$

(a) For what values of a and b is the matrix A singular?

(b) Determine the inverse of A (for those values of a and b for which A is invertible).

7. (a) Compute det $\begin{pmatrix} x^2+1 & x & 0 & 0 \\ x & x^2+1 & x & 0 \\ 0 & x & x^2+1 & x \\ 0 & 0 & x & x^2+1 \end{pmatrix}.$

(b) Compute det $\begin{pmatrix} x^2+1 & x & 0 & 0 & 0 \\ x & x^2+1 & x & 0 & 0 \\ 0 & x & x^2+1 & x & 0 \\ 0 & 0 & x & x^2+1 & x \\ 0 & 0 & 0 & x & x^2+1 \end{pmatrix}.$

(c) Looking at the results of (a) and (b), do you have any idea what the determinant of a general matrix of the above form is? If so, check your conjecture for a 8×8 matrix. If not, compute the determinants for matrices of dimension 6 and 7 to get an idea.

8. For each natural number n, the $n \times n$ matrix A_n is defined as

$$A_n(i,j) = \begin{cases} 0, & \text{if } i = j, \\ 1, & \text{if } i \neq j. \end{cases}$$

Carry out the following computations for $n = 3$, 4, and 5.

(a) Compute the determinant of A_n.

(b) Compute the characteristic polynomial of A_n.

(c) Determine all eigenvalues of A_n and determine for each eigenvalue a basis of the corresponding eigenspace.

9. For each natural number n, the $n \times n$ matrix A_n is defined as

$$A_n(i,j) = \gcd(i,j).$$

(a) Compute the determinant of A_n for $n = 1, 2, \ldots, 15$.

(b) (for the mathematicians among us) Try to find a closed formula for the general case.

10. Compute the LU decomposition of the following matrix A, taken from [50].

$$A = \begin{pmatrix} 6 & 2 & 1 & -1 \\ 2 & 4 & 1 & 0 \\ 1 & 1 & 4 & -1 \\ -1 & 0 & -1 & 3 \end{pmatrix}$$

11. Let A be the following 5×5 matrix over the field F_2 with two elements.

$$A = \begin{pmatrix} 0 & 0 & 0 & 1 & 0 \\ 0 & 0 & 1 & 0 & 1 \\ 0 & 0 & 0 & 0 & 1 \\ 1 & 0 & 0 & 1 & 0 \\ 0 & 1 & 0 & 0 & 0 \end{pmatrix}$$

Determine a transformation matrix T over F_2 such that $T^{-1}AT$ is of the form

$$A = \begin{pmatrix} B & 0 \\ 0 & C \end{pmatrix},$$

where B is a 2×2 matrix over F_2 and C is a 3×3 matrix over F_2.

19

Linear Algebra: Applications

This chapter illustrates matrix computations with five practical examples. They arc:

- Kinematics of the Stanford manipulator.

- A three-compartmental model of cadmium transfer through the human body.

- Molecular-orbital Hückel theory.

- Vector analysis.

- Moore-Penrose inverse.

In all sessions we shall assume that the `linalg` package has been loaded.

19.1   Kinematics of the Stanford Manipulator

The matrices below are so-called Denavit-Hartenberg matrices used in kinematics studies of robot manipulators; actually, we shall use the matrices A_1, A_2, ..., A_6 defining the Stanford manipulator [151]. Henceforth, we shall use in the Maple session the abbreviations $c_1 = \cos\theta_1$, $c_2 = \cos\theta_2$, ..., $s_1 = \sin\theta_1$, $s_2 = \sin\theta_2$, ...

```
>   alias( seq( c[i] = cos(theta[i]), i=1..6 ),
>     seq( s[i] = sin(theta[i]), i=1..6 ) ):
>   M := (a,alpha,d,theta) -> matrix( 4, 4, [cos(theta),
>     -sin(theta)*cos(alpha), sin(theta)*sin(alpha),
>     a*cos(theta), sin(theta), cos(theta)*cos(alpha),
>     -cos(theta)*sin(alpha), a*sin(theta), 0, sin(alpha),
>     cos(alpha), d, 0, 0, 0, 1 ] ):
>   M(a,alpha,d,theta);
```

$$
\begin{bmatrix}
\cos(\theta) & -\sin(\theta)\cos(\alpha) & \sin(\theta)\sin(\alpha) & a\cos(\theta) \\
\sin(\theta) & \cos(\theta)\cos(\alpha) & -\cos(\theta)\sin(\alpha) & a\sin(\theta) \\
0 & \sin(\alpha) & \cos(\alpha) & d \\
0 & 0 & 0 & 1
\end{bmatrix}
$$

```
>   # link length
>   a := vector([0$6]):
>   # link twist
>   alpha := vector([-Pi/2,Pi/2,0,-Pi/2,Pi/2,0]):
>   # offset distance
>   d := vector([0$6]):
>   d[2] := evaln(d[2]): d[3] := evaln(d[3]):
>   # joint angle
>   theta := vector(6): theta[3] := 0:
>   for i to 6 do
>     A[i] := M( a[i], alpha[i], d[i], theta[i] )
>   od;
```

$$
A_1 := \begin{bmatrix}
c_1 & 0 & -s_1 & 0 \\
s_1 & 0 & c_1 & 0 \\
0 & -1 & 0 & 0 \\
0 & 0 & 0 & 1
\end{bmatrix}
$$

$$
A_2 := \begin{bmatrix}
c_2 & 0 & s_2 & 0 \\
s_2 & 0 & -c_2 & 0 \\
0 & 1 & 0 & d_2 \\
0 & 0 & 0 & 1
\end{bmatrix}
$$

$$
A_3 := \begin{bmatrix}
1 & 0 & 0 & 0 \\
0 & 1 & 0 & 0 \\
0 & 0 & 1 & d_3 \\
0 & 0 & 0 & 1
\end{bmatrix}
$$

$$
A_4 := \begin{bmatrix}
c_4 & 0 & -s_4 & 0 \\
s_4 & 0 & c_4 & 0 \\
0 & -1 & 0 & 0 \\
0 & 0 & 0 & 1
\end{bmatrix}
$$

$$
A_5 := \begin{bmatrix}
c_5 & 0 & s_5 & 0 \\
s_5 & 0 & -c_5 & 0 \\
0 & 1 & 0 & 0 \\
0 & 0 & 0 & 1
\end{bmatrix}
$$

$$A_6 := \begin{bmatrix} c_6 & -s_6 & 0 & 0 \\ s_6 & c_6 & 0 & 0 \\ 0 & 0 & 1 & 0 \\ 0 & 0 & 0 & 1 \end{bmatrix}$$

The position and orientation of the tip of the manipulator is determined by the Denavit-Hartenberg parameters; it is the product of the matrices $A_1, \ldots, A_6$.

>   Tip := evalm(`&*`(seq(A[i], i=1..6))):

Let us look at the entry in the upper left corner.

>   collect(Tip[1,1], [c[1],c[2],s[1]]);

$$((-s_6\, s_4 + c_6\, c_5\, c_4)\, c_2 - c_6\, s_2\, s_5)\, c_1 + (-s_6\, c_4 - c_6\, c_5\, s_4)\, s_1$$

This is in agreement with formula 2.55 in [151]. By hand, such matrix computations take much time and are error-prone; the computer algebra system really does its work here as symbol cruncher.

An example of how computer algebra can help to solve the inverse kinematics problem, i.e., how to compute the link parameters for a given position and orientation of the tip of a robot arm, can be found in [81].

In this section, we shall study the forward kinematics problem, and more precisely, the velocities of the tip of the Stanford manipulator. Once the physical geometry of the robot arm is fixed, i.e., once d_2 and d_3 are fixed, the tip of the robot arm is a function of θ_1, θ_2, θ_4, θ_5, and θ_6. We shall determine the translational velocity v and rotational velocity ω of the tip as a function of θ_1', θ_2', θ_4', θ_5', and θ_6'. First, we split the translation part T and rotational part R of the matrix that describe the location and orientation of the tip of the robot arm. This is easily done with the procedures **subvector** and **submatrix**.

>   T := subvector(Tip, 1..3, 4);

$$T := \begin{bmatrix} c_1\, s_2\, d_3 - s_1\, d_2 & s_1\, s_2\, d_3 + c_1\, d_2 & c_2\, d_3 \end{bmatrix}$$

>   R := submatrix(Tip, 1..3, 1..3):

The information about the translational and rotational velocity is contained in the Jacobian matrix

$$J = \begin{pmatrix} J_1^v & J_2^v & \cdots & J_5^v \\ J_1^\omega & J_2^\omega & \cdots & J_5^\omega \end{pmatrix},$$

where $J = (\, J_1^v \quad J_2^v \quad \cdots \quad J_5^v \,)$ is the Jacobian matrix of the vector function that maps the kinematic parameters θ_1, θ_2, θ_4, θ_5, and θ_6 into the translational submatrix T. The J_i^ω's are 3×1 vectors defined as

$$J_i^\omega = \begin{pmatrix} \omega_{x_i} \\ \omega_{y_i} \\ \omega_{z_i} \end{pmatrix},$$

where the components can be found with respect to the kinematic parameters from the relation

$$\frac{\partial R}{\partial \theta_i} \cdot R^T = \begin{pmatrix} 0 & -\omega_{z_i} & \omega_{y_i} \\ \omega_{z_i} & 0 & -\omega_{x_i} \\ -\omega_{y_i} & \omega_{x_i} & 0 \end{pmatrix}.$$

First, we shall consider the translational part. In the `linalg` package the procedure **jacobian** already exists for computing the Jacobian matrix of a vector valued function.

```
> Jv := jacobian( T,
>    [theta[1],theta[2],theta[4],theta[5],theta[6]] );
```

$$Jv := \begin{bmatrix} -s_1\,s_2\,d_3 - c_1\,d_2 & c_1\,c_2\,d_3 & 0 & 0 & 0 \\ c_1\,s_2\,d_3 - s_1\,d_2 & s_1\,c_2\,d_3 & 0 & 0 & 0 \\ 0 & -s_2\,d_3 & 0 & 0 & 0 \end{bmatrix}$$

Next, we shall consider the rotational velocity of the tip. We start with computing the derivatives $\frac{\partial R}{\partial \theta_i}$ by mapping the procedure **diff** to all matrix coefficients.

```
> R1 := map( diff, R, theta[1] ):
> R2 := map( diff, R, theta[2] ):
> R3 := map( diff, R, theta[4] ):
> R4 := map( diff, R, theta[5] ):
> R5 := map( diff, R, theta[6] ):
```

The transpose of a matrix can be computed with — to no one's surprise — **transpose**.

```
> Rtranspose := transpose( R ):
```

Now we have all ingredients for computing the matrices J_1^ω, J_2^ω, ..., J_5^ω. As an example, we show the results for J_1^ω.

```
> evalm( R1 &* Rtranspose ):  omega := map( simplify, " );
```

$$\omega := \begin{bmatrix} 0 & -1 & 0 \\ 1 & 0 & 0 \\ 0 & 0 & 0 \end{bmatrix}$$

```
> Jomega[1] := vector([omega[3,2],-omega[3,1],omega[2,1]]);
```

$$Jomega_1 := [\, 0 \quad 0 \quad 1 \,]$$

All other vectors may be computed in a loop; and finally we can concatenate them into the requested submatrix of J with **concat** or **augment**.

```
> for i from 2 to 5 do
>    evalm( R.i &* Rtranspose ):
>    omega := map( simplify, " ):
>    Jomega[i] := vector( [ omega[3,2], -omega[3,1],
>       omega[2,1] ] ):
>    print( Jomega[i]=eval(Jomega[i]) )
> od:
```

$$Jomega_2 = [\, -s_1 \quad c_1 \quad 0 \,]$$

$$Jomega_3 = \begin{bmatrix} c_1\, s_2 & s_1\, s_2 & c_2 \end{bmatrix}$$

$$Jomega_4 = \begin{bmatrix} -c_1\, s_4\, c_2 - s_1\, c_4 & -s_1\, s_4\, c_2 + c_1\, c_4 & s_4\, s_2 \end{bmatrix}$$

$$Jomega_5 = \begin{bmatrix} s_5\, c_1\, c_2\, c_4 - s_5\, s_1\, s_4 + c_1\, s_2\, c_5 & s_5\, s_1\, c_2\, c_4 + s_5\, c_1\, s_4 + s_1\, s_2\, c_5 \\ -s_2\, c_4\, s_5 + s_5 + c_2\, c_5 \end{bmatrix}$$

```
>   Jomega := concat( seq( eval(Jomega[i]), i=1..5 ) ):
```

The translational and rotational part of J can be placed below each other in one matrix with the `linalg` procedure **stack**.

```
>   J := stack( Jv, Jomega );
```

$$J := \begin{bmatrix} & -s_1\, s_2\, d_3 - c_1\, d_2 & c_1\, c_2\, d_3 & 0 & 0 & 0 \\ & c_1\, s_2\, d_3 - s_1\, d_2 & s_1\, c_2\, d_3 & 0 & 0 & 0 \\ & 0 & -s_2\, d_3 & 0 & 0 & 0 \\ 0 & -s_1 & c_1\, s_2 & -c_1\, s_4\, c_2 - s_1\, c_4 & s_5\, c_1\, c_2\, c_4 - s_5\, s_1\, s_4 + c_1\, s_2\, c_5 \\ 0 & c_1 & s_1\, s_2 & -s_1\, s_4\, c_2 + c_1\, c_4 & s_5\, s_1\, c_2\, c_4 + s_5\, c_1\, s_4 + s_1\, s_2\, c_5 \\ 1 & 0 & c_2 & s_4\, s_2 & -s_2\, c_4\, s_5 + c_2\, c_5 \end{bmatrix}$$

Consider the translational part of the Jacobian matrix.

```
>   print( Jv = eval(Jv) );
```

$$Jv = \begin{bmatrix} -s_1\, s_2\, d_3 - c_1\, d_2 & c_1\, c_2\, d_3 & 0 & 0 & 0 \\ c_1\, s_2\, d_3 - s_1\, d_2 & s_1\, c_2\, d_3 & 0 & 0 & 0 \\ 0 & -s_2\, d_3 & 0 & 0 & 0 \end{bmatrix}$$

The maximum rank is equal to two. If for some kinematic parameters the maximum rank is not reached, then we say that the manipulator is in a singular state. Singular states are forbidden configurations of the robot arm. Let us try to find such parameter values. What happens when $s_2 = 0$ (i.e., when $\theta_2 \in \{0, \pi\}$)?

```
>   subs( s[2]=0, eval(Jv) );
```

$$\begin{bmatrix} -c_1\, d_2 & c_1\, c_2\, d_3 & 0 & 0 & 0 \\ -s_1\, d_2 & s_1\, c_2\, d_3 & 0 & 0 & 0 \\ 0 & 0 & 0 & 0 & 0 \end{bmatrix}$$

```
>   submatrix( ", 1..2, 1..2 );
```

$$\begin{bmatrix} -c_1\, d_2 & c_1\, c_2\, d_3 \\ -s_1\, d_2 & s_1\, c_2\, d_3 \end{bmatrix}$$

The determinant of this submatrix can be computed with **det** .

```
>   det(");
```

$$0$$

So, the rank is less than two and the manipulator is in a singular state. When $s_2 \neq 0$ we can use elementary row operations to inspect the row space. For example, we can add $c_2 c_1 s_2$ times the third row to the first row with **addrow**.

```
>  addrow( Jv, 3, 1, c[2]*c[1]/s[2] );
```

$$\begin{bmatrix} -s_1 s_2 d_3 - c_1 d_2 & 0 & 0 & 0 & 0 \\ c_1 s_2 d_3 - s_1 d_2 & s_1 c_2 d_3 & 0 & 0 & 0 \\ 0 & -s_2 d_3 & 0 & 0 & 0 \end{bmatrix}$$

```
>  addrow( ", 3, 2, s[1]*c[2]/s[2] );
```

$$\begin{bmatrix} -s_1 s_2 d_3 - c_1 d_2 & 0 & 0 & 0 & 0 \\ c_1 s_2 d_3 - s_1 d_2 & 0 & 0 & 0 & 0 \\ 0 & -s_2 d_3 & 0 & 0 & 0 \end{bmatrix}$$

The rank is less than two if and only if the first column is equal to zero.

```
>  { "[1,1]=0, "[2,1]=0 };
```

$$\{-s_1 s_2 d_3 - c_1 d_2 = 0, c_1 s_2 d_3 - s_1 d_2 = 0\}$$

```
>  solve( ", {s[1],c[1]} );
```

$$\{s_1 = 0, c_1 = 0\}$$

This can only be true when both $\cos\theta_1$ and $\sin\theta_1$ are equal to zero, which is by definition impossible. No additional singular states of the manipulator are detected.

19.2   A Three-Compartment Model of Cadmium Transfer

The next example comes from a case study in linear system theory. In [25, 99], structural identifiability of several time-invariant, continuous-time, compartmental models, which describe the transfer of cadmium through the human body, have been studied. Here, we shall only consider the three-compartment model shown in Figure 19.1.

The corresponding mathematical model is a system of differential equations.

$$\begin{aligned} \frac{dx(t)}{dt} &= A\,x(t) + B\,u(t) \\ y(t) &= C\,x(t) \end{aligned}$$

where

$$A = \begin{pmatrix} -a_{21} & a_{12} & 0 \\ a_{21} & -(a_{02} + a_{12} + a_{32}) & a_{23} \\ 0 & a_{32} & -(a_{03} + a_{23}) \end{pmatrix}$$

and

$$B = \begin{pmatrix} 0 \\ 1 \\ 0 \end{pmatrix}, \qquad C = \begin{pmatrix} 0 & 0 & c_3 \\ 0 & a_{02} & a_{03} \end{pmatrix}.$$

All parameters are nonnegative. Two measurements of cadmium concentrations are done: measurements in the kidney are described by

$$y_1(t) = c_3 x_3(t)$$

and measurements in urine are described by

$$y_2(t) = a_{02}x_2(t) + a_{03}x_3(t).$$

The parameter c_3 is supposed to be known and positive.

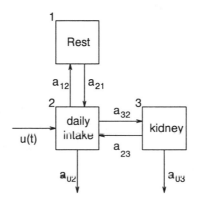

FIGURE 19.1. Cadmium transfer in the human body.

In general, a time-invariant, continuous-time, linear n-compartment model $M(\theta)$ that depends on parameters θ is described by

$$M(\theta) : \begin{cases} \dot{x}(t) &= A(\theta) \cdot x(t) + B(\theta) \cdot u(t), \quad x(t_0) = x_0, \\ y(t) &= C(\theta) \cdot x(t) + D(\theta) \cdot u(t), \end{cases}$$

where $A(\theta)$ is an $n \times n$ matrix, $B(\theta)$ is an $n \times m$ matrix, $C(\theta)$ is an $k \times n$ matrix, $D(\theta)$ is an $k \times m$ matrix, $x = (x_1, x_2, \cdots, x_n)^T$ is the state vector in $\mathbb{R}_+^n$, $u = (u_1, u_2, \cdots, u_m)^T$ is the input vector in $\mathbb{R}_+^m$, $y = (y_1, y_2, \cdots, y_k)^T$ is the output vector in R_+^k, and $\theta = (\theta_1, \cdots, \theta_r)$ is the parameter vector. Here, $\mathbb{R}_+$ denotes the set of nonnegative real numbers. The coefficients in the system matrix $A(\theta)$ satisfy

$$A_{ij} \geq 0 \text{ if } i \neq j, \quad A_{ii} \leq 0, \quad \text{and} \quad \sum_j A_{ji} \leq 0.$$

The coefficients in the input distribution matrix $B(\theta)$, the output connection matrix $C(\theta)$, and $D(\theta)$ are all nonnegative real numbers. The input and output are related through the so-called *external behavior* of the compartmental system which is defined as

$$y(t) = C(\theta) \, e^{(t-t_0)A(\theta)} \, x_0 + \int_{t_0}^{t} W_\theta(t - \tau) \, u(\tau) \, d\tau,$$

where

$$W_\theta(t) = C(\theta) \, e^{tA(\theta)} \, B(\theta) + D(\theta) \, \delta(t).$$

W_θ is called the *impulse response function* of the compartmental system. It is completely characterized by the so-called *Markov parameter matrices* $M_k(\theta)$, $k = 0, 1, 2, \ldots$ defined as

$$\begin{aligned} M_0(\theta) &= D \\ M_k(\theta) &= \frac{d^{k-1}}{dt^{k-1}} W_\theta(t) \Big|_{x=0} \\ &= C(\theta) \, A(\theta)^{k-1} \, B(\theta), \quad \text{for } k = 1, 2, \ldots \end{aligned}$$

Henceforth, we shall assume $D(\theta) = 0$.

Three notions in system theory are relevant in the study of theoretical (a priori) identifiability: *controllability*, *observability*, and *structural identifiability*. For a short introduction and the application of computer algebra, the interested reader is referred to [126, 157]. The following criteria hold:

Kalman's criterion for controllability. *The linear system is controllable iff the controllability matrix*

$$M_C = \left(B \,\middle|\, AB \,\middle|\, A^2 B \,\middle|\, \cdots \,\middle|\, A^{n-rb} B \right),$$

where $rb = \operatorname{rank}(B)$, has maximum rank n.

Kalman's criterion for observability. *The linear system is observable iff the observability matrix*

$$M_O = \begin{pmatrix} C \\ CA \\ CA^2 \\ \vdots \\ CA^{n-rc} \end{pmatrix},$$

where $rc = \operatorname{rank}(C)$, has maximum rank n.

Remark: You may always take $rb = rc = 1$ in the above criteria (e.g., if you do not know or cannot compute the rank of matrix C).

Now, the main question in parameter identifiability is roughly stated as follows.

"Is it in principle possible, given the observations of input and output, to uniquely determine the parameter values?"

Recall that the set of common zeroes of a set of polynomials is called an algebraic set. We shall use the following definitions of structural identifiability.

A model $M(\theta)$ is *structurally locally identifiable at* θ if there is an open neighborhood Ω around θ such that there is no $\theta' \in \Omega$ different from θ with the same external behavior for all identification experiments (t_0, x_0, u).

A model $M(\theta)$ is *structurally locally identifiable* if it is structurally locally identifiable for all θ outside an algebraic set.

A model $M(\theta)$ is *structurally globally identifiable at* θ if there is no θ' different from θ with the same external behavior for all identification experiments (t_0, x_0, u).

A model $M(\theta)$ is *structurally globally identifiable* if it is structurally globally identifiable for all θ outside an algebraic set.

In our model for cadmium transfer in the human body we have assumed that the system is stable and that the time horizon is relatively long compared with the dynamics of the system. So, the effect of the initial condition may be neglected. Thus, the input $u(t)$ and the output $y(t)$ are related by the convolution $y = W_\theta * u$. Below we mention three methods to determine structural identifiability.

Markov parameter matrix approach to identifiability. *Use the Markov parameter matrices* $M_1(\theta)$, $M_2(\theta)$, $\cdots$, $M_{2n}(\theta)$ *to build up the matrix*

$$
M_\theta = \begin{pmatrix} C(\theta)\, B(\theta) \\ C(\theta)\, A(\theta)\, B(\theta) \\ C(\theta)\, A(\theta)^2\, B(\theta) \\ \vdots \\ C(\theta)\, A(\theta)^{2n-1}\, B(\theta) \end{pmatrix}.
$$

The linear system is structurally globally identifiable iff for all θ outside an algebraic set $M_{\theta'} = M_\theta$ implies $\theta' = \theta$. The linear system is structurally locally identifiable iff the $2nkm \times r$ Jacobian matrix

$$
\begin{pmatrix} \dfrac{\partial M_1}{\partial \theta_1} & \cdots & \dfrac{\partial M_1}{\partial \theta_r} \\ \vdots & & \vdots \\ \dfrac{\partial M_{2n}}{\partial \theta_1} & \cdots & \dfrac{\partial M_{2n}}{\partial \theta_r} \end{pmatrix}
$$

has maximum rank for all θ outside an algebraic set.

Transfer function approach. *Define the transfer function matrix* $H_\theta(s)$ *as*

$$H_\theta(s) = C(\theta)[sI - A(\theta)]^{-1}B(\theta).$$

The linear system is structurally globally identifiable iff, for all θ outside an algebraic set, $H_{\theta'}(s) = H_\theta(s)$ implies $\theta' = \theta$. The linear compartmental system is structurally locally identifiable iff the $(2n-1)km \times r$ Jacobian matrix of the mapping of θ into the coefficients of the numerator and denominator of matrix elements of $H(s,\theta)$ has maximum rank r for all θ outside an algebraic set.

WARNING: The very popular *similarity transformation approach* only holds for general time-invariant continuous-time finite-dimensional linear systems, where state, input, and output vectors are from $\mathbb{R}$-spaces and A, B, C, and D are matrices with coefficients in $\mathbb{R}$. The similarity approach is of limited use in compartmental systems, where state, input, and output vectors are positive vectors. The following criterion is the best you can get in this approach.

Similarity-transformation method. *Let the compartmental system be structurally controllable and structurally observable for all parameters outside an algebraic set, and let the system have less than four compartments. Under these conditions the compartmental system is structurally globally identifiable at θ iff for all θ' and for all nonsingular T the system of equations*

$$\begin{aligned}
T\,A(\theta') &= A(\theta)\,T \\
T\,B(\theta') &= B(\theta) \\
C(\theta') &= C(\theta)\,T
\end{aligned}$$

has a unique solution (I, θ). If the system of equations has a finite set of solutions (T, θ), then the model is structurally locally identifiable at θ.

For systems with four or more compartments the above criterion is sufficient but not necessary. This limits its usefulness enormously.

In all the above criteria, computer algebra is the appropriate computational tool. We shall apply the criteria to our example of cadmium transfer.

First we introduce with the **macro** facility some shortcuts for various indexed names a_{ij}, b_{ij} and t_{ij}. This is done in a somewhat tricky way because of the evaluation rules of arguments of **macro**.

```
>   sequence :=
>     seq(seq( a.i.j = a[i,j], i=0..3 ), j=0..3 ),
>     seq(seq( b.i.j = b[i,j], i=0..3 ), j=0..3 ),
>     seq(seq( t.i.j = t[i,j], i=0..3 ), j=0..3 ), c3 = c[3]:
>   (eval@subs)( S=sequence, ´macro(S)´ ):
```

Next, we introduce matrices that describe the compartmental system.

```
>  A := matrix( 3, 3, [ -a21, a12, 0, a21,
>     -(a02+a12+a32), a23, 0, a32, -(a03+a23) ] );
```

$$A := \begin{bmatrix} -a_{2,1} & a_{1,2} & 0 \\ a_{2,1} & -a_{0,2} - a_{1,2} - a_{3,2} & a_{2,3} \\ 0 & a_{3,2} & -a_{0,3} - a_{2,3} \end{bmatrix}$$

```
>  B := matrix( 3, 1, [0,1,0] );
```

$$B := \begin{bmatrix} 0 \\ 1 \\ 0 \end{bmatrix}$$

```
>  C := matrix( 2, 3, [0,0,c3,0,a02,a03] );
```

$$C := \begin{bmatrix} 0 & 0 & c_3 \\ 0 & a_{0,2} & a_{0,3} \end{bmatrix}$$

```
>  AB := evalm( A &* B ):    A2B := evalm( A &* AB ):
>  MC := augment( B, AB, A2B );
```

$$MC := \begin{bmatrix} 0 & a_{1,2} & -a_{2,1}\,a_{1,2} + a_{1,2}\,\%1 \\ 1 & \%1 & a_{2,1}\,a_{1,2} + \%1^2 + a_{2,3}\,a_{3,2} \\ 0 & a_{3,2} & a_{3,2}\,\%1 + (-a_{0,3} - a_{2,3})\,a_{3,2} \end{bmatrix}$$

$$\%1 = -a_{0,2} - a_{1,2} - a_{3,2}$$

It is tempting to compute the rank of the controllability matrix M_C with the Maple procedure **rank**.

```
>  rank( MC );
```

$$3$$

But this gives only the generic rank for the matrix considered as a matrix with coefficients in the quotient field $\mathbb{Q}(a_{12}, a_{21}, \ldots, a_{32})$. This is not what we wanted! Another way of computing the rank is by fraction free **Gauss elimination**, carried out by the procedure **ffgausselim**.

```
>  ffgausselim( MC );
```

$$\begin{aligned} &\Big[1, -a_{0,2} - a_{1,2} - a_{3,2}, a_{2,1}\,a_{1,2} + a_{0,2}^2 + 2\,a_{1,2}\,a_{0,2} + 2\,a_{0,2}\,a_{3,2} \\ &\quad + a_{1,2}^2 + 2\,a_{1,2}\,a_{3,2} + a_{3,2}^2 + a_{2,3}\,a_{3,2}\Big] \\ &\Big[0, a_{1,2}, -a_{2,1}\,a_{1,2} - a_{1,2}\,a_{0,2} - a_{1,2}^2 - a_{1,2}\,a_{3,2}\Big] \\ &\Big[0, 0, -a_{1,2}\,a_{3,2}\,a_{0,3} - a_{1,2}\,a_{2,3}\,a_{3,2} + a_{3,2}\,a_{2,1}\,a_{1,2}\Big] \end{aligned}$$

```
>  map( factor, " );
```

$$\begin{aligned} &\Big[1, -a_{0,2} - a_{1,2} - a_{3,2}, a_{2,1}\,a_{1,2} + a_{0,2}^2 + 2\,a_{1,2}\,a_{0,2} + 2\,a_{0,2}\,a_{3,2} \\ &\quad + a_{1,2}^2 + 2\,a_{1,2}\,a_{3,2} + a_{3,2}^2 + a_{2,3}\,a_{3,2}\Big] \end{aligned}$$

$$[0\,,a_{1,2}\,,-a_{1,2}\,(a_{1,2}+a_{2,1}+a_{0,2}+a_{3,2})]$$
$$[0\,,0\,,-a_{1,2}\,a_{3,2}\,(a_{0,3}+a_{2,3}-a_{2,1})]$$

It follows immediately that the system is controllable iff $a_{12}\neq0$, $a_{32}\neq0$, and $a_{21}\neq a_{03}+a_{23}$. However, recall that Maple considers the matrix coefficients as elements in $\mathbb{Q}(a_{12},a_{21},\ldots,a_{32})$ so that, at each step of the fraction free Gauss elimination, it is possible that in each row the previous pivot is divided out or that the gcd of the polynomials in the row are divided out. The latter operation is not implemented in the procedure **ffgauselim**, and the former operation of dividing out previous pivots is of no harm as these pivots must be nonzero anyway in order to reach the maximum rank. If you don't want to rely on these implementation issues, then you can use the following equivalent controllability criterion.

Criterion for controllability. *The linear system is controllable iff for the controllability matrix M_C holds* $\det\bigl(M_C\,M_C^T\bigr)\neq0$ *(or* $\det(M_C)\neq0$ *when M_C is a square matrix).*

```
>   factor( det( MC ) );
```

$$a_{1,2}\,a_{3,2}\,(a_{0,3}+a_{2,3}-a_{2,1})$$

But, in general this criterion will give trickier conditions.

Observability can be checked in the same way. We shall assume that $a_{02}\neq0$ so that the matrix C has rank 2.

```
>   CA := evalm( C &* A ):
>   MO := stack( C, CA );
```

$$MO :=$$
$$[0\,,0\,,c_3]$$
$$[0\,,a_{0,2}\,,a_{0,3}]$$
$$[0\,,c_3\,a_{3,2}\,,-c_3\,(a_{0,3}+a_{2,3})]$$
$$\bigl[a_{0,2}\,a_{2,1}\,,-a_{0,2}{}^2-a_{1,2}\,a_{0,2}-a_{0,2}\,a_{3,2}+a_{3,2}\,a_{0,3}\,,$$
$$a_{0,2}\,a_{2,3}-a_{0,3}{}^2-a_{0,3}\,a_{2,3}\bigr]$$

```
>   ffgausselim( MO );
```

$$\bigl[a_{0,2}\,a_{2,1}\,,-a_{0,2}{}^2-a_{1,2}\,a_{0,2}-a_{0,2}\,a_{3,2}+a_{3,2}\,a_{0,3}\,,$$
$$a_{0,2}\,a_{2,3}-a_{0,3}{}^2-a_{0,3}\,a_{2,3}\bigr]$$
$$[0\,,a_{0,2}{}^2\,a_{2,1}\,,a_{0,3}\,a_{0,2}\,a_{2,1}]$$
$$[0\,,0\,,c_3\,a_{2,1}\,a_{0,2}{}^2]$$
$$[0\,,0\,,0]$$

So, the system is observable if $a_{02} \neq 0$ and $a_{21} \neq 0$.

In our example, the next criterion for observability leads to more difficult, but equivalent conditions.

Criterion for observability. *The linear system is observable iff for the observability matrix M_O holds $\det(M_O^T M_O) \neq 0$ (or $\det(M_O) \neq 0$ when M_O is a square matrix).*

```
> factor( det( transpose(MO) &* MO ) );
```

$$a_{0,2}^2\, c_3^2\, a_{2,1}^2 \left(a_{0,2}^2 + 2\, a_{0,2}\, a_{3,2}\, a_{0,3}^2 + 2\, a_{0,2}^2\, a_{0,3}\, a_{2,3} + a_{0,2}^2\, a_{0,3}^2 \right.$$
$$\left. + a_{0,2}^2\, a_{2,3}^2 + a_{3,2}^2\, a_{0,3}^2 + c_3^2\, a_{3,2}^2 + 2\, a_{0,2}\, a_{3,2}\, a_{0,3}\, a_{2,3} \right)$$

It looks as if an extra condition follows from the fourth factor. But when you consider it as a second-degree polynomial in a_{32} and compute the discriminant, then you come to the conclusion that this term is always negative.

```
> collect( op(4,"), a32 );
```

$$\left(a_{0,3}^2 + c_3^2 \right) a_{3,2}^2 + \left(2\, a_{0,2}\, a_{0,3}^2 + 2\, a_{0,2}\, a_{0,3}\, a_{2,3} \right) a_{3,2} + a_{0,2}^2$$
$$+ 2\, a_{0,2}^2\, a_{0,3}\, a_{2,3} + a_{0,2}^2\, a_{0,3}^2 + a_{0,2}^2\, a_{2,3}^2$$

```
> discrim(",a32);
```

$$-4 \left(c_3^2 + 2\, c_3^2\, a_{0,3}\, a_{2,3} + c_3^2\, a_{0,3}^2 + c_3^2\, a_{2,3}^2 + a_{0,3}^2 \right) a_{0,2}^2$$

Next, we shall study structural local identifiability via the Markov parameter matrix. First, we must introduce the matrix and its Jacobian in Maple.

```
> n := rowdim( A );
```

$$n := 3$$

```
> CAOB := evalm( C&*B ):
> for i from 1 to 5 do CA.i.B := evalm( C &* A^i &* B ) od:
> J := stack( seq(CA.i.B, i=0..2*n-1) ):
> J12 := map( diff, J, a12):   J21 := map( diff, J, a21):
> J23 := map( diff, J, a23):   J32 := map( diff, J, a32):
> J02 := map( diff, J, a02):   J03 := map( diff, J, a03):
> JM := augment( J21, J12, J02, J23, J32, J03 ):
> ffgausselim( JM ):
> map( factor, " );
```

$$\left[\%1, a_{0,2}\, a_{2,1} + 2\, a_{0,2}^2 + 2\, \%1 + 2\, \%3 - \%2, a_{2,1}\, a_{1,2} + 3\, a_{0,2}^2 \right.$$
$$+ 4\, \%1 + 4\, \%3 + a_{1,2}^2 + 2\, a_{1,2}\, a_{3,2} + a_{3,2}^2 + a_{2,3}\, a_{3,2} - \%2,$$
$$\left. -a_{3,2} \left(-a_{0,2} + a_{0,3} \right), 2\, a_{0,2}^2 + 2\, \%1 + 2\, \%3 + a_{0,2}\, a_{2,3} - a_{0,3}\, a_{0,2} \right.$$

$$- a_{1,2}\, a_{0,3} - 2\,\%2 - a_{0,3}{}^2 - a_{0,3}\, a_{2,3},$$
$$-a_{3,2}\,(a_{3,2} + a_{0,2} + a_{1,2} + 2\, a_{0,3} + a_{2,3})\big]$$
$$\big[0\,,\, -a_{1,2}\, a_{0,2}{}^2\,,\, -a_{1,2}\, a_{0,2}\,(2\, a_{0,2} + a_{1,2} + a_{3,2})\,,\,0\,,$$
$$a_{1,2}\, a_{0,2}\,(-a_{0,2} + a_{0,3})\,,\, a_{0,2}\, a_{1,2}\, a_{3,2}\big]$$
$$\big[0\,,0\,,\, -a_{1,2}\, a_{0,2}{}^2\,,0\,,0\,,0\big]$$
$$\big[0\,,0\,,0\,,\, c_3\, a_{3,2}\, a_{1,2}\, a_{0,2}{}^2\,,$$
$$c_3\, a_{1,2}\, a_{0,2}\,\big(a_{0,2}{}^2 + \%1 + a_{0,3}\, a_{0,2} + a_{0,2}\, a_{2,3} + \%3 + \%2\big)\,,$$
$$c_3\, a_{3,2}\, a_{1,2}\, a_{0,2}\,(a_{0,2} + a_{3,2})\big]$$
$$\big[0\,,0\,,0\,,0\,,\, c_3{}^2\, a_{3,2}\, a_{1,2}\, a_{0,2}{}^2\,,0\big]$$
$$\big[0\,,0\,,0\,,0\,,0\,,$$
$$c_3{}^2\, a_{3,2}{}^2\, a_{0,2}{}^2\, a_{1,2}\,(a_{2,3} - a_{2,1} + a_{0,3})\,(a_{2,3} - a_{2,1} - a_{1,2} + a_{0,3})\big]$$
$$\big[0\,,0\,,0\,,0\,,0\,,0\big]$$
$$\big[0\,,0\,,0\,,0\,,0\,,0\big]$$
$$\big[0\,,0\,,0\,,0\,,0\,,0\big]$$
$$\big[0\,,0\,,0\,,0\,,0\,,0\big]$$
$$\big[0\,,0\,,0\,,0\,,0\,,0\big]$$
$$\big[0\,,0\,,0\,,0\,,0\,,0\big]$$
$$\%1 := a_{1,2}\, a_{0,2}$$
$$\%2 := a_{3,2}\, a_{0,3}$$
$$\%3 := a_{0,2}\, a_{3,2}$$

The system is structurally locally identifiable iff a_{12}, a_{02}, and a_{32} are nonzero, $a_{21} \neq a_{03} + a_{23}$, and $a_{12} + a_{21} \neq a_{03} + a_{23}$. We shall also study structural global identifiability via the transfer function method.

```
> H := evalm( C &* (s-A)^(-1) &* B ):
> evalm( denom(H[1,1]) * H ) / collect(denom(H[1,1]),s);
```

$$\left(\begin{bmatrix} c_3\,(a_{2,1} + s)\, a_{3,2} \\ (a_{2,1} + s)\,(a_{0,3}\, a_{0,2} + a_{0,2}\, a_{2,3} + a_{0,2}\, s + a_{3,2}\, a_{0,3}) \end{bmatrix}\right) \bigg/$$
$$\big(s^3 + (a_{2,1} + a_{0,2} + a_{1,2} + a_{3,2} + a_{0,3} + a_{2,3})\, s^2 + \big(a_{0,2}\, a_{2,1} + a_{0,3}\, a_{0,2}$$
$$+\, a_{2,1}\, a_{3,2} + a_{0,3}\, a_{2,1} + a_{2,3}\, a_{2,1} + a_{1,2}\, a_{0,3} + a_{0,2}\, a_{2,3} + a_{1,2}\, a_{2,3}$$
$$+\, a_{3,2}\, a_{0,3}\big)\, s + a_{0,2}\, a_{2,3}\, a_{2,1} + a_{0,3}\, a_{0,2}\, a_{2,1} + a_{0,3}\, a_{2,1}\, a_{3,2}\big)$$

```
> collect( numer(H[1,1]), s );
```

$$c_3\, a_{3,2}\, s + c_3\, a_{2,1}\, a_{3,2}$$

```
> collect( numer(H[2,1]), s );
```

$$a_{0,2}\, s^2 + (a_{0,2}\, a_{2,1} + a_{0,3}\, a_{0,2} + a_{0,2}\, a_{2,3} + a_{3,2}\, a_{0,3})\, s$$
$$+\, a_{2,1}\,(a_{0,3}\, a_{0,2} + a_{0,2}\, a_{2,3} + a_{3,2}\, a_{0,3})$$

According to the transfer function criterion, structural global identifiability is equivalent to the uniqueness of the solution of the system of equations that is generated as follows.

```
>   cfs1 := { coeffs( expand(numer(H[1,1])), s ) };
```

$$cfs1 := \{c_3\, a_{2,1}\, a_{3,2}, c_3\, a_{3,2}\}$$

```
>   cfs2 := { coeffs( expand(numer(H[2,1])), s ) };
```

$$cfs2 := \{a_{0,2}, a_{0,2}\, a_{2,3}\, a_{2,1} + a_{0,3}\, a_{0,2}\, a_{2,1} + a_{0,3}\, a_{2,1}\, a_{3,2},$$
$$a_{0,2}\, a_{2,1} + a_{0,3}\, a_{0,2} + a_{0,2}\, a_{2,3} + a_{3,2}\, a_{0,3}\}$$

```
>   cfs3 := { coeffs( expand(denom(H[1,1])), s ) }
>      minus {1};
```

$$cfs3 := \{a_{2,1} + a_{0,2} + a_{1,2} + a_{3,2} + a_{0,3} + a_{2,3}, a_{0,2}\, a_{2,1} + a_{0,3}\, a_{0,2}$$
$$+ a_{2,1}\, a_{3,2} + a_{0,3}\, a_{2,1} + a_{2,3}\, a_{2,1} + a_{1,2}\, a_{0,3} + a_{0,2}\, a_{2,3} + a_{1,2}\, a_{2,3}$$
$$+ a_{3,2}\, a_{0,3}, a_{0,2}\, a_{2,3}\, a_{2,1} + a_{0,3}\, a_{0,2}\, a_{2,1} + a_{0,3}\, a_{2,1}\, a_{3,2}\}$$

```
>   cfs := `union`( cfs.(1..3) ):
>   eqns := map( x -> x = subs( a12=b12, a21=b21, a23=b23,
>     a32=b32, a23=b23, a03=b03, a02=b02, x ), cfs );
```

$$eqns := \{a_{0,2} = b_{0,2}, c_3\, a_{2,1}\, a_{3,2} = c_3\, b_{2,1}\, b_{3,2},$$
$$a_{2,1} + a_{0,2} + a_{1,2} + a_{3,2} + a_{0,3} + a_{2,3} =$$
$$b_{2,1} + b_{0,2} + b_{1,2} + b_{3,2} + b_{0,3} + b_{2,3}, a_{0,2}\, a_{2,1} + a_{0,3}\, a_{0,2}$$
$$+ a_{2,1}\, a_{3,2} + a_{0,3}\, a_{2,1} + a_{2,3}\, a_{2,1} + a_{1,2}\, a_{0,3} + a_{0,2}\, a_{2,3} + a_{1,2}\, a_{2,3}$$
$$+ a_{3,2}\, a_{0,3} = b_{0,2}\, b_{2,1} + b_{0,3}\, b_{0,2} + b_{2,1}\, b_{3,2} + b_{0,3}\, b_{2,1} + b_{2,3}\, b_{2,1}$$
$$+ b_{1,2}\, b_{0,3} + b_{0,2}\, b_{2,3} + b_{1,2}\, b_{2,3} + b_{3,2}\, b_{0,3},$$
$$a_{0,2}\, a_{2,3}\, a_{2,1} + a_{0,3}\, a_{0,2}\, a_{2,1} + a_{0,3}\, a_{2,1}\, a_{3,2} =$$
$$b_{0,2}\, b_{2,3}\, b_{2,1} + b_{0,3}\, b_{0,2}\, b_{2,1} + b_{0,3}\, b_{2,1}\, b_{3,2}, c_3\, a_{3,2} = c_3\, b_{3,2},$$
$$a_{0,2}\, a_{2,1} + a_{0,3}\, a_{0,2} + a_{0,2}\, a_{2,3} + a_{3,2}\, a_{0,3} =$$
$$b_{0,2}\, b_{2,1} + b_{0,3}\, b_{0,2} + b_{0,2}\, b_{2,3} + b_{3,2}\, b_{0,3}\}$$

```
>   vars := {b12,b21,b23,b32,b02,b03}:
>   solve(eqns,vars);
```

$$\{b_{0,2} = a_{0,2}, b_{2,1} = a_{2,1}, b_{2,3} = a_{2,3}, b_{1,2} = a_{1,2}, b_{0,3} = a_{0,3}, b_{3,2} = a_{3,2}\},$$
$$\{b_{0,2} = a_{0,2}, b_{2,1} = a_{2,1}, b_{1,2} = a_{0,3} + a_{2,3} - a_{2,1}, b_{2,3} = -(-a_{1,2}\, a_{0,2}$$
$$- a_{0,2}\, a_{2,1} + a_{0,2}\, a_{2,3} + a_{3,2}\, a_{0,3} + a_{0,3}\, a_{0,2} - a_{1,2}\, a_{3,2} - a_{2,1}\, a_{3,2})/$$
$$a_{3,2}, b_{0,3} = \frac{-a_{1,2}\, a_{0,2} - a_{0,2}\, a_{2,1} + a_{0,2}\, a_{2,3} + a_{3,2}\, a_{0,3} + a_{0,3}\, a_{0,2}}{a_{3,2}},$$
$$b_{3,2} = a_{3,2}\}$$

There are two solutions. Thus, the system is not structurally globally identifiable; it is only structurally locally identifiable.

The last result will be checked by the similarity-transformation method. First we introduce the matrices AA, BB, and CC corresponding to the same model M but with parameter values b_{12}, $b_{21}, \ldots$ instead of a_{12}, $a_{21}, \ldots$

```
> AA := subs( a12=b12, a21=b21, a23=b23, a32=b32,
>    a23=b23, a03=b03, a02=b02, eval(A) );
```

$$AA := \begin{bmatrix} -b_{2,1} & b_{1,2} & 0 \\ b_{2,1} & -b_{0,2} - b_{1,2} - b_{3,2} & b_{2,3} \\ 0 & b_{3,2} & -b_{0,3} - b_{2,3} \end{bmatrix}$$

```
> BB := copy(B):
> CC := subs( a02=b02, a03=b03, eval(C) );
```

$$CC := \begin{bmatrix} 0 & 0 & c_3 \\ 0 & b_{0,2} & b_{0,3} \end{bmatrix}$$

```
> T := matrix( 3, 3, (i,j)->t[i,j] );
```

$$T := \begin{bmatrix} t_{1,1} & t_{1,2} & t_{1,3} \\ t_{2,1} & t_{2,2} & t_{2,3} \\ t_{3,1} & t_{3,2} & t_{3,3} \end{bmatrix}$$

From the matrix operation

```
> evalm( T&*BB - B );
```

$$\begin{bmatrix} t_{1,2} \\ t_{2,2} - 1 \\ t_{3,2} \end{bmatrix}$$

follows that $t_{12} = t_{32} = 0$ and $t_{22} = 1$. Then the matrix equation $CC - C\,T = 0$ looks as follows.

```
> t12 := 0:  t32:= 0:  t22 := 1:
> evalm( CC - C&*T );
```

$$[-c_3\, t_{3,1}\,, -c_3\, t_{3,2}\,, c_3 - c_3\, t_{3,3}]$$
$$\Big[-a_{0,2}\, t_{2,1} - a_{0,3}\, t_{3,1}\,, b_{0,2} - a_{0,2}\, t_{2,2} - a_{0,3}\, t_{3,2}\,,$$
$$b_{0,3} - a_{0,2}\, t_{2,3} - a_{0,3}\, t_{3,3}\Big]$$

```
> map( factor, " );
```

$$[-c_3\, t_{3,1}\,, -c_3\, t_{3,2}\,, -c_3\,(-1 + t_{3,3})]$$
$$\Big[-a_{0,2}\, t_{2,1} - a_{0,3}\, t_{3,1}\,, b_{0,2} - a_{0,2}\, t_{2,2} - a_{0,3}\, t_{3,2}\,,$$
$$b_{0,3} - a_{0,2}\, t_{2,3} - a_{0,3}\, t_{3,3}\Big]$$

Because $c_3 \neq 0$, it follows immediately that $t_{31} = 0$, $t_{33} = 1$, and $b_{02} = a_{02}$.

```
>   t31 := 0:   t33 := 1:   b02 := a02:
>   evalm( CC - C&*T ):  map( factor, " );
```

$$\left[-c_3\, t_{3,1}, \quad c_3\, t_{3,2}, -c_3\, (-1 + t_{3,3})\right]$$
$$\left[- a_{0,2}\, t_{2,1} - a_{0,3}\, t_{3,1}, b_{0,2} - a_{0,2}\, t_{2,2} - a_{0,3}\, t_{3,2},\right.$$
$$\left. b_{0,3} - a_{0,2}\, t_{2,3} - a_{0,3}\, t_{3,3}\right]$$

If $a_{02} \neq 0$ (as is the case when the system is observable), then $t_{21} = 0$, and we have one equation left.

```
>   t21 := 0:
>   eqn1 := evalm(CC - C&*T)[2,3];
```

$$eqn1 := b_{0,3} - a_{0,2}\, t_{2,3} - a_{0,3}$$

Now we derive the nontrivial equations obtained from the similarity transformation of the A matrix.

```
>   evalm( T&*AA - A&*T );
```

$$\left[- t_{1,1}\, b_{2,1} + t_{1,2}\, b_{2,1} + a_{2,1}\, t_{1,1} - a_{1,2}\, t_{2,1},\right.$$
$$t_{1,1}\, b_{1,2} - t_{1,2}\, b_{0,2} - t_{1,2}\, b_{1,2} - t_{1,2}\, b_{3,2} + t_{1,3}\, b_{3,2} + a_{2,1}\, t_{1,2} - a_{1,2}\, t_{2,2}$$
$$\left., t_{1,2}\, b_{2,3} - t_{1,3}\, b_{0,3} - t_{1,3}\, b_{2,3} + a_{2,1}\, t_{1,3} - a_{1,2}\, t_{2,3}\right]$$
$$\left[- t_{2,1}\, b_{2,1} + t_{2,2}\, b_{2,1} - a_{2,1}\, t_{1,1} + a_{0,2}\, t_{2,1} + a_{1,2}\, t_{2,1} + t_{2,1}\, a_{3,2}\right.$$
$$- a_{2,3}\, t_{3,1}, t_{2,1}\, b_{1,2} - t_{2,2}\, b_{0,2} - t_{2,2}\, b_{1,2} - t_{2,2}\, b_{3,2} + t_{2,3}\, b_{3,2}$$
$$- a_{2,1}\, t_{1,2} + a_{0,2}\, t_{2,2} + a_{1,2}\, t_{2,2} + t_{2,2}\, a_{3,2} - a_{2,3}\, t_{3,2}, t_{2,2}\, b_{2,3}$$
$$- t_{2,3}\, b_{0,3} - t_{2,3}\, b_{2,3} - a_{2,1}\, t_{1,3} + a_{0,2}\, t_{2,3} + a_{1,2}\, t_{2,3} + t_{2,3}\, a_{3,2}$$
$$\left.- a_{2,3}\, t_{3,3}\right]$$
$$\left[- t_{3,1}\, b_{2,1} + t_{3,2}\, b_{2,1} - t_{2,1}\, a_{3,2} + a_{0,3}\, t_{3,1} + a_{2,3}\, t_{3,1}, t_{3,1}\, b_{1,2}\right.$$
$$- t_{3,2}\, b_{0,2} - t_{3,2}\, b_{1,2} - t_{3,2}\, b_{3,2} + t_{3,3}\, b_{3,2} - t_{2,2}\, a_{3,2} + a_{0,3}\, t_{3,2}$$
$$+ a_{2,3}\, t_{3,2},$$
$$\left. t_{3,2}\, b_{2,3} - t_{3,3}\, b_{0,3} - t_{3,3}\, b_{2,3} - t_{2,3}\, a_{3,2} + a_{0,3}\, t_{3,3} + a_{2,3}\, t_{3,3}\right]$$

```
>   eqn2 := map( op, convert(", 'listlist') ):
>   eqns := { eqn1, op(eqn2) } minus {0};
```

$$eqns := \left\{b_{0,3} - a_{0,2}\, t_{2,3} - a_{0,3}, -a_{3,2} + b_{3,2},\right.$$
$$-b_{0,3} - b_{2,3} - t_{2,3}\, a_{3,2} + a_{0,3} + a_{2,3},$$
$$-b_{1,2} - b_{3,2} + t_{2,3}\, b_{3,2} + a_{1,2} + a_{3,2}, b_{2,3} - t_{2,3}\, b_{0,3} - t_{2,3}\, b_{2,3}$$
$$- a_{2,1}\, t_{1,3} + a_{0,2}\, t_{2,3} + a_{1,2}\, t_{2,3} + t_{2,3}\, a_{3,2} - a_{2,3},$$
$$t_{1,1}\, b_{1,2} + t_{1,3}\, b_{3,2} - a_{1,2}, -t_{1,3}\, b_{0,3} - t_{1,3}\, b_{2,3} + a_{2,1}\, t_{1,3} - a_{1,2}\, t_{2,3},$$
$$\left. b_{2,1} - a_{2,1}\, t_{1,1}, -t_{1,1}\, b_{2,1} + a_{2,1}\, t_{1,1}\right\}$$

```
>  solve( eqns, {b12,b32,b23,b03,b21,t11,t13,t23} );
```

$\{b_{2,1} = a_{2,1}, t_{1,3} = 0, b_{2,3} = a_{2,3}, b_{1,2} = a_{1,2}, b_{0,3} = a_{0,3}, t_{2,3} = 0,$

$$b_{3,2} = a_{3,2}, t_{1,1} = 1\}, \{b_{2,1} = a_{2,1}, t_{1,3} = -\frac{-a_{1,2} - a_{2,1} + a_{2,3} + a_{0,3}}{a_{3,2}},$$

$$t_{2,3} = \frac{-a_{1,2} - a_{2,1} + a_{2,3} + a_{0,3}}{a_{3,2}}, b_{1,2} = a_{0,3} + a_{2,3} - a_{2,1}, b_{2,3} =$$

$$- (-a_{1,2}\,a_{0,2} - a_{0,2}\,a_{2,1} + a_{0,2}\,a_{2,3} + a_{3,2}\,a_{0,3} + a_{0,3}\,a_{0,2} - a_{1,2}\,a_{3,2}$$

$$- a_{2,1}\,a_{3,2}) / a_{3,2},$$

$$b_{0,3} = \frac{-a_{1,2}\,a_{0,2} - a_{0,2}\,a_{2,1} + a_{0,2}\,a_{2,3} + a_{3,2}\,a_{0,3} + a_{0,3}\,a_{0,2}}{a_{3,2}},$$

$$b_{3,2} = a_{3,2}, t_{1,1} = 1\}$$

There are two distinct solutions, which proves again that the system is not structurally globally identifiable; it is only locally identifiable.

For more complicated systems, the analysis of controllability, observability, and structural identifiability via the outlined methods will not be as easy as above. Appropriate polynomial equation solvers like elimination, characteristic sets, or Gröbner basis methods must be used to find the answers. But at least the computational work is done by the computer algebra system with its linear algebra package, equation solvers, and so on.

19.3   Molecular-Orbital Hückel Theory

The next example, molecular-orbital Hückel theory for the computation of π-electron energies and electronic charge distributions in molecules, comes from quantum chemistry. This method can be found in any book on quantum chemistry, e.g., in [24]; here we only sketch the method.

The particular molecule we shall use is azulene $C_{10}H_{10}$, a skeleton of ten carbon atoms linked by so-called σ-bonds as shown in Figure 19.2.

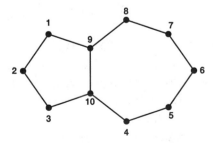

FIGURE 19.2. Azulene skeleton.

Each σ-bond contains two electrons; what remains are 10 electrons, which are called π-electrons. These π-electrons form π-bonds, which are constructed from the $2p_z$ carbon orbitals. We number each carbon atom and denote its $2p_z$ orbital as ϕ_i. The molecular orbitals are constructed from these atomic orbitals as linear combinations $\psi = c_1\phi_1 + c_2\phi_2 + \ldots + c_{10}\phi_{10}$. The coefficients $c_1, c_2 \ldots, c_{10}$ are determined by a variational method such that the energy is as low as possible. This leads to a generalized eigenvalue problem: $(H - ES)C = 0$, where H is the Hamiltonian matrix with matrix elements $< \phi_i \,|\, H \,|\, \phi_j >$, S is the overlap matrix with coefficients $< \phi_i \,|\, \phi_j >$, and C is a generalized eigenvector with generalized eigenvalue E. The following assumptions are made in Hückel theory.

- All matrix coefficients H_{ii} are equal, and are given the symbol α.

- All matrix coefficients H_{ij} are equal when atoms i and j are neighbors, and are denoted as β. When atoms i and j are not directly bonded, then $H_{ij} = 0$.

- Overlap is neglected, i.e., S is the identity matrix.

Under these assumptions we get an ordinary eigenvalue problem. The symmetric matrix H, which is called the *Hückel matrix*, for azulene is as follows.

$$\begin{pmatrix} \alpha & \beta & 0 & 0 & 0 & 0 & 0 & 0 & \beta & 0 \\ \beta & \alpha & \beta & 0 & 0 & 0 & 0 & 0 & 0 & 0 \\ 0 & \beta & \alpha & 0 & 0 & 0 & 0 & 0 & 0 & \beta \\ 0 & 0 & 0 & \alpha & \beta & 0 & 0 & 0 & 0 & \beta \\ 0 & 0 & 0 & \beta & \alpha & \beta & 0 & 0 & 0 & 0 \\ 0 & 0 & 0 & 0 & \beta & \alpha & \beta & 0 & 0 & 0 \\ 0 & 0 & 0 & 0 & 0 & \beta & \alpha & \beta & 0 & 0 \\ 0 & 0 & 0 & 0 & 0 & 0 & \beta & \alpha & \beta & 0 \\ \beta & 0 & 0 & 0 & 0 & 0 & 0 & \beta & \alpha & \beta \\ 0 & 0 & \beta & \beta & 0 & 0 & 0 & 0 & \beta & \alpha \end{pmatrix}$$

Instead of the eigenvalue problem for the Hückel matrix, we shall solve the eigenvalue problem for the corresponding topological matrix,

$$\begin{pmatrix} 0 & 1 & 0 & 0 & 0 & 0 & 0 & 0 & 1 & 0 \\ 1 & 0 & 1 & 0 & 0 & 0 & 0 & 0 & 0 & 0 \\ 0 & 1 & 0 & 0 & 0 & 0 & 0 & 0 & 0 & 1 \\ 0 & 0 & 0 & 0 & 1 & 0 & 0 & 0 & 0 & 1 \\ 0 & 0 & 0 & 1 & 0 & 1 & 0 & 0 & 0 & 0 \\ 0 & 0 & 0 & 0 & 1 & 0 & 1 & 0 & 0 & 0 \\ 0 & 0 & 0 & 0 & 0 & 1 & 0 & 1 & 0 & 0 \\ 0 & 0 & 0 & 0 & 0 & 0 & 1 & 0 & 1 & 0 \\ 1 & 0 & 0 & 0 & 0 & 0 & 0 & 1 & 0 & 1 \\ 0 & 0 & 1 & 1 & 0 & 0 & 0 & 0 & 1 & 0 \end{pmatrix}$$

The relation between an eigenvalue x of the topological matrix and the eigenvalue E is simple, viz., $E = \alpha + \beta\,x$; the corresponding eigenvectors are the same.

Let us start computing. First, we tabulate the directly bonded carbon atom pairs.

```
>  `number of C-atoms` := 10:
>  Azulene_skeleton :=
>     [ [1,2], [1,9], [2,3], [3,10], [4,5], [4,10],
>       [4,10], [5,6], [6,7], [7,8], [8,9], [9,10] ]:
```

We define the Hückel matrix as a sparse symmetric matrix.

```
>  Hueckel_matrix := array( sparse,
>    1..`number of C-atoms`, 1..`number of C-atoms` ):
>  for i from 1 to nops( Azulene_skeleton ) do
>    Hueckel_matrix[ op( Azulene_skeleton[i] ) ] := beta
>  od:
>  Hueckel_matrix := evalm( alpha + Hueckel_matrix
>    + transpose( Hueckel_matrix ) ):
>  topological_matrix := subs( alpha=0, beta=1,
>    eval( Hueckel_matrix ) ):
```

The characteristic polynomial of the topological matrix can be computed with the linalg procedure **charpoly**; the characteristic matrix can be computed by **charmat**.

```
>  factor( charpoly( topological_matrix, x ) );
```
$$(x^4 + x^3 - 3\,x^2 - x + 1)(x^6 - x^5 - 7\,x^4 + 5\,x^3 + 13\,x^2 - 6\,x - 4)$$

```
>  charmat( topological_matrix, x );
```

$$
\begin{bmatrix}
x & -1 & 0 & 0 & 0 & 0 & 0 & 0 & -1 & 0 \\
-1 & x & -1 & 0 & 0 & 0 & 0 & 0 & 0 & 0 \\
0 & -1 & x & 0 & 0 & 0 & 0 & 0 & 0 & -1 \\
0 & 0 & 0 & x & -1 & 0 & 0 & 0 & 0 & -1 \\
0 & 0 & 0 & -1 & x & -1 & 0 & 0 & 0 & 0 \\
0 & 0 & 0 & 0 & -1 & x & -1 & 0 & 0 & 0 \\
0 & 0 & 0 & 0 & 0 & -1 & x & -1 & 0 & 0 \\
0 & 0 & 0 & 0 & 0 & 0 & -1 & x & -1 & 0 \\
-1 & 0 & 0 & 0 & 0 & 0 & 0 & -1 & x & -1 \\
0 & 0 & -1 & -1 & 0 & 0 & 0 & 0 & -1 & x
\end{bmatrix}
$$

```
>  factor( det(") );
```
$$(x^4 + x^3 - 3\,x^2 - x + 1)(x^6 - x^5 - 7\,x^4 + 5\,x^3 + 13\,x^2 - 6\,x - 4)$$

Eigenvalues and eigenvectors can be computed with **eigenvalues** and **eigenvectors**, respectively.

```
>  eigenvalues( topological_matrix );
```

$$\text{RootOf}(\_Z^4 + \_Z^3 - 3\,\_Z^2 - \_Z + 1),$$
$$\text{RootOf}(\_Z^6 - \_Z^5 - 7\,\_Z^4 + 5\,\_Z^3 + 13\,\_Z^2 - 6\,\_Z - 4)$$

```
>   eigenvectors( topological_matrix );
```
$$[\,\%2, 1, \{\,[\ldots]\,\}\,], [\,\%1, 1, \{\,[\ldots]\,\}\,]$$
$$\%1 \qquad := \mathrm{RootOf}(\_Z^4 + \_Z^3 - 3\_Z^2 - \_Z + 1)$$
$$\%2 \quad := \mathrm{RootOf}(\_Z^6 - \_Z^5 - 7\_Z^4 + 5\_Z^3 + 13\_Z^2 - 6\_Z - 4)$$

We have omitted the eigenvectors. Let us consider the last element in the above sequence.

```
>   "[2];
```

$$[\%1, 1, \{[-2\,\%1 + 2\,\%1^2 - 3 + \%1^3, 0, 2\,\%1 - 2\,\%1^2 + 3 - \%1^3, -1,$$
$$\%1^2 + \%1^3 - 3\,\%1 - 1, 0, -\%1^2 - \%1^3 + 3\,\%1 + 1, 1,$$
$$\%1^3 + \%1^2 - 2\,\%1 - 1, -\%1^3 - \%1^2 + 2\,\%1 + 1]\}]$$
$$\%1 := \mathrm{RootOf}(\_Z^4 + \_Z^3 - 3\_Z^2 - \_Z + 1)$$

The first component specifies the eigenvalue associated with the eigenvector. The second component is the multiplicity of the eigenvalue. The third component is the actual eigenvector. In case of a multidimensional eigenspace, the third component would be a basis of eigenvectors. You should actually consider the above object as a description of four eigenvectors: %1 can take four values, but you must always choose the same value in one vector. Below is the one that corresponds with the eigenvalue $-\frac{1}{4} + \frac{1}{4}\sqrt{5} + \frac{1}{4}\sqrt{11 - \sqrt{5}\sqrt{2}}$.

```
>   allvalues(",`dependent`)[1];
```

$$[\%1, 1, \{\Big[-\frac{5}{2} - \frac{1}{2}\sqrt{5} - \frac{1}{2}\sqrt{22 - 2\sqrt{5}} + 2\,\%1^2 + \%1^3, 0,$$
$$\frac{5}{2} + \frac{1}{2}\sqrt{5} + \frac{1}{2}\sqrt{22 - 2\sqrt{5}} - 2\,\%1^2 - \%1^3, \ -1,$$
$$\%1^2 + \%1^3 - \frac{1}{4} - \frac{3}{4}\sqrt{5} - \frac{3}{4}\sqrt{22 - 2\sqrt{5}}, 0,$$
$$-\%1^2 - \%1^3 + \frac{1}{4} + \frac{3}{4}\sqrt{5} + \frac{3}{4}\sqrt{22 - 2\sqrt{5}}, 1,$$
$$\%1^3 + \%1^2 - \frac{1}{2} - \frac{1}{2}\sqrt{5} - \frac{1}{2}\sqrt{22 - 2\sqrt{5}},$$
$$-\%1^3 - \%1^2 + \frac{1}{2} + \frac{1}{2}\sqrt{5} + \frac{1}{2}\sqrt{22 - 2\sqrt{5}}\Big]\}]$$
$$\%1 := -\frac{1}{4} + \frac{1}{4}\sqrt{5} + \frac{1}{4}\sqrt{22 - 2\sqrt{5}}$$

Singular values of a matrix M, which are defined as the square roots of the eigenvalues of MM^T, can be computed by **singularvals**.

Numerical eigenvalues and eigenvectors can be obtained by **Eigenvals**.

```
>   eigenvalues := evalf(
>     Eigenvals( topological_matrix, ´eigenvectors´ ) );
```

$$eigenvalues := [-2.095293985 \ -1.869213984 \ -1.579218099$$
$$-.7376403029 \ -.4003923188 \ .4772599976 \ .8869752420$$
$$1.355674293 \ 1.651572314 \ 2.310276842]$$

Let us check the first eigenvector.

```
>   subvector( eigenvectors, 1..´number of C-atoms´, 1 );
```

$$[-.2590786300 \ .1881 \ 10^{-8} \ .2590786280 \ .3354972117$$
$$-.1601193962 \ -.2190 \ 10^{-8} \ .1601194004 \ -.3354972138$$
$$.5428458950 \ -.5428458923]$$

```
>   evalm( ( topological_matrix
>   - eigenvalues[1] ) &* " );
```

$$[.18 \, 10^{-8} \ .19 \ 10^{-8} \ .5 \, 10^{-9} \ .12 \, 10^{-8} \ .181 0 \, 10^{-8} \ -.4 \, 10^{-9} \ .5 \, 10^{-9}$$
$$.13 \, 10^{-8} \ .29 \, 10^{-8} \ .2 \, 10^{-8}]$$

```
>   map( fnormal, " ); # floating-point normalization
```

$$[0 \ 0 \ 0 \ 0 \ 0 \ 0 \ 0 \ 0 \ 0 \ 0]$$

We end this example with a numerical description of the π-electron energy and the π-electron density function. When the orthonormalized molecular orbitals ψ_i's are occupied by n_i π-electrons the π-electron density q_j on the carbon atom labeled j is defined as

$$q_j = \sum_{i=0}^{10} n_i c_{ji}^2.$$

We shall concentrate on the state with lowest π-electron energy.

```
>   occupation_numbers := [0,0,0,0,0,2,2,2,2,2,2]:
>   pi_electron_energy := sum( ´occupation_numbers[i]
>     * ( alpha + eigenvalues[i]*beta )´,
>     ´i´=1..´number of C-atoms´ );
```

$$pi\_electron\_energy := 10 \, \alpha + 13.36351737 \, \beta$$

In this case, no eigenvalues with multiplicities greater than 1 occur, otherwise we would have applied Gram-Schmidt orthogonalization (via the procedure **GramSchmidt** in the linalg package). Here, we only have to normalize the eigenvectors. This can be done with the **normalize** procedure.

```
>   eigenvectors := map( normalize,  [ seq(
>     subvector( eigenvectors, 1..`number of C-atoms`, i ),
>     i=1..`number of C-atoms` ) ] ):
```

We are now ready to compute the π-electron density.

```
>   electron_density := seq( sum( `occupation_numbers[i] *
>     (eigenvectors[i][j])^2`, `i`=1..`number of C-atoms` ),
>     j=1..`number of C-atoms` );
```

$$electron\_density := 1.172879340, 1.046599708, 1.172879339,$$
$$.8549456656, .9864468455, .8700013802, .9864468483,$$
$$.8549456632, 1.027427606, 1.027427605$$

For chemists, this simple model explains stereospecificity of substitution. Electrophylic substitutions (like substitution of a chlorine atom) are most likely to take place at positions of highest electron density. In the case of azulene, this is position 2. Nucleophilic substitution (e.g., of a methyl group) is most likely to take place at positions of lowest electron density, i.e., on positions 4 and 8.

19.4   Vector Analysis

Vector analysis procedures like **grad** (for *gradient*), **diverge** (short for *divergence*), **laplacian**, **jacobian**, **hessian**, and **curl** are present in the linalg package and work well for various orthogonal curvilinear coordinate systems.

```
>   alias( f=f(x,y,z), g=g(x,y,z), h=h(x,y,z), c=[x,y,z] ):
>   grad( f, c );
```

$$\left[\ \frac{\partial}{\partial x} f \quad \frac{\partial}{\partial y} f \quad \frac{\partial}{\partial z} f \ \right]$$

```
>   diverge( [f,g,h], c );
```

$$\left(\frac{\partial}{\partial x} f \right) + \left(\frac{\partial}{\partial y} g \right) + \left(\frac{\partial}{\partial z} h \right)$$

```
>   laplacian( f, c );
```

$$\left(\frac{\partial^2}{\partial x^2} f \right) + \left(\frac{\partial^2}{\partial y^2} f \right) + \left(\frac{\partial^2}{\partial z^2} f \right)$$

```
>   jacobian( [f,g,h], c );
```

$$\begin{bmatrix} \frac{\partial}{\partial x} f & \frac{\partial}{\partial y} f & \frac{\partial}{\partial z} f \\ \frac{\partial}{\partial x} g & \frac{\partial}{\partial y} g & \frac{\partial}{\partial z} g \\ \frac{\partial}{\partial x} h & \frac{\partial}{\partial y} h & \frac{\partial}{\partial z} h \end{bmatrix}$$

```
> hessian( f, c );
```

$$\begin{bmatrix} \frac{\partial^2}{\partial x^2} f & \frac{\partial^2}{\partial x\,\partial y} f & \frac{\partial^2}{\partial x\,\partial z} f \\ \frac{\partial^2}{\partial x\,\partial y} f & \frac{\partial^2}{\partial y^2} f & \frac{\partial^2}{\partial y\,\partial z} f \\ \frac{\partial^2}{\partial x\,\partial z} f & \frac{\partial^2}{\partial y\,\partial z} f & \frac{\partial^2}{\partial z^2} f \end{bmatrix}$$

```
> curl( [f,g,h], c );
```

$$\left[\left(\frac{\partial}{\partial y} h \right) - \left(\frac{\partial}{\partial z} g \right) \quad \left(\frac{\partial}{\partial z} f \right) - \left(\frac{\partial}{\partial x} h \right) \quad \left(\frac{\partial}{\partial x} g \right) - \left(\frac{\partial}{\partial y} f \right) \right]$$

```
> diverge( ", c );
```

$$0$$

```
> curl( grad( f, c ), c );
```

$$[\,0 \quad 0 \quad 0\,]$$

The last two statements are well-known properties.

Tables 19.1 and 19.2 list the main orthogonal curvilinear coordinate systems for which Maple has built-in facilities to express gradient, divergence, Laplacian, and curl. Enter **?changecoords** for a complete list and explanation of the predefined coordinate systems. The definitions of the coordinate transformations can be found in [142, 171].

Coordinates	Definition x, y, z	Maple Name
rectangular	(u, v)	cartesian
polar	$(u \cos v, u \sin v)$	polar
bipolar	$\left(\dfrac{\sinh v}{\cosh v - \cos u}, \dfrac{\sin u}{\cosh v - \cos u} \right)$	bipolar
elliptic	$(\cosh u \cos v, \sinh u \sin v)$	elliptic
parabolic	$\left(\dfrac{u^2 - v^2}{2}, uv \right)$	parabolic
hyperbolic	$(\sqrt{u + \sqrt{u^2 + v^2}}, \sqrt{-u + \sqrt{u^2 + v^2}})$	hyperbolic

TABLE 19.1. Some predefined 2D orthogonal curvilinear coordinates.

As an example, we shall show how things work for prolate spheroidal coordinates that are defined in Maple as

$$\begin{aligned} x &= a \sinh u \sin v \cos w, \\ y &= a \sinh u \sin v \sin w, \\ z &= a \cosh u \cos v. \end{aligned}$$

Coordinates	definition	Maple Name
rectangular	(u, v, w)	cartesian
circular-cylinder	$(u \cos v, u \sin v, w)$	cylindrical
elliptic-cylinder	$(a \cosh u \cos v,$ $a \cosh u \sin v,$ $w)$	ellcylindrical
parabolic-cylinder	$(uv \cos w,$ $uv \sin w,$ $\frac{u^2 - v^2}{2})$	paraboloidal
hyperbolic-cylinder	$(\sqrt{u + \sqrt{u^2 + v^2}},$ $\sqrt{v + \sqrt{u^2 + v^2}},$ $w)$	hypercylindrical
spherical	$(u \cos v \sin w,$ $u \sin v \sin w,$ $u \cos v)$	spherical
prolate spheroidal	$(a \sinh u \sin v \cos w$ $a \sinh u \sin v \sin w,$ $a \cosh u \cos v)$	prolatespheroidal
oblate spheroidal	$(a \cosh u \sin v \cos w,$ $a \cosh u \sin v \sin w,$ $a \sinh u \cos v)$	oblatespheroidal
ellipsoidal	$\left(\frac{uvw}{ab},\right.$ $\frac{1}{b}\sqrt{\frac{(u^2-b^2)(v^2-b^2)(b^2-w^2)}{a^2-b^2}},$ $\left.\frac{1}{a}\sqrt{\frac{(u^2-a^2)(a^2-v^2)(a^2-w^2)}{a^2-b^2}}\right)$	ellipsoidal

TABLE 19.2. Some predefined 3D orthogonal curvilinear coordinates.

The coordinate transformation to prolate spheroidal coordinates can be visualized by **plots[coordplot3d]**.

```
> plots[coordplot3d]( prolatespheroidal );
```

The graph is shown in Figure 19.3.

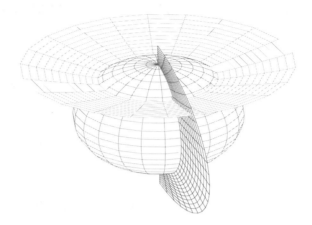

FIGURE 19.3. Graph of the coordinate transformation to prolate spheroidal co-ordinates.

The gradient, curl, divergence, and Laplacian can be computed easily by adding the options coords = *coordinate system* to the corresponding Maple commands.

```
>   alias( f=f(u,v,w), g=g(u,v,w), h=h(u.v.w), c=[u,v,w] ):
>   grad( f, c, coords = prolatespheroidal(a) );
```

$$\left[\frac{\frac{\partial}{\partial u} f}{a\sqrt{\sinh(u)^2 + \sin(v)^2}}, \frac{\frac{\partial}{\partial v} f}{a\sqrt{\sinh(u)^2 + \sin(v)^2}}, \frac{\frac{\partial}{\partial w} f}{a\sinh(u)\sin(v)} \right]$$

If you want to set the coordinate system prior to the computational work so that you do not have to repeat the name of the coordinate system each time you call a vector analysis routine, you may have a look at the source code of the **plots[changecoords]** routine and mimic the code to define the **setcoords** procedure as below.

```
>   interface( verboseproc = 2 ): # make Maple communicative
>   readlib( `plots/changecoords` ): # load library function
>   print( `plots/changecoords` );

proc(p,coord)
local c_name,a,b,c;
options `Copyright 1994 by the University of Waterloo`;
    a := 1;
    b := 1/2;
    c := 1/3;
    if type(coord,function) then
        c_name := op(0,coord);
        if nops(coord) = 1 then a := op(1,coord)
        elif nops(coord) = 2 then
            a := op(1,coord); b := op(2,coord)
        elif nops(coord) = 3 then
```

```
            a := op(1,coord); b := op(2,coord);
            c := op(3,coord)
         else ERROR(`Inappropriate number of parameters.`)
         fi
      else c_name := coord
      fi;
      if member(c_name,readlib(`plot3d/coordset2`)()) then
            `plots/changecoords/twotrans`(p,c_name,a)
      elif member(c_name,readlib(`plot3d/coordset`)()) then
            `plots/changecoords/threetrans`(p,c_name,a,b,c)
      else ERROR(`Cannot convert to coordinate system`,coord)
      fi
   end
```

The adaptation of the above Maple code is easy.

```
>   setcoords := proc( coord )
>     local c_name;
>     global curl, diverge, grad, laplacian,
>            scalefactors, `setcoords/cname`;
>     if type(coord,function) then
>           c_name := op(0,coord);
>           if nops(coord) > 3 then
>           ERROR(`Inappropriate number of parameters.`)
>        fi
>     else c_name := coord
>     fi;
>     if member(c_name,readlib(`plot3d/coordset2`)()) or
>        member(c_name,readlib(`plot3d/coordset`)())
>     then
>           `setcoords/cname` := coord,
>           unprotect( curl, diverge, grad, laplacian,
>                     scalefactors ):
>           curl := proc() linalg[curl]( args,
>                   coords = `setcoords/cname` ) end;
>           diverge := proc() linalg[diverge]( args,
>                     coords = `setcoords/cname` ) end;
>           grad := proc() linalg[grad]( args,
>                   coords = `setcoords/cname` ) end;
>           laplacian := proc() linalg[laplacian]( args,
>                       coords = `setcoords/cname` ) end;
>           scalefactors := proc() readlib(`linalg/scalefcts`)
>                          ( args, `setcoords/cname` ) end;
>           protect( curl, diverge, grad, laplacian,
>                    scalefactors )
>     else
>           ERROR(`Cannot convert to coordinate system`,coord)
>     fi
>   end:
```

Everything is ready for use now. We have even added a routine that produces the scale factors (a routine that, curiously enough, is hidden in the linalg package). For example, the scale factors can be used to determine the volume element in the new coordinate system.

```
> setcoords( prolatespheroidal(a) ):
> laplacian( f, c );
```

$$
\left(a \cosh(u)\sin(v)\,\left(\frac{\partial}{\partial u}f\right) + a\sinh(u)\sin(v)\,\left(\frac{\partial^2}{\partial u^2}f\right)\right.
$$

$$
+ a\sinh(u)\cos(v)\,\left(\frac{\partial}{\partial v}f\right) + a\sinh(u)\sin(v)\,\left(\frac{\partial^2}{\partial v^2}f\right)
$$

$$
\left. + \frac{a\left(\sinh(u)^2+\sin(v)^2\right)\left(\frac{\partial^2}{\partial w^2}f\right)}{\sinh(u)\sin(v)}\right) \Big/ \left(a^3\left(\sinh(u)^2+\sin(v)^2\right)\right.
$$

$$
\left.\sinh(u)\sin(v)\right)
$$

```
> scalefactors( c );
```

$$
\left[\, a\sqrt{\sinh(u)^2+\sin(v)^2},\, a\sqrt{\sinh(u)^2+\sin(v)^2},\, a\sinh(u)\sin(v)\,\right]
$$

```
> dV := convert( ", `*` ); # the volume element
```

$$
dV := a^3\left(\sinh(u)^2+\sin(v)^2\right)\sinh(u)\sin(v)
$$

Prolate spheroidal coordinates are used to compute the overlap integrals between Slater-Zener type atomic orbitals (q.v., [24]). In this context, these coordinates are denoted by ξ, η, and ϕ and are defined as

$$
\begin{aligned}
x &= a\sqrt{(\xi^2-1)(1-\eta^2)}\cos\phi,\\
y &= a\sqrt{(\xi^2-1)(1-\eta^2)}\sin\phi,\\
z &= a\,\xi\,\eta,
\end{aligned}
$$

where

$$
a>0,\ 1\le\xi<\infty,\ -1\le\eta\le 1,\ 0\le\phi<2\pi.
$$

You can add this new definition with the procedure **addcoords**.

```
> readlib( addcoords ):   # load the library function
> addcoords(
>   myprolatespheroidal,  # name of coordinate system
>   [xi,eta,phi],         # list of variables
>   [a*sqrt((xi^2-1)*(1-eta^2))*cos(phi),
>    a*sqrt((xi^2-1)*(1-eta^2))*sin(phi),
>    a*xi*eta ],          # the cartesian coordinates x,y,z
>                         # in terms of the new coordinates
>   [a],                  # list of names of constants
>   [[1.1],[sqrt(2)/2],[Pi/3],       # default values for
>    [1..1.2,-1..1,0..2*Pi],         # coordplot or
>    [-1.2..1.2,-1.2..1.2,-1.7..1.7]] # coordplot3d
> ):
```

However, the results are a bit complicated because Maple's **signum** and **abs** are not powerful enough to recognize signs in all cases. But we can help the system.

```
> assume( a>0, xi>=1, -1<=eta, eta<=1, 0<=phi, phi<=2*Pi );
> alias( f = f(xi,eta,phi), c = [xi,eta,phi] ):
> setcoords( myprolatespheroidal(a) ):
> grad( f, c );
```

$$
\left[\left(\frac{\partial}{\partial \tilde{\xi}} f \right) \middle/ \right.
$$

$$
\sqrt{ \frac{ a^{\tilde{}2} \left(\xi^{\tilde{}2} - 2\xi^{\tilde{}2}\eta^{\tilde{}2} + \xi^{\tilde{}2}\eta^{\tilde{}4} + \eta^{\tilde{}2} \sqrt{ -(\xi^{\tilde{}2}-1)(-1+\eta^{\tilde{}2}) } \sqrt{\%1} \right) }{ \sqrt{ -(\xi^{\tilde{}2}-1)(-1+\eta^{\tilde{}2}) } \sqrt{\%1} } } ,
$$

$$
\left(\frac{\partial}{\partial \tilde{\eta}} f \right) \middle/
$$

$$
\sqrt{ \frac{ a^{\tilde{}2} \left(\eta^{\tilde{}2}\xi^{\tilde{}4} - 2\xi^{\tilde{}2}\eta^{\tilde{}2} + \eta^{\tilde{}2} + \xi^{\tilde{}2} \sqrt{ -(\xi^{\tilde{}2}-1)(-1+eta^2) } \sqrt{\%1} \right) }{ \sqrt{ -(\xi^{\tilde{}2}-1)(-1+\eta^{\tilde{}2}) } \sqrt{\%1} } } ,
$$

$$
\frac{1}{2} \frac{ \sqrt{4} \left(\frac{\partial}{\partial \tilde{\phi}} f \right) }{ \sqrt{ a^{\tilde{}2} \sqrt{ -(\xi^{\tilde{}2}-1)(-1+\eta^{\tilde{}2}) } \sqrt{\%1} } } \Biggr]
$$

$$
\%1 := \left| \zeta^{\tilde{}2} - \zeta^{\tilde{}2} eta^2 - 1 + \eta^{\tilde{}2} \right|
$$

```
> map( simplify@combine@factor, " );
```

$$
\left[\frac{ (\tilde{\xi}-1)(\tilde{\xi}+1) \left(\frac{\partial}{\partial \tilde{\xi}} f \right) }{ a^{\tilde{}} \sqrt{ (\tilde{\xi}-\tilde{\eta})(\tilde{\xi}+\tilde{\eta})(\tilde{\xi}-1)(\tilde{\xi}+1) } }, \right.
$$

$$
- \frac{ (\tilde{\eta}-1)(\tilde{\eta}+1) \left(\frac{\partial}{\partial \tilde{\eta}} f \right) }{ a \sqrt{ (\tilde{\xi}-\tilde{\eta})(\tilde{\xi}+\tilde{\eta})(-\tilde{\eta}+1)(\tilde{\eta}+1) } },
$$

$$
- \frac{ \sqrt{\xi^{\tilde{}2}-1} \sqrt{1-\eta^{\tilde{}2}} \left(\frac{\partial}{\partial \tilde{\phi}} f \right) }{ a (\tilde{\eta}-1)(\tilde{\eta}+1)(\tilde{\xi}-1)(\tilde{\xi}+1) } \Biggr]
$$

```
> scalefactors( c ):
> map( simplify@combine@factor, " );
```

$$
\left[a^{\tilde{}} \sqrt{ \frac{ (\tilde{\xi}-\tilde{\eta})(\tilde{\xi}+\tilde{\eta}) }{ (\tilde{\xi}-1)(\tilde{\xi}+1) } }, \; a^{\tilde{}} \sqrt{ \frac{ (\tilde{\xi}-\tilde{\eta})(\tilde{\xi}+\tilde{\eta}) }{ (-\tilde{\eta}+1)(\tilde{\eta}+1) } }, \right.
$$

$$
a^{\tilde{}} \sqrt{\xi^{\tilde{}2}-1} \sqrt{1-\eta^{\tilde{}2}} \Biggr]
$$

```
> dV := simplify( convert( ", `*` ) );
```

$$
dV := (\tilde{\xi}+\tilde{\eta})(\tilde{\xi}-\tilde{\eta}) a^{\tilde{}3}
$$

Of course, you have better control over the results when you do the work yourself in smaller steps and simplify intermediate results. For example, you can start with the computation of the Jacobian matrix J of the above coordinate transformation (denoted by T).

```
>  restart; with(linalg):
```

Warning, new definition for norm
Warning, new definition for trace

```
>  assume( a>0, xi>=1, -1<=eta, eta<=1, 0<=phi, phi<=2*Pi );
>  alias( f = f(xi,eta,phi), c = [xi,eta,phi] ):
>  T := [a*sqrt((xi^2-1)*(1-eta^2))*cos(phi),
>          a*sqrt((xi^2-1)*(1-eta^2))*sin(phi), a*xi*eta ];
```

$$T := \left[a^\sim \sqrt{(\xi^{\sim 2} - 1)(1 - \eta^{\sim 2})} \cos(\phi^\sim),\right.$$
$$\left. a^\sim \sqrt{(\xi^{\sim 2} - 1)(1 - \eta^{\sim 2})} \sin(\phi^\sim), a^\sim \xi^\sim \eta^\sim \right]$$

```
>  J := jacobian(T,[xi,eta,phi]);
```

$$J :=$$
$$\left[\frac{a^\sim \cos(\phi^\sim) \xi^\sim (1 - \eta^{\sim 2})}{\sqrt{(\xi^{\sim 2} - 1)(1 - \eta^{\sim 2})}}, -\frac{a^\sim \cos(\phi^\sim)(\xi^{\sim 2} - 1)\eta^\sim}{\sqrt{(\xi^{\sim 2} - 1)(1 - \eta^{\sim 2})}}, \right.$$
$$\left. -a^\sim \sqrt{(\xi^{\sim 2} - 1)(1 - \eta^{\sim 2})} \sin(\phi^\sim) \right]$$
$$\left[\frac{a^\sim \sin(\phi^\sim) \xi^\sim (1 - \eta^{\sim 2})}{\sqrt{(\xi^{\sim 2} - 1)(1 - \eta^{\sim 2})}}, -\frac{a^\sim \sin(\phi^\sim)(\xi^{\sim 2} - 1)\eta^\sim}{\sqrt{(\xi^{\sim 2} - 1)(1 - \eta^{\sim 2})}}, \right.$$
$$\left. a^\sim \sqrt{(\xi^{\sim 2} - 1)(1 - \eta^{\sim 2})} \cos(\phi^\sim) \right]$$
$$\left[a^\sim \eta^\sim, a^\sim \xi^\sim, 0 \right]$$

In this case, the *metric tensor* g is equal to $J^T J$.

```
>  g := evalm( transpose(J) &* J ):   g := map(simplify,g);
```

$$g := \begin{bmatrix} -\dfrac{a^{\sim 2}(-\xi^{\sim 2} + \eta^{\sim 2})}{\xi^{\sim 2} - 1}, 0, 0 \\ 0, \dfrac{a^{\sim 2}(-\xi^{\sim 2} + \eta^{\sim 2})}{-1 + \eta^{\sim 2}}, 0 \\ 0, 0, a^{\sim 2} \xi^{\sim 2} - a^{\sim 2} \eta^{\sim 2} \xi^{\sim 2} - a^{\sim 2} + a^{\sim 2} \eta^{\sim 2} \end{bmatrix}$$

Next, you determine the scale factors and add them to the table that stores scale factors of various coordinate systems.

```
> h1 := sqrt( g[1,1] );
```

$$h1 := a^{\sim} \sqrt{\frac{\xi^{\sim 2} - \eta^{\sim 2}}{\xi^{\sim 2} - 1}}$$

```
> h2 := sqrt( g[2,2] );
```

$$h2 := a^{\sim} \sqrt{\frac{\xi^{\sim 2} - \eta^{\sim 2}}{1 - \eta^{\sim 2}}}$$

```
> h3 := sqrt( factor(g[3,3]) );
```

$$h3 := a^{\sim} \sqrt{\xi^{\sim 2} - \eta^{\sim 2} \, \xi^{\sim 2} - 1 + \eta^{\sim 2}}$$

```
> sftable := readlib( `linalg/scaletable` ):
> sftable[myprolatespheroidal] := subs(
>   { a=_a, xi=_x, eta=_y, phi=_z }, [h1,h2,h3] );
```

$$sftable_{myprolatespheroidal} :=$$

$$\left[\_a \sqrt{\frac{\_x^2 - \_y^2}{\_x^2 - 1}}, \_a \sqrt{\frac{\_x^2 - \_y^2}{1 - \_y^2}}, \_a \sqrt{\_x^2 - \_y^2 \_x^2 - 1 + \_y^2} \right]$$

Maple will now use these scale factors to compute the gradient, Laplacian, etc.

```
> laplacian( f, c, coords=myprolatespheroidal(a) ):
> map( combine, " ):
> collect( ", [ diff(f,xi$2), diff(f,eta$2), diff(f,xi),
>   diff(f,eta), f ], distributed, simplify );
```

$$-\frac{(\xi^{\sim 2} - 1)(\frac{\partial^2}{\partial \xi^{\sim 2}} f)}{a^{\sim 2}(-\xi^{\sim 2} + \eta^{\sim 2})} + \frac{(-1 + \eta^{\sim 2})(\frac{\partial^2}{\partial \eta^{\sim 2}} f)}{a^{\sim 2}(-\xi^{\sim 2} + \eta^{\sim 2})} - 2\frac{\xi^{\sim}(\frac{\partial}{\partial \xi^{\sim}} f)}{a^{\sim 2}(-\xi^{\sim 2} + \eta^{\sim 2})}$$

$$+ 2\frac{\eta^{\sim}(\frac{\partial}{\partial \eta^{\sim}} f)}{a^{\sim 2}(-\xi^{\sim 2} + \eta^{\sim 2})} - \frac{\frac{\partial^2}{\partial \phi^{\sim 2}} f}{a^{\sim 2}(-\xi^{\sim 2} + \eta^{\sim 2} \xi^{\sim 2} + 1 - \eta^{\sim 2})}$$

19.5 Moore-Penrose Inverse

In this book, we have not really considered Maple as a programming language allowing for extension of the built-in facilities. But sometimes programming is a big word. For example, the *Moore-Penrose inverse* A^+ of a matrix A can be computed via a limit-definition [5],

$$A^+ = \lim_{x \to 0} \left((A^T A + x^2 I)^{-1} A^T \right),$$

if the limit exists. With all the tools of the linalg package and your knowledge of Maple, you are already able to extend Maple.

```
>  MPinv := A -> map( limit, evalm(
>    evalm( (linalg[transpose](A)&*A+x^2)^(-1) )
>    &* linalg[transpose](A) ), x=0 );
```

$$MPinv := A \rightarrow \mathrm{map}(\, \mathrm{limit}, \mathrm{evalm}($$

$$\mathrm{evalm}(\, \frac{1}{(\,linalg_{transpose}(\,A\,)\,\&*\,A\,)+x^2}\,\&*\,linalg_{transpose}(\,A\,)\,), x = 0\,)$$

```
>  M := randmatrix(3,2);
```

$$M := \begin{bmatrix} -85 & -55 \\ -37 & -35 \\ 97 & 50 \end{bmatrix}$$

```
>  MPinv(M);
```

$$\begin{bmatrix} \dfrac{427}{88957} & \dfrac{2579}{88957} & \dfrac{2275}{88957} \\[2mm] \dfrac{-14093}{889570} & \dfrac{-45953}{889570} & \dfrac{-14939}{444785} \end{bmatrix}$$

```
>  poly := proc() Randpoly(2,y) mod 2 end:
>  M := randmatrix(3,2,entries=poly);
```

$$M := \begin{bmatrix} y^2 & y^2+y+1 \\ y^2+y & y^2+y+1 \\ y^2 & y^2 \end{bmatrix}$$

```
>  MPinv(M);
```

$$\left[-\frac{2\,y^4+3\,y^3+3\,y^2+2\,y+1}{y\,\%1}, \frac{y^4+y^3+3\,y^2+2\,y+1}{y\,\%1}, \right.$$

$$\left. \frac{y^3+3\,y^2+3\,y+2}{\%1} \right]$$

$$\left[\frac{2\,y^3+3\,y^2+2\,y+1}{\%1}, -\frac{y\,(\,y^2+1\,)}{\%1}, -\frac{y\,(\,y^2+2\,y+1\,)}{\%1} \right]$$

$$\%1 := 2\,y^4+4\,y^3+5\,y^2+2\,y+1$$

19.6 Exercises

1. In [152], the following Denavit-Hartenberg parameters for a PUMA robot arm can be found.

Joint	α	θ	d	a
1	$-90°$	θ_1	0	0
2	$0°$	θ_2	0	a_2
3	$90°$	θ_3	d_3	a_3
4	$-90°$	θ_4	d_4	0
5	$90°$	θ_5	0	0
6	$0°$	θ_6	0	0

Determine the position and orientation of the tip of this robot arm as a function of the kinematic parameters. Also describe the translational and rotational velocity of the tip.

2. In [180], the following Denavit-Hartenberg parameters for the IRb-6 robot manipulator can be found.

Joint	α	θ	d	a
1	$90°$	θ_1	d_1	0
2	$0°$	θ_2	0	a_2
3	$0°$	θ_3	0	a_3
4	$90°$	θ_4	0	0
5	$0°$	θ_5	d_5	0

Determine the position and orientation of the tip of this robot arm as a function of the kinematic parameters. Also describe the translational and rotational velocity of the tip.

3. Consider the four-compartmental model for cadmium transfer in the human body shown in Figure 19.4.

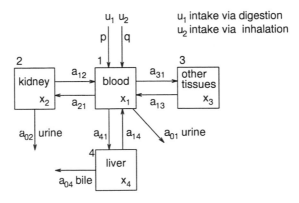

FIGURE 19.4. Cadmium transfer in the human body.

The corresponding mathematical equations are

$$
\begin{aligned}
\dot{x}(t) &= A\,x(t) + B\,u(t), \qquad x(0) = x_0, \\
y(t) &= C\,x(t),
\end{aligned}
$$

where

$$
A = \begin{pmatrix}
a_{11} & a_{12} & a_{13} & a_{14} \\
a_{21} & a_{22} & 0 & 0 \\
a_{31} & 0 & a_{33} & 0 \\
a_{41} & 0 & 0 & a_{44}
\end{pmatrix},
$$

$$
B = \begin{pmatrix}
p & q \\
0 & 0 \\
0 & 0 \\
0 & 0
\end{pmatrix},
$$

$$
C = \begin{pmatrix}
c_{11} & c_{12} & 0 & 0 \\
0 & c_{22} & 0 & 0 \\
0 & 0 & 0 & c_{44}
\end{pmatrix},
$$

with $a_{11} = -(a_{01} + a_{21} + a_{31} + a_{41})$, $a_{22} = -(a_{02} + a_{12})$, $a_{33} = -a_{13}$, $a_{44} = -(a_{04} + a_{14})$, $c_{11} = a_{01}$, and $c_{12} = a_{02}$. The parameters p, q, c_{22}, and c_{44} are supposed to be known. Use Maple to prove that this model is structurally globally identifiable.

4. The ln-tan-cylinder coordinates are defined as

$$
\begin{aligned}
x &= \frac{a}{\pi} \ln\left(\frac{\sinh^2 \eta + \sin^2 \psi}{\sinh^2 \eta + \cos^2 \psi} \right), \\
y &= \frac{2a}{\pi} \arctan\left(\frac{\sinh 2\eta}{\sin 2\psi} \right), \\
z &= z,
\end{aligned}
$$

where

$$
a > 0, \; -1 \le \eta \le 1, \; 0 \le \psi < 2\pi.
$$

Determine the scale factors of these orthogonal curvilinear coordinates and express the Laplacian operator in these coordinates.

5. Using the molecular-orbital Hückel theory, compute the π-electron energy levels of benzene. Determine also the charge distribution of state with lowest energy.

References

[1] A. Abramowitz and I. Stegun. *Handbook of Mathematical Functions.* Dover Publishers, 1970.

[2] S.A. Abromov and K.Uy. Kvashenko. Fast Algorithms to Search for the Rational Solutions of Linear Differential Equations with Polynomial Coefficients. In S.M. Watt, editor, *Proceedings of ISSAC '91*, pages 267–270. ACM Press, 1991.

[3] J.M. Aguiregabiria, A. Hernández and M. Rivas. Are We Careful Enough When Using Computer Algebra? *Computers in Physics*, 8:56–61, 1994.

[4] A.G. Akritas. *Elements of Computer Algebra.* John Wiley & Sons, 1989.

[5] A.E. Albert. *Regression and the Moore-Penrose Pseudoinverse.* Academic Press, 1972.

[6] C.M. Andersen and J.F. Geer. Power Series Expansions for the Frequency and Period of the Limit Cycle of the van der Pol Equation. *SIAM J. Appl. Math.*, 42:678–693, 1982.

[7] T. Banchoff. Differential Geometry and Computer Graphics. In W. Jäger, J. Moser and R. Remmert, editors, *Perspectives in Mathematics*, pages 43–60. Birkhäuser Verlag, 1984.

[8] D. Barton and J.P. Fitch. Applications of Algebraic Manipulation Programs in Physics. *Rep. Prog. Phys.*, 35:235–314, 1972.

[9] D. Barton and J.P. Fitch. CAMAL: the Cambridge Algebra System. *SIGSAM Bull.*, 8(3):17–23, 1974.

[10] D. Barton and R. Zippel. Polynomial Decomposition Algorithms. *J. Symbolic Computation*, 1(2):159–168, 1985.

[11] D. Barton, I.M. Willers, and R.V.M. Zahar. Taylor Series Methods for Ordinary Differential Equations — An Evaluation. In J.R. Rice, editor, *Mathematical Software*, pages 369–389. Academic Press, 1972.

[12] C. Batut, D. Bernardi, H. Cohen, and M. Olivier. *User's Guide to PARI-GP, version 1.39*. Université Bordeaux I, 1995.

[13] T. Becker, V. Weispfenning, and H. Kredel. *Gröbner Bases*. Springer-Verlag, 1993.

[14] A. Berdnikov. Private communications. RIACA, 1994.

[15] F. Bergeron. Surprising Mathematics Using a Computer Algebra System. *J. Symbolic Computation*, 15(3):365–370, 1993.

[16] E.R. Berlekamp. Factoring Polynomials over Large Finite Fields. *Math. Comp.*, 24:713–715, 1970.

[17] W. Bosma and J. Cannon. *Handbook of Magma Functions*. Univ. of Sydney, 1994.

[18] W. Bosma, J. Cannon, C. Playoust, and A. Steel. *Solving Problems with Magma*. Univ. of Sydney, 1994.

[19] A. Boyle and B.F. Caviness. Future Directions for Research in Symbolic Computation. SIAM Reports on Issues in the Mathematical Sciences, 1990.

[20] M. Bronstein, J.H. Davenport, and B.M. Trager. Symbolic Integration is Algorithmic. Tutorial, Computers and Mathematics 1989, MIT, 1989.

[21] M. Bronstein. Integration of Elementary Functions. *J. Symbolic Computation*, 9(2):117–174, 1990.

[22] M. Bronstein. Linear Ordinary Differential Equations: breaking through the order 2 barrier. In P. Wang, editor, *Proceedings of ISSAC '92*, pages 42–48. ACM Press, 1992.

[23] M. Bronstein and B. Salvy. Full Partial Fraction Decomposition of Rational Functions. In M. Bronstein, editor, *Proceedings of ISSAC '93*, pages 157–160. ACM Press, 1993.

[24] D.A. Brown. *Quantum Chemistry*. Penguin Books, 1972.

[25] C. de Bruijn. De structurele identificeerbaarheid en het schatbaar zijn van de modelparameters van het compartimentele model voor de

verspreiding van cadmium in het menselijk lichaam. Technical report, RIVM (in Dutch), 1990.

[26] B. Buchberger. Gröbner Bases: An Algorithmic Method in Polynomial Ideal Theory. In N.K. Bose, editor, *Progress, Directions and Open Problems in Multidimensional Systems Theory*, pages 184–232. Reidel Publishing Company, 1985.

[27] B. Buchberger. Applications of Gröbner Bases in Non-linear Computational Geometry. In J.R. Rice, editor, *Mathematical Aspects of Scientific Software*, IMA Volume in Mathematics and its Applications 14, pages 59–87. Springer-Verlag, 1988.

[28] G. Butler and J. Cannon. The Design of Cayley - A Language for Modern Algebra. In A. Miola, editor, *Design and Implementation of Symbolic Computation Systems*, Lecture Notes in Computer Science 429, pages 10–19. Springer-Verlag, 1990.

[29] P.F. Byrd and M.D. Friedman. *Handbook of Elliptic Integrals for Engineers and Physicists*, volume LXVII of *Die Grundlagen der Mathematischen Wissenschaften*. Springer-Verlag, 1971.

[30] J. Calmet and J.A. van Hulzen. Computer Algebra Applications. In B. Buchberger, G.E. Collins and R. Loos, editors, *Computer Algebra — Symbolic and Algebraic Computation*, pages 245–258. Springer-Verlag, 1983.

[31] J. Cannon and W. Bosma. *Cayley Quick Reference Guide*. Univ. of Sydney, 1991.

[32] J. Cannon and J. Playoust. *An Introduction to Magma*. Univ. of Sydney, 1994.

[33] D.G. Cantor and H. Zassenhaus. A New Algorithm over Large Finite Fields. *Math. Comp.*, 36:587–592, 1981.

[34] A. Capani and G. Niesi. *CoCoA User's Manual*. Univ. of Genova, CoCoA version 3.0b, 1995.

[35] J. Carminati, J.S. Devitt, and G.J. Fee. Isogroup of Differential Equations Using Algebraic Computing. *J. Symbolic Computation*, 14(1):103–120, 1992.

[36] B.W. Char, K.O. Geddes, W.M. Gentleman, and G.H. Gonnet. The Design of Maple: A Compact, Portable, and Powerful Computer Algebra System. In J.A. van Hulzen, editor, *Computer Algebra — (Proceedings of EUROCAL '83)*, Lecture Notes in Computer Science 162, pages 101–115. Springer-Verlag, 1983.

[37] B.W. Char, K.O. Geddes, and G.H. Gonnet. GCDHEU: Heuristic GCD Algorithm Based on Integer GCD Computation. *J. Symbolic Computation*, 7(1):31–48, 1989.

[38] B.W. Char, K.O. Geddes, G.H. Gonnet, B.L. Leong, M.B. Monagan, and S.M. Watt. *Maple V Library Reference Manual*. Springer-Verlag, first edition, 1991.

[39] B.W. Char, K.O. Geddes, G.H. Gonnet, B.L. Leong, M.B. Monagan, and S.M. Watt. *Maple V Language Reference Manual*. Springer-Verlag, first edition, 1991.

[40] B.W. Char, K.O. Geddes, G.H. Gonnet, B.L. Leong, M.B. Monagan, and S.M. Watt. *First Leaves: A Tutorial Introduction*. Springer-Verlag, first edition, 1992.

[41] P.L. Chebyshev. Sur l'integration des differentielles qui contienent une racine carrée d'un polynôme du troisième ou du quatrième degré. In *Oeuvres de P.L. Tchebychef*, volume I, pages 171–200. Chelsea, 1957.

[42] S.M. Christensen. Resources for Computer Algebra. *Computers in Physics*, 8:308–315, 1994.

[43] A.M. Cohen. Computer Algebra, Theory and Practice. *Nieuw Arch. voor Wisk.*, IV(7):215–230, 1989.

[44] A.M. Cohen and G.C.M. Ruitenburg. Generating Functions and Lie Groups. In A.M. Cohen, editor, *Computational Aspects of Lie Group Representations and Related Topics*, CWI Tract 84, pages 19–28. CWI, 1991.

[45] A.M. Cohen, R.L. Griess Jr., and B. Lisser. The Group L(2,61) embeds in the Lie Group of type E_8. *Comm. Algebra*, 21:1889–1907, 1993.

[46] A.M. Cohen, J.H. Davenport, and A.J.P. Heck. An Overview of Computer Algebra. In *Computer Algebra for Industry: Problem Solving in Practice*, pages 1–52. John Wiley & Sons, 1993.

[47] J.W. Cooley and J.W. Tukey. An Algorithm for the Machine Calculation of Complex Fourier Series. *Math. Comp.*, 19:297–301, 1965.

[48] R.M. Corless, G.H. Gonnet, D.E.G. Hare, and D.J. Jeffrey. On Lambert's W Function. Preprint in Maple Share Library, 1993.

[49] R.M. Corless. Simplification and the Assume Facility. *Maple Technical Newsletter*, 1(1):24–31, 1994.

[50] R.M. Corless and K. El-Sawy. Solution of Banded Linear Systems in Maple Using LU Factorization. In R.J. Lopez, editor, *Maple V: Mathematics and Its Applications*, pages 219–227. Birkhäuser Verlag, 1994.

[51] D. Cox, J. Little, and D. O'Shea. *Ideals, Varieties, and Algorithms*. Springer-Verlag, 1992.

[52] J.H. Davenport. *On the Integration of Algebraic Functions.* Lecture Notes in Computer Science 102. Springer-Verlag, 1981.

[53] J.H. Davenport, Y. Siret, and E. Tournier. *Computer algebra: systems and algorithms for algebraic computation.* Academic Press, 1988.

[54] J.H. Davenport and B.M. Trager. Scratchpad's View of Algebra I: Basic Commutative Algebra. In A. Miola, editor, *Design and Implementation of Symbolic Computation Systems*, Lecture Notes in Computer Science 429, pages 40–54. Springer-Verlag, 1990.

[55] J.H. Davenport. The Axiom System. In *Proceedings of NAGUA '91.* NAG Ltd., 1991.

[56] J. Dieudonné. *Treatise on Analysis*, volume 10-III of *Pure and Applied Mathematics.* Academic Press, 1972.

[57] A. Dingle and R. Fateman. Branch Cuts in Computer Algebra. In *Proceedings of ISSAC '94*, pages 250–257. ACM Press, 1994.

[58] W.H. Enright. The Relative Efficiency of Alternative Defect Control Schemes for High Order Continuous Runge-Kutta Formulas. Technical Report 252/91, University of Toronto, Dept. of Computer Science, June 1991.

[59] A. v.d. Essen. Polynomial Maps and the Jacobian Conjecture. In *Computational Aspects of Lie Group Representations and Related Topics*, CWI Tract 84, pages 29–44. CWI, 1991.

[60] R.J. Fateman. Advances and Trends in the Design and Construction of Algebraic Manipulation Systems. In S. Watenabe and M. Nagata, editors, *Proceedings of ISSAC '90*, pages 60–67. ACM Press, 1990.

[61] E. Fehlberg. Klassische Runge-Kutta Formeln vierter und niedriger Ordnung mit Schrittweiten Kontrolle und ihre Anwendungen in Wärmeleitungsprobleme. *Computing*, 6:61–71, 1970.

[62] R.P. Feynman, R.B. Leighton, and M. Sands. *The Feynman Lectures on Physics*, volume II. Addison-Wesley, 1964. fourth printing, pp. 22-8.

[63] J. Fitch. Solving Algebraic Problems with REDUCE. *J. Symbolic Computation*, 1(2):211–228, 1985.

[64] I. Foster and S. Taylor. *Strand — New Concepts in Parallel Programming.* Prentice-Hall, 1989.

[65] I. Frick. *SHEEP User's Manual.* Univ. of Stockholm, 1977.

[66] F.N. Fritsch, R.E. Shafer, and W.P. Crowley. Solution of the Transcendental Equation $we^w = \chi$. *Comm. ACM.*, 16:123–124, 1973.

[67] Fuchsteiner et al. *MuPAD: Multi Processing Algebra Data Tool; Benutzerhandbuch; MuPAD Version 1.1.* Birkhäuser Verlag, 1993.

[68] Fuchsteiner et al. *MuPAD: Multi Processing Algebra Data Tool; Tutorial.* Birkhäuser Verlag, 1993.

[69] W. Gander, J. Hřebíček and S. Bartoň. The Tractrix and Similar Curves. In W. Gander and J. Hřebíček, editors, *Solving Problems in Scientific Computing Using Maple and Matlab*, pages 1–14. Springer-Verlag, 1995.

[70] C.W. Gear. *Numerical Initial Value Problems in Ordinary Differential Equations.* Prentice-Hall, 1971.

[71] K.O. Geddes. Numerical Integration in a Symbolic Context. In B. Char, editor, *Proceedings of SYMSAC '86*, pages 185–191. ACM Press, 1986.

[72] K.O. Geddes and G.H. Gonnet. A New Algorithm for Computing Symbolic Limits Using Hierarchical Series. In P. Gianni, editor, *Symbolic and Algebraic Computation, Proceedings ISSAC '88*, Lecture Notes in Computer Science 358, pages 490–495. Springer-Verlag, 1989.

[73] K.O. Geddes and T.C. Scott. Recipes for Classes of Definite Integrals Involving Exponentials and Logarithms. In E. Kaltofen and S.M. Watt, editors, *Computers and Mathematics 1989*, pages 192–201. Academic Press, 1989.

[74] K.O. Geddes and L.Y. Stefanus. On the Risch-Norman integration method and its implementation in Maple. In G.H. Gonnet, editor, *Proceedings of ISSAC '89*, pages 212–217. ACM Press, 1989.

[75] K.O. Geddes. Numerical Integration using Symbolic Analysis. *Maple Technical Newsletter*, 6:8–17, 1991.

[76] K.O. Geddes, S.R. Czapor and G. Labahn. *Algorithms for Computer Algebra.* Kluwer Academic Publishers, 1992.

[77] K.O. Geddes. A Package for Numerical Approximation. *Maple Technical Newsletter*, 10:28–36, 1993.

[78] A. Giovini and G. Niesi. CoCoA: A User-Friendly System for Commutative Algebra. In A. Miola, editor, *Design and Implementation of Symbolic Computation Systems*, Lecture Notes in Computer Science 429, pages 20–29. Springer-Verlag, 1990.

[79] G.H. Gonnet and D.W. Gruntz. Algebraic Manipulation: Systems. In A. Ralston et al, editors, *Encyclopedia of Computer Science & Engineering*. Van Nostrand Reinhold, 1991.

[80] G.H. Gonnet and D.W. Gruntz. Limit Computation in Computer Algebra. Technical Report 187, Department of Computer Science, ETH Zürich, 1992.

[81] M.J. González-López and T. Recio. The ROMIN inverse geometric model and the dynamic evaluation method. In A.M. Cohen, editor, *Computer Algebra for Industry: Problem Solving in Practice*, pages 117–141. John Wiley & Sons, 1993.

[82] R.W. Gosper. Decision Procedure for Indefinite Hypergeometric Summation. *Proc. Natl. Acad. Sci. USA*, 75:40–42, 1978.

[83] X. Gourdon and B. Salvy. Computing One Million Digits of $\sqrt{2}$. *Maple Technical Newsletter*, 10:66–71, 1993.

[84] I.S. Gradshteyn and I.M. Ryzhik. *Table of Integrals, Series and Products*. Academic Press, fifth edition, 1994.

[85] J. Graf v. Schmettow. KANT - a Tool for Computations in Algebraic Number Fields. In A. Pethö, M. Pohst, H. Williams and H. Zimmer, editors, *Computational Number Theory*, pages 321–330. de Gruyter, 1991.

[86] D.R. Grayson. Macaulay 2. http://www.math.uiuc.edu/~dan/Macaulay2, 1995.

[87] A. Griewank. On Automatic Differentiation. In M. Iri and K. Tanabe, editors, *Mathematical Programming*, pages 83–107. Kluwer Academic Publishers, 1989.

[88] A. Griewank. The Chain Rule Revisited in Scientific Computing. *SIAM News*, pages 20–21 (part I), 8–9, 24 (part II), May (part I), July (part II) 1991.

[89] A. Griewank and G.F. Corliss. Automatic Differentiation of Algorithms: Theory, Implementation and Application. In *Proceedings in Applied Mathematics 53*. SIAM, Philadelphia, 1991.

[90] E. Groswald. *Bessel Polynomials*. Lecture Notes in Mathematics 698. Springer-Verlag, 1980.

[91] J. Grotendorst. A Maple Package for Transforming Series, Sequences, and Functions. *Comp. Phys. Comm.*, 67:325–342, 1991.

[92] J. Gutiérrez, T. Recio, and C. Ruiz de Velasco. Polynomial decomposition algorithm of almost quadratic complexity. In T. Mora, editor, *Proceedings of AAECC-6*, Lecture Notes in Computer Science 357. Springer-Verlag, 1989.

[93] J. Gutiérrez and T. Recio. A Practical Implementation of Two Rational Decomposition Algorithms. In P. Wang, editor, *Proceedings of ISSAC '92*, pages 152–157. ACM Press, 1992.

[94] J. Gutiérrez and T. Recio. Rational Function Decomposition and Gröbner Basis in the Parametrization of Plane Curves. In *Proceedings of LATIN '92, São Paulo, Brazil*, pages 239–245. Springer-Verlag, 1992. Springer Lecture Notes of Comput. Sci. 583.

[95] D. Harper, C. Wooff, and D. Hodgkinson. *A Guide to Computer Algebra Systems*. John Wiley & Sons, 1991.

[96] B.K. Harrison and F.B. Estabrook. Geometric Approach to Invariance Groups and Solutions of Partial Differential Equations. *J. Math. Phys.*, 12:653–665, 1971.

[97] A.C. Hearn. *REDUCE User's Manual*. The Rand Coorporation, Santa Monica, California, 1987.

[98] A.J.P. Heck. Transformation between Geocentric and Geodetic Coordinates. In A.M. Cohen, editor, *Computer Algebra for Industry: Problem Solving in Practice*, pages 203–219. John Wiley & Sons, 1993.

[99] A.J.P Heck. FORM for Pedestrians. http://www.can.nl/ SystemsOverview/General/FORM/. CAN Expertise Center & Univ. of Petrópolis, 1993.

[100] A.J.P. Heck. Computer Algebra: A Tool in Identifiability Testing. In A.M. Cohen, L. van Gastel and S. Verduyn Lunel, editors, *Computer Algebra for Industry 2: Problem Solving in Practice*, pages 267–289. John Wiley & Sons, 1995.

[101] W. Hereman. Symbolic Software for Lie Symmetry Analysis. In N.H. Ibragimov, editor, *CRC Handbook of Lie Group Analysis of Differential Equations, Vol. : New Trends in Theoretical Developments and Computational Methods*, chap. 13. CRC Press, 1995.

[102] A.C. Hindmarsh. ODEPACK: a Systemized Collection of ODE Solvers. In R. Stepleman, editor, *Numerical Methods for Scientific Computation*. North-Holland, 1983.

[103] C. Hollinger and P. Serf. SIMATH - a Computer Algebra System. In A. Pethö, M. Pohst, H. Williams and H. Zimmer, editors, *Computational Number Theory*, pages 331–342. de Gruyter, 1991.

[104] L. Hornfeldt. *STENSOR Reference Manual*. Univ. of Stockholm, 1988.

[105] E. Horowitz. Algorithms for Partial Fraction Decomposition and Rational Integration. In S.R. Petrick, editor, *Proceedings of SYMSAM '71*, pages 441–457. ACM Press, 1971.

[106] J.A. van Hulzen and J. Calmet. Computer Algebra Systems. In B. Buchberger, G.E. Collins and R. Loos, editors, *Computer Algebra*

— *Symbolic and Algebraic Computation*, pages 221–244. Springer-Verlag, 1983.

[107] A. Ivic. *The Riemann Zeta Function*. John Wiley & Sons, 1985.

[108] R.D. Jenks, R.S. Sutor, S.M. Watt. Scratchpad II: And Abstract Datatype System for Mathematical Computing. In J.R. Rice, editor, *Mathematical Aspects of Scientific Software*, IMA Volume in Mathematics and its Applications 14, pages 157–182. Springer-Verlag, 1988.

[109] Richard D. Jenks and Robert S. Sutor. *AXIOM, The Scientific Computation System*. Springer-Verlag, 1992.

[110] E. W. Johnson. *Linear Algebra with Maple V*. Brooks/Cole, 1993.

[111] W. Kahan. Branch Cuts for Complex Elementary Functions or Much Ado About Nothing's Sign Bit. In A. Iserles and M.J.D. Powell, editors, *The State of the Art in Numerical Analysis*, pages 65–212. Clarendon Press, 1987.

[112] E. Kaltofen. Polynomial Factorization. In B. Buchberger, G. Collins and R. Loos, editors, *Computer Algebra — Symbolic and Algebraic Computation*, pages 95–114. Springer-Verlag, 1983.

[113] E. Kaltofen. Sparse Hensel Lifting. In B.F. Caviness, editor, *Proceedings of EUROCAL '85*, Lecture Notes in Computer Science 204, Vol. 2, pages 4–17. Springer-Verlag, 1985.

[114] E. Kaltofen. Polynomial Factorization 1982–1986. In D.V. Chudnovsky and R.D. Jenks, editors, *Computers & Mathematics*, Lecture Notes in Pure and Applied Mathematics 125, pages 285–309. Marcel Dekker, 1990.

[115] E. Kaltofen. Polynomial Factorization 1987–1991. In *Proceedings of LATIN '92, São Paulo, Brazil*, pages 294–313. Springer-Verlag, 1992. Springer Lecture Notes of Comput. Sci. 583.

[116] M. Klerer and F. Grossman. Error Rates in Tables of Indefinite Integrals. *Industrial Mathematics*, 18, 1968.

[117] D.E. Knuth. *The Art of Computer Programming, Vol. II, Seminumerical Algorithms*. Addison-Wesley, second edition, 1981.

[118] D.E. Knuth. Problem E3335. *Amer. Math. Monthly*, 96:525, 1989.

[119] H.-P. Ko. Geometry Theorem Proving by Decomposition of Quasi-Algebraic Sets: An Application of the Ritt-Wu Principle. In D.Kapur and J.L. Mundy, editors, *Geometrical Reasoning*, pages 95–122. MIT Press, 1989.

[120] W. Koepf. Algorithms for the Indefinite and Definite Summation. Technical Report, Preprint SC 94-33, Konrad-Zuse-Zentrum Berlin (ZIB), December 94.

[121] J. Kovacic. An Algorithm for Solving Second Order Homogeneous Differential Equations. *J. Symbolic Computation*, 2(1):3–43, 1986.

[122] D. Kraft. Modeling and Simulating Robots in Maple. *Maple Technical Newsletter*, 1(2):39–47, 1994.

[123] G. Labahn. Solving Linear Differential Equations in Maple. *Maple Technical Newsletter*, 2(1):20–28, 1995.

[124] L. Lamport. *LaTeX, A Document Preparation System*. Addison-Wesley, 1988.

[125] D. Lazard and R. Rioboo. Integration of Rational Functions: Rational Computation of the Logarithmic Part. *J. Symbolic Computation*, 9(2):113–116, 1990.

[126] Y. Lecourtier and A. Raksanyi. The Testing of Structural Properties Through Symbolic Computation. In E. Walter, editor, *Identifiabilty of Parametric Models*. Pergamon Press, 1987.

[127] M.A. van Leeuwen, A.M. Cohen, and B. Lisser. *LiE: A Package for Lie Group Computations*. CAN Expertise Center, 1992.

[128] A. Lehtonen. The Klein Bottle. *The Mathematica Journal*, 1(3):65, 1991.

[129] A.K. Lenstra. Factoring Polynomials over Algebraic Number Fields. In J.A. van Hulzen, editor, *Computer Algebra — (Proceedings of EUROCAL '83)*, Lecture Notes in Computer Science 162, pages 245–254. Springer-Verlag, 1983.

[130] A.H.M. Levelt. Various Problems Solved by Computer Algebra. In A.M. Cohen, L. van Gastel and S. Verduyn Lunel, editors, *Computer Algebra for Industry 2: Problem Solving in Practice*, pages 43–59. John Wiley & Sons, 1995.

[131] B. Lisser. Kostant's Conjecture. *Maple Technical Newsletter*, pages 29–34, 1994. Special Issue: "Maple in Mathematics and the Sciences."

[132] R. Loos. Computing in Algebraic Extensions. In B. Buchberger, G.E. Collins and R. Loos, editors, *Computer Algebra — Symbolic and Algebraic Computation*, pages 173–187. Springer-Verlag, 1983.

[133] J. v.d. Lune, H.J.J. te Riele, and D.T. Winter. On the zeros of the Riemann zeta function. *Math. Comp.*, 46:667–681, 1986.

[134] M. MacCallum and J. Skea. SHEEP, a computer algebra system for general relativity. In M. MacCallum, J. Skea, J. McCrea and R. McLenaghan, editors, *Algebraic Computing in General Relativity*, pages 1–172. Clarendon Press, 1994.

[135] M.A.H. MacCallum. Using Computer Algebra to Solve Ordinary Differential Equations. In A.M. Cohen, L. van Gastel and S. Verduyn Lunel, editors, *Computer Algebra for Industry 2: Problem Solving in Practice*, pages 19–41. John Wiley & Sons, 1995.

[136] MACSYMA User's Guide. *MACSYMA User's Guiden, System Reference Manual, and Mathematics Reference Manual*. Macsyma, Inc., 1992.

[137] MathSource. http://www.wri.com/mathsource.

[138] M. Mignotte. *Mathematics for Computer Algebra*. Springer-Verlag, 1992.

[139] B. Mishra. *Algorithmic Algebra*. Springer-Verlag, 1993.

[140] R. Moenck. On Computing Closed Forms for Summation. In *Proc. MACSYMA User's Conf.*, pages 225–236, 1977.

[141] M.B. Monagan. Tips for Maple Users. *Maple Technical Newsletter*, 1(2):11–13, 1994.

[142] P. Moon and D.E. Spencer. *Field Theory Handbook: Including Coordinate Systems, Differential Equations and Their Solutions*. Springer-Verlag, 1961.

[143] J. Moses. Symbolic Integration: The Stormy Decade. *Comm. ACM.*, 14.548–560, 1971.

[144] A.H. Nayfeh and D.T. Mook. *Nonlinear Oscillations*. John Wiley & Sons, 1979.

[145] B. Noble and M.A. Hussain. Multiple Scaling and a Related Expansion Method, with Applications. Report BICOM 87/7, Brunel Univ., Uxbridge, England, June 1987.

[146] V.W. Noonburg. A Neural Network Modeled by an Adaptive Lotka-Volterra System. *SIAM J. Appl. Math*, 49:1779–1792, 1989.

[147] A.M. Odlyzko. Analytic Computations in Number Theory. In W. Gautschi, editor, *Mathematics of Computation 1943–1993: a Half-Century of Computational Mathematics*, pages 451–463. Proceedings of Symposia in Applied Mathematics, American Mathematical Society, 1994.

[148] G.J. Oldenborgh. An Introduction to FORM. Univ. of Leiden, http://www.can.nl/SystemsOverview/General/FORM/.

[149] P.J. Olver. *Applications of Lie Groups to Differential Equations*. Springer-Verlag, 1986.

646   References

[150] M.K. Paul. A Note on Computation of Geodetic Coordinates from Geocentric (Cartesian) Coordinates. *Bull. Géodésique*, 108:135–139, 1973.

[151] R.P. Paul. *Robot Manipulators: Mathematics, Programming and Control*. MIT Press, 1981.

[152] R.P. Paul. Kinematic Control Equations for Simple Manipulators. In C. Lee, R. Gonzalez and K. Fu, editors, *Tutorial on Robotics*, pages 66–72. IEEE Computer Society Press, 1983.

[153] P. Paule and V. Strehl. Symbolic Summation – Some Recent Developments. Technical Report 95-11, RISC-Linz, Johannes Kepler University, Linz, Austria, 1995. Published in *Computer Algebra in Science and Engineering – Algorithms, Systems, and Applications*, J. Fleischer, J. Grabmeier, F. Hehl, W. Küchlin (eds.), World Scientific, Singapore. In preparation.

[154] R. Pavelle. Problems sent to the USENET sci.math.symbolic bulletin board. Archived in the REDUCE network library, 1989.

[155] P.P. Petrushev and V.A. Popov. *Rational Approximation of Real Functions*. Cambridge University Press, 1987.

[156] M.E. Pohst. *Computational Algebraic Number Theory*, volume 21 of *DMV Seminar*. Birkhäuser Verlag, 1993.

[157] A. Raksanyi, Y. Lecourtier, E. Walter, and A. Venot. Identifiability and Distinguishability Testing Via Computer Algebra. *Math. Biosciences*, 77:245–266, 1985.

[158] R.H. Rand. *Computer Algebra in Applied Mathematics: An Introduction to MACSYMA*. Research Notes in Mathematics 94. Pitman Publishing, 1984.

[159] R.H. Rand and D. Armbruster. *Perturbation Methods, Bifurcation Theory and Computer Algebra*. Applied Mathematical Sciences 65. Springer-Verlag, 1987.

[160] D. Redfern. *The Maple Handbook, Maple V Release 4*. Springer-Verlag, 1995.

[161] E.Ya. Remez. Sur un procédé convergent d'approximation succesives pour déterminer les polynômes d'approximation. *Comptes Rendues*, 193:2063–2065, 1934.

[162] E.Ya. Remez. Sur le calcul effectif des polynômes d'approximation de Tschebyscheff. *Comptes Rendues*, 199:337–340, 1934.

[163] R.H. Risch. The problem of integration in finite terms. *Trans. AMS*, 139:167–189, 1969.

[164] M. Rothstein. *Aspects of Symbolic Integration and Simplification of Exponential and Primitive Functions.* PhD thesis, Univ. of Wisconsin, Madison, 1976.

[165] M. Schoenert et al. *GAP: Groups, Algorithms and Programming.* RWTH Aachen, 1994. GAP Manual Release 3.4, http://www.math. rwth-aachen.de:8000/GAP/Manual/.

[166] F.W. Schwarz. Symmetries of Differential Equations: From Sophus Lie to Computer Algebra. *SIAM Review*, 30:450–481, 1988.

[167] T.C. Scott, Y.B. Band, and K.O. Geddes. Recipes for Solving Broad Classes of Definite Integrals and Applications. *Maple Technical Newsletter*, 10:19–27, 1993.

[168] K. Siegl. Parallelizing Algorithms for Symbolic Computation Using ‖MAPLE‖. Technical Report 93-08, RISC-Linz, Johannes Kepler University, Linz, Austria, 1993. Published in: 4th ACM SIGPLAN Symp. on Principles and Practice of Parallel Programming, San Diego, CA, May 19–21, 1993.

[169] T.J. Smedley. *Fast Methods for Computation with Algebraic Numbers.* PhD thesis, Univ. of Waterloo, 1990.

[170] B.K. Spearman and K.S. Williams. Characterization of Solvable Quintics $x^5 + ax + b$. *Amer. Math. Monthly*, 101:986–992, 1994.

[171] M.R. Spiegel. *Mathematical Handbook of Formulas and Tables.* McGraw-Hill, 1968.

[172] H. Stephani. *Differential Equations: Their Solution Using symmetries.* Cambridge University Press, 1993.

[173] M. Stillman, M. Stillman and D. Bayer. *Macaulay User Manual*, 1989.

[174] J. Stoer and R. Bulirsch. *Introduction to Numerical Analysis.* Text in Applied Mathematics 12. Springer-Verlag, second edition, 1993.

[175] D. Stoutemyer. Crimes and Misdemeanors in the Computer Algebra Trade. *Notices of the AMS*, 38:778–785, 1991.

[176] D. Stoutemyer. *Derive User Manual.* Soft Warehouse, Inc., Honolulu, Hawaii, 1994. seventh edition.

[177] V. Strehl. Binomial Sums and Identities. *Maple Technical Newsletter*, 10:37–49, 1993.

[178] H. Strubbe. Manual for SCHOONSCHIP. *Comput. Phys. Commun.*, 8:1–30, 1974.

[179] R.S. Sutor (ed.). The Scratchpad II Computer Algebra System Interactive Environment Users Guide. Technical report, IBM Thomas J. Watson Research Center, Yorktown Heights, 1988.

[180] T. Szkodny. Modelling of Kinematics of the IRb-6 Manipulator. *Computers Math. Applic.*, 29:77–94, 1995.

[181] R.G. Tobey. *Algorithms for Antidifferentiation of Rational Functions.* PhD thesis, Univ. of Wisconsin, Madison, 1967.

[182] B. Trager. Algebraic Factoring and Rational Function Integration. In R.D. Jenks, editor, *Proceedings of SYMSAC '76*, pages 219–226. ACM Press, 1976.

[183] B. Trager. *Integration of Algebraic Functions.* PhD thesis, MIT, 1984.

[184] J.A.M. Vermaseren. *Symbolic Manipulation with FORM.* CAN Expertise Center, 1991.

[185] J.A.M. Vermaseren. Symbolic Heroics. *CAN Newsletter*, 11:57–58, 1993.

[186] D. Wang. An Implementation of the Characteristic Set Method in Maple. Technical Report 91-25, RISC-Linz, 1991.

[187] Waterloo Maple Inc. *The Maple Learning Guide*, 1995.

[188] Waterloo Maple Inc. *The Maple Programming Guide*, 1995.

[189] T. Weibel and G.H. Gonnet. An Algebra of Properties. In *Proceedings of ISSAC '91*, pages 352–359. ACM Press, 1991.

[190] T. Weibel and G.H. Gonnet. An Algebra of Properties. Technical report 158, Informatik ETH-Zürich, 1991.

[191] T. Weibel and G.H. Gonnet. An Assume Facility for CAS, with a Sample Implementation for Maple. In J. Fitch, editor, *Design and Implementation of Symbolic Computation Systems*, Lecture Notes in Computer Science 721, pages 95–103. Springer-Verlag, 1992.

[192] E.J. Weniger. Nonlinear Sequence Transformations for the Acceleration of Convergence and the Summation of Divergent Series. *Comp. Phys. Reports*, 10:189–371, 1989.

[193] H.S. Wilf and D. Zeilberger. Rational functions certify combinatorial identities. *J. Amer. Math. Soc.*, 3:147–158, 1990.

[194] H.S. Wilf and D. Zeilberger. Towards computerized proofs of identities. *Bull. of the Amer. Math. Soc.*, 23:77–83, 1990.

[195] F. Winkler. Computer Algebra: Problems and Developments. In A.M. Cohen, L. van Gastel and S. Verduyn Lunel, editors, *Computer Algebra for Industry 2: Problem Solving in Practice*, pages 1–18. John Wiley & Sons, 1995.

[196] S. Wolfram. *Mathematica: A System for Doing Mathematics by Computer.* Addison-Wesley, second edition, 1991.

[197] C. Wooff and D. Hodgkinson. *MuMath: A Microcomputer Algebra System.* Academic Press, 1987.

[198] P.E.S. Wormer and F. de Groot. The Potential Energy Surface of Triplet H_3^+: A Representation in Hyperspherical Coordinates. *J. Chem. Phys.*, 1989:2344, 90.

[199] Computer Algebra WWW servers, good starting points. CAIN, www.can.nl; Computer Algebra Fachgruppe, www.uni-karlsruhe.de~ CAIS; GDR MEDICIS, medicis.polytechnique.fr; RISC-Linz, info. risc.uni-linz.ac.at; SymbolicNet, symbolicnet.mcs.kent.edu.

[200] S.Y. Yan. Primality Testing of Large Numbers in Maple. *Computers Math. Applic.*, 29:1–8, 1995.

[201] R. Zippel. Rational Function Decomposition. In S.M. Watt, editor, *Proceedings of ISSAC '91*, pages 1–6. ACM Press, 1991.

[202] R. Zippel. *Effective Polynomial Computation.* Kluwer Academic Publishers, 1993.

Index